LEEDS IN THE GREAT WAR

Town Hall, Leeds, in and around which so many war activities centred.

LEEDS IN THE GREAT WAR

1914–1918

A Book of Remembrance

BY

WILLIAM HERBERT SCOTT

WITH A FOREWORD BY

A. J. GRANT,
Professor of History in the University of Leeds,

AND A ROLL OF HONOUR

COMPILED BY

C. E. MULHOLLAND.

*" Not once or twice in our fair island story
The path of duty was the way to glory."*

The Naval & Military Press Ltd

Published by

The Naval & Military Press Ltd
Unit 5 Riverside, Brambleside
Bellbrook Industrial Estate
Uckfield, East Sussex
TN22 1QQ England

Tel: +44 (0)1825 749494

www.naval-military-press.com
www.nmarchive.com

In reprinting in facsimile from the original, any imperfections are inevitably reproduced and the quality may fall short of modern type and cartographic standards.

PREFACE.

DURING the years of world conflict, from 1914 to 1918, the minds of men were often stirred by the thought that, in days to come, their children and grandchildren might require them to render an account of their deeds in the Great War. And it was some such thought that led to the writing of this book. What did Leeds do in the Great War? Should not future generations be told what their elders and forebears endured and accomplished? Moreover, if they are to be encouraged to make an end of war in the future, ought they not to know something of the bitter trials we experienced? At least it was felt that the important part taken by Leeds justified a literary memorial. And certainly in this respect the metropolis of Yorkshire has no cause to be less mindful than other large centres of population.

Within the limits of the following pages an attempt has been made to provide a comprehensive record. So much material was available for this purpose that it would have been possible to fill not one but several volumes, merely with interesting extracts from the newspapers of the period. The aim, however, was to present the outstanding features of interest in convenient as well as readable form. Accordingly there is, first, "The Story"—a general narrative of events at home; and next, "The Record," giving accounts of activities, individual and collective, the military exploits of Leeds Territorial Units naturally claiming first consideration.

The author's journalistic duties, and his close connection with affairs throughout the war period, have enabled him to write from personal observation. Nevertheless, in large measure, he has had to depend for precise details on the extremely valuable collection of Press cuttings, thoughtfully preserved by Mr. Thomas W. Hand, City Librarian, from the declaration of war until the peace. In cases where the newspaper record was found incomplete, or there was a hiatus due to the Censorship of the time, considerable research was necessary; and in this process much assistance has been given by correspondents qualified to deal with certain aspects. To all who have contributed in any way or who have supplied items of information and corrected proofs, hearty thanks are tendered. Without their help, the mass of detail comprised in " The Record " could hardly have been brought together. It is regretted that, partly for economic reasons and partly on account of difficulties of reproduction, it has not been possible to use many of the photographs kindly lent.

The accounts of military achievements have been compiled by Mr. E. Graham Walton. They are based on authoritative articles which appeared in the *Yorkshire Post* in 1919, with the addition of official information obtained since that date. In some other sections of the Record, also, use has been made of reports published in the local Press, and, for this, acknowledgments are offered to the *Yorkshire Post* and *Yorkshire Evening Post*, the *Leeds Mercury*, the *Yorkshire Observer* and the *Yorkshire Evening News*. To the services rendered by the Press in war time there is but a brief allusion in this volume. Those services were of incalculable value in many ways, and not least in steadying public opinion and fostering a spirit of determination. Yet, all the time, newspaper staffs, depleted by younger men, were working under a strain, the severity of which the general public could know nothing ; and some, even the oldest, of us, were doing our " bit " outside the regular duties of office.

The third part of the book comprises a Roll of Honour compiled by Mr. C. E. Mulholland, of whose untiring labours mention is made in a separate prefatory note. The Roll contains the names of nearly ten thousand of those from Leeds who laid down their lives.

For consistent encouragement in his task the author is greatly indebted to Professor Grant and the City Librarian, who, indeed, are jointly responsible for the first inception of the scheme. Projected early in 1921 by the Corporation Libraries and Arts Committee, of which Councillor F. Bentley is Chairman, the work as a whole received a direct stimulus from the then Lord Mayor (Alderman A. Braithwaite), and it is now brought to completion at the close of the Lord Mayoralty of Alderman Frank Fountain.

W. HERBERT SCOTT.

Leeds, October, 1923.

CONTENTS.

	PAGE
FOREWORD	.. ix.

PART I. THE STORY.

CHAPTER
I.	THE FIRST SHOCK OF WAR ..	3
II.	FACING THE SITUATION	9
III.	FOR KING AND COUNTRY	16
IV.	THE RECRUITING CAMPAIGN ..	23
V.	WAR IN EARNEST ..	31
VI.	TIGHTENING THE BELT	38
VII.	STRAIN AND STRESS	48
VIII.	NEARING THE END	58
IX.	THE ARMISTICE—AND AFTER	66

PART II. THE RECORD.

SECTION
I. ACHIEVEMENTS OF LEEDS TERRITORIALS—

1ST BRIGADE WEST RIDING ROYAL FIELD ARTILLERY	75
49TH (W.R.) DIVISIONAL SIGNALS T.A.	84
31ST DIVISIONAL ENGINEERS	86
7TH BATTALION (PRINCE OF WALES'S OWN) WEST YORKSHIRE REGIMENT	90
8TH BATTALION DO.	.. 100
THE SECOND LINE BATTALIONS	.. 108
CYCLISTS' CORPS ..	.. 110
THE LEEDS 'PALS'	.. 111
LEEDS 'BANTAMS'	.. 127
ARMY SERVICE CORPS	.. 135
ROYAL ARMY VETERINARY CORPS	.. 138
VICTORIA CROSS HEROES ..	.. 139

II. HOME DEFENCE—

THE VOLUNTEER BATTALIONS	.. 146
R.A.S.C. MOTOR TRANSPORT VOLUNTEERS	.. 152
WORK OF THE SPECIAL CONSTABLES ..	.. 158

III. WHEN ZEPPELINS CAME   .. 163

IV. TRIUMPHS OF INDUSTRY—
    THE FIRST NATIONAL SHELL FACTORY 172
        Armley, Newlay, Guns from Hunslet, Women do men's work, Gun testing, an output worth £13,000,000.
    SHELL-FILLING AT BARNBOW 182
        Women's Industry and Courage, Textile Requisites and Organisation.
    SUBSIDIARY WORK AND ARMY EQUIPMENT 188
        Leeds built battle-plane ; the Clothing Depôts.

V. HOW THE UNIVERSITY HELPED 193

VI. CARE OF THE SICK AND WOUNDED—
    MEDICAL AND HOSPITAL SERVICE 200
    2ND NORTHERN GENERAL HOSPITAL.—The Nursing Service ; East Leeds War Hospital ; Extensions at Beckett's Park ; Orthopaedic Treatment .. 204
    THE VOLUNTEER BEARER COMPANY 219
    VOLUNTARY HOSPITALS.—Harewood House ; Templenewsam ; Gledhow Hall ; Lotherton Hall ; Stapleton Park ; Ledstone Hall ; Swillington House ; Chapeltown and Roundhay 220
    MUSIC AND ENTERTAINMENT.—" Two Arts " Voluntary Effort ; " Music in War Time " ; The Wounded Warriors' Welcome 231
    LIFE IN HOSPITAL : THROUGH THE CHAPLAIN'S EYES 239

VII. MUNICIPAL ACTIVITIES—
    LORD MAYORS IN WAR TIME 247
    CORPORATION OFFICIALS' SPECIAL WORK 277
    LIBRARIES AND ART GALLERY 280

VIII. SOME ECONOMIES AND RESTRICTIONS—
    THE WAR SAVINGS MOVEMENT 282
    FUEL AND LIGHTING CONTROL 284
    FOOD CONTROL 287

IX. BENEVOLENT AGENCIES—
    THE LADY MAYORESS'S COMMITTEE .. 290
    THE HOSPITABLE Y.M.C.A. 296
    FLAG DAY COLLECTIONS 297
    WOMEN'S WAR EMPLOYMENT 299
    RELIEF OF BELGIAN REFUGEES .. 301
    THE SOCIETY OF FRIENDS 305

X. ENLISTMENTS AND EXEMPTIONS –
    THE RECRUITING EFFORT 311
    THE LOCAL MILITARY TRIBUNAL .. 314
    THE APPEAL TRIBUNAL 316
    METHODS AND PROCEDURE .. 318

PART III.

" ROLL OF HONOUR " 323

LIST OF ILLUSTRATIONS.

	PAGE
Town Hall, Leeds	Frontispiece
Leeds "Pals" Recruiting Car	13
Leeds "Pals" Advance Party at Colsterdale	33
Lieut.-Col. E. A. HIRST, R.F.A.	75
Lieut.-Col. F. MIDDLETON, R.F.A.	75
Lieut.-Col. W. F. LUCEY, R.F.A.	75
Lieut.-Col. W. HEPWORTH (Leeds Rifles) W. Yorks. Regt.	75
Lieut.-Col. A. BRAY, Royal Corps of Signals	84
Major E. HOPPER,, Divisional Engineers	84
Lieut.-Col. R. A. HUDSON (Leeds Rifles) W. Yorks. Regt.	84
Lieut.-Col. J. W. ALEXANDER (Leeds Rifles) W. Yorks. Regt.	84
Engineers (210th Company) Inspection at Ilkley	86
Officers of 7th Batt. (Leeds Rifles) W. Yorks. Regt.	89
Parade of 7th Batt. (Leeds Rifles) W. Yorks. Regt.	91
Tower of the Cloth Hall, Ypres	93
Lieut.-Col. H. D. BOUSFIELD (Leeds Rifles) W. Yorks. Regt.	98
Lieut.-Col. C. H. TETLEY (Leeds Rifles) W. Yorks. Regt.	98
Lieut.-Col. the Hon. F. S. JACKSON (Leeds Rifles) W. Yorks. Regt.	98
Lieut.-Col. A. E. KIRK (Leeds Rifles) W. Yorks. Regt.	98
Inspection of the 2/7th and 2/8th Batt. (Leeds Rifles) W. Yorks. Regt.	108
Lieut.-Col. STUART C. TAYLOR, Leeds "Pals"	111
Capt. L. BATHURST, R.A.M.C., "Leeds "Pals"	111
Lieut.-Col. J. W. STEAD, "Leeds "Pals"	111
Lieut.-Col. E. KITSON CLARK (Leeds Rifles) W. Yorks. Regt.	111
Alderman Sir CHARLES H. WILSON, Knt., M.P.	112
Parade of Army Service Corps, Leeds	135
Col. J. C. CHAMBERS, A.S.C.	136
Lieut.-Col. J. PRESTON, Leeds Volunteers, W.R. Regt.	136
Major CECIL H. TAYLOR, Leeds Volunteers, W.R. Regt.	136
Major S. R. RUSH, Leeds Volunteers, W.R. Regt.	136
Parade of Leeds Volunteer Battalions	146
W. BURNS LINDLEY, Chief Constable	158
R. NOEL MIDDLETON, Special Police	158
F. E. SAVILLE, Special Police	158
Lord MANTON, Chairman, National Shell Filling Factory	182
The Hon. RUPERT E. BECKETT	182
Sir ALGERNON FIRTH, Bart.	182
Sir JOHN McLAREN	182
Machinery Hall at Barnbow Shell-Filling Factory	184
Component Store, Cartridge Factory, Barnbow	186

	PAGE
Barnbow, Armistice Celebrations	188
A. G. LUPTON, Pro-Chancellor, Leeds University	193
Sir MICHAEL E. SADLER, Vice-Chancellor, Leeds University ..	193
Sir BERKELEY MOYNIHAN, Bart., Chairman, Army Medical Advisory Board	193
Lieut.-Col. ARTHUR SMITHELLS, F.R.S., Leeds University ..	193
Lieut.-Col. J. F. DOBSON, 1st Administrator, 2nd Northern General Hospital	200
Brevet-Col. H. LITTLEWOOD, 2nd Administrator, 2nd Northern General Hospital	200
Col. A. D. SHARP, R.A.M.C. (T.F.)	200
Lieut.-Col. H. COLLINSON, R.A.M.C. (T.F.)	200
Visit of H.M. the King to East Leeds Military Hospital ..	209
The Earl of HAREWOOD, Lord Lieutenant of the West Riding	219
Dr. HOYLAND SMITH, Commandant, Volunteer Bearer Company	219
J. W. JESSOP, Volunteer Bearer Company	219
Lady DOROTHY WOOD, Commandant, Temple Newsam V.A.D. Hospital	220
Miss E. S. INNES, Matron-in-Chief, 2nd Northern General Hospital	220
Miss E. M. CLIFF, Commandant, Gledhow Hall V.A.D. Hospital	220
Dining and Recreation Hall, V.A.D. Hospital, Temple Newsam	224
Col. Sir EDWARD A. BROTHERTON, Bart., Lord Mayor 1913-1914	251
JAMES E. BEDFORD, Lord Mayor 1914-1915	253
Alderman CHARLES LUPTON, Lord Mayor 1915-1916	259
EDMUND GEORGE ARNOLD, Lord Mayor 1916-1917	265
FRANK GOTT, Lord Mayor 1917-1918	273
JOSEPH HENRY, Lord Mayor 1918-1919	277
THOMAS B. DUNCAN, Lord Mayor 1919-1920	278
R. GEOFFREY ELLIS, M.P., Chairman of Executive, War Savings Committee	282
Rev. Canon BICKERSTETH, Hon. Chaplain, Leeds Rifles ..	282
Lord AIREDALE	282
J. B. HAMILTON, Fuel Overseer	282
JOHN GORDON, First Chairman Recruiting Committee ..	311
Alderman W. E. FARR, Chairman Recruiting Committee ..	311
Sir ROBERT FOX, Town Clerk	311
Councillor OWEN CONNELLAN, Member of Local Tribunal ..	311
Alderman FRANK FOUNTAIN, Lord Mayor 1922-1923	322

Foreword

CERTAIN English towns have already produced the history of their doings during the Great War, and it was felt by many that Leeds should not allow her great effort to pass unchronicled. These feelings were brought to a head in a letter written in October 1920, to the *Yorkshire Post*, drawing attention to the volumes of extracts from the local Press which had been prepared by Mr. T. W. Hand, the City Librarian, and urging that they should be made the basis of a history of the City during the War. The idea was taken up warmly by the City Council, and Mr. W. H. Scott was induced to undertake the task. The appearance of the book has been delayed beyond what was at first hoped by various difficulties, which were chiefly economical. But now "the end crowns the work," and the energies and sufferings of our City find a worthy chronicle.

There has been much discussion since the war as to the proper form which memorials should take. But if our object is, as the phrase implies, to save from forgetfulness the name and the memory of those who fought for us, and of the incredible efforts with which they were supported by the population that remained at home, it is clear that something is wanted besides cenotaphs, crosses, obelisks and allegorical figures; something more than the mere lists of the fallen which affection and piety have set up in public places throughout the country. The printer's art and the historian's pen must be called in to help, and while the memories of those four years are still fresh someone must transfer them to the written page, which is, strangely, more enduring than granite or bronze.

Mr. Scott's work is then, in its original impulse, one of affection and piety, and as such, we cannot doubt, it will be welcomed by a wide circle of readers in Leeds and Yorkshire. But it is something more than this; it is a valuable contribution to history, and will be of the greatest use to the historian, who undertakes to tell to a future generation the history of the Great War. As we look back on the great crises of the past we often ask, but usually in vain, what it was like to be alive then, and how the foreign struggle affected the domestic life of the country. What did Yorkshire think of the coming and the passing of the Spanish Armada? How did these great happenings affect the little group of cottages at the bottom of Briggate which was then called Leeds? They probably knew very little about the great crisis, for one of the marked changes that the progress of invention has introduced into our modern life is the closer and more immediate relation that it has permitted between the individual and the world at large. Or, to come to a later time, how interesting it would be to know from authentic sources how our community, now grown a little larger, regarded the Puritan War and the Whig Revolution: and in what way the life of our city, already an important part of the nation's life, was affected by the struggle with the French Revolution and Napoleon. But those of us who are interested in such an enquiry have to turn to collections of old letters and attempt to infuse life and meaning into the meagre notices of the contemporary Press. A century later there came upon our community, vastly grown in importance, in self-consciousness, in organisation, as well as in population, a danger far more terrible than that threatened by Philip's Spanish

Fleet or Napoleon's Army at Boulogne. The latest survivors of the Great War will be eagerly asked by the rising generation "What was it like to be alive then ? Let us see with your eyes and feel with your heart and brain the bursting of the news on a generation that hardly believed in the possibility of war, the continuous departure of the troops until all the young manhood of Leeds had gone, the return of the wounded, the arrival of the lists of those who would never return, the darkened streets, the shortened food supply, the searchlights sweeping the clouds at night, the alarm of a Zeppelin attack, the hope and the despair, and all the pathos and the riot, all the spontaneous outburst of feelings that defy analysis, when the Armistice came, and at last there was an end."

Mr. Scott's practised pen has provided an answer to these questions in this vigorous but sober narrative. I may be permitted to praise the plan he has adopted. He has divided the book into two sharply distinguished parts. First there is the continuous narrative of the war period as seen and felt in Leeds. This part is not overburdened with names or dates, which in excess make a book so difficult of digestion. Then comes the second part dealing with different aspects of the city's energies and sufferings, and here, as the subject demands, Mr. Scott has grown detailed and statistical, and gives us names and dates in plenty. Here will be found a necessarily slight record of the doings of those military units that were most closely associated with Leeds ; the organisation of medical relief ; the work of the special constables ; the tasks that fell to the lot of the Lord Mayors of the city. Here, too, will be found a long list of the fallen—a very genuine war memorial this—and of many who gained distinction, with a special note of the exploits of those who won the

Victoria Cross. Of special note, too, is the chapter which describes the work done by the Society of Friends and others for the relief of the Belgian refugees.

The book will speak for itself and I can add nothing of interest. Perhaps I may be allowed one or two reflections. I am left, as I finish reading what Mr. Scott has written, with a strong impression of the amazing energy shown, and the efficiency of the work done. I think it is worth while to emphasise this. The war is now five years behind us. There has been the inevitable crop of books by the soldiers and politicians who played a part in the struggle. The necessity for unity and for silence which the war imposed has been removed. We have had a good deal of acid criticism, of charges and replies and counter-charges ; and we may fairly say that no reputation of soldier or of statesman stands now unchallenged. The result of all this on the minds of some has been to create the impression that the whole thing was a gigantic muddle, that the talk of patriotism was only a cloak for selfish aims, and that candour looks in vain for genius or real ability among our rulers and our generals. I have certainly heard it said, and I think seen it written, that the England of the Great War compares badly in these respects with the England of the Napoleonic struggle. But all such views are really absurd. There was no such bungling either at home or abroad between 1914 and 1918 as there was during the first fifteen years of the nineteenth century. If the failures in Gallipoli and Mesopotamia receive their worst interpretation, they are still far superior in plan and execution to the Walcheren expedition of 1809 or the early stages of the Peninsula War. Nor have the statesmen of the Great War much reason to fear comparison with those of the earlier period, though the great name of Pitt is among those who fought against Napoleon. I will venture to prophesy that amongst the permanent impressions left on the pages of history by the Great War will be—the international anarchy out of which it grew and out of which other wars will grow if a remedy be not found—the unparalleled endurance of pain and suffering shown by both sides and all classes—and the wonderful power of organisation and initiative to meet unforeseen difficulties shown by our own country (though not to the exclusion of others). And for this last result we are indebted to our liberty, to our habit of criticism and discussion, and to the extent to which the executive government has "taken the people into partnership."

There is one phase of the city's life during the war, often hinted at in Mr. Scott's pages, but nowhere continuously or separately treated. I mean the effect of the war on the minds and thoughts and on the temper and convictions of men. The war novelists have given us something of this, but their books have usually been written under the influence of some overmastering passion or enthusiasm. It would be interesting to collect the opinions of ministers of religion, of social workers, of magistrates and teachers on this head. I do not know whether the city of Leeds would have anything special to contribute from her experiences. As a teacher of history at the University I seemed to see my pupils passing through various phases. There was first the mood of amazement that the thing could be. It was, said someone, as incredible as the Day of Judgment, and we looked on as if it were at the setting up of the great throne, the opening of the books and the blowing of the archangels' trumpets. That was followed by an eager desire to understand. Lectures on the origins of the war, or the history and character of the belligerent countries were well attended; any hints in elucidation of the strategy of the armies were much welcomed. But that mood passed. The war was too huge to be understood. The problems were too many for the mind to grasp. The news so often turned out false, or only partially true, that a spirit of complete scepticism was engendered. Prophecies failed so often that we hardly cared to look forward. I remember a student who had suffered the loss of many of her relations saying to me, " I seem to be losing everything ; even the power to feel." The last counter-offensive of July, 1918, did not seem to rouse among the women, who by that time formed the majority of students, the same hopes that we elders felt. I did not realise how great was the unconscious pressure on their hearts and minds until the 11th November, 1918. Lectures proceeded, but all ears were waiting for something else. Then a newspaper-boy ran down College Road shouting " Signature of the Armistice " ; and without invitation or permission the students left their laboratories and their lecture-rooms, and poured into the streets to join the general jubilation. It was no mere desire for a " rag," but the rebound from a pressure that had almost touched breaking point.

But I have no right to add my reminiscences to those that Mr. Scott has collected. I end by commending most heartily his book to the attention of the public of Leeds.

A. J. GRANT.

LEEDS UNIVERSITY.

PART I.
THE STORY.

THE STORY.

I.

THE FIRST SHOCK OF WAR.

> " Turn, turn my wheel ! What is begun
> At daybreak must at dark be done,
>   To-morrow will be another day ;
> To-morrow the hot furnace flame
> Will search the heart and try the frame,
> And stamp with honour or with shame
>   These vessels made of clay."
>
> Longfellow.

IN the experience of men, as of nations, there come days the memory of which can never be effaced. Tuesday, August the 4th, 1914, was one of them.

Cast your mind back—those who can—and try to conjure up the sensations of that eventful day, and the days which immediately preceded and followed it. Who can recall their fateful significance without some sort of inward emotion ? The dread suspense, the tense feeling of anxiety, the hopes and fears, doubts and questionings— how they crowd the mental vision as once they clouded the serenity of a summer holiday ! And yet they were but the precursor of an ordeal that with still greater severity racked the heart and tried the soul—an ordeal, too, not of days merely but of years. The strain and stress of that long period of war time can never be forgotten. Hallowed by tears, sanctified by sacrifice, it remains a haunting memory handed on to future generations by all who lived through it.

The causes of the great European conflict are now a matter of history. There is little need to dwell on them here. Our object in these pages is to review the magnificent part taken by the good city of Leeds in helping to hasten the day of victory. A glance back at the pre-war situation, however, is relevant to the story.

Consider what was happening at home and abroad. First, there was the Serajevo incident of June 28th, 1914—the murder of the heir-apparent to the throne of Austria-Hungary. The Austrian government regarded this crime as part of an organised movement by Servia. It stirred feelings of horror, true ; but Leeds people, like other inhabitants of Great Britain, felt no particular apprehension as to the ability of statesmanship to compose the differences that arose. For several weeks our public and private affairs proceeded as usual. We had our own troubles —unrest in the industrial world, grave disorders in Ireland—but even these did not divert attention from the ordinary routine of business and pleasure.

In the first week of July, King George and Queen Mary went to Scotland to fulfil a round of public engagements and, incidentally, to inspect naval and ordnance works. Little did one think how soon would be brought into action the engines of destruction and defence there exhibited! Coincident with this Royal visit, Leeds was the meeting place of the National Association for the Prevention of Consumption, and everyone's ear was sought on behalf of measures for checking the dire White Scourge. From the salving of life physically, the city, in the following week, turned to a consideration of the life spiritual, as presented by the Wesleyan Conference. Then, a few days later, the great Yorkshire Show was held at Bradford, and thither many visitors flew from Leeds by aeroplane, never dreaming on what momentous errands aircraft was ere long to be employed.

About the same time local Territorials were making ready for their annual camps, and the sport-loving populace were speculating on the ultimate result of the Cricket Championship contest. In London, on the King's return from Scotland, a conference was in progress at Buckingham Palace in the vain hope of settling grave Irish difficulties, and Parliament was showing some concern over a Housing Bill. In Leeds, also, the housing question was the subject of anxious thought at a Government Inquiry, and as the month drew to a close the city's pride was flattered by a visit paid by distinguished physicians from Continental countries (including Germany), from our colonies, and from the United States, who had heard of the fame of our General Infirmary.

In the midst of these domestic abstractions there dropped the terrible bomb of Austria's ultimatum to Serbia, and, in two or three days, it exploded with a declaration of war. Passing concern now deepened into alarm. Quickly the news came that Russia was mobilising in defence of Serbia, that martial law had been proclaimed in Germany, and that France, as Russia's ally, was preparing to ward off attack.

What did it all portend ? And what was to be the attitude of Great Britain ? Was it conceivable that we could possibly be involved in the war that threatened ? Questions like these were in everyone's mouth.

" It is unthinkable," said our pacifists : " Why should we intervene in disputes between other nations ? " Accordingly they sent their appeals broadcast urging people to do their utmost to keep England neutral.

Friday, July 31 and Saturday, August 1st, in turn, saw the crisis intensified. The Stock Market was demoralised ; the Exchanges were closed ; the price of flour rose immediately 3s. a sack ; the Bank Rate advanced, first to 8 % and then to 10 % ; children away at school in Germany were ordered to leave that country ; continental travellers tumbled over one another in the rush to get back home ; eager Bank Holiday excursionists who had started across the channel were turned back and foreigners disappeared from this country in large numbers. Whatever England's decision, it was clear that grave dangers lay ahead.

There remained one hope. Diplomacy was at work. Our Foreign Minister—then Sir Edward Grey—was all this time striving to save the peace of Europe; and indeed he explored every avenue to that end. But alas! all attempts at mediation failed. Germany was the stumbling block. " Der Tag " had arrived, and Prussian militarism was not to be turned from its tyrannous purpose. This became the more evident as the ill-omened hours passed and brought us nearer another week.

Determined holiday-makers, tempted by lavish railway facilities which still offered, had gone to the coast and the inland resorts, for the week-end, with somewhat of a feeling that, whatever happened, the customary outing must not be missed. But all had a certain foreboding and those who stayed at home, perhaps, felt the position the more keenly. On the Sunday in the churches and chapels there were prayers for peace; and invariably the first thing with which one person greeted another had some reference to the awful possibilities. Special Sunday editions of the local newspapers increased the tension and were bought up feverishly. The Leeds Rifles, marching to the railway station to entrain for the Scarborough camp, hesitated in deference to a rumour that they were to be embodied at once; but there was no confirmation of the report, and they stuck to their original programme. Meanwhile, Briggate, Boar Lane, City Square filled with anxious questioners. People gathered in groups and discussed the situation. Everywhere there was the sense of impending disaster. It was a black outlook.

Monday morning brought no relief. The suspense grew greater. The banks closed down, not for this day only but for four days on end; and a moratorium was proclaimed. Germany, it was now known, had declared war on Russia and was invading France. Liners were being recalled in mid-ocean. The shipping trade of Hull, Grimsby and other ports, was paralysed. The Bank Holiday railway excursions were suddenly cancelled— the trains had to be held in readiness for the troops. The Territorials in camp were ordered to return immediately to head-quarters.

Still there was a faint possibility that, even at the eleventh hour, the threatened catastrophe might be averted. As history will record, the British Cabinet waited until the hour of midnight on Tuesday, August 4th, hoping against hope.

Could it be believed that Germany was so dead to all feelings of shame as to persist in her high-handed course? And yet it was plain from her "infamous proposal" that the mediatory offers of Great Britain would be of no avail.

What Germany wanted was that Great Britain should consent to the violation of Belgium's neutrality—should, in fact, stand aside while Belgium was being invaded and France crushed—and, in return, should enjoy the doubtful privilege of good relations with Germany after Kaiser William had defeated France and annexed the French colonies! Germany, equally with Great Britain was pledged to respect the integrity of Belgium. To Germany, however, that pledge was, in her Chancellor's own words, merely "a scrap of paper." In response to Belgium's appeal Great Britain, in honour bound, had no option but to decline so disgraceful a bargain.

Hence the British ultimatum of August 4th to which Germany gave no answer except by forcibly violating Belgian territory.

And so it was that when we opened our newspapers on the Wednesday morning we read that Great Britain had declared war against the common enemy.

"I was sceptical about the hostile designs of Germany," wrote an eminent pacifist of that time; "then Germany by a single act reversed the moral situation. War which had so often been a crime suddenly became a duty."

Almost in a flash the nation realised that, after all, Lord Roberts had been right in the warnings he uttered long before. That great, wise and far-seeing military authority had bidden us be wary and prepared. But his voice was as of one crying in the wilderness. Some even derided him. Now, however, was no time for recriminations: the mischief was done and it could only be repaired by unity of action and steadfast endeavour.

II.
FACING THE SITUATION.

*"If it be aught toward the general good,
Set honour in one eye and death i' the other
And I will look on both indifferently."*
Shakespeare.

With no light heart, and yet with some sense of relief, Leeds entered on the tasks that patriotic sentiment prescribed. The first shock of war almost dazed our people, but by no means to inertness. Leeds was very much on the alert. It could not belie its motto. "*Pro Rege et Lege*" had now a profounder meaning than ever. A few there were whose intense hatred of war of any sort blinded them to the issues. But even those—those whose opinion was worth anything—who on the fateful eve had gone so far as to affirm utter scepticism regarding Germany's intentions, were constrained to admit that Britain's cause was just. All parties were at one in the determination to stand firm for King and Country. The whole masses of the population faced the crisis with calmness.

One topic alone now engaged public attention. People's minds seethed with a tremendous upheaval of thought and speculation. Was not the nation committed to a course the like of which was unknown in living memory? Nevertheless no faltering voice made itself heard. The Government's straightforward, honourable decision, confirmed by Parliament, inspired confidence. The national emergency measures which immediately followed were a spur to action that readily elicited a cheerful response. The King's message of pride in the Colonial offers of help, the Proclamations calling out the Army Reserve, embodying the Territorials, giving military control over the railways and otherwise safeguarding the realm—all deepened the impression created by the declaration of war.

Hurriedly returning from camp, the Territorials met with a rousing, though in no way a "Jingoist," reception, and the same fine temper marked their send-off to training centres a little later. "I am positively sure," said the Earl of Harewood (Chairman of the West Riding Territorial Association and Lord Lieut. of the West Riding) "I am positively sure that if the Germans land on our shores you will give them such a warm reception that they will never come again."

But one note of apprehension was struck. For the moment there was almost a panic caused by the sudden rise in food prices. Alarmed by the thought of a possible scarcity, many people rushed heedlessly to buy more than they required of flour, bacon and other provisions. Thus a complete dislocation of supplies threatened until, after a day or two, the Government regulated the position. There were fears of unemployment, too ; there were doubts as to the instant effect on commerce and industry ; there were difficulties foreshadowed by the calling-up of men in the police force and in the various municipal services.

Such forebodings, however, did not persist. They were speedily dispelled. Precautionary steps were taken without delay. On the day a state of war was announced, the city's General Purposes Committee at the call of its Chairman, Alderman, now Sir, Charles H. Wilson, met to prepare for eventualities, and a special meeting of the City Council was convened. The Lord Mayor, Mr. (afterwards Sir) Edward A. Brotherton set the key-note of service. "One half of my capital," he declared, "is at the disposal of my country, and one half, nay, all my income shall be given up if required." The holidays of the Corporation servants were suspended and arrangements were put in hand with the object of finding work for unemployed persons. At the same time employers of labour generally came together, on the invitation of the Lord Mayor, to devise a scheme for uniformity of action in respect of positions left vacant by men who were called up.

"Business as usual" was impossible in that eventful first week. Moreover the Banks remained closed until the Friday. Men and women of all classes were concentrating on war effort and organisation, considering how best to face new and strange responsibilities.

Almost the first definite undertaking made by Leeds was to provide 2,000 beds for the wounded. To begin with, the Training College at Beckett's Park was requisitioned as a military hospital ; and without delay was adapted and equipped for its new purpose. The required doctors, nurses, voluntary aid staff—all held themselves in readiness for duty. Leeds University students of both sexes were enrolled for voluntary aid work, and women all over the city clamoured to be made use of ; fully two thousand of them, responding to an appeal issued by the Lady Mayoress (Mrs. Charles Ratcliffe) attended a Town Hall meeting to inaugurate a movement of personal service especially directed to the provision of garments for the sailors and soldiers, a supply of hospital bandages and similar benevolent work. The question of relief and allowances to men on service also received prompt consideration, preliminaries having been arranged by the City Council with the co-operation of the Chamber of Commerce.

Meanwhile, one series of incidents crowded on another. Aliens who had failed to take out nationalisation papers had to suffer the discomfort of arrest and detention at the Town Hall, among them being some fifty or sixty Germans who were subsequently interned. Precautions, too, were taken against the sinister operations of spies, and in helping to guard the water supply at Headingley, Eccup and other points, the Boy Scouts made themselves useful. Also, twenty wireless stations owned by amateurs and students were dismantled. Crowds of young men flocked to the recruiting offices in Hanover Square, and offered themselves for service at home or abroad; and a Citizens' League was formed, prepared to carry out any essential home duties. There was no question about the splendid spirit of those early days.

Nor was there any slackening of effort as time went on.

The seriousness of the outlook was brought home more and more while the Germans were hacking their way through Belgium, bent on a hasty thrust at Paris before our forces could be ready to aid the French Army. Yet none lost faith in our arms or in our cause. Rather was zeal quickened, and one of many instances of this was the Jewish appeal for the formation of a Jewish contingent. Only the clothing operatives were greatly perturbed. There were fears that the industry—of such vital importance to Leeds—might not recover from the emphatic check of war. It's "good time," however, was not long in coming. Army orders soon gave ample employment. Contracts for boots, and for khaki cloth, too, rolled in. The early queues of workless grew smaller and smaller. Trade prospects all round brightened, though it meant a diversion of ways and means and some considerable adaptation to the novelty of the industrial situation.

In less than a month from the declaration of war, the combined energies of Leeds people were moving like a well-regulated machine oiled by the accord of all classes of the community, parties and creeds. Party politics were silenced. It was agreed there should be no contested Municipal elections. There was but one duty for all.

At the beginning of September the Leeds City (Pals) Battalion, which was destined to cover itself with glory at the Front, came into being

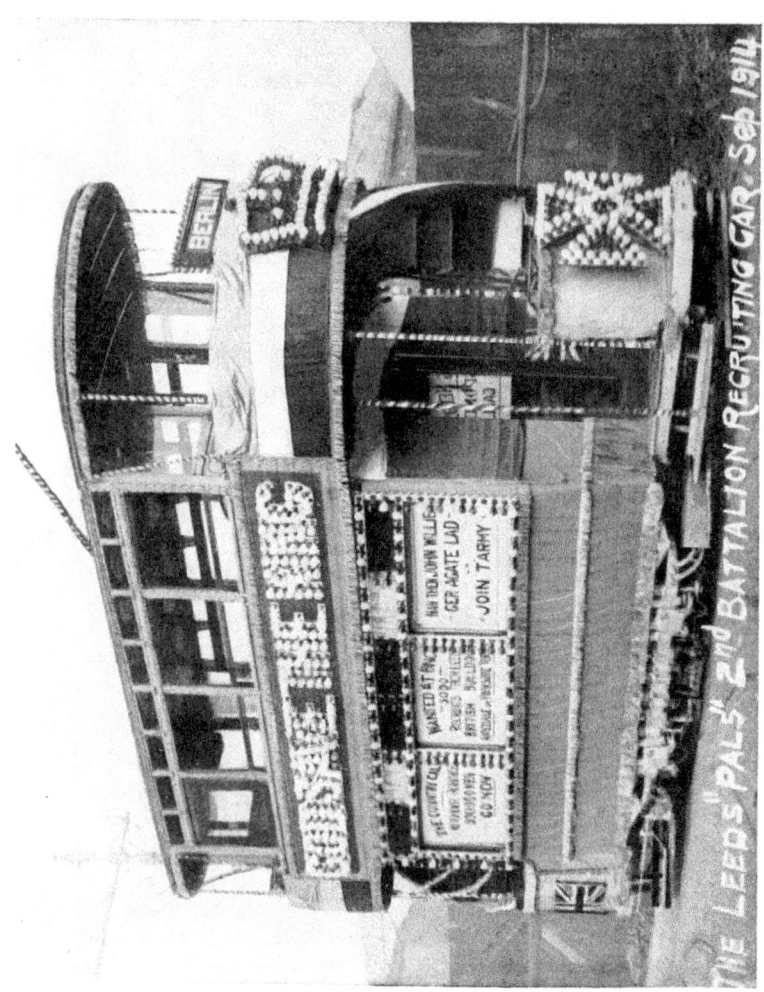

The Leeds "Pals" 2nd Battalion on Recruiting Car, 1914.

under the Command of Col. J. Walter Stead, V.D., Lord Mayor Brotherton bearing the expense of its formation, and becoming honorary Colonel. Crowded meetings were held in the Town Hall in the interest of recruiting, which also received a fillip from a nightly tour of an illuminated tramcar through all parts of the City. If anything more were needed to stir public feeling, it was surely the sight of the first batch of wounded —some 80 men—who now arrived at the Midland Railway Station in Leeds, travelling direct from the Marne battlefield, and were accommodated at Beckett's Park Hospital.

By the end of September, 5,000 recruits had joined Lord Kitchener's army in Leeds, and 1,200 had joined the " Pals " battalion ; the reserve battalions of the 7th and 8th West Yorkshires were almost completed ; the University had got to work on such matters of national importance as the testing of woollen fabrics, the provision of dyes, and so forth ; women everywhere were busily engaged under the auspices of the Lady Mayoress's Committee, carrying out their special voluntary duties—not the least noteworthy being visits to soldiers' wives in connection with the war allowance organisation. There was something for everybody to do who had a mind to help, and helpers were not lacking.

Money was forthcoming as well as personal service. At the date just mentioned a sum of £40,000 had been contributed by Leeds citizens to the Prince of Wales' National Relief Fund ; and not only offers of hospitality but the means to provide temporary homes had been received on behalf of the Belgian refugees who were now pouring into the city in their hundreds.

At the beginning of November a force of special constables was constituted, and it was about this time too, that Leeds woke up to the fact that there was more employment in its midst than had been known for many a long month. Hunslet, Holbeck, Armley and every industrial quarter shared in the improvement. Engineering and textile firms alike were working at full pressure on Government orders, one group of which, by the way, related to no less than a million uniforms. A month later, through the efforts of the new Lord Mayor (Mr. J. E. Bedford), sanction was given to the formation of a "Bantams" Battalion (the 17th West Yorkshires) to meet the case of men of small stature who wished to go on active service; and steps were taken to form a Volunteer Corps for home defence.

By the end of the year Leeds had provided 15,000 recruits, apart from those men who had joined other than purely local regiments, and not reckoning some 5,000 who were in the forces at the outbreak of war. Included in the number were nearly 900 Corporation servants of all grades and departments, a large proportion being tramwaymen whose places were soon filled by women.

Such were some of the more notable happenings and conditions as the year 1914 closed. The first shock of war had passed, but the mingled feelings of wonderment, hope and fear, solicitude and confidence, remained. The war was not over by Christmas as so many had prophesied would be the case. The Russian "steam roller" had proved a delusion. Every month has seen an extension of the conflict and the opening up of new theatres of war. If there had been any doubt regarding Lord Kitchener's estimate of a three years' struggle it was now well-nigh dispelled.

With the new year came fresh determination to play the man. The public appetite for news, which had been scarcely appeased even by Sunday war editions of the newspapers, increased from now onwards, yet so accustomed were we all to the change in our lives that, dreaded as were the reports of casualties in many a home, the whole outlook was viewed more with the steadfastness of a silent watchman than the feverishness of the alarmist.

Looking back to that early period, and remembering all that the city endured in common with other centres of population, perhaps it may be wondered if people would have kept their heads so well had they known what was yet to come. Depressed indeed were some, even to the extent of shunning all forms of entertainment. "How can we sit still enjoying ourselves when the country is in danger, and our men are falling?" Such was the plea. Others argued that it was a duty to keep cheerful; it was not good to give way to heaviness of spirit. "Some relaxation is essential," was their contention. Truly the pursuit of pleasure seemed often out of place, but who dare say it was reckless? Enough to record here that few, if any, realised how much more had yet to be accomplished over and above the early preparations, how much more had yet to happen to pain the mind and try the heart.

Still, with hope and a good courage, Leeds followed an even course in all phases of life, and at every turn of the wheel of fate and experience managed to evolve ways and means of coping with the difficulties of the situation, adapting itself to circumstances, and steeling the heart of the community to fresh impulses of derring-do.

III.
FOR KING AND COUNTRY.

" Listen, young heroes, your country is calling !
Time strikes the hour for the brave and the true !
Now, while the foremost are fighting and falling,
Fill up the ranks that have opened for you."
Oliver Wendell Holmes.

" The present state of public affairs in Europe is such as to constitute an imminent national danger." So ran one of the sentences of the King's Proclamation. Emergency measures were necessary for public safety and the defence of the realm. Of prime importance, therefore, was the embodiment of the Territorial Force and the calling up of the Army Reserve.

The need for that course struck home. In Leeds the call to arms met with a ready response. There was at once a rush to rejoin Territorial units or to enlist in the Regular or New army, and the enthusiasm during the first few days grew stronger with every movement of the men already in khaki. Leeds indeed, it was observed at the time, wore almost the aspect of a town in military occupation. Never before had such sights been seen in Fenton Street, Woodhouse Lane, Claypit Lane and Carlton Hill. Artillery, Engineers, Rifles, Hussars, all were marching hither and thither, undergoing medical examination, receiving instructions, finding billets or being quartered in barracks and schools, in readiness for training, and the central parts of the city were thronged to see and cheer them. Stirring, too, were the scenes on their departure, and inspiring were some of the words spoken by chaplains and commanding officers.

Such sights and sentiments did not fail of effect. The whole populace were stirred. Here, for example, are some scraps of talk overheard by a *Yorkshire Evening News* correspondent, on the fringe of a crowd bidding farewell to one contingent :

" I'll tell you what I think, guv'ner : this German Emperor isn't right in his napper. He's taken leave of his senses, or they've taken leave of him!" "G'luck to you, my lads!" the speaker shouted, as a party in khaki passed.

"I've got two lads i' t' army, and I wish I was young enough to join myself," said another.

"I wish they'd send t'wimmin to deal with him," (Kaiser William) cried a woman; "just fancy! he insults t'owd Empress o' Russia! He's a bonny specimen of a man, he is, and no mistake! I'd be ashamed to own him as a relation o' mine."

"That's reight, mother," rejoined her neighbour, "he owt to be flogged."

"Ay," exclaimed another dame, "he wor allus a bad 'un to his own mother, and them sort never come to onny good."

Like the sense of duty which immediatley animated so many, there was a cheerful disposition to swell the ranks of those who were eager to serve King and Country on the battlefield. At the recruiting office in Hanover Square hundreds who sought to enlist had to wait patiently in a long queue, or take their turn on the following day.

In less than a week the Northern Signal Corps (Leeds Engineers) had turned away 600 would-be recruits, and more reservists had offered themselves for service than the officials could deal with at the moment; indeed, at one stage, the difficulties actually caused some heartburning among men who had thrown up their civil occupations. Delays, unfortunately, there were at this period, and they were due largely to the lack of an adequate medical staff, the examining doctors having severe pressure put upon them in order to meet the demands of the situation and at the same time fulfil their obligations to private patients.

By the 16th of August both the 7th and 8th West Yorkshires (Leeds Rifles) had reached their full strength. The whole of the Territorial regiments of the city, in fact, had been brought up to a strength unknown before, and nearly a thousand men had enlisted in the new army founded by Lord Kitchener. The daily average of acceptances at the recruiting office was 80, and the stream of applicants still flowed steadily in. Some were rejected at first, on account of minor physical defects, as, for instance, defective teeth, but a relaxation of regulations later gave the disappointed men a chance which they did not fail to take in due time.

Of these early proceedings Dr. H. de Carle Woodcock contributes the following impression :—

"Any medical man who could spare time to examine recruits was welcomed. These boys lined up naked against the walls of the Tram Offices. How I remember them! How anxious they were to join up! A whole bunch of them swerved over to the group of medical men because we were rejecting few, and passing recruits in quickly. One drunken volunteer was turned out by an austere doctor who said the Army must not be degraded by "drink." However, the recruit came up again. I saw him enter the room, and in a few minutes he was in the Army. One old man who had been at Tel el Kebir came before me. When he was rejected as far too old he said, "You'll want me before you've finished."

"The examination was to me a strange one. Men who could jump and hop and shout, "Who goes there?" were thought by some examiners to be strong in wind and limb, strong enough to fight, whilst men with the classical faults of the recruiting tests, variocele flat foot, varicose veins, and the like, were rejected in large numbers. All these faults were subsequently ignored, and recruits who could shoot and march, whose internal organs were capable of bearing strain, were accepted.

"Undoubtedly in later days many men were admitted into the Army who were quite incapable of marching or fighting, who were indeed of no good to the Army, could not be of any good, and who were eventually rejected. In many cases they reached the Front only to be sent home.

"But in the early days, the men were on the whole the best men. If not always the best in physique, they were full of fine spirit. The policeman Bretherick standing outside the street door of the Recruiting Office was a valuable recruiting agent. Bretherick was too old to enlist but he sent his son and son-in-law. He told the crowd of waiting lads this. And his eloquence was simple and direct. "You've come here to enlist, and that's all you've come for, so march in!" And big lumps melted off the crowd and pushed through the door. Some were a little sheepish, some had flushed and some had pale faces; some were big, many were small. One thin lad was evidently suffering from phthisis—many were rejected on account of tuberculosis—"I know I am," he said to me, "but I thought I should get in, I could do something."

"As the months went by, it was evident that many unfit men had got in. I was able to compile a list of 167 who were known to the medical staff of the Tuberculosis Dispensary as tuberculous. Of these 60 to 70 were sent back during the first fifteen months, and fifty of them died. On the other hand, many sufferers from tuberculosis improved, even to the extent of apparent cure. In the Tuberculosis Hospitals, the same furor to enlist was shown and many beds were emptied, the men slipping out and slipping in to the Army. Later, the nation and the Army came to regret this, but who could blame the fiery enthusiasts who took the patriotic course?"

Lord Kitchener's special appeal undoubtedly gave an impetus to the movement, and Lord Mayor Brotherton's spirited action in regard to the proposed Leeds "Pals" battalion not only increased the enthusiasm but drew warm commendation from Lord Kitchener himself, who promptly telegraphed the following message:—

On behalf of His Majesty's Government I accept with gratitude your munificent offer to be responsible for the equipment of the Leeds Battalion. This example of generous patriotism will, I am persuaded, have a far-reaching effect. I wish the battalion every success, and shall be glad to see you if you wish to discuss matters at any time.

But there were many who, for peculiar reasons, either held back or were prevented from joining up. On the one hand there were the young men belonging to Quaker families,—though, indeed, some disregarded their Society's scruples for the sake of the common cause, and on the other hand there were those workmen who were adjudged by Lord Kitchener to be doing sufficient national service by providing the necessary equipment and munitions for the forces.

With regard to the attitude of the Society of Friends it may be sufficient to quote from a letter written by Mr. T. E. Harvey, then M.P. for West Leeds, explaining his absence from the Lord Mayor's meeting held to encourage recruiting.

"I am," he wrote under date September 10th, 1914, "at present away from London attending an ambulance training camp. I feel, however, that I ought not to make this an excuse for my absence on such an occasion. I am a Quaker, and I believe that war is contrary to the teaching of Christ, even when it is entered upon with unselfish motives and for an end which in itself is just. In this view I know that the majority of my fellow countrymen do not agree with me, but I still feel that I could not ask others to do what I myself believe to be wrong, whatever the consequences may be to my own future work. I should wish, however, to say no word to mar the sense of national unity in a time of great crisis, which has called forth a noble and inspiring stream of sacrifice from rich and poor alike. Those of us who cannot fight are, I believe, doubly bound to see that we do what we can in other ways to secure the ultimate victory, not of blood and iron or the mailed fist but of the spirit of justice and true human fellowship."

Undoubtedly a large proportion of Leeds men were exempted from service with the forces at this early date, but it must be borne in mind that Government orders of great magnitude had to be executed without delay by the civilian population. This condition of things was duly noted by the Chamber of Commerce in a report made at the close of 1914, as follows :—

"It has been suggested that recruiting in this district has not been as strong as in other parts of the country, and the Council feel it is only right to place on record their opinion that too much has been made thereof and that the recruiting in our midst, which includes recruiting not only for the special battalions and reserves but also for our several local Territorial battalions and their Reserves, as well as for Kitchener's army, compares favourably under all the circumstances with that elsewhere. It must be remembered that Leeds is a centre for the manufacture of numerous articles required for military and naval purposes, and a large demand has been made upon manufacturers in the district which could not be fully met on account of the difficulty in getting workpeople. Men employed under such circumstances are doing work which is absolutely necessary if our troops are to be equipped; and khaki cloth, uniform clothing, boots, small arms, cartridges and other munitions of war, which are made in Leeds, must be supplied if we are to succeed in defeating the enemy."

In point of fact a return issued during the first week of January, 1915, showed that Leeds was doing very creditably in the circumstances. By September 10th, 1914, the total numbers with the forces were approximately 11,000, and by the end of November these figures had been increased to 15,000. At the beginning of January, 1915, the 20,000 mark had been passed; at the end of April the figures reached 30,000, and three months later a total of over 36,000 was recorded, including 2,000 regulars.

Some idea of the progress made during the first year of war may be gathered from the annexed classification of the principal figures:—

	Nov. 1914.	Jan. 1915.	Apl. 1915.	July 1915.
Kitchener's Army	6,710	7,784	10,471	12,362
Leeds Pals	1,200	1,200	1,350	2,010
Bantams	—	1,211	1,700	1,700
Royal Engineers	833	925	1,545	2,275
R.F.A.	874	1,334	1,800	2,850
Leeds Rifles, 7th and 8th Battns.	3,324	3,940	5,000	5,900
R.A.M.C., 2nd General Northern and W.R. Clearing Hospital	1,339	1,605	2,000	2,430
R.A.S.C.	1,064	1,464	1,880	1,950
Recruited for Naval Brigade	—	50	550	1,200
Hussars and Dragoons	—	200	400	500
Nat. Reservists rejoined units away from Leeds	—	500	800	800
University O.T.C. taking service in units not recruited in Leeds	100	150	190	360

A remarkable and, in some respects, an astonishing feature of the change over from civilian life was the zest with which the recruits entered upon their new and unfamiliar duties at the training camps. This is indicated in a letter dated September 14th, 1914, from a man with the Artillery Brigade at Strensall :—

> "I am enjoying the life very well," he wrote. "As long as the weather is decent it is an ideal life, and not half as bad as it is made out to be. I am learning a varied stock of achievements, including machine gun drill and firing, rifle drill and firing, Swedish drill, riding a horse and attending to sick horses; in fact I see myself becoming quite a vet. before I have finished. The food is not half bad, and there is plenty of it, but it is served up very roughly. We usually have either fried bacon or boiled ham and bread for breakfast; roast meat or boiled meat with carrots, turnips and potatoes and bread for dinner; and either cheese and bread and jam and bread for tea. We get up about 5.30 a.m. and retire about 9 p.m. The work is not hard, and I am quite satisfied with having joined, but hope to get into more active service than at present, if it is only in the colonies. Our pay is supposed to be 8s. 5½d. a week, but we new recruits have some kit to pay for so we are on short pay, which is a bit off."

It was November, 1915, before the "Pals" were ready for active service, but meanwhile great progress had been made in regard to other units. The Bantams, nearly 1,200 strong, were in khaki in the first month of the year, and at the same time a Volunteer Training Corps movement was started which, after some vicissitudes, due to the cost of uniforms and the attitude of the War Office, materialised successfully early in the summer. Recruiting for the Leeds Rifles received an impetus in a July campaign which, in September, was followed by the building and opening of a new and commodious central recruiting office in City Square. By this time, as we have seen, between 30,000 and 40,000 men had enlisted.

Meanwhile, also, a census of businesses had been taken for recruiting purposes, and a national register had been compiled, with the result that there were ascertained to be about 50,000 men of military age yet available, a considerable proportion of whom, however, were engaged on munition work or other essential matters. Thus the way was paved for the operation of the Lord Derby scheme, which came into force in October, 1915, and for the activities of the local tribunals which thenceforward decided the fate of the registered men of military age.

IV.
THE RECRUITING CAMPAIGN.

> "Who carries the gun ?
> A lad from a Yorkshire dale.
> Then let him go, for well we know
> The heart that never will fail."
> *Conan Doyle.*

Before considering the special measures taken by the Government to increase the number of effectives in the Army, and before reviewing the military and civilian activities of Leeds in the first year of the war, it may be well to glance at a few typical happenings during the period of voluntary recruiting.

Ready as was the response made by so many to the call of Lord Kitchener, the need for more men soon became apparent, and the urgency of the case was duly emphasised by a campaign which, in various forms, impressed the importance of the matter on the public at large. Here in Leeds, almost as much as elsewhere, young men on every hand found themselves closely scrutinised and questioned. If they had not joined the colours, why not ? This was an inquiry our women folk particularly were prone to make. Football matches were brought off as usual when the season started, but not without some clear reminder of the greater opportunities awaiting both players and spectators. To one of the earliest fixtures in Elland Road for instance—the Lord Mayor and Lady Mayoress went especially to plead the needs of the nation, and in the course of half an hour they secured two hundred recruits. A ribbon of the national colours was tied round the left coat sleeve of everyone who answered the call, and the new recruits, marshalled in the centre of the field, were inspected and applauded.

Some, however, needed neither admonitions nor time for consideration. In this category was the man who dashed up to the recruiting office in a motor car ready for any emergency, and when told that he must produce his marriage lines to prove that he had a wife dependent on him, straightway returned home and fetched the lady herself; then, having passed the doctor, said good-bye to her and hurried away to the training depôt.

With regard to the type of men recruited for the Leeds " Pals " Battalion, Col. Walter Stead, the first Commanding Officer, reported that they formed "excellent material, not equalled either by the Germans or the Austrians." For the most part, he stated, they were clean, well set-up, healthy-looking young men, well educated, intelligent and vigorous, being drawn from all classes of the community, manual workers only excepted, and including ministers of religion and sons of ministers, doctors, solicitors, journalists, accountants and professional men generally, University teachers and students, public school men, merchants, manufacturers, clerks and agents. "The city," said the C.O., "may with confidence rely upon their doing their duty in whatever capacity they are called to act." Nor was this assurance in vain. The " Pals " as we shall see in due course, did the greatest credit to themselves and the city.

One of the earliest recruiting efforts was a mass meeting held in the Town Hall at which the Lord Mayor appealed for 5,000 recruits for the Kitchener Army—a figure which was reached and passed before the end of the first week in September. Another town's meeting was addressed by the Earl of Harewood (Lord Lieutenant of the West Riding), Sir Charles (afterwards Lord) Beresford and Father Bernard Vaughan; and so great was the crowd who sought admission that an overflow meeting had to be held, at which the chief speakers were the Hon. Rupert Beckett, Major Meysey-Thompson, M.P., and Ald. Charles H. Wilson, who in 1923 received the honour of knighthood and was elected M.P. for Central Leeds. But although recruits were forthcoming as a result, there was not yet a sufficient supply of khaki, and for some weeks the men had to be clothed in blue serge.

There was also a good deal of itinerant propaganda work done through the medium of a brilliantly illuminated tramcar which nightly conveyed chosen speakers to one or other populous district of the city, and served them for platform. Meetings of this kind were organised in all the Wards, north and south of the river, and Labour leaders equally with representatives of the other political parties made eloquent and forcible appeals that could not, and did not, fail to arrest attention.

So, throughout the autumn and winter, the call for more and yet more voluntary recruits resounded at street corners, at organised gatherings in City Square, in the Schools, at football matches, in fact wherever the younger men were to be found assembled. In this respect the Joint Parliamentary Committee, formed on September 11th, 1914, rendered yeoman service from their Central Offices in Boar Lane, and they were greatly helped by Major Pollard of the Northern Command.

The illuminated tram car was out and about blazing its electrical devices in deadly earnest during the dark evenings of November, for it had become apparent that the credit of the city was at stake ; the Leeds roll of recruits at this stage still fell short of the numbers recorded at one or two other populous centres. This, as has already been indicated, was due not so much to apathy as to the greater variety of essential occupations and the fact that so many workpeople were led to believe their industrial service was paramount. A fresh incentive, however, was soon given. The indignation aroused by the enemy's bombardment of Scarborough and Whitby on December 15th made for a decided quickening of the senses, and public feeling was stirred further by parades of the Caledonian Pipers and local "Pals" through the central streets. So, before the year ended, there was a steady rush of men to join the colours.

Apart from appeals by word of mouth, effective work was done by means of recruiting posters displayed on the walls and hoardings. One of the best of the local productions in this form was a coloured picture of a veteran bidding farewell to the young soldier in these words: "Good-bye, my lad! I wish I was young enough to go with you." Another, the silhouette of a man in khaki, was headed: "Think! Are you content for him to fight for you?" Yet another was inscribed with an imposing "Halt!" followed by the admonition: "Go into training and help the boys at the Front!" "What will settle the war?" asked another placard, and the reply was "Trained men, and it is your duty to become one!"

There were special reminders, too, of what the Scarborough raid connoted. One picture of the havoc wrought bore the stern question: "Men of Britain, will you stand this?" There were appeals also to employers of labour; for instance, "Have you seen that every fit man under your control has been given an opportunity to enlist? Have you encouraged these men to enlist by offering to keep them in any other way if they will serve their country?"

Before 1915 was far advanced the Recruiting Committee found their scope of operations enlarged considerably. In conjunction with the Military authorities and employers of labour they set to work to persuade all eligible men to join up. It was felt that many who were engaged in the distributing trades either did not sufficiently realise that there was an urgent need for their services, or they were fearful of losing their situations. Employers, therefore, were counselled to liberate men with a promise that their places would be kept open for them. On May 14th, 1915, for instance, it was reported that in reply to a questionnaire issued to 100 firms respecting 343 men of military age, 177 men would be released, and about a fortnight later replies came from 148 firms expressing willingness to liberate 355 out of a total of 833.

Thus, to some extent, Lord Derby's attestation scheme was anticipated, and not without reason; the outcry for voluntary recruits persisted, and in sympathy with it, Lt.-Col. Taylor, now in command of the " Pals " Battalion, made special appeals at the Empire and Hippodrome theatres. In this campaign, by the way, the Jews of Leeds were not overlooked. Rabbi Abrahams had, some months before, cited the example of Pericles who, in his reference to ancient Greece, declared, " this is a country worth dying for," and now, in answer to questions, Mr. Rosenburg announced that, of 4,000 eligible Jews in Leeds some 600 had been recruited.

A few months later (in September) more men were liberated from the clothing factories, and a Jewish V.C., Corporal Issy Smith, took a notable part in the campaign which led them to join the colours. Meanwhile, the recrudescence of effort in support of the " Pals " Battalion set in motion a travelling recruiting office, and at the same time the Rifles had another special campaign helped by tram car operations; also, the newly-formed Volunteer Training Corps supplied a few object lessons to the older men. In these respects the summer months of 1915 saw great activities; nevertheless, early in October, when the talk was of a coming necessity for compulsion, there were still from 10,000 to 15,000 eligible men who had not joined the forces. The number of " eligibles " was known in August, as a result of the National Register, and it was in October when the Derby Scheme came into operation.

By this time men everywhere were being released from industry and women were taking their places on the tramways and railways, in offices and workshops. For the moment, indeed, there was almost a glut of female labour, so willingly did the women offer their services. Most of them were married and in receipt of Government allowances or disbursements from the War Relief Fund, and they were glad enough to have the chance of supplementing their slender weekly incomes. The time soon came, however, when all such applicants obtained work at good wages, the great majority being absorbed in the Armley and Hunslet munition factories and the shell-filling factory at Barnbow, in which great enterprises Leeds was a pioneer.

Lord Derby's scheme for securing more recruits found in the Leeds Parliamentary Recruiting Committee a ready instrument of organisation. Its title was justified by the fact that all three political parties were represented, and by the mutual arrangement which enabled the staffs of the political agents to work the machinery. All that was necessary, therefore, was to form an Attestation Sub-Committee and carry out a system of voluntary canvassing; and this was done promptly with the aid of the local corps of National Motor Volunteers who collected the men together when the time came for them to join up. The scheme provided for the attestation of eligible men in groups, the first category embracing single men in groups according to age, and the second the married men in like manner, everyone being allowed to appeal to the Local Tribunal if reasons could be advanced for remaining in civil life. A time limit was fixed in each case, the period for single men expiring on March 1st, 1916.

In little more than three months after that date the Military Service Act introduced the compulsory system.

The amount of work entailed by the Derby scheme was enormous, but it was carried out with fine spirit by both men and women helpers. First, there was the numbering of the people in accordance with the plans for national registration. This task was performed by Corporation officials, school teachers, attendance officers and selected men of the Volunteer Training Corps.

Nearly 350,000 registration forms had to be distributed, filled up, and then collected. They were delivered at every house during the second week in August, and by the fifteenth of that month every person between the age of 15 and 65 had to place on record answers to questions as to name, place of abode, age, birthplace, whether married or single, number of dependents, occupation, name and business of employer, and to state if willing to undertake other work than that done habitually. There were nearly 114,000 houses visited in the course of this inquiry, and afterwards every person was supplied with a registration card, or certificate, which had to be produced and shown if required by the authorities at any time.

On the basis of this census the Derby scheme was established. Particulars relating to men between the ages of 18 and 40 were copied on to pink forms, and these forms were handed over to the Recruiting authorities. In Leeds there were something like 50,000 pink forms, which meant that there were about the same number of men of military age in the city at that time—considerably more men, in fact, than had already joined the forces. But by no means were all these men eligible or entitled to be regarded as "effectives." The eligible men numbered about 42,000, and 99 per cent. of them were duly canvassed under the auspices of the Recruiting Committee—an undertaking which involved more than 200,000 visits, paid by the voluntary workers, chiefly in the evenings and during a spell of most inclement weather towards the end of 1915.

After the canvassing the helpers had to attend at the Town Hall and there devote much time to the task of checking and tabulating the replies ; and in that process, as well as in the other work, hundreds of willing hands were engaged.

It was a complex and difficult business this preparation of analytical report for the purpose of the Derby scheme ; but it proved to be also a triumph of organisation. The late Ald. W. E. Farr, Chairman of the Committee, Mr. Harold A. Crawford and Mr. Arthur Lambert, hon. secretaries, and Mr. G. H. Pearson, for the Labour party, were at one in publicly acknowledging the great assistance rendered, and the services given by a host of voluntary workers who spent long hours at the various recruiting stations regulating and helping in the attestation of the recruits, also by the staffs of the political organisations and the local Press.

Before Christmas, 1915, under Lord Derby's Scheme, another 36,000 Leeds men had joined the forces.

V.
WAR IN EARNEST.

> " No easy hopes or lies
> Shall bring us to our goal,
> But iron sacrifice
> Of body, will and soul."
>
> *Kipling.*

Four phases of war time may be noted. Of one phase something has been written already. That early period—from the first shock of war until the end of 1915—may be likened to the moon's first quarter. Light gradually broke upon the position. It was a time of preparation, of training, of equipment; a time, also, of learning to do without things to which we had become accustomed in the old easy-going days.

In 1916 we entered the second phase. Stirred to greater activities by a crisis in the supply of munitions, we settled down to war in earnest. Our fellow Yorkshiremen were now in the thick of the fight, and we were perturbed by personal losses and bereavements. It was a time of exceptional enterprise by enemy aircraft on the Yorkshire coast. Also, the submarine menace forced us to economise in food as well as in the spending of money. National service became the duty of all, and an increase of man power grew more and more imperative.

In 1917 we tightened the belt to meet further demands. A rigid system of food and fuel control was developed. Economy was made the watchword of everyone. The restrictions were severe.

The fourth phase—in 1918—found us inured to economy and sacrifice. There was a grim determination to 'carry on'; there was hope, there was confidence to set against the war weariness of some who could not foresee the decisive finish to the conflict that came with the Armistice of November 11th, 1918.

Thus it will be seen that, trying as had been

the earlier stages of the war, there were heavier burdens yet to be borne.

Within five months from the opening of the year 1916 the groups of eligible married men had been called up and military service had become compulsory. This naturally imposed a severe strain on the wives and other female relatives of those who were engaged in industrial occupations.

With whatever degree of complacency Leeds people had regarded the outlook in 1915, they were now forced to realise that only by united effort and grim determination could the war be won. Effort had not been lacking hitherto, nor was there any lessening of the willingness to co-operate that marked the public attitude in the earlier stages. It was simply that the new and more insistent demands for increased man power raised graver questions of national import, and offered wider scope to all women as well as to those men who were deemed eligible for active service.

Up to the end of 1915, apart from recruiting efforts, civilian energies were concentrated largely on benevolent and social work, but now, in 1916, sterner duties had to be fulfilled, and everyone was made to feel that he or she, according to ability or physical strength, could take a direct part in working the gigantic and complex engine of warfare.

Meanwhile, what had happened to the men who so readily elected to serve for King and Country—the Territorials, the early recruits, those who formed part of the " First Hundred Thousand" and those who steadily followed their example and went into training ?

The Leeds Brigade of West Riding Artillery left for France in April, 1915.

A large number of men from Leeds were included in the miners' battalion raised by the West Yorkshire coal owners as a unit of the 155th Brigade of Royal Field Artillery, and went into action in January, 1916.

Advance Party of the Leeds "Pals" unloading at Colsterdale, September, 1914.

WAR IN EARNEST.

Three field companies from Leeds and a signalling company of Royal Engineers left for Egypt in December, 1915, and thence for France in the following February.

The 7th and 8th battalions of the West Yorkshire Regiment (Leeds Rifles) went to France in April, 1915, after some experiences in defending the north-east coast.

The Leeds 'Pals,' after their training at Colsterdale, Ripon and Salisbury Plain, sailed for Egypt in December, 1915, as a preliminary to their baptism of blood in France the following summer.

The 'Bantams' left for France at the end of January, 1916, and the West Yorkshire Pioneers battalion, which included many Leeds men, went out a few months later.

About the same time there was available in the West Riding a complete force of R.A.S.C. (Motor Transport Volunteers) which included a large unit of Leeds citizens (group 3), and in this year 1916, too, the Volunteer movement in Leeds culminated in the provision of three battalions which, with others in the West Riding, were taken over by the War Office. There were also bearer Companies of the Ambulance Corps not so taken over.

These stirring facts, and the knowledge that in addition to the thousands already on active service thousands more were making ready for battle, all created a profound impression.

But there were other circumstances weighing on the public mind. The fierce conflict on the Ypres in the Spring of 1915, Germany's ruthless submarine attacks, use of poison gas and dastardly sinking of the Lusitania, the air raids on Hull and Goole, our shortage of munitions and our terrible losses in the Dardanelles exploit, Italy's entrance into the war, the murder of Nurse Cavell—these were some of the events that greatly stirred, and indirectly spurred civilians to increased effort and sacrifice.

And there were even more heart-gripping incidents to come. For one thing, war was now taking heavy toll of promising young lives. For another, the burden of taxation was pressing harder, the price of food was rising and the need for economy was becoming more urgent. Also stern restrictions had to be enforced in view of threatened raids by enemy aircraft. The regulation of meatless days had been accepted as a settled system in households and public restaurants, but it soon had to give place to organised rationing, and the economical mood was reflected further in the introduction and purchase of War Savings Certificates as a means of thrift and to help provide the "sinews of war."

There was, indeed, ample reason for precautionary measures. All through the summer of 1916 our Leeds men were in the thick of the fighting on the Somme, nor did the city lack personal interest mingled with anxieties with regard to what was taking place in the more distant theatres of war.

Nevertheless the tide of life flowed on much as usual at home, excepting that in the activities of women we had episodes far out of the common. As fast as men could be spared for the forces, women and girls took their places. The new munition works at Armley, Newlay, Hunslet and Barnbow were in full swing, and women formed the great majority of the workers. Women also were employed as ticket collectors and cleaners on the railways, as tram conductors, as clerks in Banks and Insurance offices, in warehouses and in commercial and industrial establishments generally.

The idea of female tram conductors was at first esteemed lightly by the management. The pressure of contingencies, however, could not be resisted and the women acquitted themselves well.

The march of critical events gave a trend to public opinion that settled this and other matters quite naturally.

Apart from the natural instinct which forced women to offer their help, there was the strong motive power created by their close association with organisations for the relief or comfort of the sick and wounded, and the families of those men who were away at the front; and, as has been mentioned already, there was also the zeal stimulated by the now oft-recurring casualties, —the feeling that something must be done at all costs to lessen the dangers that threatened and to lighten the home tasks imposed on the country by the shortage of male labour.

In the Spring of 1915 Leeds had not far short of 10,000 women engaged in the benevolent work of visiting, advising and otherwise aiding the dependents of sailors and soldiers, for whose use, in respect of some form of help, nearly 2,000 medical books were issued entitling the recipients to medical relief. Many of these women workers also took a practical interest in the movement set on foot to provide house accommodation and hospitality for Belgian refugees, and many more devoted themselves to the work of providing clothing, medical requisites and other comforts for the troops and the disabled men, as well as British prisoners of war. This latter organisation, like that of the visiting section, was under the direction of the Lady Mayoress's Committee, and its ramifications extended over all parts of the city. In every district ladies' working parties met regularly and kept up a constant supply of the various articles, which were produced also at the distributing centre. Thus, in the first year, no fewer than 32,000 much-needed articles were forthcoming, of which 26,000 were for hospital use.

In this regard Leeds did only what was common

to other populous places. It was, nevertheless, the sort of work that not only appealed forcibly to our women folk but set the pace for war work generally.

One form of benevolent enterprise led to another. The Women's Temperance Association started a canteen at the North Eastern Railway Station where they met soldiers travelling through, and supplied them with refreshments. The Y.M.C.A. started a Club in Albion Street for men stranded on their journeys, or without homes; also a canteen in Cookridge Street. Committees were formed to organise entertainment for the wounded in the hospitals, and to supply them with cigarettes, tobacco and similar comforts. The Society of Friends, at their Meeting House in Woodhouse Lane, kept open house for Belgian refugees, nearly 1,600 of whom were now in the care of the Refugees Committee or installed in private houses as the guests of citizens.

To a large extent voluntary work of this kind was planned and carried out by people who, either by reason of their social standing or because they had the means and leisure, were able to render special help and pay close attention to the most urgent duties. But women of the artizan class, shopkeepers' wives and daughters, and many others who had little time to spare from daily industry were not inactive. Their contributions of personal service and money were considerable although less in the limelight.

Perhaps it was only characteristic of human nature that certain spectacular forms of work appealed more strongly than others to some of the younger ladies belonging to well-to-do families, but whether the attraction of a picturesque pose was real or not it did not deter them from doing their ' bit ' enthusiastically, and of those who chose the drudgery and somewhat thankless duties allotted to V. A. D. nurses, it certainly cannot be said that they failed to justify their pride in whatever glory attached to the wearing of a uniform. Their often unpleasant and always hard tasks were cheerfully performed, and deserved much fuller recognition than they received in some quarters.

With examples of energy and sacrifice such as these, it was no wonder that, when opportunity offered for an extension of effort, women in humble stations of life were found eager to undertake war work even of the most exacting nature, and ready to give up their ordinary occupations for the purpose. A large proportion were girls from the clothing factories, and domestic servants. Doubtless they were attracted by the good wages promised, and were influenced by the thought that change of occupation would impart a sense of freedom, but their willingness to take whatever risks the novel experience might bring was unquestionable. And certainly there were great risks as will be realised when the story of munition-making comes to be told. Not girls only, but married women, often the wives of soldiers, swelled the long lists of applicants. In the case of the tramway service, for instance, after 400 female conductors had been engaged in the Spring of 1916, there were still hundreds more waiting for another hundred vacancies that eventually were filled from their ranks.

VI.
TIGHTENING THE BELT.

> "Welcome fortitude and patient cheer,
> And frequent sights of what is to be borne!
> Such sights or worse as are before me here—
> Not without hope we suffer and we mourn."
> *Wordsworth.*

The war and all it connoted filled people's minds. Everything one did or read or thought was coloured by it. The war's effects at home and abroad, its bearing on the relationships of life and national affairs, its searching of the heart and stirring of the conscience, kept feeling at high tension.

Such relief as Leeds people were able to obtain from the common strain, the almost monotonous round of war work and of ordinary duties done in unaccustomed circumstances, was afforded only by fleeting hours of relaxation at theatres, cinemas and concerts, or week-ends at holiday resorts. But even then one could not get away from reminders of the world crisis, from troubled thought and conversation concerning the next thing to be done; it all weighed heavily as the burden borne by Bunyan's pilgrim when he set forth with the cry " What shall I do to be saved ?"

Many a man too old to fight, or ineligible from some other cause, and many a woman moved with a desire to help her country, rested not day or night in the endeavour to perform faithfully such tasks of national importance as were allotted to them. They had elected to do their 'bit,' and they did it wholeheartedly and thoroughly, unheeding temptations to relax at any time excepting when physical rest was positively necessary. It was different with the regular manual workers—the host of those who were helping to provide munitions and army equipment. In their case an hour or two of complete recreation seemed essential, and no one grudged them the meed of entertainment they invariably sought in their spare time. Certainly, despite some little labour and wage differences, and some individual complaints that came before the Munitions Tribunal, these workers were, in the main amenable ; they acquiesced cheerfully in the arrangement to suspend Bank Holiday in 1916 when every nerve had to be strained to meet the demand for munitions.

But there was prayer as well as work, although as the months passed, the congregations at places of worship were composed mostly of women. The psalms, hymns and prayers in common use all took on a new significance, and it was with a sincerity and fervour rarely experienced before that people joined in singing the hymn "For Absent Friends," or some other devotional petition equally suited to the times.

A national mission organised by the Church of England had by now awakened many to a fresh sense of their responsibilities and obligations, but, apart from that, the whole course of events infused the communities with feelings which called for relief not in work alone but in spiritual things, and in recognition of the bond of sympathy that made for more friendly relationship between different classes in society. Thus in churches and chapels intercessory services became the rule ; the men at the Front were remembered and interceded for, not simply in general terms through prayers and hymns, but often individually by name, and then, as time went on, here and there little shrines were erected in memory of the fallen, also Rolls of Honour that all might see and read, and so bear in mind the sacrifice which everyone was called to make in part or to the full.

One of the darkest weeks of the whole war, for Leeds, was undoubtedly that at the beginning of July, 1916, when news arrived of the battle of the Somme—the British Armies' first great onslaught on the German lines. It was a glorious victory, but at what a cost! Foremost in the fight were the Leeds " Pals." They acquitted themselves like true sons of Britain and were nearly all killed facing the enemy. But alas for those who were left to mourn! The poignant grief that afflicted so many homes is still recalled by the memorials that mark the anniversary of July 1st.

What days of brooding anxiety those were! Every morning (Sundays included), every evening, the newspapers were scanned for hopeful intelligence, but too frequently the cheery optimism which was generally maintained suffered a shock, and always a certain number of homes were darkened by reports of casualties, of which also intimation to those concerned was conveyed by telegrams from the War Office authorities. In the latter case it sometimes happened that a seriously wounded man had been removed to a base hospital, and his chance of recovery was so slight that permission was granted for a visit by his relatives. What moving scenes were then witnessed! What a rushing to and fro! The risks of the journey were overlooked in the prospect of a hopeful termination. But besides the hurried departure, a tedious inquiry in London had to be made, and there was a dangerous crossing of the Channel to be endured before suspense could be ended one way or another. Perhaps in the pressure of official work mistakes were unavoidable, but it is difficult to explain one error in a message which came to the writer's notice, and that was a telegram reporting a hospital case at the front as " serious " when the wording should have been " not serious."

Incidents like these were but one variety of many that impressed the minds of our men and women throughout the most trying period of the war. There was, indeed, so much to occupy attention that no one with an active brain or capable pair of hands found time to worry excessively or yield to depression ; a new altruism held them in sway and with it came an unconquerable desire to learn at every opportunity the fullest possible details of everything relating to the progress of events. It was largely this craving for news from day to day, and the varying degrees of satisfaction afforded by the newspaper press, that enabled the homestayers to " carry on." Curiosity, wonder, speculation as to what was really happening in the fighting zone, special interest in one or other of the enterprises that were destined to help win the war, played their part in steadying public opinion, even as did the local Press itself in responding to the desire for information and at the same time fostering a fine spirit of endurance and national endeavour.

A rigid censorship prevented publication of much of the news. Many things had to be taken for granted or never known at all. No one, however, murmured much ; the expedient was recognised as one to which patriotism must cheerfully submit. The system, of course, had its defects. Occasionally news leaked through by means of private communications or the talk of men returning from the battlefields, and sometimes it caused an erroneous impression. But enough was learned or guessed in this way to spur people on to greater endeavour or strengthen their determination in the right direction. And there was constantly the interest of local efforts, and the tightening bonds of Government restrictions to vary the occupation of mind and impress the need for fresh courage.

Our daily life thus acquired a complexion that told of humour and good temper as well as of pathos and work absorption. Men, who met together in clubs and restaurants for a midday meal found a new diversion in the choice of dishes, especially on meatless days, and the "no treating" Order was made an occasion for profound reflection when drinks had to be considered. The early closing of public houses and the limitation of hours generally provided another conundrum for those especially concerned, but the arrangement worked well enough and to the satisfaction of all reasonable persons, although it disconcerted some when the publican unexpectedly closed his doors and put out the notice "No Beer," as a sign that supplies had run short. Leeds, being a munitions area, was particularly affected by the Liquor Control, but it was the horny-handed worker employed in hard physical labour who felt the restrictions most, and it was with him not only a question of the beer's scarcity but a complaint of its low gravity or quality.

Many men—and women too—in all parts of the city were now busying themselves in their leisure hours with the cultivation of potato plots and allotment gardens on land rented from the Corporation, in the parks or other suitable places. The daylight-saving institution of "Summer Time," in 1916, was especially welcomed by those who devoted the evening to tilling and tending these acceptable aids to food production; and so enthusiastically was the allotment scheme carried out that it became a regular practice to spend part of every Sunday cultivating the plots. In the Spring of 1917 portions of the parks and golf links had been ploughed up, and many lawns and private grounds had been converted into kitchen gardens.

The need was urgent. Foodships were being sunk in greater numbers by German submarines which did not spare even hospital ships marked with the Red Cross, and before the year 1917 was over the Food Orders designed to regulate supplies developed into a drastic system of control and rationing.

The long days of "Summer Time," besides

helping people to economise in gas and electric light, imparted some sense of security in respect of air raids which were now becoming increasingly frequent. It was during the early and late months of the year that Leeds was stirred by alarms, and then on account of Zeppelin airships advancing across the north-east coast. Calm moonless nights were chosen for these sinister visitations. On such nights there were invariably to be seen flashing upwards into the sky the eerie beams of searchlights, which were installed at several points around the suburbs to act in conjunction with the anti-aircraft guns whenever active defence became necessary. But, although the enemy approached Leeds, he only passed over the city once, and then did not succeed in locating it. On other occasions the nearest he got was Collingham and Harewood where bombs were dropped harmlessly. The effective measures taken by the local authorities, the successful co-operation of the various agencies established an organisation that reduced danger to an absolute minimum. Leeds escaped attack largely if not entirely because it was enveloped in darkness on every occasion when an alarm was given. At the same time it is not at all improbable that on September 5th, 1916, when a Zeppelin came as near as Harewood, the security of the city was mainly due to the aircraft commander mistaking the River Wharfe for the River Aire. In the German version of the raid, published at Berlin, it was triumphantly proclaimed that Leeds had been bombarded and destroyed!

Month after month we grew more and more accustomed to the preponderance of women among the population moving about the city from day to day; more accustomed, also, to the sight of able-bodied men in khaki and disabled men in hospital blue. War work and war relief—these were the things that mattered. As everywhere, the needs of those engaged in navy, army or other work of national importance received prime consideration.

Visitors coming to Leeds on ordinary business were incommoded by lack of hotel and lodging room. Hotels, business premises, public buildings were, in several instances, commandeered for Government use. The Art Gallery was converted into Food Control offices. Some of the schools were utilised as municipal kitchens for the convenience of working people. The Soldiers' Field at Roundhay Park was used alternately as a drill ground for Motor and other volunteers and as a centre for testing aeroplanes. Sporting men no longer speculated on turf events—flat racing was discontinued in May, 1917; instead, some of them studied the flights of aeroplanes or the race of workers to supply munitions, or the competition between towns and cities in the raising of the War Loan. In the winter and early spring the streets after sunset were gloomy and deserted—only here and there a feeble lamplight flickered. The theatres opened and closed their doors early, and the trams ran a restricted service. As time progressed, the main streets leading out of the city showed row after row of shops vacated by men who had been called up, with frequent notices displayed as to the cause of business suspension. Roundhay Road was a conspicuous example. Confectioners, in accordance with regulations, refrained from tempting purchasers by exhibits of sweetstuffs in the windows; the few shown were but samples, as many a vendor was careful to explain. " No Chocolates " was a very common notice.

With each Christmas Day as it came round, repugnance to old-time junketting and festivity increased. How could one be jolly in circumstances that made for saddened thought, poignant grief or acute anxiety? Yet the children had to be remembered, though their joys were tempered somewhat by a lack of the accustomed luxuries and celebrations. Families who could afford it bought the best of home-made toys that were available, and in this way encouraged efforts to utilise the handicraft of disabled soldiers and sailors. Christmas cards, however, by general consent, went out of fashion. Like chocolates, they fell into the category of unnecessary items banned by the spirit of economy, and tabooed as inappropriate.

The Christmas Festival, in the main, became an opportunity for cheering the sick and suffering; the wounded service men in hospital, the convalescents, the men in training camps, the men at home on leave. Nor did Leeds forget the Canadian and Australian soldiers who found their way to the mother country. The Y.M.C.A. and private persons saw that hospitality was extended to them as far as possible. And not only at Christmas, but all through the year, the local Music-in-War-time, " Two Arts " and Wounded Warriors Welcome Committees were ready with entertainment at the hospitals and convenient meeting places, to brighten the lives of convalescents.

To the growing youth in our schools the thought of the war was a great sensation. They followed the course of events with curious interest, and were, in particular, attracted by the flying developments. Nor were they dismayed by the sights which, to so many, seemed harrowing and depressing. The schoolboys who went gleefully to help in the hayfields practised with equal gladness the drills which now took on a new meaning, and no one more ready to join up when the time came than most of these eager lads scenting the battle from afar yet innocent of war's horrors, and heedless of the dangers it might have in store for them.

Far otherwise was it with many of those on whose behalf excuses were advanced before the Tribunals set up to decide claims of exemption from service. Now it was the plea of a mother for her only son, or a father for the sole help-meet in his business, or some worker who deemed his work essential, or some pacifist who urged conscientious scruples against the taking of life. Leeds probably had no larger proportion of these cases than other towns of its size, but there were enough applications to keep the judicial body busy every week for three years inquiring into the merits of cases, fixing the period of exemption, if any, and issuing orders to join the Army.

Following are extracts from reports of the first conscientious objectors' cases, heard in March, 1916 :—

Alderman Wilson (to applicant) : " You have no conscientious objection to earning your living in this country ? "
Applicant : " I have the same right as anybody else."
" Dont you think that the country is worth fighting for ? "—
" My conscience will not allow me to do it."
The Chairman : " Supposing the Germans were going to molest your mother and sister, and you had a pistol in your hand, what would you do ? "
Applicant : " The only thing I would do would be to put myself in front of them."
Alderman Wilson : " That would not save them."
Applicant : " No, but it would save me from killing the Germans."
The Chairman : " If a man tried to steal your watch tonight, what would you do ? "
Applicant : " If I was not strong enough I would give it to him."
" Suppose you were the stronger ? "—." He would not try it on." (laughter).
The claim was disallowed.
Another claimant wanted " absolute and permanent exemption," so that he might continue his employment as a mechanical draughtsman at 15s. a week. His objection to military service arose from " a rooted belief and trust in the word of God." Quoting at some length from the Bible, he urged that he saw no reason why he should enter into the world conflict which was directly contrary to the will of God. He considered he had a covenant with God, and to go into any combatant or non-combatant force would imply unfaithfulness on his part.

One who was in almost daily attendance records a few of his impressions :—

" Experience of the internal working of the Tribunals was not infrequently lightened by humorous incidents, and occasionally

TIGHTENING THE BELT.

extraordinary reasons for exemption were advanced. One woman explained that she attended in place of her husband because he was suffering from 'illustrated throat.' A young man, prematurely bald, based his appeal on the ground that he had succeeded in securing a preparation which was rapidly restoring his lost hair, and he asked for a further three months, by which time he would be willing to serve as he was convinced that by then he would be no longer bald ! On the ground of domestic hardship a number of married men pleaded that they had to do the whole of the housework, get up in the morning and light the fire, and take a cup of tea to the wife. There certainly were a very large number of cases of grave domestic hardship, but one could not help feeling at times that this plea was greatly exaggerated, as, if all the cases were to be believed, at least a quarter of the husbands in Leeds had sick wives and other domestic troubles ! "

" The amazing feature of the whole work was the extraordinary patriotism and patience of the older men, who, with very few exceptions, submitted with wonderful cheerfulness in recognition of the country's need, and, at the bidding of the Tribunals, left business, home and family, in many cases under circumstances of great hardship. The sympathetic and patient attitude of the Tribunals themselves in dealing with cases pathetic in their human interest, with constantly growing national need for man power, and yet with great regard for cases of real hardship, is also striking, when it is borne in mind that all classes were represented on the Tribunals. The initial difficulties of procedure and relief were lightened as time passed and the needs of the country grew, and as the lists of those entitled to exemption lessened in length, but the grievous impossibility of sending older and less fit persons—frequently married men with considerable business interests and large families—rendered the Tribunals' already onerous responsibility greater. Most of the National Service representatives will remember all their lives the solemn words of Sir Auckland Geddes, in March of 1918, when he came specially to Leeds to demand a further supply of men who up to that date had been considered indispensable to industry."

In the Record of Enlistments and Exemptions will be found some further account of the procedure and of the services rendered by the members of the Tribunals. Mr. Charles Lupton, who was Lord Mayor in 1915-16, took a notable part as Chairman of the Appeal Tribunal.

VII.
STRAIN AND STRESS.

" Times go by turns, and chances change by course,
From foul to fair, from better hap to worse."
Robert Southwell.

Almost imperceptibly the national emergency net closed round the able-bodied population. Voluntary service might still be offered—was, indeed, expected from all of the male sex who were ineligible for the Navy or Army. The man who did little or nothing to help, directly or indirectly, could hardly elude observation. Shirkers certainly stood a poor chance of escaping now that the Military Tribunals had got to work.

As to those especially wanted for home service, the calling-up of single and married men under the Derby scheme reduced the force of Leeds Special Constables just as, formerly, the regular Constabulary had had their ranks depleted by enlistment. At the beginning of 1916 the strength of the special force was 1,317, but six months later it fell to 1,161, with the certain prospect of a further reduction of 400 or 500 when all the men of military age were called up. An appeal had therefore to be made for 1,500 new recruits.

How important the question of man power had become was shown by investigations which now and again took place at unexpected moments. Take, for instance, a significant street scene in Leeds, one evening in September, 1916. The main central thoroughfares were crowded. Queues were waiting at the doors of the theatres and music halls. Hotels, restaurants, cafes, were all busy. Suddenly a strong contingent of police, accompanied by a stronger force of military, drew a cordon round, and all men who looked younger than 40 years were accosted and asked to produce for examination their registration cards, exemption or rejection certificates.

Precautionary measures like these did not

fail to make an impression. It all went to emphasise the urgency of the need for national service. "Male persons between the age of 18 and 61," was the description of the volunteers asked for, in February 1917, when the application forms for national service went out. These forms made it clear that no one who volunteered would on that account be exempted from military service. The idea was to utilise to the utmost the man power of the country; and to that end—as in the case of National Registration two years earlier—particulars were required to be furnished as to age, whether the man was married or single, his occupation and average earnings, the name and address of his employer, also the work for which he considered himself especially qualified. And in order that everyone might have scope, a long list of occupations was specified for which volunteers were wanted, this list including not only various forms of munition work, but coal-mining, agriculture, engineering, quarrying, ship-building, the transport services, and other essential work.

All this time, despite a shortage of food supplies, no systematic form of control had been enforced. Rationing was largely voluntary. Only moderate amounts of certain commodities could be purchased, and a scale was fixed according to which everyone was expected to regulate their meals. Gradually, during 1916 and 1917, these allowances diminished.. In February, 1917, we were allowed 4 lbs. of bread per head per week, 2½ lbs. of meat, and ¾ lb. of sugar, and many who had not yet learned how to live frugally found the economy somewhat of a trial.

It was not until the end of 1917 that Lord Rhondda's rationing scheme matured, and we had, first, the individual ration card, with its tiny perforated squares which might be halved or presented whole to the shopkeeper with whom one registered, or the restaurant keeper; and then as an improvement on that system, the ration books which served a similar purpose for the purchase of meat and bacon, butter or margarine, lard, tea and sugar. By our womankind generally this food registration and rationing system was hailed as a relief from the earlier war experiences of housekeeping, particularly in view of the heart-burning trials to temper, and hindrances to traffic, caused by having to wait in long queues in order to secure a few ounces of margarine when only that butter substitute could be obtained. Moreover, by the exercise of economy through the earlier years of the war, most people were well prepared to make the best of reduced quantities of everything.

Even in the first year the housewife resorted to all kinds of devices to satisfy both normal and abnormal appetites with but slender portions of animal food by way of "stand by." Later, edible offal—as viands like tripe, liver, etc., were officially designated—was quite a common dish. Vegetarian fare became fashionable in the home and at the restaurants. Sausages also had a decided vogue, and they were fearfully and wonderfully made of almost everything and anything. There was even "horse beef" provided in one or two of the poorest districts of Leeds, primarily at the behest of the humbler Belgian refugees, but patronised also by others, and large quantities of oat cake were eaten instead of wheaten bread.

The introduction of the Rhondda rationing Scheme, early in 1918, made us realise as much as any other upset of house life the serious effects of the war. Think what it meant not only to the traders who had to evolve a new method of book-keeping, to keep count of every small voucher, but to every person who was thus forced to regulate his or her meals with a nicety never remembered before. It was, however, a salutary experience.

Leeds, no less than other parts of a county famed for its trencher men, and its proclivities for abundant living, learned the wisdom of abstemiousness in eating. Many persons discovered for the first time that short commons in flesh food need not prove prejudicial to good health; on the contrary they were the better for the moderate fare to which they were restricted. Special privileges were allowed only to munition workers and others engaged in severe manual tasks, and to invalids and children of tender age properly certified.

In such circumstances heavy responsibilities were laid upon housewives, and many a wife and mother felt these the more keenly because of the shortage of domestic help. The domestic servants were working in munition or clothing factories, on tramcars, on the railways, or otherwise doing men's work to which they had been attracted by high wages, no less than by the appeal that a woman must do her " bit " to help win the war. Rich and poor accordingly met on common ground in the markets and at the shops; nor was there any favour shown if customers failed to bring a bag or sheet of paper in which to wrap up the purchases, waste paper being by this time nearly as valuable as the perfect product itself.

Then, close on the heels of food rationing, came the rationing of fuel, and like restrictions in respect of the amount of gas and electricity consumed, though, almost from the first, certain economies had been exercised by the municipality by curtailing street lighting and using the by-products at the gas works for munition purposes, thus necessarily giving us an inferior kind of gas.

The Fuel Control imposed a severe trial in some cases, and means had to be devised for keeping poor households supplied with the small quantities of coal or coke to which they were accustomed, equally with the wealthier members of the community. The Control office, stationed at the Tramways Department, thus had a busy time dealing with the returns required from every house, and fixing the allowance to which householders were entitled according to the number of living rooms, the option being granted of taking some part in gas instead of coal, where gas fires were installed. Even so, difficulties and delays arose. The householder could not readily find a coal merchant who would undertake to supply him, and, as in the case of food rationing, there was no possibility of changing from one dealer to another, except for some reason deemed valid after full investigation by the Control office. And so acute was the shortage of coal that, when orders had been placed and accepted, it was often weeks before even a modest quantity could be delivered, though in times of great pressure efforts were usually made to supply at least one hundredweight for instant needs. But before any relief could be afforded, a declaration had to be made as to the quantity or lack of it in the cellars, and no one was allowed to have in stock more than their ration. Thus, during the winter of 1917-18, it was by no means possible to "keep the home fires burning" with any degree of cheerfulness, interesting as were the experiments with coal dust, etc., worked up in the form of clay balls, briquettes and the like.

Think of the general effect of restrictions like these—the cares of parents regarding their children's meals at boarding schools as well as in the home; the preparations and precautions needed when travelling any great distance by train; the trouble entailed in mastering the details of every regulation and seeing that due obedience was paid!

You were, for example, expecting a lady visitor from the other end of the county. She had to bring her ration card or book with her, and she was required to register temporarily at the local Food Control office. Her journey by rail, although not more than fifty or sixty miles, would occupy her the best part of the day, and she would travel by a slow stopping train in an overcrowded compartment, the occupants of which would be mostly, if not entirely, soldiers going to or returning from camp, and friends who had been visiting camps. If she had to break her journey at a junction she would have to rest in a comfortless, fireless waiting room, and if at night, at a darkened station. You, on your part, if you went anywhere, had a similar experience, and if you sought a bed at an hotel, you found that there was no room available, and might have to consult the police before you could obtain a night's lodging. You thought twice before arranging a holiday at the seaside, and indeed, except for the children's sake, there was little inclination to spend much time in this way, even when funds permitted. The cost of living was one bar, the discomfort and greatly increased cost of railway travelling was another.

So far as Yorkshire coast resorts were concerned—Scarborough particularly—patronage was long withheld in consequence of the raids. It was not until the summer of 1918 that confidence was restored in any degree. By then our defensive measures had improved considerably, and once more Leeds people, despite every restriction and call for economy, flocked to the coast resolved on recreating mind and body at all hazards. But still there was no escape from the prevailing topic and the war's menace. All along the coast indeed, the restrictions were severer than they were inland. There were, for instance, heavy penalties for infringement of the regulation regarding lighted windows at night. Yet in broad daylight it was not possible for some of the more sinister happenings to elude observation, and there was a peculiar and awesome fascination in watching the long convoys of merchant ships passing north and south, speculating on the appearance of destroyers and the circling round of our defensive aircraft, or trying to fathom the mysteries of German submarine exploits off Runswick.

Long before this we had grown accustomed to war-time regulations, nor did we regard as other than commonplace the censored reports in newspapers, the absence of any printed reference to the state of the weather, the ban on open-air photography and sketching, the shortage of housing accommodation, the war marriages that forced the bride to make a temporary home with her parents or parents-in-law, the shops that were closed because their tenants were away on active service, the shops which "carried on" only through the energy and enterprise of the traders' wives, daughters, or female relatives, the wearing up of old clothes to avoid the greatly increased cost of new, the irritation caused by matches that would not strike, and the indigestion due to bread which was made of many other things besides flour, the deterioration of property because there were no painters, joiners, plumbers, etc., and materials were scarce, the bad state of the tram-lines and road surface, for a similar reason, the early closing of shops and theatres, the restrictions on the use of motor cars, the untidiness of some of the streets, even the shortage of gravediggers, and the consequent strain placed on cemetery attendants, these and other extraordinary conditions were accepted as a matter of course and made the best of. There were no local elections for six years. There were no agricultural nor flower shows, no exhibitions save only those that had a direct relationship to war effort and relief work. Theatres and music-halls kept going with the help of women and exempted men, and were deemed essential as a means of keeping the

STRAIN AND STRESS.

population cheerful, and enlivening the spirits of the disabled men who now thronged the city. Lectures and meetings of various kinds there were also, but as in the case of other gatherings, women formed the great majority of those present, and they usually occupied themselves with knitting and sewing for the soldiers during the proceedings, heedless of music hall pleasantries—this, for example :—

> Sister Susie's sewing shirts for soldiers !
> Such shirts for soldiers our sister Susie sews!
> Some soldiers send epistles,
> Say they'd sooner sleep on thistles
> Than the saucy sort of shirts that sister Susie sews.

Such flights of good humour were but typical of the uniformly cheerful spirit maintained by all. But beneath the outward manifestation there lay a deep sense of the gravity of the national position, and nothing illustrated this more than the city's response to the Government's War Loan appeals. The Leeds Corporation alone invested nearly three millions of money in war securities, and towards the issue of February 1917 Leeds. as a whole subscribed over ten millions, thus ranking eighth on the list of large towns in the country. The introduction of War Savings Certificates in January, 1916, certainly found our workpeople true to their reputation for thrift, and before the war was over two and three quarter millions of money had been invested by them in this way. Altogether up to March 31st, 1920, as will be found recorded in its due place, Leeds subscribed over £42,000,000 in the form of war loan and savings certificates.

Mr. E. G. Arnold was Lord Mayor in 1917, and so firm was the resolve of the great masses of the Leeds population to carry the war through to a successful issue that neither outside revolutionary talk nor the blind theories of pacifists, and shortcomings of strikers in industrial occupations, aroused any show of public sympathy.

Early in June, 1917, a Socialist Convention was held in Leeds to "hail" the Russian Revolution with an attempt "to proclaim the dictatorship of the proletariat through the medium of workmen and soldiers' councils." It had nothing to do with organised labour in Leeds but was promoted by the United Socialist Council of the I.L.P. in London; and the Leeds Trades Council only decided to send delegates by a vote of 37 to 30, the majority being clearly attracted by the idea of international democratic control.

The Convention, however, had to reckon with public sentiment; and public sentiment was dead against them. At the same time, when, after some difficulty, the Coliseum had been secured for a Sunday meeting, no attempt at disorder was made, and the sole incident of that kind was the sinister behaviour of extremists in the meeting when one of the more moderate speakers pleaded the cause of the merchant seamen suffering from German brutality. Some notion of the attitude of the public will be gathered from the fact that a meeting in Victoria Square was banned by the police, and hotel proprietors refused accommodation to the visiting delegates—over 1,000—and they had to take refuge in private houses in Leeds and Bradford. A few who had already managed to secure rooms at one of the hotels had the unpleasant experience of finding their hats decorated with labels bearing such comments as "Are you aware there is a war on?" "Traitor!" and "What did you do in the great war?" The movement, in fact, failed to get a foothold in Leeds.

With the progress of time, jubilation at the Russian revolution died down. Bolshevism was seen in its true colours, and incurred only reproach. The vast majority of people came to realise that German militarism had to be defeated by the Allies without hope of help from so-called German democracy ; and in Leeds, during the early months of 1918, it was recorded that the supporters of proletarianism could be counted not simply on one hand but on one finger. In February, 1918, Mr. Walt Wood, one of the foremost Leeds labour leaders, conducted a large deputation of his party from various points of the Kingdom to the battle-front, and what they saw there fully impressed them with the importance of holding on against the onslaught of the common foe. Two months later, British Socialists who sympathised with Bolshevism met again in Leeds—this time at the Jewish Trades Hall—but the proceedings were remarkable for the entire absence of Leeds co-operation, and were indeed so obscure as to pass almost unnoticed.

Again, in the rare instances of strike action, just as in 1916 when a shop stewards' controversy led to a half-hearted step taken in sympathy by Leeds munition workers, so in March, 1918, a disaffection of engineers at the shell factories lasted but a couple of days. The moment it became known that the strike leader was a man of German descent, public feeling, which from the first resented the strike, attained explosive force. A mass meeting in City Square roundly condemned the lack of consideration for our men at the Front, and wounded soldiers tried to invade the strikers' meeting-place in order to protest. Fortunately, the strikers returned to their duties on receiving an assurance that an inquiry would be held regarding their grievance, which was, shortly, that some of their number had been ordered by a foreman to perform a task considered particularly dangerous. As to the amount of danger that might have been incurred, all classes in the population quietly, and with great intensity of feeling, pointed to the additional perils to which the Army would be subjected in their brave efforts to withstand the German offensive.

VIII.
NEARING THE END.

"Ever the faith endures,
England, my England!"
Henley.

ALL through the summer and winter of 1917, we had been bracing ourselves for what everyone hoped and believed would be—as indeed it proved —the final stage of the great struggle on the continent, and the crucial test of endurance at home. But that final stage in 1918 was no ordinary "last lap." Not until the fourth anniversary of the war's outbreak had been commemorated with prayer and thanksgiving did the difficulties of the situation begin to disappear, and the road to victory become straight.

The coincidence was duly noted by the spiritually-minded; it can hardly have escaped the observation of others. True to our national character of reticence and reserve, we forebore to make a mighty parade of our religious feelings; perhaps we were sickened by the ostentatious professions of the German Kaiser and his apostles of Kultur, who continually acclaimed the Almighty as their accomplice in deeds of devilry. Yet, deep down in the hearts of our people, and in Leeds fully as much as elsewhere, a belief in the Eternal verities was firmly implanted.

It was fitting, therefore, that at the opening of the year 1918 there should come from the Throne a call to Intercession in all places of worship throughout the King's dominions. Such a demonstration of national sentiment and trust in Providence was quite in accord with the people's faith in the justice of our cause. In Leeds, on the first Sunday afternoon in January, there was a most moving and memorable service held in the Town Hall, when a representative gathering occupied every seat and yard of standing room, and even overflowed on to the steps in Victoria

Square. The Lord Mayor (Mr. Frank Gott) read the King's Proclamation, and the vast concourse of people joined in the singing of the National Anthem. The President of the Free Church Council (the Rev. George Patterson), offered prayer and read that impressive chapter from Ecclesiasticus, beginning "Let us now praise famous men." The organ boomed forth the solemn tones of the Dead March; the Last Post was sounded; and with thrilling effect the congregation hymned their intercessions for Divine protection for the sailors, soldiers, sick and wounded and anxious ones at home.

A similar united service was held on Sunday, August 4th in the same place, when addresses were delivered by the Lord Mayor, the Vicar of Leeds (the Rev. Bernard Heywood) and the Rev. H. G. Haste. Prayer was offered by the Rev. W. Johnston, and the intercessions of the great gathering were led by the Rev. W. H. Draper (then Rector of Adel and afterwards Master of the Temple). Some of the words uttered by the Lord Mayor may be quoted.

> "On this remembrance day we can unanimously resolve to do all that is in our power to achieve the ideals for which the great sacrifice has been made. In unshaken faith that our cause is just and right, we ask to-day that we may be given the spirit and strength that alone can ensure victory."

On the evening of the same day the Vicar of Leeds conducted another service in the Nave of Kirkstall Abbey, which, despite cold and wet, had a singular impressiveness.

Consider the stimulating effect of such solemn interludes on the minds of people who met thus on common ground. There was some need for them apart from considerations put forward by extreme pacifists. In April 1917 the United States of America had entered the war, and in October their infantry were in action for the first time; yet, in January 1918, we had President Wilson's "14 Points" speech on the possibilities of peace, and in March the Roumanians were forced to withdraw, Russia having failed them. Months before, too, the Pope had issued a peace note, and when the Germans' great offensive on the Western front started, in March, even our own Lord Lansdowne pleaded for some *via media* whereby further wastage of life and substance might be avoided.

Certainly the situation was critical; the outlook depressing. In the autumn of 1917 a larger type of Zeppelins was being used by the enemy for air-raids, and a menacing feature was their silent action. In September, Scarborough had been again bombarded, this time by a submarine; and now, throughout the early months of 1918, daylight raids by aeroplanes were in full blast over London.

Nevertheless, it was but the darkest hour before the dawn. In April and May our Navy raided Zeebrugge, and the famous *Vindictive* exploit hammered the first big nail into the coffin of German aspirations. Before midsummer, too, our airmen had circumvented the enemy's flying tricks, and the last invasion from the air was recorded. By way of reprisals the Germans bombed hospitals at the front, but the second battle of Amiens had not long begun (early in August) before the enemy sounded a retreat and the British and French armies were advancing together over the stricken plains. Quickly now victory crowned the Allied cause. At the end of September Bulgaria surrendered. In October, the " Hindenburg line " was smashed; the Turkish Army surrendered in Mesopotamia; Ludendorff resigned, and the Austrians asked for an Armistice. Early in November Germany yielded to her fate and on the 11th day of that 11th month, at 11 o'clock in the forenoon, her fate was sealed.

During that fourth phase of the war, from 1917 to the sign ng of the Armistice, Leeds never lost heart. Trying as were local experiences of the numerous restrictions, the resolve to "carry on" was manifest in ways that have already been indicated. The visit of the King and Queen at the end of May 1918, like that His Majesty paid in 1915, had real significance, for thereby the value of the city's munitions supply, care of the sick and wounded, and war work generally, received encouraging recognition. Following the successful "Tank Week" of December 1917, there had been a further boom in war loan during the "Business Men's Week" in March 1918; and now, in July, a "War Weapons Week" provided another two millions of money. In June the contributing members of Leeds War Savings Associations alone numbered 31,800. Was not the war costing over £7,000,000 a day?

Economy? It was practised to the full at this critical period, alike by the Municipality and by the people. Had not the war to be won? Enterprises of great pith and moment—essential work on the great waterworks and sewerage schemes, tramway renewals, road repair and construction and similar undertakings—municipal obligations such as these had long been suspended; the Corporation's hands were full of more urgent business. The Government's emergency regulations imposed no light strain on members of the City Council and their officials; but every new problem was tackled manfully, and the law-abiding instincts of the citizens raised no obstacle.

The Rhondda method of rationing, now in force, was, indeed, a relief from the haphazard queue system which caused so much anxiety and complaint during the winter of 1917-18. That system aggrieved none more than the women munition workers. At one time their annoyance was such that some of them threatened to march in a body from the works to the food shops in order to protest. The threat never matured, however. It was simply grumbling born of discontent, and in no sense signified disloyalty. With the settled uniform treatment afforded by the Food Control and the Fuel Control, complaints died down. These and other tests of endurance were cheerfully accepted, although life in Leeds became strangely altered. Here, for instance, is a word picture of night scenes penned in April 1918 :—

> Now that theatres, music halls and picture houses are compelled to close at 10.30 p.m., to save gas and electricity, people are abed much earlier than before. A few popular restaurants in the centre of the city used to ply a considerable trade in late suppers, but they do this no longer. Even the fried-fish shops in back streets, the nightly resorts of thousands of working people, seem doubtful about their privileges, assuming that they have succulent comestibles to sell. Club life is dead. The business and professional man has other things to think of. The working man, having to be up early in the morning, is not tempted to linger now, when the consumption of beer "after hours" is banned by law. Many of the smaller Clubs have "gone under" altogether, and those that survive are having a precarious time. The household rationing of coal and light, shortly to be enforced, will be the last straw. It will, if anything, send people to bed sooner, and they will be all the better for it. After 10.30 when the theatres discharge their bustling crowds, Briggate and Boar Lane, except at the week end, are empty. Not quite, though. The trams are there, and lively munition girls, laughing and chatting, climb into them with their little sandwich cases, and are soon whisked off home. At 11 o'clock the streets are deserted, and the trams have only an odd passenger or two.

But neither the fuel control nor the curfew weighed the scale of fortune down as depressingly as the "last straw." The ever-present reminder of what our men were enduring at the Front checked any tendency to murmur at our home circumstances. Disabled soldiers in their regulation blue attire were everywhere to be seen—some at places of entertainment, some on fine days sunning themselves in City Square, some riding on the trams and paying visits to friends—and the sight of them compelled serious thought. As a rule they did not care to talk of the war, or of what they had been through; they much preferred to be entertained; but now and again hard facts came to light in conversation, and indirectly, too, you might learn lessons of fortitude under suffering that quite eclipsed the experiences of home-stayers. What could be more touching than the following impression communicated to the present writer by Sir Berkeley Moynihan, the eminent surgeon, whose distinguished services to the War Office reflect such honour on Leeds ?

"The thing which struck me most was the patient heroism and uncomplaining fortitude of men after being severely wounded. The single instance I chiefly recall was connected with a boy H—, who had been badly smashed about the knee joint. He lost a great deal of blood, his wounds were septic by the time he reached hospital. We tried to save his limb and his life, but gas gangrene set in, and we had to amputate the thigh at the hip joint. He was a miracle of stoic endurance and cheeriness. After the amputation it was clear he would die, for the gangrene spread on to the abdomen. When I went my "tucking-up" round at midnight he was far gone. I leaned over and said "Well, H—, old boy, how are you ?" He raised his white face till his chin was over the bedclothes and husked out "Tip-top, sir, tip-top." He was dead in less than half-an-hour.

It doesn't sound much, does it ? But nothing moved me as that did. For these boys became great friends with you in a few hectic hours, very often. And they were more than units, they were symbols."

Against reminders of the horrors of war, at this time, there were to be set the friendly visits to the city of many representatives of Allied nations, also the arrival in our midst of Americans who were in training at various places in the county, or were engaged on hospital work at Beckett's Park. These Americans were cheery souls. They showed us how to play baseball, at Roundhay Park ; and they seemed to appreciate thoroughly the organised arrangements made under the leadership of the Lord Mayor (Mr. Frank Gott) to show them hospitality. What they thought of Leeds was expressed by one of their number to an interviewer in these words :—

> "Your entire city has been to us a charm. All your men are gentlemen, and your women are as bonny in disposition as they are in feature. You have paid us the greatest compliment by taking us straight into your homes, and treating us as yourselves. We will never forget your kindness."

Some sixty of the visitors were stationed at the Military Hospitals, and many others came to Leeds on furlough. In every house, where they stayed as guests, all liquor was banned by order of the Advisory Committee.

As the summer of 1918 wore on, with its continual calls to economy, its plight of one-man businesses, salving of waste material, national kitchens, plans for training disabled service-men and similar obligations of absorbing interest—all tuning the mind up to the right pitch of war endurance—special duties were again found for our schoolboys. For example, in July, volunteers to do harvesting work in Cumberland were asked for; and the Grammar School, Boys' Modern School, Cockburn High School and West Leeds High School all sent their quota of boys who received 3d. per hour for their labour, the Ministry of National Service paying travelling expenses and making a grant of 5s. per head. Then, in August, 600 Leeds Boy Scouts, under the command of Mr. A. E. Wheeler, honorary commissioner of the local Boy Scouts' Association, went into camp at Bramham to pull flax. Very energetically they worked at this trying occupation, so essential to the Government's scheme for reviving the flax industry, and meeting the urgent demand for linen needed in the manufacture of aeroplane wings. On a like errand 110 boys from the Adel Training School went to Ulleskelf.

The month of August, as we have seen, brought

gleams of hope that the end of the war could not be far off. But still men were being called up, and the Military Tribunals were busy. As fast as the orders to join the Colours were made, men reported at the Harewood Barracks in Woodhouse Lane, and were passed on to the Gibraltar Barracks, hard by, where a rota of doctors put them through a strict medical examination. It was a novel and somewhat delicate experience for the many older men, but on the whole the arrangements worked well and considerate treatment was shown. That it was all necessary who could doubt ? The grading in itself was important ; it enabled us to secure the pick of the men for active service, and provided a guide to the utilisation of those who were graded in a lower class physically. Many of these never got to the Front. Nor were the aspirations satisfied of our youths, who, just on the point of military age when the Armistice was signed in November, were itching to bear a part in the great conflict.

IX.
THE ARMISTICE—AND AFTER.

> " The tumult and the shouting dies—
> The captains and the kings depart—
> Still stands thine ancient sacrifice,
> An humble and a contrite heart.
> Lord God of Hosts, be with us yet
> Lest we forget, lest we forget."
> *Kipling.*

It was with profound thankfulness that Leeds received the news of the signing of the Armistice. The rejoicings that immediately followed were a mere ebullition of feeling compared with the deep-seated satisfaction that now pervaded the hearts of the people. An immense load had been lifted off our minds ; it was good to awake every morning and say to oneself " the war is over at last."

For the first day or two it seemed almost difficult to believe that hostilities had really ceased. But as the weeks flew by, bringing enforcement of the victors' terms, our sense of relief and security increased ; and we turned gladly to considerations of what should be done in the form of reconstruction, and the restoration of liberties.

A delusive word, that word " reconstruction !" Too many had fondly hoped that, as the fruits of victory, there would come a Heaven upon earth, or, at least, a new and better world. But our troubles were not ended. The price of victory had to be paid in money no less than in the sacrifice of life and limb. In our efforts to repair the ravages of war we had to grapple with novel and intricate problems ; and although for a time there seemed some hope of recovering lost ground and reviving trade, those problems, in 1922 and 1923, became so serious as to arouse the gravest fears regarding the economic situation at home and in Europe.

THE ARMISTICE—AND AFTER.

This, however, affecting as it does the particular period at which these words are penned, is a matter for the historian of the future to explain.

So far as Leeds is concerned, the aftermath of war has, up to the present date, been faced with equanimity and courage; and those who have been unduly harassed by the heavy burden of taxation, the increased cost of living, the heavy expenses of producing manufactured goods, the depression of trade, the lack of employment, the irritation caused by the continuance of some bureaucratic restrictions and the difference in foreign exchanges, have not shown any very marked resentment. The Leeds crowds who filled the air with jubilation on Armistice Day can hardly have thought of such possibilities. And why should they have done? Never before had there been such a day. Restraint was cast to the winds. What one commentator at the time termed " the phlegmatic reputation of Leeds " was " entirely swept away by the torrent of enthusiastic rejoicing which deluged the city."

Certainly, for some hours after the arrival of the good news shortly after 11 o'clock on November 11th, there were unprecedented scenes in the central thoroughfares. Munition workers and University students were among the first to demonstrate. Work was suspended—in many cases by " French leave "—and, by noon, the streets were alive with merry-making crowds. In groups large and small they paraded the city, carrying little flags, wearing Union Jack helmets, singing and shouting with glee to the accompaniment of strange instruments. Shops, where anything in the form of bunting could be purchased, were besieged; the rush at one establishment was so great that an assistant had to be stationed at the doorway to cut ribbon into lengths for an eager queue. The church bells pealed, flags flew from public buildings, and even the suburbs—especially the working class districts—improvised decorations.

The most impressive features of the day's rejoicings were the scenes in Victoria Square and at the Military Hospitals. The Lord Mayor (Mr. Joseph Henry) had entered on his duties but two days before ; therefore it was with natural pride that, accompanied by the Lady Mayoress (Mrs. Hartley) and members of the City Council, he appeared on the steps of the Town Hall to address the many thousands who assembled in the Square and its approaches. It was estimated that fully 40,000 people were present. With the Police Band playing exhilarating national music, and the youngsters in the throng singing " When the boys come home," the effect on everyone was electric. Then, when night came, there were fireworks and bonfires, for the ban in respect of these was promptly withdrawn ; the shops were illuminated as they had not been for many a long month ; the hotels, restaurants and all places of amusement were crowded ; the streets were full of animated, good-humoured throngs bubbling over with excitement and yet causing no disorder.

Two nights later there were thanksgiving services in the Parish Church and some other places of worship, and, on the Sunday, a united service at the Town Hall with an overflow gathering in Oxford Place Chapel.

From now onward, a thousand and one things occupied the attention of the Civic authorities and citizens in their desire to ensure settled conditions of peace at home. Already, plans had been drawn up, and were in process of execution, for relieving the shortage of housing accommodation ; and these, together with all the many projects for getting back as far as possible to pre-war conditions, and meeting the new demands of the

THE ARMISTICE—AND AFTER.

post-war situation, gave all sections of the population, as well as the leaders of public life, plenty to think about. Quite early, too, the city's rejoicings were translated into practical steps for the national well-being. The "Thanksgiving Week," in January 1919, realised considerably over £4,600,000 as the contribution of Leeds towards paying for the war; and this financial enterprise was followed in July by a "Victory Loan" campaign which brought in nearly as much money. The new year was full of activities. Men were welcomed back from the war; trophies (including a Tank) arrived in the city, and were placed on exhibition; questions relating to the training and employment of demobilised soldiers and disabled men loomed large, and both demanded and received close consideration. The high cost of labour and materials, however, was a serious difficulty in all matters appertaining to attempted "reconstruction," and as time went on the position did not improve much. In municipal affairs, questions of the health and housing of the people were of prime importance. The progress effected may be gathered at a glance from bare statistics. The appended table, for example, is interesting as an indication of how Leeds inhabitants came through the war and its immediate effects :—

	Death rate.	Marriage rate.	Birth rate.	
1914	15.0	16.6	23.6	(1910-14)
1915	16.6	20.2	21.5	
1916	15.6	15.5	21.1	
1917	16.1	14.2	17.3	
1918	19.9	15.5	17.3	
1919	16.2	21.2	17.6	
1920	14.7	23.5	25.0	
1921	13.5	18.7	21.8	
1922	13.9	17.2	19.8	

As regards building enterprise, so long hampered, the following figures, showing the number of houses erected in Leeds, speak for themselves :—

1913-14	.. ..	287
1914-15	.. ..	228
1915-16	.. ..	146
1916-17	.. ..	51
1917-18	.. ..	5
1918-19	.. ..	4
1919-20	.. ..	7
1920-21	.. ..	196
1921-22	.. ..	1,048

In 1904 there were 2,923 houses erected but the number steadily declined yearly. In 1921-22 contracts for 2,929 Corporation houses were signed.

Some impressions of Leeds, recorded in the Spring of 1919, are a sad reminder of contrasts observed by the "boys" when they came home.

> They see no sign of the grim spectre of poverty, nor of sadness and melancholy, such as they saw abroad. Thousands of women, presumably out of work, plod daily to the Labour Exchanges, thousands of ex-soldiers (and others) go to and fro on the same errand. In the streets—thronged as perhaps they never were before—predominates the pre-war atmosphere of prosperity, even of luxury. How and why is it? There is no complaint, certainly no wailing on the part of shopkeepers. Money is about still, and apparently in plenty; if the truth were told, tradesmen were never better off, in spite of four and a half years of war. We do not yet hear of fur coats going to the pawnshop, or of the costly trinkets bought by our prosperous munitioneers finding the same resting-place. Shops, closed "for the duration," are re-opening. Places of entertainment were never doing better—even in the days when amusement taxes were unknown. And if you gain the confidence of returned soldiers they will tell you quietly of the great change which they feel has come over many of our women and girls; of their over-dress or under-dress, their giddiness and flippancy, the frequent veneer of affected masculinity. Exceptions there are, they admit. But, on the whole, they are not favourably impressed with either the tone or the manners of the majority of the girls "they left behind." The development of womanhood, in the hands of those who have professed to be its leaders, does not strike them as being on right lines. They preferred the pre-war feminine atmosphere.

The picture, though not highly-coloured then, was toned down in course of time. As khaki disappeared from the streets, thoughts of all we had endured receded into the background. War, horrid war! That was true enough, and the memory of it remained; but the aftermath had to be faced in its various phases, and many people were inclined to look upon it lightly, especially when the Peace Treaty was signed at the end of June, and when, again, there were rejoicings and thanksgivings. But soon there came the first solemn celebration of Armistice Day and, from the thrilling interval of silence that turned the busy streets of Leeds into a sanctuary of poignant memories, fresh inspiration was drawn for the common tasks of the future.

So Leeds put its hand afresh to every enterprise and movement that might be expected to relieve the necessities of its people and advance the national welfare. And while the claims of the living were thus remembered, the dead were not forgotten. One after another, in every part of the city, war memorials assumed tangible form and were dedicated to the undying memory of local heroes.

The City's War Memorial, which now occupies a commanding position on the verge of City Square, was the result of much thought and discussion. The first proposal, made when the Armistice was signed, favoured a "Temple of Fame." Later, a grandiose scheme, involving the abolition of a great mass of property opposite the Town Hall, was advocated. This, however, was rejected as being not only impracticable, and too costly, but too utilitarian to be suitable. Then an imposing symbolic structure, designed by Sir Reginald Blomfield, R.A., was provisionally approved for erection at the top of Park Row; but public opinion ruled against the selection of the site. Finally, as the outcome of a suggestion made by Col. T. Walter Harding, an old Leeds man and Freeman of the city, the beautiful cenotaph designed by Mr. H. C. Fehr came into being on its island site in City Square. Towering above a pedestal and pyramid of white marble, with their contrasted figures of War and Peace, the bronze-winged figure of Victory holds in one hand a wreath of fame and in the other droops a sword no longer needed.

The memorial, planned during the Lord Mayoralty of Mr. Albert Braithwaite, was unveiled on October 14th 1922, by Viscount Lascelles, and dedicated by the Vicar of Leeds (the Rev. Bernard Heywood) in the presence of the then Lord Mayor and Lady Mayoress (Mr. and Mrs. W. Hodgson), and a vast gathering of people, among whom were leading representatives of the city's many interests.

* * * * *

All this is but a chapter of recent history. The immediate past is too near for us to gauge its full significance or appraise the value of the lessons learned. The wounds of war still smart. The times in which these records are made are times of transition, and we must feel our way cautiously. Nevertheless, stimulated by the proud memories of all that it sacrificed and accomplished during the great conflict, Leeds may surely be trusted to make the best possible use of whatever opportunities for national service the future holds in store.

PART II. THE RECORD.

Photo by   *Bacon & Son.*
Lieut.-Col. E. A. HIRST, C.M.G., T.D.,
69th (West Riding) Brigade R.F.A.

Photo by   *Bacon & Son.*
Lieut.-Col. F. MIDDLETON, D.S.O., T.D.,
69th (West Riding) Brigade R.F.A.

Photo by   *Swaine.*
Lieut.-Col. W. F. LUCEY, C.M.G., D.S.O.,
T.D.,
69th (West Riding) Brigade R.F.A.

Photo by   *Elliott & Fry.*
Lieut.-Col. W. HEPWORTH, V.D., T.D.,
2/8th West Yorkshire Regiment,
Leeds Rifles.

THE RECORD.
I. MILITARY ACHIEVEMENTS OF LEEDS TERRITORIAL UNITS.

" They bore our banner fearless,
They lifted England peerless
To the death as to the fight,
To the old heroic height."
Gerald Massey.

LEEDS has reason to be proud of its military record. On many a battlefield in the far-flung fighting line the city's credit was worthily upheld by its heroic sons. It would be invidious to select any particular unit for especial mention. All acquitted themselves like men. To all alike is honour due for the part they bore with unflinching courage in that tremendous shock of arms. The following brief accounts of typical experiences, in training and on the battlefield, will give some idea of what every man endured who went on active service, whether with one of the local Territorial units, or in regiments other than those associated with Leeds. No precise data can be given with regard to the achievements of Leeds men who served in the Navy; but it must not be forgotten that, although their numbers were small in comparison with those who joined the Army, they performed with equal valour the duties assigned to them. Theirs was no mean contribution to the watchfulness, patience and fortitude of our first arm of defence through hundreds of dark cold nights around the coast, nor were they found wanting in the great fights and raiding expeditions in the North Sea.

LEEDS ARTILLERY.
A SPLENDID RECORD.

In the old volunteering days—long before the Territorial Force was constituted—Leeds had every reason to be proud of its artillerymen, and when war in earnest had to be faced that good credit was confirmed in every respect.

Having their headquarters at the Fenton Street Barracks, the Leeds Artillery formed the 1st Brigade of the West Riding R.F.A. Territorial Force, 49th Division. The 2nd Brigade was identified with Bradford ; the 3rd with Sheffield ; and the 4th chiefly with the Otley district. Throughout the long drawn out struggle in France and Flanders these splendid units upheld the best traditions of the British Artillery. They took part in most of the great battles, bravely enduring unimagined hardships, suffering heavy casualties, receiving hard knocks as coolly as they inflicted punishment on the enemy, and winning a wide reputation for accurate and enterprising gunnery, and for thorough efficiency in all those important matters which come under the heading of internal administration. At the very beginning, indeed, the West Riding gunners achieved renown, and throughout the campaign they steadily increased their prestige in the Army. From Divisional, Corps, and Army Commanders they received many direct messages of congratulation on their distinguished work, and they held a very high place, among all formations, in fighting efficiency. In short, they proved themselves a first-class fighting unit, and the county of their origin may justly be proud of them.

When war broke out, all four Brigades of the 49th (West Riding) Division were in camp engaged in their annual training. They returned to their respective depots on August 3rd, and on the following day received definite orders to mobilise. On the 5th they moved to their various war stations, the Leeds men going to Selby.

100 PER CENT. FOR ACTIVE SERVICE.

The 1st Brigade (Leeds) was then under the command of Lieut.-Colonel E. A. Hirst, and

MILITARY ACHIEVEMENTS.

during instruction the brigade volunteered for active service in any part of the globe, the percentage of volunteers being extremely high. A hundred per cent. of the officers offered their services, a hundred per cent. of the sergeants, and ninety-seven per cent. of the men, which probably constitutes a record in the annals of the Territorial Force. Nor could it have been otherwise with a unit having so long and honourable a history, extending back over a period of nearly 60 years.

All through the winter progressive training was carried out, and then the brigade accompanied the rest of the Division to France. They landed at Havre on April 14th, 1915, and immediately went up into the line in the Fleurbaix area. This, for a long time, was regarded as a reasonably quiet sector, but it was here they were to receive a baptism of fire. They were attached to the 8th Division, and very soon were seriously engaged, taking part on May 9th on the attack on Festubert and Aubers. In this engagement the first awards for gallantry were won, and the then rare distinction of D.C.M. was bestowed on Bombardier T. Elliott and Gunner J. Mortimer of the second battery in the 1st Brigade.

It was after this that ammunition ran so terribly short, and batteries had to suffer the intolerable restraint of being unable to reply to the enemy fire, or to give any but the smallest support to their infantry. The first officer casualty among the artillery was suffered by the Leeds Brigade on May 24th, when their gallant adjutant, Captain T. A. Abbot, R.H.A., was killed.

On July 7th, the artillery moved with the rest of the division to the extreme left of the British front, behind the canal to the north of Ypres, relieving the 4th Division. They remained for six months in this unsavoury locality, but throughout the trying time all ranks maintained remarkable cheerfulness, and a fine spirit of determination. Shells were as rare as rubies. Every round expended had to be officially accounted for, and registration had to be carried out with great exactitude and care to prevent an unnecessary round being fired. Towards the end of their stay in this sector, the 15-pounders, with which the Leeds men were armed, were gradually exchanged for the modern 18-pounders, the exchange being completely effected when the enemy tried his *tour de force* on December 19th. In the early hours of that day the divisional fronts were subjected to an immense gas attack, and it was generally agreed that our gunners won the honours of the day in repelling the attack.

The Somme Offensive.

Following this long and successful defensive struggle the division, considerably reduced in numbers, moved into rest in the first week in January, 1916, the gunners going into the Arucke and Zeggers Cappal area, north-west of Cassel. After enjoying some little but much appreciated relaxation they entrained for the Amiens area, and on February 14th went into the line in front of Martinsart, a few miles north of Albert. Here, after a few weeks of quiet the artillery units were withdrawn out of action to the beautiful country of Canaples, West of Amiens, and began to prepare themselves for the Somme offensive which was to be launched in the summer. It was during this work of intensive training in open warfare that the divisional artillery was reorganised on a more convenient basis for artillery tactics. Brigades were constituted as three batteries of 18-pounder guns, and one battery of 4.5's. This meant that the 11th Battery went to the 1st Brigade, which was re-numbered the 245th Brigade, and so remained during the rest of its war service.

MILITARY ACHIEVEMENTS.

In June the artillery went into very carefully prepared positions opposite the strongly fortified defences of Thiepval, the 245th Brigade being situated about half a mile east of Aveling village, and about two miles south-west of Thiepval. In this stage of the fighting they were brought into contact with their own infantry, the 49th Division. For three months the 49th artillery supported the numerous attacks made by their own and other divisions, and during that period, the ammunition expended by one brigade alone was over 200,000 rounds. Several officers and many men were killed or wounded by shell fire, but on the whole, and in the light of subsequent events, the gunners came out of the ordeal fairly well. In the late autumn the artillery units moved north to make new positions west of Fonquevillers, and here they participated in the severe fighting in the region of Beaumont Hamel and Serre, eventually going into rest at Lucheux, where Christmas was spent.

Next came a brief and unexciting experience south of Arras in the bitterly cold winter of the first few weeks of 1917, followed in March by a spell of quiet at Laventie. Then, early in June, the gunners moved up to the Belgian coast, near Nieuport, where both they and the infantry suffered considerably from the mustard-gas shells which were now being used by the enemy with great effect. The Leeds men had some serious losses in this area due to the wonderful counter-battery work of the German 5.9 batteries.

PASSCHENDAELE'S TRYING CONDITIONS.

Early in September, 1917, the artillery marched southward to the utterly destroyed Wytschaete area, and took part in several great attacks made by the 2nd and 5th Armies, and at the end of the same month they moved up to Wieltje, in front of Ypres, to join in the Passchendaele operations and support the magnificent attack made by the New Zealand Division on the heights west of Passchendaele. Until December 2nd the divisional artillery remained in action here, working under appalling conditions and losing nearly 900 horses and mules in the work of munitions supply. The strain was tremendous during those fateful months and inevitably the batteries suffered grave losses. The 245th Brigade lost 52 per cent. of their officers and men, killed and wounded.

At the beginning of December the brigade, which with the 246th Brigade, had been longer in the line at this vital point over a continuous period than any other divisional formations, was withdrawn badly battered but with morale still high to a rest area near Cassel to refit. It was a real rest, and the training was chiefly recreational. Prior to this, certain changes in command had taken place. Lieut.-Colonel Hirst was invalided home in 1916, and the command of the 245th Brigade was given to Lieut.-Colonel F. Middleton. Now, whilst the troops were in rest near Cassel, other changes were made. Lieut.-Colonel Middleton, who had carried the unit through many difficult and dangerous operations, was given command of the Divisional Ammunition Column, his successor in the 245th Brigade being Lieut.-Colonel W. F. Lucey, the next in seniority in the unit.

In the later part of February, 1918, the division was sent to the Ypres salient, east of Zonnebeke. The artillery brigades took part in the withdrawal from this front at the end of March, also in the very hard open fighting at Voormezeele and to the north of Kemmel. Those were especially anxious times. The officer losses included four battery commanders of the 245th Brigade : Majors Day, Clare, Jackson, and St. Paer, all of whom were killed. For several weeks in April and May the artillery covered the French infantry who had come up in force to help to stem the German tide; and in June, when the German advance was finally stopped, the divisional artillery moved north again to support their own division. Then, in August, the whole division moved south to Arras, and were for some weeks in close support to the British attack on Cambrai.

The Final Advance.

On October 7th, the artillery moved into the Bourlon Wood area, and a little later played a prominent part in the advance which ultimately destroyed the German military power. At the shortest notice the gunners were sent forward to open positions north-east of Cambrai, where they covered the attack of the 49th Divisional Infantry on the high ground at Avesnes-le-Sec and Villers-en-Cauchies. From now until November 1st the Division was continuously engaged, and on November 3rd the barrage put down by the divisional artillery was the most perfect of its type. Under its protection the infantry were able to advance down to the Rhonella river with comparative impunity. The infantry were then finally withdrawn from the line with a brilliant record, and the divisional artillery remained in action to cover the only division of the corps still functioning, namely, the 56th. Thenceforward until the Armistice was signed they made frequent and rapid advances in order to maintain close and adequate support with the quickly-moving infantry. It was about this time that Major Stewart, a tower of strength to his battery in the 245th Brigade, was killed. Throughout the period that the 49th Divisional Artillery covered the 56th Division all ranks among the gunners were imbued with the spirit of the teaching they had received in the principles of mobile field artillery training, and those lessons were put into practice with complete success.

On the day the Armistice was signed the Leeds gunners, in conjunction with their comrades of the 246th Brigade, were working with the extreme advanced guard of the British Army (the cavalry of the 16th Lancers) who on the previous evening had captured the village of Harveny, two miles south and one mile east of Mons. Accordingly, at the critical moment of the Armistice, the Leeds Brigade was further east than any other artillery of the Army. The batteries were buoyed up with intense excitement in the ardour of the advance, and the officers commanding brigades had some difficulty in restraining subordinate officers and men from continuing the attack after the time scheduled for hostilities to cease. This was partly due, perhaps, to the eager rivalry on the part of batteries to fire the last round in the war—a competition that was never satisfactorily decided.

On the Rhine and Home again.

After the Armistice the Leeds artillery rejoined their infantry in the Douai area, where, for some months, recreation and demobilisation were carried on concurrently. On the return to England of Lieut.-Colonel Lucey, the brigade was commanded by Lieut.-Colonel R. M. Horsfield, and towards the end of March, 1919, after being reconstituted and made up largely of new personnel, the unit departed from Flines, near Douai, to join the Army of Occupation on the Rhine. Officers and men thoroughly enjoyed their long march, which was delayed not disagreeably for five days, in the neighbourhood of Liege, and the brigade then became part of the Light Division, going into billets first in the Grottenheron area, and afterwards in the Solingen district. The experience of all ranks in Germany was pleasant, but amid social diversions the Brigade lost none of its old reputation for smartness and efficiency and good horse management, and they won many prizes at the Army shows that were held from time to time.

The return of the cadre of the brigade—the last of the local units of the West Riding Division on foreign service took place in November, 1919. On the 5th of that month it arrived in Leeds and was accorded a tremendous reception. The officer commanding the cadre was Lieut.-Colonel Horsfield D.S.O., who went to France with the brigade in the Spring of 1915, at which time he held the rank of captain, and it included two warrant officers, Sergeant-Major S. M. Gaines and Sergeant-Major Redgrave, who went out with the originally constituted brigade. On the day following their arrival in Leeds the men paraded at Fenton Street Barracks and marched to the Town Hall by way of the central streets of the city. They were given a civic reception at the Town Hall by the Lord Mayor (Mr. Joseph Henry), and members of the City Council, and afterwards were provided with refreshments at Fenton Street Barracks by Officers of the brigade.

Owing to the heavy casualties among officers and men in the course of the campaign, the personnel of the Leeds artillery at the end of the war was almost completely changed from that which originally went to France with the 49th Division in the early part of 1915.

The following is a list, approximately correct, of the honours won by the divisional artillery during the war :—4 C.M.G.'s, 12 D.S.O.'s, 1 D.S.O. and two bars, 42 M.C.'s, 3 M.C.'s and bar, 27 D.C.M.'s, 108 M.M.'s, 42 M.S.M.'s, 12 Croix de Guerre (French), 6 Croix de Guerre (Belgian), and 1 Medaille Militaire.

The Leeds awards included :—C.M.G., Colonel E. A. Hirst and Lieut.-Colonel F. W. Lucey; D.S.O., Lieut.-Colonel Lucey, Lieut.-Colonel F. Middleton, Lieut.-Colonel R. Horsfield and Major Petrie.

LEEDS ENGINEERS' FINE SERVICE.
THE NORTHERN SIGNAL COMPANIES.

From January, 1915, until the end of the war, there was not a single important engagement in any theatre of the war in which one or other section of the Northern Signal Companies (Royal Engineers) did not take part. Before the Territorial Army was formed, they were known as the 2nd West Yorks. Royal Engineers (Volunteers), and had been associated with Leeds for half-a-century. The Northern Signal Companies consisted of an Airline Company, a Cable Company and a Wireless Company; they were entirely Signal Companies and had no connection with Divisional Field Companies R.E.

When war was declared the Northern Signal Companies at once volunteered for active service and went to their war station at Biggleswade in Bedfordshire. Lieut.-Colonel J. W. H. Brown, T.D., was then in command. The rest of the war history of the Unit is difficult to describe, as the Companies were not taken out as a whole, but were split up into Units of different sizes, and were drafted overseas as their services were required. The Companies, at the same time, were expanded into a Training Centre called the Northern Signal Companies Training Centre—still under the command of Lieut.-Colonel Brown.

The first detail to be called upon by the War Office was a Wireless Section. This was formed, and sent out, under Lieut. N. L. Barker (who, later, became Captain and received the O.B.E.). It went to St. Omer in November, 1914, and served throughout the war in France and Belgium. Next to go was a Cable Section under Lieut. G. Bray (later, Captain, with M.C.), which went to France in January, 1915. He was followed, in September, 1915, by Lieut. J. Boyle (awarded M.C.), with No. 27 Motor Airline Section. Lieut.

Photo by   Bacon & Son.
Lieut.-Col. A. BRAY, T.D.,
49th (West Riding) Royal Corps of Signals.

Photo by   Sands
Major E. HOPPER,
O.C. Field Companies, 31st Divisional Engineers.

Photo by   Bacon & Son.
Lieut.-Col. R. A. HUDSON, D.S.O.,
8th Battalion West Yorkshire Regiment (Leeds Rifles).

Photo by   Bacon & Son.
Lieut.-Col. J. W. ALEXANDER, D.S.O., T.D.,
8th Battalion West Yorkshire Regiment (Leeds Rifles).

H. Richardson was drafted to the 8th Divisional Signal Company in February, 1915.

When the Mediterranean Expeditionary Force was formed, the Northern Signal Companies were asked to form the G.H.Q. Signal Company, consisting of Airline, Cable and Wireless Sections, and the Headquarters personnel. This Unit embarked for Gallipoli in March, 1915, under the command of Major A. Bray (now Lieut.-Colonel Commanding 49th (W.R.) Division Signals, T.A.), who was awarded the Legion of Honour for Service in Gallipoli. He had with him Major D. Hey (awarded M.C.), the second in command—who afterwards commanded Lines of Communication Companies in Egypt and Palestine—Lieut. H. McLaren (afterwards Lieut.-Colonel, D.S.O., M.C.), Lieut. W. F. Jackson (afterwards Major with M.C.), and landed with the first troops in Gallipoli at W Beach. Later, the following Officers were sent to the Mediterranean Expeditionary Force, namely, Major W. A. Stott, Capt. W. Boyle (later promoted to Major and awarded the O.B.E.), Capt. R. I. Denham (later, Major, M.C.) and Lieut. J. B. Beaumont. Major Boyle commanded the Depôt at Alexandria.

The G.H.Q. Signal Company served throughout the war in Gallipoli, Egypt and Palestine. The Unit was also represented in Mesopotamia, in the person of Lieut. P. A. Hitchcock (later, Lieut.-Colonel, and awarded the M.C.).

Throughout the war, the Northern Signal Training Centre continued in being, and trained drafts for the widespread units of Signal Service. Many of the N.C.O.'s. and men gained Commissions, were awarded honours, and otherwise distinguished themselves. It is interesting to note also that, when Tank Corps were formed, Capt. G. Bray, M.C., and Capt. W. F. Jackson, M.C. were selected to run Tank Signals.

THE DIVISIONAL FIELD COMPANIES.

It was on February 18th, 1915, that the Lord Mayor of Leeds (Mr. J. E. Bedford) received official sanction for the raising of two field companies of Royal Engineers. Prior to this the Lord Mayor's Recruiting Committee had offered to raise a second battalion of Bantams, but their offer was refused by the War Office ; instead, the suggestion was that either Artillery or Engineer units should be raised. It was then decided to endeavour to raise a body of sappers who would go to form the divisional Engineers for the new Division, of which the newly raised West Yorkshire battalions, including the Leeds Pals, formed part. One field company was asked for, but so many excellent men came forward that a second company was soon formed, and eventually there was not much difficulty in forming a Royal Engineer establishment for a division—three field companies and a signal company.

Major E. Hopper—a Leeds engineer who had had military experience in the South African war with a railway pioneer company, and was a mining engineer with experience all over the world—was put in command of the Field Companies, and the officers were all Leeds engineers of repute. On March 30th, the first of the new companies left Leeds for Ilkley to start training, and were followed later by the other units.

From Ilkley the companies went on to Ripon, and then to Fovant, on Salisbury Plain, where they became associated with many other gallant Yorkshiremen in the 31st Division. The Division marched away on December 6th, 1915, not knowing to what part of the world they were bound. Most of the Infantry sailed from Liverpool, but the Engineers embarked at Devonport, and on December 20th found themselves at Port Said. The Eastern side of the Suez Canal engaged their attention, for there was plenty of work in

Royal Engineers, 210th Company. Inspection by the Lord Mayor (Mr. James E. Bedford), at Ilkley, April 21st, 1915.

constructing defences in preparation for the attack which the Turks were expected to make. The heat of the summer made the work hard and trying, but after the fall of Erzeroum it was considered safe to reduce the Egyptian garrison considerably, and the 31st Division received orders to proceed to the Western Front.

Trench Warfare in Northern France.

The change was sudden for all concerned. Leaving Egypt on February 29th, 1916, the Division arrived at Marseilles on March 6th, and soon the Engineers had full days with the maintenance of trenches and the usual front line routine.

After remaining near Thiepval a little while the Division moved to the Courcelles district, where the Engineers were employed in constructing trenches, dug-outs, water points, ammunition stores, light railways, and a number of other necessary works in preparation for the first big Somme offensive. It was dangerous and difficult work, for the enemy were not unaware of what was forward, and plastered these areas pretty liberally with shrapnel and high explosive, causing many casualties among the field companies. Then followed the disastrous experiences of July 1st, and the 31st Division, badly shattered, was withdrawn on July 5th to the Neuve Chapelle sector, where it remained until October 6th.

By October 13th, 1916, the Division had again concentrated in the Courcelles sector, in readiness for the action now known as the battle of the Ancre, which opened at dawn on November 13th. In the assembly trenches when day broke the Engineers were gathered ready with all necessary tools to follow up the infantry and to make strong points out of the German trenches, which it was hoped to capture. Unfortunately, the infantry attack was not entirely successful and the Engineers did not come into action. They were heavily shelled, however, whilst waiting in the assembly trenches, and several casualties were reported in consequence.

In the early days of January, 1917, the Division went back to the Amiens district to rest, reinforce, and recuperate, after which it went up into the line again in the Hebuterne sector. Here the line was none too strong to meet a really hard pressed attack, and, as the enemy had shown signs of restlessness, the Engineers were called upon to accomplish some very risky work in strengthening the barbed wire in front of the trenches. The Germans, however, retired instead of attacking, and the 31st Division followed them as far as Bucquoy, the work of the Engineers being to consolidate the position behind the pursuing infantry.

Supporting the Infantry.

Later the Engineeers found themselves at St. Venant, busy with preparations for the battle of Arras, which began on April 21st, 1917. In the fierce struggles for Oppy Wood the Leeds men had a lot of wiring to do, and this cost them half a company in killed and wounded, German machine gunners having the range to an inch. When the Arras battle died down the Engineers enjoyed a period of comparative quiet, extending over some months, in the Gavrelle-Vimy sector, and when the next great test came, with the big German offensive in March, 1918, the Engineers were at Roclincourt, in General Headquarters Reserve.

The terrific onslaught of the enemy meant that every available man had to be called upon. Therefore, when the news came that our lines were being pushed back, the Engineers were rushed up in motor-'buses, a distance of 14 miles, to give what support they could to the infantry. It was work for which they had not been specially

Officers of the 7th Battalion West Yorkshire Regiment (Leeds Rifles).

trained, but officers and men fought doggedly, and earned the admiration of the most seasoned infantrymen.

On March 31st, the rush had been checked, and the Engineers were withdrawn to Marquay, near St. Pol. They were still in reserve when they were again called upon to meet a dangerous emergency, this time on the Lys. Again they went up in London motor-'buses to fill the gaps in the ranks of the infantry. Fighting " with their backs to the wall "—to quote Sir Douglas Haig's famous message—they again acquitted themselves with distinction.

At a result of the Somme operations, when the Division had to hold 9,000 yards of front, the 31st was terribly depleted, and when it was relieved on the morning of April 14th, 1918, by the 1st Australian Division, it numbered only between 4,400 and 4,500 all ranks. It remained in the Hazebrouck sector until it was withdrawn to reserve in the St. Omer district on May 23rd, 1918, and after a period of rest for refit and reinforcements the Engineers found themselves engaged in the successful operations which were brought to a close by the Armistice.

THE LEEDS RIFLES.
A SERIES OF REMARKABLE EXPLOITS.

Attention should now be directed to the 7th and 8th battalions (Leeds Rifles) of the West Yorkshire Regiment (Territorials), the history of which, from the old Volunteer days, is intimately bound up with the city of their origin.

Mobilised on the day war was declared, these two battalions went through the greater part of the war with the rest of the famous 49th Division. For most of the time their service was particularly arduous. More than once they were nearly wiped out. But, brought up to strength by re-inforcements, they again and again faced the foe with conspicuous valour. As a result of this steady feeding process the battalions to a certain extent lost their distinctively local character so far as personnel was concerned, but as units they retained their identity, and for a considerable part of the war they were fighting almost side by side.

When the storm clouds were breaking over Europe on August 2nd, 1914, the two battalions went into camp on Scarborough Racecourse for their usual annual training. They were fairly well up to strength, and there was a great keenness in all ranks, for none knew what was going to happen. They were not long kept in suspense, for on August 3rd orders came to return to Leeds immediately. The following day, coincident with the declaration of war, the Territorial Force was mobilised.

7TH BATTALION WEST YORKSHIRE REGIMENT.

In the case of the 7th Battalion, mobilisation was completed at Carlton Barracks under the command of Lieut. Col. A. E. Kirk, V.D., and the battalion moved to Selby on August 10th, where the 146th Infantry Brigade was concentrated. During the remainder of 1914 and the early part of 1915 training was carried out at Strensall and York, followed by a period of duty on the Lincolnshire coast. On April 9th, the battalion was moved to Gainsborough, and spent a very busy six days before its journey overseas. It landed at Boulogne early on the morning of April 16th, 1915, and entrained for Merville the same night. From that date to May 5th the battalion was at Merville, Estaires and Bac St. Maur, and during this period practically every man had an instructional tour of the trenches. The first great day in the history of the Leeds Rifles after their arrival in Flanders was May 5th, when the 7th Battalion went into the trenches for the first time,

Parade of the 7th Battalion West Yorkshire Regiment (Leeds Rifles), August, 1914.

relieving the 2nd Battalion Scots Guards at Fauquissart, in the Neuve Chapelle area.

One may imagine the pride of the Leeds Riflemen when they found that they were to relieve so magnificent a unit of the Old Contemptibles as the 2nd Scots Guards.

It was from this portion of the line that the British attack on the Aubers Ridge was launched on May 9th. The battalion took no part in the actual attack, but suffered a number of casualties from shell fire. The 49th Division held the front line in the neighbourhood of Fauquissart and Fleurbaix until the end of June, and it was here that Captain M. Lupton, of the 7th Battalion, son of Mr. F. M. Lupton, of Leeds, was killed, shot through the head by a sniper.

In the Ypres Salient.

The terrible Ypres salient next saw the Rifles. The 7th Battalion went into the trenches at Turco Farm on July 7th, little thinking that they were to remain in the same unhealthy neighbourhood until the end of December. It was a very warm corner, for the German position at Pilkem completely overlooked them, and the trenches were in a very bad state. On July 9th, the battalion had its first experience of gas shells. It was only in the preceding April that the Germans first started to use gas in the notorious cloud attack against the Canadians, and our anti-gas measures then were not so effective as they afterwards became. The battalion had been issued with the old P. Helmets—mere bags for the head, with eye pieces—and 13 men became gas casualties. Altogether it was a bad time in the salient, a dreary routine in and out of the trenches; and when in camp in the shell-stripped woods around Trois Tours Chateau at Brielen, the men came under very heavy shell fire, the German gunners being intent upon destroying divisional headquarters if at all possible. It was during a vigorous shelling of these woods, on July 16th, that the Divisional Commander, Major-General Baldock, was wounded.

The first decorations came to the battalion on July 29th, when they were in dug-outs under the Yser Canal bank, in the support line. The Boche took it into his head to plaster the position pretty freely with high explosives, and Lieut. Briggs, son of Mr. F. D. Briggs, of Chapeltown, Leeds, was killed in the attack, being buried by a shell explosion. Seeing what had happened, Sec.-Lieut. Glazebrook and Riflemen J. Bentley and M. Garrity went out in face of the shell fire to dig him out. They succeeded in digging out the body, and for this the officer was awarded the Military Cross and the two men the D.C.M. At the end of August Lieut.-Col. Kirk was rendered *hors de combat* by a stray bullet, and Lieut.-Col. C. H. Tetley, of Leeds, took command.

Early September brought a spell of rest, and with it visits from General Plumer, also from the Earl of Scarbrough and Brig.-General Mends, of the West Riding Territorial Association. When on September 19th the battalion resumed the old trench life it was on the extreme left of the Divisional Front at Boesinghe, next to the French. This did not last long, for on October 13th the Leeds men found themselves back in their old trenches at Turco Farm. The weather was bad, and the trenches were soon in a terrible condition, but the men kept up their spirits in a wonderful manner right up to the end of December. As much as possible was done with sand bag breastworks, but the wet ground was a severe trial, and trench feet began rapidly to lessen the rifle strength of the battalion. In one week no fewer than 99 men "went sick," but this was afterwards checked by an issue of gum boots reaching well up the thighs.

December 19th saw the Rifles in support at

Tower of the Cloth Hall, Ypres.

Elverdinghe Chateau, when, about half-past five in the morning, the Germans let loose a big gas cloud, and sent their infantry to complete the job. At 6.40 the battalion got the order to move up to the Yser Canal, but were lucky enough to escape any serious effects from the gas. The same night they relieved the 6th Battalion West Yorkshire Regiment in the front line, and the relief was carried out very well notwithstanding exceedingly difficult conditions, for there was heavy shelling and a good deal of gas still hung about.

Christmas Day, 1915, was spent as joyously as possible at Elverdinghe Chateau. The battalion went into the trenches again the same night, and remained there until December 29th when their long tour of six months in the Ypres salient came to an end. They left with no regrets, for they had had a gruelling experience. During that period they had been in what was generally admitted to be the worst part of the line. Although there had been no big battle, there had been constant activity, and life during the whole time was marked by intense discomfort.

It was with a sigh of relief, therefore, that the battalion turned their back upon the salient and departed for a rest and refit. The units had been reduced to an average of 70 per company, and the men who were left suffered so much with their feet that it was with difficulty they marched away. After a fortnight spent at Wormhoudt, during which time Leeds men from the second line came out as reinforcements, and the battalion was reorganised, the refreshed and rejuvenated battalion stepped out on a 40 miles march to Calais, which they accomplished in three days. Although the men were under canvas on the sand dunes in mid-winter they spent a jolly time at Calais, where they had a very successful though belated Christmas dinner in a hall large enough to accommodate the whole of them.

The Somme Offensive.

On February 1st, 1916, the battalion exchanged the pleasures of Calais for the stern work of preparation for the Somme offensive of that year. They moved south by train to Amiens, and after a few days in billets went into the front line at Thiepval on February 10th. The spell of duty here was short, and at the beginning of March the 49th Division was withdrawn and started training for the offensive. Then followed a variegated series of experiences—trench work, training, working parties on the new railways, and other works that were being constructed for the push, a turn at the 4th Army Infantry School, rehearsals of the attack, and so forth. Most of this period of preparation was spent in the vicinity of Vignacourt.

At eight o'clock on the morning of the 1st of July the battalion received orders to move up to the assembly trenches in Thiepval Wood. Many gallant lads went down in the dangerous crossing of the Ancre, but the battalion reached the assembly trenches, and were in support of the Ulster Division with the rest of the 146th Brigade. In the afternoon two companies were sent forward to hold the old British front line at the edge of the wood, and two other companies were sent over into the captured German trenches to assist the 9th Royal Irish Rifles, a unit of the Ulster Division. It was here that Corporal George Sanders won the V.C. for his gallant leading of a party of 40 men who got detached in the German trenches. In this fight the battalion lost 16 killed, 144 wounded and 20 missing. The battalion were withdrawn on the evening of July 2nd, and when, five days later, they went back, the battle was dying down.

A "little bombing show" which resulted in very heavy casualties, took place on July 13th. Two companies of the Seventh were ordered to clear out the enemy from some trenches in the Leipzig salient. All went well until the party was pulled up by a block in the trench. Then they were forced back, and the enemy got into our lines for a time. Eventually, however, reinforcements from the Bradford Rifles drove the enemy out. The two companies of the Seventh lost 15 killed, 92 wounded and two missing. For this bit of work the battalion received the thanks of the Divisional Commander, who said that "it materially assisted in the success of the larger operations on the British Front."

A period of very difficult trench warfare followed in the same part of the line, Thiepval being the pivot of the British attacks from the South, and the battalion were in the front line when Thiepval was captured on September 26th. It was in this affair that the Rifles had their first glimpse of the "Tanks."

The battalion next had a spell of comparatively quiet warfare at Fonquevillers and Ransart, Christmas Day of 1916 being spent in comfort well behind the line at Bouquemaison. Nothing particular happened for some time.

At the beginning of March, 1917, the battalion, back in their old trenches at Fauquissart helped to train the Portuguese Division in trench warfare, the Portuguese eventually relieving them. Then came some pleasant days of summer training on the coast of Flanders, the battalion moving from Fauquissart to Dunkirk about the middle of July. A short tour of duty in the trenches at Nieuport followed, and here the battalion had their first experience of mustard gas. On August 1st they were withdrawn, and started a period of training for the attacks on Passchendaele.

The actual attack in which the battalion participated took place on October 9th, under the worst of weather conditions, and it speaks volumes for the grit of the men that such a good advance was made in such difficult circumstances. The Brigade was congratulated by the Corps Commander on the work done "under the extremely adverse conditions." The casualties in the battalion were 14 officers and 230 other ranks.

After a month spent in training and refitting, the battalion went back into the front line on the Broodseinde Ridge, east of Ypres. The conditions at first were very bad, due to the continuous and heavy shelling of all the routes to the front line, and during four days in November sixty casualties resulted from the shelling of back areas. The tour of duty in this part of the line lasted until the beginning of April, 1918, with the exception of a month's training in the vicinity of Cassel. It was about that time, by the way, that the Seventh won the Silver Cup given by the Brigadier to the unit in the Brigade scoring the greatest number of points in a variety of athletic and military contests. Meanwhile, on February 23rd, whilst holding trenches on the Ridge, the battalion repulsed by Lewis gun and rifle fire an enemy raid, and took 15 prisoners.

Fighting in a Fog near Kemmel.

Quite suddenly on the night of April 10th, orders were received to report to the 62nd Infantry Brigade near Kemmel. The enemy were attacking all along the Messines Ridge at this time, and in the afternoon of April 11th, two companies, followed later by the rest of the battalion, were ordered to take up a position just South of Wytschaete, as the right flank of the 62nd Brigade was seriously threatened. In his report of this period the G.O.C. 62nd Brigade, used the following words about the 7th Battalion: "Under very heavy shelling the battalion moved forward splendidly, and their steadiness undoubtedly saved the situation." During the days which followed all the companies were subjected to very heavy shelling, and suffered many casualties. Then, on the night of the 15th, one Company was moved to an important part of our line, a hill named Spanbroermolen, between Wytschaete and Kemmel. They took over at 4 a.m. on the 16th, and at 5.30 a.m. the Germans made their attack on Wytschaete after a very heavy bombardment. The morning was so very foggy that it was difficult to distinguish friend from foe. In addition there was no artillery support, as the telephone wires were broken, and the S.O.S. signal could not be seen by our gunners. The enemy got round in the fog, and captured or killed 12 officers and 450 other ranks. What now remained of the Seventh was the battalion headquarters and remnants of the Companies—five officers and about 100 other ranks.

The worthy part played by the battalion was recognised in the report of the G.O.C., 62nd Brigade, in these words " :—

"On an extended front they encountered the full force of the enemy attack on the morning of the 16th, and fought most gallantly until overwhelmed by superior numbers. As in the case of other battalions, the mist placed them at an enormous disadvantage and deprived them of the full use of their fire power. There were practically no stragglers."

What remained of the battalion was formed into one company, which took a highly creditable part in the fighting on April 25th near Vierstraat.

After a period of rest for training and refitting, during which large drafts were received, the battalion went into the front line again at Potijze and Zillebeke, remaining there until the middle of August. On August 25th Lieut.-Colonel W. R. Pinwell, D.S.O., of the King's Liverpool Regiment, took command of the battalion, Lieut.-Colonel Tetley returning to England for a six months' spell of home duty.

At the end of August the 49th Division was transferred from the 2nd to the 1st Army, and after a period of intensive training for semi-open warfare, the 7th Battalion went into the front line on the River Scarpe, near Arras. Another period of intensive training was their lot at the beginning of October, and the battalion were then moved to the Cagnicourt area, where there was very little shelter of any kind, the ground having been captured recently, and all the villages razed to the ground by shell fire.

On October 11th the battalion went into action east of Naves, the final objective being the high ground east of Avesnes-le-Sec. The leading companies moved forward steadily under very heavy machine-gun fire from the front and left flank, where the enemy were still in force in the village of Iwuy, and cleared up many enemy machine-gun nests. The direct enfilade fire of the enemy machine-guns in Iwuy was particularly severe, and a counter-attack was made with five Tanks. This was at first partially successful, but the Tanks were finally driven off by rifle and Lewis gun fire, one Tank being put out of action. The casualties in the battalion amounted to about 13 officers and 400 other ranks, and the captures were 300 enemy prisoners, 12 field guns, and several machine-guns and trench mortars. Lieut.-Colonel Pinwell, who was wounded in the thigh by a machine-gun bullet, said he had never seen a battalion go over the top to an attack in better style.

Following up the retreating enemy, the battalion were again in action in an attack at Famars, in the Valenciennes direction. They were called on to reinforce the 1/5th Battalion West Yorkshire Regiment, and did very useful work in helping to repel a determined enemy counter-attack. Their casualties were five officers and 56 other ranks, but the fight was a complete success.

It is noteworthy that the 5th, 6th and 7th Battalions of the West Yorkshire Regiment finished their fighting in the great war at Famars, for

Photo by   *Bacon & Son.*
Lieut.-Col. H. D. BOUSFIELD, C.M.G.,
D.S.O., T.D.,
7th Battalion West Yorkshire Regiment
(Leeds Rifles).

Photo by   *Bacon & Son.*
Lieut.-Col. C. H. TETLEY, D.S.O., T.D.,
7th Battalion West Yorkshire Regiment
(Leeds Rifles).

Lieut.-Col. The Hon. F. S. JACKSON, M.P.,
2/7th Battalion West Yorkshire Regiment
(Leeds Rifles).

Photo by   *Chandler & Co.*
Lieut.-Col. A. E. KIRK, O.B.E., V.D.,
7th Battalion West Yorkshire Regiment
(Leeds Rifles).

MILITARY ACHIEVEMENTS.

it was here by its brilliant conduct during the French wars, 1793-4, that the West Yorkshire Regiment gained the laurels still commemorated in its regimental march "Ca Ira."

The attack by the 49th Division was largely instrumental in compelling the enemy to evacuate Valenciennes, as will appear from the following message received by the Divisional Commander from General Godley, commanding the XXII. Corps :—

"I wish to heartily congratulate you and your Division on the successful capture of all your objectives and the heavy losses inflicted on the enemy as a result of your two days' hard and gallant fighting. All three infantry brigades, your artillery and engineers, have added another page to the distinguished record of the Division."

After this came the period of occupation, and it was on Wednesday, June 25th, 1919, that the cadre of the battalion returned home to Leeds, Major Sir A. E. Dunbar being in command. They were given a hearty welcome. Headed by the regimental band, and accompanied by a strong muster of demobilised men, the cadre marched from Carlton Barracks to the Town Hall, where they were met on behalf of the city by the Lord Mayor (Mr. Joseph Henry). Lieut.-Colonel Tetley acknowledged the welcome, and paid an enthusiastic tribute to the unfailing loyalty of the battalion while under his command.

Appended is the official list of honours awarded to the 1/7th Battalion and 2/7th Battalion The West Yorkshire Regiment (Leeds Rifles) :—

Victoria Cross	1
C.M.G.	1
Distinguished Service Order	5
Bar to Distinguished Service Order	1
Military Cross	35
Distinguished Conduct Medal	29
Bar to Distinguished Conduct Medal	1
Military Medal	117
Bar to Military Medal	1
Meritorious Service Medal	5
French Croix de Guerre	7
French Medale Militaire	1
Belgian Croix de Guerre	3
Italian Bronze Medal for Military Valour	1
Russian Medal of St. George IV. Class	1

100   LEEDS IN THE GREAT WAR.

The recipient of the C.M.G. was Lieut.-Colonel H. D. Bousfield who commanded the 1/5th West Yorkshires from July 2nd, 1916 to October 9th, 1917. The D.S.O. was won by Lieut.-Colonel C. H. Tetley, Lieut.-Colonel H. D. Bousfield, Captain J. S. Hamilton, Lieutenant Edwards, and Lieutenant J. Tillotson; and the Bar to D.S.O. by Lieut.-Colonel C. K. James.

It should be added that the battalion commanded by Colonel H. D. Bousfield, comprising companies from York, Harrogate, Ripon and Selby, greatly distinguished itself in the attack on Schwaben Redoubt in September, 1916. Col. Bousfield, a member of the old Volunteer battalion of Leeds, with Territorial Decoration, gained, in addition to the honours already mentioned, the Belgian Croix de Guerre (Ordre de Division) "for devotion and ability in assisting to repel enemy attacks" on April 17th, 1918, when the English troops were associated with the French at Mont Kemmel.

8th BATTALION WEST YORKSHIRE REGIMENT.

The story of the 8th Battalion West Yorkshire Regiment is bound up to some extent with that of the 7th, but in many ways the narrative breaks fresh ground. After the rush of mobilisation, which was carried out in Green Lane Schools, under the command of Lieut.-Colonel E. Kitson Clark, the 8th moved to their first war station at Selby, together with the rest of the 146th Infantry Brigade. From August 10th the battalion were engaged in intensive training at Selby, York, and on Strensall Common, and on December 16th, they were sent to Scarborough, in view of a possible attempt at landing by the enemy.

Early in 1915 the battalion moved to Gainsborough to complete training before going overseas, and on April 15th, 1915, left for France under the command of Major (afterwards Lieut.-Col.)

J. W. Alexander, Lieut.-Colonel Kitson Clark having to remain temporarily in England as a result of a fall from his horse.

After instructional visits to the trenches, the battalion took over a sector near Fauquissart, which they held during the attack on Aubers Ridge on May 9th. They bore no active part in the attack, but suffered casualties from shell fire. A period of trench warfare followed in the same neighbourhood until the end of June, when the Division marched North to the Ypres salient where they were destined to spend six trying and arduous months. The conditions were bad, and grew steadily worse as the year went on, but in spite of great discomforts and hardships the spirit of the battalion remained of the highest order, and all fatigues were undergone with the greatest cheerfulness. The 8th Battalion were the first to see the front line, being "bussed" up to support and assist in the preparations for the attack near Pilkem, shortly after which the Division took over the sector between Turco Farm and the canal at Boesinghe.

It was near Turco Farm that the 8th got their first decorations, which were also the first in the Brigade, Second-Lieutenant Wilkinson gaining the M.C., and a rifleman the D.C.M. for an act of gallantry in bringing in a wounded comrade under heavy rifle and machine gun fire.

In the Trenches.

About the end of October, in spite of a tremendous amount of work, the condition of the trenches became very bad, and in time the communication trenches were impassable. The men were up to their thighs in mud. Strenuous efforts, however, kept the number of "trench feet" in the battalion down to one, for which special commendation was given by the Divisional Commander, Major General Perceval. This was a state of affairs very different from the experiences of the sister battalion, and it may be that this circumstance was due to the fact that the commander of the 8th—Lieut.-Colonel Alexander—was a medical man.

When the gas attack was delivered at Pilkem on December 19th, the 8th were in rest, and they were hurriedly marched up to Elverdinghe. No attack ensued there, so the battalion returned to camp and celebrated their Christmas festivities—a little prematurely, but the battalion was due to be in the front line on Christmas Day. A much-needed and frequently postponed relief took place at the end of December, and the battalion marched to Wormhoudt, and thence to Calais for a rest.

Their next tour of trench duty was opposite Thiepval, then a comparatively quiet sector, whence, after a short stay, they were sent back to Vignacourt to train for the Somme offensive.

Accordingly, the never to be forgotten July 1st, 1916, found the 8th supporting the Ulster Division in the attack on Thiepval, and although not called upon to "go over the bags," they suffered casualties to the extent of 11 officers and 191 other ranks. In the evening two companies were sent forward with another battalion to the captured German trenches, but were eventually withdrawn. Later, on July 16th, the battalion carried out a successful little attack in the Leipzig salient which yielded some very important observations. Then followed a period of lively trench warfare and the battalion were holding the front line when Thiepval was captured on September 26th. Here they first saw the Tanks in operation. A quiet period of trench warfare was their next experience, the locality being Fonquevillers and opposite Ransart, and Christmas of 1916 was celebrated in comfort behind the line.

Early in 1917, the Division moved north and took over their old trenches near Fauquissart, a sector that was enlivened by raids on both sides, successful on ours and a failure on the enemy's part. It was here that the 1st Portuguese Division were attached for instruction, and they eventually took over the sector, the 8th West Yorkshires moving to the coast under the command of Lieut.-Colonel R. A. Hudson, D.S.O., who had assumed command the previous September, when Lieut.-Colonel Alexander, D.S.O. was invalided home.

The battalion suffered severely from mustard gas in Nieuport on July 20th, and after a period of rest and refitting they went into battle again on October 9th at Passchendaele. Here, in spite of the utmost difficulties of weather and terrain and a twelve hours approach march, an advance was made, and the ground gained was held until the Division had been relieved by the New Zealand Division. In this action the 8th had 20 officers hit out of 23, and 320 casualties amongst N.C.O.'s and men. The casualties included Lieut.-Colonel Hudson by whose death the battalion lost a gallant soldier, a fine commanding officer, and a devoted friend.

The battalion were now commanded by Lieut.-Colonel S. S. Sykes, and suffered a period of difficult outpost warfare on the ridges near Passchendaele amidst great discomfort due to weather, the state of the ground, and the activities on both sides. Christmas was spent in the front line, and shortly afterwards Lieut.-Colonel Sykes went home sick, and Major Longbottom, D.S.O., assumed command, the battalion going out to rest at Staple.

On February 1st, 1918, there was a re-organisation throughout the Army, and the 7th and 8th Battalions parted company, the 1/8th being amalgamated with the 2/8th under Lieut.-Colonel A. H. James, D.S.O., in the 62nd Division. It proved a happy combination, and the battalion, still known as the 8th, went on from success to success.

When the enemy attacked in March, 1918, the battalion were holding trenches near Arras. They were hurriedly moved down to stem the attack, and on March 26th, with the 2/5th West Yorkshires on the left, and the 7th Duke of Wellington's on the right, fought off a series of hotly-pressed attacks on Bucquoy, which village formed an angle in the line and was a most vital point. In spite of the enemy's efforts, which lasted throughout the day and included attacks by the Prussian Guards, the village remained in our hands. The success, however, was dearly bought, for our casualties were very heavy, including the death of Lieut.-Colonel James, D.S.O., who was killed by a sniper whilst directing fire on to an approaching body of the enemy. He was a fine fighter, and his loss was felt throughout the battalion. Major Longbottom, D.S.O., now took command, and the battalion, after a small attack at Rossignol Wood, went back for a rest. Then, when Major Longbottom went home for six months' tour of duty, command was taken over by Lieut.-Colonel England, from the Duke of Wellington's Regiment.

How the Croix de Guerre was Won.

A period of arduous trench warfare followed at Bucquoy and the neighbouring village of Ablainqueville, alternated with short periods of rest behind the line. It was during one of these rests in July that the Division received orders to entrain for an unknown destination, which was rightly suspected to be the salient recently formed by the enemy attacks between Soissons and Rheims. After a long railway journey the 8th West Yorkshires arrived on the Marne, and after a short rest at Tours-sur-Marne, moved forward to St. Imoges, and without possibility of reconnaissance advanced to the attack. Ten days' hard fighting ensued, in which the battalion took a most gallant part, almost continuously moving or fighting, and during that brief period they captured many prisoners as well as machine guns and much material. The men never faltered, in spite of a vast concentration of enemy artillery, nests of enemy machine guns, a country made for defence, covered with woods, hills and natural defence, and with strongly held villages. Everything that the battalion were asked to do they successfully accomplished, and they crowned those magnificent achievements by carrying out unsupported a task which appeared an impossibility, in the taking of the Montaigne de Bligny—a high hill which stood up steeply at the head of a valley, commanded all approaches, and was powerfully held by the enemy's superior force.

How did they do it ? The battalion advanced through Chamuzy on the night of July 27th, and, forming up west of the village, advanced alone to the attack at 4 a.m. The hill was covered with vineyards, and honeycombed with machine gun nests, but the 8th were not to be denied. In spite of the fatigues of the previous few days, they advanced unsupported by artillery, and with magnificent valour cleared the Montaigne of the enemy. It was for this gallant action that Lieut.-Colonel England and the 8th West Yorkshire Regiment were cited in the 5th French Army Orders of the Day, gaining the Croix de Guerre avec Palme, the highest class of that Order ; and in a march past of certain units of the Division, General Berthelot, commanding the 5th French Army specially asked for the battalion that had captured the Montaigne de Bligny.

This wonderful exploit will live for ever in the annals of the Leeds Rifles. It is commemorated by the green, red and gold medal ribbon of the Croix de Guerre worn on every man's shoulder and the cockade of the same colours in the head dress.

A well-earned spell of rest and refitment at Vauchelles followed, including some days spent in marching and counter-marching to deceive the enemy as to dispositions, and then on August 24th, the battalion moved to Courcelles, occupying a railway embankment just east of that village, which was full of captured material. Next they went to Mory, and spent a few days in "peaceful penetration," and on September 1st attacked and captured the village of Vaulx, taking prisoners. Being relieved there, they moved first to Sapignes, and then to Fremicourt, whence the battalion moved on September 11th to Havrincourt Wood in support of an attack. On the 14th one company, lent to the 2/20th London Regiment, had a successful bombing attack, capturing several prisoners, and on the 16th the battalion moved to Hermies, and later to the vicinity of Vaulx Orancourt.

The next operations of importance took place on September 27th, when the battalion crossed the Canal du Nord, and attacked the trench system between Marcoing and Flesquieres. Here there was some very hard fighting, in which the battalion enhanced their reputation, two companies being especially mentioned for their gallantry in a Corps Special Order of the Day. In this action they captured 15 field guns, nine machine guns and a number of prisoners, but their casualties were very heavy, and on reorganisation into two companies, No. 1 company had two officers and 81 other ranks, and No. 2 a like number of officers and 79 other ranks, headquarters being four officers and 63 other ranks.

The following day was spent in re-organisation and then the battalion moved east of Masnieres for a further advance, which was successfully carried out in spite of troops on the left being hung up. At the end of this action only one officer was left with the companies, but after relief the battalion moved to Havrincourt.

On October 20th the 8th took part with great

success in the River Selle battle, capturing the high ground to the right of Solesmes, along with two guns, some machine guns and trench mortars, and 130 prisoners; and sustaining very few casualties. The battalion then bore their share in the final operations of the war, capturing Obies and Monplaisar, a suburb of Maubeuge, and in due course became part of the Army of Occupation in Germany.

It was on Friday, May 16th, 1919, that the cadre of the battalion, released from the Western front, arrived in Leeds. They had a great reception. Comprising about 50 officers and men, under the command of Major Brooke, they were met at the station by Brigadier General Mends and a number of other officers, and were informally welcomed to the city. Marching through the principal streets they were joined by several hundred demobilised men who had served either with the same unit or with the 7th Battalion. There was a great crowd to receive them in front of the Town Hall, including the Lord Mayor (Mr. Joseph Henry), three ex-Lord Mayors, and two of the local V.C.'s. Several speeches were made, in the course of which proud mention was made of the fact that the battalion was one of the first units to win the Croix de Guerre.

During the war, the 8th Battalion West Yorkshire Regiment—that is the 1/8th, 2/8th, and the amalgamation—gained the following honours :—

The Battalion, the Croix de Guerre avec Palme.
Individual Honours :—

Bar to D.S.O.	1
D.S.O.	4
Bar to M.C.	1
M.C.	31
D.C.M.	15
Bar to M.M.	11
M.M.	148
Croix de Guerre with palm	3
Gold Star	2
Silver Star	2
Croix de Guerre Belge	2

In addition the battalion were cited in French Army Orders and in VI. Corps Orders.

The Bar to D.S.O. was won by Colonel A. H. James. The D.S.O. was awarded to Colonel J. W. Alexander, Lieut.-Colonel R. A. Hudson, Major T. Longbottom and Lieut.-Colonel Norman England.

THE SECOND LINE BATTALIONS.

There is yet more to tell. This story of the Leeds Rifles is not complete without mention of the 2/7th and 2/8th Battalions, which landed in France on January 3rd, 1917. They formed part of the 62nd Division, which was composed of the second line units of the 49th Division.

The 2/7th, commanded by Lieut.-Colonel the Hon. F. S. Jackson, went into the front line for the first time in February, near Beaumont Hamel. The position had been captured only 48 hours before, and a long and intense frost having just come to an end, everyone had the fullest possible experience of the horrors of Somme mud. Towards the end of February, Lieut.-Colonel Jackson was invalided home, and Lieut.-Colonel C. K. James (6th Battalion Border Regiment) succeeded him. March was spent in working behind the line during the German retirement, and the beginning of April found the battalion in the front line near Bullecourt, where they remained until the end of May. Because of former heavy losses the battalion were kept in reserve during the big attack on the Hindenburg Line on May 4th, but about ten days later one company was almost wiped out in a local operation at the Crucifix, Bullecourt, only about half a dozen men—all wounded—getting back. June was spent in rest and training, and during the next four months the battalion were occupied with normal trench warfare in the Bullecourt and Noreuil sectors.

On November 20th, 1917, the battalion took

Inspection of the 2/7th and 2/8th Battalions West Yorkshire Regiment (Leeds Rifles) in Victoria Square, Leeds, by the Lord Mayor (Mr. James E. Bedford), May 15th, 1915.

part in the very successful attack on Cambrai, all troops being in the precise positions arranged beforehand by 2 p.m. After two days' rest the battalion were ordered into the line again to help to hold Bourlon Wood, and they remained there until relieved. They had been out of the line only one day when the enemy made his heavy and unsuccessful attack at Moeuvres, and his more successful attack at Gonnelieu. Thus it happened that, very tired, and having suffered very heavy casualties, the battalion had to go up into the line again, this time into support near Moeuvres. December, however, was a month of rest, after which the first three months of 1918 were spent in normal trench warfare in the Bailleul and Oppy sectors.

On March 21st, 1918, the first day of the great German offensive, the battalion were at Arleux. There was a heavy bombardment, but no attack. Three days later they marched 16 miles to Bucquoy to wait for the Boche, and from the 25th to 27th all positions were held in the face of several enemy attacks.

After a period of normal trench warfare in the Bucquoy sector, the battalion experienced the bitter blow of disbandment. The majority of the officers and men went into the 2/5th Battalion West Yorkshire Regiment, or the 8th Battalion West Yorkshire Regiment in the same Brigade. They had, however, the consolation of knowing that they had never been forced to retire from any position taken up, and had never lost a single post. In May, Lieut.-Colonel James, D.S.O., was killed. He was only 26 years of age, and had commanded the battalion for 15 months with conspicuous ability. After his death the battalion was commanded by Lieut.-Colonel L. R. Jones, M.C., until it was disbanded.

In his farewell letter to Lieut.-Colonel Jones, the G.O.C., 185th Brigade, wrote :—

" The 2/7th Battalion has invariably done everything that has been asked of it in the fighting line, and I know well that when the day comes on which the 185th Brigade meet the Germans in battle I shall long for the help of the 2/7th in whom I could always absolutely rely."

The 2/8th Battalion went out to France under the command of Lieut.-Colonel Hepworth, and gallantly shared in the difficulties and hardships at Beaumont Hamel at the end of January, 1917, and later in the action at Bullecourt. Following a period of trench warfare the battalion took part in the first battle of Cambrai, where the 62nd Division made a record advance, and established a reputation which was enhanced in later actions. At Cambrai the battalion were commanded by Lieut.-Colonel A. H. James, D.S.O., who continued in command until March, 1918. On February 1st, 1918, a reorganisation of the Army brought about the amalgamation of the 1/8th and the 2/8th in the 62nd Division, and the remainder of the story is recounted in the experiences of the 8th Battalion.

THE CYCLISTS' CORPS.

Mention also should be made of the work done by the 62nd (West Riding) Cyclist Company which was so largely recruited from Leeds. This Company was composed of men from Infantry battalions who were good cyclists, and they rendered splendid service during the long period of trench warfare on the Western Front, particularly observation work, as rearguard in the the retreat of Spring, 1918, and as advance guard in the great offensive in the Autumn. When encamped at Thoresby Park in September 1915 (Captain E. J. Clarke in command) they had a recruiting march through the West Riding, and of the 200 men wanted at that time Leeds supplied 120. The 62nd Company became one of three Companies of the 18th Corps Battalion, and in October, 1916, Captain Clarke

Lieut.-Col. STUART C. TAYLOR,
15th Battalion West Yorkshire Regiment
(Leeds "Pals").

Capt. L. BATHURST (R.A.M.C.),
15th Battalion West Yorkshire Regiment
(Leeds "Pals").

Photo by   Bacon & Son.
Lieut.-Col. J. W. STEAD, V.D.,
15th Battalion West Yorkshire Regiment
(Leeds "Pals").

Photo by   Bacon & Son.
Lieut.-Col. E. KITSON CLARK, T.D.,
8th Battalion West Yorkshire Regiment
(Leeds Rifles).

was promoted to the rank of Major. He had been seconded from the Leeds Rifles for this special service and, after commanding the Company for about a year at the Front, he was appointed on the Staff of General Maxse as A.A.Q.M.G. Then, six months later, in the summer of 1918, he was given the command of the 19th Corps Battalion. Major Clarke, who is the son of ex-Alderman W. H. Clarke, the Leeds City Coroner, was twice mentioned in despatches, and he was awarded the French Croix de Guerre, with Silver Star, in recognition of the valuable assistance rendered by his battalion in the advance.

THE LEEDS "PALS"
15th BATTALION WEST YORKSHIRE REGIMENT.

> We saw you go, your city's pride and hope,
>   From desk and class-room, office, mart, and mill,
>   And every heart extolled your resolute will,
> And cast in glowing guise your horoscope.
>
> Truest of pals, you were among the first
>   To answer gladly when the country called;
>   You never flinched; with spirit unappalled,
> You challenged fate to do its best or worst.
>
> To claims of discipline, that long foreran
>   The eventful day, we saw you patient yield;
>   Next, steeled with courage, on the battlefield,
> Forward to victory you led the van.
>
> Heroic souls! still shall your virtues glow!
>   Though many a simple cross and grassy mound
>   Blind the sad eye with tears; still, ever crowned
> In grateful hearts, we see you deathless go,
> Cherished through countless years of memory-tide,
> Your city's credit and your country's pride.
>   W.H.S.

"Four times wiped out, but fighting to the end," conveys in a sentence the glorious record of the 15th Battalion West Yorkshire Regiment, or, to give the unit its more familiar title, the Leeds Pals Battalion. Because of the circumstances in which it was recruited, and the calibre of the men who filled its ranks, the battalion made a special appeal to the city of its origin, and the splendid fighting qualities it displayed in some of the heaviest engagements on the Western front amply justified local pride.

When Lord Kitchener's call for men came in those stirring days of August, 1914, the proposal to form a city battalion of business men, in addition to the two rifle battalions, was brought forward by Col. J. Walter Stead, V.D., a Leeds Solicitor who had served his period of command in the Leeds Rifles. The idea caught on at once; it fired the popular imagination; comradeship such as a "Pals" Battalion promised provoked an immediate response from the city's young manhood. Sir Edward A. Brotherton was Lord Mayor when the proposal was made, and he not only undertook to bear the cost of equipment but threw himself heart and soul into the work of raising the battalion. Support came from all parts of the city. Alderman (now Sir) Charles H. Wilson, the leader of the City Council, himself an old volunteer, was foremost among the enthusiasts who helped, and he became the battalion's first Quartermaster. In the stress of those early days rough and ready methods were inevitable in the preliminary training, and much was left to local resource. The late Mr. Arthur Willey, M.P., then an Alderman of the City Council, was another who gave valuable help, and the Waterworks Committee, of which he was Chairman, provided the first training ground of the battalion on the Corporation Waterworks estate at Colsterdale.

Practically all the well-known families of Leeds were represented in the Pals. Lieut.-Colonel Walter Stead was appointed to the command. The second in command was Major Howard, who afterwards took command of a battalion of Northumberland Fusiliers, and was killed in action. The Adjutant was Captain Depledge. The battalion was soon over strength, and in the early days of September an advance party left for Colsterdale to prepare camp for the main body

Alderman Sir Charles H. Wilson, Knt., M.P.

which arrived on the moorland heights above Masham on Friday, September 25th, every man taking his own kit. An appeal for blankets met with a good response. The men, however, had no uniforms, but, thanks largely to the energies of Sir Edward Brotherton, these and the rest of the equipment were provided as soon as possible. In appreciation of his services, Sir Edward Brotherton had conferred upon him the distinction of hon. colonel of the battalion.

Strenuous military training during the rigours of winter on the bleak moors of Colsterdale made severe demands, but the Pals were always cheerful, and their military bearing was evident when Christmas leave came. In half battalions the men were allowed to visit Leeds, and on January 4th, 1915, they marched through the main central streets, and were accorded an enthusiastic reception. Massed in Victoria Square they were greeted by the Lord Mayor and Lady Mayoress (Mr. and Mrs. J. E. Bedford) and other leading citizens with feelings of pride at the sight of such a fine body of men. In due course the unit was taken into the Army as the 15th Battalion of the West Yorkshire Regiment, and in May, 1915, Lieut.-Colonel Stead left the battalion, exchanging command with Lieut.-Colonel S. C. Taylor, who had commanded the 13th Battalion King's Own Yorkshire Light Infantry at Harrogate. A soldier every inch of him, Colonel Taylor was an ideal man to train such a battalion, and his personality speedily stamped itself upon all ranks.

No finer tribute to the sterling quality of the battalion could be paid than the fact that during the time it was in England many of the men were picked out for commissions in other units. Before the battalion left England between 400 and 500 men from its ranks had received commissions. This steady process of attrition, however, interfered with training, and great as was the compliment,

Colonel Taylor had at last to put a check to the movement.

On June 3rd the "Pals" visited Leeds on a recruiting mission; and then, a few days later, they marched from Colsterdale to Ripon, where they became part of the 93rd Brigade of the 31st Division, the Brigade commander being Brigadier General Molesworth. Whilst at Ripon Camp Captain Charles H. Wilson unfortunately had a riding accident which necessitated his relinquishing his appointment as Quartermaster, and he retired with the honorary rank of Captain, subsequently being promoted Major in command of the Leeds group of Motor Volunteers.

FROM SALISBURY PLAIN TO EGYPT.

On leaving Ripon the battalion moved to Fovant, on the edge of Salisbury Plain, where intensive field training was carried out. At the time it was expected that the next move would be to France. But the plans were changed. On December 4th, 1915, the 31st Division left Salisbury Plain, and two days later embarked at Liverpool for Egypt, the whole of the 93rd Brigade with the brigade staff sailing in the "Empress of Britain."

This initial venture into the war zone was full of incident, for the German submarine menace was making itself apparent, and the transport had to take a course well out into the Atlantic to avoid peril. After passing the Straits of Gibraltar as many men as possible slept on deck, and all wore life belts as a precaution against torpedo attack. On the second night in the Mediterranean the "Empress of Britain," sailing, of course, without lights, crashed clean through a small French steamer which was returning to France from Salonica. The survivors, 60 or 70 in all, were picked up, and the transport ran into Malta for repairs. Possibly this delay enabled the enemy to acquire some information, for soon after the transport left Malta it was attacked by two submarines, which were, however, beaten off by the ship's 6-inch gun.

The brigade arrived safely at their destination, and Christmas, 1915, was spent at Port Said. There, they relieved the Gurkhas, who were guarding the Suez Canal. The Pals headquarters were at Kantara, and the four companies were disposed along the Canal bank. Early in the New Year the whole Division moved out into the Sinai desert, and constructed a defensive line of trenches. The Pals had their first casualty when a private was accidentally shot at a picket post in the desert.

All this time events were shaping themselves on the Western Front, and, as one result of the first big German attack on Verdun, orders were received in Egypt for the division to proceed to France.

Arrival in France.

The Leeds Pals sailed from Port Said on February 28th, 1916, on the S.S. Ascania, and after a pleasant and uneventful voyage of eight days found themselves at Marseilles. Thence two-and-a-half days' train journey through the heart of France brought them to Pont Remy, near Abbeville, at the mouth of the Somme.

The sudden change from the warm sunshine of Egypt to the snow and slush of mid-winter in Northern France caused a good deal of sickness in the form of colds and influenza, and among the victims to pneumonia was the Brigadier, who died in this district. He was succeeded by Brigadier-General Ingles, who commanded the brigade through some of its most trying times.

After a fortnight's rest the Division marched up to the line in the last week of March, the Leeds Pals taking over a sector of trenches at Mailly-Maillet, opposite Beaumont Hamel. At first the battalion experienced a quiet time, and, during its first spell of eight days in the trenches, had but two casualties—one man wounded in the foot and another killed accidentally whilst cleaning a machine gun. From now until after the opening of the Somme battle on July 1st the battalion headquarters were at Bus-le-Artois, a big straggling village a few miles behind Mailly-Maillet. As the weather improved there was more artillery activity on both sides and the quiet period in the trenches was not prolonged. The battalion's first real taste of serious warfare took the form of a raid by the Boche on the Pal trenches on May 22nd. After some stiff fighting the raiders were beaten off, and few, if any, got back to their own lines. On the other hand our casualties were heavy. A working party from C company was doing work "on top" and became heavily involved in the German barrage. This raid brought the first decoration to the battalion, the Military Cross being awarded to Lieut. Oolans.

For a month or so afterwards the Pals were engaged in intensive preparations for the fateful First of July, but meanwhile casualties were accumulating. Lieut.-Colonel Taylor had been wounded in the leg and invalided to England; and shortly afterwards the Second-in-Command, Major Dewhirst, was wounded by a shell which killed the Adjutant, Captain Depledge.

The Attack on the Somme.

The eve of July 1st found the Pals fully prepared for their first big battle. They spent the night in the battered trenches waiting anxiously for the "zero" hour, and what should have been a beautiful summer evening on the banks of the Somme was turned into a devilish inferno by the thunder of the artillery.

At length the decisive moment came. The attack, so far as the 31st Division was concerned, was entrusted to the 93rd and 94th Brigades, the former, on the right, being led by the 15th West Yorkshires, who were followed by the 16th and 18th Battalions of the same regiment. The remaining unit, the 18th Durham Light Infantry, were held in reserve, though a party of them took a splendid share in the assault and actually penetrated some depth into the enemy lines. On the left, the Sheffield battalion went over first, alongside the Leeds men, and they were supported by the Barnsley and East Lancashire Pals.

Of the Leeds Pals, C. and D. Companies led the way, the immediate objective being the village of Serre, about a quarter of a mile distant on the opposite slope of the valley. Fruitless though it unhappily proved, it was a magnificent exhibition of coolness and discipline, and worthily maintained the highest traditions of British pluck and courage. The men went over in " waves " with the precise orderliness of a parade ground manœuvre. But as our artillery barrage lifted from the Germans' front line innumerable machine guns appeared immediately on their trench parados. In face of the terrible hurricane of machine gun bullets, which swept across the open, our men went down like ripe grain before the sickle, and in almost as short a time as it takes to tell all was practically over.

How near those splendid fellows came to achievement of success may be reckoned from the fact that one party actually reached the village of Serre, and gallantly fought their way out again. Every officer except one who went "over the top" was either killed or died of wounds; every sergeant-major, including the regimental sergeant-major, was killed; and of the rank and file only a handful—47 N.C.O.'s and men—was left out of 800. A pioneer battalion of Castleford and district miners—the 12th K.O.Y.L.I.—when they saw what was happening " downed tools " and heroically rushed in to help.

TRIBUTES TO VALOUR.

News of the disaster filtered slowly through to the homeland, and the publication of the casualty lists plunged hundreds of Leeds homes into mourning. Writing to the Lord Mayor of Leeds (Mr. Charles Lupton) a week after the opening of the Somme offensive, Lieut.-Colonel Taylor, who was still an inmate of an English hospital, sent the following message of sympathy with regard to the Pals losses :—

"SIR,—As I am still in hospital, and consequently some time must elapse before I am able to obtain all the addresses of the relatives of the officers and soldiers of the 15th Battalion West Yorkshire Regiment who have recently fallen in action in France, I would ask you to grant me a little space to make known personally to all those relatives the deep sympathy I feel for them in the irreparable losses they have sustained.

For myself I mourn the loss of tried comrades and dear friends, men with whom I have been closely associated day and night, in sunshine and storm, for the past fourteen months. But with my sorrow is mingled an immense pride, a great gladness, as I hear from all sources of the magnificent bearing and heroic conduct of our dear lads who have cheerfully given their lives for their King and country. The tidings of their gallant conduct and courageous deeds causes me no surprise, as I well knew how splendidly they would stand the test when the supreme call was made upon them. To those who are left behind to mourn their loss may God grant consolation in the sure knowledge of their dear ones' valiant death. For the wounded I pray earnestly for a speedy return to health and strength. For myself my only wish is that I had been able to be with the battalion in their great and glorious attack."

This tribute from the battalion's commanding officer was supplemented by further messages which the Lord Mayor received from high officers at the Front, and which he read at a meeting of the Leeds City Council in August, 1916. The Lord Mayor explained that he had received a letter from the Brigadier-General commanding the Brigade in which the Pals were fighting, conveying the Brigadier's testimony to the work done by the battalion, and to their most gallant behaviour in their first serious engagement. The Brigadier wrote :—

"Though I have been a very short time in command of the brigade, from the first I knew from the military bearing and the keenness of all ranks that when the time did come to which they were all looking forward with such fervour they would render a good account of themselves. The opportunity came on July

1st, and right gallantly every officer, N.C.O., and man behaved. I would, however, add how deeply I sympathise with the parents, wives and families of all those gallant men who have lost their lives. I also sympathise very sincerely with all those gallant men who have been wounded, and although I know the brigade will not, unfortunately, have the honour of getting them all back, I hope that the very great majority will return to us to help to accomplish what their and our hearts desire, namely, victory and all that it means for Great Britain and our gallant Allies."

The General commanding the Army Corps also issued a message speaking in the highest terms of the conduct of the men under his command, and another superior officer sent the following message :—

" Just a line to say how sorry we are to hear of the losses which your magnificent Corps has recently suffered in its gallant fighting in the German trenches. They are indeed heroes, and their name will live for ever."

Meanwhile, following upon their disastrous experience of July 1st, the remnant of the battalion had returned to headquarters to refit, and in a fortnight the unit had been brought up to 500 strong from the general pool of new drafts. It was then sent back into the line in the Festubert section, and assumed responsibility for this part of the line until the end of the year. During this period the battalion was getting up to establishment and training the new drafts as they came along.

In the New Year, 1917, the division was moved back to the Somme, and the Pals found themselves beside their Territorial comrades from Yorkshire, the 49th Division. Whilst in this sector near their old battle-ground opposite Serre, the men of the 15th came across grim reminders of the previous July 1st, in the shape of the remains of a number of gallant officers and men who fell in that struggle, and whose bodies could not be recovered at the time. Amongst those whose fate was thus put beyond doubt were Captain Whittaker, Lieut. Tolson, and Lieut. Major Booth, the Yorkshire county cricketer. Lieutenant Booth's remains were identified by a cigarette case given to him by the M.C.C. as a member of the team which toured South Africa. This relic which was picked up in a shell-hole, was sent to Lieutenant Booth's sister.

Epic Struggle at Vimy Ridge.

In March 1917, the division moved to fresh quarters, going viâ Bethune to Bethonsart, nine miles from Arras, as reserve for the 1st Army in the Vimy Ridge operations. Here another terrible ordeal awaited them. On May 1st, Vimy Ridge had been captured by the Canadians, and the line was being pushed forward. At 5.30 on the morning of May 3rd, the battalion went over in the Gavrelle sector to complete the operations, but the whole thing was a glorious failure. The Germans had fallen back on strong defensive lines, and although the Pals fought with reckless bravery, Colonel Taylor, who had now returned to the command, had the sad experience of seeing his battalion practically wiped out for the second time. Twenty officers were either killed or wounded and missing, and about 700 other ranks were casualties. It was impossible to send relief, and Colonel Taylor and his gallant remnant had to hang on to their dangerous position. This they did for five days.

It was an epic struggle against heavy odds. Colonel Taylor collected and organised pioneers, engineers, transport men, batmen and cooks—anybody and everybody he could find—and put them into the trenches to repel counter-attacks. For this service Colonel Taylor was given the Distinguished Service Order. Here, too, Regimental Sergeant-Major Wilson won the M.C. Company Sergeant-Major Joe Jones, the champion heavyweight wrestler of Yorkshire, won the D.C.M. for his work on May 3rd. An expert bayonet fighter, he found himself surrounded by the enemy. He bayoneted four and got a fifth, but could not withdraw his bayonet quickly enough to defend himself, and was in turn severely wounded. Jones was one of the original Pals, and had given up a job at the Army School, preferring fighting with his beloved battalion to teaching at the base.

After this spell of heavy fighting the battalion, with its losses made good, enjoyed a prolonged period of comparative quiet. The battalion remained in the Gavrelle sector, holding the trenches for some months, until it was moved to Neuville St. Vaast to set free the 2nd Canadian Division for the terrible struggle which took place soon afterwards in the "No Man's Land" north of Lens. At the beginning of November the 31st Division went back to the Vimy Ridge sector, and the 15th Battalion was specially selected by the Divisional Commander to undertake a number of raids, some of which were quite brilliant little affairs. The next move was to the Roolincourt-Ecurie sector, north of Arras, and here, towards the end of November, the Leeds Bantams (17th Battalion West Yorkshire Regiment) were amalgamated with the Pals.

Christmas, 1917, was spent at Ecurie as happily as possible. As the Pals were required to take over a sector of trenches on Christmas Eve, the season's festivities had to be postponed, but when the spell of trench duty finished on December 29th the festival was celebrated with great heartiness, the presents sent out from Leeds being much enjoyed, particularly the cigarette cases. After a great Christmas dinner the day finished up with a grand pantomime in the battalion's marquee. The producer was Lieutenant Ashford, well-known in the theatrical world, and the pantomime did him credit. The big tent, known amongst the troops as "The Circus" rang with laughter. Sergeant Bristow, who was afterwards killed in action, was the principal boy, and Sergeant Hague the principal "girl." Other Leeds men who took part were Sergeant Walter

Helliwell, and Privates Bunting, Ward, Gande, Thompson and Watson Walker. Easy times followed until towards the end of March, 1918, when the Germans made their great bid for Amiens and the Paris main line.

On the Somme Again.

The Battalion was resting near Cacourt on March 22nd, 1918, when at ten o'clock at night urgent orders were received to proceed to the Somme. Five hours later the battalion had packed itself into motor 'buses, reaching Moyenville at ten o'clock on the morning of the 23rd. After marching forward for nearly two miles the men received orders to dump their packs by the side of the road, and be ready to meet the Boche at any minute. The transport got some of the men's belongings away, but a great deal was lost. The Pals were soon at close grips with the advancing enemy, and were pushed back to Monchy. It was a desperate rearguard action, and, as was inevitable, confusion reigned supreme. Parties were cut off and left behind; wounded men had to be left where they fell; and units got terribly mixed as position after position was held for a time to delay the enemy's advance, and then hastily evacuated.

It was during this confused fighting that Sergeant Mountain, who came to the Pals from the Bantams, won the Victoria Cross. Finding himself cut off he selected a good defensive position, from which he thought he could worry the enemy. He collected three other stragglers from other units, and the four held their little fortress for 28 hours. When the post was relieved by a counter-attack, about 130 dead Germans were counted in front of it. Mountain's brave and cool action had a great effect upon the situation, and the heroic sacrifice of the whole battalion undoubtedly saved the 31st Division from disaster.

For the Pals this was an even worse experience than July 1st, 1916. In a desperate rearguard action over seven or eight miles the Pals had orders to "hang on" to the last man, and they did so. All that remained were about 45 men, and the greater number of these received decorations for their gallantry. Afterwards 65 prisoners taken by the Germans were accounted for. Not one officer was left. The Commanding Officer, Colonel Twis, of the East Yorkshires, was taken prisoner, and the adjutant, Captain Harold Smith, M.C., died of wounds. Captain Smith, who was formerly manager of the Leeds Corporation Cleansing Department, had risen from the ranks, and for his gallantry in the fight he was awarded a bar to his Military Cross. Colonel Taylor was on leave in England at the time of this third disaster to his battalion, and he was recalled to command the 93rd brigade. That the French appreciated the devotion of the Leeds Pals was shown by a very sympathetic and eulogistic article published in the *Echo de Paris*.

The remnants of the battalion returned to Cacourt to refit, and here a draft of 500 was received, composed entirely of lads under 19 years of age, it evidently being the intention that the battalion should have a rest from the battle line. On April 11th it moved to the Hazebrouck sector. The enemy had opened his Northern offensive, and had forced Bailleul, but the attack was apparently dying down. The 15th were sent to Merris to oppose any further advance, but it was supposed to be a quiet part of the line. About midnight one night, however, a message came through from brigade headquarters to say that the Germans had broken through on this particular sector, and the Pals had to go into action at once. They were called upon to defend an important line of railway.

It was about this time that Lord Haig's

famous message to the Army, "We are fighting with our backs to the wall," was issued, and the Leeds Pals, true to their old traditions, grasped the true inwardness of the message, and fought gloriously to the last man.

Again history repeated itself. Everybody who could fire a rifle was thrown into the terrible melée. It was open, man-to-man fighting, and though only a few men remained of the battalion the Germans did not pass. Lieut.-Colonel Coles, of the Royal Fusiliers, was wounded and invalided home, and his place was taken by Lieut.-Colonel Norton, a Huddersfield accountant, and a West Riding Territorial officer.

Another rest for refit and reinforcements followed, and then the battalion was engaged with the 31st Division in the successful operations which led to the armistice.

Welcome Home.

On Monday, May 26th, 1919, the cadre of the Pals Battalion came to Leeds, and were accorded a hearty welcome by thousands of the citizens. The cadre—consisting of five officers—Lieut.-Colonel F. Walton, M.C., in command; Captain A. V. Brightwell; Captain and Quartermaster J. Farnworth; Second-Lieut. T. W. Raithby, D.C.M.; and Second-Lieut. R.S. Douglas—and about 40 men, arrived at the new station from York and were received by Col. Sir Edward Brotherton, M.P. (Hon. Colonel of the battalion), Lieut.-Colonel J. W. Stead (the first Commanding Officer), Major C. H. Wilson (first Quartermaster), Captain R. J. Anderson and others. "See the Conquering Hero Comes," was played by the Leeds Police Band as the cadre alighted from the train, and rousing cheers greeted the men as they marched into the station yard and took up a position in front of some 200 demobilised members of the battalion. Through streets elaborately decorated with flags the troops marched between thick lines of people to Victoria Square, where a civic reception was accorded them.

On the steps of the Town Hall stood the Lord Mayor (Mr. Joseph Henry), the Lady Mayoress (Mrs. A. E. Hartley), and the Town Clerk (Sir Robert Fox), and others present in addition to members of the City Council were Mr. (afterwards Sir) Michael Sadler, Vice-Chancellor of the University of Leeds, the Vicar of Leeds (the Rev. Bernard Heywood), Mrs. Charles Ratcliffe (who was Lady Mayoress at the time the battalion was formed), Alderman Charles Lupton, and Mr. J. E. Bedford (two ex-Lord Mayors).

The Lord Mayor, welcoming the cadre home, said that Leeds would always be proud of the Pals Battalion, proud of their record and of the valour they displayed in desperate situations on the field of battle. They had upheld the honour of the city and helped to defend the nation.

Colonel Sir Edward Brotherton thanked the Lord Mayor and citizens for their welcome, and in a few words to the troops, said : " We tender to you our gratitude and our appreciation of all you have done and dared for the sake of your country. We thank you for the dangers and hardships you have endured. You have indeed added fresh laurels to the glorious achievements of a great regiment. We think of the fate which would have befallen our country had you not stood firm and steadfast against the blackest menace that ever threatened to overwhelm freedom and civilisation. We think of those who have returned, weakened, alas ! in health, or broken in body, and our thoughts go out to those you have left behind sleeping their last sleep in other lands. These thoughts fill our hearts with a deep sense of sorrow. But to-day we are very proud and happy in having you with us once again.

Your victory won ; your warfare done.

Colonel Walton, in responding, expressed thanks to the Leeds Flag Committee for the comforts sent from home, and said how much their efforts had been appreciated by the battalion.

Afterwards the Lord Mayor entertained the troops to tea, and the cadre subsequently returned to York for demobilisation.

Had the cadre visited Leeds a few days earlier they would have been able to participate in a great reunion of the Pals which took place in the Town Hall on Wednesday, May 21st, 1919, when 1,237 guests were entertained to dinner by their hon. colonel, Sir Edward Brotherton. A distinguished company assembled in honour of the event, the host being supported by the Lord Mayor, General Sir John Maxwell, G.O.C., Northern Command, the Vicar of Leeds, Major General Sir Berkeley Moynihan, and many other prominent Leeds citizens. Tribute to the Pals was paid by Sir Edward Brotherton, who said it was one of his proudest recollections that he had been able to have some share in raising the battalion, and Mrs. Charles Ratcliffe (Dorothy Una Ratcliffe, the Yorkshire poet and former Lady Mayoress) recited some touching verses which she had written " In Memory of the 1st of July, 1916," and dedicated " To the Mothers, Wives, and Sweethearts of the Leeds Pals."

With a record of valour so conspicuous, the Pals also had a sporting and athletic record which few, if any, units of the New Army could equal. Nearly twenty silver cups or similar trophies testify to their prowess in this direction. Whilst training at Colsterdale, the members of the Battalion " swept the decks " at the Northern Command Cross-Country Meeting at Newcastle. At Fovant, in the autumn of 1915, they gathered in every prize at the Southern Command Athletic Meeting. In January 1917, in France, the Battalion won the 31st Division Cross-Country

Championship, and was awarded the divisional silver cup. In June 1917, at the Divisional athletic sports, the Pals had to stop at the Brigade stage because the Division was moved. They, however, won the Brigade silver challenge cup, and took 16 events out of 20. About this time Army Horse Shows were arranged in France to encourage the care of transport and riding animals, and at the Brigade show the 15th carried off all honours except one in eleven events. At the Divisional Show they repeated the performance, and at the Army Show they won seven events and carried off two silver cups. They also won a Divisional cross-country championship, and eventually sent three competitors to the great contest open to the whole of the Army in France. All three competitors finished in the first ten.

LEEDS " BANTAMS."
17th BATTALION WEST YORKSHIRE REGIMENT.

" Little but good " sums up the qualities of those men of small stature, who, because of this disqualification, were unable to join existing units when the call came for recruits. Their flame of patriotism burned no less brightly although they were under regulation Army height ; and many a story could be told of a heart-wearying search in those early days of the war for an opportunity of service, to be met time after time with the recruiting sergeant's somewhat sarcastic " Not big enough, my lad." Here, however, was good material going a-begging, and when the need for men became clamant the Army Council gradually relaxed its regulations, until permission was given for the formation of Bantam battalions.

The opportunity thus afforded was speedily taken advantage of in many centres up and down the country, and Bantam battalions at once began to assume shape. A new unit, the 17th West Yorkshire Regiment, was assigned to Leeds, and recruiting started late in 1914 under the ægis of the Lord Mayor (Mr. J. E. Bedford).

In two or three months' time there was a full complement, and after a short spell of training at Leeds, Ilkley and Skipton, the battalion went under canvas at Masham. They were afterwards in camp at Chisledon (near Swindon), and later at Perham Down. It was whilst in camp at Chisledon that the battalion paid its farewell visit to the city of its origin before plunging into the welter of war on the Western front.

On Wednesday, November 3rd, 1915, Leeds citizens gave a very cordial reception to the Bantams when they arrived from camp on four days' leave.

The Lord Mayor offered welcome on behalf of the citizens, who, he said, were proud of their patriotic example. He was sure they would do credit to the city when at the Front, as the men of Leeds, already fighting their country's battle, were doing. He had heard a good deal of how bravely the Leeds Rifles were acquitting themselves, and how they had been described as equal to the Guards. He ventured to prophesy that the Bantams would be likened to the Gurkhas when their time came.

The Lord Mayor's prophesy was amply fulfilled when the battalion came to grips with the enemy.

The battalion sailed for France on January 31st, 1916, in the troopship "La Marguerite"—a vessel well-known in pre-war days both in the English Channel and on the Liverpool-Llandudno service. It was a cold, dreary crossing, and there were genuine expressions of pleasure when Havre was reached and the battalion finally encamped at Harfleur, in readiness to proceed up the line. Attached to the 35th (Bantam) Division, the Leeds men were the only Yorkshire battalion. Their colleagues in the 106th Brigade were the Royal Scots, Highland Light Infantry, and the Durham Light Infantry.

The period of waiting was not prolonged. After a twenty hours' railway journey the battalion found itself near St. Omer, and until early in May it was deputed to hold certain sectors between Armentieres and Givenchy. In comparison with later events the battalion had a quiet time hereabouts, but there was plenty of work to be done. In this part of the line trenches were more or less an unknown quantity, the defences in nearly all cases being breastworks. The upkeep of these, as compared with trenches, was much more onerous, and officers and men had no time on their hands.

Unfortunately the weather was very bad during the battalion's first few weeks in the line, and the work, which was exceptionally hard, had to be performed under very trying conditions. Laventie, Fleurbaix, Neuve Chapelle, Givenchy, and Richbourg were in turn the homes of the 17th West Yorkshires during the early part of their fighting days in France, and the experience gained there, both as regards hard work and living under trying conditions proved invaluable later in the campaign.

Subsequently the battalion was billeted at Bethune, which in those days was practically intact. Then began the preparations for the great Somme offensive in which the Bantam Division was allotted its due task. A short train journey, followed by several days' route marching brought the Division to Carnoy, a mile or two behind Montauban, and here, just before the Bantams went into action, the officers of the Division were addressed by the G.O.C., whose tribute to the rank and file was "they are little men, but they have stout hearts." Their valour was soon proved to the hilt, for, although badly battered in the terrific fighting, they emerged from the task with a record creditable to themselves, their country and the city of their birth.

Terrible Experiences on the Somme.

Although for a period the Leeds Bantams were in support they were in the thick of things, and in one day behind Maltz Horn Farm the casualties were as big as, if not bigger than, they were during the whole of the time spent in the trenches before the Somme battle. Bernafay Wood, too, took a sad toll of the Bantams a few days later, and 71 N.C.O.'s, particularly the sergeants, suffered very heavily in that never-to-be-forgotten wood, which, like its neighbour, Trones Wood, acquired such a terrible reputation. In one company three platoon sergeants out of four met their death within an hour, and one platoon was reduced to one officer, a lance-corporal, and a handful of men. The intensity of the fighting, the incessant rain of shells, the countless wounded, and all the other terrible happenings, made the experience a fearful one. Relieved in the middle of the night, the battalion marched back to " camp "—a disused trench a mile or two in the rear—and for practically the whole distance they were compelled to wear gas helmets, for the countryside reeked with the horrible stuff. It was a fitting climax to the trials the battalion had been undergoing.

A tour of the line behind Guillemont followed the experiences in and about Bernafay Wood, and it was with sadly depleted ranks that the battalion eventually left the district and went back to the " Happy Valley " for a much-needed rest. Those days on the Somme were days of terribly hard work, ghastly experiences and unending privations, but the manner in which these splendid little fighters bore themselves was indicated in special congratulations sent to the G.O.C. Bantam Division on their share in the attack west of Guillemont.

The Leeds Bantams were reinforced and brought up to something like normal strength during the time of waiting for orders to take up a position in the line, and after this spell of rest and recuperation the battalion entrained and was carried north.

It was in the Arras sector that the battalion was destined to stay for the next three months, and during the whole of that period its frontage remained the same—in front of Roclincourt, embracing Kent, Katie, Kite, and Kick craters. Although, so far as actual warfare was concerned, little happened out of the common, the work was exceptionally hard, possibly the most arduous during the Bantams' stay in France. To a large extent it was a return to pre-Somme conditions, and it involved a tremendous amount of manual labour. The routine will not soon be forgotten by those who lived through it—six days in the front line, six days in support, and six days in reserve.

The spell in the front line invariably meant very strenuous work, much of which arose from the persistent manner in which the enemy blew the trenches in with heavy trench mortars. When relieved, the battalion took up positions in the rear, and spent the next six days providing working parties to assist in maintaining the front line trenches, wire, etc.

During the third period the battalion was billeted in Arras, and both by day and by night every available man was utilised for some kind of constructive work. Every day thus brought the same hard, monotonous task; and there was a sigh of relief when news arrived that the 9th Division were to take over the whole sector early in December, 1916. The actual relief took place on December 2nd.

Whilst in this sector the battalion accomplished a successful little raid. Every object was achieved without one casualty to the Bantams.

After a quiet period, the battalion was transferred to a sector a good deal further south—the sector just west of Chaulnes. This was in March, 1917. The state of the trenches they took over was appalling ; they were knee-deep, and in some places almost waist-deep, in thick gluey mud that made progress almost impossible. Happily there came relief from these deplorable conditions, for the German retreat early in 1917 brought the days of the battalion in this sector to a premature end.

In keeping with his wily ways the retreat of the Boche was a stealthy affair, and it was a feather in the cap of the Leeds Bantams that one of their officers, accompanied by a sergeant and a man, was instrumental in getting back news to their division that the last of the enemy had gone from the sector. This was the result of increasing vigilance, and the officer in question—Second-Lieut. A. D. Rose—was warmly congratulated by the higher authorities on his untiring efforts and very valuable information.

The spring and summer of 1917 were spent in various sectors. Guillemont Farm and the Knoll were very warm spots, especially the last-named. Here, at the end of August, the battalion was badly pounded by the enemy who poured every conceivable kind of high explosive into our lines. The casualties were very severe, especially among the officers. It was in this sector that Second-Lieut. Rose, previously mentioned, met his death.

Drafted to the "Pals."

The latter days of the battalion were spent in Flanders, near Langemarck, where the Bantams Division had much arduous work to do. Owing to the fact that the disbanding of the battalion was now contemplated, reinforcements were not forthcoming, and during the last week or so in the fighting zone the ranks were seriously depleted.

MILITARY ACHIEVEMENTS.

Then came the breaking up of the battalion, for in common with several other battalions of the West Yorkshires, notably the 12th, 16th, and 18th, the Leeds Bantams were disbanded in the winter of 1917. It was a sad day for everyone when it was known that the War Office had decided upon this step. There was one consolation, however ; many of the officers and practically all the men were drafted to the 15th, and so were able to assist the Pals in keeping the old flag flying. In their new surroundings the men carried on with the same pluck and determination, the same bravery and skill which had made the name of the Leeds Bantams a household word in the city.

In addition to the V.C. won by Private Butler in September, 1917, and the V.C. won by Sergeant Mountain in March, 1918, after the Bantams had been amalgamated with the Pals battalion, many honours were conferred, notably Sergeant Percival, the well-known boxer, who received both the D.C.M. and the M.M. The battalion was fortunate in its commanding officers—the late Lieut.-Colonel F. St. J. Atkinson, who was in command during the battalion's first year in France ; Lieut.-Colonel P. S. Hall, D.S.O., a later commanding officer, and Major J. H. Gill, D.S.O. They were beloved by all ranks, and will never be forgotten.

Yet again Leeds heard of its Bantams' Battalion as a distinctive unit, for on Wednesday, December 15th, 1920, there took place with much ceremonial the dedication and reception of the battalion's colours. The first part of the proceedings took place in the Leeds Town Hall. Members of the battalion to the number of about 200 assembled in Victoria Square, and then marched into the Victoria Hall, where the colours, a silken Union Jack similar to all the colours presented by the King to service battalions, rested upon a table on the platform. The colour party consisted of

Lieut. W. Redman, Regimental Sergeant-Major W. Douglas, Regimental Sergeant-Major G. Roberts, Sergeant A. Mountain, V.C., and Acting-Sergeant W. B. Butler, V.C. Distinction was lent to the proceedings by the presence of the Judges attending the Assizes at the time: Mr. Justice Salter and Mr. Justice Rigby Swift. Mr. Commissioner Greaves Lord, K.C., also attended, and the High Sheriff of Yorkshire (Sir Dennis Readett-Bailey), who represented Lieut.-General Sir Ivor Maxse, G.O.C., Northern Command, was also present. As the senior representative of the King present, Mr. Justice Salter presided, and he was supported among others by the Lord Mayor (Mr. A. Braithwaite), The Town Clerk (Sir Robert Fox), the Vicar of Leeds (the Rev. Bernard Heywood), the Rev. H. J. Glennie (formerly chaplain to the battalion) and members of the City Council.

The proceedings began with the singing of "O God, our help in ages past." The audience next repeated the Lord's Prayer, and the Vicar of Leeds, in a few sentences, offered a dedicatory Prayer, and a thanksgiving for the glorious dead. The Rev. H. J. Glennie, in the course of a short address, said their's was no conscript battalion. The Bantams had an earlier and better history than that. They were men who made their own free choice, and who toiled hard under gallant and devoted officers to make themselves efficient and effective. They had gone through the thick of the fighting with credit and distinction, and had received what few battalions received—two Victoria Crosses.

The Lord Mayor, alluding to the battalion's proud record, mentioned that one of the battalion winners of the V.C. was, at the time he won the coveted honour, serving under his own son, Major Braithwaite. The battalion was one of Leeds' own, and they were proud of the men who, whatever

Parade of West Riding Divisional Army Service Corps at Leeds, April 23rd, 1915.

they lacked in inches, made up for in Yorkshire grit. The Lord Mayor then presented the colours to Lieutenant Redman.

The battalion, which was in charge of Major Gill, D.S.O., afterwards formed up in Calverley Street, and, headed by the colour party and the Leeds City Police Band, marched to the Parish Church, where the colours were placed permanently.

LEEDS TERRITORIAL ARMY SERVICE CORPS.

When the West Riding Territorial Division was mobilised in August, 1914, as the 49th Division, it found a very efficient divisional train in the Leeds Territorial Army Service Corps, to the organisation of which Lieut.-Colonel J. C. Chambers had given painstaking care over a number of years.

Colonel Chambers had a long record of service with the Leeds Rifles, but, with the coming into being of the Territorial Force, a transport service had to be created for the West Riding Territorial Division, and Colonel Chambers gave up infantry work to organise the new body, a task he accomplished with great success. Formed in 1908 the corps steadily prepared itself for any contingency, and when the call came in those early days of August, 1914, it found the Corps well up to strength, thoroughly trained in its duties, ready and willing to take up the task of supplying the various units comprising the 49th Division with the necessaries of life.

In two hours after the order to mobilise, all the officers were out on their specially allotted jobs. There was no confusion. Horses had been ear-marked for the use of the column, and the register had been kept well up-to-date. Officers knew just where to go to collect horses and vehicles, and billets were all arranged, as well as dumps for the stores. On that first night and until the corps moved to its War Station, Doncaster, the officers and men slept at Harewood Barracks and in empty premises adjoining; from the first morning the necessary materials began to come in. Within a week of mobilisation the adjutant and instructors were recalled to the Regular Army, and their posts had to be filled by members of the Corps. Captain J. Milner was appointed Adjutant, the duties of which he carried out efficiently and was, later, rewarded with the M.C.

The important part motor transport was destined to play made a new demand upon the resources of the Corps; a Motor Lorry Column had to be formed forthwith. For this 350 technically qualified motor men were enrolled; and later, when the Division embarked for France, this Motor Lorry Column became a separate command under Major H. V. Kitson, who in June 1916 was promoted Lieut.-Colonel, and later appointed D.A.D. of T. of the southern lines of communications; and in 1918, A.D. of T. of the northern lines of communication; mentioned in despatches and awarded the O.B.E. Very appropriately the command of the Divisional Train was retained by Lieut.-Colonel Chambers. The duty of the motor drivers was to convey stores from rail-head to the divisional dump, whilst the horsed transports of the divisional train distributed the stores to the various units forming the division.

Under the mobilisation scheme Doncaster was the war station of the West Riding Division, and there it remained from August, 1914, until April of the following year, putting in a strenuous winter's work divided between garrisoning the North Lincolnshire coast and preparing for the testing days in France.

It was on April 15th, 1915, that the Division embarked at Southampton for Havre. Landing

Photo by　　　　Bacon & Son.
Col. J. C. CHAMBERS, C.B., T.D.,
49th Div. Train A.S.C.

Photo by　　　　Bacon & Son.
Lieut.-Col. J. PRESTON,
2nd Battalion (V.B.) West Riding Regiment.

Major CECIL H. TAYLOR,
3rd Battalion (V.B.) West Riding Regiment.

Major S. R. RUSH,
12th and 5th Battalions (V.B.) West Riding Regiment.

on French soil a move was made for Merville, where a week's breathing space was given so that the Division might grow accustomed to the changed surroundings. The next move was up the line to take over trenches at Fleurbaix. Stations were occupied here until July 14th, when the Division moved onward to the terrible Ypres salient. Here it remained until New Year's Day, 1916, and, although during this six months there was no big attack in the salient, there was plenty of " liveliness."

In the wet weather of the autumn, and the trying storms and frost of the winter, the work of the Army Service Corps was carried on under conditions of great difficulty. The enemy artillery continually ranged on all the practicable roads leading towards the front line, and as our labour and road-mending services were not then organised to the degree of perfection that marked them later in the war, the convoys had some exciting times and trying experiences with shell holes. There were heavy losses amongst the horses and mules, and casualties also occurred amongst the men, but the work was efficiently carried on in all circumstances, and the infantry of the 49th Division enduring the hardships of winter in the Ypres salient had every reason to be grateful to the Leeds men who formed their transport and supply column.

Leaving the Ypres salient on the first day of 1916, the Division had a month's rest, and then marched south to the Somme, where preparations were being made for the big attack on July 1st.

Up to this stage in the war the unit had succeeded in pretty well preserving its original character. Casualties amongst the men had been made good by reinforcements from Leeds. The second line was in England training with the 62nd Division, and there was a third line, which was done away with when the 62nd Division went out. The exigencies of the service, and especially the requirements of the Army commanders for the Somme push, led to a number of Army Service Corps men being transferred to the infantry, and their places being filled by others not so fit for the actual work of fighting the enemy hand-to-hand. These later men were recruited from all over the kingdom, and were posted as required. Thus, the 49th Divisional Train began to lose its distinctively Leeds character. Colonel Chambers, who for his splendid work was given the C.B. and mentioned in despatches, came home, handing over the command to Major Haigh, of Wakefield. Many of the officers were also transferred to the infantry, until only two of the band of officers that left Leeds remained at the close of fighting, and probably only about 20 other ranks.

ROYAL ARMY VETERINARY CORPS.

Great as was the importance of motor transport in the war, the Army still needed horses; and Leeds, the centre of a far-famed horse-breeding county, did its share in meeting requirements. Of heavy horses alone, thousands went from this district to supply the wants of the Artillery and the R.A.S.C.

Both at home and at the front valuable service was rendered in this matter by Leeds Veterinary Surgeons. Mr. A. W. Mason—a retired Major, who had been with the Army in India, and who was for some years attached to the Leeds Artillery, went out to France as Lt.-Col. A.D.V.S., and was awarded the O.B.E. for his good work there, from April 1915 to April 1919. Mr. H. G. Bowes, Lecturer in Veterinary Science at the Leeds University, made more than one journey across the Atlantic in connection with the inspection and purchase of remounts. On his second voyage to Canada, in September 1915, his vessel—the " Hesperian "—was torpedoed by the enemy, and he, together with his wife and daughter, had a narrow escape from drowning. He joined the Army as Lieutenant in the following month, and was for a time with the Yorkshire Dragoons. Then, in October 1917 he was gazetted Lt.-Col. and went to the United States as Inspecting Veterinary Officer. Millions of horses and mules were purchased in America.

Officers of the R.A.V.C. were attached to any unit that required such an Officer; therefore there were frequent changes. Others who went from Leeds were Major Dixon (also of the Leeds Artillery) who served in France, and Capt. Frank Somers. Capt. Somers had a varied experience; and he was much over military age when he offered his services. Attached to the 62nd Division at Doncaster in 1915, he was, later, at Newcastle-on-Tyne and Morpeth (with the Cheshire Yeomanry, Shropshire Yeomanry and Welsh Border Regt.), and at Darlington (with the 207th Infantry Brigade). In 1917 he was at Welbeck Camp and was then transferred as Brigade Veterinary Officer to Lincolnshire Coast Defences, stationed at Mablethorpe with charge of Army horses for forty miles of the coast. Later still, he became Veterinary Officer to the Honourable Artillery Company at Chapeltown Barracks, Leeds, and afterwards was with the Remount Department at Fulford Barracks, York, until demobilised in 1919.

VICTORIA CROSS HEROES.

SERGEANT GEORGE SANDERS.

7th Batt. West Yorkshire Regt. (Leeds Rifles).

Sergeant Sanders was awarded the V.C. while a corporal in the Leeds Rifles on July 1st, 1916. He was the first Leeds citizen and Territorial to win this great honour in the European War.

Isolated with a party of thirty men, he organised his defences and the mere handful of men with him, impressed them with the conviction that it was their duty to hold the position at all costs, drove off several enemy attacks, rescued some prisoners whom the enemy had captured, and after holding the position until relief came, marched his victorious party—now nineteen—back to our trenches.

For thirty-six hours he and his men were without food and water, as they had given all their own supplies to succour their wounded comrades.

Only twenty-two years of age, Sergeant Sanders was, before the war, a fitter at the Airedale Foundry, Hunslet, living with his parents at 3, Shand Grove, Holbeck, and was a member of the choir at St. John's Church up to the time of his enlistment. He received a civic welcome home in the presence of a big crowd in Victoria Square, on November 17th 1916, when the Lord Mayor, the Vicar of Leeds, and others publicly congratulated him.

Sergeant-Major John Crawshaw Raynes.
Royal Field Artillery.

Awarded the V.C. on November 18th, 1915, for most conspicuous bravery and devotion to duty.

On October 11th, 1915, at Fosse de Bethune his battery was being heavily bombarded by armour-piercing and gas shells. On cease fire being ordered, Sergeant Major Raynes went out under an intense shell fire and assisted Sergeant Ayres, who was lying wounded forty yards away. He bandaged him and returned to his gun when it was again ordered into action. A few minutes later "cease fire" was again ordered, owing to the intensity of the enemy's fire, and Sergeant-Major Raynes, calling two gunners to help him (both of them were killed shortly afterwards) went out and carried Sergeant Ayres into a dug-out. A gas shell burst at the mouth of the dug-out, and Sergeant-Major Raynes once more ran across the open, fetched his own smoke helmet, put it on Ayres, and then, himself badly gassed, staggered back to his gun.

On the following day, October 12th, at "Quality Street," a house was knocked down by a heavy shell and four men were buried in the house, while four others were buried in the cellar. The first man rescued was Sergeant-Major Raynes, wounded in the head and leg, but he insisted on remaining under heavy shell-fire to assist in the rescue of all the other men. Then, after having his wounds dressed, he reported himself immediately for duty with his battery, which was again being heavily shelled.

Sergeant-Major Raynes was a Leeds policeman, and the Force marked their sense of honour by presenting him with a gold watch and chain.

Sergeant Fred McNess.
Scots Guards.

"During a severe engagement," says the official description, "he led his men on with the greatest dash in face of heavy shell and machine-gun fire. When the first line of enemy trenches was reached, it was found that the left flank was exposed, and that the enemy was bombing down the trench. Sergeant McNess thereupon organised a counter-attack, and led it in person. He was very severely wounded in the neck and jaw, but went on passing through the barrage of hostile bombs in order to bring up fresh supplies of bombs to his own men. Finally he established a "block," and continued encouraging his men, and throwing bombs till utterly exhausted by loss of blood."

Sergeant McNess lived at 39, Eightlands Lane, Bramley. He was born on January 22nd, 1890, and prior to enlisting in January, 1915, was employed as a carter by Mr. Joseph Henry Boan, carrier, of Bramley. After the war he started in business for himself in Woodhouse Lane, Leeds. He was the second Leeds-born man to win the V.C. in the Great War.

PRIVATE WILFRID EDWARDS.
King's Own Yorkshire Light Infantry.

Awarded the V.C. for most conspicuous bravery when under heavy machine gun and rifle fire from a strong concrete fort.

Having lost all his company officers, he dashed forward at great personal risk and without hesitation, bombed through the loop-holes, surmounted the fort and waved to his company to advance. By his splendid example he saved a most critical situation at a time when the whole battalion was held up and a leader urgently needed. Three officers and thirty other ranks were taken prisoner by him in the fort. Later, Private Edwards did most valuable work as a runner and he eventually guided most of the battalion out over very difficult ground. Throughout he set a splendid personal example to all, and was utterly regardless of danger.

Although a native of Norwich, Leeds has a right to claim him, for it was in the West Riding city that he was brought up from childhood and learned his trade—that of a tailor. In July, 1918, he was gazetted Second-Lieutenant in the 4th Battalion of the regiment with which he won his award of V.C.

PRIVATE WILLIAM BOYNTON BUTLER.
17th Batt. West Yorkshire Regt. (Bantams).

Private William Boynton Butler was a miner, living with his parents at 5, Royal Terrace, Hunslet Carr, when war broke out. He was awarded the V.C. in September, 1917, for most conspicuous bravery at Guillemont Farm when in charge of a Stokes Gun in trenches which were being heavily shelled. Suddenly one of the fly-off levers of a Stokes shell came off and fired the shell in the emplacement. Private Butler picked up the shell and jumped to the entrance of the emplacement, which at that moment a party of infantry were passing. He shouted to them to hurry past as the shell was going off, and, turning round, placed himself between the party of men and the live shell, and so held it till they were out of danger. He then threw the shell on to the parados and took cover in the bottom of the trench. The shell exploded almost on leaving his hands, greatly damaging the trench. By extreme good luck his great presence of mind and disregard of his own life saved the lives of the officers and men in the emplacement, and the party which was passing at the time.

As in the case of the other V.C.'s he was given a civic welcome on arrival in Leeds.

Later in the war Private Butler received from the French High Command the Croix de Guerre awarded "for coolness and gallantry in the execution of exacting and perilous duties as a despatch rider."

SERGEANT ALBERT MOUNTAIN OF THE "BANTAMS."
15th Batt. West Yorkshire Regt. (Leeds Pals).

Awarded the V.C. for most conspicuous bravery and devotion to duty during an enemy attack on the Somme in March, 1918, after the "Bantams" had been amalgamated with the "Pals." His company were in an exposed position on a sunken road, having hastily dug themselves in, but, owing to the intense artillery fire, they were obliged to vacate the road and fall back. The enemy in the meantime was advancing in mass, preceded by an advanced patrol about 200 strong. The situation was critical, and volunteers for a counter-attack were called for. Sergeant Mountain immediately stepped forward, and his party of ten men followed him. He then advanced on the flank with a Lewis Gun and brought enfilade fire to bear on the enemy patrol, killing about a hundred. In the meantime the remainder of the company made a frontal-attack and the entire enemy patrol was cut up, and thirty prisoners taken. At this time the enemy main body appeared, and the men who were numerically many times weaker than the enemy, began to waver. Sergeant Mountain rallied and organised his party, and formed a defensive position from which to cover the retirement of the rest of the company and the prisoners. With this party of one non-commissioned officer and four men he successfully held at bay 600 of the enemy for half an hour, eventually retiring and rejoining his company. He then took command of the flank post of the battalion, which was "in the air," and held on there for twenty-seven hours until finally surrounded by the enemy. Sergeant Mountain was one of the few who managed to fight their way back. His supreme fearlessness and initiative undoubtedly saved the whole situation.

Private Arthur Poulter.
West Riding Regiment.

For most conspicuous bravery when acting as a stretcher-bearer. On ten occasions, at Kemmel on April 10th, 1918, Private Poulter carried badly wounded men on his back to a safer locality, through a particularly heavy artillery and machine gun barrage. Two of these were hit a second time whilst on his back. Again, after a withdrawal over the river had been ordered, Private Poulter returned in full view of the enemy, who were advancing, and carried back another man who had been left behind wounded. He bandaged up over forty men under fire, and his conduct throughout the whole day was a magnificent example to all ranks. This gallant soldier was subsequently seriously wounded when attempting another rescue in the face of the enemy.

Private Poulter who had his home at New Wortley, Leeds, was one of nine sons, all of whom saw service in the war. He was aged 24 at the time of his brave exploit. In recognition of his heroism the Society of Yorkshiremen in London presented him with a silver watch suitably inscribed.

Sergeant Laurence Calvert.
King's Own Yorkshire Light Infantry.

Awarded for most conspicuous bravery and devotion to duty in attack, when the success of the operation was rendered doubtful owing to severe enfilade machine gun fire. Alone and single handed, Sergt. Calvert, rushing forward against the machine-gun team, bayoneted three and shot four. His valour and determination in capturing single-handed two machine guns and killing the crews thereof, enabled the ultimate objective to be won. His personal gallantry inspired all ranks.

A native of Leeds, Sergeant Calvert was the son of a tinsmith in Hunslet, and was educated at the Rowland Road and Cockburn Higher Grade Schools. After his father's death in 1910 he removed to Conisborough with his mother, and joined the Doncaster Battalion of the King's Own Yorkshire Light Infantry in April 1914.

II. HOME DEFENCE.

*" Blow, wind ! Come, wrack !
At least we'll die with harness on our back."*
Shakespeare.

THE VOLUNTEER BATTALIONS.

AN account of the services rendered by the Volunteer Regiments raised in 1914 and 1915 is certainly worthy of permanent record.

The first impulse to do something in Leeds came from several independent sources. There was, for example, the influence of the Citizens' League which had come into being during the Municipal strike of 1913, with Major W. W. Macpherson at its head. There was the stimulus of the Rifle Clubs. There was the eagerness of the National Reserve. But as much as any other, perhaps, it was the organised bodies of athletes that gave a spur to definite action.

Soon after the outbreak of war, in response to an appeal from Mr. S. F. Edge (sent out by Major S. R. Noble, secretary of the National Cyclists' Union) athletes began to organise themselves into Volunteer Training Corps, and, in Leeds, a body was formed under the chairmanship of Mr. (afterwards Captain) Arthur Mosley (President of the Yorkshire branch of the Amateur Swimming Association) and the vice-chairmanship of Mr. Arthur Blakeborough (who became Captain, and second-in-command of the 6th Volunteer Battalion) with Mr. A. Goodall as honorary secretary. What were for a time known as the 11th and 13th Battalions of the West Riding Volunteer Regiment were the direct outcome of the early work of this body.

The 12th Battalion (afterwards styled the 5th) owed its origin independently to a North Leeds movement and its early interests were looked after by a committee of which Mr. J. S. Moxon was

First Public Parade of the Leeds Volunteer Battalions on Woodhouse Moor, March 13th, 1915.

chairman. Besides these there were smaller bodies formed—one an organisation of teachers, another of tramway workers, a Press platoon, and several sections from outlying villages.

All these efforts combined produced what was for a short period known as the Leeds Volunteer Training Corps, the 1st Battalion of which was commanded by Mr. (afterwards Major) D. W. Mitchell, who had seen service to his credit in the South African war; the 2nd Battalion by Captain (afterwards Lt.-Col.) Preston, of the Territorial Force Reserve; and the 3rd by Mr. (afterwards Major) Cecil H. Taylor, who had served $11\frac{1}{2}$ years with the 1st Devons at home and in India and Egypt. In 1917 the Volunteer Battalions were given the territorial designations, according to the Territorial Army Scheme. The Leeds units thus became Volunteer Battalions of the West Yorkshire Regiment.

At first the administration was carried out through committees. Members paid an entrance fee and a weekly subscription, and bought their own uniforms; and arrangements were made for drill in suitable schoolrooms. This system, however, was not altogether satisfactory. Accordingly, the then Lord Mayor (Mr. James E. Bedford) and the Town Clerk (Sir Robert Fox) were approached with a view to getting the Force adopted by the City Council; and the Lord Mayor having satisfied himself as to the value of the movement, the City Council gave such liberal financial support as enabled the three battalions to be raised and equipped. Fourteen different units were represented at an inaugural meeting held in January, 1915, and Mr. Bedford as Lord Mayor, headed the subscription list with £200. In all, the grants of money made by the City Council amounted to about £5,000, and this sum formed the basis of the Corps' finance apart from Government grants.

In an historical sketch of the movement, Mr. A. G. Baker has pointed out that great care was taken at this time to avoid making the Volunteer Force into a harbour of refuge for those who should have been in the Regular Army. Every man was required to sign an undertaking to do certain definite military work, as, for instance, to do night or day patrol work, to go away for a week at a time at his own expense, to serve in any part of Yorkshire in case of invasion, or, if necessary, in any part of the United Kingdom. With these requirements quite a number of men felt unable to comply. A recruiting campaign was therefore instituted by Major Taylor, one effect of which was to draw into the Force many youths just below military age; and later on, these lads gave an exceedingly good account of themselves when called on for active service in connection with East Coast defence.

So far from the Volunteers competing with Army recruiting, in Leeds at any rate, the battalions acted as feeders for the Army. The recruiting office at Priestley Hall was staffed very largely by the 12th Battalion beforementioned, members of which also helped to compile the National Register. Again, all the Volunteer units in Leeds threw themselves heartily into the work of the Derby Scheme. One part of this scheme was to give preliminary training to men in certain groups, and this the Volunteers did, holding parades for the purpose every day of the week, including Sunday. For a period they had a very busy time. Thousands of men passed through their hands.

The headquarters of one Battalion (afterwards known as the 5th) were at Carlton Barracks. The other units, which finally became the 6th Battalion, had headquarters at the old Eccentric Club in Albion Street until they were transferred to the Gibraltar Barracks in Claypit Lane.

It was in June, 1915, that the whole Force had their first big ceremonial parade. They were then inspected in the Soldiers' Field at Roundhay Park, by the Earl of Harewood. A year later, they were reviewed at the same place by H.R.H. the Duke of Connaught who, in the meantime, had been appointed General Officer Commanding the Volunteer Force.

In 1916, the Volunteer Forces of the country were taken over completely by the War Office, and all officers were given Army rank. The West Riding Volunteers were commanded by Brigadier General Sir Alington Bewicke-Copley, C.B., and Captain Preston was promoted to the rank of Lt.-Colonel and placed in command of the Leeds group of three battalions with Capt. Ivimy (an official of the Leeds Corporation Electricity Department) as his adjutant. Major S. R. Rush, adjutant of the old 12th Battalion, became commanding officer of that unit, and he had as adjutant, Capt. C. W. Banks of the Leeds Bantams, the second-in-command being Capt. T. A. Hall, of Horsforth, with Lieut. Holliday as Quartermaster. The Company Commanders were Captain H. K. Kitchen, Captain W. H. Sharp, Capt. A. E. Bates, and Lieut. A. Dawson.

When the battalions were inspected by Earl French on the Knavesmire, at York, in the autumn of 1916, they had become fairly accustomed to their duties. Every night, at the request of the Leeds Corporation, a guard had long been furnished for certain unprotected parts of the city's water supply—work which was done quite voluntarily. But there was even more important work to be done. There was the guarding of lines of communication—the railways between Leeds and Selby, Doncaster and York, and other branches; and all this entailed a great deal of sacrifice. Special schemes approved by the higher military authorities had been prepared for this purpose, and tested with the assistance of the Motor Transport Volunteers, under the eye of the Brigadier General, with the result that each battalion knew exactly what would be required in case of emergency. Thus there was ensured a concentration of troops, along a line running through the Eastern Midlands, ready to proceed at once to any threatened part of the East Coast.

And what of the preparations for such a contingency? Under an affiliation scheme, each Volunteer battalion was linked up with a unit at a training centre. Two of the Leeds Battalions were fortunate in coming under the care of the 4th (Reserve) Battalion of the Black Watch at Ripon, commanded by Colonel Sir Robert Moncrieff. The officers of this famous Scottish Regiment provided instructors highly-skilled in the various specialized branches of modern warfare, and they gave to every Volunteer officer and N.C.O. who visited the camp for training the heartiest possible welcome. The third Volunteer Battalion underwent training with the Argyll and Sutherland Regiment, also at Ripon.

From now onwards the Leeds Volunteers furnished men at night for the manning of some of the anti-aircraft guns which protected Leeds, and they also did guard work around the city.

About the same time, one of the battalions having become somewhat depleted in numbers, it was amalgamated with the 12th, which now became the 5th Battalion under the command of Major S. R. Rush, with Major D. W. Mitchell, second-in-command, and Captain Wilcher, adjutant. It was formed as a five company battalion, having three companies in Leeds, one at Pudsey, and one in the Micklefield and Kippax districts. The remaining battalion now became the 6th, still under the command of Major Taylor.

It was in the early part of June, 1918, when Foch was preparing his great push and the country was being drained of available fit men for the Regular Army, that the call came for the Volunteers to guard our coast. The West Riding Regiment were asked to provide 1,000 men for coast defence, and in less than three weeks that force was in position. The West Riding Volunteers, indeed, were the first to offer two complete companies; and Leeds had the distinction of providing both those companies, which were also the strongest companies at the end of the three months service.

The special service company from the 5th Battalion (the 42nd) was stationed at Whitby, with detachments at Robin Hood's Bay and Sandsend, the officers being Major S. R. Rush, Captain A. E. Bates, Lieut. H. Tidswell, Lieut. A. Wormald, and Lieut. W. T. Wallbank. The company furnished by the 6th Battalion also went to Whitby, but for by far the greater part of the time they garrisoned the outlying station of Runswick, where the camp was pitched on the top of the cliffs in the face of all the winds that blew. Major Taylor commanded this, the 43rd Special Service Company, and the other officers were Lieut. A. G. Baker (Second-in-Command), Lieut. W. Hodgson and Second-Lieuts. F. McManus and J. F. Harvey. Of the 6th Battalion's experiences it has been recorded that "during the first month things were fairly enjoyable, but afterwards the weather broke, and towards the end life in the rain-sodden, wind-swept camp was one continual hardship, borne, however with a spirit of indomitable cheerfulness." Coast defences were found to be in a very neglected state, and there was much heavy digging and concreting to be carried out, as well as the laying of miles of barbed wire. Besides this, ceaseless vigilance had to be maintained in guarding the coast especially during the hours of darkness, and the work of the sentries and patrols on the paths up and down the face of the cliffs was frequently perilous. Two officers of the company performed special duties : Lieut. Baker was appointed Station Intelligence Officer, and Lieut. Hodgson was taken on to the staff of the C.R.E. at Scarborough.

Similar duties were fulfilled with great credit by the 5th Battalion Service Company at Whitby, Sandsend, and Robin Hood's Bay, where they were almost equally exposed to the rigours of the North Sea, notwithstanding that it was the summer season of the year. In the case of both Service Companies a high standard of efficiency and discipline was maintained, with results that evoked special thanks and congratulations from the General Officer Commanding the Yorkshire Coast Defences.

In the latter part of its career the following were the officers of the 5th Battalion :—Commanding Officer : Major S. R. Rush ; Second-in-Command, Major D. W. Mitchell ; Quarter Master, Lieut. C. H. Holliday ; Assistant Adjutant and Musketry Instructor, Lieut. A. K. Legg ; Machine Gun Officer, Lieut. E. R. Phillips. "A" Company : Captain H. Kitchen, Lieuts. E. B. Nicholson, H. Tidswell, H. I. Bowring, S. Boyes and Garstang. "B" Company : Captain W. H. Sharp, Lieuts. Libby, A. Dawson, H. Thornton, C. W. Wade, and H. Turner. "C" Company : Captain A. E. Bates, Lieuts. J. Lyon, A. Wormald, W. T. Wallbank, G. Coxon and P. Farrar. "D" Company : Captain A. Mosley, Lieuts. Hall, C. Lee, S. Smith, MacGrath and Hutchinson. "E" Company : Captain Spring, Lieuts. Thompson, Rushton and Coltman.

WEST RIDING R.A.S.C. MOTOR TRANSPORT VOLUNTEERS.

This organisation began as a section of the National Motor Volunteers, with a strength of twenty and a small Committee. When it became known that Alderman Charles H. Wilson would be gazetted out of the 15th Battalion Prince of Wales' Own West Yorkshire Regiment, he was invited to take command of the Leeds Group on the 12th October, 1915, and it soon grew into a useful and powerful unit. Under various names, and several formations, nearly 700 men were enrolled. Of these, 150 passed into regular units, several obtaining Commissions, and many becoming non-commissioned officers.

The following Officers passed the required tests and were granted Commissions :—

Major Charles H. Wilson, Officer Commanding ; Captain Urban Aspey, Jr., Adjutant ; Lieut. John Monteith, Quarter Master ; Lieut. Clarence R. Foster, Works Officer ; Captain Ernest A. White, Medical Officer ; Captains Ernest B. Laycock, Wilfred S. Scarr and Charles G. Gibson, Company Commanders ; Lieutenants Fred Bentley (Signalling Officer), Herbert Laycock, J. Leonard Firth, Fred Firth, Matthew E. Walker, Edwin Airey, E. G. Allen, Charles G. Henzell, Ernest Self, Edward P. Morton, Edward T. Broadbridge, Victor Robinson and John F. Strother (Petrol Officer).

These officers attended two great camps at Burton Agnes and Ripley Valley, and, in addition, served for a period in the Royal Army Service Corps, being attached to a Company stationed in Leeds under Captain S. Newman. For some time this force was not formally recognised by the War Office, and, no special duties being allotted to it, the O.C. was told to " carry on," and find such work as could usefully be done. Later, when the Unit had demonstrated what it could do, one celebrated General Officer declared that, if he could have his way, it should never be demobilised.

Many thousands of convalescent wounded, accompanied by sisters and nurses, were conveyed week by week to gentlemen's country houses around Leeds, where they received a welcome and were cared for. Large numbers, too, were brought from the hospitals to entertainments in the City, and returned safety to their billets. All this gave the transport officers and men considerable practice in taking up and setting down troops.

Over and over again the roads were explored, and occasional drills in the great parks helped to vary the proceedings. At the same time the wounded men benefited by a change of scene. Every journey meant an exercise in quick concentration. That was certainly so when the call came to carry troops from Leeds to guard the railways. The infantry were transported to their allotted stations, and brought back, without hitch, entirely to the satisfaction of the Brigadier-General, Sir A. Bewicke-Copley, C.B., and his staff.

Perhaps the most interesting service performed continuously was the calling out and transporting of the Telephone staffs to their respective post-offices. Only half-an-hour was allowed, from the time of the call to landing the telephonists at their stations, but the O.C. many times saw cars arrive, with their loads, in twelve minutes. These calls were issued every time an air raid was notified, and the officers and men stood by all night, assisting the police in putting out lights, carrying messages, etc., and eventually conveying the telephonists to their homes. When it is remembered that they had to drive in the dark, and that there was no serious accident to report, it must be admitted that they enjoyed a certain measure of good fortune. On one occasion there was, at some large works, a great fire which could not be put out ; it could be seen for miles, yet the Zeppelins did not come near ; evidently the enemy regarded the blaze as a trap.

Another service cheerfully performed was to attend at the railway stations in the small hours of Sunday morning to meet men arriving by train from the South, and then to whisk them off to towns and villages all over the West Riding. In this way, men on leave were enabled to secure a better holiday than if they had to wait until the following morning for a train to take them the remainder of their journey. Before this arrangement was made considerable hardships were suffered; men, carrying full kit, had to walk long distances to reach their homes. One case was reported of a man who could not afford to pay a fare of £4 demanded by a taxi-driver, and who walked from York to Oswaldkirk. When his wife opened the door he fell, fainting, to the floor.

This Unit unofficially provided also most of the owner drivers who met the Hospital trains, and conveyed the wounded to Beckett's Park and other Hospitals. Many trains arrived in the course of a month, and the work was of a heavy and continuous character. Several of the Unit regularly manned some of the ambulances used at the Northern Base Hospital. The Fenton Street Barracks were made the Headquarters, and they were afterwards shared with Major Taylor's Infantry Battalion. Harrogate and Ripon supplied a certain number of men and vehicles. Altogether, some 600 motor cars, motor cycles and Motor lorries were enrolled, worth over £700,000. They were of all makes, sizes and shapes. At an inspection held at Headquarters by Major-General D. C. F. Macintyre, C.B., over three hundred vehicles were passed in review covering a distance, spaced out according to regulations, of four and a half miles. There were, however, as many more vehicles in reserve, so that the total length of the Leeds Group transport was about nine miles.

The Unit volunteered to serve the First Line Coast Defence from Middlesbrough to Hull, and was accepted. Accordingly, numerous runs were made to the coast and to several camps, including Clipstone, in order that officers and men might know the roads, to whom to report, where to park, receive stores and many other duties. In addition, sailors were conveyed long distances from railway stations to coal pits, to look after pumping engines.

Troops were moved from stations to Barracks. (On one occasion when a sudden call came, at 1.30 p.m., to arrive at a certain place by 5 p.m. most of the transport required was in the Barrack Square at 3.30 p.m.). Infantry Officers, drilling or inspecting their outlying Companies, were frequently carried out and back.

At Headquarters, both Infantry and R.A.S.C. drills were ceaselessly practised, on Sundays and weekdays. Lieut. (now Sir) Edwin Airey gave two hundred stand of Arms, and all the Officers subscribed for a Trumpet Band. Officers and men subscribed regularly, as well as when anything was specially needed. And it should be noted, also, that every gallon of petrol used was paid for by the Unit.

The O.C. arranged with the Brigadier-General to address the City Council, with the result that the Leeds Volunteers generally benefited from the grants made by the Corporation. They would not, otherwise, have been so well equipped.

The Miniature Rifle Ranges at Headquarters, and at the Tramways Depot in Swinegate, were used by all officers and men; and their shooting was greatly improved. Also, under the Signalling Officer, Lieut. Fred Bentley, officers and men obtained a high degree of efficiency in various methods of signalling, including Morse, Semaphore and Sounding. For the latter purpose instruments were fitted by the Adjutant, Captain N. Aspey, Jr. This Officer took the Guards' Course for six weeks at Chelsea, at his own expense. The three Company Commanders, Captains E. B. Laycock, Wilfred S. Scarr and O. G. Gibson, assisted ably by their junior officers, kept their men well occupied with drill; and the Officers underwent a course of Swedish drill under Mr. Mason Clarke. The Quarter-Master, Lieut. John Monteith, soon had stores of considerable dimensions with a very efficient staff, and the Medical Officer, Captain

Ernest A. White, regularly lectured on First Aid and other subjects. The Works Officer, Lieutenant Clarence R. Foster, gave instructions on Repairs and Renewals, whilst Lieut. J. F. Strother dealt with the petrol stores. Map reading was one of the most useful forms of Instruction; lectures were given on this subject by Mr. Thornton, of Halton.

Before the Unit was run on Military lines a considerable amount of good work was done by Messrs. Tom G. Porter, Rowland Winn, J. B. Hamilton, Oliver Swithenbank, W. Hodgson (afterwards Lord Mayor), William Heaton, J. W. Haigh and S. A. Albrecht. It should be mentioned, too, that, although not officially recognised by the War Office, a section of lady owner-drivers, under Mrs. A. Hoyland Smith, rendered active and useful service throughout the whole period.

After their time of probation, the five West Riding Groups were placed under the Command of Lt.-Col. Hoyle (now Sir Emanuel Hoyle) of Huddersfield, and, with the advantage of his active oversight, they grew and prospered exceedingly, all difficulties being cheerfully tackled and successfully overcome. A task of peculiar interest had to be performed when the British prisoners of war returned home and were conveyed, with their luggage, to the great Camp at Ripon, there to prepare for demobilisation. Very expeditiously were they carried to their destination. Many were deeply impressed when they saw the procession of brilliantly-lighted cars coming to meet them. A frequent remark was "This is some reception." The narrow streets of Ripon were crowded with thousands who had travelled long distances to see the war-worn prisoners return, and they were wild with joy. Driving at this time was dangerous, but all passed off happily.

On the initiation of the Secretary of State for

War, the Officer Commanding this Unit was mentioned in despatches.

WORK OF THE SPECIAL CONSTABLES.
(By an Ex-Officer of the Force).

The ardent and loyal men who formed a Citizens' League to help the municipality to fight local disorder in the days before the war, little dreamt of the notable national part they were destined to take. Those, in authority, as is sometimes their way, were rather shy of what they regarded as a merely amateur, and perhaps a little fussy, organisation. But when, in the dread autumn and winter of 1914 the call came for the establishment of Special Constabulary throughout the land, Leeds found a skeleton force ready to hand in its Citizens' League. It was from that body, aided by some members of the National Reserve, that its first officers were obtained.

The batches of eager men were sworn in rapidly, and on an appointed day formed up in somewhat uneven ranks before the Chief Constable (the late Mr. W. Burns Lindley) and members of the Watch Committee—a display in miniature of the unity which bound the nation. Magistrates, bankers, solicitors, artisans, clerks, side by side —masters and men of all ages, except the merely youthful, faced the drill instructors, most of them for the first time in their lives. To some of us it appeared that drill was a very secondary thing, almost a superfluity ; but it was impressed upon us that if we were to act together as a force we must know how to act together on the parade ground. And surely no body of men ever had more adequate or more patient drill instructors than Sergeant (afterwards Inspector) Hemsley of the regular police, and Superintendent Dalton.

From the men and officers of the Regular

Photo by   *Bacon & Son.*
W. BURNS LINDLEY,
Chief Constable.

R. NOEL MIDDLETON,
1st Chief Administration Officer,
Special Police.

Photo by   *Scrimshaw.*
F. E. SAVILLE, O.B.E.,
2nd Chief Administration Officer,
Special Police.

Police the Special Constables received unvarying courtesy and all the help it was possible to give. If the impression ever prevailed that our duties were to be merely nominal it was quickly dispelled, for as the nation's need grew greater the drafting of able-bodied Regular police into the Army proceeded more rapidly until the force was reduced to about half its normal strength. Night after night during the dreariest hours in that dreary winter of 1914-15 the Specials, surrendering sleep and comfort, often at an age when these can be sacrificed only at a costly price in health, tramped in mud and slush and fog around the Headingley Pumping Station, Woodhouse Moor Reservoir, the Olympia Works in Roundhay Road, Messrs. Braime's Works in Hunslet, and the Corporation Electricity Works in Whitehall Road.

Then came the call to even sterner duties. In June 1915 an observation post was established at the very top of the Town Hall dome, and there, night after night in two-hour "shifts," men watched that no glaring lights proclaimed to prowling enemy aircraft the city's position. In the same year the Auxiliary Fire Brigade was established which, with Mr. J. G. Roper as Chief Officer, and Mr. G. R. Gaunt as Chief Superintendent, gave valuable assistance to the regular brigade.

In October, 1916, point duty began, which brought the Special police more prominently before the public, and in November certain suburban beats were taken over. That beat duty meant often the loss of a night's sleep, but it was patiently, and, on the whole, uncomplainingly performed. It was in December of the same year that the highest daily strength of the force was reached—about 2,200 men and officers.

The air-raid nights were probably the most trying of all. Men were summoned to their stations at all hours of the night; sometimes they were out almost the whole of the night. It is no unfair claim to make for the Special police that in assisting the Regular force to ensure the complete darkening of Leeds, they saved the city from air-raid damage. When the signal was sent out and the "snowball call" set rolling, men on their way to their stations extinguished the street lamps, and warned householders against displaying lights. From the observation post above the Town Hall clock word went forth by telephone if a bright light showed itself in any area. All over the city patrols were posted. Word of the presence of a light was sent to the nearest police station; from there the word was passed on to the patrol; and in less than ten minutes from its detection that light was out.

What knowledge of criminal law most of us gained we got from the able lectures to the force given from time to time by Superintendent Dalton, for it was necessary that we should know at any rate something of the difference between a felony and a misdemeanour, and have some glimmering notion imparted to us of the value of evidence. One wonders if the public ever knew the hidden hours that were consumed in this way.

In their own two Chief officers the Special force were fortunate. The first Chief Administration Officer was Mr. R. Noel Middleton, who subsequently resigned and joined the Army. He was succeeded by Mr. F. E. Saville, who gave unstinted energy and devotion to the work until the disbandment of the force. He had as his deputy Mr. R. A. Wilson, and around them an efficient band of superintendents in Messrs. W. Carby Hall, K. Wilkinson, R. C. Beevers, A. Hart, W. H. Beckwith, E. S. Sneath, J. C. Town, J. F. Syme, H. D. Middleton, J. P. Lee, F. S. Stephenson, E. Pickersgill, W. A. Borland, H. Clifford Bowling, N. Hurtley, C. F. Clark, and N. W. Morrison, with

Mr. Charles Scriven as Chief Inspector, Observation Section.

Several other influential business men of the city held appointments in the lower ranks of the Special Constabulary at their own request. Mr. C. F. Haigh served as a constable up to the date of his appointment as Chairman of the Watch Committee, and although he relinquished his appointment as a Special Constable on taking up this duty, yet on every occasion when the Special Constabulary were called upon for duty Mr. Haigh attended at the police headquarters and showed an active interest in the welfare of this important section of the public. Mr. E. E. Lawson (the former Chairman) also served as constable during the period of the war, and officers of the Regular Leeds City Police Force who acted in an administrative capacity were Mr. Kirk Handley (Deputy Chief Constable), Mr. R. L. Matthews (Superintendent and Chief Clerk), who in 1923 became Chief Constable, Superintendent Blakey, and Inspector (afterwards Superintendent) E. E. Dalton.

In due course quite a large proportion of the Specials joined the forces, and when the Derby Scheme came into operation not only did the Chief Administrative Officer (Mr. Middleton) attest, but he started a recruiting campaign through which over 700 men were enrolled before he left for France. From the first he took steps to prevent any reproach that the Special Constabulary were accepting men fit to serve in the army; no one was accepted as a Special without strict inquiry conducted by one or more members of the Army Recruiting Committee sitting in conjunction with Inspector Dalton and Mr. Middleton. The policy thus pursued by the Chief Administrative Officer also took into consideration the fact that men accepted as Specials would, by reason of their training for that duty, be all the better fitted to serve in the Army. Long route marches, drills, rifle instruction and gymnastic exercises all formed part of the plan, and their great value was proved when the time came for service at the front.

The total number of men sworn in between November 16th, 1914, and November 15th, 1918, was 3,277, of which the following resigned for the reasons stated :—

Enlisted in Army or Navy	724
Munitions or Government Work	79
Ill health	160
Left Leeds	137
Died	28
Business and other reasons	310

Of the 724 who enlisted in the Army or Navy nine were killed in action ; two died of wounds ; and one was reported missing and presumed dead.

The following decorations were gained for Army Service :—D.C.M., 2 ; M.M., 1 ; Italian Decoration, 2 ; Total, 5.

One other thing remains to be recorded. There were more or less pleasant parades for Royal Visits and other civic functions ; and by concerts, a flag day, and in various other ways, the Special Constabulary raised £9,814 for charities —£1,698 for the Northern Police Orphanage, and £8,116 for the Leeds General Infirmary.

It was a source of regret to many of us when, parading on Woodhouse Moor on the 27th July, 1919, the force was formally disbanded. Long service medals were, later, distributed to many members who had served practically throughout the war ; but even more valuable than these were the friendships which had been formed among men of all grades of society giving free service to the community in the time of need.

III. WHEN ZEPPELINS CAME.

" Fire comes, and crash and wreck, and lives are shed
As if the Eternal Will Itself were dead."
Lewis Morris.

HOW LEEDS ESCAPED ATTACK.

Germany's air raids on England ranged over nearly the whole of the war period. The London district suffered most from these bombing expeditions. Yorkshire, however, attracted a full share of the enemy's attention and Hull bore the brunt of the attack. But, while the raiders managed to get inland over Nottingham, Retford, Sheffield, Derby and Burton, and even as far west as Walsall, Bolton and Wigan, at all of which places they did damage and destroyed life, they never succeeded in locating Leeds. Nevertheless, from the time of the first raid—that on the Northumberland coast in April, 1915—we were not free from alarms. Whenever Zeppelins were reported to be approaching the North-Eastern coast, warning was given, and due precautions had to be taken. There were, for instance, at least six serious raids on Hull, resulting in great damage to property and loss of life, and on every occasion there was the possibility of an advance on Leeds. On three occasions, indeed, the enemy reached York and found their way further west; and twice they passed within a dozen miles of Leeds.

Only in the case of the first raid—that on the Northumberland coast—were details published in the newspapers. Thereafter a policy of silence was enforced by the censorship, and ample justification for this course was found in the claims of the enemy's official reports. These reports indulged in the wildest surmises as to the places visited by the raiders, who, it was clear, dropped their bombs indiscriminately without certain knowledge of their whereabouts, thus attacking undefended towns, killing and maiming thousands of civilians, and destroying many dwelling-houses, largely of the humble artisan type. The whole story of the German air-raids indeed, has been well described as one of the blackest chapters in Germany's black book of crime on land and sea.

In the summer of 1915, Hull, Tyneside, and Goole suffered particularly. In the early part of 1916 the Midlands were raided; and during the summer and autumn of the same year there was a succession of attacks on the North-East coast and places inland. This, in fact, was the year of the enemy's greatest activity by Zeppelins. After the raids of November 27th, 1916, the North-East coast enjoyed a nine months respite. Then, in the autumn of 1917, Hull was again bombed and Lancashire was visited. In the meantime the enemy concentrated on London and the South-East coast by means of Gotha aeroplanes, for our powerful defences against Zeppelins had proved too much for them. One monster airship was brought down in flames at Cuffley, north of London, on September 2nd, 1916; two were similarly wrecked in Essex a little later; another met with a like fate at Potter's Bar on October 1st, and in November others were fired at and brought down in the sea at Hartlepool and off the Norfolk coast.

How was it that Leeds escaped? The general public did not know precisely until after the Armistice, and the facts were then revealed by the *Yorkshire Post*. In a word, perfect darkness, secured by efficient organisation, saved the city. Even before instructions were issued from Government departments Leeds was placed in darkness as soon as it was known that Zeppelins were about. The Government scheme aimed at darkening the landscape so that the enemy could not distinguish large cities and towns, but with the proviso that munition works must avoid stoppage until the last moment; and upon this scheme the Leeds Chief Constable (the late Mr. W. Burns Lindley) built his scheme of organisation, which affected both the members of his regular force and the Special Constabulary.

It was known as the "Snowball" scheme among the "Specials," because men, summoned to the telephone and told that a raid was impending, knew that it was their duty to warn so many other of their comrades. A similar system warned the members of the Auxiliary Fire Brigade, who, to the number of a hundred or more, paraded immediately for duty at the Fire Station with auxiliary tenders and other cars. Members of the St. John Ambulance Association, summoned by the police, paraded at their headquarters in Albion Place, and the Leeds Volunteer Bearer Company, under Dr. Hoyland Smith, were at once on duty with their numerous ambulances, and dispersed to different parts of the city where casualties might conceivably occur. There was a Salvage Corps, also, under the City Engineer (Mr. W. T. Lancashire), and the local section of the R.A.S.C. Motor Volunteers, under Major C. H. Wilson, ready to go swiftly on any duty at a second's notice.

Co-operating with these agencies, were the anti-aircraft defences, and a wonderful system of telephonic communication above as well as underground. High up, in the "Crow's Nest" of the Leeds Town Hall, as well as at other favourable observation points, special constables were on duty with signalling apparatus—often in hail, rain, and snow—while a mounted section was detailed below for closing all traffic in and out of the city.

When a warning was received, forges and furnaces were notified, then the factories, and after them the Electricity and Gas departments, so that the lighting supplies could be cut down. At the same time, care had to be taken that there was no interference with the railway companies, who worked to an order of their own, or with the chemical manufacturers who were busy on continuous processes. The Corporation tramways officials had also to be told quickly, and, by a curious system of signalling, tramcar drivers on outlying routes knew at once what was afoot, while places of amusement of every kind exhibited by arrangement a screen with the letter "S" on it, for the information of any special constables who happened to be present.

The darkening of the streets presented difficulties because of the different methods of lighting in the city, and this required considerable organisation ; while in the interests of humanity it was necessary for the police to acquaint the infirmaries, hospitals, and similar institutions, as well as the divisional police surgeons, who "stood by" in case their services were needed. The number of firemen on duty may appear large, but on two occasions at night, when air-raid warnings had gone forth, fires actually broke out in the city, and if they had not been tackled by trained men the flames would have proved of great use to the enemy as a guide. From midsummer of 1916 to the signing of the Armistice the city's precautionary machinery, here described, was in motion on thirteen different occasions, varying in point of time from nine o'clock at night until four o'clock in the morning.

The regulations issued by the Chief Constable for observance by Leeds citizens, ran as follows :—

> The electric current which provides light for the greater part of the city will be switched off, and the pressure of gas reduced to a minimum.
>
> Theatres and music halls will be given notice of this intention a quarter of an hour before it is carried into effect, but cinema theatres will not receive a previous warning.

Hospitals, the Infirmary, and munition works, will not have their lighting affected, but will be expected to reduce their illumination.

Light everywhere in the city must be rigidly screened.

Street electric lights will be switched off, and the gas lamps put out by lamplighters and special constables as quickly as possible.

Tramcars will be stopped and their lights extinguished, and passengers will perforce have to get home as best they can.

On the nights of Monday, September 25th, 1916, and Monday, November 27th, 1916, the Zeppelin raiders came very near Leeds. On each occasion it meant an abrupt ending of the entertainment which so many people were enjoying at theatres and music halls. Warned by signal from the coast, the police set in motion the precautionary machinery, not the least effective of which was the switching off of the electric light. The places of amusement were prepared for such a contingency, and the sudden change from brilliant illumination to the feeble glow of oil lamps, told at once what danger was to be apprehended. Warned by the pre-arranged signal, special constables in the audience hastened to their post of duty; gatherings of one sort and another dispersed as quickly as possible; and people in general, unless compelled to stay in town on business, hurried off homewards on foot, for by this time the trams were stopped or being returned to the depots as rapidly as possible. Thus time was taken by the forelock, and the nearer the enemy approached the quieter grew the streets, and the deeper the darkness.

Take, for instance, that dark tranquil night in September. It was about eleven o'clock when the first alarm was given. It was a little after midnight when, on the outskirts of Leeds, secure in their darkened homes, people waited and listened almost breathlessly for that uncanny sound in the air above, which nearly all had read of, but never heard. They could not help knowing and feeling the approach of the " terror that flieth by night," for from the moment the special constables were called up these indefatigable gentlemen never ceased their expeditions, up and down the streets in all directions, knocking at doors of houses and calling to residents to extinguish all lights. And when finally silence reigned, how weird was the sensation as one peered out into the darkness of the calm night and wondered what would happen next! Many people went to bed and thought nothing more of the incident, but curiosity was strong in most, and, with the certain knowledge that a Zeppelin was on its way towards Leeds, they sat up and waited for events. Those of us at Roundhay who did this were rewarded between one and two o'clock by the distant sight of an airship in the gleam of one of the searchlights out Collingham way. The huge thing looked like a cigar all aglow hovering backwards and forwards. For a minute or two it swung in sight and then suddenly disappeared. This was all that Leeds saw of the Zeppelin invasion.

Another occasion when a Zeppelin airship came anywhere near Leeds—the night of Monday, November 27th, 1916—its presence was made known by the sound of bombs dropped indiscriminately in Pontefract Park, twelve miles away, and the dull boom of the explosions was heard plainly on the north side of Leeds. The warning given to the city in this case was earlier than that of the September visitation, and many people spending the evening in town had scarcely reached their homes on the outskirts when, just at the hour of midnight, the explosions broke the silence of the night. It was not known until next day—and then only through gossip locally— that the alarm was caused by two Zeppelins which had been careering around the Barnsley district and were making their way back to the coast. One airship went off in the direction of Ferrybridge, and the other in a more northerly direction, passing over the V.A.D. hospital at Ledstone Hall, and creating a diversion for the convalescent soldiers, many of whom turned out of bed to see all that was to be seen. Several incendiary bombs were dropped in Pontefract Park and the neighbourhood, and some slight damage was done to property, but there were no casualties.

Nor was there any damage of moment done on the former visitation in September, when, as already stated, a Zeppelin passed over Collingham. Before reaching that rural spot, on its way to the coast, the invader had penetrated as far inland as Ripon, but was evidently unaware of the big military camp in its proximity and did not discharge any bombs until returning over the village of Wormald Green, near Harrogate. Here, and later on, near Weeton and Harewood, bombs were dropped in the fields.

"We can never, of course, know what was in the mind of the officer in charge of the bomb dropping gear," wrote a *Yorkshire Post* correspondent afterwards. "He may have thought that he was over some of the big works of Leeds—only about ten miles away—or he may merely have been in a hurry to finish his work and get home to breakfast. At any rate, in quick succession he rained incendiary bombs upon the unoffending turf of Harewood Park; and when day broke most of these were pulled up out of the damp soil like ripe turnips and formed a most interesting exhibition in the coach-house of the Harewood Arms. At the time, it was suggested that the commander of the Zeppelin knew more than he was generally credited with, and that in dropping these bombs he was merely endeavouring to carry out the principles of Applied Kultur, Harewood House being then in use as a Red Cross Hospital. The Germans probably knew that it was not defended by anti-aircraft guns, as were the arsenals of Leeds.

"Having successfully disturbed the turf in the Park, and, by then, having only a few more bombs left, the raider turned eastwards for home. He may or may not have been able to see the houses of the hamlet. At any rate, as he was crossing the main road near to the principal gates of the Park, he dropped another incendiary bomb This fell on the corner of the roof of a cottage, but with such ill-luck from the enemy's point of view that on going through the tiles it sank into the water cistern, and was immediately extinguished. The impact of the falling bomb destroyed the cistern and flooded the bedroom below, but such damage can hardly be said to be worth even the cost of the bomb. The Zeppelin's farewell to Harewood was another incendiary bomb which dropped into an empty hen-house belonging to Dr. Matthews."

"Over the line of Harewood Avenue, the Zeppelin came within view of the anti-aircraft gun station between East Keswick and Collingham, was picked up by the seachlight, and was fired upon, though without result. By way of acknowledgment the Zeppelin dropped its last two incendiary bombs, both of which fell in the field in which the gun was placed. An incendiary bomb dropping into a soft, damp meadow is not a very terrifying thing, and here, again, beyond a couple of holes in the turf, the Germans achieved nothing. Perhaps the greatest things that they might claim for their enterprise were that they had dropped quite a large weight of bombs on the estate of the Lord Lieutenant, the representative of the King in the West Riding, and had avoided running any very great risk themselves."

That Leeds escaped was the more remarkable because on the same night a fire broke out at the Kirby Banks Screw Works, near Meadow Lane, and although soon subdued, was at its brightest when the Zeppelin was hovering over Wharfedale. It was, indeed, the flares which had been lit in Pontefract Park, to guide our aeroplanes there, that attracted so much attention in that particular neighbourhood. The night was exceedingly still; the sky was clear and star-lit; but the darkness which had been systematised all over the city ensured protection.

IV. TRIUMPHS OF INDUSTRY.

THE FIRST NATIONAL SHELL FACTORY.

> "The country owes a great debt of gratitude not only to the various groups of National Shell Factories, but, above all, to the mind that originated them...What those factories did will never be fully realised. They were responsible for one quarter of the total output of shells in the country, and so far as heavy shells were concerned, from March 1916 until March 1917, the National Factories produced one third."

In these words Major R. Harrison Archbald has indirectly paid tribute to the notable and indeed leading part played by Leeds in providing munitions of war. The quotation is taken from his voluminous unpublished "Record of the National Ordnance Factories in Leeds," and the following outstanding facts and figures, extracted from its pages, show that, in this matter of shell-making, the city of Leeds can justly claim distinction.

For access to the "Record" mentioned, the present writer is indebted to the courtesy of Sir Algernon Firth, Bart., who was President of the Associated Chambers of Commerce when the National Shell Factory movement started in March 1915.

What was the position then ? "Shells, shells, and yet more shells," was the cry that went forth. But how were these shells to be supplied ? When war broke out the British firms producing armaments could be numbered on the fingers of one hand, and the output was inappreciable. Imagine the strain placed on those establishments in the early months of the war ! The arsenal at Woolwich was soon overwhelmed with work ; the private factories had to meet greater demands than they could fulfil. Something had to be done without delay to relieve the situation. Mr. Lloyd George showed the way by introducing, and getting passed, legislation giving the Government power to take over and utilise engineering works in which war material was not then being produced. Two days sufficed for this important step, and a week later Lord Kitchener pressed home the importance of the matter by warning the country that unless the whole nation worked together in supplying the necessary arms, munitions, and equipment, our warlike preparations would be very seriously hampered and delayed.

Precisely at the moment when the famous Field Marshal made his momentous appeal, the Associated Chambers of Commerce were holding their annual conference in London under the presidency of Sir Algernon Firth, with the Hon. Rupert Beckett as senior vice president. So it happened that a West Riding manufacturer, and the head of the great banking firm at Leeds, each in his respective sphere, seized the opportunity provided by the crisis. Speaking on behalf of the meeting, the president declared that the traders of the country would be prepared to co-operate heartily and to the fullest possible extent in producing the munitions required.

In confirmation, Mr. Beckett at once invited representatives of the principal engineering firms in Leeds to meet him and Sir Algernon, and to consider what should be done here. On March 22nd this meeting took place, and laid the train for the splendid achievements which are now recorded. First, there were negotiations, interviews and inquiries; the country was divided into areas in order to make the best use of the various engineering centres; but in the meantime the Leeds Munitions Committee got to work promptly, found out how shells were manufactured, and at the Leeds Forge made preliminary experiments.

Thus, on May 20th, the management board of the Leeds National Shell Factory came into being by authority of the Army Council, its members being Mr. (afterwards Sir) John McLaren, Mr. Bernal Bagshawe, Mr. A. H. Meysey-Thompson, Mr. Christopher James, and Mr. Alexander Campbell, and thus, as the War Office acknowledged, Leeds was the first of the new districts to be organised on the basis of a national factory for the production of munitions.

ARMLEY FACTORY.

As a beginning, the Leeds Forge Company placed suitable premises at the disposal of the Government Committee under the control and direction of the five gentlemen just named who were, by the way, appointed by the Engineering Employers' Association, and gave their services voluntarily. The "point shop" of the Leeds Forge Company, at Armley, was the first of the three large ordnance factories organised, and as Major Archbald mentions in his review of the enterprise, it came into being even before the Ministry of Munitions was instituted. Certainly it was used as a centre to which reference was made for information by other factories as they got to work. Here a start was made with the production of 4.5 shells, the adjoining stables being temporarily converted into offices. Captain Dewar was the Superintendent ; Mr. Hopper, the works manager ; Mr. Walford, manager of the fuse and gauge department, and Mr. Charles Dawson, the secretary. Here, too, men were trained for the other factories which sprang up.

By August, 1915, the first shell had been produced, and in November the requirements of the Ministry of Munitions were not only being met but were exceeded by 50 per cent. That is to say that, every week, 5,000 high explosive 4.5 shells, Mark V., were asked for, and 7,500 were being made. Four months later shell manufacture here was at its height, and in the week ending March 29th, 1916, a record output of 10,128 was reached.

There were difficulties, of course, but not such as determination could not overcome. Machines had to be reset to cope with the changing requirements; new machinery had to be installed. It was a novel industry to Leeds; there were complex technicalities to be mastered, and ways and means devised whereby the production of faulty shells could be reduced to a minimum. At one time no fewer than 20,000 faulty 4.5 shells had to be laid aside, but within three months this type of shell was being passed for use at the rate of 10,000 a week, and on at least one occasion 2,000 were turned out in the course of a single day. At first the space taken up by the factory extended over 22,400 square feet, but, with the addition of another shop, the area eventually covered 128,180 square feet.

Labour troubles caused little delay. There was, in the early stages, some slight dispute with regard to piece work; there was a joiners' strike; and there were workers' grievances on the subject of dilution of male labour; but conferences, investigations and advanced pay, smoothed the way for increased activity. Female labour was introduced in November, 1915. In this year there were 670 women employed, as compared with 1,320 men and boys, and in the following year 1,940 men and boys were at work as compared with 820 women; but in 1917 the women were in the majority and continued so to the end, the figures being :—

    1917—Men and Boys, 942; Women, 1,390.
    1918—Men and Boys, 681; Women, 1,658.

The average wage was from 35s. to 28s. a week.

What perhaps interfered with output as much as anything was the prevalence of influenza in 1918; though at every alarm of an approaching air-raid much time was lost through suspension of operations. In the summer of 1918 many men, women and boys were unable to "carry on" because of illness. On one day over a hundred workpeople had to be removed from the factory suffering from the dreaded influenza scourge, and a large number of cases unfortunately proved fatal. On the other hand there was remarkable freedom from accidents.

NEWLAY WORKS.

But there were ordnance factories also—at Newlay and Hunslet.

The Newlay works were projected only a few weeks later than the Armley factory, and by March, 1916, had started operations, the special object in view being the production of 9.2 shells at the rate of 5,000 a week. For this purpose a site of fourteen acres was secured. Progress was delayed, however. The shortage of labour, the scarcity of materials, the sodden state of the riverside ground—the workmen were often nearly knee-deep in mud—the torpedoing of a vessel which was bringing essential machinery—things like these handicapped the project somewhat seriously.

In these circumstances it was June before even an output of 1,000 shells a week was attained. But two months later, that number was doubled; and in September the factory was extended. The record output in any one week was achieved in May, 1918, when 4,611 shells were produced. After this, in accordance with instructions from London, the production was reduced. From first to last, 360,652 shells were made at Newlay, their value being estimated at £3,500,000.

Mr. Hopper was the first deputy superintendent and on his transfer to the Hunslet factory his duties were taken over by Mr. F. H. Bingham. Mr. Thomas Burns was the works manager.

Almost the only labour trouble was that caused

by the employment of unskilled hands, coupled with the early difficulty of finding women workers. In June, 1916, 90 per cent. of the workers were men. A year later the proportion was 883 women to 864 men, and in March, 1918, 945 women to 779 men. The skilled men received £4 4s. 2d. a week, the unskilled £2 12s. 6d., and the women (unskilled, of course) £1 17s. 6d. Piece workers' pay, on the other hand averaged £10 a week, and women engaged on copper band turning were able to earn on an average £7 weekly. Happily, so it is recorded, there was satisfactory co-operation by the men when ample female labour was obtained, and the skilled hands took a pride in the achievements of the women under them.

Guns from Hunslet.

Still more serious problems had to be solved at the beginning of 1916, when it was decided to equip a factory at Hunslet. There was a pressing need at that time for shells of a large calibre—huge things weighing 1,200 lbs. each, the forgings for which would weigh something like twice as much.

Such shells could not be produced without special plant; no ordinary engineering shops could tackle the job. Moreover, there was no time to set about the construction of buildings; delay might have been fatal; the business had to be put in hand at once. Delays enough there were, as it happened, when the scheme materialised, for although, fortunately, premises were available at the old works of Tannett, Walker & Co., in Goodman Street, Hunslet, they were in such disorder that some time elapsed before the necessary overhauling paved the way for adaptation, and then further delay was caused in the production of 9.2 shells by the sinking of the vessel which was bringing the special machine tools from America. But even this did not daunt the management ; ordinary purpose lathes were at once adapted and made to serve the required purpose. For the 15 in. shells, by the way, the machinery was British made, and the first shell was forged and machined by the end of June, 200 a week being turned out soon after that date, and in one week as many as 333.

The work on 9.2 shells suffered several hindrances. More than once contracts were cancelled, and the machines had to be dismantled, the variation being due first to excess of supply and then to unexpected shortage.

In spite of all difficulties, the factory turned out 5,633 15 in. Howitzer shells and 38,897 9.2 shells, besides rectifying many thousands of others.

But there was another reason for the dismantling process just mentioned. While the supply of shells was increasing, our guns at the front were deteriorating. So from shells, Hunslet was switched on to gun-making. The proposition was the re-lining of 800 guns a month. Accordingly special visits to Woolwich were paid to find out how the thing was done ; the 15 in. shell shop was shut down, and machinery installed to carry on the new work. On May 18th, 1917, the first 18 pounder field gun was delivered re-lined, and two months later two guns every twenty-four hours were being dealt with ; this rate increasing until, during the four weeks ending February 21st, 1918, 208 guns were turned out.

Altogether, when work stopped after the Armistice the Hunslet factory had accounted for nearly 2,500 guns. Had the war continued, the department would have extended its operations considerably, for, following the crisis of March, 1918, a gun carriage shop was in course of construction to meet the heavy demands of the artillery at that time. Besides shells and guns, the factory did a vast amount of general engineering work—made, for instance, hundreds of thousands of brass bushes for fuses, and tens of thousands of parts for mine sinkers.

WOMEN DO MEN'S WORK.

As will be surmised, the successive variations, alterations and adaptations, proved somewhat trying not only to the management but to the workpeople. On the one hand the overhead charges were increased ; on the other, the labour arrangements had to undergo various modifications to suit the class of work required. Apart from these difficult conditions there was little trouble beyond some objections which the skilled men raised to the dilution of labour, and which they upheld by a strike, external influence compelling the management to give in to them. The trouble, it is recorded, was engineered by a few dissatisfied workers and not by the whole body. The maximum number of men employed at one time on shell production was 1,591, and of women, 916 ; while on gun production the figures were 1,253 men, 740 women. Their wage rates were the same as at the other factories.

Remarkable as their achievements seemed, experience nevertheless led to the conclusion that semi-skilled men and women could be employed as successfully on most of the operations in gun repair as on shell filling. Once a full degree of confidence was acquired the mechanic came to look upon his job as ordinary engineering repetition work.

Generally, the women attained satisfactory results ; one female operator became so proficient that she could rifle an 18 pounder gun in 2 hours 40 minutes. Great attention, by the way, was given to the women's welfare, and not the least of the acts of consideration shown by Mrs. Margaret Jackson, the Lady Superintendent, was her example set in the wearing of the " boiler suit," which, on being unanimously followed, enabled the workers to avoid accidents when in contact with the machinery. A high distinction was conferred on this band of female munition workers when three of their number—Mrs. Edith Butler, Mrs. Stanyon, and Miss Vera Holdsworth—were selected as the first factory recipients of the Order of the British Empire.

The guns were tested at Meanwood, about four miles from the centre of the city, where a disused quarry offered suitable scope for such an important operation. The task of converting the place into a gun proofing range, with sand butt 200 yards from the firing point, was the biggest piece of constructional work undertaken by the Board. It was, too, the first range set up for the use of a National Ordnance Factory, and thus served as a model for similar enterprises elsewhere in the country. In all, throughout the period the range was in use, during 1917 and 1918, 4,884 guns were proofed, some 20,000 rounds of ammunition being fired to that end. Leeds residents, therefore, occasionally received audible demonstration of what the booming of the guns sounded like on the battlefield.

An Output worth £13,000,000.

The organisation that admitted of all these strenuous activities was, of necessity, on a vast scale and complete in every detail. To each member of the Board were allotted special directorial duties and every department had its competent and responsible chief. Some idea of the various ramifications of the undertaking may be gathered from the fact that the secretarial department numbered no fewer than 300 officials (including 80 at headquarters) all under the control of Mr. Ben Day. A raw materials department dealt with forgings, castings, etc., to the value of over four millions sterling. (The shell forgings alone weighed, in the aggregate, about 150,000 tons). The traffic department handled 320,000 tons of materials and products, bringing or removing which between 40 or 50 railway trucks were in use daily at the busiest times, in addition to more than a score of motor lorries going to and from five different goods stations. There was a warehouse in Great Wilson Street, and another in Wellington Road ; and Marshall's Mills in Holbeck were requisitioned for the assembling of fuses. A labour department, housed at the Hotel de Ville under Mr. J. S. Hepper, dealt with 40,000 employees' applications, and an Inspection department acted as a buffer between the ordinary shop inspection and that carried out by the Government officials. There was also a Tool and Gauge department ; there was a Contract and Fuses department ; and a Welfare and Canteens department.

The shells produced reached a total of over 1,500,000 ; the fuses dealt with ran into thousands of millions ; and the numerous other components and sub-components, into tens of millions more. The value of the building and plant at all the factories was estimated at £800,000 ; the stocks at little short of a million sterling ; the total output at £13,000,000 ; and, after allowing for a loss of nearly £35,000 during the first year at Armley, there was a net profit of £533,000. Major Dewar was largely responsible for getting the factories to work, and he was succeeded in November, 1916, by Major Morgan, who was, in turn, succeeded by Captain Ovans in April, 1917, Mr. Peter Burt being chief engineer. When at their fullest capacity, the factories were the second largest group in the kingdom.

Thoroughness characterised the business of munition making in Leeds. Not only were shells made here ; they were filled also, and many millions of other shells as well.

SHELL FILLING AT BARNBOW.

No sooner had the Armley Ordnance Factory started operations than its promoters decided to carry the work a stage further by setting up a filling factory. To this end an independent Directing Board was appointed under the chairmanship of Mr. Joseph Watson (afterwards Lord Manton). The other members of the Board—all Leeds Citizens—were Mr. T. L. Taylor (deputy-chairman), the Hon. Rupert Beckett, Mr. Bernal Bagshawe, Mr. Arthur G. Lupton, and Major G. Yewdall (secretary). In August, 1915, they selected a site and let contracts for the new works, and before Christmas a start had been made with shell filling.

The undertaking was one of the largest of its kind in the kingdom. First of all, it involved the acquisition of some 400 acres of farm land at Barnbow, between Crossgates and Garforth on the outskirts of the city, where every possible convenience had to be provided *ab initio*. Roads, trolley tracks, railways connecting with the adjoining North Eastern system, gas, water and electricity supplies, sanitation—all these and other auxiliary services had to be provided in addition to long ranges of factory buildings. Nevertheless, such was the progress made that in the course of a few months, namely, in April, 1916, the first section of the Amatol plant was completed, and 4.5 shells were being filled, the output thereafter soon rising to 6,000 shells a day. Meanwhile, the buildings requisite for the manufacture of cartridges had been erected and brought into use, and a little later a breech loading extension and a box factory were built, together with a second Amatol factory. To these structures, in due course, others were added, until eventually the transformed fields of Barnbow had a roof area of 127,000 square feet.

Photo by   *Swaine.*
The Right Honourable LORD MANTON,
Chairman of the Board, National Shell
Filling Factory, Barnbow.

Photo by   *Bacon & Son.*
The Hon. RUPERT E. BECKETT, D.L., J.P.,
Member of the Board, National
Shell Filling Factory, Barnbow.

Photo by   *Swaine.*
SIR ALGERNON FIRTH, BART., J.P.,
President of the Association of Chambers
of Commerce.

Photo by   *Fielding.*
SIR JOHN MCLAREN,
Member of the Board, Leeds National
Shell Factory.

"Assembly" rooms, component stores, explosive magazines, fuse and gaine rooms, finished ammunition magazines, a big melting house building, a huge press factory, canteen and administration buildings, bulk stores, guard rooms, and so forth, all went to the making of this hive of industry which, when work was in full swing, in 1917 and 1918, with its host of workers and its efficient services, resembled nothing so much as a well ordered small manufacturing town.

In the official record of this enterprise—"The Story of Barnbow"—the present writer has already narrated in detail how successfully the work was carried on, and what remarkable results were achieved. It may, however, be well here to note a few of the statistics collected by Mr. R. H. Gummer, the chief engineer, and embodied in the above mentioned book. Not far short of six million bricks, and 5,400 tons of cement were used on the buildings. The service mains (water, sewage, and fire) wound in and out all over the place for a distance of 33 miles. The electric power and distributing cables extended for $28\frac{1}{2}$ miles, and the steam and hot water piping for 60 miles. There were $13\frac{1}{2}$ miles of wide gauge railway track and there were ten miles of narrow trolley track. At one period, when activities were at their height, over 16,000 workers were employed, some 93 per cent. being women and girls.

Woman's Industry and Courage.

Female labour predominated. Even the loading and storing of the various explosives, also, towards the last, the unloading of coal, was done by women and girls. Only male labour, however, was employed on the heaviest manual tasks, such as the breaking up of the ammonium nitrate, and the duties of shunters, engine men, boilermen, and the like. About one-third of the women came from Leeds, and for the convenience of these, and the workers from outlying places, 38 special trains were run daily. There was no lack of candidates for the many risky tasks which had to be performed. No fewer than 130,000 female applicants were interviewed. It was not until the summer of 1917 that the number of operatives substantially declined, and then only because the scheme of operations had become more systematic and effective.

When the work finished in November 1918, it was recorded, among other striking statistics, that over 36,000,000 breech loading cartridges had been charged and nearly 25,000,000 shells filled, apart from 19,250,000 shells completed with fuses and packed in boxes, making a grand total of 566,000 tons of finished ammunition despatched overseas. Of 18-pounder shells alone, 9,250,000 were dealt with—enough, if laid end to end, to measure as far as from London to New York, a distance of 3,200 miles.

This enormous output would not have been possible had not every contingency been carefully thought out beforehand, and due arrangements made for the expeditious performance of duties and for ready transport, together with precautions against accident and measures for the health, feeding, clothing, and comfort of the thousands who were engaged on the operations.

That it was dangerous work was unfortunately demonstrated on three occasions. The first and most serious explosion took place on the night of December 5th, 1916, in one of the fusing rooms. A shell placed in position on one of the machines used for screwing in the fuse suddenly burst and affected other projectiles close at hand, with the immediate result that 35 young women were killed. But for the sandbags and protecting shields which were in regular use the disaster would have been much more serious. Naturally,

Photo by *Pickard.*

No. 1. National Shell Filling Factory, Barnbow, Leeds. View of Box Factory, Machinery Hall.

great alarm was caused throughout the factory at the time, nevertheless work was continued courageously, and not only so, but within a few hours girls were found volunteering to work in the very room where the accident happened. The actual cause of the mishap could only be conjectured. Part of the fuse was supposed to be faulty. But it was not one that had been made in Leeds.

Although the censorship forbade publication of this item of news, and the matter therefore became exaggerated in local gossip, it travelled quickly to the British battle front and, without reference to the locality, was cited by the Commander-in-Chief in a special Order of the Day as a splendid example of the loyalty and determination with which munition workers were helping towards victory.

Barnbow's second explosion occurred about three months later, causing the death of two girls, and the third on May 31st, 1918, when three men were killed, ten others sustained injury, and one of the mixing sheds was wrecked. The shift was being changed at the time, otherwise the casualties might have been greater. This last accident happened on the day when the King and Queen were visiting Leeds, and His Majesty at once telephoned sympathetic inquiries, which were followed by a gracious gift of flowers for the injured from Queen Mary. Happily, all three disasters were restricted in effect by the precautionary measures taken. If Barnbow had blown up to any extent there would probably have been very few windows left unshattered in Leeds.

Risky work indeed! Think only of the enormous tonnage of explosive substances that had to be handled! At the Amatol factory 12,000 tons of T.N.T. were incorporated with 26,350 tons of ammonium nitrate to form the high explosive known as Amatol. In the cartridge factory more than 61,000 tons of propellant (N.C.T. and cordite) were made into breech-loading charges. And all this dangerous material had to be weighed on scales in ounces and drachms.

But, as already indicated, all available means were adopted in order to ensure a reasonable degree of safety. There was a fire brigade, the equipment including a specially constructed reservoir of 300,000 gallons of water; there was a steam siren to sound an alarm; there were sprinklers and drenchers attached to the magazines; there were fireproof doors and protective earthworks. Elaborate arrangements, too, were made for warming and ventilating the workshops, and eliminating the danger of poisoning; and, in general, by the provision of medical and nursing services, the health and comfort of everyone about the place received full attention. Similarly, in the matter of food supplies and catering, the huge canteens were equipped with every convenience and labour saving appliance. Barnbow even had a milk supply from its own cows, its slaughter-house and butcher's shop, its bacon factory, and vegetables from its own kitchen gardens.

TEXTILE REQUISITES AND ORGANISATION.

No small part of the organisation of this gigantic enterprise was concerned with textile wares, of which immense quantities were used in the process of manufacturing munitions. For example, nearly 87,000,000 cartridge bags and 26,000,000 exploder bags had to be handled, and these requisites, as well as the smaller components, were made almost entirely in Leeds. The textile stores occupied six acres of floor space at four warehouse premises in Wellington Street, Leeds, and thus constituted a separate department, which, by the way, formed the main distributing centre for all the filling factories in the kingdom. Here,

Photo by   No. 1 National Shell Filling Factory, Barnbow, Leeds.   View of Component Store, Cartridge Factory.   Pickard.

among other things, the Directing Board's staff dealt with well over 27 million yards of textile materials in the piece, nearly 142 million yards of braids and tapes, 150 tons of sewing threads, and 9,354 tons of millboard and strawboard, etc.

This branch of work, under the special direction of Mr. A. G. Lupton, also gave employment to the local printing trade, and it led, incidentally, to the introduction of a new system of printing on the bag material.

From end to end of the extensive range of factory buildings activity was the order of the day and the night alike. Heavily-laden railway trucks coming and going constantly; motor lorries bringing supplies from outlying stores; magazines and stores continually being fed and, in turn, disgorging their contents for purpose of manufacture—such was the daily condition of affairs while, all the time, busy hands and deft machinery fulfilled their allotted and essential tasks. Nearly every day scores of train-loads of ammunition were marshalled and despatched. In the year 1916 some 150 trucks a day were handled, and before the autumn of 1918 came that number had more than quadrupled.

The general management, as may be guessed, imposed no light responsibility. At least once a month the Directing Board met to review the position disclosed in reports presented by the heads of departments, but apart from that, there was individual attention given by the members, two of whom were in daily attendance from the time work started in 1915 until the Armistice was signed in November, 1918. It was no wonder that, as a result of this enterprise, resourcefulness and industry, the cost of producing ammunition at Barnbow was found to compare favourably with any other factory in the Kingdom. That this was so was due not only to the thoroughness of the work, but in no small measure to the useful economies effected, as, for instance, the saving of £12,000 by the sale of waste material and the utilisation of scrap.

Barnbow, in short, maintained to the last its reputation as the premier National Shell-Filling Factory, helped in notable fashion to win the war, and reflected the greatest credit on its Leeds origin and the business men and workers who were at the back of it.

SUBSIDIARY WORK AND ARMY EQUIPMENT.

Apart from the gigantic operations already noted, Leeds attained distinction through the enterprise of firms like Kitson's, Fowler's, Fairbairn-Lawson's and others who adapted or extended their works in order to meet the demand for munitions and other war essentials. Leeds, in short, manufactured practically every weapon of war from cartridges and bombs to big guns, "tanks," and battle aeroplanes. The city was the head-quarters of the West Riding Munitions Area, comprising 1,730 firms with offices at Quebec Chambers, where Captain Peter Thomas (a former Leeds solicitor) was installed as organising secretary.

An enormous amount of useful subsidiary work was done not only by the various branches of the engineering trade but by other industries whose normal productions were now of small importance in comparison with the special requirements of war time. One firm, for instance, diverted its attention from printing machinery making to the manufacture of shells as a feeder to the big ordnance factories; another changed over from lamp manufacture to the production of submarine mines, and another from motor cars to the construction of ambulances; while yet another concentrated on the manufacture of artificial limbs. Indeed, in a very special sense,

Photo by No. 1 National Shell Filling Factory, Barnbow, Leeds. Armistice Celebrations. *Pickard.*

Leeds provided facilities that redounded to its credit as a great engineering centre. The local output of steel cases for submarine mines was large enough to encircle the coast of Great Britain.

Other Leeds productions included such things as copper tubes and shell bands, parts for fuses, aeroplane parts and complete aircraft, burners for lamps used on all kind of transport vehicles, the parts of motor engines, gauges for fuses and shells, and rifle cartridges. More rifle cartridges were produced by Greenwood and Batley, of Armley, than by any other firm in the country; and Samuel Butler and Company, of Stanningley, machined, hardened, and tested the steel plates which formed the armour of 65 per cent of the "Tanks," the principal makers of which, in Leeds, were Kitson & Co. R. W. Crabtree and Sons, of Holbeck, manufacturers of printing presses, made shell components, including eight million gaines (special containers) and fuses at the rate of thousands weekly, also "Tank" gears; and George Bray and Company, manufacturers of gas fittings, made millions of essential parts for shell fuses, in addition to parts for aero engines and burners for lamps. T. F. Braime and Company, of Hunslet, led the way in the production of copper shell bands by means of presses, thereby winning enconiums from the Ministry of Munitions for their adaptability and inventiveness, such fittings having before been mostly made from copper tubes supplied by the tube manufacturers. Altogether, this firm turned out about eight million shell-bands, and so notable was the enterprise that firms in other parts of the country were sent to Leeds to study the process, with the result that the manufacture was extended elsewhere and an uninterrupted supply became available throughout the war.

Leeds took no small interest in the efficiency of the air service. Many an aeroplane was built at the Olympia Works in Roundhay Road; and it was a Leeds-built battleplane that the Chamber of Commerce presented to the Government of India, in April, 1917, as the nucleus of an Imperial Air Fleet. The ceremony of handing over this gift took place at Roundhay, when the Lady Mayoress (Mrs. E. George Arnold) broke a bottle of wine over the nose of the aeroplane and named it "Leeds," and also attached as a mascot a facsimile of the Star of India given by Miss Calvert. General Sir David Henderson, G.O.C., Royal Flying Corps, took charge of the machine for use on the Western Front, and it was accepted as a gift to the Indian Government by Lord Islington, Under Secretary of State for India, at the hands of Lord Desborough, President of the Imperial Air Fleet Committee.

As to the supply of Navy and Army equipment, every cloth mill, clothing factory, tannery and boot factory, contributed its quota to swell the tremendous output which went from Leeds, and the big contracts placed here by the Admiralty and War Office were carried out with an expedition and thoroughness that not only justified the confidence reposed in local capabilities, but pleasantly surprised the Government and evoked admiration on all sides.

The Clothing Depôts.

The Northern Area Army Clothing Department, centred in Leeds, dealt with and distributed an enormous quantity of goods. In the last year of the war the number of garments officially inspected averaged 750,000 a week. At first the Tramway Shed in Swinegate was taken over, but the goods came through so quickly that in the course of two or three weeks the adjacent King's Mills had to be requisitioned. But still the business developed and further accommodation had to be provided. In May, 1915, the Cattle Market buildings in Gelderd Road came into use as a store, and were filled from end to end with 9,000,000 yards of cloth. Later, additional premises were acquired to meet the need for increased accommodation. In a great warehouse belonging to the Aire and Calder Navigation over 3,000,000 garments could be stored in bales. Room was also found in the basement of Messrs. J. & W. Campbell's clothing factory in Hunslet, the arches under the North-Eastern Railway Station and a temporary structure adjoining, also at premises in Call Lane, at the Gibraltar Barracks in Claypit Lane and a building in Park Row, where every week 80,000 shirts underwent official inspection.

In 1917 branches were opened at Huddersfield and Halifax, and in the last year of the war there were no fewer than 42 such depôts in the West Riding, all of them under the jurisdiction of the Northern Area which, with its headquarters in Leeds, comprised Yorkshire, Lancashire and Scotland. The woollen and cotton materials received at the depôts in 1915 aggregated nearly 33,000,000 yards at a total value of $8\frac{3}{4}$ million pounds sterling —of which 20,000,000 yards were issued to clothing contractors in the district. These figures increased in the following year about 25 per cent. and thereafter, so enormously did the operations develop that in 1918 the weekly average inspection covered 6,000,000 yards, equivalent to over 312,000,000 yards in the year. Altogether, the Department issued over 53,000,000 shirts, 21,000,000 pairs of service trousers and a like number of jackets, 8,000,000 pairs of pantaloons for the mounted forces and nearly 10,000,000 great coats and British warms, apart from over 30,000,000 pairs of boots, 24,000,000 puttees and 89,000,000 pairs of socks.

The Department was organised by Lt.-Col. W. A. Malcolm of the Special Reserve of Officers, Highland Light Infantry, and he had the advantage of expert advice voluntarily given by Mr. David Little and Mr. George Brown, two well-known representatives of the Leeds Clothing Industry. Valuable services were also rendered by Mr. E. F. Chard and Mr. H. F. Odroft, trained civilian officials who were both more than once "mentioned in despatches," and by Mr. J. Hawkesford, assistant Inspector of Clothing.

Photo by   *Bacon & Son.*
A. G. LUPTON, J.P.,
Pro-Chancellor, Leeds University
Member of the Board, National Shell
Filling Factory, Barnbow.

Photo by   *Rosemont.*
Sir MICHAEL E. SADLER, K.C.S.I., C.B.,
LL.D.
Vice-Chancellor, Leeds University.

Photo by   *Fielding.*
Sir BERKELEY MOYNIHAN, BART.,
K.C.M.G., C.B.
Chairman of the Army Medical Advisory
Board.

Photo by   *Elliott & Fry.*
Lieut.-Col. ARTHUR SMITHELLS, C.M.G.,
F.R.S., B.Sc.,
Professor of Chemistry, Leeds University.

V. HOW THE UNIVERSITY HELPED.

"Let reason go before every enterprise, and counsel before every action."—*Ecclesiasticus.*

OF the several industrial efforts described as "of national importance" none more truly merited that designation than the war work done by the University of Leeds. It was rendered in a great variety of ways, for the whole resources of the University were placed at the disposal of the Government. From the moment war broke out, when members of the Officers' Training Corps volunteered for active service, until after the armistice, when the need for educating Ex-Service men became pressing, the University through all the trying period of depleted staffs, reduced finances, and general disturbance of arrangements, grappled unceasingly and successfully with many a complex scientific problem and urgent educational task in order that the war might be crowned with victory for the Allied cause.

In little more than a year from the outbreak of hostilities no fewer than 415 members of the University O.T.C. had received commissions, while, in addition, a large number of other members of the University were serving in the Army or Navy. In the autumn of 1915, in fact, one third of the members of the teaching and administrative staff, and about the same proportion of undergraduates of the year 1913-14, were on active service—nearly a thousand all told. During the whole war period, 1,596 members of the University were on active service, and of these, 1,435 held commissioned rank. The casualties numbered 501, classified thus :—202 killed, 40 missing, 259 wounded ; and the distinctions gained (including one Victoria Cross) numbered 165.

Coincident with other steps taken on the outbreak of war to render national service the

University regulations were modified so that no disadvantage might befall undergraduates who volunteered for the defence of the country, and nine months later a new Ordinance was approved which definitely secured elasticity and discretionary power in this matter.

One of the first effects of the war was a demand for the services of members of the Faculty of Medicine. The then Dean of the Faculty, Professor de Burgh Birch, became Assistant Director of Medical Services (Reserve) West Riding Division Territorial Force; and other members took up duties at Beckett's Park and Beckett Street Military Hospitals, or were engaged actively in the medical examination of recruits.

At the same time training classes for Voluntary Aid Detachments were organised under the direction of Professor Arthur Smithells, F.R.S., and Professor de Burgh Birch; a staff of expert linguists undertook to act as interpreters, where necessary, and to assist in the correspondence of the wounded; ladies connected with the University set about providing garments and medical comforts; a hospitable scheme was devised and carried out in the interest of Belgian refugees of the educated classes, the undergraduates contributing in monthly subscriptions about £200 a year to the cost; and in many other directions plans were laid and promptly executed with a view to meet emergencies.

In the matter of the nation's food supply, for instance, the Agricultural Department of the University lost no time in issuing throughout the country handbills and pamphlets on the subject of farm, allotments and poultry management, besides giving advice to the Belgian refugees who started horticultural operations at Killingbeck, training women at Garforth for farm work and sending a member of the staff to give instruction in farriery at the camps of the Northern Command.

Throughout the war, indeed, the University Agricultural Department was in close co-operation with the War Agricultural and Executive Committees set up by the Board of Agriculture and Fisheries, and the expert advice of its staff was freely given to those committees and the farming community. Professor R. S. Seton, head of the Department, added to his onerous duties those of the Board's Commissioner for Yorkshire ; the professor of Agricultural Chemistry (Dr. C. Crowther) became a member of the Consultative Staff instituted in connection with the Food Production Branch of the Board ; and Mr. A. S. Galt, lecturer in horticulture, rendered special service as organiser in regard to the cultivation of allotments. Again, by the Board's utilisation of the University Flax Experiment Station at Selby, a considerable increase in the production of flax was secured at a time when it was most needed by the Royal Air Service.

How many-sided was the University's war work may be gathered from the following summary of its main activities :—

    Experiments in connection with the manufacture of explosives.

    Testing high explosives.

    Analysing coal tar for toluene and benzine.

    Advising in regard to the shortage of chemical products.

    Researches in aid of the establishment of a national dye industry.

    The manufacture of antiseptics and anaesthetics and the preparation of bacterial culture media.

    The testing of metals and aeroplane spars.

    Preparing models of military bridges.

    The testing of Army cloths and aeroplane fabrics.

    The testing of optical instruments.

    The testing of varnishes used in shell manufacture.

Instruction in elementary machine work for intending munition workers.

The organisation of lecture courses on war subjects and special advice and assistance in agricultural problems.

Even the bare mention of such things as these will convey some idea of the far-reaching importance of the work. Its value was certainly appreciated, and on one memorable occasion—September 27th, 1915—His Majesty King George paid the University a visit of inspection, and saw for himself what was being done. The Department of Organic Chemistry, for instance, under Professor Cohen, F.R.S., successfully overcame all difficulties in the production of the anaesthetic Novocaine, a drug formerly made under patent in Germany, and involving a long, complex and costly process. Here, too, at the request of Dr. Dakin (D.Sc. of Leeds University) a hundred different compounds underwent experimental trial as antiseptics, and the material known as hypochlorite antiseptic was prepared for distribution among the hospitals of the country. Again, in the direction of life saving, the researches of Professor Proctor, of the Leather Industries Department, were a notable factor. His new process of chrome leather tanning enabled boots and other light leather equipment for the allied armies to be provided with the least possible delay.

In regard to munitions, the work of the Coal Gas, and Fuel Industries Department, under Professor Cobb, was especially useful through its systematic control of the process of extracting toluene from coal gas, thus helping to maintain a regular supply of the high explosive T.N.T. (trinitotoluene). This, in addition to the inspection and testing of the lyddite, T.N.T., and ammonium nitrate produced in Yorkshire. Explosives were also investigated by the Department of Tinctorial Chemistry and Dyeing, under Professor Arthur

G. Green, and his successor, Professor A. G. Perkin, and a new process of manufacturing lyddite was worked out which rendered that product independent of the supply of carbolic acid.

Both the Textile Industries Department, under Professor Barker, and the Colour Chemistry Department, were of the greatest utility in helping the Government to meet emergencies in respect of fabrics and dyes. The resources of the latter department (then known as the Tinctorial Chemistry and Dyeing Department) were placed at the disposal of the nation quite early in the war when the Government appointed a Chemical Trades Committee, under Lord Moulton, to investigate the question of dyestuffs and explosives, and the scientific researches carried out in connection with the production of dyes proved of inestimable value in fostering a revival of the British Dye Industry and impressing its national importance in relation to the supply of explosives. One member of the Textile Department—Mr. T. Hollis—filled the important post of manager of the Textile Store of the Leeds National Shell Factory.

Professor Goodman and the staff of the Engineering Department, with the help of Professor Bragg and members of the Department of Physics, were engaged in special work, in which the laboratories of the Department had full play ; and the general public were kept informed of European history in relation to the war through courses of lectures delivered by Professor A. J. Grant, while the troops in training camps were instructed on poison gas warfare by Professor Arthur Smithells, F.R.S., who became Chief Chemical Adviser to the War Office (G.H.Q. Home Forces) being gazetted with the rank of Lt.-Colonel.

The University Annual Reports show also that four Professors—viz., Professors Barbier, Gordon, Macgregor, and Priestley—served in France ;

Professor Raper did experimental work for the R.A.M.C.; Professor Crowther's services were monopolised by the Department of Food Production; and Major T. Wardrop Griffith (Professor of Medicine) acting as honorary secretary for the lectures on Venereal Diseases to the troops in the Northern Command, with the co-operation of Professor Johnstone Campbell and Major Rawdon Veale, imparted instruction on this subject to 160,000 officers and men. Again, the members of the Dental School of the University assisted in the dental treatment of recruits and wounded soldiers; many medical men connected with the University served abroad in the R.A.M.C.; members of the staff of the Agricultural Department helped at the various centres through Yorkshire in the training of women for farm work; women students took active part in the organisation of the National Register, and the reception and care of refugees from Belgium and Serbia; the Department of Modern Languages supplied interpreters, and the Department of Classics furnished from its staff an officer who possessed special local knowledge of Salonika and the district.

These and other worthy records may be found enshrined in the printed Reports of the University. What it all entailed few knew but those who were charged with the task of "carrying on" the University during the war years. We read that "The absence of so many members of the staff on service, and the claims of the various branches of war work done in the University itself, involved a great strain on the remainder of the teaching staff. The work of the administrative staff was also greatly increased. In some departments the continuance of the ordinary teaching was only rendered possible by outside help."

For nearly two years—from **1917** to **1919**—the University was without the services of its Vice-Chancellor, Mr. (afterwards Sir) Michael Sadler, who, at the request of the Secretary of State, and of the Government of India, undertook the duties of President of the Calcutta University Commission. During his absence his home duties were discharged by the then Pro-Vice Chancellor, Professor C. M. Gillespie, upon whom especially heavy responsibilities devolved during the winter following the armistice, when the University had to meet a great influx of students from among the men released from military service. That session of 1918-19, it is recorded, was a period of unprecedented growth. It not only saw the return of members of the staff and undergraduates from active service, but the enrolment of many demobilised officers and men for courses of training, and the beginning of a rapid increase in the number of new students. Accommodation was thus taxed to the extreme limit, and hundreds seeking admission had to be turned away. The number of students taking full-time courses at the University rose from **778** in the session **1918-19** to **1,389** in the spring of **1920**.

VI. CARE OF THE SICK AND WOUNDED.

" We live in deeds, not years ; in thoughts, not breaths ;
In feelings, not in figures on a dial.
We should count time by heart-throbs. He most lives
Who thinks most, feels the noblest, acts the best."
P. J. Bailey.

MEDICAL AND HOSPITAL SERVICE.

One of the brightest chapters in the history of Leeds in war time must ever remain that which records the steady, faithful, and useful work done for the relief of the sick and wounded. A great deal of what was accomplished, and the self-sacrificing zeal it entailed, will never be fully known, and a great deal more can only be guessed by reading between the lines of statistical information.

True to its great reputation as a home of medical and surgical science, Leeds promptly met the war's demand for hospital accommodation and for the services of the most skilled in every department.

It was with thoroughness and efficiency that Leeds carried out those measures of hospital treatment which were so essential to the interests of the nation. This was due alike to the ability and resource of the medical profession, the devotion of trained and voluntary nurses, and the help of citizens both rich and poor, who, in a variety of ways, contributed their quota to the working of the scheme. In money alone Leeds and the neighbouring districts supplied funds amounting to over £50,000 for extensions at Beckett's Park Military Hospital, where ultimately 3,200 beds were available. But, besides this important centre—in 1917 it was made the Orthopædic centre of the whole Northern Command —there was the East Leeds War Hospital, and there were auxiliary hospitals in quite a number

Photo by   *Surelle.*
Lieut.-Col. J. F. DOBSON,
1st Administrator, 2nd Northern General
Hospital.

Photo by   *Bacon & Son.*
Brevet-Colonel H. LITTLEWOOD, C.M.G.,
2nd Administrator, 2nd Northern General
Hospital.

Photo by   *Elliott & Fry.*
Col. A. D. SHARP, C.B., C.M.G., K.H.S.,
T.D.,
O.C. 1st West Riding Field
Ambulance, R.A.M.C., (T.F.).

Lieut.-Col. H. COLLINSON, C.B., C.M.G.,
D.S.O.,
O.C. 2nd West Riding Field
Ambulance R.A.M.C., (T.F.).

of other places, so that altogether Leeds found 6,500 beds, and in the course of the five years provided treatment for over 100,000 patients.

At Beckett's Park Hospital alone no fewer than 57,200 cases were admitted during the five years of war, and there were only 226 deaths, while the surgical operations numbered :—general, 9,670 ; jaws, 2,024 ; total 11,694.

Nor were achievements like these confined to the city ; many a medical man from Leeds rendered service in camps, at the base hospitals, and at the Front, those who had private practices being relieved at home by older men who voluntarily assumed the responsibility of caring for civilian patients. In due course, also, several of the Military Hospital staff undertook onerous tasks in France and the other theatres of war. A notable example was the eminent surgeon Sir Berkeley Moynihan, whose great work in abdominal surgery is world-famed. Throughout the war his talents and services were placed unreservedly at the disposal of the War Office.

When war broke out Sir Berkeley Moynihan was one of the *a la suite* staff at Beckett's Park Hospital, with the rank of Major ; and when the East Leeds War Hospital was organised, a few months later, he took temporary charge of the surgical side there. Meanwhile—in November, 1914—he had been appointed Consultant Surgeon in France, with the rank of Colonel A.M.S., and was mentioned in despatches. In April, 1915, he was appointed Consultant to the Northern Command, but the increasing pressure of war's claims soon necessitated his return to the front, and the great Somme battle of July, 1916, found him again actively engaged as Consultant to the British Army in France. In February, 1917, he became Chairman of the Council of Consultants in the British Army, once more being mentioned in Despatches ; the military Order of C.B. was conferred on him, and he was appointed British Representative at the Inter-Allied Surgical Conference. A few months later, after America's entry into the war, he was sent across the Atlantic at the request of the United States Government to deliver addresses on war surgery. Returning in December, 1917, he was promoted to the rank of Surgeon General A.M.S. and, two months later to the rank of Major-General, being also appointed to the chairmanship of the Army Medical Advisory Board, which office he still holds. In June, 1918, the King conferred on him the honour of K.C.M.G., and, in 1922, a Baronetcy.

And what of those officers and men of the Field Ambulance Corps whose patriotic action also reflected credit on Leeds? From the brief accounts of military achievements already given it will have been gathered that over and over again the heroic Ambulance Corps were called on to work under extreme pressure in most difficult conditions, in the midst of grave risks and in imminent peril of life. In this noble work the 1st and 2nd West Riding Field Ambulance R.A.M.C. (T.F.) commanded by Leeds surgeons, and comprising no small proportion of Leeds men, played a noteworthy part, and, it was fitly acknowledged by the high honours conferred on the Commanding officers, Colonel A. D. Sharp and Colonel H. Collinson. Both these corps were attached to the 49th Division and went through the fierce Somme battle and experiences in the Ypres salient, having left for France in April, 1915. When the Territorials were mobilised on August 4th, 1914, Colonel Sharp took command of the 1st W.R. Field Ambulance R.A.M.C. He then held the rank of Major, and was promoted Lieut.-Colonel the following month. Similarly, Colonel Collinson, then second-in-command of the 2nd Field Ambulance, with the rank of Major, was promoted Lieut.-Colonel at Christmas and

CARE OF THE SICK AND WOUNDED.

went to France in April, 1915 as O.C. How thoroughly well both C.O.'s justified the trust reposed in them will be seen from the following outline of subsequent events and honours won.

Colonel A. D. Sharp—July to December, 1915, Ypres salient. December 19th, 1915, appointed A.D.M.S. 49th (W.R.) Division and promoted temporary Colonel A.M.S. January, 1916, awarded C.M.G. and mentioned in Despatches. May, 1916, promoted to permanent rank of Colonel. July to September, 1916, Battle of the Somme. January, 1917, mentioned in Despatches. 1917, Defence of Nieuport. October to December, 1917, Passchendaele battle. January 7th, 1918, awarded C.B., and mentioned in Despatches. January to March, 1918, Ypres salient. April, 1918, German offensive, Mont Kemmal. September, 1918, A.D.M.S., Kent Force. 1919, awarded the Territorial Decoration; appointed a member of the War Office Committee for Reorganisation of the Territorial Army Medical Service; awarded the Military Order of Aviz, Portugal, Commander. 1920, appointed A.D.M.S. 49th (W.R. Division) 1922, appointed Hon. Surgeon to the King.

Colonel H. Collinson—July to December, 1915, Ypres salient. January, 1916, mentioned in Despatches. July to September, 1916, battle of the Somme. November, 1916, transferred as O.C. to No. 7 Casualty Clearing Station. January, 1917, awarded D.S.O. Mentioned in Despatches. May, 1917, transferred to the 62nd (W.R.) Division as A.D.M.S. with temporary rank of Colonel A.M.S. November, 1917, battle of Cambrai. January, 1918, mentioned in Despatches. March, 1918, German offensive, Bucquoy. June, 1918, awarded C.M.G. and mentioned in Despatches. July, 1918, second battle of the Marne; awarded Croix de Chevalier, Legion of Honour. August to November, 1918, British offensive. December, 1918 to March 1919, with the British Army of

Occupation in Germany. June, 1919, awarded C.B., and mentioned in Despatches. 1922, awarded the Territorial Decoration.

THE 2ND NORTHERN GENERAL HOSPITAL.

A review of the general situation as regards Leeds hospital work cannot but excite admiration for the prescience and energy of the local R.A.M.C. When the Territorial forces came into being in 1908, and arrangements were made for hospitals to be started in various centres of medical education, Leeds was selected as the location for the 2nd Northern General Hospital, and a plan was elaborated which involved the taking-over of the Leeds Institute buildings and certain schools for the accommodation of 500 beds in case of emergency. On Colonel Trevelyan's death in 1912, Major J. F. Dobson, who succeeded to the command, carried the scheme a step further. After paying a visit to Netley Hospital with Major J. A. Coupland, he formed the opinion that the Cookridge Street proposal was unsuitable and inadequate. Accordingly he devised another plan, none other than the utilisation of the newly-erected Training College at Beckett's Park, and no opposition being offered by the Leeds Education Committee, it was this plan (which, with great forethought, Major Dobson had worked out in every detail) that finally received the approval of the Military Authorities when war was declared.

Thus it happened that, on August 7th, 1914, 300 beds were in readiness, apart from 100 beds which the General Infirmary offered, and that, in less than a fortnight from the outbreak of war, 600 beds were available with 92 fully-trained nurses prepared to take duty. At the same time an appeal issued by Dr. Mary Phillips, under the auspices of the Lady Mayoress (Mrs. Charles Ratcliffe) drew a warm-hearted response from Leeds women anxious to render voluntary aid.

At Beckett's Park, to begin with, 46 beds were provided in the Central Hall, 16 in the Library, 26 in the Women's Common Room, and others in smaller rooms, but by degrees other buildings were taken over until, ultimately, all the hostels but one—seven in number—were occupied. Major (afterwards Lieut.-Colonel) J. F. Dobson was the first Administrator ; Major J. A. Coupland, Registrar ; Lieut.-Colonel A. G. Barrs, and Lieut.-Colonel (later Brevet Colonel) H. Littlewood, were in charge of the Medical and Surgical Departments of the Hospital, assisted by other members of the *a la suite* staff ; and the first sixty beds set apart for sick officers were in charge of Major Knaggs. In April, 1915, Lieut.-Colonel Dobson had a serious illness and Major Coupland acted as Administrator. On his leaving for duties in France in June, 1915, Lieut.-Colonel Littlewood became Administrator and carried on the work until May, 1919, when Lieut.-Colonel C. E. Ligertwood, D.S.O., was appointed his successor. It was in June, 1915, too, that Major (afterwards Brevet Lieut.-Colonel) G. W. Watson was appointed Registrar, which post he filled with conspicuous ability until June, 1919. Miss E. S. Innes, R.R.C. (Matron of the Leeds General Infirmary) was Matron-in-Chief, and Miss Hill the first Matron of the Hospital, succeeded on her appointment to France in May, 1915, by Miss M. Whiffin.

THE NURSING SERVICE.

With regard to the nursing service, Miss Innes has kindly supplied the following interesting memoranda :—

"In 1909 the Territorial Force Nursing Service was formed as an auxiliary to the Territorial Army, and all over the country hospitals were selected and a nursing staff booked for each one so that, in the event of war, everything could quickly be ready for the reception of the wounded. There were 23 hospitals : four in London, fifteen in the provinces, and four in Scotland. Every hospital had a Principal Matron who was responsible for finding the staff of nurses considered necessary for her hospital. Before the war a staff of 92 trained nurses was considered the right number for 500 beds, but each Principal Matron was required to have 121 on her books in readiness to fill any gaps that might occur. This staff consisted of two matrons, 30 sisters, 88 nurses and one principal Matron. The ranks of the 92 members to be called up for duty were—one Matron, 22 Sisters, and 68 nurses. These were all fully trained.

"On August 4th, 1914, by the request of the Commanding Officer, I visited the Training College at Beckett's Park to consider what class-rooms would make the best wards, kitchens, etc. The first member to be called up for duty was Miss Jessie Hills, Matron of the Royal Infirmary, Halifax, who came over on August 6th to visit Beckett's Park, and therefore on that day became the first Matron of the 2nd Northern General Hospital. On the evening of Thursday, August 6th, I received a telephone message from Hull asking for nurses to be sent there at once, if possible, as a battle was said to be in progress off the coast. This, fortunately, did not prove true, but at the time one did not know what to think. I spoke to the officer-on-duty at the barracks and we decided not to send any nurses to Hull, but to telegraph for thirty to report at Beckett's Park the next day (Friday). This they all did quite early; in fact one arrived at midnight on Thursday, and accommodation had to be found for her.

"These thirty nurses formed the nucleus of the nursing staff of the 2nd Northern General Hospital, and others up to the number of 92 were gradually called up during August and September. The first Matron was Miss J. E. Hills, and the first Assistant Matron, Miss F. H. Tomlin, who was afterwards Matron of East Leeds War Hospital. The Sisters who arrived on August 7th were Miss Gertrude Bullman, Miss Margaret Hughes, and Miss Anne Simpson, and the remainder of the thirty were staff nurses. Within the next few days others were added to the number. The nursing staff was composed only of trained nurses until the end of April, 1915, when the first contingent of V.A.D.'s were called up for duty.

"On October 9th, 1914, we sent out our first members for service in France and Belgium, namely Miss Caroline Bayly, Miss Mary Wharton, Miss Anne E. Roberts, Miss Elinor Sheard, and Miss Amy Relph. They were followed as time went on by many others who all distinguished themselves by their excellent work.

The great work of conveying the sick and wounded from the railway stations, and to and from the various auxiliaries, was a remarkably efficient organisation, carried out entirely by voluntary workers and voluntary funds, between £8,000 and £9,000 being subscribed. In addition, ambulances were given by Mr. Harold Nickols and Mr. Kitson, and some were lent by Sir William Middlebrook, Messrs. Albrecht and others. In the end there was a fleet of 25 ambulances available. The scheme was started by the Administrator, who was ably assisted, first by Mr. F. C. Appleton and later by Mr. J. S. Mathers, in whose hands were placed the entire working of the transports ; and no more unselfish work has ever been done by men who were all over military age, or in other ways unfit for general military service.

Discerning people must have realised this when they saw the frequent comings and goings through the streets of the city. And there were certainly some stirring sights witnessed. Public feeling, for instance, was profoundly moved by the arrival of the first convoy. A civic welcome was extended by the Lord Mayor (Col. Sir Edward Brotherton, Bart.), who met the ambulance train in person at the Midland Station, and a dense crowd assembled in City Square to cheer the patients as they passed on their way to Beckett's Park. About three weeks later, another and larger convoy arrived, including a greater proportion of serious cases, and the city's greeting was again most cordial and sympathetic. In City Square alone the throng of onlookers numbered some 5,000 or 6,000 and almost the whole route to Far Headingley was lined with spectators who voiced their sympathy in cheers and showed their goodwill by throwing packets of tobacco or cigarettes to the men.

From now onwards, these experiences grew familiar, and the tax on accommodation became

"In May, 1915, Miss Hills was seconded to France to be Matron of the First Territorial Force hospital there, and Miss Mabel Whiffin was appointed to the 2nd Northern in her place. About the same time the East Leeds War Hospital was opened with Miss Tomlin as Matron, and further additions to the nursing staff were made from time to time until a staff of well over 400 was reached."

As with all other Territorial hospitals, the Leeds Military hospitals were used to their full extent for wounded men from the Front. For some time Leeds and Sheffield were the chief Hospitals in the West Riding, but soon Leeds arranged for Auxiliaries in Bradford, Huddersfield, Halifax, Keighley, and Dewsbury ; and later on all these towns had their own War Hospitals with an average of considerably over 1,000 beds. Other auxiliaries were started voluntarily in the neighbourhood of Leeds, and in different parts of Yorkshire, so that ultimately the number of beds under the Leeds Administrator totalled 6,500.

The number of beds in these Auxiliary Hospitals varied from 30 to 200, and they were inspected by the Administrator or one of his staff monthly. It is impossible to praise too highly this auxiliary work, some account of which is given in another chapter. The medical men in the districts attended to the patients and the nursing was mainly done by the V.A.D.'s. Great credit is due to the Commandants, and everyone who helped to make these hospitals a success.

The first convoy of wounded from the Front, numbering nearly 90, arrived in Leeds on September 17th, 1914. Most of them had taken part in the fighting at Mons. Later, the wounded came practically from every battle field in the various theatres of the war. In November, 1914, 90 wounded Belgians and 16 Belgian Officers were admitted to the Hospital. Many of these were serious cases, but all recovered and all the officers ultimately returned to duty in France.

Visit of H.M. The King to the East Leeds Military Hospital, Beckett Street 28th September, 1915.

such as to render an extension of premises imperatively necessary. Accordingly, early in 1915, it was decided to establish a new centre in East Leeds, and for this purpose part of the Workhouse in Beckett Street was taken over, 500 beds being provided at first. Later, extensions at Killingbeck, Harehills Council School, etc., increased the accommodation to over 2,000 beds.

East Leeds War Hospital.

The whole of this additional accommodation was known as the East Leeds War Hospital extension of the 2nd Northern General Hospital, a separate organisation but under the control of the Administrator at Beckett's Park, the nursing staff also being controlled by the Matron-in-Chief (Miss Innes). Major Jamieson (afterwards Lieut.-Colonel) Professor of Anatomy in the University of Leeds, was appointed Registrar, and he acted as Assistant Administrator. He did most excellent work ; spared no pains to make the organisation as perfect as possible ; and was placed in entire charge when Colonel Littlewood retired in May, 1919, holding that position until the Hospital was finally closed in September, 1919. At the outset, Lieut.-Colonel Sir Berkeley Moynihan (afterwards Major-General) and Lieut.-Colonel Maxwell Telling took charge of the Surgical and Medical Divisions, but when, in April, 1915, Sir Berkeley Moynihan was appointed Consulting Surgeon to the Northern Command, Lieut.-Colonel Walter Thompson took charge of the surgical side. Other members of the staff were either transferred from Beckett's Park or were members of the *a la suite* staff that had not yet been called up. Miss Tomlin was appointed Matron, and N.C.O.'s and men were also transferred from Beckett's Park.

The importance of keeping the patients cheerful was not forgotten, and in that regard generous help was soon forthcoming. On November 23rd,

1915, a large recreation hall, thoroughly furnished and equipped with a complete Cinema apparatus was opened at Beckett's Park by the Grand Duchess George of Russia. It was the gift of the wholesale clothiers of Leeds, and cost £1,200. This welcome provision was extended later by the Y.M.C.A., at a cost of £600 and played a very important part in the hospital organisation. Here concerts, lectures, dramatic entertainments, billiard tournaments, and other forms of recreation were enjoyed by the men regularly. About the same time a similar institution was founded and opened at East Leeds, a large hall in the workhouse having been handed over by public subscription. Mr. A. G. Lupton, then Pro-Chancellor of the Leeds University, was foremost in supporting the movement. Later, at Killingbeck, another recreation hall was provided by the Y.M.C.A.

Extensions at Beckett's Park.

In this month of November 1915, also, definite arrangements were made for structural additions to the Hospital at Beckett's Park. Still more beds were required, and it was deemed wiser to centralize at Beckett's Park instead of distributing patients in various schools or other buildings. The matter had been under consideration by Major Dobson a few months earlier, when he was laid aside by illness for some months, and it was now taken in hand by his successor, Colonel Littlewood who, by the way, on the outbreak of war had hastened back from his Norfolk home (where he had retired from practice) in order to look after the surgical cases at Beckett's Park. With great energy Colonel Littlewood set to work and enlisted influential interest in an extension scheme, consulting with the Lord Mayor, Alderman Charles Lupton, Treasurer of the Leeds Infirmary, who at all times gave valuable help and advice in hospital organisation and management ; and discussing the matter also with the Hon. Rupert Beckett, Mr. Joseph Watson (afterwards Lord Manton), Mr. F. J. Kitson, and Alderman F. Kinder. All these gentlemen gave practical support to the movement, and with the approval of the War Office they were constituted a committee to carry out the proposed extension scheme. In less than a month £26,000 was publicly subscribed —very largely by Leeds citizens—and building operations started, Mr. F. Broadbent, Architect to the Leeds Education Committee, acting as honorary architect. The scheme provided for 700 additional beds, new kitchens, stores, etc., in a group of temporary structures forming an annexe to the permanent buildings, and when complete it became a model which was copied by many other centres.

In a letter to the Lord Mayor (Mr. Charles Lupton) with reference to the funds raised, Sir Alfred Keogh, Director General Army Medical Department, wrote : " What a splendid record Leeds has made ! It is a truly magnificent and I do most warmly congratulate you. Lord Kitchener has heard of the magnificent response to your efforts with the greatest satisfaction and pleasure."

The extension was opened on March 30th, 1916, by Major General H. M. Lawson, General Officer Commanding in Chief Northern Command, in the absence of Lord French who was unavoidably prevented from being present.

The increasing number of patients brought heavier responsibilities and still more arduous duties. New departments of work had to be taken in hand, and the whole range of operations enlarged. Major Wilfrid Vining, the Pathologist to the hospital, was very early placed in charge of cerebrospinal fever cases, tetanus and other infections in the West Riding area of the Command ; and these cases with their contacts were admitted to Killingbeck. At times the work was very hard and exacting, but it was always done with enthusiasm and painstaking accuracy. Captain M. Stewart, the Professor of Pathology at the Leeds University, attached to the East Leeds Staff, had charge of the cases of typhoid, dysentery, malaria, etc., and did a great amount of useful and important bacteriological work.

In May, 1916, a department for the treatment of injuries to the jaws and face was opened at Beckett's Park with 150 beds, and here all cases of this class of injury were sent from the hospitals in the Northern Command. The Administrator acted as Consulting Surgeon and was assisted by Captain Mumby, as Surgeon, and Captain Alan Forty as Dental Surgeon until his retirement in 1917 when Captain Shefford succeeded him. The department did excellent work and treated over 2,000 patients.

In June, 1916, there was started at the East Leeds Hospital a Dental Mechanical Department where dentures were fitted for the whole of the Command. The arrangements and organisation of this new development stand entirely to the credit of Major Jamieson, and he was ably assisted by Captain Child, the Surgeon-Dentist in charge. When the department was in full swing more than 100 mechanics were working, and altogether over 60,000 dentures were sent out.

ORTHOPÆDIC TREATMENT.

A month or two before this the Orthopædic Department at Beckett's Park had been established. As the war progressed and the number of soldiers with healed wounds increased, it was evident that a large class was developing who were left with residual disabilities following their war wounds. Injuries of nerve trunks, stiff and distorted joints, bony defects and deformities all called for the special kind of treatment called orthopædic, which was not available in many of the hospitals which had sprung into being throughout the kingdom. By 1916 the problem had become urgent, and early in that year Beckett's Park was chosen as one of the centres dealing with cases of this kind. A ward of about 50 beds was set aside for the purpose, and a massage and physical exercises department was organised to supplement the operative and other treatment carried on in the ward. This accommodation, however, was soon found to be totally inadequate to deal with the ever-increasing number of the crippled, and fresh wards were gradually allotted to the work.

In 1917, as we shall see presently, the whole hospital was converted into a Special Surgical Hospital for the treatment of these cases, and it constituted one of the largest in the kingdom, with over 2,000 beds. Meanwhile, experience had shown that exercises with a definite object were less tedious and more useful therapeutically than those which were purely mechanical, and a Curative Workshop had been added which, in its turn, was increased in size and scope until a large number of useful occupations could be carried on and taught with the object of getting the disabled to learn in an interesting manner how to regain their lost usefulness.

There can be no doubt of the great value of the principle of Curative Workshops (1) physically, in leading gradually and almost unconsciously to increased use of stiff joints and crippled limbs ; (2) morally, in taking the patients out of a life of complete idleness and in restoring their zest for useful work. Of the results of orthopædic treatment as a whole, it is possible to speak only briefly. Nerve suture was performed on a scale unknown before. Within limitations now well recognised, the results were remarkably good. Reconstructed work to make good defects by bone grafting was done on a large scale with inestimable advantage to a great number of patients. By these and other means the activity and wage-earning capacity of very many men was restored or enhanced, and the whole movement was carried out whole-heartedly and with enthusiasm.

When, in March 1917, it was decided to set apart 500 beds at Beckett's Park for Orthopædic patients doing reconstruction work—a project which entailed another extension of wards, with workshops, massage and electrical departments, baths, new operation theatres and X-ray rooms, etc.—the Administrator again approached the Lord Mayor (now Mr. E. George Arnold) on the subject of ways and means. Thereupon the committee of the first extension scheme, with the addition of Major-General Sir Berkeley Moynihan met to discuss the possibility of a further appeal for funds from the generous people of Leeds and the surrounding districts. It was agreed to make such an appeal, and the result was that £16,000 was raised by March 15th, 1917, £2,000 being given by a lady anonymously, for the new operating theatres. The buildings were formally opened on October 11th, 1917, by Dr. Walter Hines Page, the American Ambassador, in the presence of a distinguished company, including the Lord Mayor and Lady Mayoress, the Earl and Countess of Harewood, and General Sir John Maxwell, G.O.C. in Chief, Northern Command. The Administrator acted as Consulting Surgeon, assisted by Captains Daw, Richardson, W. and Alf. Gough. There were also appointed two American Surgeons, Captains Fayerweather and Spencer.

It is but fair to record that the anonymous donor of £2,000 was Mrs. Currer Briggs, the widow of a former Lord Mayor of Leeds, and a lady whose philanthropy will be well remembered in connection with child welfare. Thereby hangs a tale. When this second hospital extension was undertaken Sir Berkeley Moynihan was compelled officially to condemn the proposed operation theatre as too small, and he therefore at once appealed to Mrs. Currer Briggs to get the women of Leeds to supply the deficiency. Her generous gift, immediately promised, enabled him to build the very satisfactory theatre block which is still in use and which, with some modification, has become the Army standard. The whole of the designs for this building were worked out by Sir Berkeley Moynihan with the assistance of Colonel Littlewood.

It was on the opening of the workshops extension that the whole hospital was converted into an Orthopædic Hospital, with the exception of 150 beds for jaw cases, and 60 beds for sick and wounded officers. The number of beds at this time at Beckett's Park was 2,200. Later, the X-Ray rooms were equipped with the latest forms of apparatus by the people of Ilkley at the request of Captain Stansfield, who was in charge of the department, on the condition that when Beckett's Park ceased to be a hospital these should be transferred to the Ilkley Hospital.

This conversion of Beckett's Park Hospital into the orthopædic centre of the Northern Command meant a complete re-organisation of the work. All the auxiliary hospitals were handed over to the East Leeds branch of the 2nd Northern General Hospital, and here all the convoys of wounded sent to Leeds were afterwards received.

Major W. A. Stott, R.E., a medical man who had served in Egypt and elsewhere, was appointed Officer-in-Charge of the Workshops. He worked with painstaking enthusiasm and ability and soon popularised the various sections in the shops, as for instance, splint-making, basket-making, weaving, blacksmith's work, tailoring, shorthand and typewriting, shoe-making, and mending—all of which proved a real boon to the patients.

But now, as several of the staff were anxious

to go abroad, and Captain Daw had retired owing to ill-health, eight additional American surgeons were placed on the hospital staff. At one time, indeed, there was only one English surgeon of consulting rank in addition to the Administrator. The American surgeons were a great help ; in fact the hospital could not have been carried on without them. They worked at Beckett's Park for about eighteen months. At times the personnel changed, some going to France while others were appointed to take their places.

In November, 1917, Major Coupland, the first Registrar, returned from France to take charge of the surgical work of the Hospital, and so relieved the Administrator of the surgical responsibilities which he had borne in addition to his other duties for more than six months. A Gymnasium, Massage and Electrical Departments and Baths were organised, and at one period 70 masseurs were kept at work under the guidance of Lieut.-Colonel T. Wardrop Griffith, who was later succeeded by Major E. Solly. Baths of all descriptions were arranged for. The new paraffin baths were first started here and they proved of great value as a preparation for massage and electrical treatment, and for painful conditions of limbs and joints. Up to the beginning of August, 1919, as many as 394,700 treatments by massage were given.

Captain Burrow was re-called from Egypt for the electrical work, in which he was assisted by Captain Carter. In this department careful records of all nerve lesions were taken and the electrical treatment carried out. Some 5,000 cases of nerve injury were admitted and the great majority were operated on by the surgical staff. There were 25,000 neurological examinations made, and 255,100 electrical treatments carried out. Dr. Morton (later Lieutenant and C.B.E.) organised a special department for a number of cases requiring re-education of muscles. He achieved conspicuous success and attracted many medical men from all parts to see his work.

A Ladies' Committee, which was started in May, 1915, did invaluable work, helping the Sisters and nurses to make the wards cheerful with flowers and other decorations, and in teaching the men handicrafts suitable to their physical condition. This was done in all the hospitals. Miss D. Hepton was chiefly responsible for East Leeds, and Miss M. Middleton for Beckett's Park. Lady visitors also rendered good service to anxious Leeds families by inquiries among the patients for news of missing men.

In December 1917, classes were started for the training of some of the junior American medical officers. A six weeks' course was arranged, consisting of lectures and demonstrations in medicine, surgery, applied anatomy, pathology and bacteriology. In connection with these classes a school of sanitation was organised under the able direction of Captain Dawkes, and it soon attained a wide reputation. In addition to the American surgeons a number of R.A.M.C. officers, N.C.O.'s and men, attended for short courses of training, and every apparatus and appliance was demonstrated, dealing with the problems of sanitation and health of our troops in every theatre of War. It was a masterly organisation. Altogether, 203 American Officers took advantage of these classes.

Another notable feature was the treatment of pensioners. Many patients who had been discharged from the Army, required further operative and other surgical treatment. A clinic was established by the Administrator to interview all patients sent by the Local Pensions Committee and to advise them as to the necessity or otherwise of further treatment, and an office was opened where Mrs. Alane Coupland spent most of the day seeing patients who left the Hospital and advising them what to do as regards pensions, getting work and other important problems. Her work was greatly appreciated, and the patients were very grateful; they felt that they had a friend who was interested in their future welfare.

In September, 1918, a Cardiac centre was opened in connection with the East Leeds Hospital. Lieut.-Colonel Griffith was placed in charge, with power to equip and organise the department, and he arranged for 50 beds at the Leeds Infirmary, where an Electric-Cardiograph was installed. At Killingbeck also there were placed at his disposal 200 beds under the immediate care of Captain Edgecumbe and a specially selected staff of experts in this work.

There were Royal visits to Beckett's Park Hospital on several occasions. On September 27th, 1915, H.M. the King came privately, made a tour of the Wards and spoke to most of the patients. H.R.H. Princess Victoria and the Grand Duchess of Russia paid a visit at the same time, and the Matrons and several nurses had the honour of being presented to His Majesty. On the following day His Majesty paid a like visit of inspection to the East Leeds Hospital. Then, on May 31st, 1918, the Queen accompanied the King on His Majesty's second war visit to Leeds, when he invested several officers with decorations and medals. After the investiture both their Majesties inspected the Hospital and Curative Workshops, and further presentations were made. On June 7th, 1918, H.R.H. the Duke of Connaught was a visitor, and after delivering a short address to the American Officers he spent a considerable time in the School of Sanitation. Visits were paid also by King Manuel, and by Lord French and other distinguished men. The Ex-King of Portugal, who came early in 1917, was specially interested in the Orthopædic Department.

Appended is the original list (1914) of Officers

Photo by   *Dickinson.*
The Right Honourable The
EARL OF HAREWOOD, G.C.V.O., D.L.,
J.P.,
Lord-Lieutenant of the West Riding of
Yorkshire.

Photo by   *Bacon & Son.*
HOYLAND SMITH, M.R.C.S.,
Commandant, Leeds Volunteer Bearer
Company.

Photo by   *Bacon & Son.*
J. W. JESSOP,
Leeds Volunteer Bearer Company.

at the 2nd Northern General Hospital R.A.M.C. (T.):—

Lieut.-Colonel J. F. Dobson (Administrator), Major J. A. Coupland (Registrar), Lieut.-Colonel A. G. Barrs (in charge of Medical Division), Lieut.-Colonel H. Littlewood (in charge of Surgical Division), Major G. W. Watson, Major R. L. Knaggs, Major A. L. Whitehead, Major R. A. Veale, Major C. W. Vining (Pathologist), Captain E. W. Bain, Captain G. P. Anning, Captain S. W. Daw, Captain J. F. Stansfield (X-Ray Department), and Captain J. le F. C. Burrow.

THE VOLUNTEER BEARER COMPANY.

Until midsummer of 1916 the task of conveying the wounded from the railway stations to hospital devolved entirely on the R.A.M.C., of whose special services mention has already been made. In July of that year, however, a Volunteer Bearer Company was formed which in due time released regular R.A.M.C. men for duties at the Front. The Bearer Company sprang chiefly from West Leeds, where it, early, received encouragement by a motor ambulance presented by Mr. J. W. Jessop in July, 1915. At first it numbered some fifty or sixty specially trained men, but gradually the numbers swelled until there were five hundred on the books, all volunteers and mostly disqualified for active service, though some eventually went into the army and others, the older men, undertook ward and orderly duties in the hospitals.

During the two years or more that such services were needed, the Bearer Company met 212 ambulance trains and handled no fewer than 36,000 patients. Difficult as so many of the cases were—especially those of spinal trouble—the work was so well done that an American Army surgeon, who had witnessed similar operations on the continent, paid the Bearer Company the compliment of saying that it was one of the best organised companies he had seen. "Leeds," said he, "ought to be proud of such a fine body of men." Not only did these voluntary stretcher bearers handle their charges with skill, sympathy and care but they were ever ready with cigarettes for "Tommy Atkins," and with postcards so that he might drop a line home.

Apart from station and hospital duties, this Bearer Company's services were found of great use to the city, when emergency required. In times of threatened air raids, as well as on the occasion of explosions at local munition factories, the members all paraded with stretchers, surgical appliances and bandages, ready to succour and help. And everything was done self-sacrificingly without cost either to the State or to the ratepayers. The leaders in this praiseworthy enterprise included Dr. Hoyland Smith of Armley, the Commandant; Mr. A. Sheard, Adjutant; Mr. J. Penny, Quartermaster; and Mr. J. W. Jessop, Mr. H. M. Hepworth and Mr. S. B. Heaps who acted as transport officers.

VOLUNTARY HOSPITALS.

Commodious as were the military hospitals, they were not big enough to house the increasing numbers of stricken men who needed treatment and rest. Happily this contingency was foreseen. With a patriotism that redounds to their credit, owners of great houses, quite early in the war, offered accommodation in their own homes; and the Leeds district was in no way behind other parts of the country in making such provision. The voluntary hospitals thus available in this district were auxiliary to the 2nd Northern General Hospital at Beckett's Park, except that each auxiliary hospital was responsible for its own finances, a War Office grant of from two to three shillings per day per person being allowed. Not only were

Photo by   Yevonde.
The Hon. LADY DOROTHY WOOD,
Commandant, Templenewsam V.A.D.
Hospital.

Miss E. S. INNES, R.R.C.,
Matron-in-Chief, 2nd Northern General
Hospital.

Photo by   Hartnell.
Miss E. M. CLIFF, O.B.E.,
Commandant, Gledhow Hall V.A.D.
Hospital.

auxiliary hospitals opened, but V.A.D. nurses were ready to take duty. Long before the war broke out thousands of ladies all over the country had received a certain amount of training, either in St. John Ambulance work or in the scheme of Voluntary Aid Detachments which had been set on foot in more recent years ; and so thorough was the organisation in the great majority of cases, Leeds included, that hardly any change in personnel became necessary. Doctors and nurses almost automatically stepped into the positions assigned to them.

In his introduction to the West Riding Auxiliary Hospitals Record, which was printed for private circulation, Colonel C. W. E. Duncombe, C.B.E. (Red Cross County Director, 1916-1919) testified to the value of the splendid word done. During his term of office the number of hospitals in the West Riding increased from 27 to 45, and the number of Voluntary Aid Detachments from 97 to 119. This, however, he notes, was only possible because of the admirable organisation which existed before war broke out, and the details of which were evolved by Brigadier-General H. Mends, C.B.

Between August, 1914, and the time of closing, 51,610 patients were treated in the West Riding Auxiliary Hospitals. The demands on the V.A.D.'s were heavy and continuous. A very large number volunteered in response to calls for service overseas, or in military hospitals at home, as nursing or general service members ; and recruits had to be found to fill the vacancies—this at a time when the establishment of equipped beds was gradually rising from the 1,228 registered in the year 1916 to the 3,200 which marked the maximum in the summer of 1918.

In this connection the services rendered by the Men's Detachments should not be forgotten. As Colonel Duncombe reminds us, the reception of convoys and the removal of the wounded to the hospitals was almost entirely in their hands. A very large proportion of West Riding members joined the R.A.M.C. or the fighting units, but the minority, who remained at home, spent long and tiring days; frequently they had to meet ambulance trains arriving very late at night or in the small hours of the morning.

Harewood House.

One of the first benevolent offers made to Leeds was that of the Earl of Harewood, Lord Lieutenant of the West Riding, who set aside part of Harewood House for the reception of wounded soldiers during their period of convalescence. It was on January 5th, 1915, that an auxiliary hospital was opened here, provision being made for 50 patients. Later, tent accommodation allowed an increase to 61 beds. As the length of stay varied from about two weeks to four months, many hundreds of sick and wounded men enjoyed the benefit of residence and treatment at the Yorkshire home of the Lascelles family, combined with life in the open air amid some of the most picturesque scenery in the North of England. The hospital was closed on January 27th, 1919, having treated 1,269 patients.

The men were proud to know that they were dwelling under a roof that had sheltered the King himself. Harewood House, indeed—one of the stateliest of the stately homes of England—has entertained Royalty on many occasions.

Among the meadows, groves, and glades of the charming park, the soldiers were allowed to wander at will. But they were by no means restricted to the park. There was the prettily-situated village, with its pleasant walk through meadows overlooking the winding Wharfe and the famous Harewood Avenue. In winter, when outdoor recreations were necessarily limited, the men were given an ample supply of books, and they could find diversion at a billiard table in the temporary wooden structure adjoining the house, or with cards and other games. At least once a week a concert party from Leeds came to entertain them, and every Saturday the patients who were well enough were taken to the city in motor cars for a specially arranged entertainment.

The thousands of people who, before the war, through the kindness of Lord Harewood, visited Harewood House, probably never dreamed that some of the large lofty and artistically furnished and decorated apartments, with their valuable pictures and beautifully painted ceilings, would one day be transformed into hospital wards. The dining-room and the music-room formed the two principal wards, together containing 28 beds; while smaller wards completed the total provision for half a hundred patients. Usually there were only a small proportion of bed cases; the majority of the patients were able to get out and about. In addition to the matron, Mrs. Battrum—during whose absence through illness the duties were discharged with unremitting care by Mrs. Birkmyrl, of Inghamthorpe Hall, the staff consisted of two trained sisters and six V.A.D. nurses. The Harewood doctor, Captain Matthews, R.A.M.C., invalided home from France, had medical charge of the hospital, and both the Earl and Countess—her Ladyship being Commandant—took a sympathetic interest in the work and in individual cases. Mrs. Maurice Lascelles served as Quartermaster and the Vicar of Harewood (the Rev. Maurice Lascelles) was a constant visitor.

Templenewsam.

Another historic country house devoted to the work of mercy was Templenewsam, now the property of the City of Leeds. Here, while Major the Hon. Edward Wood, M.P., was away fighting for his country, Lady Dorothy Wood supervised the nursing back to health and vigour of some thirty disabled men sent from Leeds. The whole of the south wing, which was built by Viscountess Irwin in the 18th century, was set apart as a V.A.D. hospital. It was opened on October 29th, 1914, first of all for the accommodation of wounded Belgian soldiers; and with the exception of the second half of the year 1916, when it was closed, it continued as an auxiliary to the 2nd Northern General Hospital, Beckett's Park until November 23rd, 1917. Lady Dorothy Wood combined the duties of Commandant and Quartermaster, and in 1916 the duties of Matron were taken over by Miss Roff. The staff included two trained nurses, and five V.A.D. nurses who in their house duties were assisted by Lady Dorothy's household staff. Useful help was also rendered by Miss Bennett, Major Wood's secretary; and Dr. Bean, of Crossgates, visited the hospital regularly, giving his services freely. Altogether, 615 patients were treated here.

As at Harewood, the wounded warriors moved about in rooms and corridors that Royalty had trodden from time to time. But, even centuries ago, Templenewsam was a place of repute. In one of the apartments there was born Lord Darnley, husband of Mary Queen of Scots, and father of James I. Among such interesting associations the patients found shelter and treatment. Large, lofty, well-lighted bedrooms were assigned to them, and the big main entrance hall made a splendid recreation room, its fine pictures by old masters, collections of armour, great vases, and massive chimney piece lending rare distinction to the scene on cold winter days and nights, when the men sat round the glowing fire recounting their adventures, quietly reading, or listening to Leeds concert parties. A whist drive was a frequent item in the amusement programme, and a cinematograph, personally

Dining and Recreation Hall, V.A.D. Hospital, Templenewsam.

managed by Lady Dorothy, proved an unfailing source of entertainment and instruction. A full-sized billiard table provided by a kind friend was exceedingly popular, and during the summer months there was ample provision for outdoor recreation in the gardens and park.

GLEDHOW HALL.

Lord Airedale also, quite early in the war, offered his Leeds residence, Gledhow Hall, to be used as a V.A.D. hospital, and when the house was full, hut accommodation was provided in the grounds, thus increasing the original number of 50 beds to 138. Miss E. M. Cliff, O.B.E. (hon. Serving Sister of the Order of St. John of Jerusalem) a cousin of Lord Airedale, performed the duties of Commandant, Mrs. F. J. Kitson was the Honorary Secretary, Miss K. Sykes the Quartermaster and Dr. Eustace Carter, O.B.E., Medical Officer. There were twelve V.A.D. nurses who did the work of ward and surgery nurses, parlour maids and house maids, together with two trained sisters and five servants. Afterwards, in addition to the honours just noted, official recognition was made of the services of Sister L. Roscoe, R.R.C., Miss S. Powys, Miss Sykes and Miss Mannaberg—all four " mentioned."

Alike within the house and out in the secluded park the men's welfare received consideration. A special feature of the work was the hut treatment established in the grounds for the worst cases, seven huts being erected on a lawn which the nurses could reach by a temporary covered way from the house. There were two beds in each hut, and between the beds a radiator so that the occupants were fairly well fortified against cold weather. In making this provision Gledhow Hall was one of the first, if not actually the pioneer, among V.A.D. Hospitals. Other serious cases were accommodated on the ground floor of the house, the second floor being allotted to convalescents who were able to leave their beds every morning, visit the recreation rooms or take exercise in the open air. Particular attention was paid to amusements, indoor and out. The motor garage was converted into a billiard room, and the walls were hung with crayon sketches of celebrities by a visiting cartoonist ; silver cups were given for competition by ward teams ; there was a cinematograph on the premises and a canteen furnished like a dainty café, where patients and staff entertained their friends. When the hospital closed on March 31st, 1919, it had treated 2,250 cases.

LOTHERTON HALL.

Only a few miles away, in the peaceful heart of the ancient Kingdom of Elmet of which old Leeds formed part—at Aberford, renowned in earlier times for its health-giving properties— Colonel and Mrs. Trench Gascoigne kept open house for more wounded soldiers. Their beneficent work at Lotherton Hall started on November 21st, 1914, eighteen beds being provided until July, 1916, when the number was increased to thirty-five, with the result that a hundred men found accommodation and treatment here in the six weeks immediately following. When the hospital closed on March 28th, 1919, 655 patients had been treated.

Colonel and Mrs. Gascoigne not only equipped the place as a hospital but bore the whole expense of maintenance. The nursing staff comprised two trained nurses and two V.A.D. nurses, with a trained masseur and a ward maid, and the domestic duties were performed by the regular house staff. Valuable voluntary help was given by the local medical men ; Dr. Abbott, M.B.E., and Dr. Sykes, M.B.E., were regular visitors, and visits were also paid by Dr. Pickersgill and Dr. Scatcherd. Mrs. Gascoigne enhanced the value of her distinction as a Lady of Grace of the Order of St. John of Jerusalem not only by her general supervision as Commandant but by personal service ; Miss Routledge was Quartermaster and Miss Thompson (mentioned) the Matron. Such was the hospitable feeling and cheerfulness of the place that it speedily became known as " a home in every sense of the word."

The sunny south side of the house was given up to the patients, who occupied the best bedrooms. These rooms looked over the beautiful gardens and park, gave direct access to the patients' dining room, and were conveniently near a stairway lending to the recreation room in the Court yard, and to the entrance hall where every other Sunday afternoon service was conducted by the Rev. B. W. S. Walwyn, Vicar of Aberford. In the same hall meetings were arranged *en famille* for whist drives, concerts, and dramatic entertainments organised by Miss Gascoigne, and always there was a variety of recreation possible, even a chance sometimes of going out shooting with Colonel Gascoigne when he came back from the Front. That the men relished it all was shown by the many thankful letters received from them after they left.

In the Souvenir Record, compiled by Colonel C. W. E. Duncombe, County Director, Lotherton is described as " the most valuable contribution of its kind made by any private individual in the West Riding to the cause of the sick and wounded soldiers."

Stapleton Park.

Farther afield, in Stapleton Park, four miles south of Pontefract, was another V.A.D. hospital associated with Beckett's Park. It began operations on February 20th, 1915, with 50 beds, increased later to 74, and was closed December 21st, 1918. Here, at the Yorkshire seat of Mr.

and Mrs. H. J. Hope-Barton, with Mrs. Hope-Barton herself as Commandant and Quartermaster, 1,437 patients enjoyed rest and careful nursing, with opportunities for cricket and tennis in the summer, concerts all the year through, and motor drives whenever petrol was available. The Commandant—a Lady of Grace of the Order of St. John of Jerusalem—received the O.B.E. Many ladies of the district gave loyal support as nurses and attendants, the staff all told, including a skilled masseuse, numbering over twenty.

LEDSTONE HALL.

From April 11th, 1915, to December 18th, 1918, beginning with 33 beds and afterwards extending to 55 beds, admirable accommodation was provided by Major G. C. H. Wheler, M.P., and Mrs. Wheler, O.B.E. at Ledstone Hall, near Castleford. This picturesque Elizabethan mansion, with its memorials of the pious and charitable Lady Betty Hastings—a Lady Bountiful of olden times in Leeds—was indeed a fitting centre for the benevolent work of its 20th century owners; and the charming surroundings and prospects made a strong appeal to the many disabled men who were sequestered here. There were 800 patients during the whole period.

Order, harmony, and peace were characteristics of this pleasantly-situated voluntary hospital. Both on the ground and first floors convenient accommodation was provided, one oak-panelled ward being the transformed dining-room, and another the main entrance hall. Close at hand, the drawing room, used as a day room, allowed space for recreation as well as for meals. At one end a stage was erected for concerts and other entertainments, many of which were organised by the Misses Ruth and Opal Hugonin (nieces of Mrs. Wheler) with the co-operation of the men. Here, too, fancy dress balls and whist drives were held, and in the proper season lawn tennis, bowls, and croquet could be played in the ground.

As Commandant, Mrs. Wheler was assisted by two trained nurses, two V.A.D. nurses, and three other helpers. The medical officers were Dr. Blomfield and Dr. Hillman, and the chaplain, the Rev. G. E. Warlow, Vicar of Ledsham. Every morning, prayers were said in the ancient chapel attached to the house, where, on one occasion, many soldier patients were confirmed by the Archbishop of York (Dr. Lang), and the Bishop of Beverley (Dr. Crosthwaite).

Swillington House.

A little nearer Leeds, Swillington House, the home of the Yorkshire Lowthers, was placed at the disposal of the authorities by Sir Charles Lowther, Bart., in June, 1915, and was kept going without grant until January 21st, 1919, the total number of patients being 980. This auxiliary hospital also was attached to Beckett's Park, but was worked by the Pontefract and Castleford Voluntary Aid Detachment under Miss F. S. Garforth as Commandant. The spacious rooms on the ground floor made a compact hospital of 60 beds, and it was found to be a great advantage from an administrative point of view to have all the arrangements carried out on the same level. Out of doors, the well-wooded park and the gardens were greatly appreciated by the patients, and no less can be said of the indoor amusements, particularly billiards. Matches were played against teams of convalescents from other hospitals, and so expert did the Swillington men become that they proved the winners in a cup competition at the Gambit Café, Leeds.

Chapeltown and Roundhay.

At Allerton House, Leeds (lent by Mr. T. G. Mylchreest, of Thorner), a hospital was opened on March 30th, 1916, with accommodation for 35 beds, afterwards increased to 57 beds; and before it closed on April 17th, 1919, as many as 1,320 patients had been treated. Excepting during the first three months this hospital was reserved entirely for jaw cases. The Commandant was Mrs. Harding Churton, Hon. Serving Sister of the Order of St. John (upon whom the O.B.E. was conferred) with Captain Munby, Medical Officer. Besides the honour just named, mention was made of the services of Miss H. Mann (Matron), Miss Pflaum (Quartermaster), Miss Lofthouse (twice mentioned), Miss Chapman, Miss Aspey, and Miss Mary Glover.

At Roundhay there were two auxiliary hospitals, both used chiefly in the later war period. A commodious house (lent by Mr. Thompson), near Gledhow Lane, treated about 400 patients during part of 1915, and it was re-opened on March 10th, 1917, with 50 beds, increased by hut accommodation to 82 subsequently, and closed on January 22nd, 1919, having served the needs of 630 patients. Mrs. Kitson, an Hon. Serving Sister of the Order of St. John, performed the duties of Commandant and received official mention. The Quartermaster was Mrs. A. B. Hudson, and the Medical Officer Dr. Carter. St. Edmund's Parish Hall was the other Roundhay auxiliary hospital. Here, Mrs. A. S. Davis acted as Commandant, and she with three of her helpers, viz., Mrs. C. O'Connor Fenton, Miss M. J. Chadwick, and Miss Atkinson, received mention. Mrs. A. K. Wilkinson was the Quartermaster, and Dr. H. M. Robertson, the Medical Officer. This hospital started with 30 beds in December, 1916, and closed on February 10th, 1919, with 50 beds, the increase being rendered possible by open air hut accommodation. In all 459 patients received treatment.

Other auxiliary hospitals attached to Beckett's Park were Beaulieu, at Harrogate, lent and equipped by Mr. and Mrs. Lund, of Becca Hall,

CARE OF THE SICK AND WOUNDED. 231

where 1,002 patients were treated; the private houses known as Boothroyde and Longroyde at Brighouse (1,975 patients); Darrington Hall, Pontefract, lent by the Rev. Estcourt Grey (406 patients); Grove House, Harrogate, lent by Mr. W. Fox, where 1,372 patients were treated under Miss Evelyn Lascelles as Commandant; Hopton Grove, Mirfield, lent by Mr. and Mrs. Sutcliffe (193 patients); Ilkley Convalescent Home (3,212 patients); Saltaire Hospital (438 patients); Guiseley Town Hall (St. John's Hospital) where 493 patients were treated; Wentworth House, Wakefield, (3,131 in-patients and 297 out-patients); Parochial Hall, Halton, with Mrs. E. M. Marsden as Commandant (456 patients).

In addition to these and many other auxiliary hospitals open for longer or shorter periods throughout the West Riding, provision was made for officers at North Deighton Manor, Wetherby, by Mrs. Adolphus Duncombe, also at Oulton Hall (lent by Major H. W. Calverley) which was used as a base hospital for neurasthenic cases.

MUSIC AND ENTERTAINMENT.

It was early recognised in Leeds that the soldier wounded in this war needed something which the military hospitals did not provide. In the regular military hospital as it existed when Britain went to war the treatment was sound and good, but there was little or nothing to relieve monotony. The citizen-soldier now brought into being presented a problem different from his long-service prototype. Soldiering was not his trade, and he had not developed that patience under restraint which helps men to bear monotony. The strain of this war, too, was greater than that of any which had gone before, and worn nerves called for some distraction. Even the hard German disciplinarians recognised this fact before the war was very old, and Ludendorff tells in his memoirs of the concerts organised, by his desire, for the German troops on the Russian front. Music and entertainment have, indeed, a direct healing and therefore a direct military value.

"Two Arts" Voluntary Effort.

All sections of the community contributed in one way or another to brighten the lot of the sick and wounded, and members of the musical and theatrical professions rendered especially welcome help. Mr. Clifford Bowling was one of the first to show practical sympathy. His action led to the organisation of the Leeds War Hospital Entertainments Scheme which was established as a registered charity on October 4th, 1916, the committee consisting of Lieut.-Colonel Littlewood (Administrator of the 2nd Northern General Hospital) Miss Innes (Superintendent Territorial Nursing Staff), and Lady Moynihan, with Mr. Bowling as honorary secretary.

Before the date mentioned Mr. Bowling made himself responsible for the necessary funds, which he raised partly by the sale of his war cartoons and partly by private subscriptions. Soon after the first contingent of wounded arrived in Leeds he took Miss Carrie Tubb and other well-known singers to Beckett Park Hospital, and at Christmas time in 1914 he arranged a special concert by the Leeds Philharmonic Society's chorus, conducted by Mr. H. A. Fricker, and accompanied by Mr. H. H. Pickard. Then, when the East Leeds Military Hospital was opened, the Philharmonic Society visited that institution also. Meanwhile arrangements were made for two entertainments weekly, with the co-operation of theatrical companies visiting the city, and there were alternate visits paid to both hospitals by entertainers from the Empire and Hippodrome.

At the General Infirmary, too, the Killingbeck branch hospital, and the auxiliary hospitals of

Leeds and district there were entertainments organised at frequent intervals, until in 1916 ten or eleven entertainments were being provided every week, the performers all giving their services and receiving only an allowance for out-of-pocket expenses. Altogether about 400 were engaged, more than half the number being vocalists, 90 instrumentalists, 115 accompanists, 90 elocutionists and 40 dancers, besides comedians, ventriloquists, conjurors, mimics, jugglers, cartoonists, sword experts, and other variety entertainers. In the end over 1,000 entertainments were provided.

The expenses in connection with an organised scheme like this were necessarily considerable, and the larger proportion was entailed by the cost of conveyances to and fro. In the early days of the war it was possible to borrow motor-cars and other vehicles, but with the growth of military demands and the tightening of restrictions difficulties arose. Practically all private cars came under the military regime, and the Corporation had even to withdraw the free use of the Red Cross 'bus which had been used to convey concert parties to the outlying V.A.D. Hospitals. The committee, however, raised the money required by promoting what were known as "Two Arts" concerts, which proved very popular, and from the gross receipts found they were able to make an allocation of £600 surplus to the permanent local charities.

Under the chairmanship of Mr. J. S. R. Phillips in 1917, the work of the Fund was greatly extended. On his death on November 5th, 1919, Sir Berkeley Moynihan was appointed president, with Mr. George A. Blackburn as the Chairman of Committee—a most enthusiastic and loyal worker to the last. After the Armistice, public interest in war charities diminished, and it became increasingly difficult to obtain subscriptions, so much so that the receipts dwindled until the committee were left with a debit balance at the bank. Fortunately, the late Mr. Thomas Henry Kirkbride, of Leeds, had made provision for the movement under his will, and in May 1923, the debt was cleared off. At the same time the registered scheme was closed, for, apart from the difficulty of carrying on without adequate funds, the committee felt that the post-war needs as regards hospital entertainments were being admirably met by the Wounded Warriors' Welfare Committee.

"Music in War Time."

This movement was begun in London in the early days of the war, its object being twofold: (1) to afford entertainment to soldiers or sailors in camp, hospital, or elsewhere, and (2) to give professional musicians, hard hit by this war, a little assistance by the payment of modest fees—usually a guinea a concert. The movement was introduced to Leeds by Miss Paget, who, accompanied by Mr. Sydney Nicholson (now organist of Westminster Abbey) spoke at a meeting in the Hall of Leeds University, and brought some musicians who gave a sample concert. On October 28th, 1915, a committee was formed (affiliated to the Leeds Lady Mayoress's Committee) under the presidency of Mr. Herbert Thompson, the other members being Miss Edith Baines, Miss Elizabeth Ford, Mr. Willoughby Williams, Mr. H. A. Fricker, and Mr. H. Percy Richardson, with Mr. H. Bacon Smith as honorary secretary, and later, Dr. E. C. Bairstow, and Dr. A. C. Tysoe were added to the committee.

Besides the objects already mentioned the committee sought to provide music of high-class character as it was felt that the provision of variety concerts and lighter forms of entertainment was adequately covered by other organisations. The music chosen was of a popular nature, but good; and experience proved that it was not necessary to play to the gallery as much as some perhaps imagined. Indeed, as time passed, requests in overwhelming numbers were received from military centres for concerts of "real music."

The first concert was given in Cookridge Hospital. Thereafter, from 1915 to 1921, nearly 2,000 concerts were held for which some 5,000 fees were paid to professional musicians. Assisted by capable amateurs who gave their service in order to complete concert parties, over 12,000 engagements were negotiated, and it is needless to add that in the aggregate the audiences numbered hundreds of thousands. At the Royal Bath Hospital, Harrogate, a concert was given every Friday night for four years. The soldiers in Leeds Infirmary were catered for every week, and the great camp at Ripon was provided with a series of first-class concerts twice a week, in different centres on each visit. Altogether about sixty hospitals in various parts of the county were visited, and concerts were organised even as far afield as Clipstone (Notts), and Newcastle. Special oratorio concerts were given in Leeds Town Hall when the audiences consisted entirely of men in khaki and blue. The Leeds Choral Union and Philharmonic Society provided the chorus, and the performances were given with organ and full orchestra and special soloists. These concerts were especially appreciated by the men from overseas. Realising they were in the Musical Festival City of Leeds they eagerly embraced the opportunity of hearing our famous local choruses in the actual hall where the Triennial Festival is held, a fact recorded with pride by many in their letters home. Under Mr. Fricker's guidance a small select "Music in War Time" chorus visited Beckett's Park and other hospitals on many occasions.

The Fund to carry on so extensive a work was raised by donations and subscriptions ; collections at concerts (many of the leading musical societies gave facilities for these yearly during the war); and by concerts arranged by artists who devoted the entire proceeds to the Fund. Many eminent musicians gave recitals entirely at their own expense. Mr. Frederick Dawson, the famous pianist, was indefatigable in this matter, and his splendid efforts resulted in considerable additions to the Fund. The Fund also received considerable support from the British Red Cross Society.

After the Armistice many requests were made for a continuation of the concerts ; for a short time, therefore, the Committee supplied parties to the hospitals and camps for the entertainment of thousands of soldiers awaiting demobilisation. It is worthy of note that the choristers of Leeds Parish Church (many of whom appeared as soloists at the soldiers' concerts) raised over £100 for the fund by concerts of their own. Chamber music, too, was frequently given, and Mr. John Dunn, the well-known Yorkshire violinist, was in great demand and gave much valuable support to the work.

The success of the organisation was due in very large measure to the untiring devotion of Mr. H. Bacon Smith, the honorary secretary. He personally organised and superintended about 1,600 concerts, in and about Leeds ; chiefly in hospitals and camps. After he had accomplished his 1,000th concert his friends gave him a token of their appreciation, in the shape of a pair of silver candlesticks, the inscription on which briefly records the circumstance in which they were given.

THE WOUNDED WARRIORS' WELCOME.

The "Wounded Warriors' Welcome" effort had its origin at the house of Mrs. Richardson in Roundhay where the manager of the "Gambit" Café met some men from Beckett Street Hospital who were being entertained by her. As a result regular gatherings of the men were instituted at the café on the invitation of a body of gentlemen who took up the work zealously and formed an organisation, the difficulty of providing ways and means being overcome by the generous contributions of citizens and the help of voluntary workers. Where so many gave willing service it is almost invidious to mention names, but among those prominently identified with the movement were Mr. J. A. Brown, Mr. R. H. Brown, and Mr. Thomas Gordon. The gatherings were held on Saturday afternoons, and up to the time of the Armistice the number of men entertained reached the enormous total of over 200,000. Also the leading political clubs threw open their doors to gatherings of the men; on one day as many as 1,250 were entertained.

In the summer of 1916, when the hospitals were beginning to be crowded with the wounded from the series of great battles which opened with the Somme, a great scheme of open-air treats in the parks started. In this work the Leeds Volunteer Motor Corps, under Major C. H. Wilson, bore a leading part, especially valuable help being given by Messrs. Oliver Swithenbank and Sam Watson. They undertook the transport of the men from the various hospitals, and this, for the motorists, in itself formed a valuable exercise in quick concentration—an operation which would have been of prime importance if the enemy had at any time succeeded in throwing an invading force across the North Sea. In this way, as long as petrol was available, parties were conveyed to very many places within a radius of 25 miles from Leeds during the summer months of 1916 and 1917. The biggest gathering was on one Saturday afternoon in 1917, when 500 men were transported to Lotherton Hall. Other places to which outings were arranged were Ribston, Grimston, Bolton Woods, Harrogate, Wetherby, and Monk Fryston.

With the progress of the submarine campaign,

and its effect upon petrol supplies, summer outings became less practicable, and the Headingley Cricket Ground was placed by the directors at the disposal of the wounded. Many afternoon gatherings were held at the grounds and these continued right up to the summer of 1919. In 1917, the committee of the Leeds Institute granted the free use of the Albert Hall and its crypt, and thousands of men assembled for the Saturday afternoon entertainments held there during the winters of 1917, 1918 and 1919, a successful tombola run by Messrs. T. Porter, W. Roscoe and J. Haigh providing funds for carrying out the work.

Thus Leeds efforts on behalf of the wounded did not cease with hostilities. In consequence of the closing down of various outlying hospitals and the concentration of Yorkshire victims at Beckett's Park, Oulton, and Darrington, the number of patients under treatment continued very large, and a small body of men and women made it their care to see that the brave fellows were not forgotten. Most of these workers were members of the Wounded Warriors' Welfare Committee, a body formed in 1921, but, in addition, a number of devoted people came and went regularly, carrying flowers or other simple offerings to help the men to bear the long days and nights of confinement, and proving that in Yorkshire hearts, sufferings borne in defence of country have as their just guerdon remembrance, sympathy and love.

Even at the time this Record passes through the press (October, 1923) the need for sympathetic help continues. There are still about 400 patients in the hospital at Beckett's Park, and 150 more at Oulton and Dorrington. Besides these, there are some 2,000 out-patients who visit Beckett's Park at intervals, for advice and treatment, and, almost any day, 200 belonging to Leeds and the district may be seen in waiting.

LIFE IN HOSPITAL.
THROUGH THE CHAPLAIN'S EYES.
(By Lt.-Col. J. F. Phillips, C.F., R.A.M.C. (T.), Chaplain, 2nd Northern General Hospital, Leeds. 1914-1916).

When the war broke out we had in Leeds a very complete and popular organisation of the Army Medical Services with their headquarters at Harewood Barracks. The three companies of Field Ambulance, as their name implies, were in case of war destined for service in the Field, the other arm of the organisation was to form and provide the staff for a Military Hospital at home. One who had occupied the post of Chaplain to the combined services for more than fifteen years could hardly do otherwise than apply for permission to go out with one of the Field Ambulance Corps, for it with these he had his chief association and duties. The answer to my application came on October 5th, 1914, from the Headquarters of the 3rd W.R. Division, saying the Brigade Chaplain had been appointed and asking me to take on the duty of chaplain to the 2nd Northern General Hospital (Leeds). As this Hospital was in charge of our own organisation I had, while waiting for my answer, done what duty I could there.

Lieut.-Colonel Dobson was in command at the Hospital, or what was to be the Hospital, and by his genius for seeing the whole and not overlooking the working details, the enormous work of adapting the appropriated buildings of the Training College and equipping for their new use was accomplished with surprising speed and completeness. The stimulus was the immediate and urgent demand for such accommodation.

It was not long after the Declaration of War before heavily laded trains were bearing the the wounded and sick to various parts of the Kingdom. Speedy as was the transformation at

Beckett's Park there was no marking time before the first convoy arrived from the battlefields of France. They came with the soil of France upon their great-coats, a few with support walked from the Ambulance to the wards, the rest the stretcher-bearers carried, some were entirely covered from view and of these some would not have been recognised by those who knew them best. That first arrival sent a thrill through Leeds and it was not least felt by the Officers, Nurses and Ward Orderlies at the Hospitals. Other convoys arrived in quick succession and in a short time building on a large scale had to be undertaken to supply additional accommodation.

For the first two years there was one resident Chaplain of the Church of England; Dean Shine was chiefly responsible for ministry to the Roman Catholic patients, and the Free Churches were represented by the Rev. W. Johnston, Rev. G. Patterson and Rev. G. Hooper. It was never a difficult matter for a minister of any denomination to obtain a permit to visit the Hospital and a large number availed themselves of the privilege.

The Church of England had its early Sunday Service of Holy Communion in the Administrator's Room. Messrs. Barraclough kindly lent the vessels necessary for this service. The morning service was held in the large hall, which was also the principal ward. Attendance was not compulsory, except for those confined to the Ward, and it was as a rule excellent. The well known hymns were sung with great spirit, and the whole of the brief service was marked by attentiveness and reverence. The hall had the advantage of a fairly powerful organ, and when it was in the humour it added much, under the skill of Mr. Percy Richardson, to the swing of the service. On Sunday evening we had hymns chosen by the men, the programme was often varied by a soloist, vocal or instrumental, and in providing these Miss Maud Middleton was an invaluable help. On one Christmas Eve the choir of St. Michael's Church, on another that of St. Chad's, paraded the corridors singing carols and hymns : the effect in the distance and within the wards was noticeably impressive. Almost regularly on the Sunday afternoon chosen members of the Leeds Choral Societies sang selections from oratorios and other sacred music, from positions which enabled them to be heard by the largest number in the wards.

The chief interest and means of influence for the Chaplain was his personal contact with the individual. Conversation was hardly ever difficult and it was as seldom ordinary. These men had been in, and gone through, events which all the world watched from a distance with intense and intimate anxiety. They were as a rule intelligent and observant, and the story of their experiences needed no special gifts in the telling. They said a good deal about the conditions of dirt and danger men had to endure, both before and after trench warfare began. But a man rarely allowed you to single him out as an example of the courage and endurance he had spoken of ; he was no hero or else all who fought had an equal claim. In my two years' service there were a number who had won distinctions, but I remember only one who readily talked of what he had done, he " had been told " that he had been recommended, but as far as I could learn the distinction never materialised. Those who had shown conspicuous bravery had, according to their own account, " only done what anyone would have done in the circumstances," and the usual explanation of their honour was that their act happened to have been seen and reported, but there were many deeds done by others as much or more worthy which had not come under the eye of an authority competent to report them. One felt the modesty of genuine courage, and although their statement was probably true in many instances this did not take from its generosity. A message of the King to the Army about this time, "The Whole Army is Illustrious" spoke the mind of those who came under our care, and not least the mind of those who had been especially chosen for distinction.

The glamour of the Service and eagerness to join up were strong in those days, and we had our examples of those who had flagrantly tampered with their age. There were a few lads, pitifully young, who had to bear suffering that would have taxed the fortitude of mature manhood, and their main support, the fact that they had already done a man's part, helped them wonderfully to keep up appearances. We had also those who had as clearly defied the limit in the opposite direction and whose acceptance for service told as much of the blindness of the official as of the determination of the recruit ; unless, as was no doubt the truth in some cases, the candidate got himself up ingeniously for the official examination. The eagerness to go out was evidently genuine and widespread, but I heard little in the Hospital to confirm statements made at the time of men's eagerness to return to the fighting line. On the contrary, the sort of remark was common enough that anyone who had been in it and professed an anxiety to get back was a humbug. It was more than probable that most of our patients would go back, and they said they would go without grousing or complaint, but there would be a vast deal more of duty than desire in it. It required a soberer, less romantic courage to return to the conditions men knew than was necessary for the first venture.

There was another form of courage—we had many examples of it—a courage which refuses to be damped by suffering, does its utmost to make light of pain, knows of a coming ordeal more or less critical and would make you believe the patient was hardly concerned. It was often a brave front put on to conceal anxiety, the more anxious he was the more he tried to hide it, he might speak of his visit to the Operating Theatre as "going to see the pictures" but it only meant that he was not wearing his heart on his sleeve. A wound or pain was rarely so bad that there were not "a lot worse cases than mine," and with sadly little sign of it there was the cheery claim to be "in the pink." Officers and nurses, one felt, had here whatever help the hopefulness and good spirit of patients could render to their efforts.

The war had not gone on long before one became aware of the large number who returned with a strong bias towards Fatalism. The way to such belief is in reality prepared by the training and position of a soldier: his doings and place are fixed for him, he has no escape nor appeal from his orders, he is at best the agent, he may easily regard himself as the instrument of a superior rank and force. It needed only the extension of his trained habits to bring him the conception of an authority which ordered and compelled all events, and was responsible for the results. What was to be would be, and he took the doctrine to himself; what would happen to him was fixed and determined, it could not be avoided and to bother over it was worse than useless. It was evidently a belief for the field of action, we saw little of its attitude in the Hospital, there was no sign of mere submissiveness to a fixed decree as to whether a man would recover or not, he fought for health and grappled with what often seemed the sure order of fate. Fate was usually "It," a vague but determining something, not a Personality, and therefore did not seem to suggest or imply a will and purpose.

We heard much in those days of eager, crowded religious services at the Front, and great hopes were expressed that religion was, by means of the war, to gain a deeper, wider hold upon the lives of men. The tone of our men did not at any time convey this impression of eagerness and enthusiasm, and perhaps one's knowledge of human nature should have prevented the feelings of disappointment that these qualities were not in evidence at the Hospital as they were at the Front. These men were mostly young, they lived very much in the moment, and they took their tone readily from their surroundings. In their experiences at the Front, whatever belief they adopted for their support and relief, they were not unaffected by the hardships or dangers which were constantly there, and it was not to be wondered at that, in circumstances so novel and perilous, they sought in services and prayers the answer to their pressing needs. It was just as natural that when they left the Field and its strain and threats they would leave behind the motives and feelings which lived by and depended upon the conditions in the Field. There were also those who in the calm of safety got surer hold of the permanent values which the experiences at the Front had only indicated.

With few exceptions the men spoke well and appreciatively of their Padre. He was a good fellow, he saw to their wants and when possible their comforts and recreation, he fared with them, they gave instances of his courage, and not seldom as a special tribute they added "he did not talk religion." In this last item he was probably as wise as in the others. To show himself a man and their friend, one who shared their risks and thought for them was a way (it may have been the only way) to win their esteem and commend to them the religion he stood for. I had qualms at times as to whether my conversations with the men were as definitely religious as they should be, and I made attempts to lead or turn them in that direction. It was not often a success. When the man became aware of my object he would draw into himself, there was the consciousness of constraint, and then, if persisted in, a very one-sided talk. On one occasion I did persist and for several days I could not find that man awake. Some excellent people, I believe, thought that one only had, in most favourable conditions, to go straight to the point and drive home the lessons sensitive minds had so lately been impressed with, but our soldier friend had his methods of defence against the incautious as he had against vaporous sympathy. There were also those who presented no difficulty of approach, ready and frank or responsive to suggestion, and I had many a talk on problems, troubles, beliefs of the highest as well as the deepest interest.

We had, in proportion to the number of our patients and the nature of their wounds, very few losses. A funeral was marked by the whole Hospital's reverence, one felt it in the wards and saw it in the quiet lines at attention through which the procession passed from us. It was always as fully military as it was possible to procure, the gun-carriage, escort, buglers and other essentials being supplied by the various units stationed in Leeds. The Authorities at Lawnswood Cemetery set apart a plot for the burial of soldiers, and here most of those we lost were laid.

The Chaplain's duties included the provision and arrangement of entertainments. The first need in this direction was a suitable place for the purpose, and here as in many other requirements, we were most indebted to Mr. G. W. Brown and Mr. David Little ; by their exertions among the wholesale clothiers we were early in possession of our commodious and well-furnished Recreation Hall with its piano, billiard tables and cinematograph apparatus. The managers of the Empire and Hippodrome made themselves responsible for an afternoon each during the week, and they did not often fail to bring a representative number of their visiting company. There were very few artistes of note in the Theatrical, Operatic or Music Hall world who did not visit us and give us of their best. Picture Houses readily lent us films, and we never lacked an expert Operator. Amateur companies and individuals were not behind in their kindly offers and it was often difficult and sometimes impossible to avail ourselves of their kindness.

In many directions the Hospital afforded an opportunity and an object for gratitude to express itself, feeling ran high in those first two years, and Leeds people, rich and poor, rose to the occasion with splendid generosity.

VII. MUNICIPAL ACTIVITIES.

> " Men in great place are thrice servants
> —servants of the Sovereign or State,
> servants of Fame, and servants of business ;
> so as they have no freedom, neither in their
> persons, nor in their actions, nor in their
> times."—*Bacon.*

THE LORD MAYORS IN WAR TIME.

IT will be obvious to anyone who reads this volume that the Leeds City Council, through its members and officials, contributed notably to the successful operation of the varied war efforts. The willing hands of the Municipal authorities may be discerned at every turn of the abnormal situation.

The lead given by the several Chief Magistrates claims first attention. Upon every Lord Mayor of Leeds, throughout the war years, arduous and exacting duties devolved, and by all of them were those duties carried out with the greatest credit to the city. Each one in turn, too, was nobly supported by his Lady Mayoress, who—in respect of women's work particularly—fulfilled with courage and assiduity the prominent part assigned to her—Mrs. Charles Ratcliffe (niece of Sir Edward Brotherton) in 1913-14 ; Mrs. J. E. Bedford in 1914-15; Mrs. Charles Lupton in 1915-16 ; Mrs. E. G. Arnold in 1916-17 ; Mrs. F. Gott in 1917-18 ; and Mrs. Hartley (daughter of Mr. Joseph Henry) in 1918-19.

Who and what were the holders of the high office of Lord Mayor, some future generation may ask ? Brief details regarding them follow, together with some impressions or reminiscences of the year of office—in one or two cases personally contributed.

Colonel Sir Edward Allen Brotherton, Bart., was Lord Mayor of Leeds when war broke out. He was then plain Mr. Brotherton. On the formation of the City " Pals " Battalion (15th

West Yorkshires), which he equipped at his own expense, he was appointed its Hon. Colonel; and in 1918 his public and national services were recognised by the honour of a Baronetcy. The controlling head of the largest chemical undertaking of its kind in the kingdom, he brought to bear on his public service a business acumen eminently adapted to the unprecedented situation. Moreover, although not an elected member of the City Council, he had had experience of municipal work as Mayor of Wakefield in 1901, and for many years he represented that city in Parliament. His many benefactions are well known. To the Prince of Wales' War Relief Fund he gave £5,000, and to the Leeds University he gave £20,000 for the development of bacteriological study and research in the interests of public health. In 1923 the University conferred on him the honorary degree of Doctor of Laws.

Mr. James Edward Bedford, F.G.S., F.S.A., whose year of office began on November 9th, 1914, also had a close association with the chemical industry. He had retired from business in the month before war broke out, and was thus able to devote his whole time and energy to the duties of Lord Mayor. Nor did he spare himself although then in his 60th year. Mr. Bedford came of a family that had been established in Leeds since the early days of last century, and, like his father before him, he took a keen interest in public affairs. Although a City Councillor for only three years before being invited to become Chief Magistrate, he had held office as President of the Leeds Chamber of Commerce, President of the Leeds Philosophical and Literary Society (to the Museum Collection of which he contributed generously), President of the Institute, and President of the School of Art. The old Mechanics' Institute was entirely re-organised during his presidency and on his initiative, and he originated the scheme of a Commercial Library which is now so valuable an adjunct to the Reading Room at the City's Central Public Free Library. As will be seen later, he had an eventful Mayoralty and his record is one for pride and satisfaction. In September, 1915, he had the honour of receiving the King on His Majesty's visit to the Military Hospitals.

Mr. Charles Lupton, M.A. (Camb.), a well-known Solicitor and member of one of the oldest and most highly esteemed Leeds families, filled the office of Lord Mayor from November 1915 to November 1916, a year full of incident and anxiety. For many years, until the war was over, he held the position of Honorary Treasurer and Chairman of the Leeds General Infirmary; accordingly the extension scheme at Beckett's Park Military Hospital made a special appeal to him. No better testimony to his services could be made than the following tribute paid in November 1919, when he was presented for the honorary degree of Doctor of Laws at the Leeds University :—

> "He has laboured to alleviate the lot of the soldiers and sailors disabled in the war, by supplementing the accommodation and equipment of the great military hospitals established in our midst, and by securing to those discharged from His Majesty's forces with wounds or other disabilities adequate medical treatment and efficient training. As member of the Council of the University he has taken part in every movement to improve the standards of professional education in the arts of medicine and law; to him are due, in large measure, the close co-operation between the University and the Infirmary so necessary to the welfare of the School of Medicine, and the foundation and maintenance of the School of Law in the University in conjunction with the Yorkshire Board of Legal Studies."

Mr. Edmund George Arnold, the youngest of the Lord Mayors in war time, took office in November 1916 at the age of 51. A native of North Devon, he had been resident in Leeds from boyhood and was educated at the Leeds Grammar School. He succeeded his father as head of a great local printing and publishing business, and from 1916 to 1918 was President of the Federation of Master

Printers of Great Britain and Ireland. During the war, too, he presided over the committee for the release of printers' metals, large quantities of which were used for munitions purposes, and was chairman of the fund for distressed French printers. Also, as chairman of the Leeds Y.M.C.A. Area Board and in other directions, educational and benevolent, he did a great amount of useful public work. In 1921 he was elected Pro-Chancellor of the University of Leeds, in succession to Mr. A. G. Lupton. It is a noteworthy fact that, out of 179 men of military age employed by Mr. Arnold's firm when war broke out, 167 volunteered for active service, encouraged by the directors who promptly decided to make allowances to the dependents. His very busy year as Lord Mayor fell in a particularly depressing period of the war, but his cheerful spirit never flagged.

Mr. Frank Gott, who was Lord Mayor during the last year of the war, belonged to a family which, for more than a century before, had taken a leading part in the industrial and social life of Leeds, and had, moreover, given to the town one of its best-known vicars, who afterwards became Bishop of Truro. Mr. Gott unfortunately succumbed to a serious illness in 1920, and the reminiscences of his year of office which follow are kindly supplied by his widow, whose services in the realm of education and charity were hardly less distinguished than his. A land agent by profession, the late Mr. Gott still found time to perform more or less public duties in connection with the Parish Church, the Infirmary, the Chamber of Commerce, Church Extension Society, Thoresby Society and other organisations, but he had no direct experience of municipal service until he accepted the position of Lord Mayor. He discharged the obligations of that office with unfailing courtesy and tact, and he maintained at a high level the prestige of Leeds in what was, perhaps,

Photo by   *Bacon & Son.*
Col. Sir EDWARD A. BROTHERTON, BART., LL.D.,
Lord Mayor, 1913-1914.

the most trying period of the war. In June 1918 he had the honour of receiving the King and Queen, when their Majesties visited the city to inspect Beckett's Park Hospital and the munition works.

Mr. Gott was succeeded on November 9th, 1918, by Mr. Joseph Henry, who, as will be found recorded on another page, had the privilege of announcing publicly the signing of the Armistice.

A MEMORY OF THE FIRST MONTHS.
(BY SIR EDWARD BROTHERTON, BART.)

I welcome the invitation to write something about that portion of my year of office as Lord Mayor of Leeds which coincided with the first months of the Great War, because it enables me to place on permanent record the profound and lasting impressions which the magnificent patriotism of all classes of citizens made upon me at the time—impressions that strengthen rather than diminish with the passage of time.

When war broke out, my activities as Lord Mayor were directed primarily to two things—the obtaining of recruits for the Forces and the continued provision of employment for the wage earners. In connection with the latter, I convened a meeting at the Town Hall of a number of the leading employers of labour, and various suggestions were made and considered. What the future would bring forth was hidden from us, but in order to prevent distress through lack of work we all undertook to keep our factories going at least half time. It is to be remembered that when war was declared there was an immediate cessation of the general demand for goods. How, subsequently the demand for war material of one kind and another took the place of ordinary requirements is a matter of history, but the extent of this demand could not then be foreseen. The industrial outlook in the early days was dark and uncertain, and I recall the determination of the employers of Leeds to "carry on" as one of many evidences of the spontaneous patriotism of the citizens.

Another, and not the least important, manifestation of the fine spirit animating all classes was the splendid service rendered by the Banks to both the Government and private individuals. It was a time of great uncertainty and unsettlement. As an indication of the bewilderment in the minds of many, I remember instances of people refusing even Bank of England Notes, and insisting upon payment in gold. At such a time and in such an atmosphere, the attitude of the Banks was of incalculable importance, and the manner in which they readily granted required credits assisted materially in maintaining stability and confidence.

But the deepest and most abiding impression that remains with me from my civic office in the early days of the War is that left by the magnificent devotion and patriotism of the men who responded to the call to the Colours. It is impossible to find words that adequately express one's feelings of pride and admiration as the mind dwells on the wonderful demonstration of intense love of country and noble eagerness for service. I felt then, I feel even more strongly now, that no praise or thanks can be too high for the greatness of spirit shown by the men of the city. They came to the Town Hall, pressing forward, literally tumbling over each other in a fervour of impatience to be enrolled for service.

The battalion with which I became most closely associated was the 15th Battalion West Yorkshire Regiment, which soon became known as the "Leeds Pals," and of which I had the great honour to be appointed Honorary Colonel by Lord Kitchener. In my efforts in connection with the "Pals," I gladly recognise the splendid

Photo by *Bacon & Son.*
JAMES E. BEDFORD, F.G.S., F.S.A.,
Lord Mayor, 1914-1915.

assistance I received from many leading citizens. Both in the recruits and in those who helped in the organisation was prominently displayed the spirit of patriotic service. Everyone desired to do all he could for his country. The 15th Battalion came to be known as the "Pals" because the men were more or less acquainted with one another, and the idea of serving with friends undoubtedly made a strong appeal.

The story of the Leeds men generally on the battlefields is told in this volume. Though my few words of recollection relate to the early war months of my Lord Mayoralty, I cannot close without some reference to the subsequent events in which the men with whom I was associated were so closely concerned. The "Pals" proved themselves to be one of the finest battalions that even this country had ever raised. Going gallantly into action on 1st July, 1916, the battalion was annihilated. Our young men sealed their patriotism with their blood. This service and sacrifice will ever be a proud memory to the people of our city, and an example of duty noble rendered, of faithfulness "even unto Death."

EDWARD ALLEN BROTHERTON.

EXTRACTS FROM THE DIARY OF MR. J. E. BEDFORD, 1914-15.

In taking the reins of office from Colonel Sir Edward Brotherton in the first months of the war, namely on November 9th, 1914, Mr. James Edward Bedford was confronted with tasks of exceptional weight and importance. An admirable lead had already been given to citizens, and a splendid spirit was shown but, naturally, there was much still to be done in respect of organisation and the co-ordination of war efforts. To the work of two important committees already active —the Parliamentary Recruiting Committee, and the General Purposes Committee—there was now added a variety of movements which appealed at once to citizens, *e.g.*, the Belgian Refugees Committee, the Joint Recruiting Committee, the Bantam Battalion Equipment and Housing Committees, the Lord Mayor's Refugee Fund Committee, the Serbian Relief Committee, the Leeds Volunteer Training Corps Committee, the Leeds Special Constables' Committee, the Leeds Munitions of War Committee, a branch of the War National Relief Fund, and another of the British Red Cross Society, the Leeds Brigade National Reserve Committee, the Leeds War Savings Committee, the Pioneer Battalion Joint Committee and the Lady Mayoress's Committee co-ordinating work on behalf of the service men.

Besides helping to promote the efficiency of the Pals Battalion, established by his predecessor in the Mayoral chair, Mr. Bedford set to work and secured the formation of the Bantam Battalion, by which name we designated the men of small stature who had been rejected because they did not come up to the Army height standard. One of his first acts after taking office was to inquire into the possibilities of raising such a unit, and in less than a month plans were laid, and as a result of his personal applications to General Plumer at York and the War Office in London, the roll of names swelled until, on December 24th, the battalion had a strength of 500 ; on January 13th it numbered 1,200, and on January 16th marched through the streets of Leeds 1,290 strong. The enrolment was completed in six weeks, when a strength of 1,330 was attained under the command of Major Pollard.

Other units equipped and trained during Mr. Bedford's Mayoralty were the Pals, and the 7th and 8th second line Battalions of the Rifles (West Yorkshire Regiment). The Leeds Educational Service Company and Brigade Bearer Company of the Volunteer Training Corps were started in the same period, when, also, two companies of Royal Engineers went into training at Ilkley alongside the Bantams ; and the 11th Divisional Ammunition Column of R.F.A., the 21st Service Battalion West Yorkshire Textile Pioneers and West Riding Cyclist Corps for the 62nd Division were formed.

From a diary, which Mr. Bedford kept during his year of office, the present writer has extracted a number of entries which indicate what demands were made continuously on his time. The diary bristles with engagements from week to week— recruiting meetings, war relief committee meetings. interviews with military, volunteers and police representatives, munitions committee meetings and similar engagements ; only in the latter part of August did he and the Lady Mayoress secure a comparatively quiet interval. One of the earliest demands made on him, by the way, was that of the following telegram which he received from the War Authorities at York : " Purchase ten tons of barbed wire, and forward by first passenger train ! "

In the first two months the Lord Mayor's attention was largely occupied with questions of Belgian refugee relief, formation of the " Bantams " Battalion, the Volunteer Corps Movement and the National War Relief Fund. Thereafter the work increased. January 1915, was a typical month. Here are a few of the entries :—

1915. January 1st.—Cabled the American Minister at the Hague, asking him to intervene and save the life of Private Lonsdale, of Leeds, a prisoner in Berlin, condemned to death for striking a prison warder.

January 2nd.—Received cable from American Minister as follows : " Have requested American Ambassador in Berlin to do everything possible for Private Lonsdale.—Van Dyke, American Minister." Also the following telegram · " War Office to Lord Mayor of Leeds. Thank you, on behalf of regiment for steps you have taken to save life of Private Lonsdale. I sincerely hope you will be successful. General Belfield, Colonel of Wellington Regiment."

(NOTE.—Private Lonsdale's life was saved).

January 4th.—Lord Mayor received the Pals Battalion in Victoria Square and, later, entertained the Officers to luncheon.

Meeting of the Volunteer Corps Committee in Lord Mayor's Rooms.

January 10th.—Archbishop of York addressed meeting in Coliseum, Lord Mayor presiding. The Archbishop came to " tell the men their duties."

January 13th.—Journeyed to York in reference to the appointment of a Colonel for the Bantams (2nd) Battalion.

January 16th.—Bantams (1st) Battalion paraded in Victoria Square; Lord Mayor took the salute. Tea given to Belgian children by Lady Mayoress.

January 20th.—Lord Mayor's Luncheon to Officers of the Bantams.

January 23rd.—Bantams Battalion marched to Town Hall and were received officially by the Lord Mayor in Victoria Square. After the parade 40 recruits joined, making the total 1,330; only 20 more required to complete the strength. The time occupied from the appointment of Colonel Pollard and commencement of recruiting was exactly six weeks : an excellent result.

NOTE.—Five British Warships engage German Fleet in North Sea about this date.

During February we find the Lord Mayor on one day opening a Soldiers' Club, and on another entertaining the Chief Constables of Yorkshire and attending a meeting of the Volunteer Corps Sub-Committee. On the 17th he interviewed applicants for appointment as Major of the Engineers' Corps, and on the 27th attended a concert in aid of the Belgian Refugee Fund.

In March he devoted several days to Committee work in connection with the appointment of Special Constables, visited Ilkley to inspect the Bantams in training and also inspected the Volunteer Training Corps on Woodhouse Moor and attended a luncheon given by the Hon. Rupert Beckett to Sir Algernon Firth and the Leeds Engineering Employers to consider the question of munition manufacture, and, on the 29th, took the salute at an Inspection of the 1st Company of Royal Engineers in Victoria Square. On the 30th a " Government appeal to women " meeting was held in the Town Hall, the Lady Mayoress presiding.

April and May were also very busy months; and so it continued through the summer. In April there was a conference with General Molesworth respecting the Bantams, and a meeting of engineering employers in the Lord Mayor's Rooms on the subject of munitions, with regard to which the Corporation General Purposes Committee were considering inquiries for workmen by the Local Government Board. In the same month the Lord Mayor inspected the new Artillery Ammunition Column in City Square, and both in April and May paid several visits to Ilkley to inspect the Territorial units, besides delivering addresses at various places in furtherance of recruiting. On April 23rd he inspected the local Army Service Corps in Victoria Square, and on the 28th received the Serbian delegates.

Under date May 10th the Diary contains the entry "Steamship Lusitania torpedoed by German devils, and 1,142 lives lost." On the 11th the Lord Mayor presided at a Munitions Committee meeting, and the next day motored to Colsterdale to inspect the Pals Battalion. On the 15th Colonel F. Stanley Jackson and two double companies of the 7th and 8th Battalions (West Yorkshire Regiment) Leeds Rifles arrived from Doncaster and paraded in Victoria Square. The Lord Mayor took the salute and entertained the senior officers to lunch. On the 17th he presided over a Serbian Relief Committee meeting, and on the 19th received delegates from the National Council on Housing and Town Planning and afterwards visited the homes for the Belgians. The formation of the Coalition Government about this time is also noted in the Diary. On the 27th he received a call from Lord Allerton in response to an invitation to attend a Munitions Committee meeting which met on the 31st in the Lord Mayor's Rooms to appoint an Advisory Committee.

Among other engagements of particular interest noted during the rest of the year were :—

June 9th.—Educational Service Corps parade in City Square. Officers entertained by Lord Mayor.

June 12th.—Volunteer Training Corps paraded in Roundhay Park. Also attended by Lord Allerton and Lord Airedale.

June 17th.—Lady Mayoress presided at concert in aid of Motor Ambulances.

July 5th.—Lady Mayoress presented to the Queen at Buckingham Palace, at review of the Lady Mayoresses' fleet of ambulances. At the Mansion House, London, Mr. Bedford replied to the toast of the guests. (Leeds presented two ambulances; the Lady Mayoress collected the sum of £1,600 for that purpose).

July 17th.—Attended Parade and Inspection of Leeds Cadet Imperial Yeomanry, Roundhay Park.

July 27th.—Lady Mayoress presided at meeting of National Union of Trained Nurses.

August 4th.—Military Parade in Victoria Square on first anniversary of the war. Lord Mayor addressed the gathering.

August 11th.—Lord Mayor presided at French Relief Fund Meeting.

September 4th.—Munitions Management Committee presented Lord Mayor with a 4.5 howitzer shell (now in the Leeds Museum), and sent a similar one to Mr. Lloyd George On the same day, at the Empire Theatre, delivered an address on "Our Lads at the Front."

September 7th.—Attended Bradford Conference re proposed Wool Textile Pioneers' Battalion.

September 8th.—Entertained Belgian Commission to luncheon.

September 10th.—Lord Mayor and Lady Mayoress visited Prince Ranjitsinhji in a Leeds nursing home. The Prince presented a cheque for a hundred guineas to the fund for " Our Lads at the Front."

September 13th.—General Mends, of the Northern Command, called on his return from the Front and gave a splendid account of the Leeds men. He said the Leeds Rifles were equal to the Guards. Together with the Lord Mayor he visited the Shell Factory.

September 18th.—Lord and Lady Mayoress opened the Soldiers' Institute, North Camp, Ripon.

September 27th.—The Lord Mayor received the King at the railway station, Leeds, on his Majesty's visit to Beckett's Park Military Hospital. The King expressed to the Lord Mayor his satisfaction with the visit.

September 28th.—Committee meeting in Lord Mayor's Rooms to promote 21st Service Battalion West Yorkshire Wool Textile Pioneers.

September 29th.—Addressed recruiting meeting for 62nd Division West Riding Cyclist Company.

October 1st.—Opened Sale of Work for the Red Cross.

October 2nd.—Great Recruiting Rally. Addressed gathering in Victoria Square.

October 19th.—Opened new Recruiting Office, City Square, and entertained officers of the Northern Command to luncheon.

November 3rd.—Farewell to Bantams' Battalion. Inspection in Victoria Square.

November 5th.—Conversazione given by Lord Mayor and Lady Mayoress in the Philosophical Hall to members of committees organised for war work.

Were space available, the reproduction of all the entries in this Diary would be in the nature of a revelation regarding the numerous calls on the Chief Magistrate of the City, not only in 1915 but in every year of the war.

Photo by   Alderman Charles Lupton, D.L., M.A., J.P.,   *Fielding*
Lord Mayor, 1915-1916.

REMINISCENCES OF 1915-16.
(By Mr. CHARLES LUPTON).

The municipal year from 1915-16 was one of great interest to those who shared in its activities, but has perhaps fewer landmarks to make it memorable than the year which ended in November 1914, or some of the later years of the war. The country had become accustomed to the fact that we were in for a long and hard struggle, and was beginning to take the steps which such a struggle required and which ultimately led us to victory.

The first and perhaps the most obvious was the better supply of munitions of war. Strictly speaking this was not a municipal activity at all, but Leeds men took such a great part in it, and workers from Leeds and the neighbourhood effected such remarkable results, that no record of the year would be complete without some reference to this department of war work. Leeds was one of the first places to divert its great engineering resources to this work, and the plan proved most successful and set up an example which was followed in many other large centres.

Another side of the question—that of supplying new men for the fighting lines—was one which had naturally engaged the attention of Leeds from the commencement of the war, and both Sir Edward Brotherton and Mr. Bedford had taken a leading part in raising new battalions. By November 1915, this effort had largely spent itself, and except for visiting the training camps in Nottinghamshire, and using any influences which were available to encourage recruiting, the Lord Mayor (Mr. Charles Lupton) could effect very little in this direction until Lord Derby's Recruiting scheme with its concomitant tribunals came into work in the Spring of 1916. After this, however, he spent two or three days every week in acting as chairman of the Military Appeal Tribunal for the N.W. Division of the West Riding, a most difficult and responsible duty which was happily lightened by the high quality of the tribunal itself, and by the confidence which the public showed in the fairness of its decisions. It is perhaps invidious to mention names where all worked so smoothly together, but the work done by Mr. Slingsby, as chairman of the second court, with Major Dent as his chief colleague, and the highminded line adopted by Mr. Fountain (Lord Mayor, 1922-23) and by Mr. Mulholland, who has since done such excellent work as Secretary of the War Pensions Committee, should not be forgotten.

It has been pleasant to learn in the years which have passed since the tribunal concluded its labours that many even of those we sent into the fighting line were satisfied with the decisions of the Tribunal, and it was often remarked at the time that the men who came before it were more often the victims of conflicting duties than shirkers who wished to avoid all service for their country.

Another subject which was taken up in this year was the question of employing women to take over the work which had hitherto been done by men in factories, bakeries, etc. This was a most difficult problem and might have proved insoluble if the hearty support of the employers and Labour Leaders had not been freely given. A series of committees were organised, composed of men selected for the purpose by the various trade and labour organisations and which also contained factory inspectors and other persons interested in the welfare of the workers as well as persons who had devoted themselves to various branches of philanthropic work. These committees made many valuable suggestions which proved more and more useful as the war dragged on, and it is interesting to note that the lines on which these committees were framed met with such approval in London that they were adopted as the model for other committees to do the same work which were afterwards set up in other places.

During the autumn of 1915 it had become evident that the hospital accommodation for wounded soldiers was very much below the requirements, and Lieut.-Colonel Littlewood, who had returned to Leeds from his retirement in Norfolk to take charge of the surgical work at the hospital established at the commencement of the war in the Training College buildings at Beckett's Park, had urged that Leeds with its great medical, surgical and nursing resources, ought to make a great effort to help to supply this need. The suggestion was at once taken up, and a committee consisting of Mr. Littlewood, the late Lord Manton, the Hon. Rupert Beckett, Mr. F. J. Kitson, the late Alderman Kinder, and the Lord Mayor, with Mr. Box as honorary secretary, was formed to carry it out. This committee decided that any help which they could give should be directed to concentrating the resources at their command rather than to increasing the number of existing hospital units, which up to then had been the plan usually adopted. They did this because they saw that as more and more of the experienced physicians and surgeons and nurses were drained off to the Front it would be increasingly difficult to give adequate supervision to units which were small and isolated. They therefore set aside proposals which had been made to utilise the Leeds Grammar School and other buildings as auxiliary hospitals, and advocated a great extension of Beckett's Park Hospital which had been established and worked so successfully under Lieut.-Colonel Dobson.

The War Office approved the suggestion and promised to bear the cost of equipment if Leeds would build an extension for 750 beds and a large kitchen. The £25,000 needed for the building was subscribed in a very few days by Leeds and other friends in the county, the money pouring in so fast that the list was closed down before the first replies were exhausted. Owing to the inclemency of the winter of 1915-16 the erection of this addition took longer than was anticipated, and its opening ceremony on March 29th, 1916, was marred by the absence of Lord French, who had promised to take the chief part in the opening ceremony, but was detained in the Midlands by a severe snowstorm which cut off all communication between Leeds and the country south of Doncaster for several days. Lord French, however, visited Leeds and inspected the hospital later in the year.

In result the new building proved most satisfactory and, before the end of 1916, another large addition was commenced to the ward accommodation at Beckett's Park, which included a block of operation rooms and X-ray rooms (provided by the liberality of Mrs. Currer Briggs), Leeds and the neighbourhood providing £10,000 towards the cost of the wards, and the War Office the rest; whilst Leeds also provided on its own initiative and at its sole expense a separate building at the cost of £5,000 in which the soldiers were trained to do various kinds of useful work which were suited to their incapacities or state of convalescence. So useful did these various extensions become that they are still (five years after) in full use for soldiers who have to receive continuous or recurrent treatment for the injuries they received during the war.

The results of this unification proved so valuable that practically all the War Hospitals in Leeds were put under the command of Lieut.-Colonel Littlewood, who had succeeded to the position of Lieut.-Colonel Dobson on the latter's retirement owing to overwork and ill-health, whilst all the Leeds nursing arrangements were put under the charge of Miss Innes, the Lady Superintendent of the Leeds Infirmary. In this connection neither the splendid efforts of the women of Leeds in organising and running numerous convalescent hospitals in various suburbs of the city, nor the efforts of the motor owners in arranging an excellent system of ambulances from the stations to the various hospitals, nor the efforts of the Leeds Wholesale Clothiers' Association in building and running a recreation hall at Beckett's Park, nor those of the "Two Arts" Club and the "Music in Wartime" branch of the Lady Mayoress Committee should be forgotten.

Closely following on the provision of hospitals for the wounded came the necessity of pensions for those who were disabled by the war and for the families which had lost their bread-winners. The Government passed an Act in 1916 arranging that this work (except for a million pounds which was to be given by the State to help the country districts) should be carried through with funds raised by the municipalities and Local Government units in the Kingdom by voluntary effort. It was at once realised to be hopelessly inadequate and an agitation led by the Lord Mayors of Liverpool and Birmingham, supported by all the chief cities in the United Kingdom, resulted in a very large and influential deputation to the Chancellor of the Exchequer to urge that this was a national duty and should be undertaken by the State. The Government at once acceded to the demand and voted £5,000,000 for the purpose. This was the commencement of the present War Pension Scheme, and was at once followed by the establishment of the network of War Pension Committees which did such notable work during the rest of the war.

Side by side with this work an immense amount of home visiting was done by a branch of the Lady Mayoress's Committee, which contributed material assistance where it was needed and gave very valuable help by advice and encouragement to mothers and others who were left in positions of great difficulty. Other branches of the Lady Mayoress's Committee provided homes for children who had lost their mothers whilst their fathers were at the war, supplied comforts and necessaries for the troops abroad in conjunction with Sir Edward Ward's national organisation for this purpose, and assisted the West Riding War Fund, which by arrangement with Sir Edward Ward had special charge of the West Riding regiments in despatching large quantities of boots, clothing, and other necessaries to the West Riding regiments on the various Fronts.

Another subject which engaged much attention at the beginning of the year was the better protection of the home population against air raids. Before November 1915, it had become evident that something was urgently needed, but the shortage of guns at the Front was so great that none could be spared for home defence. Other defensive efforts were therefore considered and it was decided that the complete darkening of the city on nights when raids were threatened afforded the best security available. The objection to this was that it involved the owners of large furnaces and other similar works in great expense in suddenly damping down their fires, and that to secure safety they must often be damped down when this was ultimately unnecessary. The question was, however, carefully considered at a meeting of the owners and managers of large works, collieries, etc., held at the Lord Mayor's Rooms, and it was unanimously decided that the line of greatest safety for the population should be adopted ; and the extraordinary freedom of Leeds and its neighbourhood from air raid injuries may be largely traced to the loyalty and unselfishness of the individuals on whom its

Photo by   Bacon & Son.
EDMUND GEORGE ARNOLD,
Lord Mayor, 1916–1917.

success depended. Towards the end of 1916 guns became easier to obtain, and stations equipped with searchlights and anti-aircraft guns were set up round Leeds. Fortunately, these did not come into active operation against the enemy.

I fear that I have already filled more than my allotted space, and so cannot do more than refer to the efforts which were made to assist our Belgian and other Allies and to arrange for the collection of the funds needed for all these efforts, as well as to induce those who were temporarily benefited by the high wages engendered by the war to set aside some of their surplus savings for war purposes or for their own use in the bad times which would follow it.

The year was one of great activity, and one felt that people of all classes were determined to help each other and the State to the utmost limit of their capacity, and that no reasonable claim could be made upon them without meeting an adequate response. CHARLES LUPTON.

WAR-TIME IMPRESSIONS, 1916-17.
(By Mr. E. G. ARNOLD).

When asked to write an article giving my war-time impressions during the twelve months I was at the Town Hall, I can but feel the enormous difference between then and now. The tendency of all of us is to forget the strain, the anxiety, the lack of war-progress, which prevailed during the twelve months referred to, the depression resulting from the submarine menace. In short, 1916-17 was, without doubt, the most dismal and depressing period of the whole of the war.

Amongst many recollections, memories that fill one with pride, and memories which fill one with grief and regret, the following stand out prominently :—

Extension of Beckett's Park Military Hospital.—Towards the end of 1916, the Military Hospitals

Extension Committee, consisting of the Ex-Lord Mayor (Mr. Charles Lupton), the Hon. Rupert Beckett, Sir Berkeley Moynihan, Major Watson, Mr. F. J. Kitson, the late Alderman Kinder, the late Lord Manton, and the late Colonel Littlewood, began to prepare schemes for additional accommodation for wounded soldiers at Beckett's Park.

To visit Beckett's Park Military Hospital was a revelation of organisation under the guidance and control of modern medical science. It was a wonderful place, but most pathetic, many of the cases being so terrible, but the all-prevailing cheerfulness of the "boys" was most touching. The general body of citizens could have no idea of what the military hospitals were like, there being several others than Beckett's Park, and from the nature of the work carried on therein it was impossible to afford any opportunity for inspection. Colonel Littlewood, who did so much to make these hospitals successful, has since passed away.

In March, the City Council relinquished several more Hostels at Beckett's Park for use as military hospitals, as did also the Leeds Guardians at Beckett Street. Another V.A.D. Hospital was opened at Roundhay, and on the 14th March, 1917, an appeal was launched for still further military hospital accommodation at Beckett's Park, £14,270 being promised before the appeal was actually made public on March 14th—a most gratifying result. On the 4th May, 1917, H.R.H. the Duke of Connaught paid an official visit to Beckett's Park Hospital, and when going through the wards displayed that kindly, genial graciousness which is such a marked characteristic of our Royal House.

Entertainments.—There were many activities for entertaining and amusing the wounded soldiers in hospital, and concerts were held at various public halls to entertain those disabled men who were able to attend. One theatrical entertainment stands out vividly—a free matinée at the

Grand Theatre to soldiers' children. The house was packed with little ones, all of whose fathers were on service. Their joy was altogether delightful to see, and it was a wonderful occasion.

Welcome to V.C.'s.—Three of the Leeds V.C.'s, Sergeants Sanders and McNess and Private Evans, were officially welcomed by the Lord Mayor on the steps of the Town Hall, the utmost interest being taken by the general citizens in the arrival of these heroic men.

Medal giving.—During the year, there were two or more public distributions of Medals to soldiers and sailors who had earned them, the Victoria Hall being crowded with men on service, wounded soldiers and sailors, and the widows or parents of those who had fallen and who were entitled to medals. These ceremonies were most heartening in the testimony they gave to the valour of the young men who had been on service, but they were also pathetic in the extreme on account of those who had fallen, and whose widows and parents came for their medals.

The Air Force.—As the British aeroplanes increased in number, and, alas, as the casualties increased also, the demand came for greater numbers of well-educated youths to occupy the position of Officers in the Air Force, and large numbers of young men joined up for this purpose at Leeds.

Food restrictions.—The intensity of the submarine campaign, which increased very seriously as the year went on, led to the need of more severe food restrictions in all directions. The citizens nevertheless submitted admirably to the restraint. While exercising to the full their right to grumble, they loyally did their best to help their country in the manner required. As the submarines sank more and more ships, the food supply became shorter and shorter, and the need for still greater restrictions grew and grew.

A movement developed, and was very successful, for increasing the number of women to work on the land. It had been initiated in the previous year, but was developed materially during the period under review.

In May, 1917, the restrictions of the Ministry of Food in connection with the flour supply brought about such a shortage at Leeds that a hurried visit had to be paid to headquarters and permits for the release of greater quantities had to be demanded. The request was granted after some difficulty. One method of attempting and undoubtedly achieving economy in the use of food supplies was the institution of communal kitchens. There were many of these in different parts of the city, and they were unquestionably of the greatest use. In June, 1917, an Exhibition of appliances and arrangements for war economy in its various forms, principally food, was held under official auspices, and was so well supported by the citizens that a handsome profit resulted.

Sugar Control.—Like most other food-stuffs, sugar was under control throughout the year and could only be supplied in limited quantities of fixed prescribed weight. The Local Food Control Committee did wonderful work in this connection. They organised classes, consisting of hundreds of women and girl workers who packeted the sugar when it arrived from the Ministry, in packets of the prescribed size.

Allotments.—Owing to the food scarcity, the allotment movement, which had commenced in the previous year, grew enormously. Many fields and such pieces of waste land as were suitable were taken for the purpose all over the city, the most noticeable example being the western side of Woodhouse Moor, upon which hundreds of allotments developed. Not only did the allotment movement serve to reduce the food shortage, but it gave to thousands of town-dwelling men the interest and the joy of having a little vegetable garden of their own. To grow one's own vegetables and to realise their superiority to any that could be bought was a revelation to many, and, terrible as the war was, yet one of the good things that has come out of it has been the growth of the allotment movement, which continues, happily, in the majority of cases to this day.

Entry of U.S.A. into the War.—On April 6th, 1917, the United States of America entered into the war, and the effect on the public mind was electrical. For so many months prior to their entry there had been on land a position of stalemate ; on the sea incessant sinking of ships with fearful loss of life, non-combatant as well as naval ; in the air, air raid after air raid: and the public mind, although fully determined to go on and " see the thing through," was depressed from the lack of any sign of gaining an advantage. The entry of the U.S.A. changed all that. The general feeling now was that this event was the beginning of the end.

Effects of Russian Revolution.—Towards the end of May, 1917, a most regrettable strike of male munition workers occurred, numbers of them leaving work for some fancied grievance. Their action was roundly condemned by the general body of citizens, who remarked, justly, that as these were young able-bodied men they should either be made to go on with their work or sent out to the firing line. After a few days, the strikers realised that public opinion was entirely against them, and one after another they returned to work.

In June, the extremists promoted a series of outdoor meetings in connection with the revolution in Russia, but the Watch Committee very wisely prohibited the holding of these meetings, and nothing happened.

National Service.—As the need increased for more and more troops, there had to be a great increase in the " combing out," and the voluntary Committees that undertook the work of finding additional men for the army had much difficulty in deciding as to what were and what were not essential trades, who were and who were not " key " men, and they incurred much odium in the discharge of their very responsible, and somewhat unpleasant, national duties. Taken all round, the number of slackers and " sheltered " men was negligible compared with the enormous numbers who rushed to the colours.

Combination in Industry.—In view of the increased shortage of men, it became more and more difficult to carry on businesses in which the product of labour was the chief factor, and many arrangements, both public and private, were made in order that business could be carried on under the increasing shortage of male workers of all kinds. Some of the developments arising from these movements were worthy of note. For instance, the boot repairers throughout the city pooled all their businesses in order that the work might be carried on and the citizens kept dryshod in consequence.

Air Raids.—Owing to the wise precautions of the Watch Committee, carried out so thoroughly by the then Chief Constable, Mr. W. Burns Lindley (since deceased), Leeds was mercifully spared from the horrors of air raids, although enemy aircraft were much nearer to the city than was generally known.

Leeds was most fortunate in this connection, as it would appear to have been a comparatively easy matter to follow the river from the coast. This, however, did not happen.

The services rendered to the community by the Special Constables and the Voluntary Fire Brigade were beyond praise, the former admirably taking the place of the large number of Police Constables who had gone on service.

Coal Control.—Throughout the year the handling and supplying of Coal was under control, and as the number of miners on service increased and increased, and as the need of coal for military and naval purposes—to say nothing of the supplies sent to our Allies—became greater and greater, the amount available for industrial and domestic purposes decreased more and more.

The citizens submitted to the control as being inevitable and a result of the national emergency.

Visit of the American Ambassador.—One of the greatest events of the year was the visit of the American Ambassador (Mr. W. H. Page), since, alas, deceased. The public took the greatest interest in his visit, arising from the entry of the U.S.A. into the war a few months before. His Excellency visited Beckett's Park in the afternoon of Wednesday, 10th October, 1917, and inspected the whole premises, chatting genially with many of the wounded, after which the official opening of the new wings and extensions took place. His speech on the war position in general was intensely interesting and of the highest order. Opportunity was taken, while his Excellency was at Beckett's Park, to present the survivors of that fast-diminishing band of Crimean and Indian Mutiny veterans who live at Leeds.

At night, his Excellency was present and spoke at a private dinner in the Lord Mayor's rooms—a dinner given in accordance with the necessities of food control and war-time restraint. His speech on the Allied cause will never be forgotten by those who heard it.

Benevolent War Work.—The pitiful cases of blinded soldiers at St. Dunstan's Hospital were well supported through the St. Dunstan's Lottery and by private subscriptions, substantial amounts being raised.

During the year also there were many " Flag

Day" movements, in order to raise funds for military and naval charities and other war purposes, substantial amounts resulting. The general citizens appeared to regard the Flag Days as rather a nuisance, but supported them heartily nevertheless, because their promoters were working for those who were fighting for their country. The classes at which bandages of many kinds were made for the military hospitals rendered invaluable work, and the output was valuable and very great.

Amongst the many activities for obtaining funds for comforts for the troops and other war purposes were free matinées, concerts, etc., organised by the theatres, music halls, cinemas and the like, the Managements defraying all the expenses and handing over the funds to the movements concerned.

Incessant activity of the Lord Lieutenant.—The activities of the Lord Lieutenant (The Earl of Harewood) and the Countess of Harewood were innumerable and unceasing. Meeting after meeting, both public and Committee, gathering after gathering, civic functions, military functions, etc., made up their life from one day to another. And all the time railway travelling was much restricted and very uncomfortable, while motor travelling was almost impossible, in that supplies of petrol could only be obtained to a very limited extent, if at all, and private motors had to be driven by gas power. When it is remembered that they must have been most anxious concerning their son, Viscount Lascelles, who was on active service, there can be but one feeling towards the Lord Lieutenant and his gracious Lady—a grateful sense that they did their utmost and set a magnificent example.

Conclusion.—Looking back on the twelve months ending 9th November, 1917, the outstanding characteristic of the period seems to be that, on all hands and with everybody, there was

Photo by Bacon & Son.
FRANK GOTT,
Lord Mayor, 1917–1918.

one great, fixed, all-prevailing principle, which was that "Britain must see this thing through."

The fact of the long-continued stalemate was depressing in the extreme, and, remembering that the war had been in progress from two-and-a-half to three years, without any apparent advantage having accrued to the Allied cause, one could but be very proud of a community that was so determined to go on in spite of the apparently insuperable difficulties. It is true that here and there the little voices of little men were raised in favour of a compromise, of the Russian Revolutionists, and the like, but their number was negligible and their influence amounted to nothing at all. E. G. ARNOLD.

MR. FRANK GOTT'S MAYORALTY, 1917-18.

Mr. Gott's Mayoralty coincided with the most critical days of the war, when the success of the submarine campaign, the consequent shortage of food, the general unrest and depression caused by the ever-increasing numbers of wounded men to be seen everywhere, the retreat during the Spring of 1918, the queues of anxious women outside food shops, and the knowledge that only a few weeks' supply lay between the country and starvation, gave intense anxiety to those in responsible positions who realised how small a spark might easily cause a great conflagration.

All these facts naturally coloured Mr. Gott's term of office to an even greater extent than that of his immediate predecessors. Apart from the duty of presiding at meetings, holding interviews and fulfilling other engagements which form the normal routine of Lord Mayors in peace and war alike, his time was devoted to questions of food supplies, munitions, hospitals, war savings and kindred subjects which could in any way further the efforts of those directly responsible for winning the war.

The first weeks of his year of office were largely occupied in dealing with the evils of queues, paying visits to London to study the working of National Kitchens and the various means adopted in order to regulate the food supply until rationing became universal, and the limits of 1 oz. of tea, 4 oz. margarine, etc., at least did away with any suspicion that one class was getting more than its share. The public kitchens which had been started by the Lady Mayoress's Committee were then taken over by the City, and large and fully-equipped kitchens were opened in Beckett Street and Park Lane.

During the later months of 1917 much curiosity was aroused by the enclosure of Meanwood woods and quarries so long a favourite Sunday walk, by high barbed-wire fencing, park-like roads replacing the old stone tracks, but in January 1918 curiosity was allayed; the Lord Mayor opened in the centre of the wood a gun-testing station, and from now till the end of the war, the dull roar of heavy guns, and the vibration of all the houses near, became an everyday event which soon only attracted the attention of strangers.

The War Savings campaign started under Mr. Charles Lupton in 1916 was carried on with increasing success. On December 3rd, 1917, the Attorney General (Mr. F. E. Smith, now Lord Birkenhead) addressed a large gathering in the Town Hall; and during Tank Week, held shortly afterwards, a sum of £1,651,000 was subscribed. In July, 1918, following a meeting addressed by Sir Thomas Mackenzie, High Commissioner of New Zealand, War Weapon Week raised £2,085,892. Mr. Gott took an active part in every detail of this work, which was so ably organised by the City Treasurer (Mr. Mitchell) and his deputy (Mr. Kendall).

Various Services of Intercession for those fighting were held about this period, and will never be forgotten by those who took part in them, especially one Service in the Town Hall, when a great crowd filled the building to overflowing and representatives of all the Churches took part ; and one, on a gloomy wet night during the darkest days of the war held in the great nave of Kirkstall Abbey.

In September, 1918, the Rev. H. S. S. Woollcombe, the present Suffragan Bishop of Whitby held (what has now become an annual event) a service on Armley Feast Ground for those taking part in the Feast, when the Lord Mayor spoke on the sacrifice men and women were making for us, and urged all present to make their lives worthy of such sacrifices.

On a lovely day at the end of May, the King and Queen came to Leeds to visit the munition works. They were received at the Town Hall by a representative gathering of citizens, while children from the elementary schools voiced their greetings in delightful songs, which brought a gleam of real pleasure to the sad and tired face of the King and he asked for them to be repeated. In the afternoon their Majesties visited the War Hospital at Beckett's Park and went through all the wards and curative workshops. On the same occasion the King distributed medals and V.C.'s to a group of wounded soldiers, and to the wives and mothers of those who had not survived to receive them personally.

In July, Mr. Gott welcomed and entertained the famous Band of the 1st Regiment of Zouaves, in the course of their tour of the provinces on behalf of the French Red Cross Fund.

One of the most interesting features of the year was the visits of delegates, from other countries involved in the war, who were entertained at the Town Hall, where representatives of all sides of Leeds life were invited to meet them. The visitors included the Serbian Industrial and

Commercial Mission, delegates from the Italian Universities and the Greek Chamber of Commerce, and two members of the American Mission (Mr. Meredith, Director of the Chamber of Commerce, U.S.A., and the Hon. Mrs. Grenfell, Chairman of the State Board of Correction of Colorado). Among men of note whom the Lord Mayor entertained during the year were Sir Thomas Mackenzie, High Commissioner of New Zealand; Mr. Hughes, Prime Minister of Australia; Sir Martin Conway, Lord Denbigh and Lord Birkenhead (all of whom addressed large meetings in the Town Hall), also Sir William Robertson, besides daily visits and conferences with Government officials connected with the war, or the health and welfare of the community, of whom not the least interesting was Dr. Truby King, with his schemes for infant welfare.

The entry of America into the war brought many Americans to Leeds for short courses at Beckett's Park Hospital, and on July 4th, 1918, the Lord Mayor gave a big reception in their honour, when a large number of citizens were invited to meet them, and a hospitality committee was formed to organise further opportunities for their welcome. In the same month he opened the new Commercial and Technical Library, established by the City Council—one of the first four to be formed in England.

Housing even then was much to the fore, and the purchase of the Middleton, Wyther and Hawksworth estates was carried through, partly as the result of a suggestion from Mr. Gott. The Pious Uses Trust were approached and they added a public park. Again, allotments were a subject to which in the course of his professional career Mr. Gott had given much time and thought; and he did all in his power to encourage their development during the war. The increase in the number of allotments provided by the Corporation Parks Committee, and the wonderful

Photo by *Bacon & Son.*

JOSEPH HENRY, J.P.,
Lord Mayor, 1918–1919.

shows of produce grown on them in the autumn of 1918, when over 40 tons of vegetables were exhibited at the Town Hall, indicated how greatly this war-time effort was adding to the health of citizens.

On Mr. Gott also devolved the duty—in June—of opening publicly the Automatic Telephone Exchange in Basinghall Street—the largest in Europe at that time—which has since proved so successful and has been extended to London.

MR. JOSEPH HENRY, 1918-19.

Mr. Joseph Henry, who succeeded Mr. Gott as Lord Mayor on November 9th, 1918, had the happy experience of announcing the signing of the Armistice two days after he took office. Great rejoicings followed both then and in the succeeding months, when the Lord Mayor had the honour of welcoming home, in the name of the city, returning and repatriated soldiers, and helping to provide entertainment for them. He himself took part in seven street processions during the year and attended a great many meetings and functions more or less connected with the war's aftermath, besides continuing the mayoral interest in benevolent work which still remained to be done. A native of Leeds, Mr. Henry raised himself from a very humble position, and he was over 70 years of age when he accepted office as Lord Mayor. Almost from his boyhood he had been in touch with public affairs, and for a long period a member of the City Council, having close associations with Holbeck, where he was the head of a large iron foundry. He was succeeded in November, 1919, by Mr. T. B. Duncan, the first Labour Lord Mayor of Leeds.

CORPORATION OFFICIALS' SPECIAL WORK.

Outstanding examples of war work done by representatives of the Municipality are given in their proper place—in earlier and later chapters—

but there were others not so conspicuous which nevertheless served a useful purpose in the national interest.

Several Leeds Corporation officials had the distinction of performing special duties on behalf of the Government. The Town Clerk (Sir Robert Fox) was, in 1915, appointed a member of the National Registration Committee set up by the Local Government Board to report as to the best means of utilising information obtained by means of the National Register, then in course of compilation ; and when the Military Tribunals were instituted, as will be found recorded later, Sir Robert took over the responsibility for the duties of clerk and secretary with the assistance of trusted members of his staff.

At the request of the Admiralty, the question of loaning the services of other officials came before the City Council on January 3rd, 1917, and was referred approvingly to the General Purposes Committee who at once made the desired arrangements. The first selected was Mr. W. D. Leech, General Manager of the Gas Works, who was placed in charge of the Shipyard Labour Department in the Hull area, and, later, appointed Technical Officer and Superintendent of the Labour Dispute Section of the Shipyard Labour Department at the Admiralty. Mr. Leech served thus for fifteen months, and was only released in 1918 by reason of the urgency of Corporation work then demanding his attention.

Mr. J. B. Hamilton, Géneral Manager of the Tramways and Commercial Manager for the city, was—also in January 1917—invited to undertake the duties of Director of Trades Regulations under the Admiralty. He held that office for ten months, at the end of which term his services were requisitioned by the Board of Trade, and—as noted on another page—were of especial value in connection with the Fuel Control.

Photo by   THOMAS B. DUNCAN, J.P.,   *Rosemont.*
Lord Mayor, 1919-1920.

At the same time, Mr. R. B. Holt, Highways and Permanent Way Engineer, and Mr. H. G. Jeken, the Electrical Engineer, went to act voluntarily as District Director in the Hull and Newcastle areas, respectively, of the Admiralty Labour Department, and were so employed up to the end of January, 1919.

From March 1917, to January 1919, also, Mr. G. A. Hart, the Sewerage Engineer, voluntarily fulfilled the duties of Chief Labour Organisation Officer in the Leeds Area of the Admiralty Labour Department.

In respect of the valuable services rendered by all these Corporation officials special letters of thanks and appreciation were received from the Lords Commissioners of the Admiralty.

Then there was the work of special Committees. The General Purposes Committee of the Corporation dealt with questions of employment, received registrations of applications for work, and instituted works for relief of unemployment, from August 1914 to January 1915, after which time the army requirements led to a scarcity of labour. After the war, however, the Committee's activities were renewed and work was found for thousands of unemployed men on park improvements, the construction of bowling greens, tennis courts, golf courses, new roads, etc.

The War Pensions Committee covered the period from May 17th, 1915 to June 12th, 1922, and from June 1916, their duties included the relief of local distress which before had been administered by the Local Committee in connection with the National Relief Fund.

Apart from these and kindred matters, dealt with in another part of this volume, Corporation officials were continuously employed in carrying out Government requirements of one sort or another to meet the emergencies of the time. Thousands of printed circulars of instructions were issued and circulated to the Police and Fire Brigade, the Special Constabulary and Salvage Corps, the Voluntary Ambulance Detachment, Munition Works, etc., and in respect of public health, water, gas and electricity supplies unusual tasks were laid upon the responsible heads of departments.

Activities of the Libraries.

The Leeds Corporation Public Libraries served a singularly useful purpose all through the war. At the outset an exhibition of books, illustrating the history and policy of the nations involved, was brought together and arranged in show cases. In addition, a complete classified list was compiled of all works in the Reference Library, and the Central and Branch Libraries, bearing in any way on military matters and the countries concerned.

Of these facilities the public took full advantage, and the same may be said of the opportunities afforded for the acquisition of knowledge on technical matters relating to war work, and industry generally. But, apart from this, the Libraries all over the city were used extensively for the circulation of placards, pamphlets and leaflets in connection with the Recruiting Campaign, and movements for the encouragement of thrift. Also, thousands of publications, issued by the Central Committee of National Patriotic Organisations, were distributed, leading people to study the deeper causes of the war ; and, similarly Government circulars were passed on to the troops in camp and on active service. A notable work, too, was the daily collection of newspaper cuttings from the local Press, dealing with the city's activities in war-time. These cuttings, pasted into fourteen huge scrap books, number many thousands. They include reproductions of interesting photographs, as well as items of news which passed the Censorship at the time. Thus, thanks to the foresight of the City Librarian (Mr. Thomas W. Hand), a valuable series of local records is available for reference at the Central Public Library.

Further, the Libraries had a benevolent side. Books, disused magazines and other periodicals were regularly sent to the Military Hospitals, and also distributed among soldiers at the Front and in training camps at home. Large numbers of these gifts were contributed by the general public, who were invited to bring them to the Libraries.

The Art Gallery in War-Time.

Good use was made of the City Art Gallery. When the Belgian refugees began to come with a rush, in October 1914, it provided temporary accommodation for three hundred of them. Two rooms were converted into dormitories for women and girls; two other rooms, along with the balcony vestibule, were allotted to the men and boys; meals were served in the Sculpture gallery; and a space was cleared in the central hall as a playground for the children. Later on, many of the permanent exhibits in the Gallery had to be stored away; the whole of the ground floor was granted for the use of the Local Food Control Committee and their large staff. Before then, however, several exhibitions were held—all having some relation to the war. In place of the usual Autumn Exhibition, in 1914, an illuminating exposition of German brutality in Belgium was organised by Miss Bertha Bennet Burleigh, who had spent three months in Belgium during the German occupation. The exhibits—proclamations, photographs and similar evidences of ruthlessness—were of painful interest and helped to stimulate recruiting. Other exhibitions, held subsequently, were of women's war work, war trophies, and photographs from the Imperial War Museum.

VIII. SOME ECONOMIES AND RESTRICTIONS.

"Wisdom reacheth from one end to another mightily: and sweetly doth she order all things."—Solomon.

THE WAR SAVINGS MOVEMENT.

STARTED in February, 1916, as an incentive to thrift and a means of financing the war through the medium of small as well as large investments, the National War Savings Movement met with ready support from Leeds citizens. In the four years ending in March 1920, they subscribed well over £42,000,000, a considerable proportion of which sum was in the form of 15s. 6d. Savings Certificates, each yielding £1 at the end of five years. Up to December, 1918—the month following the Armistice—the amount was £32,173,757, including £2,798,759 in war savings certificates.

The various campaigns which led to this result received the primary impetus in March 1916, when the then Lord Mayor (Mr. Charles Lupton) convened a meeting of members of the City Council, Leeds Munitions Advisory Committee, representatives of the local Banks, Religious Bodies, Friendly Societies and Trade Unions, to consider what organised step should be taken. As an immediate outcome a strong committee, styled the Leeds War Savings Committee, was appointed under the chairmanship of the Lord Mayor, with Mr. R. Geoffrey Ellis (of the banking firm of Beckett & Co.) as chairman of the Executive, and this committee continued in being throughout the period under the chairmanship of the Lord Mayor in office. With the approval of the National War Savings Committee, a Leeds Deduction Scheme was adopted whereby War Savings Associations formed in factories and workshops were affiliated to the Leeds Local Committee who became responsible for contributions received from,

R. GEOFFREY ELLIS, M.P., D.L.,
Chairman of the Executive, Leeds War
Savings Committee.

Photo by   *Bacon & Son.*
Rev. Canon BICKERSTETH, D.D.,
Hon. Chaplain, 7th Battalion Leeds Rifles,
1905–16.

Photo by   *Vandyk.*
The Right Honourable LORD AIREDALE.

Photo by   *Elliott & Fry.*
J. B. HAMILTON, C.B.E.,
Director of Trades Regulations under the
Admiralty. Fuel Overseer.

and securities purchased for, members of the Association. The Chairman of the Leeds Corporation Finance Committee (Alderman Charles H. Wilson) agreed to allow the administrative work done by the Local Committee to be carried out in the City Treasurer's office without charge to the National Funds; accordingly the City Treasurer himself (at that time Mr. William Derry) was appointed honorary treasurer, and Mr. S. Kendall joint honorary secretary, with Mr. J. A. Purchas of Beckett's Bank.

In October, when the National War Savings Committee issued an urgent appeal to the nation for assistance, the chairman of the National War Savings Committee (Sir Robert Kindersley) visited Leeds and addressed a meeting of members of the Leeds Chamber of Commerce, who decided heartily to support the movement. At the same time the Local Committee invited the secretaries of all affiliated associations to become members of the committee. Mr. J. P. Spetch was appointed joint honorary secretary in place of Mr. Purchas, resigned, and in January, 1917, Mr. J. Mitchell succeeded to the position of honorary treasurer on the death of Mr. Derry.

The Leeds Local Committee carried on several successful campaigns in the furtherance of the War Savings movement, public meetings being held at which speeches were delivered by Lord Finlay (then Lord Chancellor), Lord Birkenhead (then Attorney General), Sir Robert Kindersley, Sir William Theodore Chambers, Sir William Schooling and other prominent personages. During the Victory Loan Campaign a Tank was presented to the City of Leeds by the Army Council; was formally handed over at a demonstration in City Square, on June 30th, 1919, by Lieut.-General Sir Ivor Maxse, K.C.B., C.V.O., D.S.O., Commander-in-Chief of the Northern Command, and was accepted by the then Lord Mayor (Mr. Joseph Henry).

In February, 1919, the National War Savings Committee notified Local War Savings Committees that the War Office had placed at their disposal a number of captured German rifles which were to be awarded to War Savings Associations whose members had contributed not less than £5 per member for the year ended 30th September, 1919, or whose returns showed an increase of 50 per cent. on their own Association's contributions for the previous year. Ninety-one, or 31 per cent. of the Associations affiliated to the Leeds Local Committee, had complied with the conditions, and, on March 11th, 1920, at the Town Hall, the rifles were presented to the representatives of the winning associations by the Lo:d Mayor (Mr. T. B. Duncan).

STATEMENT showing the amount subscribed in Leeds through the War Savings Movement up to March 31st, 1920:—

TITLE.	DATE.	AMOUNT RAISED. £
War Loan Campaign	February, 1917	10,250,000
Tank Week	December 17th-22nd, 1917	1,651,000
Business Men's Week	March 4th-9th, 1918	2,218,038
War Weapons Week	July 8th-15th, 1918	2,085,892
Thanksgiving Week	January 13th-18th, 1919	4,623,227
Victory Loan Campaign	June 30th-July 12th, 1919	4,398,026
		25,226,183
Other Investments		17,033,630
		£42,259,813

FUEL AND LIGHTING CONTROL.

The Household Fuel and Lighting Order, which came into operation in June, 1918, provided for the control, regulation and allocation of fuel supplies to merchants, dealers and consumers, also supplies of gas and electricity for domestic and quasi-domestic purposes. It involved a tremendous amount of work and necessitated a staff which, during the preliminary stage, numbered 143, most of whom were recruited temporarily

SOME ECONOMIES AND RESTRICTIONS.

from the Education and Tramway Departments of the Corporation.

Mr. J. B. Hamilton, C.B.E. (Tramways and Commercial Manager), was appointed Fuel Overseer, his office being at No. 1, Swinegate. The work to be done included the registration of all householders, industries, institutions, etc., in the city, as well as coal dealers and merchants (about 700 in all); the allocation of the quantity of fuel to be consumed during the period of twelve months; and the issuing of certificates authorising supplies of coal in accordance with the quantities allocated. This work, by the way, was rendered most arduous by the special demands of necessitous cases, such as institutions, food-producing industries, household sickness, etc., in respect of which additional allowances were sanctioned.

The extent of the operations may be gathered from the fact that no fewer than 109,573 separate requisition forms were issued to householders, a proceeding altogether apart from the attention given to personal inquiries which came in a constant stream.

The quantity of coal allocated amounted to 558,031 tons. This gave, on an average, a supply of 1 ton 4 cwts. per head of the Leeds population. The average amount per requisition was 5 tons 1 cwt., and the number of rateable premises concerned was 129,939. The various matters arising out of the Order were dealt with by a Fuel and Lighting Committee consisting of the following:—

Alderman Charles H. Wilson (Chairman), Aldermen W. H. Clarke, T. Oldroyd, and R. A. Smithson, Councillors Connellan, Eddison, Arnott and Gibson, Alderman Penrose-Green (Chairman of the Gas Committee), Councillor Hugh Lupton (Chairman of the Electricity Committee), Mr. Armour (representing the Co-operative Society), Mr. J. B. Hamilton, C.B.E. (Tramways and Commercial

Manager, and Local Fuel Overseer during the whole period of control), Mr. F. Townson (nominated by the Coal Merchants' Association to act as Coal Merchants' Supervisor), Mr. J. E. Wiltshire (Coal Dealers' Representative). Mr. Townson and Mr. Wiltshire acted in an advisory capacity to the Local Fuel Overseer, and the former gave invaluable assistance on matters connected with the Trade.

In the matter of supplies Leeds was in a very favourable position as compared with other cities, thanks to the foresight of the General Purposes Committee and the energy of the Local Fuel Overseer and coal merchants. The reserve stock of coal secured amounted to over 8,000 tons.

In regard to prices the Fuel Overseer was responsible for the fixing of the retail charges. He had first to ascertain prices of the various qualities of coal at the pit-head, the railway and handling costs and the profits of merchants and dealers ; and then he had to see that the charges he fixed for the various groups were not exceeded. Not only were such measures enforced during the last year of war, owing to the serious coal shortage caused by the withdrawal of skilled miners for the Army and the necessity of supplying our Allies with coal, but they were imperative in the year following the Armistice until June 1920. Also, towards the close of that year, and again from April to July 1921 in consequence of coal strikes, similar duties were imposed on the Local Authority ; and in the last period great assistance was given by a Local Emergency Coal Committee composed of representatives of the Coal Merchants' Association under the chairmanship of Mr. Hargreaves, acting with Mr. Edgar Lupton, president of the Chamber of Commerce, and Mr. Hamilton. Of this Committee, Mr. F. Marshall, Chief Assistant to the Commercial Manager, acted as secretary.

Throughout the whole period of control no

serious cases of infringement of regulations were reported—a fact which says much for the method of administration and the citizens' loyal acceptance of a trying position.

FOOD CONTROL.

When Lord Rhondda's rationing scheme had to be tackled, at the close of 1917, the whole ground floor of the Leeds City Art Gallery was converted into a Food Control Office. Here, a large staff of clerks engaged by the Town Clerk, (the Executive Officer), were continuously employed answering inquiries as well as sending out and dealing with the many thousands of cards and books that had to be issued. So exacting were these duties that the staff of 41 in January 1918, had to be increased to 68 four months later. The Control was directed by Mr. J. A. Greene, and Mr. W. Carby Hall was concerned with the co-ordination and administration for the whole of Yorkshire.

The scheme was welcomed because it put an end finally to the discomforts caused by the queues at the shops. Its novelty, however, led to another form of queue, and every day the Food Control Department was besieged by people in doubt or difficulty as regards the filling up of application forms, transference from one residence to another, claims for extra allowances of food or other questions. Hundreds, and on some days, thousands of inquiries had to be satisfied on points like these.

Unfortunately few statistical records as to the magnitude of the task have been preserved. A certain amount of information, however, is available and was noted at the time in the Press. For instance, in May, 1918, 429,758 ordinary ration cards were issued, together with 47,260 forms to be filled up by men who, by reason of their heavy manual national work, were entitled to supplementary rations ; 1,989 certificates were given to retailers of tea and butter, and 1,780 to dealers in margarine. Every week, by the way, the Executive Officer had consigned to him about 44 tons of margarine, and this had to be apportioned among the traders. At the same time, 2,000 applications from householders who wanted the special allowance of sugar for jam-making had to be dealt with ; and there were 60 applications from fruit-dealers also to be considered in this connection. Again, there were some 400 applications for permission to preserve eggs for domestic use, fifty eggs per head being allowed.

Matters of this kind, apart altogether from the organisation of meat supplies by 466 butchers in the city, and the judicial settlement of all questions arising out of the administration of affairs, imposed a continuous strain on the officials, but, as the population grew accustomed to the procedure, the scheme worked smoothly, and when ration cards had to be exchanged for ration books everyone acquiesced cheerfully, and readily followed the new instructions. For this later scheme, which came into force in July, 1918, 120,000 households in Leeds were supplied with ration books.

At a meeting of the City Council on September 5th, 1917, the following were appointed to be the Food Control Committee for Leeds :—

>The Lord Mayor of Leeds for the time being.
>Alderman J. R. FORD.   Alderman G. RATCLIFFE.
>Alderman F. FOUNTAIN.   Alderman C. H. WILSON.
>Alderman C. LUPTON.   Councillor CONNELLAN.
>Mrs. L. COHEN (nominated by the Leeds Trades and Labour Council).
>>Mr. J. C. GRATION (nominated by the Leeds Industrial Co-operative Society Ltd.).
>>Mr. T. H. S. HODGE (nominated by the Leeds Master Bakers' Wholesale Association and the Leeds and District Master Bakers' and Confectioners' Association).
>>Mr. ISAAC STEPHENSON (nominated by the Leeds and District Butchers' Association).
>>Mr. J. W. JESSOP (nominated by the Leeds and District Grocers and Provision Dealers' Association).

In November, Alderman Lupton resigned, and Alderman Willey was appointed in his place; and in March 1918, the following other members of the Committee were appointed, namely:—Mr. A. Gill and Mr. M. Sclare (Representatives of Labour suggested by the Leeds Trades and Labour Council), Councillor Moses Myers (representative of the Jewish population of the city). The Executive Officer was Sir Robert Fox (Town Clerk), the Deputy Executive Officer: Mr. S. Kendall (Deputy City Treasurer), and the Assistant Executive Officer: Mr. John W. Smith of the Town Clerk's Office. Valuable assistance was rendered by a Distribution Advisory Sub-Committee, under the chairmanship of Mr. S. Lineham, who, with Mr. W. H. Clarke and Mr. C. E. Penfold were delegates from the wholesale provision trade.

IX. BENEVOLENT AGENCIES.

" For his bounty,
There was no winter in't ; an autumn 'twas,
That grew the more by reaping."
Shakespeare.
" Best it is indeed
To spend ourselves upon the general good."
Lewis Morris.

WOMAN'S co-operation, conspicuous in industry, in hospital service and in other special departments of war work, was accorded with unfailing devotion in support of the many benevolent movements which went to relieve the hardships of war. Typical examples of this will be found in the pages immediately following.

Apart from the enormous value of personal service and private gifts in one form or another, it is computed that Leeds, largely with the aid of its women, subscribed at least a quarter of a million of money to various local funds for war relief, £74,000 alone being raised for the Leeds National Relief Fund and over £40,000 for local military hospital extension. Nor were the needy among our Allies forgotten. Belgians, French, Serbians, Russians, Roumanians, Italians, as well as our own soldiers and sailors and prisoners of war and our poorer children, received their quota of help.

THE LADY MAYORESS'S COMMITTEE.

It is difficult to describe in words alone the immense amount of social work accomplished in Leeds during the war years, and the great wave of loving sympathy that prompted women of all shades of opinions and experiences to unite in this work. The call to arms, on that fateful 4th of August, 1914, brought with it a crop of problems for the solution of which help was needed from voluntary organisations, quite apart from what the Government, involved in stupendous military and naval undertakings, could accomplish. How nobly the women came forward in this emergency constitutes one of the brightest chapters of the war's history. It is to the credit of Leeds that a definite lead was given by an organisation which sprang into being in those early days of the war, and in its general application became known as the Leeds Lady Mayoress's Committee.

Starting operations in temporary rooms at the Town Hall, and removing first to offices in East Parade and then to Basinghall Buildings, a general committee of sixty ladies, with an Executive of half that number, were finally installed in commodious premises at No. 4, Park Row. Here, with a devoted and untiring energy worthy of the highest praise, they adhered to their self-imposed task until the victory of the allied armies made it possible for them to close their many activities in the early summer of 1919.

Begun under the chairmanship of the then Lady Mayoress, Mrs. Charles Ratcliffe, the work developed on a large scale and resulted in great practical benefits to the fighting men and many less directly connected with the war. Each successive Lady Mayoress in turn—Mrs. J. E. Bedford in 1914-15, Mrs. Charles Lupton in 1915-16, Mrs. E. George Arnold in 1916-17, Mrs. Frank Gott in 1917-18, and Mrs. A. E. Hartley in 1918-19 —gave the support of her position to the Committee, and their self-sacrificing efforts were an inspiration to all the workers.

Following upon the organisation of Beckett's Park Training College as a great Military Hospital one thing obviously was at once needed, namely, hospital garments for the wounded men who began to arrive in the city from the Flanders front. The Committee were able to supply a considerable number of garments for the first batch of men admitted to hospital, and shirts and socks were also supplied to many men who were newly enrolled for training. In those early days Government stocks of clothing were wholly inadequate to meet the needs of all who rallied to the colours, and such help as was afforded by the Lady Mayoress's Committee was highly appreciated by those who were fortunate to receive it.

Working at high pressure, practically all hours of the day and night, the Committee steadily developed their activities, until by the end of July, 1916, a truly remarkable achievement was recorded. Six wheel chairs had been sent to the hospitals and two motor ambulances to the Front; 68,000 garments had been provided for the troops and 174,000 bandages and hospital requisites supplied; 1,000 pairs of boots had been given by Leeds boot manufacturers and presented to soldiers' and sailors' children; twenty beds for soldiers' and sailors' children had been provided at the Wyther Babies' Home, five "Lord Roberts" Clubs opened, 1,920 women and girls enrolled in the League of Honour, 34 prisoners of war regularly supplied with parcels of food, 90 concerts given to soldiers in hospitals and camps under the "Music-in-Wartime" Committee, one-and-a-quarter tons of tin foil collected and sold for the benefit of disabled soldiers, 14,200 visits a month paid to the wives and dependents of soldiers and sailors, and a register of lodgings for women munition workers compiled.

From this time onward the work continued steadily to increase, being divided under various sub-committees that were energetically managed and administered. Of these many activities considerable importance was attached to the work of the Visiting Committee, some 2,000 workers visiting every soldier's family in the city once a fortnight in order to give help, advice and encouragement, and thus maintain that close touch with the home that is necessary in any scheme of assistance. For this purpose the city was divided into 32 districts. In many cases the visitor's interest was the means of reporting irregularities in the payment of allowances and of having such defects rectified ; also of getting women and children sent to holiday homes, and motherless babies cared for. Much valuable work was thus accomplished.

The Local War Pensions Committee took over the control and responsibility for these visits from July, 1916. Mrs. E. E. Lawson was at the head of the dependents' branch of the committee which, by March, 1918, had to deal with 30 or 40 applicants for advice daily, more than 30,000 families being at that time under observation. Suitable employment was found for discharged soldiers and sailors by the Soldiers' and Sailors' Help Society, who made advances on account of delayed pay or pensions, and gave monetary assistance according to a scale agreed upon with the National Relief Fund. This work, too, the War Pensions Committee absorbed.

The Lady Mayoress's Committee as an organisation was recognised by the Government in their scheme of co-ordination established under Sir Edward Ward, Director-General of Voluntary Organisations, the first outcome of which was an urgent appeal for 500 mufflers and 1,000 pairs of mittens. Between 40 and 50 working parties in different parts of the city sent in goods regularly to the distributing centre, and about 60,000 garments were despatched yearly to meet the appeals.

In 1916-17 the Clothing and Hospital Needs Sub-Committee supplied 31,552 articles—almost double the previous year's figures, and the total number of articles made by the Bandages Section in the same period was 34,211, an increase of several thousands on the previous year's figures. This number did not include 5,336 gifts received from working parties in the outlying districts. The register showed also that the workers at the Park Row rooms made 7,435 attendances. The members of the War Hospital Supply Depot increased in numbers in that year to 408, and since the beginning of their work they had sent out 150,000 articles and had supplied hospitals on every battle front.

The Military Hospitals Committee, affiliated to the Lady Mayoress's Committee, also had a central depôt in Park Row, and here goods were received for all the military hospitals, being collected from country depôts and distributed by motor car. From this depôt were organised regular hospital visits by a band of ladies who arranged flowers, mended linen and generally supplied all the extra comforts needed by the men in the hospitals. A very popular scheme arranged by the Committee was the teaching of handicrafts to wounded men. In this same year of 1916-17 nearly 400 concerts were given through the agency of the affiliated " Music in War-Time " Committee, who, as already stated on another page, thus provided a great deal of entertainment for thousands of hospital inmates, and at the same time found employment for professional musicians who were suffering from causes of the war.

For the year ended August 1918, there was a still further extension of the work of the Lady Mayoress's Committee, and among the most valuable of the services rendered was the supplying of authentic information to the relatives of prisoners of war. The assistance which was given almost daily to numerous anxious inquiries was gratefully acknowledged. During that year 26,472 garments were made, and the Bandages Section, with the help of the outlying working parties, produced 44,984 articles. The War Hospital Supply Depôt, under the able direction of Mrs. A. R. Bingham, the honorary organising secretary, sent out about 131,130 articles. After July of the same year the depôt was recognised as an independent organisation. In the same period over 300 concerts were given, and nearly £900 expended in fees for professional artists, fares, transport and other incidentals.

Brief as is the foregoing summary of the Committee's activities, the remarkable figures recorded will indicate the untiring devotion of the enthusiastic and patriotic women who threw the whole of their energies into the work. Such results could only have been achieved by close and whole-hearted co-operation, and it is only right to acknowledge the services unsparingly given by Mrs. Charles Lupton, the honorary secretary of the Committee during the earlier period, and to mention the splendid work performed in special departments by Mrs. Powell Williams, Mrs. Breach and Mrs. Bingham. Mrs. Powell Williams, who had charge of the Bandages Section, was in constant attendance at the workroom in Park Row throughout the war, not missing a single day, and under her direction 200,000 dressings were provided for the wounded. In recognition of her powers of organisation and devotion to duty, the many voluntary workers whom she had supervised made a suitable presentation to her when the Committee's work finished in May, 1919.

In addition to the parcels of clothing, cigarettes and comforts of every kind which were sent for distribution among the men at the Front and British prisoners of war, a great deal of work, as will be seen presently, was done in the city for the benefit of men arriving in Leeds, or passing through on leave. A canteen in the London and North Eastern Station, maintained by the Women's Temperance Association, was of the greatest assistance to men who were stranded in the city for a few hours between trains, a day and night service meeting all necessary needs. In Albion Street, the Y.M.C.A. managed a club and canteen, and many voluntary helpers made the centre a popular rallying point for soldiers or sailors who found themselves in Leeds for the time being. In other directions, notably in promoting economy and saving, the Yorkshire Ladies' Council of Education and the Charity Organisation Society conducted successful campaigns ; and the Y.W.C.A. lent useful assistance, apart from their efforts in getting young women to join the Women's Army Auxiliary Corps and the Land Army, or to undertake other strenuous forms of war work.

THE HOSPITABLE Y.M.C.A.

The sign of the Red Triangle is a constant reminder of the good work done by the Y.M.C.A. for the welfare of the Forces, whether in camp, on leave, or in the fighting line.

The Committee of the Leeds Branch embraced the earliest opportunity of rendering service. Up to the end of June 1915, the institution in Albion Place supplied home comforts to all men seeking refuge when passing through the city, but by that time the accommodation was found inadequate. Accordingly the Leeds clothiers provided a hut at Beckett's Park Hospital, and the Y.M.C.A. Committee not only supplemented that effort by an extension but, in December 1915, opened premises in Albion Street which were especially serviceable to men arriving at the railway stations who required a night's lodging, or a few hours' rest, recreation and refreshment during the day. Here they received the personal attention of lady helpers, some 250 of whom had volunteered for the duties. There were also about fifty male helpers who kept a look-out for the visitors, met them at the trains, gave them advice or information according to their needs, and, where necessary, arranged for their conveyance by the Volunteer

Motor Service within a radius of twenty miles of the city.

The zest with which the work was done is evidenced by a record kept for five months in 1917. During that period the station patrol put in 845 attendances, met 2,401 trains, and dealt with 5,180 men of whom close on 1,600 were taken to the very hospitable canteen provided at the North Eastern Station by the local branch of the British Women's Temperance Association.

It was estimated that 2,000 sailors and soldiers visited the Albion Street Hut every twenty-four hours in 1918. The total number of visitors was well over 2,000,000. All were welcome, not only men of the Home Forces, but those from Overseas and from Belgium; indeed, so greatly was the place appreciated that the upper room reserved as sleeping quarters soon proved too restricted and the gymnasium at the Albion Place institution was therefore, in June 1917, converted into a dormitory where two thousand men every month were able to obtain a night's rest.

FLAG DAY COLLECTIONS.

The Leeds Flag Days' Committee, which started operations in July 1915, raised, in the course of three years £33,520 17s. 2d. Of this sum £15,276 1s. 11d. went to buy comforts of various kinds for Leeds Units at the Front, and the remainder was allocated to a number of local charities and war benevolent funds.

The Flag Day method was adopted because it offered exceptional opportunities to the very poor and those who felt that they could not afford to contribute to a subscription list; and, besides street collections on fixed days, arrangements were made for the distribution of collecting boxes in large works, licensed houses and other places. To a very considerable extent the street collecting was done by school children, indeed, the amount obtained through the Educational services averaged about 60 per cent. of the whole sum raised. In the counting and banking of the money the schoolmasters and the staff of the Leeds, Skyrac and Morley Savings Bank, in Bond Street, lent valuable assistance, and they were on many occasions, helped by the Tramways Committee and their counting staff—a matter of no small moment considering the weight of currency handled. The first collection, for instance, produced not less than 2 tons 5 cwts. of copper, apart from silver, notes and even gold.

The work was supervised by a committee consisting of Mr. W. P. Bowman, Mr. James Graham, Mr. J. B. Hamilton, Mr. Thomas Robinson, Dr. Sydney Rumboll, Mr. H. B. Snell, Councillor N. G. Morrison, and Mr. J. W. Jacob, with Mr. Herbert Denison and Mr. James Wardle as joint honorary secretaries and treasurers. Captain W. A. Ibbitson was also a member of the Committee at the first, but retired when he took up recruiting work. Mr. Frank Galsworthy provided office room rent free at No. 17, Wellington Street, until the premises had to be vacated to suit the convenience of the Ministry of Munitions, and then Mr. Joseph Pickersgill came to the rescue with similarly liberal provision at No. 9, Infirmary Street. Mr. James E. Bedford was the Lord Mayor at the inception of the movement, and he headed the deputation which secured the Watch Committee's approval of the scheme ; and Alderman R. A. Smithson, F.C.A., gave his services as honorary auditor of the accounts.

The selection of comforts for men at the Front was decided after inquiries from officers and men as to what articles would be most acceptable, and in the end the committee were satisfied by the letters of appreciation and thanks they received that the work had been worth undertaking. The goods were despatched in bulk, and by the aid of the military authorities, distributed among the men with their rations so that everyone knew of the distribution, and was able to claim his share.

Many and varied were the requirements, ranging from things useful or entertaining to little luxuries in the form of eatables or sweets. Here is a list of some of the principal items :—Cigarettes, 5,914,730 ; matches, 433,068 boxes ; letter pads, 139,307 ; soap, 84,956 pieces ; boot laces, 27,640 pairs ; candles, 13,092 lbs. ; sardines, 37,374 tins ; biscuits, 7,028 lbs. ; Yorkshire parkin, 9,538 lbs. ; chocolate, 3,860 lbs. ; mint humbugs, 10,115 lbs. ; other sweets, 16,517 lbs. ; apples, 21,168 lbs. ; Yorkshire Relish, 100,516 bottles.

The objects to which other funds were devoted included the following, the amounts received being net proceeds :—

	£		£
Leeds Children's Charities	2,280	British Red Cross	1,283
British Prisoners of War	2,080	Y.M.C.A. War Work	1,123
Sailors and Minesweepers	1,881	Blinded Soldiers and Sailors	956
Soldiers and Sailors	1,602	Roumanian Relief	908
Russian Wounded	1,588	Italian Relief	714
Serbian Relief	1,345		

WOMEN'S WAR EMPLOYMENT COMMITTEE.

In the latter part of 1915, a Women's War Employment Committee was formed under the chairmanship of the Lord Mayor (then Mr. Charles Lupton), the members being Mrs. Kitson Clark, Miss Beatrice Kitson, Mrs. Grosvenor Talbot, Miss I. O. Ford, Mrs. Butler, Miss Holmes, Mrs. Arnott, Mrs. Cohen, Mr. James Graham, Mr. J. A. Mackay, Mr. Henry Barran, Mr. Frank Chadwick, Mr. J. R. Cross, Mr. Sykes, Mr. F. Fountain and Mr. Owen Connellan. Officials from the Home Office and Ministry of Labour were in attendance at all meetings, and efforts were made to secure the substitution of female for male labour in trades and industries where the enlistment of men had depleted the staffs. To this end conferences were held from time to time both in 1916 and in 1917 (when Mr. E. G. Arnold was Lord Mayor and Chairman of the Committee). Also a mass meeting was held in the Town Hall and an appeal made to the women of Leeds to enrol for war work, the late Sir John McLaren presiding. The two main industries dealt with were dyeing and finishing, and the wholesale bakeries.

Later on, the question of providing a recreation club for the workers (particularly the munition workers) engaged the attention of the committee, and at the end of 1917 when Mr. Frank Gott, as Lord Mayor, became chairman, both he and Mrs. Gott threw themselves whole-heartedly into the scheme. Eventually it was decided to open a mixed club. Then came the question of funds. At a meeting of business men Mr. Gott headed the list with £100 ; Mrs. Kitson Clark gave another £100, and all the large and many small firms contributed, some giving an amount to cover all their workers at a given sum per head (*e.g.*, a firm employing 1,000 workers gave at the rate of 1/- per head). In the raising of funds, as well as in visiting factories, a great work was done by Mr. Gott, Mr. Henry Barran and Mr. J. A. Mackay.

Premises, however, were difficult to obtain, and after spending many days visiting apparently suitable places, it was decided to take a building in Vicar Lane. Here there was ample space for dancing, concerts, refreshments and, for those who preferred quiet, reading rooms. The committee spent many anxious hours trying to cater for all tastes and to make everything a success, and none displayed more active personal interest than Mr. and Mrs. Gott, whose thoughts were all for the workers' comfort and pleasure.

Under the name of "The Three R's" (Rest, Recreation and Refreshment), the club was opened in September 1918, by Field Marshal General Robertson, and was for many months a great success. It was only in the latter part of 1919, after the munition workers had returned to their homes, that the attendances fell off, and the work ended.

Lt.-Col. Chambers gave very valuable help after the opening. In the canteen a hot meal was provided every mid-day, besides refreshments. Baths were available for the women members. Dances and games were held most evenings in the week, and billiards could be played on three large tables. Concerts were held on Sundays, and occasionally performers from the theatres and music halls would give their services.

RELIEF OF BELGIAN REFUGEES.

The work of the Lord Mayor's Belgian Relief Committee was inaugurated at a meeting of citizens held on September 17th, 1914, when it was resolved to offer hospitality to 1,000 refugees. The response made to the appeal issued by the Committee was, however, so generous that it was possible to meet the needs of a very much greater number; and at various dates throughout the war period the Committee had the care continuously of an average of 1,550 refugees.

On the day following the formation of the Relief Committee 80 refugees arrived in the city; on October 3rd, 138, and on October 13th as many as 600, although only 180 were expected. This sudden influx made the initial work very difficult, but the crisis was surmounted. The Society of Friends, some of whose members had already arranged for private hospitality, came to the rescue by providing temporary accommodation at the Friends' Meeting House in Woodhouse Lane for 150 of the new arrivals; and further accommodation for 300 was provided at the City Art Gallery, until house room could be found. The Committee's appeals for offers of hospitality, furniture and clothing elicited a liberal response; but the work at this early stage was unexpectedly on so large a scale that the helpers were almost overwhelmed by it; and it was further complicated by the great difficulty of obtaining a satisfactory Register of all the Belgians, inasmuch as many had been invited by private persons, and some had been sent by the Catholic Women's League in London, and other organisations.

The Committee endeavoured to house every family separately, and in this effort it was greatly helped by local committees and hosts who took charge of and provided maintenance for one or more families. The total number of houses occupied was 288, and the Committee undertook the inspection and visiting of all these. In January 1915, a hostel was opened for the reception of unmarried Belgians and discharged soldiers, and this did useful work until closed in February 1919.

As a rule, where only house-room was provided, the Committee supplied the means of maintenance. The Committee was in constant touch with all occupants through visitors who made friendly inquiries, as, for instance, in reference to questions of possible employment and so forth. The majority of the exiles were of the artisan and peasant class—women and children—and until local knowledge had been obtained by them much advice and guidance was necessary. Where needs were pressing, gifts of food and clothing were made from a Store established by the Committee at No. 16, Swinegate, and utilised until April, 1916, after which date this part of the work was carried on at the premises provided by the Leeds Education Committee in Great George Street. The refugees were housed in all quarters of the city on the family plan, and wherever any dissatisfaction was apparent the visitors' call enabled it to be removed.

As regards immediate employment, workshops were fitted up in the Highways Department, Kirkstall Road, and men were employed for a few weeks in making furniture until they could get other work; an upper storey at King's Mills, Swinegate, was turned into a boot repairing factory for the repair of boots of Belgians; and the Corporation placed at the disposal of the Committee ten acres of land at Killingbeck which were cultivated on the intensive system and produced good results—the vegetables were sold to the refugees at a cheap rate. Eventually all able-bodied men, and many of the women, were employed in works in the city.

In February 1916 there were 1,600 Belgians in Leeds, of whom 219 were men, and all but a dozen were in regular employment in a variety of trades. Many families included more than one worker each in the position of drawing from £4 to £6 weekly in wages. Accordingly the calls on the local fund gradually declined until about £50 a week was being paid to soldiers' wives and dependents, and old folk unable to work. Most of the children were educated in the public elementary schools, some in the secondary schools, and all learned to speak English.

The total amount received in subscriptions by the Central Committee was £10,714 10s. 5d. This does not represent by any means the actual sums raised and expended for the Belgians, as there were 165 local Committees who for the first two or three years separately financed those in their charge. From September 1916 onwards, owing to the fact that the local funds had been expended, Government grants amounting to £11,258 4s. 6d. were received for the maintenance of the Refugees. The Fund was administered, and the work carried on by a General Committee under the chairmanship of the Lord Mayor, and by a sub-committee of the officers which sat weekly during the greater part of the war and until the summer of 1919, Mr. J. C. Jackson, Chartered Accountant, officiating as Secretary.

The General Committee comprised the following :—

> The Lord Mayor (Chairman), the Lady Mayoress, the Vicar of Leeds (Dr. Bickersteth), the Very Rev. Dean Shine, the Rev. Father Butler, the Rev. Father Vermeire, Councillor Arnott, Mr. A. B. Balfour (Belgian Consul), Mrs. Rowland Barran, Mrs. Bickersteth, Colonel Sir Edward A. Brotherton, Mrs. Currer Briggs, Councillor Owen Connellan, Mr. H. A. Crawford, Mr. J. B. Hamilton, Mr. W. Harvey, Mr. H. E. Harwood, Mr. F. M. Lupton (Vice-Chairman), Miss Mahony, Mr. A. N. Mason, Mr. T. Moore, Mr. K. Ostler, Miss Owen, Councillor Owen, Mrs. Charles Ratcliffe, Mr. J. Town, Mr. R. Valentine and Mr. H. I. Bowring (Hon. Treasurer).

The audited accounts, to the date when the fund closed in June 1920, show that £17,573 was expended in weekly allowances, apart from the cost of administration and the many incidental items such as employment, house furnishing, repairs, boots and clothing, medical attendances, funerals, railway fares, etc., all of which absorbed £4,435.

What was achieved, however, could hardly have been possible but for the generous support given by the many lady helpers—too numerous to mention individually—who worked voluntarily and devotedly at the offices and the Food and Clothing Store, and by others who, in gifts and personal service, enabled the Committee to fulfil its beneficent purpose.

About 500 Belgian families, including some 1,700 persons, were repatriated in 1919. The first party, numbering 200, left Leeds on February 12th and by the end of May the majority had departed. The last family under the care of the Central Committee left on March 31st, 1920. On January 23rd, 1919, there was an interesting ceremony at the Town Hall, when Mr. G. Van Vyve, on behalf of the Refugees as a whole, handed to the Lord Mayor (Mr. Joseph Henry) a tangible token of their gratitude for the hospitality shown by the city. It took the form of a silver tea and coffee service, for use at civic functions, suitably inscribed and engraved with the

Belgian and British national emblems and the Leeds coat of arms. The Belgians, said Mr. Van Vyve, had found that, under what might be called an apparent coldness, the English heart was the warmest, truest and most sympathetic in the world. "You should," he said, "be proud of your country; it stands higher to-day in the estimation of the nations of the world than ever before."

WORK OF THE SOCIETY OF FRIENDS.
By One of Them.

The war years opened out many fields of activity for members of the Society of Friends in Leeds, mainly in the direction of the relief of human suffering. The position of the Society at large was in accordance with their fundamental principles respecting the unity of mankind, namely that they could make no distinction between peoples—our own, allied, enemies or neutral. The demand from our own country, from the actual field of conflict, from the desolated areas of the continent and from segregations of refugees, was insistent, and a large number of Leeds Friends became actively engaged soon after the outbreak of war.

The earliest work undertaken by the Society was in relief of the sufferings of aliens in our midst—Germans, Austrians, and others—most of whom were domiciled in this country, and in a large number of cases were married to English wives, and for the most part law-abiding British citizens, becoming workless through no fault of their own and speedily reduced to penury. Headquarters of relief were opened in August 1914, in London, under the Friends' Emergency Committee, with branches in the provinces. A branch with a local committee was formed in Leeds in October, 1914, and during the first year the number of cases dealt with was about 100 representing, with wives and children, about 350 persons. These were kept in close touch with the Committee—composed mostly of ladies—by visitation, work parties and social gatherings, financial help in many cases supplementing the meagre Government allowances, British or German. During four years over £200 was thus disbursed, contributed by sympathisers in the city. The following, taken from the Leeds Committee's report, summarises the forms of practical help given :—

(1) Small supplementary grants, mainly for special purposes, such as arrears of rent, removal expenses, purchase of household articles, boot repairs, etc.

(2) Endeavours, sometimes with success, to secure release of prisoners whose *bona-fides* was unquestionable, and against whom no police objections were raised, and also to obtain situations for released men.

(3) Efforts to secure work for wives whose home circumstances permitted their taking employment.

(4) Letters written to husbands in camps informing them of visits to their families.

(5) The holding of a weekly sewing party and social gatherings, aliens' wives being invited, at which winter garments were made for the children.

The position of very many families of aliens in the country was rendered more acute owing to the internment of the bread-winners; and the mental suffering of the men interned was often very great. The Emergency Committee was permitted by the Government to extend its operations to the camps themselves, including those not for civilians only but for military prisoners. In addition to the worth of the social visits paid, valuable industrial work was organised in the camps and the necessary equipment installed, giving useful occupation to a large number of men. The good effect of this camp work upon the morale was recognised by none more than, generally speaking, the commandants and officials. The Leeds Committee, of which Mr. William Harvey was treasurer and Mr. William Whiting secretary, was associated with this work through one of their members who was a regular visitor to several camps.

The second large field of service entered upon by the Society was in the establishment of the Friends' Ambulance Unit, and many young men members, whose principles forbade their fighting, yet who were eager for some useful service for their fellows, involving hardship and danger, joined the Unit at different periods, including 24 from Leeds. Amongst these were Mr. Ernest Dodgshun, who held a position as censor, Mr. Oliver S. Hopkins, despatch rider, and Mr. Gervase L. Ford, Administrative Officer at Dunkirk. The Unit worked and staffed twelve hospitals, including Dunkirk and Ypres, 12,000 in-patients being treated at the former place, which was in continual danger from air-raids and shells. Three ambulance convoys and three trains were staffed by the Unit and worked in Belgium and Northern France, carrying nearly 800,000 cases. Civilians were innoculated against typhoid, and water purification and milk distribution were organised.

Sir George Newman, the Unit chairman, at the close of the work said that the members of the committee had without exception, steadfastly set their face against the direct military control of the Unit, and against enlistment or the bearing of arms, and he added in his address to the men:—

> "You began with 43 men, and finished with 1,800. You began with a donation of £100, and finished having received £140,000. You began having never served a wounded man, and finished having served an innumerable host of many races, men, women and children caught in the trammels of war, and in a land of darkening shadow, all in a voluntary unit, unenlisted, unarmed and unpaid."

The third big enterprise, entered upon by direct invitation of the French Government in October 1914, was the Friends' War Victims' Relief Committee, which followed the lines of the similar organisation in the Franco-Prussian war of 1870. An early pioneer for the purpose of preliminary inquiry was Mr. T. Edmund Harvey, and before many weeks were over a large staff of doctors, nurses and relief workers were occupied in the Marne battlefield attending to the pitiable condition of the peasantry, the erection of shelters and the provision of a Maternity Home. As the tide of war rolled on, this work, with the addition of agricultural help, such as the provision of seeds, farm implements and live stock, extended to other areas. Several Leeds Friends were engaged for a long time in this effort, including Mr. and Mrs. Roger Soltau ; and after the war, as is well known, the operations of the Relief Committee were extended to Germany, Austria, Russia, Poland and the Near East.

The Society of Friends in Leeds also took a prominent part in providing hospitality and relief for the Belgian refugees who began to reach our shores in ever-increasing numbers in the Autumn of 1914. Some two or three weeks before the Leeds Civic Hospitality Committee was formed, a few local Friends had taken action on their own account. Leeds, and the chief port of arrival, Folkestone, were linked up. Generous private hospitality was obtained, and in the course of a week or ten days a steady stream of refugees, almost entirely of the educated class and numbering over a hundred had reached the city. Early in October the Lord Mayor's Committee was formed and, acting in conjunction with it, the Friends' Meeting House in Woodhouse Lane was offered for the temporary use of the increasing crowds of refugees arriving in the city. On October 10th a train-load of 150 Belgians were taken from the station to the Meeting House in a fleet of private motor cars, generously lent. The incidents attending the arrival are thus described by a member of the committee :—

> " It would be ten o'clock in the dark of night before the throbbing of the first motor-car told the waiting group of helpers that their Belgian guests were arriving. A vast crowd of onlookers had for several hours gathered around the Meeting House gateway, and as motor after motor drew up at the entrance, ready hands opened the car doors, others took the various assortment of bundles which comprised the scanty luggage, and the most

fortunate of helpers received jolly little Belgian children into their arms. Before long the last party had been safely escorted up the stairs. They were all comfortably seated at tables in the upper Schoolroom, refreshed with a good supper consisting of coffee, bread and butter, cheese, and biscuits.

Then came the registering of the large company. This took place in the small Meeting House. It was a somewhat protracted proceeding as, with the help of interpreters, every man, woman and child, had to be duly registered by officials from the Lord Mayor's Committee. After this the luggage was claimed by the various families and individual members of the party, and then, about midnight, all made themselves ready for sleep. The women and children found the forms—placed in pairs, face to face, and lined with cushions, rugs and pillows, improvised for the most part out of hassocks—converted into comfortable beds on the ground floor; while the men on the shelved floors of the gallery, screened off by a canvas wall stretched from pillar to pillar, looked particularly comfortable. Sacks filled with straw made good mattresses, and there were plenty of rugs and blankets for all.

Four helpers who through the night took charge of this peaceful scene were privileged to partake of a unique experience. Imagine the situation ! The interior of the Meeting House looked immense in the dimness of the one unextinguished light, with so many little mounds of humanity dotted about in various reposeful attitudes ; and to add to the effect, the deep rhythmical breathing of 150 sleepers. It was most impressive, and brought feelings too deep for words."

The school premises were shortly afterwards furnished and thrown open as a Social Institute for the use of all Belgians located in Leeds, the small Meeting House being set apart for concerts and dramatic performances. In connection with the Lord Mayor's Committee, a house was taken and furnished by Friends, where a party of Belgians were provided with hospitality for ten months. The secretary of the Local Friends' Committee was Mr. J. J. Wood, and the treasurer Mr. Edwin Rowntree.

In September, accommodation on the Meeting House premises was offered to the St. John Ambulance Association, and a central store opened for the collection and distribution of hospital requirements. For some two years this was continued, enlisting the voluntary services, whole and part-time, of a number of young Friends.

It was not only to this country that Belgian refugees fled. In much larger numbers they flocked across the frontier into Holland where, without privacy of family life, they were massed together in large camps and wooden barracks. To relieve these terribly depressing and demoralising conditions, Friends devoted themselves, and a number from Leeds, of both sexes, gave their ready service. Huts on an extensive scale were erected, and various industries, such as brush-making, rug-making and embroidery, were initiated and social and recreative amenities set on foot. It should be added that a considerable number of the young men of the Society in Leeds who shared in the work of the Friends' Ambulance Unit, the War Victims' Relief Committee, and the Emergency Committee, were those who on conscientious grounds were allotted alternative service by the Tribunals, and made choice of one or other of these fields of work.

Photo by   *Elliott & Fry.*
JOHN GORDON, J.P.,
Chairman, Leeds Parliamentary Recruiting Committee.

Photo by   *Lafayette.*
Alderman W. E. FARR, C.B.E., J.P.,
Chairman, Leeds Parliamentary Recruiting Committee.

Photo by   *Bacon & Son.*
Sir ROBERT FOX,
Town Clerk,
Clerk to the Local Tribunal, and Secretary of the Appeal Tribunal.

Photo by   *Fielding*
Councillor OWEN CONNELLAN, J.P.,
Member of Local Tribunal.

X. ENLISTMENTS & EXEMPTIONS.

" Let our strength be the law of justice."
The Book of Wisdom.

WORK OF THE MILITARY TRIBUNALS.

FROM official records and careful estimates it is computed that Leeds sent well over 82,000 men to swell the fighting forces of the country. This figure is probably below the mark, for, in addition to those who passed through the hands of the authorities locally, or were on the rolls of the Territorial units in Leeds, many Leeds men enlisted in other centres and joined other than Yorkshire regiments.

Returns compiled by the Town Clerk (Sir Robert Fox) show the following interesting details :—

Enlistments from August 4th, 1914, to July 15th, 1915	36,000
Enlistments between July 15th and August 15th, 1915, when the National Register came into operation, together with numbers on the rolls of Territorial units, reservists (Naval and Military), also enlistments in other towns, and naval ratings not included above	11,000
Enlistments under National Regulation Acts between August, 1915, and December, 1918	35,479
	82,479

It will thus be seen that by far the greater proportion of the man power which Leeds can claim to have supplied was made up of voluntary enlistments.

The proportion compelled to serve was approximately one-sixth. About 27,000 men were dealt with by the Local Military Tribunal after the Derby Scheme was adopted, and when the Military Service Act came into operation ; and in respect of those 27,000 men there were 55,101 applications for exemption, of which 13,897 were dismissed.

THE RECRUITING EFFORT.

An earlier chapter in this book deals generally with the Recruiting Campaign which, immediately following the outbreak of war, did so much to encourage voluntary enlistments ; but, by way of supplement to what is there narrated, a brief summary of events compiled from official documents is worthy of record.

The movement set on foot by the Leeds Joint Parliamentary Recruiting Committee had its origin at a meeting of representatives of the two great political parties held at the Leeds and County Conservative Club on September 11th, 1914, when there were present Mr. John Gordon, Mr. Alfred Hobson, Alderman C. H. Wilson, Mr. Arthur Lambert, Mr. Moses Gaunt, Mr. Overend, Mr. Rowland Barran, M.P., Mr. Joseph Henry, Mr. W. E. Farr, Mr. Harold Crawford, Mr. J. W. Harland, Mr. Ernest Roscoe and Mr. Frankland. On the motion of Mr. Barran, Mr. John Gordon was voted to the chair, and arrangements were made straightway for a series of meetings in various parts of the city, the expenses to be defrayed by the two political parties in equal proportions. In the course of the next six weeks, however, the Labour Party joined the movement, and it was reported on October 30th that they had paid their share of the expenses of the opening campaign. The Labour members attending the committee meeting on October 30th were Mr. G. H. Pearson, Mr. D. B. Foster, Mr. Bert Killip and Mr. F. H. Gath.

Events now moved rapidly. A recruiting office was opened ; voluntary offers of motor cars for the conveyance of recruits were secured ; a supply of recruiting literature was obtained from London ; and the co-operation of various bodies was invited with the object of facilitating appeals to eligible young men all over the city. In December and in the early part of 1915 the committee took an active part in promoting the formation of the " Bantams " Battalion. That, however, was but one of the many efforts put forth in different directions to increase our man power. Meanwhile the committee's membership swelled, and Mr. John Gordon was succeeded in the chairmanship of Sir Rowland Barran, and he in turn succeeded by Mr. William E. Farr, who had been performing secretarial duties ; Mr. Harold A. Crawford became joint honorary secretary with Mr. A. Lambert ; and Mr. Alexander O. Joy was appointed honorary treasurer.

Until the time came when the committee took up the scheme of National Service, at least one meeting was held every month, and in the intervals members were busily engaged on propaganda work all over the city. In addition, during the last quarter of 1915, between thirty and forty meetings of the canvassing sub-committee were held and active steps taken, as recorded on an earlier page, to secure trustworthy returns of men willing to serve. The canvass arranged by the committee in November, 1915, showed that 10,675 promised to enlist. Of these, 5,655 were married men, and 5,020 single. On the other hand 14,070 gave various reasons why they should or could not enlist (9,442 married and 4,628 single). Against these figures, however, is set the record that 35,750 actually enlisted in the Derby groups, 37 per cent. of whom were single men and 63 per cent. married, while in addition 4,500 had enlisted after registration in August.

Nor did the committee's activities end here. They were merged into the work of an Advisory Committee, a body which afforded unique assistance in connection with the Derby grouping and Military Service Acts. Its efforts were a natural sequel to a conference of traders and professional men which the Recruiting Committee convened in May, 1915, when a resolution was passed urging all trades to make a special effort to so readjust their business arrangements as to liberate every possible man and keep open his place for him. It was indeed, in effect, another Military Tribunal and, as already acknowledged in these pages, relieved the official Tribunals of very much laborious enquiry, for wherever exemptions were recommended by the Advisory Committee, the Tribunals knew full well that those recommendations were the outcome of thorough investigation.

The Advisory Committee, consisting of two panels, sat four afternoons a week for two years and, on an average dealt with about eighty cases at a sitting. One panel comprised representatives of the wholesale and manufacturing trades; the other, representatives of the retail and distributive trades; and on each panel Labour had a voice. They met at the Poor Law Offices in South Parade, where the Board Room was assigned to their use by the Guardians, and here applicants attended regularly to be examined, the military representative being also present and often a solicitor on behalf of claimants for exemption. So searching was the examination that, as a rule, only doubtful cases and men who it was thought should go into the Army were required to appear before the Military Tribunal. The general public knew little of this quiet unobtrusive work at the time, but there is no doubt it gave great satisfaction, established confidence in the methods by which increased man power was secured, and helped the local war-work machine to run smoothly—such was the attention given by the members of the committee, all of whom ungrudgingly sacrificed their leisure in the cause.

The Local Tribunal.

The work of the Military Tribunal began, of course, with the special steps taken by the Government to increase our man power. On the introduction of the group system in October, 1915, Alderman Charles H. Wilson, Alderman George Ratcliffe, Councillor John Buckle, Mr. John Gordon, and Mr. F. J. Kitson were appointed as the first Local Tribunal, their duty being to decide questions which might arise with regard to " starred " men, that is those who were barred from enlistment and men whose skill and knowledge rendered them indispensable to the trades and undertakings in which they were employed. Later, the membership of the Tribunal was increased from time to time in order to cope with the situation caused by demands under the Military Service Acts, as indicated by the following table of dates :—

October 25th, 1915.—Group System introduced.

March 2nd, 1916.—Military Service Act for single men.

June 24th, 1916.—Military Service Act for married men.

July 10th, 1917.—Military Service Act to carry out mutual arrangements with allied countries as to military service obligations.

April 18th, 1918.—Military Service (No. 2) Act, extending obligation to military service to 51 years of age, and 56 years of age in specified cases.

The members of the Tribunal appointed, in addition to those whose names have already been mentioned, were :—

November 9th, 1915.—Alderman W. H. Clarke, Alderman F. Kinder, Councillor Owen Connellan, and D. B. Foster.

April 5th, 1916.—Alderman W. Penrose-Green, Alderman D. B. Wilson, Alderman Herbert Brown, Councillor G. H. Pearson, Sir George Cockburn, and Mr. T. Rushton.

August 9th, 1916.—Alderman R. Pickersgill, Alderman T. Oldroyd, Councillor T. O. Vause, Councillor A. B. Hunter, Mr. W. Cottam, and Mr. J. W. Verity.

Several changes, however, must be recorded. In April, 1916, Mr. Foster resigned and his place was taken by Councillor Escritt ; similarly in August, 1916, Alderman Midgley took the place of Alderman Kinder ; in June, 1917, Mr. R. M. Lancaster was appointed to a vacancy caused by Councillor Pearson's resignation ; and in July, 1917, Councillor Leigh in place of Alderman Clarke, who resigned.

Besides the Tribunal proper, a special tribunal had to be set up in August 1917, to deal with applications for exemption made in respect of Russian subjects in the Leeds area. Of this body, Sir George Cockburn was chairman, the other members being Councillors Escritt and Hunter, Messrs. F. J. Kitson, T. Rushton, R. M. Lancaster, N. Cohen and J. Cohen.

The total number of cases dealt with by the Leeds Tribunal was 55,101, representing 27,089 men. Of the applications for exemption 13,897 were dismissed, and in 41,204 cases exemption was granted or the case withdrawn. The periods of exemption varied from two to six months.

Appeals against the decision of the Local Tribunal were made by or on behalf of men in 4,755 cases. Of these, 3,374 appeals were dismissed and 223 were withdrawn. The appeals made by the Military Representative or the National Service representative numbered 153, of which 81 were dismissed, 14 were withdrawn and 12 not proceeded with.

Owing to the frequent revision of Government regulations, to meet the changing position, no fewer than 244 Instructions and Circulars as to procedure were issued by the Local Government Board ; and, altogether, the Tribunal, meeting in three sections, held 435 sittings between October, 1915, and the signing of the Armistice on November 11th, 1918. Mr. John Gordon presided over the First Section ; Alderman Kinder, Alderman Penrose-Green, and Alderman Ratcliffe were, in turn, chairmen of the Second Section ; and Mr. Buckle was chairman of the Third Section.

The Appeal Tribunal.

The appeals, to which reference has already been made, were heard by a Tribunal whose jurisdiction covered the whole Northern district of the West Riding ; and of the 200 sittings no fewer than 196 were held at Leeds. The members of this Appeal Tribunal (appointed in March,

1916), were Mr. Charles Lupton (Lord Mayor of Leeds), Mr. A. W. Bain, Mr. A. B. Bonwell, Major J. W. Dent, Mr. Ernest H. Foster, Alderman Frank Fountain, Mr. C. E. Mulholland, Mr. J. A. Slingsby and Mr. G. Wilson. On the death of Mr. Foster in January, 1917, Mr. J. C. Atkinson was appointed a member. Mr. W. J. Armstrong took the place of Mr. Mulholland who resigned in December, 1917, and Mr. Armstrong was succeeded on his resignation in June, 1918, by Mr. S. Lodge.

According to an official statement the appeals in this northern area of the West Riding numbered 8,403, affecting 8,101 persons, and in 2,246 cases exemption was granted. There were 6,157 cases dismissed or withdrawn. For renewal or variation of certificates 2,589 applications were received, of which 1,885 were granted and 704 refused. The Tribunal dealt with 547 applications for withdrawal of exemptions made by the National Service Representative, 397 of them being granted. In 35 cases leave was granted to appeal to the Central Tribunal, and in 18 of them the decision of the Appeal Tribunal was confirmed.

Delicate questions regarding medical re-examinations and the grading of men for military service also came within the purview of the Appeal Tribunal after November 3rd, 1917. Between December 6th, 1917, and October 24th, 1918, they received 618 applications on these points, with the result that in 259 cases permission was granted for examination by the Medical Assessors; 129 were ordered re-examination by National Service Medical Boards; 197 applications were refused, and 33 withdrawn. In 113 cases the grading was confirmed; in 101 it was reduced, and in 15 it was raised.

Sir Robert E. Fox, Town Clerk of Leeds, officiated as Clerk to the Local Tribunal and Secretary of the Appeal Tribunal, the Assistant Secretary being the late Mr. W. B. Hesling (Chief

Committee Clerk). The Assistant Clerk to the Local Tribunal was Mr. A. T. Wilson, then the Deputy-Chief Committee Clerk.

METHODS AND PROCEDURE.

The work of the Appeal Tribunal, sitting in Leeds, was conducted in two Courts. These sat on the average two days a week, and the proceedings occupied the whole of the day. The clerical and enquiry work necessitated the services of the National Service Representatives at least two more days, and their clerks every day of the week. A sitting had been fixed for November 11th, 1918, and it was with feelings of profound thankfulness that the court heard Mr. Slingsby's announcement that all applications were adjourned *sine die*. The Tribunal did not meet again.

There was happily a full spirit of camaraderie between the National Service Representatives, whether Appeal or Local, and you frequently found one of them doing duty for another, the claims of whose private business or health prevented his attendance. An honest attempt was made to treat applicants with that spirit which is the essence of English justice and to admit anything in the applicant's favour without unduly emphasising the claims of the nation.

The wonderful voluntary service of the gentlemen comprising the Tribunals must not be overlooked. Day after day they devoted hours of their time to the work, many of those sitting on the Appeal Tribunal having to travel a considerable distance from their places of residence. With exemplary patience and, on the whole, with great fairness they held the balance between the demands of war and business.

The inside working of the Tribunal was never without interest. In an average day perhaps 120 cases would be dealt with by the two Courts of the Appeal Tribunal. The court met at 11 o'clock and appellants appeared in person, frequently represented by solicitors and counsel. There were many able advocates of the men's cases and reputation. Most of these gentlemen rarely overstated a case and they were prepared with strong evidence in support of their contentions. An adjournment of one hour for lunch was made at 1 p.m. and frequently the work of the day was not concluded before six in the evening.

As regards the Local Tribunal, it should be remembered that all the cases brought before them had previously been considered by the Advisory Committee whose members were chosen from the principal industries in the city, and only where the Advisory Committee considered that no good case for exemption had been made out was it necessary for the applicants to appear before the Tribunal. The Advisory Committee proved of tremendous assistance to the Tribunals and the National Service Representatives in considering the cases of employees of large firms, and in arranging schemes with the employers whereby a certain percentage of men engaged in a particular process were released for service with the forces.

Sittings of the Local Tribunal usually commenced about four o'clock in the afternoon and frequently lasted until eight o'clock, but of course these Tribunals sat several times a week. During the intervals between the sittings a mass of detail work and correspondence fell on the National Service Representatives and their clerks, who will long be remembered with gratitude by the gentlemen they so ably assisted. The duties of clerks to the respective Tribunals were undertaken by officials from the Committee Department of the Leeds Corporation. Mr. R. G. Emsley and Mr. F. W. Gillespie, who were the first Military, or National Service, Representatives appointed for Leeds, were responsible for the settlement of the forms of notices and orders which were afterwards universally adopted, and this work of theirs rendered the later appointees' duties infinitely easier and simpler.

In the early work of the Appeal Tribunal the Government appointed as Military Representatives Captain Alexander and Captain Freedman, both barristers-at-law; and both had the voluntary help of Mr. W. E. Farr and Mr. C. Scriven, each of whom received the Order of the British Empire. Then, during the last year and a half, Mr. Farr and Mr. Scriven voluntarily performed the whole of the work. It is an interesting fact, and one not generally known, that, when early in 1918 recruiting was taken out of the hands of the War Office and a new Ministry of National Service was formed, the Military Representatives became National Service Representatives, and they and their clerks who were members of the Forces were ordered not in any circumstances to wear uniform when on duty, though they were given leave to wear it when not on duty. As a result it was no unusual thing for them to be told by disappointed applicants that they ought to be in the Army, and it was only those who were familiar with the conditions who could appreciate the joke. It should be added that all Military Representatives and clerks who were members of the Forces were unfit for foreign service.

The Appeal Tribunal were called upon to decide a great many cases of farmers and agricultural workers from the surrounding districts, and for this purpose the wide knowledge and experience of two or three of their members who were themselves directly interested in agriculture was of the greatest assistance. In addition, a representative of the Agricultural Committee was allowed to appear before the Tribunal and to express his views as to whether applicants could be spared from the land for Army service.

It is impossible to conclude this account without

paying a tribute to the extraordinary patience of Mr. Charles Lupton (Chairman of the first Court of the Appeal Tribunal) in his consideration of the cases brought before him. Nothing was too much trouble to him if it assisted in getting a true view of the facts. He was in the habit of taking extensive notes of each case and frequently surprised applicants who applied for a further extension of time by referring to some statement they had made at the previous hearing. When one remembered that he was himself a great sufferer in the loss of his son on active service, the patience and courtesy he displayed in dealing with cases where the ground of application must have appeared frivolous to him was remarkable.

LIBRARIES AND ARTS COMMITTEE.
1922-1923.

THE RIGHT HONOURABLE THE LORD MAYOR
(Alderman Frank Fountain, J.P.)

Chairman :
COUNCILLOR FRED BENTLEY.

Deputy-Chairman :
COUNCILLOR JOHN LAMBERT.

Alderman :
ROBERT PICKERSGILL, J.P.

Councillors :

LACEY BATHURST.	PERCIVAL TOOKEY LEIGH.
THOMAS HARDING CHURTON.	RICHARD LOWE.
ERIC J. CLARKE.	FRED BROWN SIMPSON.
JOHN WILLIAM DAWSON.	JOHN WORMALD.
EDWIN HAWKESWORTH.	

Officers :

City Librarian ..	.. THOMAS W. HAND, F.L.A.
Deputy Librarian	.. ROBERT McLEANNAN.

Photo by   Alderman FRANK FOUNTAIN, J.P.,   *Fielding*
Lord Mayor, 1922-1923.

PART III.
LEEDS ROLL OF HONOUR

PREFATORY NOTE.

The following list of Leeds men who were killed in action, or died as the result of service in the Great War, has been compiled by Mr. C. E. Mulholland, Secretary of the Leeds War Pensions Committee, who was formerly a member of the Leeds City Council as a representative of the Labour Party. Mr. Mulholland was assisted in his arduous task by members of the War Pension Staff who, for a considerable period, devoted nearly the whole of their spare time to the work. An enormous amount of correspondence was entailed in the effort to obtain the fullest possible information and to ensure accuracy of statement; even so, it may be found that some name has eluded investigation, so numerous were the outside Units to which Leeds men were attached, and so difficult was the work of tracing them all.

Altogether, 9,640 names are recorded, practically all having been ascertained from official sources. The recorders were also helped in their quest by paragraphs which appeared in the local Press, and by the willing co-operation of many persons possessed of authoritative information. Letters relating to a considerable number of the details in the list came from all parts of the world; there are included nearly eighty Colonials who belong to Leeds. As regards the local Territorial Units a very large proportion of the names—nearly one-third—are those of officers and men in the several Leeds battalions of the West Yorkshire Regiment. Over and over again it was found that three members of a family had made the supreme sacrifice, and there are many cases of four, and even five, of the same family whose loss is mourned.

In compiling the Roll, it has been found necessary to use abbreviations in order to save space. The following is a list :—

A.B.	..	Able Bodied Seaman.
A.F.A.	..	Australian Field Ambulance.
A.M.	..	Air Mechanic.
A.P.C.	..	Army Pay Corps.
A.P.W.O. Yorks.		Alexandra, Princess of Wales' Own.
A/Sgt.	..	Acting Sergeant.
Air Cfm.	..	Air Craftsman.
Austr. F. Ambul.		Australian Field Ambulance.
Bdr.	..	Bombardier.
B'dsm'n	..	Bandsman.
Bglr.	..	Bugler.
B.Q.M.S.	..	Battery Quarter-Master Sergeant.
C.E.R.A.	..	Chief Engine-Room Artificer.
C.Q.M.S.	..	Company Quarter-Master Sergeant.
C.S.M.	..	Company Sergeant-Major.
C/Sgt.	..	Colour Sergeant.
Can. M. Rifles		Canadian Mounted Rifles.
Ck's Mte.	..	Cook's Mate.
Clk.	..	Clerk.
Cpl.	..	Corporal.
D. a. Dis.	..	Died after Discharge.
D.C.M.	..	Distinguished Conduct Medal.
D.S.O.	..	Distinguished Service Order.
Died P.O.W.		Died Prisoner of War.
D. of W.	..	Died of Wounds.
Disp'sr	..	Dispenser.
Drmr.	..	Drummer.
Dvr.	..	Driver.
E.R.A.	..	Engine-Room Artificer.
E.R. Yeomanry		East Riding Yeomanry.
E. Kent	..	East Kent Regiment.
E. Yorks.	..	East Yorkshire Regiment.
Engr.	..	Engineer.
F. Cad.	..	Flying Cadet.
Flt./Sgt.	..	Flight-Sergeant.
Fmn.	..	Trimmer.
Gdsmn.	..	Guardsman.
Gnr.	..	Gunner.
H.A.C.	..	Honourable Artillery Company.
K.O.Y.L.I.		King's Own Yorkshire Light Infantry.
K. in A.	..	Killed in Action.
L/Bdr.	..	Lance-Bombardier.
L/Cpl.	..	Lance-Corporal.
L/S	..	Leading Seaman.
L/Sgt.	..	Lance-Sergeant.
L.Stkr.	..	Leading Stoker.
M.C.	..	Military Cross.
M.M.	..	Military Medal.
O.S.	..	Ordinary Seaman.
P.O.	..	Petty Officer.
Pnr.	..	Pioneer.
Pte.	..	Private.
Q.M.S.	..	Quarter-Master Sergeant.
R.A.M.C.	..	Royal Army Medical Corps.
R.A.O.C.	..	Royal Army Ordnance Corps.
R.A.S.C. (M.T.)		Royal Army Service Corps Motor Transport.
R.F.A.	..	Royal Field Artillery.
R.G.A.	..	Royal Garrison Artillery.
R.S.M.	..	Regimental Sergeant-Major.
Rfm.	..	Rifleman.
S.B.	..	Second Boatswain.
S/Sgt.	..	Staff-Sergeant.
S/Sgt./Mjr.	..	Staff Sergeant-Major.
S/Smith		Shoeing Smith.
Sdlr.	..	Saddler.
Sgt.	..	Sergeant.
Sgt.-M.	..	Sergeant-Major.
Shipwt.	..	Shipwright.
Sig.	..	Signaller.
Smn.	..	Seaman.
Spr.	..	Sapper.
Stkr.	..	Stoker.
Stwd.	..	Steward.
Teleg.	..	Telegraphist.
Tpr.	..	Trooper.
Trmr.	..	Trimmer.
V.C.	..	Victoria Cross.
W. Riding	..	West Riding Regiment.
W. Yorks.	..	West Yorkshire Regiment.
York & Lancs.		York & Lancaster Regiment.

Leeds Roll of Honour

" Shall I mourn for those who are not ?
Nay, while love and regret
Still linger within our souls,
They live with us yet."—Lewis Morris.

Name	Rank	No.	Regiment.	Honours	How Died
Abbishaw, Harold H.	Pte.	19147	1st Royal Scots Fusrs.	—	K. in A.
Abbott, Allen	Pte.	52164	Middlesex	—	K. in A.
Abbott, C. H.	Pte.	8/19283	Gordon Highlanders	—	K. in A.
Abbott, Charles	Rfm.	306565	2/8th W. Yorks.	—	K. in A.
Abbott, George	Pte.	353331	Gloucesters	—	K. in A.
Abbott, Harry	Pte.	27996	12th W. Yorks.	—	Missing
Abbott, Sydney C.	Sgt.	28615	York. & Lancs.	—	K. in A.
Abbott, Thomas	Pte.	4318	W. Yorks.	—	Died
Abbott, V. H. C.	Pte.	646187	29th Canadians	—	D. a. Dis.
Abbott, William	Gnr.	166559	R.G.A.	—	Died
Abe, Frank	2nd Lieut.		8th W. Yorks.	—	K. in A.
Abell, Arthur A.	Pte.	236018	9th W. Yorks.	—	K. in A.
Abrahams, Myer	Cpl.	34185	15th W. Yorks.	—	Missing
Abrahams, Sam	Pte.	25351	W. Yorks.	—	K. in A.
Ackroyd, Ernest	Pte.	7558	2nd Yorks.	—	Missing
Ackroyd, Henry	Pte.	41640	W. Yorks.	—	Died
Ackroyd, Irvine	Pte.	165218	R.A.S.C.	—	D. a. Dis.
Ackroyd, Matthews	Pte.	315644	Northumberland Fusrs.	—	K. in A.
Adams, Clement R.	Gnr.	185937	R.F.A.	—	K. in A.
Adams, Ernest V.	Pte.	201693	Seaforth Highlanders	—	K. in A.
Adams, George	Pte.	2830	10th Royal Hussars	—	K. in A.
Adams, John	Pte.	203657	R.F.A.	—	K. in A.
Adams, Wm. T. F.	A/Cpl.	245866	Royal Air Force	—	Died
Adamson, Robert	L/Cpl.	10158	2nd W. Yorks.	—	K. in A.
Adamson, Sam	Dvr.	34652	R.F.A.	—	K. in A.
Addis, John H.	Spr.	193545	Royal Engineers	—	K. in A.
Addy, Cecil	L/Cpl.	23788	2nd W. Yorks.	—	K. in A.
Addy, Frank	Pte.	34433	9th York. & Lancs.	—	K. in A.
Addy, Fred	Pte.	98551	Machine Gun Corps	—	Died
Addy, J. W.	Pnr.	117161	Royal Engineers	—	D. a. Dis.
Adgie, Cecil	Rfm.	1455	8th W. Yorks.	—	Missing
Ager, Arthur	Sgt.	7933	10th Essex	—	K. in A.
Aggas, Walter	Pte.	24196	7th Yorks.	—	D. of W.
Ainley, Harold	Pte.	24964	W. Yorks.	—	Died P.O.W.
Ainscow, Peter B.	Pte.	20641	South Lancs.	—	K. in A.
Ainsley, Donald	Pte.	12341	10th K.O.Y.L.I.	—	K. in A.
Ainsley, George	Pte.	9338	2nd York. & Lancs.	—	Missing
Ainsley, Howard L.	Pte.	267155	10th W. Yorks.	—	K. in A.
Ainsworth, Harold	L/Cpl.	91877	R.A.M.C.	—	D. a. Dis.

LEEDS ROLL OF HONOUR.

Name	Rank	No	Regiment	Honours	How Died
Ainsworth, James E.	Cpl.	654	R.A.M.C.	—	Died
Airey, James H.	Sgt.	1579	15th W. Yorks.	—	K. in A.
Airlie, James	Pte.	24436	3rd W. Yorks.	—	K. in A.
Airton, George B.	Sgt.	1343	16th W. Yorks.	—	K. in A.
Akeroyd, John Wm.	Pte.	37291	E. Yorks.	—	K. in A.
Akeroyd, Leonard	Rfm.	1568	1/8th W. Yorks.	—	K. in A.
Alcock, Arthur R.	2nd Lieut.		7th E. Yorks.	—	K. in A.
Alden, Thomas	Pte.	265883	W. Yorks.	—	K. in A.
Alderman, Percy Wm.	Pte.	55327	21st Northumberl'd Fusrs.	—	Killed
Aldersley, Ernest	Pte.	154978	Machine Gun Corps	—	Died
Alderson, Charles	Pte.	267065	W. Yorks.	—	K. in A.
Alderson, Clifford	Pte.	20209	K.O. Scottish Bordrs.	—	D. a. Dis.
Alderson, Cyril L.	Pte.	1787	15th W. Yorks.	—	Missing
Alderson, George	Rfm.	2753	1/7th W. Yorks.	—	K. in A.
Alderson, Harry	Pte.	62483	K.O.Y.L.I.	—	Died
Alderson, Henry	Pte.	34182	W. Yorks.	—	K. in A.
Alderson, Henry	Pte.	19821	13th W. Yorks.	—	D. of W.
Alderson, Horace	Gnr.	74822	R.G.A.	—	Killed
Alderson, Mark	L/Cpl.	12158	12th W. Yorks.	—	K. in A.
Alderson, William	Rfm.	4121	1/7th W. Yorks.	—	K. in A.
Aldous, Arthur	Pte.	15604	9th W. Yorks.	—	Missing
Alexander, Arthur	Pte.	13082	10th W. Yorks.	—	K. in A.
Alford, J. Ed.	Pte.	9831	3rd W. Yorks.	—	Died
Allan, Charles	Pte.	11608	10th W. Yorks.	—	K. in A.
Allan, Harold	Pte.	1570	19th W.. Yorks.	—	K. in A.
Allan, John	Pte.	634426	20th London	—	Died
Allan, William	Pte.	350426	Highland Lt. Infantry	—	K. in A.
Allanby, J. E.	Pte.	12740	10th Royal Warwick	—	K. in A.
Allanson, Chas. Wm.	Gnr.	173934	R.F.A.	—	D. of W.
Allanson, E. V.	Pte.	9651	Royal Fusiliers	—	K. in A.
Allanson, Thomas	Pte.	33384	Royal Defence Corps.	—	D. a. Dis.
Allcock, Geo. Wm.	Pte.	140200	Machine Gun Corps	—	K. in A.
Allcock, H. E.	Pte.	6774	2nd York. & Lancs.	—	K. in A.
Allcock, James	Pte.	13443	W. Yorks.	—	D. of W.
Allen, Cyril	Gnr.	128068	R.F.A.	—	K. in A.
Allen, Fred	Rfm.	1594	1/8 W. Yorks.	—	K. in A.
Allen, Harry	Pte.	55610	Northumberland Fusrs.	—	Died
Allen, James	Pte.	4986	Royal Defence Corps.	—	Died
Allen, Percy A. G.	Sgt.	775006	R.F.A.	—	K. in A.
Allen, Walter	Rfm.	305870	1/8th W. Yorks.	—	Died
Allenby, Chas. Ed.	Pte.	900	W. Yorks.	—	D. a. Dis.
Allerton, Joseph	Pte.	Ply/S/41	2nd Royal Marine L.I.	—	K. in A.
Allinson, Chas. Hbt.	C.Q.M.S.	13497	Royal Irish Fusiliers	—	K. in A.
Allinson, David	Pte.	17554	14th Coldstream Guards	—	K. in A.
Allinson, Robt. Hy.	Pte.	9873	1st W. Yorks.	—	Died
Allinson, W.	Pte.	21986	W. Yorks.	—	K. in A.
Allison, James	Pte.	7505	2nd K.O. Scottish Bordrs.	—	K. in A.

LEEDS ROLL OF HONOUR.

Name	Rank	No.	Regiment	Honours	How Died
Allison, W. Hy.	1 A/M	4947	Royal Air Force	—	K. in A.
Allman, Francis W.	A/Cpl.	263617	R.A.S.C.	—	Died
Allman, Thomas	Pte.	17935	1st W. Yorks.	—	K. in A.
Allot, Dawson	Pnr.	18617	Royal Engineers	—	Killed
Allworthy, A.	Rfm.	608012	18th London	—	Missing
Almgill, Arthur	Pte.	79836	R.A.M.C.	—	Died
Almond, Chas. A.	Pte.	55333	21st Northumberl'd Fusrs.	—	Killed
Almond, Charles	Pte.	450033	Labour Corps	—	Died
Almond, H.	Pte.	451992	Labour Corps	—	Died
Alnwick, Geo. A.	Pte.	1417	15th W. Yorks.	—	K. in A.
Alpine, Walter	Pte.	24511	W. Riding	—	K. in A.
Alston, James	Pte.	4934	W. Riding	—	Died
Althorp, Albert Ed.	L/Cpl.	15	15th W. Yorks.	—	Killed
Altoft, Fred	Pte.	307380	W. Yorks.	—	Died P.O.W.
Ambler, George	Spr.	1770	Royal Engineers	—	Died
Ambler, Geo. B.	Pte.	24694	13th Yorks.	—	Died
Ambler, Harry	Pte.	11181	19th W. Yorks.	—	Died
Ambler, Harold	Pte.	50581	10th Cheshire	—	D. of W.
Ambler, Irvine	Pte.	683	W. Yorks.	—	Died
Ambler, Joseph	Pte.	2138	21st W. Yorks.	—	K. in A.
Ambler, T. W.	L/Cpl.	S/5842	Rifle Brigade	—	K. in A.
Ambridge, Albert	Pte.	25081	1st Liverpool	—	K. in A.
Ames, Charleston	Rfm.	3090	7th W. Yorks.	—	K. in A.
Amos, Fredk...	Pte.	23892	York. & Lancs.	—	K. in A.
Andaer, Fred	L/Cpl.	25269	1st W. Yorks.	—	D. of W.
Anderson, George	Cpl.	29878	R.G.A.	—	Killed
Anderson, Harry	Pte.	41123	11th W. Yorks.	—	K. in A.
Anderson, Harry	Pte.	16332	3rd W. Yorks.	—	D. of W.
Anderson, Herbert	Dvr.	40849	Royal Engineers	—	Died
Anderson, Joe	L/Cpl.	484156	Royal Engineers	—	D. a. Dis.
Anderson, John	Pte.	4526	King's Royal Rifles	—	Died
Anderson, John	Sgt.	5771	4th W. Yorks.	—	K. in A.
Anderson, J. W.	Pte.	484283	Labour Corps	—	Died
Anderson, J. W.	Pte.	24669	Army Vetery. Corps	—	Died
Anderson, Wilfred	Pte.	38251	1st E. Yorks.	—	Killed
Anderson, William	Rfm.	266429	W. Yorks.	—	K. in A.
Andrew, Harry	Spr.	521955	Royal Engineers	—	K. in A.
Andrews, Alfred	Sgt.	19989	3rd Dragoon Guards	—	K. in A.
Andrews, J.	Rfm.	9980	Irish Rifles	—	Died
Angue, John Ed.	2A/M	47406	Royal Air Force	—	Died
Annal, Richard	Pte.	42659	4th South Staffs.	—	Died
Annall, Robert	L/Sgt.	3787	2nd W. Yorks.	—	D. a. Dis.
Annenberg, Israel	Pte.	41506	17th W. Yorks.	—	D. of W.
Ansell, Arthur R.	Rfm.	307044	1/7th W. Yorks.	—	D. a. Dis.
Anson, Herbert	Gnr.	348598	R.G.A.	—	K. in A.
Appleby, George	Pte.	20726	16th Cheshire	—	D. of W.
Appleby, H.	Pte.	7236	1st W. Yorks.	—	K. in A.

LEEDS ROLL OF HONOUR.

Name	Rank	No.	Regiment	Honours	How Died
Applegarth, Thos. F.	2nd Lieut.		6th Durham Lt. Inftry.	—	K. in A.
Appleton, Albert	Rfm.	2666	1/7 W. Yorks.	—	K. in A.
Appleton, Harry	Pte.	31171	1st E. Yorks.	—	Missing
Appleyard, Arthur	Gnr.	146747	R.G.A.	—	K. in A.
Appleyard, Clifford E.	Bmbr.	775885	R.F.A.	—	D. of W.
Appleyard, Fred	Rfm.	305138	2/8 W. Yorks.	—	K. in A.
Appleyard, Geo. Hy.	Pte.	22300	2/6 Royal Sussex	—	Died
Appleyard, Harry	Pte.	26291	Durham Light Infantry	—	Died
Appleyard, Harry	L/Cpl.	1564	1/8th W. Yorks.	—	K. in A.
Appleyard, Herbert	Pte.	52207	Lincoln	—	K. in A.
Appleyard, Hilton	A.B.	J/63202	H.M.S. " Hindustan "	—	K. in A.
Appleyard, James	Pte.	35009	E. Yorks.	—	K. in A.
Appleyard, Jas. A.	Pte.	39273	W. Yorks.	—	Died
Appleyard, John Wm.	Pte.	40248	1/5th W. Yorks.	—	Died P.O.W.
Appleyard, Percy	Cpl.	38289	Yorks. & Lancs.	—	K. in A.
Arch, Henry	Pte.	29030	E. Yorks.	—	K. in A.
Archer, Albert	Pte.	17899	Hussars	—	K. in A.
Archer, Alfred	Pte.	21028	K.O.Y.L.I.	—	K. in A.
Archer, Ben	Sgt.	1605	2/8th W. Yorks.	—	K. in A.
Archer, Cliff. O.	Pte.	66955	R.A.M.C.	—	Died
Archer, Dick	Pte.	43350	Lincoln	—	K. in A.
Archer, George	Dvr.	95970	R.F.A.	—	Died
Archer, Jas. Wm.	Pte.	43426	2nd W. Yorks.	—	Missing
Archer, John B.	Pte.	15676	9th W. Yorks.	—	K. in A.
Archer, Samuel	Pte.	268398	1/6th W. Riding	—	K. in A.
Armatage, Walter	Pte.	1647	15th W. Yorks.	—	K. in A.
Armin, Stanley G.	Pte.	14663	14th T. Res.	—	Died
Armistead, Arthur	Rfm.	4583	3/7th W. Yorks.	—	K. in A.
Armistead, Wm. H.	Pte.	55	21st W. Yorks.	—	K. in A.
Armistead, Richard	Rfm.	2962	1/8th W. Yorks.	—	D. a. Dis.
Armitage, Albert	Pte.	32207	3rd W. Yorks.	—	K. in A.
Armitage, Alec.	Gnr.	152294	R.F.A.	—	K. in A.
Armitage, Chas. Wm.	Cpl.T/252573		R.A.S.C.	—	Died
Armitage, Clarence	Pte.T/389768		R.A.S.C.	—	Died
Armitage, Edward	Pte.	17408	E. Yorks.	—	K. in A.
Armitage, Ernest G.	2nd Lieut.		Royal Engineers	—	K. in A.
Armitage, Fred	Pte.	525649	Labour Corps	—	Died
Armitage, George	Pte.	10331	9th W. Yorks.	—	K. in A.
Armitage, George	Pte.	14762	K.O.Y.L.I.	—	K. in A.
Armitage, George	Cpl.	28779	15th W. Yorks.	—	K. in A.
Armitage, Geo. H.	L/Cpl.	39483	4th W. Yorks.	—	K. in A.
Armitage, Joseph	Pte.	15240	W. Riding	—	K. in A.
Armitage, John Hy.	R.S.M.	5245	9th Northumb'l'd Fusrs.	M.C.	D. of W.
Armitage, John	Pte.	106523	Royal Fusiliers	—	D. a. Dis.
Armitage, Robert	Pte.	779	17th W. Yorks.	—	K. in A.
Armstrong, Frank	Pte.	32194	8th E. Lancs.	—	K. in A.
Armstrong, J. H.	Pte.	122298	Machine Gun Corps	—	K. in A.

LEEDS ROLL OF HONOUR.

Name	Rank	No.	Regiment	Honours	How Died
Armstrong, Thos. A.	Cpl.	10864	King's Royal Rifle Cps.	—	Missing
Arnold, A. C.	Cpl.	1913	1/8th W. Yorks.	—	D. of W.
Arnold, Chas...	A/B	J/20511	Royal Navy	—	D. a. Dis.
Arnold, George	Pte.	15843	11th W. Yorks.	—	K. in A.
Arnold, George	Pte.	13454	9th W. Riding..	—	K. in A.
Arnold, Joseph	2nd Lieut.		1/5th Manchester	—	K. in A.
Arnold, T. R...	L/Cpl.	22726	93rd Machine Gun Cps.	—	D. of W.
Artis, Walter	Pte.	31132	E. Yorks.	—	K. in A.
Arundel, Percy	Pte.	37527	W. Yorks.	—	D. of W.
Asche, Tom B.	Pte.	15676	9th W. Yorks.	—	Missing
Ash, Leonard	L/Sgt.	1642	3rd Dragoon Guards	—	K. in A.
Ashby, J. T. ..	Pte.	6213	W. Riding	—	Missing
Ashby, Percy	L/Cpl.	6151	King's Royal Rifle Cps.	—	Missing
Ashby, Sydney	O.S.	J/19260	H.M.S. " Formidable "	—	K. in A.
Ashby, Thomas	Rfm.	3605	1/7th W. Yorks.	—	K. in A.
Ashcroft, Chas.	Pte.	325828	9th Royal Scots Fusrs.	—	Missing
Ashcroft, Chas.	Pte.	5170	Border Regiment	—	D. a. Dis.
Asher, Hyman	Pte.	301392	Royal Scots Fusiliers ..	—	Died.
Ashforth, Fred V.	C.Q.M.S.	305742	8th W. Yorks.	—	K. in A.
Ashmell, Arthur E.	L/Cpl.	24537	W. Yorks.	—	K. in A.
Ashmell, John F.	Gnr.	72988	R.F.A. ..	—	Died
Ashton, H. V.	Cpl.	12739	Royal Warwicks	—˙	Died
Ashton, Harry	Rfm.	14910	8th W. Yorks.	—	K. in A.
Ashton, Wm. F.	L/Cpl.	15949	9th W. Yorks.	—	K. in A.
Ashwell, Arthur	L/Cpl.	24537	W. Yorks.	—	Died
Ashworth, Herbert	Pte.	1313	15th W. Yorks.	—	Missing
Ashworth, Thos. J.	L/Cpl.	2041	W. Yorks.	—	K. in A.
Ashworth, Walter	L/Cpl.	1379	17th W. Yorks.	—	K. in A.
Askam, William	Sgt.	266039	W. Yorks.	—	D. a. Dis.
Askam, Wm. H.	Spr.	252009	Royal Engineers	—	Died
Aspin, Benj. ..	Pte.	700247	Labour Corps ..	—	D. a. Dis.
Aspinall, Ernest	Pte.	40752	12th Suffolk	—	K. in A.
Aspinall, Harold J.	Pte.	670	21st W. Yorks.	—	D. of W.
Aspinall, Herbert R.	Pte.	55329	21st Northumberl'd Fusrs.	—	K. in A.
Aspinall, John F.	Pte.	34	15th W. Yorks.	—	K. in A.
Asquith, Jas. T.	Pte.	202400	2/5th Royal Warwicks	—	Died
Asquith, Walter	A.B.	77	Royal Naval Division	—	D. a. Dis.
Atack, G. E. ..	Sgt.	202139	7th W. Yorks.	—	D. a. Dis.
Atack, Harry	Pte.	29379	R.A.M.C.	—	Died
Atha, Albert ..	Pte.	13606	8th K.O.Y.L.I.	—	K. in A.
Atha, Charles..	Pte.	24484	1/6th W. Riding	—	K. in A.
Atha, James ..	L/Cpl.		11th W. Yorks.	—	K. in A.
Atha, John	Pte.	37315	11th W. Yorks.	—	K. in A.
Atha, Walter			1/7th W. Yorks.	—	D. of W.
Atkin, George	Rfm.	8242	7th W. Yorks.	—	D. of W.
Atkin, Tom	Pte.	25457	W. Yorks.	—	K. in A.
Atkins, George	Pte.	33117	Lincoln	—	Died

LEEDS ROLL OF HONOUR.

Name	Rank	No.	Regiment	Honours	How Died
Atkinson, Albert	Gnr.	58284	R.G.A.	—	D. of W.
Atkinson, Albert	Pte.	1807	15th W. Yorks.	—	K. in A.
Atkinson, Albert W.	Pte.	82080	20th Durham Lt. Infty.	—	K. in A.
Atkinson, Alfred	Pte.	37975	10th W. Yorks.	—	Died
Atkinson, Chas. H.	Pte.	260036	1/6th W. Yorks.	—	K. in A.
Atkinson, E.	Pte.	42605	K.O.Y.L.I.	—	Missing
Atkinson, E. D.	Pte.	1652	15th W. Yorks.	—	Died
Atkinson, Eric	Rfm.	305207	2/8th W. Yorks.	—	K. in A.
Atkinson, Ernest	L/Cpl.	37722	2/6th W. Yorks.	—	K. in A.
Atkinson, F.	Pte.	34270	Royal Lancs.	—	K. in A.
Atkinson, Frank	Pte.	19091	E. Yorks.	—	K. in A.
Atkinson, Fred	Pte.	62353	R.A.M.C.	—	Died
Atkinson, Fred	Pte.	8847	2nd Border	—	K. in A.
Atkinson, Fredk.	L/Cpl.	7505	Yorks.	—	Died
Atkinson, Fred	Pte.	266600	W. Yorks.	—	K. in A.
Atkinson, Fredk. Wm.	Pte.	376385	Durham Light Infantry	—	K. in A.
Atkinson, George	Pte.	25147	W. Yorks.	—	K. in A.
Atkinson, George	L/Cpl.	306399	2/8th W. Yorks.	—	K. in A.
Atkinson, Geo. F.	L/Cpl.	7505	2nd W. Yorks.	—	K. in A.
Atkinson, Geo. M.	Sgt.	27206	Royal Engineers	M.M.	K. in A.
Atkinson, Harry	A/Cpl.	2968	8th Northumberl'd Fusrs.	—	K. in A.
Atkinson, J: W.	Pte.	14	17th W. Yorks.	—	K. in A.
Atkinson, John	Pte.	47992	16th Northumberl'd Fusrs.	—	K. in A.
Atkinson, John C.	Pte.	8050	17th Manchester	—	K. in A.
Atkinson, John W.	Pte.	868	5th W. Yorks.	—	Died
Atkinson, Jos. J.	Pte.	52355	N. Staffs.	—	Killed
Atkinson, Marshall	Spr.	155089	Royal Engineers	—	Died
Atkinson, Paul	Pte.	41837	Northumberland Fusrs.	—	K. in A.
Atkinson, Robert J.	L/Cpl.	28802	14th W. Yorks.	—	K. in A.
Atkinson, Sam G.	Pte.	401041	R.A.M.C.	—	Died
Atkinson, Sam S.	L/Cpl.	9642	10th W. Yorks.	—	K. in A.
Atkinson, Stanley	Pte.	38831	16th W. Yorks.	—	K. in A.
Atkinson, T.	Pte.	7505	W. Yorks.	—	K. in A.
Atkinson, T.	Pte.	12975	3rd W. Yorks.	—	K. in A.
Atkinson, T. P.	Pte.	195681	Labour Corps	—	Died
Atkinson, Thos.	Pte.	25535	W. Riding	—	K. in A.
Atkinson, Tom	Gnr.	152814	R.F.A.	—	Killed
Atkinson, Tom	Dvr.	169314	R.F.A.	—	K. in A.
Atkinson, W. E.	Pte.	41051	7th Leicester	—	K. in A.
Atkinson, Walter	L/Cpl.	266962	2/5th W. Yorks.	—	K. in A.
Atkinson, Wm.	Pte.	12599	10th W. Yorks.	—	Died
Atkinson, Wm. A.	Pte.	26286	15th W. Yorks.	—	K. in A.
Attwood, Albert	Pte.	24486	1st Yorks.	—	K. in A.
Audaer, Ernest C.	2nd Lieut.		15th Lancs. Fusiliers	—	Missing
Ault, Wm.	L/Cpl.	9931	Yorks. & Lancs.	—	Killed
Austen, Wm.	Pte.	10756	K.O.Y.L.I.	—	Died P.O.W.
Austin, Frank	Cpl.	2163	Household Cavalry	—	K. in A.

LEEDS ROLL OF HONOUR.

Name	Rank	No.	Regiment	Honours	How Died
Austwick, Henry	L/Cpl.	2390	King's Royal Rifle Cps.	—	K. in A.
Auty, Herbert	Pte.	11514	Liverpool	—	Killed
Auty, Stanley	L/Cpl.	480126	Royal Engineers	—	K. in A.
Averback, Israel	Spr.	476540	Royal Engineers	—	K. in A.
Avery, Chas.	Gdsmn.	6298	Scots Guards	—	D. of W.
Avery, Walter	Pte.	21699	K.O. Scottish Bordrs.	—	K. in A.
Aveyard, Jesse	L/Cpl.	6008	2nd W. Yorks.	—	K. in A.
Ayres, Alb. A.	Sgt.	5115	R.A.S.C.	—	Died
Babb, R. N.	2nd Lieut.		W. Riding	—	D. of W.
Backhouse, Clarence	L/Cpl.	17881	York. & Lancs.	—	K. in A.
Backhouse, George	Pte.	6662	W. Riding	—	K. in A.
Backhouse, Isaac	Pte.	7475	E. Yorks.	—	K. in A.
Backhouse, John R.	E.R.A.	33124	H.M.S. "Tiger"	—	Died
Bacon, Harold	S/Sgt.	128153	15th London	—	Missing
Bacon, John	Pte.	25589	K.O.Y.L.I.	—	K. in A.
Baddon, W.			Machine Gun Corps	—	
Baggins, R.	Pte.	8252	South Wales Borderers	—	K. in A.
Bagnall, Samuel	Pte.	9632	19th Yorks.	—	K. in A.
Bagshaw, Albert	Pte.	76299	Durham Light Infty.	—	K. in A.
Bagshaw, Geo. H.	Pte.	33049	W. Riding	—	D. of W.
Bailes, Clifford	Pte.	26634	K.O.Y.L.I.	—	K. in A.
Bailes, Eric	Gdsmn.	19044	Coldstream Guards	—	K. in A.
Bailey, Arthur	Rfm.	307087	1/8th W. Yorks.	—	Missing
Bailey, Arthur	Pte.	8911	2nd W. Yorks.	—	K. in A.
Bailey, Ernest	Dvr.	19380	R.F.A.	—	K. in A.
Bailey, Fredk. E.	Pte.	41799	21st W. Yorks.	—	Died
Bailey, Fredk. M.	Gdsmn.	7325	1st Scots Guards	—	Missing
Bailey, Geo. W.	Pte.	2662	3rd York. & Lancs.	—	K. in A.
Bailey, Hampton	Pte.	124657	Machine Gun Corps	—	Died
Bailey, Horace	Pte.	9163	2nd W. Yorks.	—	K. in A.
Bailey, Herbert	Pte.	475008	Canadian Exp. Force	—	Died
Bailey, Percy V.	Pte.	252483	Manchester	—	Died
Bailey, Stanley	L/Cpl.	33188	1/8th W. Yorks.	—	K. in A.
Bailey, Thos.	Pte.	46128	Yorks.	—	K. in A.
Baines, F. O.	Pte.	40695	K.O.Y.L.I.	—	K. in A.
Baines, Harry	Pte.	71	11th E. Yorks.	—	Died
Baines, Jas.	Pte.	25242	Royal Defence Corps.	—	K. in A.
Baines, M.	Pte.	1387	17th W. Yorks.	—	Died
Baines, Selwyn	Pte.	25574	6th K.O.Y.L.I.	—	K. in A.
Baines, Wm.	Rfm.	266310	2/7th W. Yorks.	—	Died
Baines, Wm.	Rfm.	3707	7th W. Yorks.	—	Died
Bairstow, Thos. H.	Spr.	398843	Royal Engineers	—	Died
Baker, A.	Pte.	201471	1/4th Seaforth Highdrs.	M.M.	K. in A.
Baker, Albert	Pte.	47665	W. Yorks.	—	K. in A.
Baker, Fredk.	Rfm.	4763	King's Royal Rifle Cps.	—	K. in A.
Baker, George	Rfm.	12621	Rifle Brigade	—	K. in A.

LEEDS ROLL OF HONOUR.

Name	Rank	No.	Regiment	Honours	How Died
Baker, Geo. W.	Pte.	53656	W. Yorks.	—	Missing
Baker, John	Pte.	12783	15th W. Yorks.	—	Died
Baker, John W.	Dvr.	96614	R.F.A.	—	D. of W.
Baker, N.	Rfm.	276228	2/7th W. Yorks.	—	K. in A.
Baker, R. W.	Pte.	46996	7th Leicester	—	K. in A.
Baker, Thos.	Pte.	51984	11th E. Yorks.	—	K. in A.
Baker, W.	Pte.	15896	11th W. Yorks.	—	Missing
Balderston, Roy	Pte.	32837	1st Welsh	—	K. in A.
Baldwin, Chas.	Pte.	61588	9th W. Yorks.	—	K. in A.
Baldwin, Clifford	Sgt.	1347	8th W. Yorks.	—	K. in A.
Baldwin, H.	Pte.	105144	5th Canadians	—	K. in A.
Baldwin, J.	Spr.	83845	Royal Engineers	—	Died
Baldwin, Jos. W.	Cpl.	18772	W. Yorks.	—	Died
Baldwin, Walter	Dvr.	2751	1/1 W. Riding R.F.A.	—	D. of W.
Baldwin, Wm.	Pte.	1523	W. Yorks.	—	K. in A.
Baldwin, Wm.	Pte.	7897	1st W. Yorks.	—	Died P.O.W.
Baldwinson, Arthur	Pte.	15115	9th W. Riding	—	Missing
Baldwinson, Harry	Pte.	25311	Machine Gun Corps	—	K. in A.
Baldwinson, J.	Sgt.		Machine Gun Corps	—	
Baldwinson, John A.H.	Pte.	242422	2/6th W. Yorks.	—	K. in A.
Baldwinson, Tom	Cpl.	598	17th Northumb'l'd Fusrs.	—	K. in A.
Ball, Edward	Rfm.	307057	2/8th W. Yorks.	—	K. in A.
Ball, Enoch	Pte.	19477	W. Yorks.	—	Died
Ball, Fred	Rfm.	59119	8th W. Yorks.	—	K. in A.
Ball, Geo.	Stkr.	19982	H.M.S. " Invincible "	—	Died
Ball, John W.	Spr.	98487	Royal Engineers	—	Drowned
Ball, Joseph	Pte.	5136	Northumberland Fusrs.	—	K. in A.
Ball, Sydney		1427	10th W. Yorks.	—	K. in A.
Ballantine, Geo. N.	Pte.	1491	6th Manchester	—	Missing
Balme, Edward	Spr.	2005	Royal Engineers	—	Died
Balmforth, Christian	Pte.	35013	10th E. Yorks.	—	Missing
Balmforth, Joseph	Pte.	13619	K.O.Y.L.I.	—	K. in A.
Balmforth, S. R.	Pte.	42157	1st Royal Irish Fusrs.	—	K. in A.
Balmforth, Thos.	L/Cpl.	202927	1/5th W. Yorks.	—	K. in A.
Bambrook, Wilfred	L/Cpl.	1974	1/7th W. Yorks.	—	Killed
Bamfield, Fredk.	Pte.	095687	R.A.S.C.	—	K. in A.
Bamford, E. S.	Dvr.	252501	R.A.S.C.	—	Died
Banks, Arthur	L/Cpl.	6740	1st W. Yorks.	—	K. in A.
Banks, Harold B.	Pte.	62683	W. Yorks.	—	Died
Banks, John J.	Rfm.	7788	Rifle Brigade	—	D. of W.
Banks, Thos.	Cpl.	202241	Royal Welsh Fusiliers	—	K. in A.
Bannister, Chas.		150	15th W. Yorks.	—	D. of W.
Bantick, John Wm.	Pte.	4955	1/6th W. Yorks.	—	Died
Bapty, Walter	Pte.	40064	Royal Defence Corps	—	D. a. Dis.
Barber, Clifford	Rfm.	265527	1/7th W. Yorks.	—	K. in A.
Barber, Fred W.	Pte.	32533	5th Ox. & Bucks.	—	Killed
Barber, Geo. F.	Pte.	899	Royal Marine Lt. Infty.	—	K. in A.

LEEDS ROLL OF HONOUR.

Name	Rank	No.	Regiment	Honours	How Died
Barber, John W.	Pte.	38833	2/7th Lancs. Fusiliers	—	Died
Barber, Wm.	L/Cpl.	20504	Northumberland Fusrs.	—	K. in A.
Barclay, Albert E.	Pte.	326251	Royal Scots Fusiliers	—	Died
Barclay, Arthur	Pte.	4505	W. Yorks.	—	D. of W.
Barclay, Jas. A.	Pte.	130485	R.A.S.C.	—	Died
Barclay, Wm.	Pte.	12016	Royal Irish Fusiliers	—	K. in A.
Barcroft, Jas. S.	Q.M.S.	8948	9th W. Yorks.	—	Missing
Barden, Conrad E.	Sgt.	9603	Royal W. Kent.	—	K. in A.
Bardgett, J.	Pte.	15309	11th Border	—	Missing
Bardsley, R. H.	Q.M.S.	265862	R.A.S.C.	—	D. a. Dis.
Barff, Tom	Pte.	34031	3rd W. Yorks.	—	K. in A.
Barfield, Fredk.	Pte.	29457	W. Yorks.	—	D. of W.
Bargate, John	Pte.	61590	W. Yorks.	—	K. in A.
Barkby, H. T.	Pte.	263034	1/6th W. Yorks.	—	K. in A.
Barker, A.	Pte.	38829	Somerset Lt. Infantry	—	K. in A.
Barker, Albert	Pte.	28043	11th W. Yorks.	—	K. in A.
Barker, Albert	Pte.	21737	Leicesters	—	K. in A.
Barker, Alfred	Pte.	34361	York. & Lancs.	—	Missing
Barker, Alfred	Ftr.	156664	R.F.A.	—	K. in A.
Barker, Archibald	Pte.	8503	2nd W. Yorks.	—	D. of W.
Barker, Arthur	2nd Lieut.		1/5th W. Yorks.	—	K. in A.
Barker, Arthur	Pte.	29560	1st W. Yorks.	—	Died
Barker, C. J.	Capt. & Adjut.		Royal Engineers	—	K. in A.
Barker, Ed. L.	Gnr.	74048	R.F.A.	—	K. in A.
Barker, Ernest	Pte.	266059	W. Yorks.	—	K. in A.
Barker, F.	Pte.	10710	2nd W. Riding	—	Killed
Barker, Frank	Pte.	7756	King's Royal Rifle Cps.	—	K. in A.
Barker, Fred	Pte.	18593	9th W. Yorks.	—	K. in A.
Barker, Fred C.	Pte.	37455	2/5th W. Yorks.	—	K. in A.
Barker, Fred E.	2nd Lieut.		10th W. Yorks.	—	K. in A.
Barker, Geo.	Rfm.	C/12621	King's Royal Rifle Cps.	—	K. in A.
Barker, Geo. W. J.	Pte.	13614	K.O.Y.L.I.	—	K. in A.
Barker, Harry	Pte.	40022	9th Royal Irish Fusrs.	—	K. in A.
Barker, Harry	L/Cpl.	24620	W. Yorks.	—	K. in A.
Barker, Harry	Pte.	21482	2nd Northumberl'd Fusrs.	—	K. in A.
Barker, Hedley	Pte.	54540	R.A.M.C.	—	Died
Barker, Henry	Pte.	43910	Royal Irish Fusiliers	—	K. in A.
Barker, Hy. R.	Sgt.	148061	Machine Gun Corps	—	D. of W.
Barker, Jas. W.	Pte.	34571	Loyal N. Lancs.	—	K. in A.
Barker, John	L/Cpl.	10249	2nd Yorks.	—	K. in A.
Barker, John	Pte.	57219	W. Yorks.	—	Died
Barker, John Ed.	Pte.	18989	8th K.O.Y.L.I.	—	K. in A.
Barker, John H.	Cpl.	29019	W. Yorks.	—	D. a. Dis.
Barker, R.	Pte.	266535	W. Yorks.	—	Died
Barker, R. J. E. C.	Pte.	241255	3/5th Seaforth Highdrs.	—	K. in A.
Barker, R. T.	Pte.	45704	13th Northumb'l'd Fusrs.	—	Killed
Barker, Stephen	Pte.	36600	W. Yorks.	—	D. of W.

LEEDS ROLL OF HONOUR.

Name	Rank	No.	Regiment	Honours	How Died
Barker, Sydney	Pte.	1236	15th W. Yorks.	—	Missing
Barker, Sydney	Pte.	26513	W. Yorks.	—	K. in A.
Barker, Sydney	Pte.	24410	1st W. Yorks.	—	K. in A.
Barker, W.	A/Sgt.	598	22nd Northumb'l'd Fusrs.	—	Missing
Barker, Walter	Pte.	S4/146377	R.A.S.C.	—	Died
Barlow, Ernest	Pte.	202436	Durham Light Infantry	—	Died
Barlow, F.	Pnr.	98471	Royal Engineers	—	D. a. Dis.
Barlow, R. W.	Pte.	52348	Cheshire	—	K. in A.
Barlow, Tom	Pte.	263120	Border	—	D. a. Dis.
Barmforth, Harry	Pte.	41467	17th W. Yorks.	—	K. in A.
Barnable, Ed. B.	Pte.	28041	Lincolns	—	K. in A.
Barne, Ed.	Spr.	2005	Royal Engineers	—	K. in A.
Barnes, Fred	Pte.	14191	W. Yorks.	—	Missing
Barnes, Harry	Pte.	305308	W. Yorks.	—	K. in A.
Barnes, Jackson	Rfm.	43739	1/8th W. Yorks.	—	K. in A.
Barnes, Stephen	Pte.	42116	S. Staffs.	—	K. in A.
Barnes, Wm.	Rfm.	2377	1/7th W. Yorks.	—	K. in A.
Barnes, Wm. Hy.	Pte.	2447	2/5th York. & Lancs.	—	K. in A.
Barnet, G. M.	2nd Lieut.		5th W. Riding	—	K. in A.
Barnett, Geo.	Pte.	532892	15th London	—	K. in A.
Barnett, Wm.	R.Q.M.S.	203921	2/4th Yorks.	—	K. in A.
Barnfather, Harry	Rfm.	3930	1/8th W. Yorks.	—	K. in A.
Barnfather, John	Pte.	77118	W. Yorks.	—	D. a. Dis.
Barnham, C.	Pte.	18004	W. Yorks.	—	K. in A.
Barnham, Geo.	Pte.	25548	6th K.O.Y.L.I.	—	K. in A.
Barnley, C. H. A.	Pte.	305714	1/8th W. Yorks.	—	K. in A.
Baron, John T.	Pte.	28086	Machine Gun Corps	—	Died
Baron, Walter	Pte.	253890	R.A.S.C.	—	D. of W.
Barr, F. B.	Pte.	20668	K.O. Scottish Bordrs.	—	K. in A.
Barr, Fredk. G.	Pte.	44904	2/4th K.O.Y.L.I.	—	K. in A.
Barr, Harold	Pte.	235250	10th York. & Lancs.	—	K. in A.
Barr, John Wm.	Pte.	240618	2/5th K.O.Y.L.I.	—	Died P.O.W.
Barr, John Wm.	2nd Lieut.		5th Royal Highlanders	—	K. in A.
Barraclough, Arthur	Gnr.	36048	R.F.A.	—	K. in A.
Barraclough, Edwin	L/Cpl.	16576	7th K.O.Scottish Bdrs.	—	D. of W.
Barraclough, Ellis	Pte.	18393	10th W. Yorks.	—	K. in A.
Barraclough, Geo.	Pte.	9699	E. Yorks.	—	Died
Barraclough, Harry	Pte.	80333	Machine Gun Corps	—	Died
Barraclough, Herbert	A/Sgt.	9258	1st W. Yorks.	—	Missing
Barraclough, Isaac	Bmbr.	26590	R.F.A.	—	K. in A.
Barraclough, Jas.	Sig.	6321	1st W. Yorks.	M.M.	K. in A.
Barraclough, John M.	Pte.	41957	E. Yorks.	—	K. in A.
Barraclough, Lawrence	Gdsmn.	8945	Scots Guards	—	Missing
Barraclough, Frank	Pte.	41084	8th R. Lancs.	—	K. in A.
Barran, Herbert	Gdsmn.	12620	2nd Irish Guards	—	K. in A.
Barran, M.	Pte.	202224	4th Lincolns	—	K. in A.
Barrand, Arthur	Pte.	40112	Royal Scots Fusiliers	—	K. in A.

LEEDS ROLL OF HONOUR.

Name	Rank	No.	Regiment	Honours	How Died
Barrand, Sydney	Lieut.		1st King's Royal Rifle Cps.	—	K. in A.
Barrass, Fred.	Pte.	45453	K.O.Y.L.I.	—	Died
Barrass, Geo.	Dvr.	251963	R.A.S.C.	—	K. in A.
Barrass, Jas.	Pte.	17912	3rd E. Yorks.	—	K. in A.
Barrett, Alex.	Gdsmn.	26483	1st Grenadier Guards	—	K. in A.
Barrett, C. H.	Pte.	37970	Machine Gun Corps	—	Missing
Barrett, Chas.	A.B.	R.521	Royal Naval Division	—	Killed
Barrett, Frank	Dvr.	34084	3rd W. Yorks.	—	K. in A.
Barrett, F.	Pte.	32742	1st Yorks.	—	K. in A.
Barrett, Fred	Pte.	203503	W. Yorks.	—	D. a. Dis.
Barrett, Fredk.	L/Cpl.	79	11th E. Yorks.	—	K. in A.
Barrett, Fredk.	O.S.	803	H.M.S. "Bayano"	—	Killed
Barrett, James	Pte.	440208	R.A.S.C.	—	Died
Barrett, S.	Pte.	19130	W. Yorks.	—	K. in A.
Barrett, Stephen	Rfm.	12623	King's Royal Rifle Cps.	—	K. in A.
Barrett, William	Pte.	21155	4th K.O. Scottish Bdrs.	—	K. in A.
Barrow, Edw. S.	Rfm.	49009	1/8th W. Yorks.	—	Missing
Barrow, Morris	Pte.	136	20th W. Yorks.	—	Missing
Barrow, W.	Gnr.	72911	R.G.A.	—	K. in A.
Barry, David	Pte.	4246	Royal Munster Fusiliers	—	Killed
Barry, Hy. J.	Pte.	662771	Labour Corps	—	Died
Barry, J. V.	Pte.	305517	1/6th W. Yorks.	—	Died
Barry, John E.	Pte.	23189	10th Yorks.	—	K. in A.
Barry, Philip	Cpl.	265555	1/7th W. Yorks.	—	Killed
Barry, Thos.	Pte.	72188	84th T. Res.	—	K. in A.
Barsby, Hy.	Pte.	18933	Somerset Lt. Infantry	—	K. in A.
Barthorpe, P. C.	Pte.	23224	Duke of Cornwall's L.I.	—	K. in A.
Barthram, Harold	Pte.	24059	10th W. Yorks.	—	D. of W.
Bartlam, Jas. E.	Pte.	60726	13th Northumb'ld' Fusrs.	—	K. in A.
Bartlam, Thos.	Pte.	20652	King's Shrops. Lt. Infty.	—	K. in A.
Bartle, Alfred	Rfm.	4910	2/7th W. Yorks.	—	K. in A.
Bartle, Geo. S.	Pte.	1507	Lincoln	—	Killed
Bartle, Harry S.	Pte.	47500	1st Leicester	—	K. in A.
Bartle, Jas. A.	Sgt.	7629	2nd Yorks.	—	K. in A.
Bartle, John	Pte.	95045	Royal Fusiliers	—	K. in A.
Bartle, Rowland	Rfm.	203839	2/8th W. Yorks.	—	D. of W.
Bartley, David	Pte.	18672	1st E. Yorks.	—	K. in A.
Bartley, Edward	Gnr.	785879	R.F.A.	—	D. of W.
Barton, Fred	Pte.	19382	16th W. Yorks.	—	K. in A.
Barwick, Ernest	Rfm.	266490	1/7th W. Yorks.	—	K. in A.
Barwick, Herbert	Pte.	177907	R.A.S.C.	—	Died
Bashforth, J.	L/Cpl.	52338	N. Staffs.	—	K. in A.
Baskerville, Fred	Pte.	186638	Royal Air Force	—	K. in A.
Bass, G. T.	2A/M	165985	Royal Air Force	—	Killed
Bastide, Chorley	Rfm.	3827	8th W. Yorks.	—	D. of W.
Bastin, Albert	Pte.	3/1926	York. & Lancs.	—	Died
Bastow, Chas. R.	Rfm.	5293	1/8th W. Yorks.	—	Missing

LEEDS ROLL OF HONOUR.

Name	Rank	No.	Regiment	Honours	How Died
Bastow, M. W.	L/Cpl.	2324	11th City of London	—	D. of W.
Bate, Harry	Rfm.	1656	1/7th W. Yorks.	—	D. of W.
Bateman, Fred	Gnr.	133341	R.G.A.	—	K. in A.
Bates, Geo.	Pte.	9675	3rd Cheshire	—	Missing
Bateson, E.	Pte.	2370	6th Manchester	—	Killed
Bateson, Harold	Pte.	11786	1st S. African Infantry	—	Killed
Bateson, John W.	Sgt.	21756	K.O.Y.L.I.	—	K. in A.
Bateson, Jos.	Pte.	664	21st W. Yorks.	—	Killed
Batley, Clifford	L/Cpl.	1399	15th W. Yorks.	—	Missing
Batley, Ernest	Pte.	307558	2nd W. Yorks.	—	Missing
Batley, Harold	Rfm.	268266	2/8th W. Yorks.	—	K. in A.
Battersby, Chas. H.	L/Cpl.	265211	W. Yorks.	—	K. in A.
Battersby, Percy R.	Rfm.	265572	1/7th W. Yorks.	—	K. in A.
Battle, John P.	Pte.	8557	4th W. Yorks.	—	K. in A.
Batty, Ben	Pte.	8075	W. Yorks.	—	Died.
Batty, Edgar	Pte.	33760	15th W. Yorks.	—	Missing
Batty, Ed. L.	A/Cpl.	171	19th W. Yorks.	—	K. in A.
Batty, Fred	Pte.	268430	1/6th W. Riding	—	D. of W.
Batty, Jas.	C.Q.M.S.	22225	R.A.S.C.	—	Died
Batty, Percival	Pte.	36580	11th W. Yorks.	—	K. in A.
Batty, Wm.	Pte.	S/255105	R.A.S.C.	—	K. in A.
Bawn, J. P.	Pte.	19136	Yorks.	—	Died
Baxter, Alfred	Pte.	16615	5th Manchester	—	K. in A.
Baxter, Alfred	Sgt.	6832	9th Yorks.	—	K. in A.
Baxter, Bromwell	Pte.	41941	Worcester	—	D. of W.
Baxter, Ernest	Pte.	19991	12th W. Yorks.	—	Died
Baxter, Frank M.	Gnr.	95879	R.F.A.	—	K. in A.
Baxter, Fredk.	Rfm.	306362	1/8th W. Yorks.	—	Died
Baxter, Harold	Pte.	7352	W. Yorks.	—	D. a. Dis.
Baxter, Joseph	Pte.	65071	16th Lancs. Fusiliers	—	K. in A.
Baxter, Samuel	Pte.	34363	York. & Lancs.	—	K. in A.
Baxter, Walter	Pte.	50526	Lancs. Fusiliers	—	D. of W.
Baxter, Wm. Hy.	Pte.	15871	9th W. Yorks.	—	K. in A.
Bayldon, George	Gdsmn.	6134	Scots Guards	—	D. of W.
Bayldon, Richard	Pte.	8799	2nd Northumberl'd Fusrs.	—	K. in A.
Bayliss, Wm.	Pte.	PO/19586	Royal Marine Lt. Infty.	—	K. in A.
Baynes, Brixon	Sgt.	16644	York. & Lancs.	—	Killed
Beadnell, T.	Pte.	27832	2nd W. Yorks.	—	Died P.O.W.
Beal, F.	Pte.	307707	1/6th W. Yorks.	—	K. in A.
Beal, Wm. A.	Stkr.	8664	Submarine E.3	—	Drowned
Bean, Willie	Sig.	4418	3/8th W. Yorks.	—	K. in A.
Beanland, Louice	Pte.	21236	1st W. Yorks.	—	K. in A.
Beanland, Joseph	Pte.	44923	2/4th K.O.Y.L.I.	—	K. in A.
Beard, Frank	Pte.	28943	20th Hussars	—	K. in A.
Beardsley, Isaiah	Pte.	4941	3/7th W. Riding	—	Died
Beardsley, Samuel	Rfm.	6652	1/8th W. Yorks.	—	K. in A.
Bearpark, Arthur	Sgt.	13715	10th W. Riding	—	K. in A.

LEEDS ROLL OF HONOUR.

Name	Rank	No.	Regiment	Honours	How Died
Bearup, John Wm.	B.Q.M.S.	55338	R.H.A.	—	D. of W.
Beasley, Chas. T.	Pte.	60815	25th Northumberl'd Fusrs.	—	K. in A.
Beasley, Walter	Pte.	202636	West Yorks.	—	K. in A.
Beattie, Arthur B.	Rfm.	41661	8th W. Yorks.	—	K. in A.
Beattie, Reginald	Pte.	17201	Canadian Regiment	—	K. in A.
Beaumont, Albert	Pte.		2nd W. Yorks.	—	K. in A.
Beaumont, Alfred	Pte.	31965	12th York. & Lancs.	—	K. in A.
Beaumont, Arthur	Drv.	695	R.A.S.C.	—	Died
Beaumont, Ernest	Pte.	41461	17th W. Yorks.	—	Died
Beaumont, Fred	L/Cpl.	55157	2nd Canadian Div.	—	K. in A.
Beaumont, H.	Pte.	19727	10th York. & Lancs.	—	K. in A.
Beaumont, Harry	Pte.	36705	14th Northumberl'd Fusrs.	—	K. in A.
Beaumont, Harry	Pte.	9517	2nd W. Yorks	—	D. of W.
Beaumont, John	Rfm.	306796	2/8th W. Yorks.	—	K. in A.
Beaumont, Joseph	Pte.	242190	2/5th K.O.Y.L.I.	—	K. in A.
Beaumont, L.	Cpl.	11846	8th W. Yorks	—	D. of W.
Beaumont, Samuel	Pte.	38439	7th Yorks.	—	K. in A.
Beaumont, Thos.	Pte.	114492	Machine Gun Corps	—	K. in A.
Beaumont, Wm.	Pte.	302	2nd W. Yorks.	—	Died
Beck, Amos	Pte.	37765	2nd W. Yorks.	—	Missing
Beck, Horace	L/Cpl.	36860	Durham Light Infty.	—	Died
Beckett, B.	Pte.	13022	K.O.Y.L.I.	—	D. of W.
Beckton, John	Pte.	15/1674	West Yorks.	—	K. in A.
Beckwith, Harry	Pte.	200227	1/4th K.O.Y.L.I.	—	K. in A.
Beckwith, Harry	Pte.	76339	R.A.M.C.	—	K. in A.
Beckwith, Herbert W.	Rfm.	266138	2/7th W. Yorks.	—	K. in A.
Beckwith, J. A.	Pte.	44459	13th Northumberl'd Fusrs.	—	Missing
Beckwith, James E.	L/Cpl.	3028	1/7th W. Yorks.	—	K. in A.
Beckwith, John W.	Pte.	43908	14th Durham Lt. Infty.	—	D. of W.
Beckwith, Thos.	Rfm.	1430	1/7th W. Yorks.	—	Died
Bedford, Albert E.	Pte.	41117	York. & Lancs.	—	D. a. Dis.
Bedford, Chas.	Pte.	5784	1/5th Lancs. Fusrs.	—	Died
Bedford, Chas. J.	Pte.	202870	6th Lancs. Fusrs.	—	K. in A.
Bedford, Frank	Pte.	201245	Seaforth Highlanders	—	K. in A.
Bedford, L.					K. in A.
Bedford, Percy	Pte.	279902	R.A.S.C.	—	Died
Bedford, Ralph G.	Spr.	398829	R.E.	—	K. in A.
Bedford, Robert	Gnr.	127969	R.F.A.	—	K. in A.
Bednall, John G. W.	Pte.	55069	8th N. Staffs.	—	K. in A.
Bee, Herbert	Pte.	24430	1st W. Yorks.	—	D. of W.
Beeby, Louis	Pte.	39895	W. Yorks.	—	Died
Beech, Edward	Gnr.	80687	R.G.A.	—	K. in A.
Beech, Milburn	Pte.	384791	Labour Corps	—	D. a. Dis.
Beech, Norman W.	2nd Lieut.		1/5th W. Yorks.	—	K. in A.
Beecham, Jesse	Pte.	44776	8th Royal Berks.	—	K. in A.
Beecham, Wm. Hy.	Rfm.	307474	8th W. Yorks.	—	K. in A.
Beecroft, C. B.	Gnr.	797064	R.F.A.	—	K. in A.

LEEDS ROLL OF HONOUR.

Name	Rank	No.	Regiment	Honours	How Died
Beecroft, Walter	Pte.	57400	Northumberl'd Fusrs.	—	K. in A.
Beedie, Robt. S.	Rfm.	6435	2nd King's R. Rifle Cps.	—	Missing
Beeston, Albert	Pte.	15726	W. Yorks.	—	K. in A.
Beeston, Alfred	Drv.	95988	R.F.A.	—	K. in A.
Beevers, A. A.	Pte.	28175	12th W. Yorks.	—	K. in A.
Beevers, H.	Pte.	10605	Yorks.	—	K. in A.
Bell, Albert	Pte.	24049	11th W. Yorks.	—	K. in A.
Bell, C. H.	Gnr.	219831	R.F.A.	—	K. in A.
Bell, C. S.	Pte.	36351	8th Northumberl'dFusrs.	—	K. in A.
Bell, Edgar A.	L/Cpl.	242985	1/6th South Staffs.	—	Died
Bell, Eric	Gnr.	155018	R.F.A.	—	Died
Bell, Fred	Pte.	52188	Middlesex	—	K. in A.
Bell, G. H.	Pte.	242693	4th Northumberl'dFusrs.	—	K. in A.
Bell, Harold	Pte.	267410	W. Riding	—	D. a. Dis.
Bell, Harry	Pte.	805	17th W. Yorks.	—	K. in A.
Bell, James	Pte.	269/010	1/4th W. Riding	—	K. in A.
Bell, Jim	Pte.	19536	11th W. Yorks.	—	K. in A.
Bell, Joseph	Pte.	8902	Royal Warwicks	—	Died
Bell, Joseph	Pte.	19072	Liverpool Regt.	—	K. in A.
Bell, Lionel	Pte.	24195	2nd W. Yorks.	—	K. in A.
Bell, Reginald	Pte.	22276	2nd Border	—	K. in A.
Bell, Saml.	Cpl.	9818	Royal Irish Rifles	—	K. in A.
Bell, Thos.	A/L/Cpl.	266949	1/7th W. Yorks.	—	D. a. Dis.
Bell, Thos.	Pte.	6/11749	E. Lancs.	—	D. a. Dis.
Bellamy, Raymond	Pte.	42029	13th Northumb'l'd Fusrs.	—	K. in A.
Bellerby, Albert	Pte.	5740	8th E. Yorks.	—	K. in A.
Bellerby, W. E.	Pte.	250773	20th Durham Lt. Infty.	—	K. in A.
Bellfield, Rbt.	Pte.	89419	Northumberland Fusrs.	—	D. a. Dis.
Bellhouse, Harry	Pte.	40724	Lancs. Fusiliers	—	K. in A.
Bellhouse, James	Pte.	13298	K.O.Y.L.I.	—	K. in A.
Bellwood, Arthur	Rfm.	267569	3/7th W. Yorks.	—	K. in A.
Bellwood, Edwin	Pte.	13972	Machine Gun Corps	—	K. in A.
Bellwood, Rbt. Hy.	Pte.	13029	W. Yorks.	—	K. in A.
Bellwood, Wm.	L/Cpl.	15817	W. Yorks.	—	K. in A.
Belt, Chas. D. B.	Bdr.	38550	R.H.A.	—	K. in A.
Belt, Joseph	Pte.	32605	8th York. & Lancs.	—	K. in A.
Belton, Frank	Rfm.	1590	1/8th W. Yorks.	—	Died
Belwalford, Chas. T.	Pte.	19307	Labour Corps	—	Died
Beman, Percy	Pte.	14794	Norfolk	—	Died
Bendelow, Edmond	Pte.	11701	2nd K.O. Scottish Bordrs.	—	K. in A.
Benge, K. L.	Sgt.	11541	2nd Durham Lt. Infty.	—	K. in A.
Benjamin, Harry	Pte.	12029	7th Norfolk	—	D. of W.
Benjamin, Keber	Pte.	32321	W. Yorks.	—	K. in A.
Benn, James	Pte.	29199	W. Yorks.	—	Missing
Bennett, A.	Pte.	266729	W. Yorks.	—	Died
Bennett, Albert	Pte.	11838	7th Yorks.	—	K. in A.
Bennett, Albt. Ed.	Pte.	11316	6th Yorks.	—	K. in A.

LEEDS ROLL OF HONOUR.

Name	Rank	No.	Regiment	Honours	How Died
Bennett, Arthur	O/S	12834	H.M.S. "Victory"	—	Died
Bennett, Arthur E.	Rfm.	266517	1/7th W. Yorks.	—	K. in A.
Bennett, Dan	Pte.	3/9049	3rd W. Yorks.	—	Missing
Bennett, Ernest	L/Cpl.	140902	Machine Gun Corps	—	Died
Bennett, F.	Pte.	15121	10th W. Yorks.	—	K. in A.
Bennett, H.	L/Cpl.	14989	10th W. Yorks.	—	K. in A.
Bennett, Harry	Cpl.	370001	9th Manchester	—	K. in A.
Bennett, James A.	Cpl.	4236	E. Kents	—	Died
Bennett, Sylvester	Rfm.	7395	King's Royal Rifle Cps.	—	Died
Bennett, T. W.	Pte.	18721	9th W. Yorks.	—	Died
Bennett, Wm.	Pte.	41831	Northumberland Fusrs.	—	D. a. Dis.
Bennett, Fred J.	Pte.	15/1201	W. Yorks.	—	Died
Bennett, Wm. P.	Pte.	11677	10th W. Yorks.	—	K. in A.
Bennington, John	Pte.	8670	3rd W. Yorks.	—	D. of W.
Bennison, James A.	Pte.	G/52222	Middlesex	—	Missing
Benson, Clarence	Pte.	1203	Royal Marine Lt. Infty.	—	K. in A.
Benson, Jesse	Pte.	56445	W. Yorks.	—	K. in A.
Benson, John	Pte.	4/8342	W. Yorks.	—	D. of W.
Benson, Wm.	Pte.	18156	Essex	—	K. in A.
Benstead, Thos. B.	Pte.	M/296387	R.A.S.C. (M.T.)	—	D. a. Dis.
Bent, Milner W.	Pte.	72568	W. Yorks.	—	K. in A.
Bentley, Benj.	Drv.	72090	Royal Engineers	—	K. in A.
Bentley, Chas. H.	Cpl.	3390	2/8th W. Yorks.	—	K. in A.
Bentley, Lewis	Pte.	18771	9th W. Yorks.	—	K. in A.
Bentley, Tom	Pte.	49476	2/5th W. Yorks.	—	K. in A.
Bentley, Walter	Pte.	40889	Northumberland Fusrs.	—	K. in A.
Bentley, Wm. A.	Pte.	41294	Leicester	—	K. in A.
Bentley, Wm. H.	A/Cpl.	97972	Machine Gun Corps	—	K. in A.
Benton, D. McC.	Pte.	219554	Labour Corps	—	Died
Benton, Geo. C.	Gnr.		R.F.A.	—	K. in A.
Benton, Hubert	Pte.	15804	1st W. Yorks.	—	D. of W.
Benton, John W.	2nd Lieut.		14/11th Notts. & Derby	—	K. in A.
Benton, Wm.	Pte.	41302	Leicester	—	Died
Benton, Willie	Pte.	306485	W. Yorks.	—	K. in A.
Benyon, John T.	Pte.	97262	W. Yorks.	—	Died
Bernard, Arthur	Tpr.	4875	9th Lancers	—	K. in A.
Bernasconi, James	Spr.	132108	Royal Engineers	—	K. in A.
Bernhardt, Adolph	Pte.	12830	9th Lancers	—	K. in A.
Bernstein, Jacob	Pte.	29444	10th W. Yorks.	—	K. in A.
Bernstein, Sam	Pte.	J698	39th Royal Fusiliers	—	Died
Berriff, Bruce	Sgt.	72366	Royal Engineers	—	K. in A.
Berriman, Fred	L/St.	310977	H.M.S. "Invincible"	—	Drowned
Berry, Albert	Sgt.	12710	11th W. Yorks.	—	K. in A.
Berry, Alfred	Pte.	28074	12th W. Yorks.	—	D. of W.
Berry, Frank	Pte.	6724	1st E. Yorks.	—	D. a. Dis.
Berry, H.	Pte.	200577	R.A.S.C.	—	Died
Berry, Harry	Pte.	23344	2nd W. Riding	—	K. in A.

LEEDS ROLL OF HONOUR.

Name	Rank	No.	Regiment	Honours	How Died
Berry, Harry	Cpl.	41412	W. Yorks.	—	K. in A.
Berry, Herbert	L/Cpl.	201395	3/4th Seaforth Highldrs.	—	K. in A.
Berry, J. T.	Pte.	1696	R.A.M.C.	—	K. in A.
Berry, R.	Gnr.	111980	R.F.A.	—	K. in A.
Berry, Walter	Pte.	1703	17th W. Yorks.	—	D. of W.
Berson, David	L/Cpl.	266074	2/7th W. Yorks.	—	K. in A.
Bes, Archibald	Pte.	29072	Border	—	K. in A.
Best, Albert F.	Rfm.	268885	2/6th W. Yorks.	—	K. in A.
Best, George H.	Tpr.		Yorks. Hussars	—	K. in A.
Best, Harry M.	Gnr.	775797	R.F.A.	—	K. in A.
Best, Henry	Pte.	26844	6th Yorks.	—	K. in A.
Best, John Chas.	3A/M	277546	Royal Air Force	—	D. a. Dis.
Best, T. E.	Cpl.	17/1565	15th W. Yorks.	—	Missing
Best, Thos. E.	Lieut.		8th W. Riding	—	K. in A.
Best, Wilfred R.	Lieut.		9th W. Riding	—	K. in A.
Best, Wm. W.	Pte.	14477	K.O.Y.L.I.	—	K. in A.
Bestington, Mark	Pte.	266504	9th W. Yorks.	—	K. in A.
Betteridge, J. T.	Pte.	10834	Royal Defence Corps	—	K. in A.
Betteridge, Lawrence	Pte.	28260	1st Northumberl'd Fusrs.	—	K. in A.
Bettles, Lawrence E.	Rfm.	306852	2/8th W. Yorks.	—	Died
Betts, James A.	Pte.	45447	K.O.Y.L.I.	—	Died
Betts, Samuel	Spr.	2197	Australians	—	K. in A.
Beverley, Bernard	Pte.	8497	15th W. Yorks.	—	K. in A.
Beverley, Robt.	P.O.	J15794	H.M.S. "Hampshire"	—	Drowned
Beverley, Wm.	Rfm.	2685	8th W. Yorks.	—	K. in A.
Bexon, Harry	Pte.	22361	2nd Highland Lt. Infty.	—	K. in A.
Bickerdike, A.	Pte.	14232	12th W. Yorks.	—	Missing
Bickerdyke, F.	Pte.	1018530	Canadians	—	K. in A.
Bickerdyke, Jas. R.	Pte.	34841	W. Riding	—	K. in A.
Bickerdyke, Thos.	Pte.	265308	W. Yorks.	—	Died
Bickerton, George W.	Pte.	34443	Northumberland Fusrs.	—	K. in A.
Biddle, Wm.	L/Cpl.	72217	Royal Engineers	—	Died
Biggins, Frank	Pte.	34674	W. Yorks.	—	K. in A.
Bilbrough, George	Pte.	242423	2/6th W. Yorks.	—	Missing
Bilbrough, Harry	Rfm.	306812	2/7th W. Yorks.	—	K. in A.
Billing, Chas.	Sgt.	237010	360th Res. Labour Corps.	—	D. a. Dis.
Billington, Wm.	Pte.	25088	8th K.O.Y.L.I.	—	Missing
Bills, John Thos.	Gnr.	28714	R.F.A.	—	D. of W.
Billsbury, John	Pte.	38853	1/4th Northants.	—	D. a. Dis.
Bilson, John A.	Pte.	21423	1st W. Yorks.	—	K. in A.
Biltcliffe, Joe Wm.	Pte.	27195	W. Yorks.	—	K. in A.
Bilton, George	Pte.	24004	W. Yorks.	—	K. in A.
Bilton, Parkinson	Rfm.	306017	2/8th W. Yorks.	—	K. in A.
Bilton, Stewart	Cpl.	201431	Seaforth Highlanders	—	Died
Bimrose, Alfred	Rfm.	300105	1/7th W. Yorks.	—	K. in A.
Bimrose, Chas.	2nd Lieut.		1/6th Notts. & Derbys.	M.C.	K. in A.
Binge, Thos.	Pte.	28852	E. Yorks.	—	K. in A.

LEEDS ROLL OF HONOUR.

Name	Rank	No.	Regiment	Honours	How Died
Binks, A.	Gnr.	111981	R.F.A.	—	K. in A.
Binks, Albert	Pte.	12/24	K.O.Y.L.I.	—	K. in A.
Binks, Arthur	Pte.	331104	Royal Scots Fusiliers	—	K. in A.
Binks, Frank	Sgt.	47790	Yorks.	—	Died
Binks, George	Pte.	202202	1/5th W. Yorks.	—	K. in A.
Binks, George	Pte.	307091	W. Riding	—	K. in A.
Binks, Herbert	Cpl.	139989	Machine Gun Corps	—	D. a. Dis.
Binks, Joshua	Pte.	49127	3rd Northants.	—	K. in A.
Binks, M.	Pte.	16676	2nd K.O.Y.L.I.	—	Missing
Binks, Ralph	Pte.	29313	Border	—	Died.
Binks, Robt.	Pte.	3899	2nd King's R. Rifle Cps.	D.C.M.	K. in A.
Binks, S.	Gnr.	1845	Machine Gun Corps	—	K. in A.
Binnington, Wilfred	Pte.	466	3rd Manchester	—	D. of W.
Binns, Arnold	Pte.	13109	10th W. Yorks.	—	K. in A.
Binns, Daniel	Rfm.	266586	7th W. Yorks.	—	D. a. Dis.
Binns, Edwin	Pte.	45335	Highland Lt. Infty.	—	K. in A.
Binns, Ernest	Rfm.	2845	7th W. Yorks.	—	K. in A.
Binns, Fred	Pte.	31148	E. Yorks.	—	K. in A.
Binns, George Wm.	Pte.	8121	1st W. Yorks.	—	K. in A.
Binns, John	Pte.	21545	9th W. Yorks.	—	D. of W.
Binns, John R.	Pte.	33111	18th W. Yorks.	—	Missing
Binns, Reginald	Pte.	24048	2nd Royal Scots Fusrs.	—	Missing
Binns, Thos. Hy.	Rfm.	306606	1/8th W. Yorks.	—	Died
Binns, Walter	Rfm.	305819	1/7th W. Yorks.	—	Died
Binns, Wm. B.	Pte.	38856	Yorks.	—	K. in A.
Birch, Ernest	Pte.	26395	3rd W. Yorks.	—	Died
Birch, Thos.	Pte.	209	21st W. Yorks.	—	K. in A.
Birchley, F.	Gdsmn.	12164	Grenadier Guards	—	Died
Bird, Victor	Pte.	39128	2nd W. Yorks.	—	K. in A.
Bird, Walter E. W.	Rfm.	4055	King's Royal Rifle Cps.	—	K. in A.
Birds, Fredk. A.	Gnr.	165332	R.F.A.	—	Died
Birdsall, Frank	Pte.	684195	Labour Corps	—	D. a. Dis.
Birdsall, Harry	Rfm.	1459	7th W. Yorks.	—	K. in A.
Birdsall W. A.	Spr.	197179	R.E.	—	D. a. Dis.
Birkby, Tom	Pte.	308100	Tank Corps	—	Died
Birkett, Edward	Pte.	25558	13th Yorks.	—	K. in A.
Birkett, Horace	L/S.	K/11086	Royal Navy	—	Died
Birkett, Wm. M.	L/Cpl.	40644	12th Middlesex	—	D. of W.
Birkhead, Jos.	Pte.	24202	3rd W. Yorks.	—	K. in A.
Birkin, Arthur	Pte.	11050	8th Gordon Highdrs.	—	K. in A.
Birkinshaw, John	L/Cpl.	16887	Highland Lt. Infantry	—	Died
Birkinshaw, L.	Pte.	72562	W. Yorks.	—	K. in A.
Birtley, Chas. E.	Pte.	25290	14th W. Yorks.	—	K. in A.
Birtwhistle, H.	L/Cpl.	202175	Leicester	M.M.	K. in A.
Black, Louis	Pte.	J/332	Royal Fusiliers	—	Died
Blackburn, Arthur	Pte.	77822	W. Yorks.	—	Died
Blackburn, Bertie M.	Pte.	24418	3rd W. Yorks.	—	K. in A.

LEEDS ROLL OF HONOUR.

Name	Rank	No.	Regiment	Honours	How Died
Blackburn, C.	Pte.	12105	Labour Corps	—	Died
Blackburn, C. J. C.	Capt.		1/5th W. Yorks.	—	K. in A.
Blackburn, Edward	Sgt.	34328	R.F.A.	—	D. of W.
Blackburn, Eli S.	Pte.	15711	10th York. & Lancs.	—	K. in A.
Blackburn, Ernest	Pte.	25080	9th King's R. Rifle Cps.	—	K. in A.
Blackburn, Harry	Pte.	175	Royal Scots Fusrs.	—	Died
Blackburn, Herbert	Rfm.	34009	2/7th W. Yorks.	—	K. in A.
Blackburn, H. C.	2nd Lieut.		1/7th W. Yorks.	—	Killed.
Blackburn, Jim	Pte.	170087	7th H.S. Labour Corps	—	D. a. Dis.
Blackburn, John T.	Pte.	10230	2nd W. Yorks.	—	Killed
Blackburn, Layton	L.S.	217575	Royal Navy, Sub. E.10	—	Killed
Blackburn, Leonard	Cpl.	306137	W. Yorks.	—	D. a. Dis.
Blackburn, Thos.	Rfm.	305921	2/8th W. Yorks.	—	Missing
Blackburn, Wilfred	Pte.	25443	2nd W. Yorks.	—	K. in A.
Blackburn, William	Pte.	59933	1/5th Northumb'l'd Fusrs.	—	K. in A.
Blackburn, William	Pte.	203833	7th Yorks.	—	K. in A.
Blackburn, Wm. Hy.	Rfm.	306987	8th W. Yorks.	—	K. in A.
Blacker, Edward A.	Pte.	37786	W. Yorks.	—	Died
Blackett, Alfred J.	Pte.	44743	Lincoln	—	Missing
Blackie, Wm.	Pte.	61584	Royal Defence Corps.	—	Died
Blackwell, Leonard	Pte.	42119	South Staffs.	—	D. of W.
Blagg, Wm. H.	Rfm.	63769	8th W. Yorks.	—	K. in A.
Blake, Geo. Hy.	M.B.	4794	R.A.S.C.	—	Died
Blake, J. J.	Lieut.		Royal Engineers	—	Died
Blakeborough, Ernest	Pte.	28998	2nd W. Yorks.	—	K. in A.
Blakeborough, Harry	Rfm.	306593	1/8th W. Yorks.	—	D. of W.
Blakeborough, Wm. A.	Gnr.	801894	R.F.A.	—	K. in A.
Blakeley, Herbert	Pte.	21513	W. Yorks.	—	Missing
Blaker, Albert	Pte.	3496	2nd S. Lancs.	—	K. in A.
Blaker, F.	Pte.	39865	Lancs. Fusiliers	—	Died
Blakes, Wm.	Pte.	252017	Labour Corps	—	Died
Blakey, Harry	A/Sgt.	265810	W. Yorks.	—	D. a. Dis.
Blakey, James H.	O.S.	J49849	H.M.S. "Tipperary"	—	Died
Blakey, John	Pte.	1049	Royal Marine Lt. Infty.	—	Died
Blakey, Walter	Pte.	4785	3/7th W. Riding	—	Died
Blanchard, John Wm.	Pte.	17461	9th W. Riding	—	K. in A.
Bland, Benjamin	Pte.	93	15th W. Yorks.	—	K. in A.
Bland, George	Cpl.	3412	2/5th Northumb'l'd Fusrs.	—	K. in A.
Bland, George	Sgt.	403105	R.A.M.C.	—	K. in A.
Bland, J.	Gnr.		Canadians	—	Died
Bland, P.	Pte.		Loyal North Lancs.	—	K. in A.
Bland, Thos.	L/Cpl.	12016	10th W. Yorks.	—	K. in A.
Blanshard, Ernest	L/Cpl.	242551	W. Yorks.	—	Died
Bligh, James R.	Spr.	398842	Royal Engineers	—	D. a. Dis.
Blocksidge, James	Sgr.	7112	1st W. Yorks.	—	K. in A.
Blocksidge, Thos. M.	Gnr.	84937	R.F.A.	—	Died
Bloomfield, Albert	Pte.	37680	9th K.O.Y.L.I.	—	K. in A.

LEEDS ROLL OF HONOUR.

Name	Rank	No.	Regiment	Honours	How Died
Bloomfield, Cyril	Pte.	63804	K.O.Y.L.I.	—	Died
Blore, Wm. J.	Q.M.S.	8307	6th Yorks.	—	K. in A.
Bluett, Fredk. J.	Pte.	79704	Durham Lt. Infty.	—	K. in A.
Blumson, Wm.	Sgt.	111602	Labour Corps.	—	K. in A.
Blythe, J. B.	Pte.	281744	R.A.S.C.	—	D. a. Dis.
Boal, Wm.	2nd Lieut.		Northants.	—	K. in A.
Boam, Charlie	Pte.	82647	8th York. & Lancs.	—	K. in A.
Boddy, Albert	Cpl.	12159	King's Royal Rifle Cps.	—	K. in A.
Boddy, Frank W.	Sgt.	9124	1st W. Yorks.	—	K. in A.
Boddy, George	Pte.	21721	1st K.O.Y.L.I	—	K. in A.
Boden, Wm.	Pte.	18286	W. Yorks.	—	D. of W.
Bogg, John Wm.	Pte.	21350	2nd Northumberl'd Fusrs.	—	Died
Bogg, Mark	L/Sgt.	8559	1st W. Yorks.	—	D. of W.
Boggin, Richard Wm.	Pte.	8252	South Wales Borderers	—	K. in A.
Boland, Joseph	Pte.	268437	W. Yorks.	—	K. in A.
Boland, T.	Pte.	39461	2nd W. Yorks.	—	K. in A.
Boldison, Mark	Cpl.	7524	1st W. Yorks.	—	K. in A.
Boldwinson, Hilton	Pte.	6071	2/6th W. Yorks.	—	K. in A.
Bollon, George	Pte.	204348	Norfolk	—	K. in A.
Bollon, Harry	Cpl.	775050	R.F.A.	—	D. of W.
Bolton, C. A. R.	Pte.	27566	1st Royal Irish Rifles	—	Missing
Bolton, Edward	Pte.	17429	8th Northumberl'd Fusrs.	—	D. of W.
Bolton, Fred	Ptc.	178	19th W. Yorks.	—	K. in A.
Bolton, James	Pte.	14149	W. Riding	—	K. in A.
Bolton, John H.	Cpl.	265474	W. Yorks.	—	Died
Bolton, Wm. B.	L/Cpl.	13458	W. Yorks.	—	K. in A.
Bonaquisto, Casey	Pte.	26303	Loyal N. Lancs.	—	Missing
Bond, Francis C.	Pte.	32570	8th York. & Lancs.	—	Missing
Bond, Percy G.	Pte.	159	W. Yorks.	—	K. in A.
Bond, Wm. A.	Pte.	138826	R.A.S.C.	—	Died
Bonner, Arthur J. T.	Pte.	242687	W. Yorks.	—	K. in A.
Bonner, Thos.	Pte.	17394	York. & Lancs.	—	Missing
Boocock, Clifford	Cpl.	2413	York. & Lancs.	—	D. of W.
Boocock, E.	Pte.	13102	10th W. Yorks.	—	K. in A.
Boocock, J.	Pte.	44677	4th Lancs.	—	K. in A.
Booker, Arthur	Pte.	753	17th W. Yorks.	—	K. in A.
Booker, Harry	Pte.	306675	W. Yorks.	—	Died
Booker, Harry	Pte.	24834	Northumberland Fusrs.	—	K. in A.
Boot, G. H.	Pte.	512	17th W. Yorks.	—	K. in A.
Booth, Benjamin	Pte.	25660	13th W. Yorks.	—	D. of W.
Booth, Ernest	Pte.	25146	11th K.O.Y.L.I.	—	Died
Booth, Fred	Gnr.	173884	R.F.A.	—	K. in A.
Booth, Harold	Rfm.	265215	7th W. Yorks.	—	K. in A.
Booth, Jeremiah	Pte.	81	Rifle Brigade	—	Died
Booth, John	Spr.	108898	Royal Engineers	—	Died
Booth, Louis	Pte.	41824	1st Northumberl'd Fusrs.	—	K. in A.
Booth, Sydney	Pte.	326041	15th Royal Scots Fusrs.	—	Died

LEEDS ROLL OF HONOUR.

Name	Rank	No.	Regiment	Honours	How Died
Booth, Thos.	Rfm.	266806	1/7th W. Yorks.	—	K. in A.
Booth, Walter	Sgt.	14825	10th K.O.Y.L.I.	—	D. of W.
Booth, Wilfred L.	Pte.	21698	W. Yorks.	—	K. in A.
Booth, Wm.	Pte.	106687	Notts. & Derby	—	K. in A.
Booth, Wm.	Pte.	24547	3rd W. Yorks.	—	K. in A.
Boothman, W.	Gnr.	107649	R.F.A.	—	Died
Boreham, Chas. Wm.	1stC. Stkr.		H.M.S. " Good Hope "	—	Drowned
Boshell, Harry	Pte.	40730	N. Staffs.	—	Missing
Boshell, Irwin	Rfm.	2824	1/8th W. Yorks.	—	K. in A.
Bosomworth, Hbt. R.	Rfm.	4772	2/7th W. Yorks.		
Boswell, James	Major & Q.M.		R.A.M.C.	—	Died
Bottomley, Albert	Pte.	7174	2nd Dragoon Guards	—	D. of W.
Bottomley, John C.	2nd Lieut.		1/8th W. Yorks.	—	K. in A.
Bottomley, Percy	Rfm.	4581	2/8th W. Yorks.	—	K. in A.
Bottomley, T. W.	Pte.	142715	Machine Gun Corps	—	K. in A.
Boucher, Fred	Pte.	3/9024	W. Yorks.	—	K. in A.
Boulby, Ernest	Pte.	13299	2/4th K.O.Y.L.I.	—	K. in A.
Boulby, J. O.	Spr.	95523	Royal Engineers	—	K. in A.
Boulton, Ernest	Pte.	42151	K.O.Y.L.I.	—	K. in A.
Boulton, James E.	Pte.	34973	3rd W. Yorks.	—	K. in A.
Boulton, Sam	Pte.	8081	K.O. Scottish Bordrs.	—	K. in A.
Bousfield, Ernest	Pte.	98873	Machine Gun Corps	—	Died
Bouskill, Herbert	Pte.	242813	K.O. Scottish Bordrs.	—	K. in A.
Bowe, Frank	Rfm.	266692	1/7th W. Yorks.	—	K. in A.
Bowen, Alfred	Gdsmn.	16753	3rd Scots Guards	—	Died
Bowen, Herbert Wm.	Cpl.		Australian Lt. Infty.	—	Missing
Bower, Frank B.	Cpl.	106587	Royal Engineers	—	K. in A.
Bower, Harry	Pte.	16467	W. Riding	—	K. in A.
Bower, Joseph L.	Pte.	10089	2nd Yorks.	—	K. in A.
Bowen, Leonard	Gdsmn.	21540	Grenadier Guards	—	K. in A.
Bower, Thos.	Cpl.	3057	2nd Seaforth Highdrs.	—	K. in A.
Bowerbank, John P.	Pte.	153167	R.A.M.C.	—	Died
Bowerbank, Wilfred	Pte.	37259	W. Yorks.	—	K. in A.
Bowers, Albert	Pte.	62841	R.A.M.C.	—	K. in A.
Bowers, Arthur	Rfm.	4368	1/8th W. Yorks.	—	D. of W.
Bowers, J.	Pte.	8100	Yorks.	—	K. in A.
Bowers, Jack	Pte.	13106	10th W. Yorks.	—	K. in A.
Bowes, Rbt. E.		L5306	H.M.S. " Hague "	—	K. in A.
Bowey, W. H.	Pte.	307000	W. Yorks.	—	Died
Bowick, Wm.	S.M.	2947	K.O.Y.L.I.	—	K. in A.
Bowker, Joseph	Gnr.	84878	R.F.A.	—	K. in A.
Bowker, Richard	L/Sgt.	35782	15th Durham Lt. Infty.	—	K. in A.
Bowkett, John Hy.			Aust. Imp. Force (13th M.G.C.)	—	D. of W.
Bowland, H.	Pte.	21738	1st K.O.Y.L.I.	—	K. in A.
Bowling, Norman	Pte.	3/9077	3rd W. Yorks.	—	Died
Bowman, A. E.	L/Sgt.	25957	Worcesters.	—	Died

LEEDS ROLL OF HONOUR.

Name	Rank	No.	Regiment	Honours	How Died
Bowman, Alan	Sig.	C/12022	10th King's R. Rifle Cps.	—	K. in A.
Bowman, Archie	Pte.	5616	2nd E. Yorks.	—	Missing
Bowman, Arthur	Pte.	267498	1/5th W. Yorks.	—	K. in A.
Bowman, David C.	Pte	15/76	W. Yorks.	—	K. in A.
Bowman, Ernest	Pte.	7650	9th York. & Lancs.	—	K. in A.
Bowman, Geoffrey G.	Flight-Lieut.		Royal N. Air Service	—	K. in A.
Bowman, Jas. W.	Pte.	41303	6th Leicester	—	K. in A.
Bowman, T.	Pte.	42221	2nd K.O.Y.L.I.	—	Died.
Bowman, Stanley	Rfm.	3829	1/8th West Yorks.	—	Died.
Bowman, Wm. P.	Flight-Lieut.		R.A.F.	—	K. in A.
Bowyer, George	Pte.	4/8453	W. Yorks.	—	K. in A.
Boyall, A.	Pte.	51703	20th Manchester	—	Missing
Boyce, Albert	Tpr.	2075	Royal Horse Guards	—	Died
Boyce, Henry	Pte.	25243	58th Royal Defence Cps.	—	Died
Boyd, Frank	Dvr.	5368	R.A.S.C.	—	K. in A.
Boyd, Joseph	L/Cpl.	271854	Labour Corps	—	D. of W.
Boyd, T. R.			Canadians	—	Died
Boyer, Thos. Wm.	Cpl.	16083	10th Royal Warwicks.	—	K. in A.
Boyes, Douglas	Rfm.	33487	King's Royal Rifle Corps	—	K. in A.
Boyes, Harry	Dvr.	231905	R.F.A.	—	K. in A.
Boyes, Herbert A.	2/A.M.	42524	Royal Air Force	—	Died
Boyes, Herbert A.	O.S.	140636	H.M.S. "Vanguard"	—	Died
Boyes, James A.	Cpl.	265163	W. Yorks.	—	K. in A.
Boyes, W.	Pte.	22121	W. Yorks.	—	K. in A.
Boyington, Fred	Pte.	7797	1st W. Yorks.	—	K. in A.
Boyington, George	Pte.	7554	1st W. Yorks.	—	Died
Boyle, F.	Sgt.	82793	Machine Gun Corps	—	K. in A.
Boyle, James	Pte.	13613	King's Liverpool	—	K. in A.
Boyle, Robt.	Pte.	3435	17th W. Yorks.	—	K. in A.
Boyle, Thos.	Pte.	6410	Connaught Rangers	—	Died
Boyne, Thos. I.	Rfm.	305386	8th W. Yorks.	—	D. of W.
Brabbs, Ernest	Pte.	11589	K.O.Y.L.I.	—	K. in A.
Brace, Alfred	Pte.	59661	1st Northumb'l'd Fusrs.	—	K. in A.
Brace, Henry	Pte.	39745	15th Lancs. Fusiliers	—	K. in A.
Bracewell, Richard	Bdr.	775484	R.F.A.	—	K. in A.
Bradbury, James Ed.	Pte.	305233	W. Yorks.	—	K. in A.
Bradd, George	Pte.	14710	12th W. Yorks.	—	Missing.
Bradley, Arthur	Pte.	021242	R.A.S.C.	—	K. in A.
Bradley, C.	Pte.	50356	Northumberland Fusrs.	—	D. a. Dis.
Bradley, Crowther S.	Pte.	39535	W. Yorks.	—	K. in A.
Bradley, Fred	Pte.	11318	4th W. Yorks.	—	K. in A.
Bradley, F. W.	Pte.	41406	6th Leicesters	—	Died P.O.W.
Bradley, George A.	Pte.	4900	3/5th W. Yorks	—	K. in A.
Bradley, Harry	Spr.	84143	Royal Engineers	—	K. in A.
Bradley, Horace	Pte.	37282	11th W. Yorks.	—	K. in A.
Bradley, J. W.	Pte.	202678	W. Yorks.	—	D. a. Dis.
Bradley, James A.	Pte.	241828	K.O.Y.L.I.	—	Died

LEEDS ROLL OF HONOUR.

Name	Rank	No.	Regiment	Honours	How Died
Bradley, James L.	Pte.	35096	1st W. Yorks.	—	D. a Dis.
Bradley, John	Pte.	14781	Scottish Rifles	—	K. in A.
Bradley, Josh. K.	Pte.	8281	1st W. Yorks.	—	K. in A.
Bradley, Leonard	Gnr.	50706	R.G.A.	—	Died
Bradley, Thos.	L/Cpl.	305527	8th W. Yorks.	—	Died
Bradshaw, A...	Rfm.	3376	2/7th W. Yorks.	—	D. of W.
Bradshaw, George	Cpl.	164795	R.A.S.C.	—	Died
Bradshaw, Wm.	Cpl.	28014	12th W. Yorks.	—	Died
Bradstock, Harold	Cpl.	2944	7th W. Yorks.	—	K. in A.
Brady, James	Rfm.	306051	2/8th W. Yorks.	—	Missing
Brady, Joseph	Pte.	50936	E. Yorks.	—	Died
Braginton, Henry T.	Pte.	8279	Royal Defence Corps.	—	Died
Braham, John	Pte.	81466	Royal Fusiliers	—	K. in A.
Braithwaite, Albert	Pte.	29384	R.A.M.C.	—	Died
Braithwaite, Chas.	Pte.	27998	12th W. Yorks.	—	Missing
Braithwaite, Harry	Pte.	40986	Cameron Highlanders	—	K. in A.
Braithwaite, James E.	Pte.		5th W. Yorks.	—	K. in A.
Braithwaite, James W.	Pte.	14764	K.O.Y.L.I.	—	Missing
Braithwaite, M.	Pte.	35628	16th W. Yorks.	—	Missing
Braithwaite, Samuel	Pte.	21371	7th E. Yorks.	—	K. in A.
Bramham, Wm.	Pte.	13128	10th W. Yorks.	—	K. in A.
Bramley, Chas.	Cpl.	49754	2nd Lincoln	—	K. in A.
Bramley, Frank	Pte.	8172	2nd W. Yorks.	—	K. in A.
Bramley, G.	Cpl.	120	13th W. Riding	—	Died
Bramley, George	Sgt.	7287	4th W. Yorks.	—	Died
Bramley, George	Rfm.	9149	12th King's R. Rifle Cps.	—	K. in A.
Brammer, Arthur A.	Pte.	3618	1st York. & Lancs.	—	Missing
Brannan, Nicholas	Pte.	9312	W. Yorks.	—	K. in A.
Brannan, Thos.	Rfm.	24180	7th W. Yorks.	—	Missing
Bray, Arthur	Pte.	20667	K.O.Y.L.I.	—	D. of W.
Bray, Clifford	Pte.	98042	Notts. & Derby.	—	K. in A.
Bray, Clifford	Pte.	202679	2nd W. Yorks.	—	K. in A.
Bray, George Wm.	Pte.	10/855	E. Yorks.	—	K. in A.
Brayshaw, Wm.	Spr.	388676	Royal Engineers	—	D. a. Dis.
Brayshay, Albert Ed.	Pte.	306847	2/5th W. Yorks.	—	Died
Brayshay, W. S.	Capt.		Royal Air Force	—	K. in A.
Brayshay, Wm. W.	Cpl.	28878	6th W. Yorks.	—	K. in A.
Brazeas, Frank	Pte.	59936	Northumberland Fusrs.	—	K. in A.
Brear, Walter	L/Cpl.	10544	K.O.Y.L.I.	—	K. in A.
Brearley, Ernest W.	Pte.	21120	8th Canadian Infantry	—	K. in A.
Brearley, Harold	Pte.	19970	26th Royal Fusiliers	—	K. in A.
Brearley, Percy	Rfm.	62687	1/7th W. Yorks.	—	K. in A.
Breckin, A.	Pte.	20739	Cheshire	—	Died
Bree, Daniel	Gnr.	174508	21st R.H.A.	—	K. in A.
Breed, Fred	Pte.	41076	Scottish Rifles	—	Died
Breed, J. B.	Lieut.		R.G.A.	—	K. in A.
Breese, W.	Pte.	13584	6th Royal W. Surrey		Missing

LEEDS ROLL OF HONOUR.

Name	Rank	No.	Regiment	Honours	How Died
Brennan, Daniel	Cpl.	24869	Training Reserve	—	D. a. Dis.
Brennan, Edward	Pte.	13894	7th K.O.Y.L.I.	—	K. in A.
Brennan, R. March	Gnr.	76428	R.F.A.	—	Died
Brennand, Arthur	Gnr.	135213	R.F.A.	—	Missing
Breintnall, C. J.			R.F.A.	—	Died
Bretherick, Herbert	Pte.	24006	8th W. Riding	—	D. of W.
Brewer, Joseph	Pte.	27657	9th Lancs. Fusiliers	—	Missing
Brewer, Sydney	Pte.	41382	K.O. Scottish Bordrs.	—	Died
Brice, Arthur J.	Dvr.	28879	R.F.A.	—	K. in A.
Bridge, Louis	L/Cpl.	268072	1/7th W. Yorks.	—	K. in A.
Bridgeman, Thos. L.	Pte.	143561	Machine Gun Corps	—	K. in A.
Brierley, Arthur	Rfm.	1541	1/7th W. Yorks.	—	K. in A.
Brierley, George W.	Cpl.	78560	R.A.M.C.	—	Died
Briggs, Alfred	Pte.	27852	12th W. Yorks.	—	K. in A.
Briggs, C.	Gnr.	16649	R.F.A.	—	K. in A.
Briggs, Edward	Bugl.	S/11375	Rifle Brigade	—	Missing
Briggs, Edwin	Pte.	58772	18th Liverpool	—	K. in A.
Briggs, Ernest	Pte.	242738	K.O.Y.L.I.	—	K. in A.
Briggs, Fred	Sgt.	7493	1st Lincoln	—	D. of W.
Briggs, George	Pte.	33102	18th W. Yorks.	—	Died
Briggs, H.	2/Clk.	225714	Royal Air Force	—	Died
Briggs, H.	A/Cpl.	320643	Royal Engineers	—	K. in A.
Briggs, Harry G.	Pte.	32928	9th W. Yorks.	—	D. of W.
Briggs, Henry	Pte.	9828	Royal Fusiliers	—	Died
Briggs, Herbert	Pte.	58679	10th W. Yorks.	—	D. of W.
Briggs, Horace L.	L/Cpl.	72	15th W. Yorks.	—	K. in A.
Briggs, James	Pte.	4743	W. Yorks.	—	K. in A.
Briggs, Joseph	Pte.	372667	Labour Corps	—	D. a. Dis.
Briggs, Orrie	A/Capt.		8th Somerset Lt. Infty.	—	K. in A.
Briggs, Richard S.	Lieut.		1/7th W. Yorks.	—	K. in A.
Briggs, W.	Pte.	21057	10th W. Yorks.	—	K. in A.
Briggs, W. H.	Cpl.		15th W. Yorks.	—	K. in A.
Briggs, Walter	Pte.	23490	Labour Corps	—	Died
Brigham, John Wm.	Pte.		W. Yorks.	—	Died
Brigham, Geo. H. M.	L/Cpl.	33574	Border	—	K. in A.
Brigham, Gervase W.	Gnr.	137281	R.F.A.	—	K. in A.
Brigham, Norman		R1661	Royal Naval Division	—	K. in A.
Brigham, Samuel	Pte.	511049	Labour Corps	—	Died
Bright, Norman H.	L/Cpl.	2647	1/4th Lincoln	—	D. of W.
Brindley, R.	Gnr.	781208	R.F.A.	—	K. in A.
Brining, Edwin	Pte.	60299	Royal Defence Corps	—	K. in A.
Briscombe, Herbert	Pte.	43181	W. Yorks.	—	Died
Bristow, Edmund	C.S.M.	1244	W. Yorks.	—	K. in A.
Brittain, Harry L.	Pte.	48890	W. Yorks.	—	K. in A.
Britten, Wm.	Sgt.	51351	R.H.A.	—	K. in A.
Britton, Clifford	Cpl.	18442	8th K.O.Y.L.I.	M.M.	K. in A.
Britton, Chas.	L/Cpl.	398450	Labour Corps	—	D. a. Dis.

LEEDS ROLL OF HONOUR.

Name	Rank	No.	Regiment	Honours	How Died
Britton, Harry	Pte.	27773	W. Yorks.	—	K. in A.
Britton, James Wm.	Sgt.	15529	W. Yorks.	—	K. in A.
Britton, John A.	Pte.	319714	R.A.S.C.	—	D. a. Dis.
Britton, L.	L/Cpl.	17522	Northumberland Fusrs.	—	Missing
Britton, Walter	L/Cpl.	12/99	K.O.Y.L.I.	—	K. in A.
Broadbelt, Chas.	Pte.	21240	9th W. Yorks.	—	D. a. Dis.
Broadbelt, Leonard	Rfm.	266097	2/7th W. Yorks.	—	Died
Broadbent, Albert	Cpl.	8464	2nd Leinster	—	K. in A.
Broadbent, Arthur	Gnr.	194811	R.H.A.	—	K. in A.
Broadbent, Bertie	Gnr.	775906	R.F.A.	—	K. in A.
Broadbent, Clifford	L/Cpl.	11937	K. O. Scottish Bordrs.	—	D. of W.
Broadbent, Clifford	Rfm.	5295	1/8th W. Yorks.	—	D. of W.
Broadbent, D.	Pte.	30047	Labour Corps	—	D. a. Dis.
Broadbent, Edmund	Pte.	39751	South Wales Borderers	—	K. in A.
Broadbent, G.	Pte.	118375	R.A.M.C.	—	D. a. Dis.
Broadbent, Henry	Pte.	438858	Canadian Exped. Force	—	D. of W.
Broadbent, Lawrence F.	Cpl.	265536	Royal Engineers	—	K. in A.
Broadbent, Leonard	Pte.	27202	12th W. Yorks.	—	K. in A.
Broadbent, Oscar B.	Pte.	38012	R.A.M.C.	—	K. in A.
Broadbent, Samuel	Pte.	11619	K.O.Y.L.I.	—	K. in A.
Broadbent, Wm.	Pte.	2420	4th K.O.Y.L.I.	—	Missing
Broadbent, Wm.	Cpl.	8788	2nd W. Yorks.	—	K. in A.
Broadhead, Albert E.	Rfm.	305734	2/8th W. Yorks.	—	D. a. Dis.
Broadhead, Joseph	Pte.	47352	Durham Lt. Infantry	—	Died
Broadhead, Willie	L/Cpl.	32807	Royal Scots	—	Died
Broadhurst, Thos.	Pte.	120218	R.A.S.C.	—	D. a. Dis.
Broadhurst, Wm.	Pte.	265889	1/5th W. Yorks.	—	K. in A.
Broadley, Albert	Pte.	10090	2nd W. Yorks.	—	K. in A.
Broadley, Harry	Capt.		2nd R. Irish Fusiliers	—	K. in A.
Broadley, James	Rfm.	265808	2/7th W. Yorks.	—	Missing
Broadley, John E.	Rfm.	41287	1/8th W. Yorks.	—	Missing
Broadley, Robt.	Pte.	300001	5th W. Yorks.	—	D. a. Dis.
Broadley, W.	L/Sgt.	7930	1st W. Yorks.	—	K. in A.
Broadley, Wm.	Pte.	306705	W. Yorks.	—	K. in A.
Broadley, Wm.	Pte.	14541	8th K.O.Y.L.I.	—	K. in A.
Broadley, Wm.	Sig.	246702	R.F.A.	—	Died
Broadwith, James A.	Pte.	64250	W. Yorks.	—	Died
Brock, Herbert	Sig.	200255	1/4th K.O.Y.L.I.	—	Died
Brockhouse, Horace	Pte.	27836	9th Lancs. Fusiliers	—	K. in A.
Brodie, Wm.	Pte.	27132	W. Yorks.	—	Died
Brogden, G. H.	Pte.	23428	9th Yorks.	—	K. in A.
Brogden, J. W.	Pte.	22476	W. Yorks.	—	Died
Brogden, Joseph	Pte.	9243	2nd W. Yorks.	—	K. in A.
Bromley, Fred	Rfm.	3357	2/7th W. Yorks.	—	K. in A.
Bromley, Tom	Pte.	201806	Royal Scots	—	D. of W.
Brook, Arthur H.	Pte.	40902	9th K.O.Y.L.I.	—	Missing
Brook, Cecil F.	2nd-Lieut.		8th E. Yorks.	—	Died

LEEDS ROLL OF HONOUR.

Name	Rank	No.	Regiment	Honours	How Died
Brook, Claude	Pte.	229135	1st London	—	Died
Brook, Cyril	Pte.	241146	2/6th W. Yorks.	—	Missing
Brook, Henry	Rfm.	2518	7th W. Yorks.	—	Died
Brook, Herbert	Pte.	34365	8th York. & Lancs.	—	K. in A.
Brook, Herbert	Pte.			—	Died
Brook, Herbert	Pte.	145	15th W. Yorks.	—	Died
Brook, Herbert	Pte.	64119	W. Yorks.	—	Died
Brook, James	L/Sgt.	265355	7th W. Yorks.	—	Died
Brook, Joseph	Pte.	45464	Royal Defence Corps	—	Died
Brook, Mortimer	Gnr.	73980	R.F.A.	—	K. in A.
Brook, Leonard	Pte.	21/674	W. Yorks.	—	Died
Brook, Samuel	Pte.	1581	15th W. Yorks.	—	K. in A.
Brook, Stephen	Pte.	4967	Machine Gun Corps	—	K. in A.
Brook, Wm.	Pte.	34061	1st W. Yorks.	—	K. in A.
Brooke, Clarence	2nd Lieut.		13th E. Yorks.	—	Missing
Brooke, Cyril	Pte.	260059	York. & Lancs.	—	K. in A.
Brooke, George E.	Pte.	28951	10th W. Yorks.	—	K. in A.
Brooke, Harold W.	Captain		7th E. Yorks.	—	K. in A.
Brooke, J. B.	Pte.	1126	Royal Marine Lt. Infty.	—	K. in A.
Brooke, John J.	Pte.	114	15th W. Yorks.	—	K. in A.
Brooke, Percy	Captain		12th W. Yorks.	—	K. in A.
Brooke, Wm.	Pte.	48003	Royal Inniskillen Fusrs.	—	K. in A.
Brooke, Wm.	Pte.	401615	R.A.M.C.	—	Died
Brookes, Arthur R. M.	Gnr.	73980	R.F.A.	—	K. in A.
Brookes, Benjamin	A/Sgt.	403502	R.A.M.C.	—	K. in A.
Brookes, J.	Pte.	2971	2nd Northumb'l'd Fusrs.	—	Missing
Brookes, Walter	Pte.	20441	1st K.O.Y.L.I.	—	K. in A.
Brophy, Martin	Pte.	8280	Royal Defence Corps..	—	D. a. Dis.
Brophy, Martin	Spr.	273892	Royal Engineers	—	K. in A.
Brophy, Wm.	Pte.	9785	2nd K.O.Y.L.I.	—	Missing
Broscombe, Arthur	Pte.	9799	K.O.Y.L.I.	—	K. in A.
Brosgall, Wm.	R.M.	307067	12th W. Yorks.	—	K. in A.
Brotherton, Wm.	Pte.		Machine Gun Corps	—	D. of W.
Brough, G. C.	L/Cpl.	17683	1st W. Yorks.	—	K. in A.
Brough, Samuel	Pte.	53379	13th W. Yorks.	—	K. in A.
Broughton, James	Pte.	10955	8th W. Riding	—	Missing
Broughton, John Wm.	Pte.	53053	W. Riding	—	Died
Brown, A.	Pte.	122296	Machine Gun Corps	—	Died
Brown, Abraham	Pte.	1448	8th E. Yorks.	—	K. in A.
Brown, Albert	Pte.	3974	W. Yorks.	—	D. a. Dis.
Brown, Alfred	Pte.	38194	15th W. Yorks.	—	Missing
Brown, Arthur	Gnr.	152552	R.F.A.	—	Died
Brown, Arthur	Rfm.	5300	1/7th W. Yorks.	—	K. in A.
Brown, Benjamin	Dvr.	204843	R.F.A.	—	K. in A.
Brown, C.	L/Cpl.	12765	10th W. Yorks.	—	K. in A.
Brown, Charles	Pte.	41980	Northumberland Fusrs.	—	K. in A.
Brown, Charles	Pte.	31398	14th Northumb'l'd Fusrs.	—	K. in A.

LEEDS ROLL OF HONOUR.

Name	Rank	No.	Regiment	Honours	How Died
Brown, Charles	L/Cpl.	12765	10th W. Yorks.	—	K. in A.
Brown, Charles Ed.	Pte.	42470	2nd W. Yorks.	—	K. in A.
Brown, Chas. Hy.	Dvr.	74007	R.F.A.	—	Died
Brown, Chas. Wm.	Pte.	10350	4th W. Yorks.	—	Missing
Brown, Clifford	Pte.	24080	13th W. Yorks.	—	Died
Brown, David C.	Dvr.	39661	R.F.A.	—	K. in A.
Brown, David	Pte.	58737	Machine Gun Corps	—	K. in A.
Brown, Ernest	Pte.	205038	W. Yorks.	—	K. in A.
Brown, Ernest	Sgt.	12474	12th W. Yorks.	—	K. in A.
Brown, Ernest	Rfm.	266082	1/7th W. Yorks.	—	Missing
Brown, F. E.	Bdr.	21982	R.F.A.	—	K. in A.
Brown, Francis C.	Pte.	3212	55th Aust. Imp. Force	—	K. in A.
Brown, Frank R.	Pte.	34209	18th W. Yorks.	—	K. in A.
Brown, Fred	Pte.		Canadians	—	Died
Brown, Fredk.	Pte.	24489	2nd W. Yorks.	—	K. in A.
Brown, G. Byron	Sgt.	659	K. African Rifles	—	Died
Brown, George	Pte.	268193	17th W. Riding	—	K. in A.
Brown, George	Gnr.	80726	R.F.A.	—	Drowned
Brown, George	Gnr.	21769	R.F.A.	—	Died
Brown, George E.	Pte.	40282	W. Yorks.	—	K. in A.
Brown, Geo. Fred	Pte.	4250	K.O.Y.L.I.	—	K. in A.
Brown, Geo. W.	L./Cpl	21652	K.O. Scottish Bordrs.	—	K. in A.
Brown, H.	Major		Yorkshire	D.S.O., M.C. Croix de Guerre.	K. in A.
Brown, Harry	L/Cpl.	266539	1/7th W. Yorks.	—	K. in A.
Brown, Harry H.	Pte.	46093	2nd York. & Lancs.	—	D. of W.
Brown, J. W.	Gnr.	776038	R.F.A.	—	K. in A.
Brown, James	Pte.	9147	3rd W. Yorks.	—	Died
Brown, James	Pte.	4/7629	W. Yorks.	—	K. in A.
Brown, James	Rfm.	34064	2/8th W. Yorks.	—	K. in A.
Brown, James	Pte.	3864	2nd Northumb'ld Fusrs.	—	K. in A.
Brown, John	Cpl.	38685	1st W. Yorks.	—	Missing
Brown, John	Pte.	40477	Northants.	—	D. of W.
Brown, John	L/Cpl.	30607	Machine Gun Corps	—	K. in A.
Brown, John	Spr.	61572	Royal Engineers	—	Died
Brown, John B.	Gdsmn.	7659	1st Scots Guards	—	Died
Brown, John Chas.	Rfm.	6292	1/8th W. Yorks.	—	K. in A.
Brown, John W.	Pte.	018863	R.A.O.C.	—	Died
Brown, John Wm.	Pte.	235400	Yorks.	—	K. in A.
Brown, Lawrence	Pte.	1444	15th West Yorks	—	K. in A.
Brown, M. F.	Pte.	50950	Cheshire	—	D. of W.
Brown, Martin P.	Rfm.	4073	3/8th West Yorks.	—	K. in A.
Brown, Percy	Pte.	8165	2nd W. Riding	—	K. in A.
Brown, Robt.	Pte.	S/2876	2nd Royal Highlanders	—	Died
Brown, S. L.	Pte.	865	W. Yorks.	—	Died
Brown, Squire	Pte.	71022	Durham Lt. Infantry	—	K. in A.
Brown, Stephenson W.	Boy 1	J41400	H.M.S. " Invincible ".	—	Drowned

LEEDS ROLL OF HONOUR.

Name	Rank	No.	Regiment	Honours	How Died
Brown, Thos.	Pte.	10074	1st W. Yorks.	—	K. in A.
Brown, Thos.	Dvr.	796140	R.F.A.	—	K. in A.
Brown, Thos. E.	Pte.	41207	Northants	—	K. in A.
Brown, Thos. Wm.	Cpl.	266730	W. Yorks.	—	D. a. Dis.
Brown, W.	Pte.	15/1291	W. Yorks.	—	D. a. Dis.
Brown, Walter	Pte.	1291	15th W. Yorks.	—	K. in A.
Brown, Walter	Rfm.	3069	1/7th W. Yorks.	—	K. in A.
Brown, Walter R.	2nd-Lieut.		2/7th W. Yorks.	M.C.	K. in A.
Brown, Wm.	Pte.	222	Royal Munster Fusrs.	—	K. in A.
Brown, Wm.	Pte.	12311	4th W. Yorks.	—	K. in A.
Brown, Wm. H. S.	Cpl.	13075	10th W. Yorks.	—	K. in A.
Brown, Wm. Hy.	Pte.	19434	10th K.O.Y.L.I.	—	K. in A.
Browne, John C.	Pte.	24478	2nd W. Yorks.	—	K. in A.
Browne, Wilfred H.	L/Cpl.	20024	Royal Scots Fusiliers	—	Died
Browning, Wm.	L/Cpl.	32533	Highland Lt. Infantry	—	K. in A.
Brownridge, Arthur	A.B.		H.M.S. " Queen Mary "	—	K. in A.
Brownridge, Fredk.	Pte.	21393	R.A.S.C.	—	D. a. Dis.
Bruce, Alfred	Pte.	59661	1st Northumb'l'd Fusrs.	—	K. in A.
Bruce, Fred M.	Pte.	32272	K.O.Y.L.I.	—	Missing
Bruce, G. L.	Gnr.	2713	R.F.A.	—	K. in A.
Bruce, Harold	L/Cpl.	241709	Yorks.	—	Died
Bruines, Bertie	Pte.	25334	15th W. Yorks.	—	Missing
Brundred, J. Samuel	L/Cpl.	15878	Yorks.	—	Died
Brundred, Wm.	A.M.	329969	R.A.F.	—	Died
Brunskill, Thos.	Pte.	15151	10th W. Yorks.	—	K. in A.
Bryan, Philip	Pte.	13054	W. Riding	—	Died
Bryans, John	Pte.	43215	13th Durham Lt. Infty.	—	Died
Buck, Thos. Wm.	Cpl.	48205	27th Northumb'l'd Fusrs.	—	K. in A.
Buckbrough, Percy			22nd W. Yorks.	—	K. in A.
Buckingham, Frank	Pte.	3604	3/4th Seaforth Highdrs.	—	K. in A.
Buckingham, George A.	Pte.	19977	K.O. Scottish Borderers	—	K. in A.
Buckle, Albert	Rfm.	4383	3/7th W. Yorks.	—	K. in A.
Buckle, Chas F.	Pnr.	84170	Royal Engineers	—	K. in A.
Buckle, Henderson	Pte.	18762	9th W. Yorks.	—	K. in A.
Buckley, Alfred	Pte.	1116	W. Yorks.	—	D. of W.
Buckley, Edgar	O.S.	J65625	H.M.S. " Victory "	—	Died
Buckley, Frank	Sig.	19997	K.O. Scottish Borderers	—	Missing
Buckley, Wm. L.	Pte.	72806	Royal Welsh Fusiliers	—	K. in A.
Buckridge, Leonard G.	Pte.	63771	W. Yorks.	—	K. in A.
Buckroyd, John Ed.	A.B.	J28417	H.M.S. " Stephen Furness "	—	K. in A.
Buckton, Herbert J.	Dvr.	222267	R.F.A.	—	K. in A.
Buckton, Thos. L.	Dvr.	2557	R.F.A.	—	K. in A.
Bucktrout, Chas. A.	Rfm.	4107	1/8th W. Yorks.	—	K. in A.
Bufton, Joseph	Pte.	17606	K.O.Y.L.I.	—	Died
Bull, James L.	Rfm.	305401	1/8th W. Yorks.	—	K. in A.
Bullen, J. R.	Pte.	45926	12th W. Yorks.	—	K. in A.

LEEDS ROLL OF HONOUR.

Name	Rank	No.	Regiment	Honours	How Died
Buller, Oliver	Pte.	408335	R.A.M.C.	—	Died
Bullock, Frank	Pte.	301775	Tank Corps	—	K. in A.
Bullock, Thos.	Pte.	7901	2nd Yorks.	—	K. in A.
Bullough, Albert	Pte.	8189	2nd W. Yorks.	—	K. in A.
Bullough, Maurice J.	Pte.	57406	R.A.M.C.	—	K. in A.
Bulmer, Herbert	Pte.	15785	10th York. & Lancs.	—	K. in A.
Bulmer, Isaac	Rfm.	266528	1/7th West Yorks.	—	K. in A.
Bulmer, Joseph E.	Dvr.	98852	Royal Engineers	—	D. of W.
Bulmer, Thos. E.	Pte.	49188	R.A.M.C.	—	K. in A.
Bulmer, Wm.	Rfm.	1645	2/8th W. Yorks.	—	K. in A.
Bumby, Francis L.	Spr.	36250	Royal Engineers	—	Died
Bumby, Fredk. A.	Pte.	45174	7th South Staffs.	—	K. in A.
Bunce, Herbert W.	Cpl.		R.A.S.C., M.T.	—	Died
Bunce, John Ed.	Pte.		R.A.S.C.	—	Died
Bungey, Sidney T.	Gnr.	8101	R.G.A.	—	K. in A.
Bunkall, Richard	Gnr.	6362	R.G.A.	—	Died
Bunting, Enos S.	Pte.	202680	W. Yorks.	—	K. in A.
Bunting, George A.	Rfm.	3814	2/7th W. Yorks.	—	Missing
Bunyan, John	Dvr.	035631	R.A.S.C.	—	K. in A.
Burdekin, Wm. H.	Rfm.	266935	1/7th W. Yorks.	—	D. of W.
Burdett, Harry	L/Cpl.	12988	4th W. Yorks.	—	K. in A.
Burdett, Samuel	Pte.	12944	K.O.Y.L.I.	—	Died
Burdett, Walter	Pte.	202220	2/4th Lincoln	—	D. of W.
Burgess, George A.	Dvr.	21/649	21st W. Yorks.	—	K. in A.
Burgess, Harold	Pte.	33153	8th York. & Lancs.	—	D. of W.
Burhouse, H. J.	Pte.	41888	Leicester	—	Died
Burke, Edmund	Pte.		W. Yorks.	—	Died
Burke, Geo. E.	Spr.	247486	Railway Ordnance Dep.	—	Died
Burke, James	Pte.	9478	3rd Yorks.	—	Died
Burke, John	Cpl.	19876	Cheshire	—	K. in A.
Burke, John	Pte.	27670	Yorks.	—	D. of W.
Burke, John	Pte.	60388	Royal Defence Corps	—	D. a. Dis.
Burke, Michael M.	Pte.	3401	7th Leinster	—	K. in A.
Burke, Patrick	Pte.	3479	2/8th W. Yorks.	—	Missing
Burke, Robt.	Rfm.	2/1212	Rifle Brigade	—	Died
Burke, Thos.	Pte.	3817	1st W. Yorks.	—	K. in A.
Burke, Thos.	Pte.	33670	Royal Defence Corps	—	D. a. Dis.
Burke, Walter	Sgt.	9879	2nd York. & Lancs.	—	K. in A.
Burke, Wm.	Pte.	606043	W. Yorks.	—	Died
Burke, Wm. Hy.	Pte.	36162	20th Northumb'l'd Fusrs.	—	K. in A.
Burks, Wm. T.	Pte.	4887	W. Yorks.	—	K. in A.
Burn, D.	Pte.	25160	Royal Air Force	—	D. of W.
Burn, Ernest	Pte.	266082	1/7th W. Yorks.	—	Missing
Burn, Reg. J.	Pte.	64112	1st W. Yorks.	—	K. in A.
Burnand, Harry	Pte.	26458	Machine Gun Corps	—	K. in A.
Burnell, Arnold	Pte.	13109	W. Yorks.	—	Died
Burnell, Roland	Pte.	70588	Royal Defence Corps	—	Died

LEEDS ROLL OF HONOUR.

Name	Rank	No.	Regiment	Honours	How Died
Burnett, Arthur	Pte.	267417	W. Yorks.	—	D. a. Dis.
Burnett, Arthur	Pte.	1666	2/7th W. Yorks.	—	Died
Burnett, Edward	Pte.	18568	12th W. Yorks.	—	K. in A.
Burnett, Ernest	Pte.	41112	11th W. Yorks.	—	K. in A.
Burnett, John C.	Pte.	53018	Durham Light Infantry	—	Died
Burnham, Geo.	Pte.	8014	Durham Light Infantry	—	Died
Burniston, Harry	Pte.	64	15th W. Yorks.	—	K. in A.
Burns, Robt.	Pte.	9485	1st W. Yorks.	—	K. in A.
Burns, Wm.	Pte.	16787	8th York. & Lancs.	—	K. in A.
Burras, James Wm.	Pte.	18768	3rd W. Yorks.	—	K. in A.
Burrell, Fred Geo.	Pte.	8548	2nd Royal Sussex	•—	K in A.
Burrell, James S.	L/Sgt.	6818	12th W. Yorks.	—	K. in A.
Burrill, A.	Pte.	58173	Middlesex	—	K. in A.
Burrow, Wilfred	Pte.	1317	15th W. Yorks.	—	K. in A.
Burrows, Cyril	Pte.	23783	11th W. Yorks.	—	K. in A.
Burrows, J. W.	Pte.	34680	2nd W. Yorks.	—	Missing
Burrows, Thos.	Pte.	46566	10th Northumb'l'd Fusrs.	—	Died
Burrows, W.	Sgt.	76480	R.F.A.	—	K. in A.
Burrows, Wm.	Pte.	7/2221	Royal Munster Fusrs.	—	K. in A.
Burstall, Walter	Pte.	142713	Machine Gun Corps	—	K. in A.
Burtle, Wm.	Rfm.	266870	1st W. Yorks.	—	K. in A.
Burton, Arthur	Pte.	238022	22nd Northumb'ld Fusrs.	—	K. in A.
Burton, Chris. C.	Pte.	19163	Yorks. & Lancs.	—	K. in A.
Burton, David	Gnr.	223156	R.F.A.	—	Died
Burton, Edgar	Pte.	37858	9th W. Yorks.	—	D. of W.
Burton, Harold	Pte.	78402	R.A.M.C.	—	K. in A.
Burton, Harold	Pnr.	357706	Royal Engineers	—	K. in A.
Burton, Herbert	2nd Lieut.		1/5th York. & Lancs.	—	K. in A.
Burton, Lawrence E.	Pte.	266817	1/7th W. Yorks.	—	K. in A.
Burton, Wm.	Pte.	10550	3rd E. Surrey	—	K. in A.
Burton, Wm.	Pte.	32572	8th Yorks. & Lancs.	—	K. in A.
Burwell, James H.			Royal Naval Division	—	K. in A.
Burwen, Frank	Pte.	19086	8th Northumberld Fusrs.	—	Missing
Bury, Wm.	Pte.	215777	W. Yorks.	—	K. in A.
Busfield, Robt. P.	Pte.	45000	K.O.Y.L.I.	—	Missing
Busk, Edwin	Sgt.	3233	Yorks.	—	D. a. Dis.
Butler, Albert	Pte.	11888	8th York. & Lancs.	—	K. in A.
Butler, Arthur W.	C.S.M.	5613	1st Royal W. Surrey	—	D. of W.
Butler, Clifford	Pte.	34517	W. Riding	—	K. in A.
Butler, E.	Pte.	446417	56th Canadians	—	K. in A.
Butler, Edgar	Sgt.	775072	R.F.A.	—	D. of W.
Butler, F.	Pte.	18675	1st K.O. Scottish Bordrs.	—	K. in A.
Butler, Harry	Pte.	1401	15th W. Yorks.	—	Missing
Butler, James	Pte.	1060	17th W. Yorks.	—	K. in A.
Butler, John S.	Spr.	239441	Royal Engineers	—	D. of W.
Butler, Lawrence	Dvr.	1321	W. Riding Fld. Amb.	—	Died
Butt, Edward	Pte.	18512	1st W. Yorks.	—	Died

LEEDS ROLL OF HONOUR.

Name	Rank	No.	Regiment	Honours	How Died
Butterfield, J.	L/Cpl.	4228	1/4th Seaforth Highdrs.	—	Missing
Butterick, Thos. W.	Pte.	41693	W. Yorks.	—	K. in A.
Butters, Geo. A.	Pte.	62812	R.A.M.C.	—	K. in A.
Butterwood, Arthur	Cpl.	16767	11th York. & Lancs.	—	D. of W.
Butterworth, Archie	Cpl.	1574	11th W. Yorks.	—	K. in A.
Butterworth, Ernest	Rfm.	305271	8th W. Yorks.	—	K. in A.
Butterworth, Herbert	Pte.	11631	8th W. Riding	—	Missing
Butterworth, Wm. B.	Pte.	24493	2nd W. Riding	—	K. in A.
Buttery, J. E.	Pte.	28196	15th Durham Lt. Infty.	—	Died
Buttery, Richard	Sgt.	15862	W. Yorks.	—	Died
Buttery, Thos. F.	Sgt.	306795	8th W. Yorks.	—	K. in A.
Buttery, Wm.	Pte.	68891	Royal Fusiliers	—	Died
Button, Sydney V.	L/Cpl.	12117	W. Yorks.	M.M.	K. in A.
Buxton, Frank	L/Cpl.	10936	10th W. Yorks.	—	K. in A.
Buxton, Samuel L.	Pte.	1337	15th W. Yorks.	—	K. in A.
Bye, Geo. H.	Cpl.	39992	13th York. & Lancs.	—	K. in A.
Bygott, Frank	Cpl.	74	15th W. Yorks.	—	K. in A.
Byron, James	Pte.	31225	1st E. Yorks.	—	K. in A.
Bywater, James	Pte.	09317	R.A.O.C.	—	Died
Bywater, John	Pte.	8167	1st W. Yorks.	—	K. in A.
Bywater, Wm.	Spr.	84040	Royal Engineers	—	Died
Bywater, Wm.	Pte.	54008	W. Yorks.	—	K. in A.
Cable, Fredk.	Spr.	72136	Royal Engineers	—	Died a. Dis.
Cable, John	L/Cpl.	3540	1/7th West Yorks.	—	K. in A.
Cade, F.	Pte.	49704	9th Liverpool	—	K. in A.
Cahill, Jos.	Pte.	10771	K.O.Y.L.I.	—	K. in A.
Cahill, Wm.	Pte.	24064	2/6th West Yorks.	—	K. in A.
Cain, Sml. L. P.	L/Cpl.	23947	9th West Yorks.	—	K. in A.
Cain, Stanley J.	Pte.	25577	2nd West Yorks.	—	K. in A.
Cairns, Daniel	Pte.	14526	Scots Guards	—	K. in A.
Cairns, Harold	Pte.	139239	Machine Gun Corps	—	K. in A.
Caizergues, Jos.	Rfm.	5827	King's Royal Rifle Corps	—	Died
Calderhead, Cliff	Pte.	1584	15th West Yorks.	—	K. in A.
Callaghan, Ernest	Gnr.	113893	R.G.A.	—	K. in A.
Callaghan, F.	Pte.	710601	Labour Corps	—	Died
Callaghan, J.	Pte.	37500	K.O.Y.L.I.	—	Died
Callaghan, John	Pte.	38295	10th York. & Lancs.	—	K. in A.
Callaghan, John	Dvr.	5733	R.H. & R.F.A.	—	Died
Callaghan, Jos.	Pte.	55511	10th Welsh	—	K. in A.
Callan, Richard	Sgt.	11127	K.O.Y.L.I.	—	K. in A.
Callis, Arthur	Rfm.	4015	1/8th W. Yorks.	—	K. in A.
Calton, Alfred	Pte.	26959	1st W. Yorks.	—	D. of W.
Calverley, F. G.	Pte.	24819	1st W. Yorks.	—	K. in A.
Calverley, Fred	Pte.	305272	11th W. Yorks.	—	K. in A.
Calverley, Geo. H.	Rfm.	2819	8th W. Yorks.	—	K. in A.
Calverley, James	A.B.	342978	H.M.S. "Aboukir"	—	K. in A.

LEEDS ROLL OF HONOUR.

Name	Rank	No.	Regiment	Honours	How Died
Calverley, M. A.	Pte.	38463	8th Gloucester	—	D. of W.
Calverley, Tom	Pte.	1886	15th W. Yorks.	—	K. in A.
Calvert, Arthur	Pte.	13021	1st W. Yorks.	—	Missing
Calvert, Arthur	Rfm.	4758	1/8th W. Yorks.	—	K. in A.
Calvert, Geoff. C.	Lieut.		K.O.Y.L.I.	—	Died
Calvert, George	Pte.	2947	Northumberland Fusrs.	—	K. in A.
Calvert, Harry	Pte.	65271	2/4th K.O.Y.L.I.	—	K. in A.
Calvert, Harry	Pte.	170	15th W. Yorks.	—	K. in A.
Calvert, Henry	Pte.	115218	Labour Corps.	—	D. a. Dis.
Calvert, Herbert	Pte.	34482	18th W. Yorks.	—	K. in A.
Calvert, James A.	Rfm.	4758	1/8th W. Yorks.	—	K. in A.
Calvert, John C.	Pte.		5th R. Hdrs. Canada	—	Died
Calvert, Reg. C.	Capt.		Leeds Rifles	—	Died
Calvert, Squire J.	Pte.	48709	4th W. Yorks.	—	K. in A.
Calvert, Thos.	Pte.	14215	11th W. Yorks.	—	K. in A.
Cambridge, Henry	Cpl.	11853	6th K.O. Scottish Brdrs.	—	D. of W.
Cambridge, Norman	Pte.	29643	R.A.S.C.	—	D. of W.
Cameron, Colin H.	Pte.	46882	61st Machine Gun Corps	—	Died
Cameron, Cyril	Dvr.	274208	R.F.A.	—	Died
Cameron, Fred	Pte.	54249	5th W. Riding	—	K. in A.
Cameron, John	Pte.	376512	Durham Light Infantry	—	K. in A.
Cameron, Percy	Stkr.	109411	H.M.S. "Black Prince"	—	K. in A.
Cameron, Thomas	Pte.	4240	W. Yorks.	—	Died
Cames, Geo.	Cpl.	173	15th W. Yorks.	—	K. in A.
Campbell, Chas. D.	Pte.	14478	14th Austr. F. Ambul.	—	D. of W.
Campbell, G. E.	Pte.	45811	Royal Berks.	—	K. in A.
Campbell, John R.	Pte.	20008	Essex	—	K. in A.
Campbell, Thos. H.	Spr.	36251	Royal Engineers	—	Died
Campleman, Chas. R.	Pte.	1331	15th W. Yorks.	—	K. in A.
Cane, Walter	Pte.	337834	R.A.S.C.	—	Died
Canning, Wm.	Sgt.	8262	6th Yorks.	—	K. in A.
Cannon, John N.	Pte.	99605	King's Liverpool	—	Died
Cannon, Jos. N.	Pte.	12730	12th W. Yorks.	—	D. of W.
Cantral, Edward	Pte.	5204	W. Yorks.	—	K. in A.
Cape, Arnott	Pte.	11903	Machine Gun Corps	—	K. in A.
Capp, Albert	Pte.	11542	Durham Light Infantry	—	K. in A.
Carding, Wm.	Sgt.	6040	K.O.Y.L.I.	—	K. in A.
Cardis, Albert	Rfm.	266871	1/7th W. Yorks.	—	K. in A.
Careless, Fred	Pte.	3604	Grenadier Guards	—	K. in A.
Carling, Harold	Rfm.	4219	7th W. Yorks.	—	D. of W.
Carlisle, Harold	Gnr.	32717	R.F.A.	—	K. in A.
Carlisle, Wm. E.	Pte.	2730	Durham Light Infantry	—	D. of W.
Carlton, Arthur	Dvr.	775794	R.F.A.	—	Died
Carlton, Edwin A.	Pte.	6501	London Scottish	—	K. in A.
Carney, John	Pte.	10649	W. Riding	—	Died
Carney, Wm.	Pte.	43834	West Yorks.	—	K. in A.
Carnley, Carl A.	Rfm.	35714	1/8th West Yorks.	—	K. in A.

LEEDS ROLL OF HONOUR.

Name	Rank	No.	Regiment	Honours	How Died
Carr, Chas.	Pte.	175944	R.A.S.C. (M.T.)	—	Died
Carr, G. W.	Pte.	34628	2nd Yorks.	—	Missing
Carr, Herbert	Sgt.	58727	Machine Gun Corps	—	K. in A.
Carr, J.	Pte.	42364	Machine Gun Corps	—	Died
Carr, James	Pte.		W. Riding	—	K. in A.
Carr, Jerry	Pte.	6838	4th W. Yorks.	—	Died
Carr, Percy	Spr.	99259	Royal Engineers	—	Died
Carr, Walter	Pte.	35623	15th W. Yorks.	—	Missing
Carr, Wm.	Pte.	8493	W. Yorks.	—	K. in A.
Carrack, Albert	Pte.	19578	Leicester	—	K. in A.
Carrack, J.	Pte.	257708	Labour Corps	—	Died
Carrack, Joshua	Pte.	14656	E. Kent	—	K. in A.
Carrier, Stanley C.	L/Cpl.	35966	Northumberland Fusrs.	—	Died
Carrigan, Ernest	Gnr.	113893	R.G.A.	—	Died
Carrigan, Patrick	Pte.	25083	Coldstream Guards	—	Died
Carrington, Fred B.	L.Stkr.	310977	H.M.S. " Invincible "	—	K. in A.
Carritt, Edward	Pte.	12954	7th K.O.Y.L.I.	—	Missing
Carritt, J. W.	Pte.	29829	King's Liverpool	—	K. in A.
Carroll, F. J.	Pte.	62683	K.O.Y.L.I.	—	K. in A.
Carroll, Harry	Pte.	41090	K.O.Y.L.I.	—	Missing
Carroll, John	Pte.	9872	1st W. Yorks.	—	D. of W.
Carroll, John	Cpl.	7486	1st W. Yorks.	—	Missing
Carroll, John W.	Pte.	316415	Labour Corps	—	D. a. Dis.
Carroll, Patrick	Pte.	7062	1st E. Yorks.	—	K. in A.
Carroll, Peter	L/Cpl.	8373	7th W. Yorks.	—	K. in A.
Carruthers, J. W.	Pte.	330866	Royal Scots Fusiliers	—	K. in A.
Carswell, Walter	Bdr.	46548	R.F.A.	—	D. of W.
Carter, Albert	Pte.	30144	Loyal N. Lancs.	—	Missing
Carter, Albert N.	Pte.	205113	W. Yorks.	—	K. in A.
Carter, Chas.	Pte.	36833	15th W. Yorks.	—	Died
Carter, Eric H.	Pte.	39551	K.O.Y.L.I.	—	Died
Carter, Fredk.	Pte.	11334	7th Yorks.	—	K. in A.
Carter, Harry	Pnr.	24019	Royal Engineers	—	D. a. Dis.
Carter, Harry	Rfm.	306802	1/8th W. Yorks.	—	D. of W.
Carter, Jabez	Pte.	38796	W. Yorks.	—	Died
Carter, James	Rfm.	5841	11th Rifle Brigade	—	K. in A.
Carter, John E.	Pte.	15484	13th W. Yorks.	—	Missing
Carter, John M.	Gnr.	96731	R.G.A.	—	K. in A.
Carter, John R.	Pte.	268551	2/6th W. Yorks.	—	K. in A.
Carter, Thos. C.	Pte.	37345	2nd W. Yorks.	—	K. in A.
Carter, W.	L/Cpl.	65476	Northumberland Fusrs.	—	K. in A.
Carter, Wm.	Pte.	13574	9th K.O.Y.L.I.	—	K. in A.
Carter, Wm. C.	Pte.	41806	K.O.Y.L.I.	—	D. of W.
Cartledge, John	Pte.	7649	North Staffs.	—	K. in A.
Cartmell, Rbt. W.	Pte.	36187	Northumberland Fusrs.	—	K. in A.
Cartwright, T.	Pte.	15298	York. & Lancs.	—	Died
Carty, D.	Pte.	1153	W. Riding	—	D. a. Dis.

LEEDS ROLL OF HONOUR.

Name	Rank	No.	Regiment	Honours	How Died
Carver, David	Pte.	11300	7th Yorks.	—	K. in A.
Carver, Thos.	A.B.	8561	Royal Naval Division	—	K. in A.
Casburn, Ernest	Pte.	642	W. Yorks.	—	K. in A.
Casey, Edward	Pte.	27752	W. Yorks.	—	K. in A.
Casey, Thos.	Pte.	6410	Connaught Rangers	—	Died
Cass, Francis	Pte.	8952	11th W. Yorks.	—	K. in A.
Cass, Frank	A/Bdr.	34661	R.F.A.	—	K. in A.
Cassidy, John	Spr.	279128	Royal Engineers	—	D. a. Dis.
Cassidy, Jos.	Pte.	21704	13th W. Yorks.	—	D. a. Dis.
Casson, Harry	Pte.	180	15th W. Yorks.	—	K. in A.
Cast, —		25866	3rd E. Yorks.	—	K. in A.
Castle, Herbert	Pte.	2353	York. & Lancs.	—	K. in A.
Cater, Geo.	Pte.	18604	York. & Lancs.	—	D. a. Dis.
Cathcart, Gavin B.	Pte.	2724	W. Yorks.	—	Died
Catherall, Geo.	Pte.	13023	K.O.Y.L.I.	—	Missing
Catherall, Herbert	Pte.	42760	Leicester	—	K. in A.
Caton, Fredk.	2nd Lieut.		Royal Air Force	—	D. of W.
Caton, Robert	Pte.	38857	2nd Yorks.	—	K. in A.
Cattle, Harry	Stkr.	100138	Royal Navy	—	Died
Catton, A. C.	Dvr.	18969	R.F.A.	—	Died
Catton, Alfred	Pte.	24853	W. Yorks.	—	D. of W.
Catton, Walter	Pte.	20809	Cheshire	—	D. of W.
Catton, Wm.	Pte.	1352	17th W. Yorks.	—	K. in A.
Catton, Wm. L.	Gnr.	127184	R.G.A.	—	Died
Caufield, John	Rfm.	2619	1/7th W. Yorks.	—	K. in A.
Caunt, Harry	Rfm.	267078	2/7th W. Yorks.	—	D. of W.
Cavanagh, Frank R.	Pte.	305	17th W. Yorks.	—	Died
Cave, Alfred T.	Pte.	33281	10th W. Yorks.	—	K. in A.
Cave, James A.	L/Cpl.	41907	Northumberland Fusrs.	—	K. in A.
Cawood, Arthur	Pte.	24016	K.O.Y.L.I.	—	Died
Cawood, Charlie	Rfm.	306895	2/8th W. Yorks.	—	K. in A.
Cawood, Fred	Pte.	1121	15th W. Yorks.	—	K. in A.
Cawood, Owen B.	L/Cpl.	83648	Royal Engineers	—	Died
Cawood, Walter	Pte.	266184	10th W. Yorks.	—	Missing
Cawood, Wilfred	Pte.	10770	W. Yorks.	—	Missing
Cawood, William	Pte.	15673	Labour Corps	—	Died
Cawson, Albert	Pte.	46878	Durham Light Infantry	—	K. in A.
Cawtheray, William	Pte.	21407	K.O.Y.L.I.	—	K. in A.
Cawthorne, Norman B.	Pte.	81757	Durham Light Infantry	—	K. in A.
Cawthorne, Tom	Sgt.	54507	Machine Gun Corps	—	K. in A.
Caygill, Fred	Pte.	201947	Scottish Rifles	—	K. in A.
Chadwick, A.				—	Died
Chadwick, Andrew	Spr.	276472	Royal Engineers	—	Drowned
Chadwick, Arthur	L/Cpl.	456164	Labour Corps	—	Died
Chadwick, Charles	Pte.	37656	9th W. Yorks.	—	D. of W.
Chadwick, Ernest	Pte.	18496	11th W. Yorks.	—	K. in A.
Chadwick, F. P.	Pte.	36055	E. Surrey	—	K. in A.

LEEDS ROLL OF HONOUR.

Name	Rank	No.	Regiment	Honours	How Died
Chadwick, Fred	Pte.	28022	15th W. Yorks.	—	Missing
Chadwick, Fredk.	Sgt.	8932	1st W. Yorks.	—	D. of W.
Chadwick, Fredk. W.	Pte.	36865	W. Yorks.		D. of W.
Chadwick, Harry	Pte.	8441	R.A.O.C.	—	Died
Chadwick, Herbert	L/Cpl.	8133	1st W. Yorks.	—	K. in A.
Chadwick, Herbert	Pte.	1934	17th W. Yorks.	—	D. of W.
Chadwick, J. M.	Pte.	27954	W. Yorks.	—	Died
Chadwick, James	A.B.	TZ7519	Royal Naval Division	—	K. in A.
Chadwick, John	Cpl.	1240	Machine Gun Corps	—	K. in A.
Chadwick, Louis	Pte.	54150	18th Canadians	—	K. in A.
Chadwick, Percy	Pte.	201453	2/5th W. Yorks.	—	K. in A.
Chadwick, Walter	Pte.	13315	Yorks.	—	K. in A.
Chadwick, William	Pte.	49063	1/5th W. Yorks.		Missing
Chadwick, William	Pte.	9276	9th W. Yorks.	—	Died
Chafer, Samuel	Rfm.	4006	1/7th W. Yorks.	—	K. in A.
Chaffer, Albert	A/Sgt.	017904	R.A.S.C.	—	Died
Chaffer, Jas. C.	O.S.	J55091	H.M.S. " Opal "	—	K. in A.
Challans, Clifford	Pte.	31156	1st E. Yorks.	—	K. in A.
Challinor, Wm. J.	Pte.	10275	W. Yorks.		K. in A.
Challis, Bertie	Pte.	291671	Northumberland Fusrs.		Died
Challis, James	Dvr.	42455	R.F.A.	—	Died
Challons, Clifford	Pte.	31156	1st E. Yorks.	—	K. in A.
Chaloner, Ed. P.	Sgt.	307820	1/8th W. Yorks.		K. in A.
Chamberlin, J.	Sgt.	8906	2nd W. Yorks.	—	K. in A.
Chambers, Albert	Pte.	14241	10th W. Yorks.	—	K. in A.
Chambers, Alfred G.	L/Cpl.	305194	1/8th W. Yorks.	—	K. in A.
Chambers, Arthur	Pte.	40252	18th W. Yorks.	—	K. in A.
Chambers, Arthur L.	Pte.	375522	1/8th Durham Lt. Infty.	—	K. in A.
Chambers, F.	Pte.	44596	Lincoln	—	Died
Chambers, Frank	Stkr.	K24928	H.M.S. " Victorious "	—	Died
Chambers, John H.	Pte.	187	15th W. Yorks.	—	Missing
Chambers, Joseph	L/Sgt.	266612	1/7th W. Yorks.	—	K. in A.
Chambers, Samuel	Pte.	28243	12th W. Yorks.	—	Missing
Chambers, Thomas	Rfm.	3849	1/8th W. Yorks.	—	K. in A.
Champlin, Henry	Pte.	27197	12th W. Yorks.	—	K. in A.
Champlin, Wm.	Sgt.	9139	K.O.Y.L.I.	—	K. in A.
Chandler, Jas. W.	Pte.		R.F.A.	—	K. in A.
Chaplin, Arthur	Pte.	4716	3/7th W. Yorks.	—	Died
Chaplin, Charles	Pte.	201809	1/5th Royal Scots Fusrs.	—	Died
Chapman, Alfred H.	Pte.	38959	Durham Light Infantry	—	Died
Chapman, Arthur A.	Lieut.		7th W. Riding	—	K. in A.
Chapman, Bernard	Pte.	7921	2nd Yorks.	—	K. in A.
Chapman, Chas. E.	A.B.	J43746	Royal Navy	—	K. in A.
Chapman, Claude F.	Spr.	172616	Royal Engineers	—	Died
Chapman, Clifford		7824	Scots Guards	—	Died
Chapman, Eric	Cpl.	2209	1/8th W. Yorks.	—	K. in A.
Chapman, F.	Pte.	13689	K.O.Y.L.I.	—	Died

LEEDS ROLL OF HONOUR.

Name	Rank	No.	Regiment	Honours	How Died
Chapman, G.	Sgt.	267467	2/6th W. Yorks.	—	K. in A.
Chapman, George	Pte.	51950	K.O.Y.L.I.	—	K. in A.
Chapman, Harry	Cpl.	14752	K.O.Y.L.I.	—	K. in A.
Chapman, Herbert D.	Pte.	191	15th W. Yorks.	—	Missing
Chapman, Horace	Pte.	38597	Lincoln	—	Died
Chapman, Lawrie	Pte.	20399	R.A.O.C.	—	K. in A.
Chapman, Nathan	Pte.	7745	Northumberland Fusrs.	—	K. in A.
Chapman, Percy	Rfm.	2116	7th W. Yorks.	—	K. in A.
Chapman, Robert	Pte.	265802	Royal Air Force	—	Died
Chapman, Stanley W.	Cpl.	777170	R.F.A.	—	K. in A.
Chapman, Walter	Pte.	702187	Labour Corps	—	D. a. Dis.
Chapman, Wilfred	Pte.	170844	A.S.C. (M.T.)	—	K. in A.
Chappell, Arthur R.	Pte.	4778	K.O.Y.L.I.	—	K. in A.
Chappell, Geo.	Pte.	13234	K.O.Y.L.I.	—	D. of W.
Chappelow, Thomas H.	Cpl.	2233	8th W. Yorks.	—	K. in A.
Charles, Hy. R.	Gnr.	1286	Royal Marine Artillery	—	K. in A.
Charlesworth, H. H.	Pte.	60329	Northumberland Fusrs.	—	Died
Charlesworth, Jas. A.	Pte.	34082	1st W. Yorks.	—	K. in A.
Charlesworth, John	E.R.A.		H.M.S. " Resolute "	—	Drowned
Charlesworth, Tom	L/Cpl.	3173	W. Yorks.	—	Died
Charlesworth, Walter	Pte.	52607	K.O.Y.L.I.	—	Died
Charlton, George E.	L/Cpl.	10571	12th W. Yorks.	—	Missing
Charnley, R.	Pte.	13473	Lancs. Fusiliers	—	Died
Charters, Fred R.	Pte.	37626	12th W. Yorks.	—	K. in A.
Chatburn, Bartle	Pte.	39394	2nd W. Yorks.	—	K. in A.
Chatsworthy, Jos. H.	Art.	2529	Royal Naval Reserve	—	K. in A.
Cheatter, W. F.	Pte.	268505	6th W. Yorks.	—	K. in A.
Cheetham, Albert	O.S.	J50123	Royal Navy	—	K. in A.
Cheetham, Ernest	Pte.	60965	W. Yorks.	—	K. in A.
Cheetham, Herbert	Lieut.		W. Yorks.	—	K. in A.
Cheesman, Fred	Rfm.	42023	Royal Irish Rifles	—	K. in A.
Chennell, Thomas L.	Pte.	23512	Labour Corps	—	Died
Cherman, Solomon	Rfm.	5151	8th W. Yorks.	—	K. in A.
Chew, Harold	Pte.	82983	R.A.M.C.	—	D. a. Dis.
Chew, Joseph	Gnr.	62002	R.G.A.	—	Died
Child, Clifford	Pte.	9990	2nd W. Yorks.	—	K. in A.
Child, Jas. W.	Pte.	12534	Durham Light Infantry	—	D. of W.
Child, Joseph	Pte.	351764	Royal Scots	—	K. in A.
Child, Joseph A.	L/Cpl.	266131	10th W. Yorks.	—	K. in A.
Child, Regd. V.	Pte.	29338	Border	—	Died P.O.W.
Child, Walter	Pte.	13918	4th R. Irish Drag'n Gds.	—	K. in A.
Child, William	Pte.	23650	2nd W. Yorks.	—	K. in A.
Childe, Norman E.	Rfm.	41972	7th E. Yorks.	—	Missing
Chippendale, James	Pte.	10210	1st E. Yorks.	—	K. in A.
Chippendale, Samuel	Pte.	2393	6th W. Yorks.	—	K. in A.
Chitham, Charles	Pte.	36715	W. Yorks.	—	Died
Chorley, Arthur R.	Captain		K.O.Y.L.I.	—	D. of W.

LEEDS ROLL OF HONOUR.

Name	Rank	No.	Regiment	Honours	How Died
Christie, Geo. H.	Cpl.	070312	R.A.S.C.	—	Died
Christie, John	Cpl.	42450	K.O.Y.L.I.	—	K. in A.
Church, Albert A.	Pte.	047204	R.A.S.C.	—	Died
Church, Harold	Cpl.	205	21st W. Yorks.	—	K. in A.
Clancy, Michael	Pte.	9428	Irish Guards	—	Died
Clapham, Arthur C.	Pte.	17871	10th W. Riding	—	K. in A.
Clapham, Joseph	Pte.	95127	Royal Fusiliers	—	K. in A.
Clapham, Reg. A.	Gnr.	1717	R.F.A.	—	D. of W.
Clapham, Rowland H.	L/Cpl.	3280	9th W. Yorks.	—	K. in A.
Clapham, Thomas	Cpl.	22908	6th W. Yorks.	—	Died
Clark, Albert	Pte.	15424	Coldstream Guards		K. in A.
Clark, Edward	Pte.	236864	Labour Corps.	—	K. in A.
Clark, Frank	Pte.	4830	Scots Guards	—	K. in A.
Clark, Frank	Cpl.	775205	R.F.A.	M.M.	D. of W.
Clark, Fredk.	Pte.	28404	6th S. Lancs.	—	K. in A.
Clark, Fredk.	Pte.	18803	K.O.Y.L.I.	—	K. in A.
Clark, George	Spr.	256264	Royal Engineers	—	D. a. Dis.
Clark, George	2/AM.	32897	Royal Air Force	—	K. in A.
Clark, Gus. E.	Pte.	38257	W. Yorks.	—	K. in A.
Clark, Harold	Pte.	82106	Durham Light Infantry	—	Died
Clark, Harry	A.B.	J6351	H.M.S. "Black Prince"	—	K. in A.
Clark, J. P.	Pte.	1759	5th Yorks.	—	K. in A.
Clark, John	Pte.	6487	2nd Life Guards	—	K. in A.
Clark, John E.	Pte.	46748	1st W. Yorks.		Missing
Clark, John W. H.	Rfm.	13103	8th W. Riding	—	K. in A.
Clark, Joseph	Pte.	30638	1st E. Yorks.	—	Died P.O.W.
Clark, Osmond	Pte.	33342	W. Yorks.	—	K. in A.
Clark, Regd. Geo.	Pte.	234311	52nd Canadian Infty.	—	K. in A.
Clark, Richard	Pte.	41771	Leicester	—	K. in A.
Clark, Tom	Rfm.	306122	8th W. Yorks.	—	Died
Clark, Walter	Pte.	14473	2/4th Yorks. & Lancs.	—	K. in A.
Clark, William	Pte.	2288	W. Yorks.	—	K. in A.
Clark, Wm. H.	Pte.	32333	15th W. Yorks.	—	Missing
Clarke, Alfred	Pte.	307373	W. Yorks.	—	K. in A.
Clarke, Alg. C.	Gnr.	222955	R.F.A.	—	K. in A.
Clarke, Archibald T.	Pte.	200	15th W. Yorks.	—	K. in A.
Clarke, Arthur	Pte.	13890	8th K.O.Y.L.I.	—	K. in A.
Clarke, Ernest A.	L/Cpl.	2057	2/7th W. Yorks.	—	K. in A.
Clarke, Fredk.	Pte.	21536	9th W. Yorks.	—	K. in A.
Clarke, Harry V.	Pte.	76369	Notts. & Derby.	—	K. in A.
Clarke, Jas.	Pte.	9436	Lincoln	—	K. in A.
Clarke, John	Pte.	17248	1st W. Yorks.	—	K. in A.
Clarke, John T.	Gnr.	365440	R.G.A.	—	Died
Clarke, M.	Sgt.	11319	Yorks.	—	Died
Clarke, R. L.	Pte.	04456	R.A.S.C.	—	Drowned
Clarke, W. E.	Rfm.	4309	7th W. Yorks.	—	K. in A.
Clarke, William	Pte.	164916	R.A.S.C. (M.T.)	—	Died

LEEDS ROLL OF HONOUR.

Name	Rank	No.	Regiment	Honours	How Died
Clarkson, Alfred	Pte.	17071	12th W. Yorks.	—	K. in A.
Clarkson, Arthur	Pte.	24929	K.O.Y.L.I.	—	K. in A.
Clarkson, F.	Pte.	13121	W. Yorks.	—	Died
Clarkson, Frank	Pte.	24042	W. Yorks.	—	K. in A.
Clarkson, G.	Pte.	33090	18th W. Yorks.	—	K. in A.
Clarkson, G. T.	Pte.	32988	W. Yorks.	—	K. in A.
Clarkson, George	Pte.	17238	W. Yorks.	—	Drowned
Clarkson, Geo. A.	Pte.	408325	R.A.M.C.	—	Died
Clarkson, James	Pte.	12217	10th W. Yorks.	—	K. in A.
Clarkson, James	Pte.	47215	W. Yorks.	—	Died
Clarkson, James	Pte.	15619	11th W. Yorks.	—	K. in A.
Clarkson, James L.	Pte.	1586	R.F.A.	—	Died
Clarkson, John	Pte.	53281	K.O.Y.L.I.	—	Died
Clarkson, John C.	Sgt.	30509	Border	—	K. in A.
Clarkson, John W.	Pte.	2528	W. Yorks.	—	D. of W.
Clarkson, Morris	Rfm.	14668	King's Royal Rifle Cps.	—	K. in A.
Clarkson, Robert C.	Pte.	149770	Machine Gun Corps	—	D. a. Dis.
Clarkson, Thomas	Pte.	1898	15th W. Yorks.	—	D. of W.
Clarkson, Thomas A.	Pte.	51343	1st E. Yorks.	—	K. in A.
Clarkson, Thomson W.	Pte.	37029	4th W. Yorks.	—	K. in A.
Clarkson, William	L/Cpl.	6828	2nd W. Yorks.	—	K. in A.
Clasper, Thomas S.	Spr.	49069	Royal Engineers	—	Died
Claughton, A. W.	Pte.	268791	12th W. Yorks.	—	Died
Claughton, Arthur	Gnr.	94334	R.G.A.	—	Died
Claughton, Garnet	Pte.	260046	Northumberland Fusrs.	—	K. in A.
Clay, Ernest	Gnr.	123476	R.G.A.	—	K. in A.
Clay, John	Pte.	10649	W. Riding	—	Died
Clayford, Douglas	Pte.	37890	10th E. Yorks.	—	Died
Clayford, Ernest	Pte.			—	K. in A.
Clayford, Willie	Pte.	40934	27th Northumb'l'd Fusrs.	—	K. in A.
Clayforth, Charles	Pte.	32491	3rd Yorks.	—	K. in A.
Clayforth, Chas. E.	Pte.	265624	W. Yorks.	—	Died
Clayforth, Ernest	Pte.	87835	2nd W. Yorks.	—	Died
Clayforth, Harry	Pte.	41320	Leicesters.	—	K. in A.
Clayton, A. W.	A/Cpl.	013156	R.A.O.C.	—	D. a. Dis.
Clayton, Clarence	A/Cpl.	26273	7th W. Yorks.	—	Died
Clayton, Frank	Sgt.	209	15th W. Yorks.	—	K. in A.
Clayton, Geo. W.	Pte.	1447	1st. W. Yorks.	—	K. in A.
Clayton, H.	A. L/Cpl.	306886	8th W. Yorks.	—	K.in A.
Clayton, Herbert	L/Cpl.	9056	W. Riding	—	Died
Clayton, J. W.	Rfm.	2198	1/8th W. Yorks.	—	K. in A.
Clayton, Jas.	Pte.	59971	Machine Gun Corps	—	Died
Clayton, Joe	Sgt.	7195	1st Scots Guards	—	Died
Clayton, John W.	L/Bdr.	31854	R.F.A.	—	Died
Clayton, Percy	Pte.	26221	W. Yorks.	—	Died
Clayton, Percy	Pte.	32701	9th York. & Lancs.	—	Missing
Clayton, Wm.	Pte.	344013	R.A.S.C.	—	Died

LEEDS ROLL OF HONOUR.

Name	Rank	No.	Regiment	Honours	How Died
Clegg, Geo.	Dvr.	252503	R.F.A.	—	K. in A.
Clegg, Henry E.	Pte.	21825	W. Yorks.	—	D. of W.
Clement, Elliott	Rfm.	14652	Scots Guards	—	K. in A.
Clement, John H.	Pte.	24533	16th W. Yorks.	—	K. in A.
Clemishaw, Wm.	Pte.	7482	H.A.C.	—	K. in A.
Clibbins, Wm.	L/Cpl.	9680	2nd W. Yorks.	—	K. in A.
Clibbins, Wm. G.	Pte.	37348	10th W. Yorks.	—	K. in A.
Cliff, H.	Major		W. Yorks.	—	K. in A.
Cliff, Herbert	Pte.	5482	2nd Royal Warwicks.	—	K. in A.
Cliff, Jas.	Pte.	61000	W. Yorks.	—	K. in A.
Cliff, Walter	Cpl.	8748	Border	—	K. in A.
Cliff, Walter	Rfm.	306022	1/8th W. Yorks.	—	K. in A.
Cliffe, Geo. E.	Dvr.	72267	R.F.A.	—	Died
Cliffe, Joseph	Pte.	10161	2nd W. Yorks.	—	K. in A.
Clifford, A.	Pte.	25260	12th E. Surreys	—	K. in A.
Clifford, Harold	Pte.	50288	10th Lancs. Fusiliers	—	K. in A.
Clifford, John W.	Pte.	31300	8th E. Yorks.	—	K. in A.
Clough, Albert E.	Pte.	23967	9th W. Yorks.	—	Missing
Clough, C. W.	Sgt.	390596	10th London	—	K. in A.
Clough, Jonathan	Rfm.	32269	2/8th W. Yorks.	—	K. in A.
Clough, Joseph	Spr.	361414	Royal Engineers	—	K. in A.
Clough, Norman H.	Pte.	28259	1st W. Yorks.	—	K. in A.
Clough, Wm.	Pte.	21791	13th W. Yorks.	—	Died
Cloutt, Harry	Pte.	34376	1st W. Yorks.	—	Missing
Clowerey, Alec.	L/Cpl.	57787	York. & Lancs.	—	K. in A.
Clowes, Peter	Spr.	158380	Royal Engineers	—	Missing
Cluderay, Thos.	Pte.	49105	W. Yorks.	—	Missing
Clutterham, Harry	Pte.	62635	Yorks.	—	Died
Clynes, John	Pte.	25448	9th Yorks.	—	K. in A.
Coates, A.	Pte.	34405	W. Yorks.	—	K. in A.
Coates, A.	Pte.	57017	W. Yorks.	—	K. in A.
Coates, Albert	Pte.	41534	8th Lincoln	—	K. in A.
Coates, Chas. M.	Pte.	33114	31st Northumb'l'd Fusrs.	—	Drowned
Coates, Ed. C.	L/Cpl.	10381	7th Munster Fusiliers	—	K. in A.
Coates, Fred	Pte.	24499	2nd W. Riding	—	D. of W.
Coates, Harry	Pte.	15431	9th W. Yorks.	—	Missing
Coates, John	Pte.	45719	20th Northumb'l'd Fusrs.	—	K. in A.
Coates, Lawrence	Rfm.	865	1/8th W. Yorks.	—	K. in A.
Coates, P.	2nd Lieut.		Royal Engineers	—	K. in A.
Coates, Wm.	Pte.	43149	13th Essex	—	Died P.O.W.
Coatham, Jas. R.	Pte.	1119	18th Durham Lt. Infty.	—	K. in A.
Cockayne, John	Pte.	21322	3rd W. Yorks.	—	K. in A.
Cockburn, John P.	Pte.	266637	1/6th Gordon Highdrs.	—	K. in A.
Cockroft, Geo. W.	Pte.	66	R.A.M.C.	—	K. in A.
Cockroft, Jas. Hy.	Pte.	78529	Durham Light Infantry	—	K. in A.
Cockerham, Harry	L/Clp.	268854	1/8th W. Yorks.	—	K. in A.
Cockerham, J. W.	Pte.	37620	W. Yorks.	—	K. in A.

LEEDS ROLL OF HONOUR.

Name	Rank	No.	Regiment	Honours	How Died
Cockerill, Jas.	Pte.	17922	Yorks. & Lancs.	—	Died
Cockshott, Morrell H.	Pte.	2357	Yorks. Hussars	—	Died
Coe, Wm.	Pte.	27722	9th Lancs. Fusiliers	—	K. in A.
Cogan, Jos. F.	Pte.	41975	Worcester	—	Died
Coggzan, Geo.	C.S.M.	20674	13th Royal Scots	—	Died
Coggill, Harold	Cpl.	215	15th W. Yorks.	—	Died
Coggill, Tom	Pte.	33259	W. Yorks.	—	K. in A.
Coggings, W.	Rfm.	48658	1/8th W. Yorks.	—	K. in A.
Coggins, John S.	Pte.	21508	2nd Northumb'l'd Fusrs.	—	K. in A.
Coghill, Herbert	Pte.	20738	W. Yorks.	—	Died
Cohen, Abraham	Pte.	307060	W. Yorks.	—	Died
Cohen, Abraham	Cpl.	14347	2nd Welsh	—	Died
Cohen, Abraham	Pte.	25070	Northumberland Fusrs.	—	K. in A.
Cohen, Adolphus B.	Lieut.		17th W. Yorks.	—	K. in A.
Cohen, Harry	Pte.	9998	1st Cheshire	—	K. in A.
Cohen, Jack	Pte.	24008	W. Riding	—	K. in A.
Cohen, Morris	Pte.	241285	Seaforth Highlanders	—	Died
Cohen, Morris	Rfm.	13469	9th King's R. Rifle Cps.	—	K. in A.
Coghlan, W. Humphrey	Lieut.		R.F.A.	—	K. in A.
Colby, Cliff	Pte.	17732	2nd W. Yorks.	—	K. in A.
Colcroft, G. W.	Pte.	216	W. Yorks.	—	K. in A.
Colden, Hbt. Wm.	L/Cpl.	19927	6th K.O.Y.L.I.	—	K. in A.
Coldham, Harold	Pnr.	98378	Royal Engineers	—	K. in A.
Cole, Ernest	Pte.	4128072	R.A.S.C.	—	Died
Cole, Jos.	Bdr.	1432	R.F.A.	—	K. in A.
Cole, Tom	Pte.	264750	R.A.S.C.	—	K. in A.
Colebrook, Alfred	Dvr.	L/16692	R.F.A.	—	K. in A.
Colebrook, Wm.	Pte.	579572	125th Labour Corps	—	D. a. Dis.
Colehan, Desmond	Pte.	322003	R.A.S.C. (M.T.)	—	D. a. Dis.
Coleman, Albert	Pte.	13769	W. Yorks.	—	D. a. Dis.
Coleman, Fred	Pte.	28015	14th W. Yorks.	—	K. in A.
Coley, Arthur	Cpl.	10042	1st Northumberl'd Fusrs.	—	K. in A.
Colledge, Herbert	Pte.	15261	Yorks.	—	Died
Collett, Alb. E.	Dvr.	327134	R.A.S.C.	—	Died
Collett, John E.	Pte.	40682	23rd Northumb'l'd Fusrs.	—	K. in A.
Collett, R.	Rfm.	266415	2/7th W. Yorks.	—	K. in A.
Colley, David	L/Cpl.	2254	7th Royal Munster Fusrs.	—	K. in A.
Colley, Harry	Rfm.	306315	1/8th W. Yorks.	—	K. in A.
Colley, Robt.	Pte.	31191	1/5th E. Lancs.	—	D. of W.
Collier, Edward	Cpl.	1583	2nd W. Yorks.	—	K. in A.
Collier, Geo.	Pte.	1759	R.A.M.C.	—	K. in A.
Collier, Wm.	Rfm.	2677	1/8th W. Yorks.	—	K. in A.
Collings, Arthur	Pte.	2509	W. Yorks.	—	D. of W.
Collins, Austin	Gnr.	776033	R.F.A.	—	D. of W.
Collins, Francis	Rfm.	304045	5th London	—	Missing
Collins, G. W.	Pte.	13762	10th W. Yorks.	—	K. in A.
Collins, Harold B.	Gnr.	58744	R.G.A.	—	K. in A.

LEEDS ROLL OF HONOUR.

Name	Rank	No.	Regiment	Honours	How Died
Collins, Harry	Rfm.	266145	2/7th W. Yorks.	—	Missing
Collins, James	Pte.	1641	W. Yorks.	—	Died
Collins, James	Pte.	12709	Labour Corps	—	K. in A.
Collins, John W.	Pte.	10345	2nd Yorks.	—	K. in A.
Collins, John	Pte.	8160	Royal Defence Corps	—	Died
Collins, Joseph	Spr.	145814	Royal Engineers	—	K. in A.
Collins, Patrick	Pte.	17189	1st W. Yorks.	—	K. in A.
Collins, Richard	Pte.	6645	11th W. Yorks.	—	D. of W.
Collins, Tom	Pte.	13557	K.O.Y.L.I.	—	D. of W.
Collinson, Ernest	3A.M.	281940	Royal Air Force	—	Died
Collinson, J. A.	Sgt.	40539	2nd South Staffs.	—	K. in A.
Collinson, J. W.	Cpl.	217	15/9th W. Yorks.	M.M.	K. in A.
Collis, Geo. W.	Pte.	13493	10th W. Yorks.	—	K. in A.
Coultate, Frank	Pte.	306107	W. Yorks.	—	K. in A.
Commons, John	Pte.	1630	1/4th K.O.Y.L.I.	—	K. in A.
Compton, Thos. Wm.	Pte.	28695	Royal Warwick	—	Died
Comstive, Percy	Pte.	25857	W. Yorks.	—	K. in A.
Conalty, Bernard	Pte.	149705	Labour Corps	—	Died
Conlan, Wm. A.	Pte.	8149	Royal Defence Corps	—	Died
Conlan, Edward	Pnr.	160878	Royal Engineers	—	Died
Conlan, Robt. E.	Pte.	21482	1st W. Yorks.	—	K. in A.
Conley, Austin	Pte.	45926	5th Yorks.	—	Died
Connell, David	Pte.	4622	1st W. Yorks.	—	K. in A.
Connell, Harold	Sgt.	21424	2nd Royal Dublin Fusrs.	—	Died
Connell, John Wm.	Pte.	40278	W. Yorks.	—	K. in A.
Connelley, Thos.	Pte.		W. Yorks.	—	Died
Connor, Albert	Gdsmn.	1088	4th Dragoon Guards	—	Died
Connor, George	Pte.	34315	Lincoln	—	Died
Connor, John	Pte.	20862	K.O. Scottish Bordrs.	—	K. in A.
Connor, Martin	Pte.	205377	297th Labour Corps	—	Died
Connor, T.	Pte.	20749	16th Cheshires	—	K. in A.
Connor, Thos.	Pte.	15845	11th W. Yorks.	—	K. in A.
Connors, John E.	Pte.			—	K. in A.
Conolly, Chas. W.	L/Cpl.	51189	4th Northumberl'd Fusrs.	—	Died
Constantine, John	Pte.	10770	8th W. Riding	—	K. in A.
Convey, Albert	Pte.	7691	4th W. Yorks.	—	K. in A.
Conway, Harry	Pte.	238036	21st Northumb'l'd Fusrs.	—	Died
Conway, N.	Pte.	138009	Machine Gun Corps.	—	Died
Conway, Thos.	Pte.	14155	7th Yorks.		K. in A.
Conway, Wm.	Pte.	29502	14th Highland Lt. Infty.	—	K. in A.
Conyers, Leon J.	Spr.	244219	Royal Engineers	—	D. of W.
Conyers, W.	Sgt.	222	15th W. Yorks.	—	K. in A.
Cook,				—	Died
Cook, Albert	Pte.	38782	Northumberland Fusrs.	—	K. in A.
Cook, Clifford	Pte.	4547	2/8th W. Yorks.	—	K. in A.
Cook, Ernest A. L.	Major		R.F.A.	M.C.	K. in A.
Cook, J. A.	Pte.	32785	W. Yorks.	—	K. in A.

LEEDS ROLL OF HONOUR.

Name	Rank	No.	Regiment	Honours	How Died
Cook, John	L/Cpl.	16696	York. & Lancs.	—	K. in A.
Cook, John Edwd.	L/Cpl.	8113	1st W. Yorks.	—	D. of W.
Cook, Jos.	S.S.	775015	Royal Air Force	—	D. a. Dis.
Cook, Lawrence	Pte.	408003	R.A.M.C.	—	Died
Cook, R.				—	K. in A.
Cook, Wm. Arthur	Pte.		2nd York. & Lancs.	—	K. in A.
Cooke, Charles	Pte.	20633	9th K.O.Y.L.I.	—	Missing
Cooke, Jas. E.	Rfm.	4419	1/7th West Yorks.	—	K. in A.
Cooke, Jas. Wm.	Pte.	16783	14th York. & Lancs.	—	K. in A.
Cooke, Wm. Arthur	Pte.	7662	2nd York. & Lancs.	—	K. in A.
Cooke, Wilf. Henry	Pte.	90004	Machine Gun Corps	—	K. in A.
Cooke, Williamson	Pte.	29497	W. Yorks.	—	K. in A.
Cookson, John F.	Sgt.	19324	24th Labour Corps	—	K. in A.
Cookson, Jos...	Pte.	1663	17th W. Yorks.	—	K. in A.
Coomer, Percy	Pte.	267005	2/5th West Yorks.	—	Died
Cooney, Steven	Pte.	40250	1st W. Yorks.	—	K. in A.
Coop, Arthur				—	Died
Coop, John				—	Died
Cooper, Alf.	Pte.	40007	Royal Welsh Fusiliers	—	D. a. Dis.
Cooper, Ernest	Pte.	6527	Rifle Brigade	—	Died.
Cooper, Frank	Gnr.	207669	R.G.A.	—	Died
Cooper, Frank A.					Died
Cooper, Geo.	A.B.	Tl./5718	Royal Naval Division	—	K. in A.
Cooper, Geo. N.	Pte.	32688	1st W. Yorks.	—	K. in A.
Cooper, Geo. T.	Pte.	63416	2nd W. Yorks.	—	K. in A.
Cooper, Harold	Pte.	5545	York. & Lancs.	—	K. in A.
Cooper, Harry	Pte.	33826	1st West Yorks.	—	K. in A.
Cooper, Henry D.	Pte.	19509	Royal Marines	—	K. in A.
Cooper, Jas. W.	Rfm.	2795	1/8th W. Yorks.	—	K. in A.
Cooper, John W.	L/Cpl.	1512	7th W. Yorks.	—	K. in A.
Cooper, Jos.	Pte.	4367	3/4th Seaforth Hghdrs.	—	K. in A.
Cooper, Jos.	Pte.		Labour Corps.	—	Died
Cooper, Reg. J.	L/Cpl.	403564	R.A.M.C.	—	K. in A.
Cooper, Walter	Pte.	42513	1st East Yorks.	—	K. in A.
Cooper, Wm.	Spr.	82772	Royal Engineers	—	K. in A.
Cooper, Wm.	Pte.	28794	K.O.Y.L.I.	—	D. of W.
Coote, Clifford	Pte.	24753	10th W. Yorks.	—	Missing
Coote, Walter	L/Cpl.	6188	2nd K.O.Y.L.I.	—	D. of W.
Copeman, Oswald	L/Sgt.	12357	6th E. Yorks.	—	K. in A.
Copeman, Saml.	Pte.	2041	2/1st S. Notts. Hussars	—	K. in A.
Corbett, Geo.	Pte.	19947	6th York. & Lancs.	—	K. in A.
Corcoran, James	Pte.	16571	7th K.O. Scottish Brdrs.	—	K. in A.
Corcoran, Luke	Pte.	4808	West Yorks.	—	Died
Corcoran, Matthew	Pte.	10238	9th W. Yorks.	—	K. in A.
Cordingley, Harold	Pte.	268895	1/5th W. Yorks.	—	K. in A.
Cordingley, Hbt.	Pte.	11646	3rd Scots. Guards	—	D. of W.
Cordukes, Geo. Wm.	Pte.	1411	Royal Marine Lt. Infty.	—	K. in A.

LEEDS ROLL OF HONOUR.

Name	Rank	No.	Regiment	Honours	How Died
Corker			10th Aust. Light Horse	—	K. in A.
Corker, H. R.	Pte.	12476	8th Royal Welsh Fusrs.	—	K. in A.
Corlett, Cliff N.	Pte.	28342	Loyal N. Lancs.	—	Died
Corner, Tom	Pte.	10937	9th W. Yorks.	—	K. in A.
Cornforth, Norman L.	2nd Lieut.		Royal Air Force	—	K. in A.
Cornish, J. S.	1st A.M.	103264	Royal Air Force	—	D. a. Dis.
Cornwall, Arthur	Pte.	1815	12th K.O.Y.L.I.	—	K. in A.
Cory, Harry	Rfm.	5015	1/7th W. Yorks.	—	K. in A.
Cossins, Chas. Wm.	Pte.	19483	K.O.Y.L.I.	—	K. in A.
Costello, James	Pte.	10176	W. Yorks.	—	Died
Costello, John	L./Cpl.	17265	W. Yorks.	—	K. in A.
Cottan, Chas. T.	Pte.	189	13th York. & Lancs.	—	K. in A.
Cotterill, W. H.	Gnr.	113677	R.G.A.	—	Died
Cotton, Wilf.	Gnr.	127184	R.G.A.	—	Died
Coulson, David	L./Cpl.	41447	E. Yorks.	—	K. in A.
Coulson, Geo.	L./Cpl.	7886	9th W. Yorks.	—	Missing
Coultas, Walter	Pte.	242513	1/6th W. Yorks.	—	Died
Coultate, Clifford	Cpl.	40299	1st Royal Highlanders	—	K. in A.
Coultate, Geo.	Pte.	8463	9th Yorks.	—	K. in A.
Coultate, T.	Pte.	340	17th W. Yorks.	—	K. in A.
Coultate, Thos.	Pte.	1506	9th W. Yorks.	—	K. in A.
Coulthard, Jas.	Pte.	7163	3rd Royal Welsh Fusrs.	—	K. in A.
Coults, Arthur	A.B.	84201	Royal Naval Division	—	Died
Couplan, Jos.	Spr.	476478	Royal Engineers	—	K. in A.
Couplan, Maurice	Sgt.	10917	1/7th W. Riding	—	D. of W.
Coupland, John	Pte.	18435	9th W. Yorks.	—	K. in A.
Cousins, Jos.	Dvr.T/	4249764	R.A.S.C.	—	Died
Coutts, Arthur	A.B.	8420	Royal Naval Division	—	Died
Coward, James	Rfm.	4190	1/8th W. Yorks.	—	K. in A.
Cowell, Frank	Dvr. T/	329758	R.A.S.C.	—	Died
Cowell, Wilfred	Gnr.	5770	R.F.A.	—	Died
Cowl, Geo.	Gnr.	47981	R.F.A.	—	K. in A.
Cowling, Jas.	Gnr.	88399	R.F.A.	—	Died
Cowling, Wm. Henry	2/AM.	13959	Royal Air Force	—	Died
Cowlisham, Elijah	L/Cpl.	125478	Royal Fusiliers	—	Died
Cox, Alfred	A/Sgt.	P/6145	Military Foot Police	—	Killed
Cox, Arthur	Pte.	398377	Labour Corps	—	Died
Cox, Arthur	Gnr.	134835	R.F.A.	—	K. in A.
Cox, Chas. F. A.	L/Cpl.	237	15th W. Yorks.	—	K. in A.
Cox, Geo.	Pte.	41742	9th Essex	—	K. in A.
Cox, Harold	Sgt.	305820	1/8th W. Yorks.	—	K. in A.
Cox, Henry	Pte.	98808	Northumberland Fusrs.	—	Died
Cox, Hbt.	Pte.	307140	W. Yorks.	—	Missing
Cox, John	Rfm.	3246	1/7th W. Yorks.	—	K. in A.
Cox, John Patrick	Pte.	2/075973	R.A.S.C. (M.T.)	—	Died
Cox, Robert	Pte.	19297	K.O.Y.L.I.	—	K. in A.
Cox, Wm.	Gnr.	J/17266	H.M.S. " Vanguard "	—	K. in A.

LEEDS ROLL OF HONOUR.

Name	Rank	No.	Regiment	Honours	How Died
Coyle, A.	Pte.	106725	Notts. & Derby.	—	Missing
Coyle, D.	Pte.	242448	Labour Corps	—	Died
Coyne, Wm.	Pte.	307491	1/6th W. Yorks.	—	K. in A.
Coyne, Wm.	Pte.	13797	W. Yorks.	—	D. of W.
Crabtree, Angus	Pte.	263031	W. Riding	—	K. in A.
Cracknell, Alfred	Pte.	21818	10th W. Yorks.	—	K. in A.
Craddock, James	Pte.	15408	6th Yorks.	—	K. in A.
Craig, John	Pte.	7998	6th Yorks.	—	K. in A.
Crampton, Thos.	Pte.	28949	W. Yorks.	—	Died
Crampton, Wm.	Pte.	740458	Gordon Highlanders	—	D. of W.
Crane, Jas.	Pte.	34708	23rd Northumb'l'd Fusrs.	—	K. in A.
Crann, Fred	Pte.	45264	1/6th Northumb'l'd Fusrs.	—	Missing
Crannage, Harry	P.O.	R12239	H.M.S. "Adamant"	—	Drowned
Crashley, J.	Pte.	41930	10th Northumb'ld' Fusrs.	—	K. in A.
Craven, Albert	Pte.	35366	2nd W. Yorks.	—	D. of W.
Craven, Arthur	Pte.	41312	Leicester		K. in A.
Craven, Bingley	Pte.	30512	Border	—	D. a. Dis.
Craven, Ernest	Pte.	242	15th W. Yorks.	—	K. in A.
Craven, Gilbert	Rfm.	62709	1/7th W. Yorks.	—	K. in A.
Craven, Harold	Pte.	266689	Gordon Highlanders	—	K. in A.
Craven, Harry	Dvr.	80957	R.F.A.	—	Died
Craven, Hbt.	L/Cpl.	9792	W. Yorks.	—	K. in A.
Craven, Henry M.	Pte.	17970	9th W. Yorks.	—	K. in A.
Craven, James	Pte.	3150	7th W. Yorks.	—	K. in A.
Craven, Thos.	Pte.	28806	K.O. Scottish Bordrs.	—	K. in A.
Craven, Wm.	Pte.	13062	11th W. Yorks.	—	K. in A.
Craven, Wm. Henry	Spr.	174730	Royal Engineers	—	K. in A.
Craven, Wm. V.	Dvr.	2407	R.F.A.	—	Died
Crawford, Harold	Pte.	1139	12th E. Yorks.	—	K. in A.
Crawford, John Fredk.	Sgt.	266160	2/7th W. Yorks.	—	K. in A.
Crawford, Richard	Pte.	35866	K.O.Y.L.I.	—	K. in A.
Crawford, William	Pte.	305859	1/5th W. Yorks.	—	Missing
Crawley, Alfred	Pte.	34517	11th K.O.Y.L.I.	—	K. in A.
Crawshaw, Wm.	Pte.	76613	11th Welsh	—	K. in A.
Crayton, Michael	A.B.	KP103	Royal Naval V. Reserve	—	K. in A.
Creed, Ernest	L/Cpl.	18087	Royal Engineers	—	Died
Creek, Clifford	Pte.	38812	W. Yorks.	—	K. in A.
Creighton, John	Pte.	506371	3rd W. Yorks.	—	K. in A.
Creswick, Wm.	Sgt.	776830	R.F.A.	M.M.	D. of W.
Crew, Ben	Pte.	754	1st W. Yorks.	—	K. in A.
Crick, Arthur	A/Cpl.	264401	Labour Corps	—	Died
Critchley, Harry	Pte.	42018	10th Northumb'l'd Fusrs.	—	K. in A.
Crockett, Lionel	Pte.	3801	3/5th W. Yorks.	—	K. in A.
Croft, Cyril	L/Cpl.	266368	8th W. Yorks.	—	K. in A.
Croft, Geo.	A/Sgt.	2631	Northumberland Fusrs.	—	Killed
Croft, John	Pte.	11706	10th W. Yorks.	—	K. in A.
Croft, Wm.	Pte.	51	17th W. Yorks.	—	D. of W.

LEEDS ROLL OF HONOUR.

Name	Rank	No.	Regiment	Honours	How Died
Cromack, Chas.	Pte.	439299	Labour Corps	—	Died
Cromack, Cyrus	Pte.	179459	743rd Labour Corps	—	K. in A.
Cromack, Lawrence	Pte.	39063	R.A.S.C.	—	Died
Cromack, S.	Pte.	5638	Yorks.	—	K. in A.
Cromark, John	Pte.	266613	W. Yorks.	—	K. in A.
Crombie, Robt.	Pte.	260066	York. & Lancs.	—	Missing
Crompton, Chas. S.	Pte.	9708	H.A.C.	—	Missing
Cropper, Wm.	2nd Lieut.		6th London	—	K. in A.
Crook, Charlie	Gnr.	66685	R.F.A.	—	D. of W.
Crook, G. A.				—	Died
Crook, Harry	Pte.	1589	1st W. Yorks.	—	Missing
Crook, John	Pte.	12669	10th W. Yorks.	—	Died
Crooks, Harry	Gnr.	66343	R.F.A.	—	K. in A.
Crooks, Henry	Pte.	31144	E. Yorks.	—	K. in A.
Croon, F. J.	Spr.	72923	Royal Engineers	—	Died
Crosby, Arthur	Pte.	36572	W. Yorks.	—	Died
Crosby, George	Pte.	16572	W. Riding	—	Died
Crosby, J. E.	L/Cpl.	4615	Connaught Rangers	—	Died
Crosby, John Jos.	Pte.	22092	Lancs. Fusiliers	—	Died
Crosfill, Geo.	Pte.	305922	W. Yorks.	—	K. in A.
Crosland, Herbert	Pte.	84	13th York. & Lancs.	—	K. in A.
Cross, John	Gnr.	800886	R.F.A.	—	K. in A.
Cross, Samuel	L./Sgt.	307880	W. Riding	—	Died
Crossfield, Wilfred	Pte.	7321	1st Scots Guards	—	D. of W.
Crossland, Chas.	Gnr.	39197	R.G.A.	—	D. of W.
Crossland, Harry	Sgt.	1321	8th W. Yorks.	—	K. in A.
Crossland, John	Pte.	1375	15th W. Yorks.	—	Died
Crossland, John Hy.	A.B.	334	H.M.S. " Good Hope "	—	Drowned
Crossland, Robt.	Pte.	248	15th W. Yorks.	—	Died
Crossley, F.	Pte.	33957	9th W. Yorks.	—	K. in A.
Crossley, George	Pte.	41986	10th Northumb'l'd Fusrs.	—	Died
Crossley, Henry S.	Pte.	2088	3rd K.O.Y.L.I.	—	K. in A.
Crossley, Herbert	Pte.	710	W. Yorks.	—	K. in A.
Crossley, Leonard	Pte.	43917	1st Royal Inniskillen Fusrs.	—	K. in A.
Crossley, Robert	Sgt.	8685	K.O. Scottish Bordrs.	—	Killed
Crossley, Stanley	Pte.	56235	R.A.M.C.	—	K. in A.
Crossley, Wilfred	Pte.	249	15th W. Yorks.	—	Missing
Crossman, George	Cpl.	10802	Devon	—	Died
Crosthwaite, Stanley	Pte.	201510	Royal Scots Fusiliers	—	K. in A.
Crowe, Cyril D.	Pte.	5727	5th W. Yorks.	—	Died
Crowe, L.	Pte.	328033	Lancs. Fusiliers	—	Killed
Crowther, Albert	Cpl.	1879	W. Yorks.	—	K. in A.
Crowther, Arthur	Pte.	86801	11th Machine Gun Cps.	—	Killed
Crowther, C. E.	Pte.	19666	4th York. & Lancs.	—	K. in A.
Crowther, Chas. Edwin	Pte.	13000	3rd W. Yorks.	—	K. in A.
Crowther, Clifford	Pte.	25802	13th Yorks.	—	K. in A.
Crowther, Henry	Pte.	39427	2nd W. Yorks.	—	K. in A.

LEEDS ROLL OF HONOUR.

Name	Rank	No.	Regiment	Honours	How Died
Crowther, J. E.	Pte.	32543	8th York. & Lancs.	—	K. in A.
Crowther, Jack	Rfm.	8958	7th King's R. Rifle Cps.	—	Missing
Crowther, Jos. Charles	Cpl.	10816	Royal Defence Corps	—	Died
Crowther, Wm.	Pte.	14281	12th W. Yorks.	—	K. in A.
Crowther, Willie	Pte.	36799	16th W. Yorks.	—	Died
Crozier, Fred Jas.	Rfm.	3722	2/8th W. Yorks.	—	K. in A.
Cuckson, Alfred	Pte.	103431	R.A.M.C.	—	K. in A.
Cuddy, Jos.	Pte.	26628	1st W. Yorks.	—	Died
Cudworth, Harold	S/Sgt.	T/1363	R.A.O.C.	—	Died
Cudworth, Rudolph C.	A.B.		H.M.S. " Indefatigable "	—	K. in A.
Cullen, Wilfred	Gnr.	167607	R.G.A.	—	K. in A.
Cullen, Wm. L.	L/Cpl.	29373	E. Surrey	—	K. in A.
Culley, Leonard	Pte.	58775	W. Yorks.	—	K. in A.
Cullingworth, Ellis	Pte.	41616	17th W. Yorks.	—	K. in A.
Cullingworth, J.	Pte.	68393	4th London	—	K. in A.
Cullingworth, Jas. L.	Pte.	302682	13th Durham Lt. Infty.	—	K. in A.
Culloden, Arthur	Pte.	41747	W. Yorks.	—	K. in A.
Cullum, James	Pte.	284789	124th Labour Corps	—	Died
Cummings, Bertie	Dvr.	99284	R.F.A.	—	D. of W.
Cummings, Jas. Henry	Pte.	45	17th W. Yorks.	—	K. in A.
Cundale, Frank Rbt.	L/Cpl.	305783	W. Yorks.	—	Died P.O.W.
Cundall, Rbt.	Pte.	S/39	H.M.S. " Victory "	—	K. in A.
Cundell, Wm.	Spr.	83806	Royal Engineers	—	Died
Cunliffe, Ellis M.	Pte.	306067	W. Yorks.	—	Died
Cunningham, Harry	Dvr.	75066	R.F.A.	—	K. in A.
Cunningham, J.	Stkr.	00003	H.M.S. " Macedonia "	—	Died
Cunningham, Jos. G.	Pte.	22282	1st W. Yorks.	—	K. in A.
Cunningham, Jos. P.	Pte.	40338	12th R. Scots	—	D. a. Dis.
Curling, Cecil W.	Pte.	68003	R.F.A.	—	K. in A.
Curnock, Bernard	Pte.	306294	W. Yorks.	—	K. in A.
Currie, Donald	Pte.	26166	1/4th E. Yorks.	—	K. in A.
Currier, Stanley C.	L/Cpl.	35966	Northumberland Fusrs.	—	Died
Curry, Owen	Pte.	9446	2nd W. Riding	—	K. in A.
Curtis, J. N.			W. Yorks.	—	Died
Curtis, W. S.	Pte.	2962	15th London	—	K. in A.
Cushin, Ernest	Gnr.	76824	Tank Corps	—	K. in A.
Custance, Stanley	Pte.	35075	24th Northumb'l'd Fusrs.	—	K. in A.
Cusworth, Geo.	C.S.M.	265073	W. Yorks.	—	Died
Cuthbert, Harry	Pte.	34633	Manchester	—	K. in A.
Cutler, T.	Pte.	79917	31st Canadians	—	K. in A.
Cutts, Jas. Wm.	Pte.	18990	9th W. Yorks.	—	K. in A.
Cutts, Kelvin E.	Pte.	3162	1/5th W. Riding	—	D. of W.
Daccus, Edmund F.	Pte.	44828	9th Manchester	—	K. in A.
Dacre, John Wm.	Pte.	50291	Lancs. Fusiliers	—	D. of W.
Dadswell, Chas.	Pte.	7375	7th R. Sussex	—	K. in A.
Dagless, John J.	Rfm.	266422	1/7th W. Yorks.	—	K. in A.

LEEDS ROLL OF HONOUR.

Name	Rank	No.	Regiment	Honours	How Died
Dailey, Thos.	A.B.	8209	Royal Naval V. Reserve	—	K. in A.
Dains, Herbert	Rfm.	4989	3/7th W. Yorks.	—	K. in A.
Daker, H.	Pte.	1942	R.A.M.C.	—	K. in A.
Dalby, Arthur	Pte.	39480	W. Yorks.	—	K. in A.
Dalby, Arthur	Pte.	36864	15th W. Yorks.	—	K. in A.
Dalby, Douglas	Pte.		R.A.S.C. (M.T.)	—	K. in A.
Dalby, John	Pte.	49029	W. Yorks.	—	K. in A.
Dalby, Richard	Sgt.		1/7th W. Yorks.	—	K. in A.
Dale, C. F.	Pte.	43141	Scottish Rifles	—	K. in A.
Dale, Edgar	Pte.	4656	3/5th Seaforth Hdrs.	—	K. in A.
Dale, J. W.	Pte.	43510	4th Bedfords	—	K. in A.
Dale, Matthew		1626	1st Northumb'l'd Fusrs.	—	K. in A.
Dale, Robt. Hy	Pte.	12748	10th W. Yorks.	—	K. in A.
Daley, Bernard	Pte.	40984	W. Yorks.	—	K. in A.
Daley, John	Pte.	17592	Machine Gun Corps.	—	K. in A.
Daley, John Thos.	L/Cpl.	5240	2nd Yorks.	—	K. in A.
Daley, H.	Pte.	268401	W. Riding	—	K. in A.
Dalton, Clifford	Rfm.	3289	1/8th W. Yorks.	—	Died
Dalton, H. E.	L/Cpl.	41852	Northumberland Fusrs.	—	K. in A.
Dalton, Horace M.	2nd Lieut.		E. Yorks.	—	K. in A.
Dalton, James F.	Rfm.	1527	1/8th W. Yorks.	—	K. in A.
Dalton, John Ed.	Pte.	15479	8th R. Scots Fusiliers	—	D. of W.
Dalton, Wilfred	Pte.	40129	Royal Scots Fusiliers	—	Died
Daly, Francis	Rfm.	4114	1/8th W. Yorks.	—	K. in A.
Daly, Peter	Pte.	36599	1st S. Staffs.	—	Died
Daly, Wm.	Pte.	9476	2nd W. Yorks.	—	K. in A.
Danby, Fred	Pte.	202136	1st Leicester	—	K. in A.
Danby, George	Rfm.	386	King's Royal Rifle Corps	—	K. in A.
Dancer, J. E.	Rfm.	266208	7th W. Yorks.	—	Died
Daneygar, Louis	Cpl.	20944	7th K.O. Scottish Brdrs.	—	K. in A.
Dangerfield, Ernest	L/Cpl.	25890	15th Yorks.	—	K. in A.
Daniels, Harold	Pte.	50292	10th Lancs. Fusiliers	—	K. in A.
Daniels, James	Pte.	11441	Manchester	—	K. in A.
Daniels, W.	Gnr.	58661	R.G.A.	—	K. in A.
Danley, F.	Pte.	202136	Leicester	—	Died
Danvers, M.	C.Q.M.S.	1109	Royal Lancs.	—	K. in A.
Daper, H.	Pte.	1942	R.A.M.C.	—	D. of W.
Darby, Chas. F.	A.B.	—	H.M.S. " Iron Duke "	—	Died
Darbyshire, Clifford	Pte.	818	2nd W. Yorks.	—	K. in A.
Darbyshire, Frank	Pte.	245114	1/5th Durham Lt. Infty.	—	D. of W.
Darbyshire, Wm.	Pte.	21407	10th York. & Lancs.	—	K. in A.
Darcy, Geo. A.	Pte.	25874	9th York. & Lancs.	—	K. in A.
D'Arcy, Michael J.	Sgt.	7677	Royal Inniskilling Fusrs.	—	K. in A.
Darfield, Arthur	Pte.	12724	16th W. Yorks.	—	K. in A.
Darley, Percy R.	Pte.	75710	Tank Corps	—	Died P.O.W.
Darwell, Wm. G.	Cpl.	103345	R.A.S.C. (M.T.)	—	K. in A.
Davey, Edgar	Sgt.	13093	W. Yorks.	—	K. in A.

LEEDS ROLL OF HONOUR.

Name	Rank	No.	Regiment	Honours	How Died
Davey, Fred	Pte.	7500	W. Riding	—	D. a. Dis.
Davey, Harry	Pte.	45494	1/9th K.O.Y.L.I.	—	K. in A.
Davey, John	L/Sgt.	6007	W. Riding	—	K. in A.
David, Lionel A. D.	2nd Lieut.		7th Yorks.	—	K. in A.
Davidson, Chas.	Rfm.	4451	3/8th W. Yorks.	—	K. in A.
Davidson, George	Pte.	40952	Cameron Highlanders	—	K. in A.
Davidson, John A.	Rfm.	201299	Rifle Brigade	—	Died
Davies	Pte.	33899	25th Northumb'l'd Fusrs.	—	Died
Davies, Alfred	Pte.	30679	Lancs. Fusiliers	—	K. in A.
Davies, Ernest	Pte.	21214	K.O.Y.L.I.	—	K. in A.
Davies, J. E.	Pte.	62332	2nd K.O.Y.L.I.	—	D. of W.
Davies, James S.	Pte.	307138	11th W. Yorks.	—	K. in A.
Davies, John	Pte.	52039	K.O.Y.L.I.	—	K. in A.
Davies, Leonard	L/Cpl.	024466	R.A.O.C.	—	Died
Davies, Myer	1/A.M.	20834	Royal Air Force	—	K. in A.
Davies, Richard	Dvr.	092279	R.A.S.C.	—	K. in A.
Davies, W.	Pte.	42360	2/6th W. Yorks.	—	K. in A.
Davies, Walter	Rfm.	4279	1/7th W. Yorks.	—	K. in A.
Davies, Walter H.	Sig.	203958	2nd Worcester	—	K. in A.
Davill, Harry	Pte.	9289	Seaforth Highlanders	—	K. in A.
Davis, —	Rfm.	4989	3/7th W. Yorks.	—	Died
Davis, Amos	Spr.	79219	Royal Engineers	—	K. in A.
Davis, Geo. W.	Pte.	19701	W. Yorks.	—	K. in A.
Davis, Isaac	Dvr.	158939	R.H.A.	—	K. in A.
Davis, Tom	Pte.	38891	Northumberland Fusrs.	—	K. in A.
Davis, Wm. C.	Pte.	267	15th W. Yorks.	—	K. in A.
Davison, Christopher	Pte.	1592	15th W. Yorks.	—	K. in A.
Davison, F.	Sgt.	9802	W. Riding	—	K. in A.
Davison, Herbert	Cpl.	98589	Royal Engineers	—	K. in A.
Davison, J.	Spr.	343237	Royal Engineers	—	Died
Davison, J.	Pte.	49464	W. Yorks.	—	D. a. Dis.
Davison, J. W.	L/Cpl.	12903	8th K.O.Y.L.I.	—	Missing
Davy, Albert	Pte.	140574	Machine Gun Corps	—	Died
Dawe, Robt.	Pte.	17/259	W. Yorks.	—	K. in A.
Dawes, Fred	Rfm.	4016	1/7th W. Yorks.	—	K. in A.
Dawkins, Chas.				—	
Daws, Harry	A/Bdr.	293721	R.G.A.	—	K. in A.
Dawson, A.	Pte.	458453	60th Canadians	—	K. in A.
Dawson, Chas.	Gnr.	71774	R.F.A.	—	Died
Dawson, Clarence	Pte.	30142	E. Yorks.	—	K. in A.
Dawson, Ernest A.	Gnr.	110078	Tank Corps	—	Died
Dawson, Fred	Gdsmn.	19304	Coldstream Guards	—	K. in A.
Dawson, Fred M.	Sig.	123112	R.G.A.	—	K. in A.
Dawson, George K.	Pte.	T/410981	R.A.S.C.	—	Died
Dawson, Harold	Pte.	31974	12th York. & Lancs.	—	Died
Dawson, Harry	Pte.	21577	18th Highland Lt. Infty.	—	K. in A.
Dawson, Harry	Pte.	15055	26th Labour Corps	—	K. in A.

LEEDS ROLL OF HONOUR.

Name	Rank	No.	Regiment	Honours	How Died
Dawson, Harry	Pte.	268515	W. Yorks.	—	K. in A.
Dawson, Harry V.	Cpl.	266287	W. Yorks.	—	K. in A.
Dawson, Herbert	Pte.	17907	Labour Corps	—	Died
Dawson, Herbert H.M.	2nd Lieut.		R.F.A.	—	K. in A.
Dawson, J.	Pte.	263143	Border	—	D. a. Dis.
Dawson, J. H.	Pte.	20043	Northumberland Fusrs.	—	Died
Dawson, James		S/10567	2nd Royal Highlanders	—	K. in A.
Dawson, John	Rfm.	266256	2/7th W. Yorks.	—	K. in A.
Dawson, Percy	Pte.	39481	2nd W. Yorks.	—	Died
Dawson, Robert	Gnr.	165580	R.F.A.	—	K. in A.
Dawson, Sydney	Lieut. Adjt.		8th York. & Lancs.	—	K. in A.
Dawson, Thos.	Pte.	12022	1st Highland Lt. Infty.	—	K. in A.
Dawson, Wm.	Sig.	1655	1/5th W. Yorks.	—	K. in A.
Day, Alfred	Rfm.	4371	1/8th W. Yorks.	—	K. in A.
Day, Chas.	Pte.	27940	Lancs. Fusrs.	—	K. in A.
Day, Chas. Wm.	Pte.	8633	Liverpool	—	D. a. Dis.
Day, Ed. A.	Cpl.	252282	R.A.S.C.	—	D. a. Dis.
Day, Ernest	Pte.	37521	W. Yorks.	—	K. in A.
Day, Ernest B.	Pte.	3/8966	Dorset	—	Died
Day, George	Pte.	622534	Canadian Infantry	—	K. in A.
Day, Herbert	Gnr.	140980	R.F.A.	—	D. of W.
Day, Richard	Major		R.F.A.	M.C. and Bar	K. in A.
Deacon, John	Pte.	306269	2/5th W. Yorks.	—	K. in A.
Deacon, Wm.	Pte.	13987	12th W. Yorks.	—	K. in A.
Dean, Arthur	Pte.	19262	K.O.Y.L.I.	—	K. in A.
Dean, Chas. Wm.	Pte.	G/52169	Middlesex	—	Died
Dean, Fred	Pte.	113918	Durham Lt. Infantry	—	D. a. Dis.
Dean, G.	L/Cpl.	303454	1/4th Northants	—	Missing
Dean, Harold	Pte.	53124	11th Manchester	—	K. in A.
Dean, Harry	Sgt.	43289	R.A.S.C.	—	K. in A.
Dean, Herbert L.				—	
Dean, J. G.	Pte.	306597	W. Yorks.	—	K. in A.
Dean, Joseph	Rfm.	55076	1/7th W. Yorks.	—	Missing
Dean, Leonard	Pte.	266782	1/5th W. Yorks.	—	K. in A.
Dean, Michael	Pte.	10844	Royal Defence Corps	—	D. a. Dis.
Dean, Thos.	Pte.	34326	2nd W. Yorks.	—	K. in A.
Dean, Thos. C.	Pte.	24094	10th W. Yorks.	—	K. in A.
Deans, Harold	Pte.	2127	1/5th W. Yorks.	—	K. in A.
Dearden, Frank	Rfm.	1767	8th W. Yorks.	—	K. in A.
Dearden, Lawrence B.	Cpl.	2549	Royal Munster Fusrs.	—	Died
Dearden, Wm.	Pte.	28214	W. Yorks.	—	Died
Dearlove, Arthur	Pte.	297981	R.A.S.C.	—	Died
Dearlove, Ed. Albert	Pte.	7509	1st W. Yorks.	—	K. in A.
Dearlove, Fred	Rfm.	3303	8th W. Yorks.	—	K. in A.
Debenham, Chas. Fred	Gnr.	25800	R.F.A.	—	K. in A.
DeBussey, W.	Pte.	457466	Labour Corps	—	K. in A.
DeBussey, Walter	2nd Lieut.		Royal Air Force	—	K. in A.

LEEDS ROLL OF HONOUR.

Name	Rank	No.	Regiment	Honours	How Died
Deherr, H.	Pte.	199013	Royal Air Force	—	Died
Deighton, James	1/Stkr.	K25339	Royal Navy	—	D. a. Dis.
Deigman, R.	Pnr.	83942	Royal Engineers	—	Died
Deitz, F.	Pte.	10702	E. Lancs.	—	Died
Delahanty, Richard	Pte.	18136	9th W. Yorks.	—	K. in A.
Delaney, James	Pte.	10766	12th W. Yorks.	—	K. in A.
Delaney, Richard	Pte.	5536	11th Northumb'l'd Fusrs.	—	K. in A.
Demaine, Leonard E.	Rfm.	4945	2/8th W. Yorks.	—	K. in A.
Dempsey, Tom	Gnr.	152726	R.F.A.	—	K. in A.
Denby, Isaac C.	2nd Lieut.		1/4th W. Riding	—	K. in A.
Denham, Frank	Rfm.	4297	3/8th W. Yorks.	—	K. in A.
Denham, John	Pte.	200996	W. Riding	—	K. in A.
Denison, Harry	Sgt.	111852	R.F.A.	—	D. of W.
Denison, Joe M.	Pte.	PO1271	Royal Marine Lt. Infty.	—	K. in A.
Denison, John	Pte.	8908	W. Yorks.	—	Died
Dennell, James W.	Rfm.	5483	1/8th W. Yorks.	—	K. in A.
Dennis, Arthur	Pte.	12457	8th K.O.Y.L.I.	—	Missing
Dennis, Walter	Pte.	1596	15/17th W. Yorks.	—	K. in A.
Dennis, Walter	Pte.	2618	18th Q.M.O. Hussars	—	Died
Dennison, Austin	Pte.	1374	15th W. Yorks.	—	K. in A
Dennison, Ernest	L/Cpl.	266299	W. Yorks.	—	K. in A
Dennison, Ernest	Gnr.	81259	R.F.A.	—	K. in A.
Dennison, Harry V.	Pte.	62515	K.O.Y.L.I.	—	K. in A.
Dent, Wm.	Rfm.	1593	8th W. Yorks.	—	D. of W
Denton, Edgar F.	Rfm.	267688	8th W. Yorks.	—	K. in A.
Denton, Geo.	Sgt.	1226	1/8th W. Yorks.	—	K. in A.
Denton, Geo.	Pte.	13088	11th W. Yorks.	—	Missing
Denton, H.	Pte.	60746	7th Northumberl'd Fusrs.	—	K. in A.
Denton, Harry	Pte.	21346	1/5th W. Yorks.	—	K. in A.
Denton, Joseph	Bdr.	775108	R.F.A.	—	Died
Derbyshire, Fred	Pte.	543952	Labour Corps	—	Died
Derbyshire, Harry	Pte.	35129	Yorks.	—	K. in A.
Derbyshire, Henry	Dvr.	4280	R.A.S.C.	—	Died
Derrick, James	L./Cpl.	83850	Royal Engineers	—	K. in A.
Devine, John	Pte.	5009	Royal Defence Corps	—	Died
Dewes, Chas.	Pte.	4793	1/4th Seaforth Highdrs.	—	K. in A.
Dews, Albert	Gdsmn.	13685	1st Scots Guards	—	K. in A.
Dexter, Geo. A.	Rfm.	235266	8th W. Yorks.	—	K. in A.
Diamond, Richard	Gdsmn.	7993	1st Scots Guards	—	D. of W.
Dibnah, Harry	O.S.	3363	Royal Navy	—	Died
Dickenson, Arthur	Pte.	12348	6th E. Yorks.	—	K. in A.
Dickenson, Fred	Pte.	35067	24th Northumb'l'd Fusrs.	—	K. in A.
Dickenson, Harry	Pte.	8239	2nd W. Yorks.	—	K. in A.
Dickenson, Joseph	Pte.	18714	3rd W. Yorks.	—	K. in A.
Dickenson, Richard	Pte.	13192	1st E. Yorks.	—	K. in A.
Dickenson, Thos.	Pte.	17255	Machine Gun Corps	—	D. of W.
Dickenson, Walter	Pte.	62637	K.O.Y.L.I.	—	Died

LEEDS ROLL OF HONOUR.

Name	Rank	No.	Regiment	Honours	How Died
Dickenson, Wm. A.	Rfm.	204607	1/8th W. Yorks.	—	K. in A.
Dickinson, Albert	Gnr.	111283	R.F.A.	—	Missing
Dickinson, Alexander	Pte.	307088	W. Riding	—	K. in A.
Dickinson, Alfred	L/Cpl.	1454	8th W. Yorks.	—	K. in A.
Dickinson, Arthur R.	Pte.	235108	1/4th Leicester	—	K. in A.
Dickinson, Arthur	Pte.	37039	3rd W. Yorks.	—	D. a. Dis.
Dickinson, Arthur	Gnr.	112264	R.F.A.	—	K. in A.
Dickinson, Edward	Pte.	14297	13th W. Yorks.	—	K. in A.
Dickinson, Edward F.	Cpl.	59133	11th Royal Scots Fusrs.	—	K. in A.
Dickinson, Francis E.	Pte.	42010	1st Leicester	—	D. of W.
Dickinson, George	Pte.	820	17th W. Yorks.	—	Died
Dickinson, Geo. W.	Pte.	36697	Northumberland Fusrs.	—	D. of W.
Dickinson, Harry	Spr.	263477	Royal Engineers	—	D. a. Dis.
Dickinson, Jeffery	Pte.	47265	12th W. Yorks.	—	K. in A.
Dickinson, John Wm.	Pte.	13447	11th W. Yorks.	—	K. in A.
Dickinson, Joseph	Pte.	266649	6th Gordon Highdrs.	—	Died
Dickinson, Leonard	Rfm.	2526	1/7th W. Yorks.	—	K. in A.
Dickinson, Sydney	Pte.	277	15th W. Yorks.	—	K. in A.
Dickinson, Wm.	Pte.	45947	Northumberland Fusrs.	—	K. in A.
Dickson, Geo.	Gnr.	99308	R.F.A.	—	K. in A.
Dickson, John	Pte.	5445	1st Cameron Highdrs.	—	Died P.O.W.
Diffley, Geo.	Gdsmn.	4399	2nd Scots Guards	—	K. in A.
Digby, Joseph	Pte.	36967	1/4th Essex	—	K. in A.
Dilley, H.	Pte.	13867	6th Northants.	—	Missing
Dillon, Joe Fredk.	Pte.	1344	Royal Fusiliers	—	K. in A.
Dillon, Thos.	Pte.	2238	W. Yorks.	—	K. in A.
Dimbleby, Frank	Pte.	50433	Lancs. Fusiliers	—	K. in A.
Dimery, Geo W.	2nd Lieut.		15th W. Yorks.	—	K. in A.
Dinsdale, Herbert J.	Pte.	8224	9th W. Yorks.	—	K. in A.
Dinsdale, James	Pte.	306380	W. Yorks.	—	K. in A.
Dinsdale, T. A.	Pte.	11484	1/4th K.O.Y.L.I.	—	Missing
Dinsdale, Wm. H.	Gnr.	221913	R.F.A.	—	D. of W.
Dixon, Albert	Pte.	203070	1/5th W. Yorks.	—	K. in A.
Dixon, Arthur H.	Pte.	1059	10th E. Yorks.	—	K. in A.
Dixon, Benjamin	Pte.	27193	1st W. Yorks.	—	K. in A.
Dixon, Chas.	Pte.	1653	17th W. Yorks.	—	Died
Dixon, F.	Pte.	41842	10th Northumb'l'd Fusrs.	—	K. in A.
Dixon, Frank	Pte.	21512	9th W. Yorks.	—	K. in A.
Dixon, Fred	Pte.	40612	6th K.O.Y.L.I.	—	Died
Dixon, Geo.	Pte.	678617	29th Middlesex	—	Died
Dixon, Geo.	L/Sgt.	10403	9th W. Yorks.	—	K. in A.
Dixon, Geo. T.	Pte.	3421	27th Northumb'l'd Fusrs.	—	K. in A.
Dixon, Harry Y.	2nd Lieut.		11th York. & Lancs.	—	K. in A.
Dixon, Henry	Pte.	40978	6th Cameron Highdrs.	—	K. in A.
Dixon, Henry	Pte.	7122	W. Yorks.	—	K. in A.
Dixon, Herbert	Pte.	16206	7th W. Riding	—	K. in A.
Dixon, J. W.	Pnr.	274639	Royal Engineers	—	K. in A.

LEEDS ROLL OF HONOUR.

Name	Rank	No.	Regiment	Honours	How Died
Dixon, James	Rfm.	4833	8th London	—	K. in A.
Dixon, John	Pte.	21247	9th Northumb'l'd Fusrs.	—	Died
Dixon, Joseph E.	Rfm.	5154	2/7th W. Yorks.	—	K. in A.
Dixon, Joshua	Rfm.	4902	2/8th W. Yorks.	—	K. in A.
Dixon, Kenneth	2nd Lieut.		7th W. Riding	—	D. of W.
Dixon, Newton	Stkr.	116854	H.M.S. " Hyacinth "	—	K. in A.
Dixon, R.	Pte.	7695	1st W. Yorks.	—	K. in A.
Dixon, Ralph	Pte.	28218	12th W. Yorks.	—	K. in A.
Dixon, Robert	Pte.	21913	14th W. Yorks.	—	K. in A.
Dixon, Robert	L./Cpl.	20382	K.O. Scottish Borderers	—	D. of W.
Dixon, Walter	Pte.	235455	Lincoln	—	K. in A.
Dixon, Wm.	Rfm.	46942	Rifle Brigade	—	K. in A.
Dobbie, Geo.	Pte.	1616	R.A.M.C.	—	K. in A.
Dobbie, Leonard	Pte.	37482	9th W. Yorks.	—	K. in A.
Dobson, Albert	Pte.	10583	9th W. Yorks.	—	Missing
Dobson, Albert	Rfm.	26050	1/7th W. Yorks.	—	Died P.O.W.
Dobson, Arthur	Rfm.	13203	9th King's R. Rifle Cps.	—	K. in A.
Dobson, Arthur S.	Pte.	281	15th W. Yorks.	—	K. in A.
Dobson, Chas.	L./Cpl.	8169	2nd W. Yorks.	—	K. in A.
Dobson, Chas.	Pte.	14343	Royal Army Vet. Corps	—	Died
Dobson, Frank	Pte.	201722	Northumberland Fusrs.	—	K. in A.
Dobson, G. E.	Pte.	27877	15th W. Yorks.	—	Died P.O.W.
Dobson, Geo. W.	Pte.	271947	Labour Corps.	—	Died
Dobson, Harry	Rfm.	305251	8th W. Yorks.	—	K. in A.
Dobson, Herbert H.	Gnr.	154388	R.G.A.	—	K. in A.
Dobson, John Hy.	Rfm.	4444	1/8th W. Yorks.	—	K. in A.
Dobson, Joseph	Gnr.	81429	R.F.A.	—	K. in A.
Dobson, Walter	Rfm.	5414	W. Yorks.	—	D. a. Dis.
Dobson, Wm.	Pte.	13841	12th W. Yorks.	—	K. in A.
Dodds, Andrew	L/Cpl.	2069	7th W. Yorks.	—	K. in A.
Dodgson, Chas. Hy.	O.S.	J65012	H.M.S. " Penn "	—	Drowned
Dodgson, E.	Pte.		W. Yorks.	—	K. in A.
Dodgson, F.	Pte.	42569	Manchester	—	Died
Dodgson, Wm.	Pte.	37896	17th W. Yorks.	—	K. in A.
Dodson, Herbert	Pte.	14522	K.O.Y.L.I.	—	Died
Dodsworth, Thos.	Pte.	52608	K.O.Y.L.I.	—	Died
Doherty, Wm.	Pte.	242913	W. Yorks.	—	K. in A.
Dolan, Albert	Pte.	3/9173	2nd W. Yorks.	—	K. in A.
Dolan, James	Pte.	50895	11th E. Yorks.	—	K. in A.
Donald, Geo. E.	Pte.	60131	1st W. Yorks.	—	Died
Donlan, Joe	Pte.	484273	R.A.S.C.	—	Died
Donlan, John	Pte.	13054	King's Own R. Lancs.	—	K. in A.
Donley, James	Pte.	1078	17th Labour Corps	—	K. in A.
Donnelly, Stephen	Pte.	285	15th W. Yorks.	—	Died
Donnelly, Wm.	Pte.	28628	2/5th Norfolk	—	Died
Donovan, F.	Sgt.	9802	W. Riding	—	K. in A.
Donovan, J. W.	L/Cpl.	12903	8th K.O.Y.L.I.	—	Missing

LEEDS ROLL OF HONOUR.

Name	Rank	No.	Regiment	Honours	How Died
Dooks, Harold	Gnr.	203773	R.F.A.	—	Died
Doolan, John	Sgt.	1007	17th W. Yorks.	—	K. in A.
Dooley, Thos.	Pte.	23857	2nd East Lancs.	—	Missing
Doran, Richard	Pte.	10414	2rd Yorks.	—	Died
Doran, Wm.	Pte.	399	17th W. Yorks.	—	K. in A.
Dordick, Abraham	Pte.	556748	Labour Corps.	—	Died
Doughty, Harry	Rfm.	305616	2/8th W. Yorks.	—	Missing
Doughty, John C.	Pte.	286	15th W. Yorks.	—	K. in A.
Dougill, Fred	Cpl.	201124	Seaforth Highlanders	—	K. in A.
Douglas, Chas.	Pte.	38591	W. Yorks.	—	K. in A.
Douglas, John J.	Rfm.	266422	1/7th W. Yorks.	—	K. in A.
Douglas, John R.	Pte.	21410	2nd Royal Scots	—	K. in A.
Douglas, Wm.	Pte.	104356	R.A.M.C.	—	D. a. Dis.
Douglass, John G.	Gdsmn.	20111	2nd Coldstream Guards	—	D. of W.
Dove, Walter	Pte.	10675	K.O.Y.L.I.	—	K. in A.
Dovener, Cyril H.	Tpr.	330076	Yorks. Hussars	—	K. in A.
Dover, Herbert	Pnr.	83750	Royal Engineers	—	D. of W.
Dovill, Harold	Pte.	9289	7th Seaforth Highdrs.	—	Died
Dowgill, Fred	Cpl.	201124	Seaforth Highlanders	—	K. in A.
Dowgill, Richard	L/Cpl.	35729	9th K.O.Y.L.I.	—	K. in A.
Dowgill, W. T.	Pte.	52461	Middlesex	—	K. in A.
Dowling, W. A.	Rfm.	·	W. Yorks.	—	K. in A.
Dowling, Wm.	Pte.	396132	10th W. Yorks.	—	Died
Downes, Wm.	Pte.	29614	1st W. Yorks.	—	Died
Downie, Benjamin	L/Cpl.	19037	York. & Lancs.	—	K. in A.
Downing, A. Harry	Gnr.	2666	R.F.A.	—	K. in A.
Downing, Herbert	Dvr.	96490	R.F.A.	—	K. in A.
Downing, Tom	Pte.	8861	2nd W. Yorks.	—	D. of W.
Doyle, Arthur	Pte.	309	17th W. Yorks.	—	K. in A.
Doyle, Chas.	Pte.	11/1194	17th W. Yorks.	—	D. of W.
Doyle, James	Pte.	20582	2nd Royal Scots	—	K. in A.
Doyle, James	Pte.	18937	W. Yorks.	—	K. in A.
Doyle, Joseph	Pte.	8359	4th W. Yorks.	—	K. in A.
Drake, Herbert	Pte.	446721	Labour Corps	—	D. a. Dis.
Dransfield, Ernest	2/Cpl.	84094	Royal Engineers	—	K. in A.
Draper, Alan	Pte.	12754	W. Yorks.	—	K. in A.
Draycott, Benjamin	Rfm.	306299	2/8th W. Yorks.	—	K. in A.
Draycott, E.	Pte.		2nd K.O. Scottish Bordrs.	—	K. in A.
Draycott, John Ed.	Pte.	37729	12th W. Yorks.	—	K. in A.
Drewery, Walter	Pte.	105696	Liverpool	—	K. in A.
Drewry, Geo.	Pte.	287	15th W. Yorks.	—	K. in A.
Drewry, Robt. Wm.	Pte.	288	15th W. Yorks.	—	K. in A.
Driffield, Richard	Pte.	1372	W. Yorks.	—	K. in A.
Driver, Joseph	Pte.	266649	6th Gordon Highdrs.	—	K. in A.
Drury, A. T.	Dvr.T4/044969		R.A.S.C.	—	K. in A.
Drury, Albert	L/Cpl.	4501	1/7th W. Yorks.	—	K. in A.
Drury, Harry	Pte.	27795	2nd W. Yorks.	—	K. in A.

LEEDS ROLL OF HONOUR.

Name	Rank	No.	Regiment	Honours	How Died
Drye, John Wm.	Pte.	34191	7th S. Lancs.	—	Missing
Duce, Harry	Sgt./M.	816	17th W. Yorks.	—	K. in A.
Duckett, John E.	Rfm.	C/12355	21st King's R. Rifle Cps.	—	D. of W.
Duckett, Wm.	Pte.	41252	W. Yorks.	—	K. in A.
Duckett, Wm. Hy.	Spr.	34961	Royal Engineers	—	D. a. Dis.
Duckham, Samuel	Pte.	16392	K.O. Scottish Bordrs.	—	K. in A.
Duffy, Edward	Pte.	21214	3rd W. Yorks.	—	D. a. Dis.
Duffy, John	Pte.	8694	W. Riding	—	Died
Dufton, Lawrence	Pte.	40125	7th Royal Scots Fusrs.	—	Missing
Dufton, Wm.	Pte.	202184	W. Yorks.	—	Died
Dufton, Wm. A.	Pte.	41749	12th W. Yorks.	—	K. in A.
Dugdale, H.	Dvr.	85677	R.F.A.	—	K. in A.
Dukes, Norman	L./Cpl.	266844	1/8th W. Yorks.	—	K. in A.
Dukes, T.	Sgt.	2016	1/7th W. Yorks.	—	Died
Duncalfe, John F.	Dvr.	53430	Royal Engineers	—	K. in A.
Duncan, Alan B.	Pte.	075833	Army Pay Corps	—	D. of W.
Duncan, Fred C.	Pte.	24716	W. Yorks.	—	K. in A.
Duncan, J. H.	Pte.	268176	Cheshire	—	Died
Dunderdale, James	Pte.	31132	10th Hussars	—	K. in A.
Dunhill, E.	Pte.	71893	Canadians	—	K. in A.
Dunn, Chas. E.	Pte.	12174	7th E. Yorks.	—	K. in A.
Dunn, Ernest	Pte.	41779	Leicester	—	Died
Dunn, James	1/Stkr.	116520	H.M.S. " Queen Mary "	—	K. in A.
Dunn, John	Pte.	33364	3rd W. Yorks.	—	Missing
Dunn, John Wm.	Pte.	305166	W. Yorks.	—	K. in A.
Dunn, Robert	Pte.	21367	Northumberland Fusrs.	—	D. of W.
Dunn, Thos.	Pte.	32008	21st Northumb'l'd Fusrs.	—	K. in A.
Dunne, John F.	Rfm.	267285	2/7th W. Yorks.	—	K. in A.
Dunne, W.	Pte.	33910	Leicester	—	Died
Dunning, J.	Pte.	114	Labour Corps Canadns.	—	Died
Dunning, John Wm.	Pte.	56475	W. Yorks.	—	Died
Dunnington, G.	1/Stkr.	302957	H.M.S. " Alert "	—	Died P.O.W.
Dunwell, Arthur	Pte.	62475	W. Yorks.	—	K. in A.
Dunwell, Clifford	Pte.	294	15th W. Yorks.	—	Missing
Dunwell, David	Gnr.	34460	R.F.A.	—	K. in A.
Dunwell, Walter	Rfm.	266379	2/7th W. Yorks.	—	K. in A.
Durant, Clarence	Pte.	170210	R.A.S.C.	—	Died
Durban, Alfred	Pte.	17211	14th Gordon Highders	—	K. in A.
Durham, Albert	Pte.	36606	11th W. Yorks.	—	K. in A.
Durham, Chas.	Pnr.	83702	Royal Engineers	—	Died
Durham, Geo.	Pte.	28933	8th Yorks.	—	K. in A.
Durham, John Wm.	Pte.	22928	8th Yorks.	—	Missing
Durkin, Bart.	Pte.	5/54125	83rd Training Res. Bat.	—	Died
Durrant, A. F.	Sgt.	305720	W. Yorks.	—	K. in A.
Durrant, Clifford	Pte.	3380	1/1st Yorks. Hussars	—	K. in A.
Durrant, E.	Cpl.		8th W. Yorks.	M.M.	K. in A.
Durrant, James Wm.	Pte.	31351	Labour Corps	—	D. of W.

LEEDS ROLL OF HONOUR.

Name	Rank	No.	Regiment	Honours	How Died
Duthoit, Cyril	Dvr.	96491	R.F.A.	—	K. in A.
Duthoit, H.	Pte.	37280	16th W. Yorks.	—	Died P.O.W.
Duthoit, John A.	Pte.	263020	1/6th W. Yorks.	—	K. in A.
Duxbury, Joe K.	Pte.	2545	6th Yorks.	—	K. in A.
Duxbury, Edward	B.S.M.	776113	R.F.A.	—	K. in A.
Duxbury, James	L/Cpl.G/18836		Royal Fusiliers	—	K. in A.
Dye, Fredk.	Pte.	2235	W. Yorks.	—	K. in A.
Dye, Harry	Pte.	44194	K.O.Y.L.I.	—	D. of W.
Dye, Osbourne	Pte.	1428	Royal Marine Lt. Infantry	—	K. in A.
Dyer, Chas.	Pte.	27221	W. Riding	—	K. in A.
Dyer, Daniel	Rfm.	3807	1/8th W. Yorks.	—	D. of W.
Dyer, Henry	Pte.	77339	Durham Light Infantry	—	K. in A.
Dykes, Edward	Sgt.		17th W. Yorks.	—	K. in A.
Dyson, H. F.	Sgt.	3/7527	1st W. Yorks.	—	Died
Dyson, Horace A.	Pte.	38300	10th York. & Lancs.	—	K. in A.
Dyson, John B.	Sgt.	32018	R.G.A.	—	Died
Dyson, Leonard	Pte.	62070	W. Yorks.	—	K. in A.
Dyson, Thos. A.	Pte.	21/520	21st W. Yorks.	—	K. in A.
Dyson, Walter	Rfm.	307001	2/8th W. Yorks.	—	K. in A.
Dytch, Arthur J.	Pte.	40619	6th Middlesex	—	Died
Eaddie, Herbert	Rfm.	3595	2/8th W. Yorks.	—	K. in A.
Eagin, Archie	Sig.		W. Yorks.	M.M.	Died
Ealand, James	Pte.	15/1658	2nd W. Yorks.	—	K. in A.
Eales, John	Pte.	3989	W. Yorks.	—	Died
Eames, Phillip E.	Pte.	21168	Labour Corps	—	D. a. Dis.
Eamonson, Arthur	Pte.	36091	W. Yorks.	—	K. in A.
Earl, Clifford	Dvr.	2/096837	R.A.S.C. (M.T.)	—	K. in A.
Earle, Fredk.	Pte.	12866	12th W. Yorks.	—	K. in A.
Earles, Michael	Pte.	11849	Northumberland Fusrs.	—	K. in A.
Earnshaw, J. T.	L/Cpl.	21194	8th York. & Lancs.	—	Missing
Eary, Walter	Pte.	25942	W. Riding	—	Died
Easby, Norman G.	Gnr.	71697	Machine Gun Corps	—	K. in A.
Eason, Henry	Gdsm.	15083	Scots Guards	—	D. a. Dis.
Eastwell, Geo.	Rfm.	300004	8th W. Yorks.	—	D. a. Dis.
Eastwell, Herbert T.	Pte.	4421	1/8th W. Yorks.	—	Died
Eastwood, Chas.	Pte.	7668	W. Yorks.	—	K. in A.
Eastwood, Geo. A.	Sgt.	266478	W. Yorks.	—	Died
Eastwood, Harold	Pte.	29014	13th W. Yorks.	—	Missing
Eastwood, James A.	1 Clk.	62253	Royal Air Force	—	Died
Eastwood, Robert	Pte.	23449	Yorks.	—	Died
Eastwood, Tom	Pte.	15/1511	1st W. Yorks.	—	K. in A.
Easy, Geo. F.	Sgt.	302	15th W. Yorks.	—	K. in A.
Easy, John Wm.	Pte.	25950	7th Cameron Highdrs.	—	Missing
Eaton, J.	Pte.	238024	19th Lancs. Fusiliers	—	K. in A.
Eaton, John	Rfm.	1592	W. Yorks.	—	Died
Eccles, Thos.	Pte.	47011	K.O. Scottish Borderers	—	Died

LEEDS ROLL OF HONOUR.

Name	Rank	No.	Regiment	Honours	How Died
Eccles, Wm.	Pte.	40510	3rd York. & Lancs.	—	Died
Eddie, Herbert	Rfm.	3595	2/8th W. Yorks.	—	K. in A.
Eddison, James	Pte.	1025	15th W. Yorks.	—	D. of W.
Eden, Fredk.	Pte.	351700	Labour Corps	—	Died
Eden, Geo. F.	Cpl.	PO/1270/S	Royal Marine Lt. Infty.	—	K. in A.
Edge, John	Pte.	19759	K.O.Y.L.I.	—	Died
Edmanson, Joe	2nd Lieut.		7th K.O.Y.L.I.	—	K. in A.
Edmondson, Arthur	Gnr.	175085	R.F.A.	—	K. in A.
Edmondson, James A.	Pte.	235788	York. & Lancs.	—	Died
Edmondson, John	Pte.	98879	Machine Gun Corps	—	Died
Edmondson, Thos. E.	Pte.	38784	2/5th W. Yorks.	—	K. in A.
Edmondson, Walter	Pte.	201692	5th W. Yorks.	—	D. a. Dis.
Edmunds, Thos. P.	Pte.	516	12th E. Yorks.	—	Missing
Edmunds, W. H.	Cpl.	202677	2nd Cheshire	—	D. a. Dis.
Edon, Cecil	Pte.	28224	17th W. Yorks.	—	K. in A.
Edon, Walter	Gnr.	76285	R.F.A.	—	K. in A.
Edson, Ernest	Pte.	86298	Machine Gun Corps	—	K. in A.
Edwards, Alfred W.	Sgt./M.	15005	R.F.A.	—	K. in A.
Edwards, George	Pte.	261828	R.A.S.C. (M.T.)	—	Died
Edwards, J. E.	Pte.	16923	18th W. Yorks.	—	K. in A.
Edwards, Walter	Pte.	21464	W. Yorks.	—	K. in A.
Egan, Michael	Pte.	7201	19th Yorks.	—	K. in A.
Elder, T. H.	Pte.	31979	10th York. & Lancs.	—	K. in A.
Eldin, James A.	Pte.	56109	W. Yorks.	—	K. in A.
Ellenier, James	Rfm.	24493	1/7th W. Yorks.	—	K. in A.
Elkins, David W.	Pte.	8974	W. Yorks.	—	K. in A.
Elkins, Stephen	Rfm.	3811	3/8th W. Yorks.	—	Died
Ellershaw, Sidney	Cpl.	16003	9th Yorks.	—	K. in A.
Ellett, Geo. H.	Pte.	413961	Labour Corps	—	D. a. Dis.
Elliff, Chas.	L./Cpl.	23981	15th W. Yorks.	—	Missing
Elliott, C.	L./Cpl.		15th W. Yorks.	—	K. in A.
Elliott, Edwin	Bdr.	21091	R.F.A.	—	K. in A.
Elliott, Fred	Pte.	33235	5th K.O.R. Lancs.	—	K. in A.
Elliott, Geo.	2A.M.	21618	Royal Air Force	—	Died
Elliott, Geo. L.	Sub-Lieut. Eng.		H.M.S. " Laurentia "	—	Died
Elliott, Harry	Pte.	1423	15th W. Yorks.	—	Died
Elliott, Harry	Pte.	23/410	2nd Durham Lt. Infty.	—	K. in A.
Elliott, Harry S.	Pte.	97390	Notts. & Derby.	—	Missing
Elliott, John	Rfm.	307041	2/8th W. Yorks.	—	K. in A.
Elliott, John E.	Pte.	1037	Durham Lt. Infantry	—	Died
Ellis, Abraham	Pte.	16488	K.O. Scottish Bordrs.	—	K. in A.
Ellis, Albert E.	Pte.	S/11848	Royal Hussars	—	K. in A.
Ellis, Alfred	Pte.	12735	4th W. Yorks.	—	D. of W.
Ellis, Arthur G.	Pte.	49495	21st W. Yorks.	—	K. in A.
Ellis, Cecil A.	Pte.	16503	K.O. Scottish Bordrs.	—	D. of W.
Ellis, David	Pte.	35103	Lincoln	—	K. in A.
Ellis, David	Rfm.	265571	7th W. Yorks.	—	K. in A.

LEEDS ROLL OF HONOUR

Name	Rank	No.	Regiment	Honours	How Died
Ellis, E.	Gdsmn.	27713	3rd Grenadier Guards	—	K. in A.
Ellis, Edgar	Pte.	56002	W. Yorks.	—	K. in A.
Ellis, Ernest	Pte.	84057	R.G.A.	—	K. in A.
Ellis, Geo.	L/Cpl.	265103	W. Yorks.	—	K. in A.
Ellis, Geo. H.	Pte.	34389	4th W. Yorks.	—	Died
Ellis, Geo. S.	Pte.	G/37127	1/6th Royal Sussex	—	K. in A.
Ellis, Geo. W.	A/Cpl.	15133	25th Royal Fusiliers	—	Died
Ellis, Harry	Pte.	26688	K.O. Scottish Bordrs.	—	Died
Ellis, Harry	Pte.	4379092	1st Green Howards	—	Died
Ellis, Herbert	Pte.	36996	2nd W. Yorks.	—	K. in A.
Ellis, Herbert W.	Pte.	306402	W. Yorks.	—	Died
Ellis, James	Pte.	21993	K.O.Y.L.I.	—	D. of W.
Ellis, James	Rfm.	55846	16th King's R. Rifle Cps.	—	K. in A.
Ellis, James H.	A/Sgt.	305519	1/8th W. Yorks.	—	K. in A.
Ellis, John J.	Pte.	21992	1st K.O.Y.L.I.	—	K. in A.
Ellis, John R.	Pte.	37395	10th W. Yorks.	—	K. in A.
Ellis, John Thos.	Pte.	3470	1/6th Northumb'l'd Fusrs.	—	K. in A.
Ellis, Leslie	Pte.	41291	18th W. Yorks.	—	Missing
Ellis, Norman	Spr.	224547	Royal Engineers	—	Died
Ellis, Rowland	Pte.	565105	Labour Corps.	—	Died
Ellis, Sargent	Pte.	11509	W. Riding	—	K. in A.
Ellis, Septimus	Pte.	27810	13th W. Yorks.	—	D. a. Dis.
Ellis, Thos.	Pte.	972	18th Hussars	—	K. in A.
Ellis, Wilfred	Gdsmn.	8876	Scots Guards	—	K. in A.
Ellis, Wm.	Gdsmn.	16785	Coldstream Guards	—	K. in A.
Ellis, Wm. H.		15950	H.M.S. " Invincible "	—	Drowned
Ellis, Wm. R.	Pte.	65459	Royal Fusiliers	—	Died
Ellison, Arthur B.	Pte.	37749	1st W. Yorks.	—	K. in A.
Ellison, Geo. E.	Pte.	6722	5th Lancers	—	K. in A.
Ellison, John	Pte.	268400	W. Riding	—	K. in A.
Ellison, Robert	Pte.	31158	1st E. Yorks.	—	K. in A.
Ellyard, Roland	L/Sgt.	266732	2/8th W. Yorks.	—	K. in A.
Elmer, Fred	Spr.	98529	Royal Engineers	—	D. a. Dis.
Elmer, Wm.	Pte.	39959	10th Worcester	—	K. in A.
Elstub, Geo.	Gnr.	795958	R.F.A.	—	K. in A.
Elstub, Maurice	Pte.	203074	1/4th E. Yorks.	—	K. in A.
Elsworth, Chas.	Cpl.	266407	2/7th W. Yorks.	—	K. in A.
Elsworth, Ernest E.	L/Cpl.	3263	Northumberland Fusrs.	—	K. in A.
Ely, Fred	Rfm.	3337	2/7th W. Yorks.	—	Died
Ely, Henry	Pte.	16938	Labour Corps	—	Died
Emery, Robt.	Bdr.	64490	R.F.A.	—	K. in A.
Emmerson, Chas. N.	Pte.	19124	7th Yorks.	—	K. in A.
Emmerson, Samuel	Pte.	2672	9th W. Yorks.	—	Missing
Emmett, Willie	Rfm.	266123	1/8th W. Yorks.	—	Died
Emmonds, Alfred	Rfm.	1682	2/7th W. Yorks.	—	K. in A.
Emmott, Clifford	L/Cpl.	3536	21st Lancers	—	Died
Emmott, Walter	Pte.	351698	Labour Corps	—	D. a. Dis.

LEEDS ROLL OF HONOUR.

Name	Rank	No.	Regiment	Honours	How Died
Emms, F.	Sgt.	15760	8th W. Yorks.	—	K. in A.
Empey, H. S.	Pte.	76132	29th Canadians	—	Died
Emsley, Alfred	Rfm.	2040	2/8th W. Yorks.	—	D. of W.
Emsley, Alfred	Cpl.	9634	W. Yorks.	—	D. a. Dis.
Emsley, Alfred	Pte.	2040	W. Yorks.	—	Died
Emsley, Alfred	Rfm.	305393	2/8th W. Yorks.	—	D. of W.
Emsley, Frank	Pte.	33846	1/5th K.O. Royal Lancs.	—	K. in A.
Emsley, Geo.	Pte.	19677	W. Yorks.	—	Died
Emsley, Willis	Pte.	32313	9th W. Yorks.	—	Died
Endeacott, Chas.	Pte.	38837	Northumberland Fusrs.	—	Died
Enderby, Harry	Pte.	268433	2/7th W. Riding	—	Missing
Endersley, Geo. W.	Pte.	270242	11th Royal Scots	—	K. in A.
England, Albert	Pte.	21337	W. Yorks.	—	Died
England, Arthur	Rfm.	266601	1/7th W. Yorks.	—	K. in A.
England, John					
England, John H.	Gdsm.	7845	Coldstream Guards	—	Died
England, Levi	Pte.	43913	14th Durham Lt. Infty.	—	K. in A.
England, Wm.	Pte.	21435	W. Yorks.	—	Died
Essam, Alfred	L/Cpl.	24353	2nd W. Yorks.	—	D. of W.
Essex, Henry	Pte.	31963	W. Yorks.	—	Died
Etherington, Joseph	Pte.	40326	Royal Scots	—	Died
Etherington, Joseph	Pte.	44303	Durham Light Infantry	—	Died
Eteson, Harold	Cpl.	645	12th York. & Lancs.	—	Died
Ettershank, Thos. W.	L/Cpl.	1163	6th K.O.Y.L.I.	—	Died
Evans, Albert	Dvr.	99904	R.F.A.	—	D. a. Dis.
Evans, Alfred	Pte.	12132	10th W. Yorks.	—	K. in A.
Evans, Ernest	Pte.	61056	23rd Lancs. Fusiliers	—	K. in A.
Evans, Fred H.	Lieut.		W. Yorks.	—	K. in A.
Evans, Harry	Pte.	25175	K.O.Y.L.I.	—	D. of W.
Evans, James	Pte.	26727	Lincoln	—	K. in A.
Evans, Lewellyn	L/Cpl.	75281	Machine Gun Corps	—	K. in A.
Evans, Norton	Pte.	4368	Seaforth Highlanders	—	K. in A.
Evans, Theodroe	Pte.	37990	2nd York. & Lancs.	—	K. in A.
Evans, Thos.	L/Cpl.	14746	8th Northumb'l'd Fusrs.	—	Died
Evans, Thos.	Pte.	23569	6th Dorset	—	K. in A.
Evans, W. Gilbert	Rfm.	306170	2/8th W. Yorks.	—	K. in A.
Evans, Wm.	Rfm.	202429	9th King's R. Rifle Cps.	—	K. in A.
Evans, Wm. H.	Pte.	265574	12th W. Yorks.	—	Died
Everall, Geo.	Pte.	10307	6th E. Yorks.	—	Missing
Everett, Wilfred	Dvr.	72320	R.F.A.	—	K. in A.
Evers, A.	Sgt.	306699	2/8th W. Yorks.	—	K. in A.
Evers, Thos. L.	L/Cpl.	38587	2/7th W. Riding	—	K. in A.
Evinson, Claude W.	Pte.	1880	12th K.O.Y.L.I.	—	K. in A.
Ewart, Harry	A.B.	J8799	H.M.S. "Goliath"	—	Drowned
Ewart, James	Spr.	83753	Royal Engineers	—	K. in A.
Ewart, John S.	Cpl.	314	15th W. Yorks.	—	K. in A.
Ewbank, John W.	Pte.	82124	20th Durham Lt. Infty.	—	K. in A.

LEEDS ROLL OF HONOUR.

Name	Rank	No.	Regiment	Honours	How Died
Ewing, Harry	Sgt.	578524	7th W. Yorks.	—	D. a. Dis.
Ewington, Ernest	Rfm.	3643	Royal Irish Rifles	—	Missing
Exley, Ernest	Pte.	52662	1st W. Yorks.	—	Missing
Exley, Ernest	Spr.	154254	Royal Engineers	—	K. in A.
Exley, Henry	Rfm.	2469	1/8th W. Yorks.	—	K. in A.
Exton, Arthur	Pte.	127002	Machine Gun Corps	—	K. in A.
Eyre, Tom	Pte.	4/8238	9th W. Yorks.	—	K. in A.
Fairbrother, Arthur	Sgt.	7510	1/3rd W. Yorks.	—	K. in A.
Fairbrother, R. R.	Sgt.	21165	6th Dragoons	—	K. in A.
Fairburn, G. S. H.			W. Yorks.	—	
Fairburn, J.	Gnr.	201394	R.F.A.	—	K. in A.
Fall, Reg.	Pte.	140903	Machine Gun Corps	—	K. in A.
Fallen, Michael	Pte.	31202	York. & Lancs.	—	K. in A.
Fannon, Wm. E.	Dvr.	81696	R.F.A.	—	D. a. Dis.
Fanton, Wm.	Sgt.	82918	R.G.A.	—	Died
Fare, Fred	Pte.	242542	W. Yorks.	—	K. in A.
Farley, Jas. W.	Pte.	10514	10th W. Yorks.	—	K. in A.
Farley, John W.	Rfm.	9547	King's Royal Rifle Cps.	—	K. in A.
Farne, Walter	Dvr.	169884	Royal Engineers	—	Died
Farnell, Geo.	Pte.	44040	Lincoln	—	D. of W.
Farniss, John W.	Cpl.	305197	8th W. Yorks.	—	Died
Farr, Edward	Pte.	17096	2nd W. Yorks.	—	K. in A.
Farr, Robert	Pte.	24102	10th W. Yorks.	—	K. in A.
Farrand, L. W.	Pte.	6276	Lancers	—	K. in A.
Farrar, A.	Pte.	3642	26th W. Yorks.	—	K. in A.
Farrar, Edgar	Pte.	7600	4th W. Yorks.	—	K. in A.
Farrar, Geo. W.	Cpl.	3756	1/7th W. Yorks.	—	K. in A.
Farrar, Gofton	Sgt.	13146	11th W. Yorks.	—	D. a. Dis.
Farrar, Harry	Rfm.	34125	3/8th W. Yorks.	—	Died
Farrar, Harry	Gnr.	776842	R.F.A.	—	D. of W.
Farrar, Leonard	Pte.	39445	2nd W. Yorks.	—	K. in A.
Farrar, Percival	Cpl.	98881	Machine Gun Corps	—	K. in A.
Farrar, Thos.	Pte.	27163	1st W. Yorks.	—	K. in A.
Farrar, Thos.		K17662	Royal Navy	—	D. a. Dis.
Farrar, Thos. O.	Rfm.	267114	2/7th W. Yorks.	—	K. in A.
Farrar, Walter	Pte.	28840	W. Yorks.	—	K. in A.
Farrar, Wm.	Whlr.	63137	R.F.A.	—	K. in A.
Farrell, J.	Pte.	305952	W. Yorks.	—	K. in A.
Farrell, John E.	Sig.	1907	1/7th W. Yorks.	—	Missing
Farrell, W. T.	Gnr.	620	R.F.A.	—	Died
Farrer, Albert	Rfm.	3642	2/8th W. Yorks.	—	Died
Farrer, Ramsden	Pte.	3189	Yorks. Dragoons	—	Died
Farrer, Thos.	Stkr.	K17662	Royal Navy	—	Died
Farrer, Wm. R.	Pte.	38645	10th W. Yorks.	—	K. in A.
Farrow, J. H.	Pte.	35930	Northumberland Fusrs.	—	K. in A.
Fase, A. A. H.	Pte.	S1355	Royal Marine Lt. Infty.	—	K. in A.

LEEDS ROLL OF HONOUR.

Name	Rank	No.	Regiment	Honours	How Died
Fatkin, W. A.	Pte.	65703	R.G.A.	—	K. in A.
Fawcett, Benj.	Pte.	238023	26th Northumb'ld Fusrs.	—	K. in A.
Fawcett, Fred	Pte.	201709	2/5th W. Yorks.	—	K. in A.
Fawcett, Geo. A.	Pte.	169187	Machine Gun Corps	—	D. a. Dis.
Fawcett, Harry	Pte.	PO1280/S	Royal Naval Division	—	K. in A.
Fawcett, M.	Pte.	14606	Labour Corps	—	D. a. Dis.
Fawcett, Tom	Pte.	7695	Seaforth Highlanders	—	K. in A.
Fawcett, Wm.	Pte.	66614	Royal Engineers	—	Died
Fawcett, Wm.	Pte.	12984	10th York. & Lancs.	—	Missing
Fear, Wm. H.	R.S.M.	3940	1/8th W. Yorks.	M.C.	K. in A.
Fearby, Wm.	Pte.	341522	R.A.S.C.	—	K. in A.
Fearn, B.	Pte.	12297	W. Yorks.	—	D. of W.
Fearn, Geo.	Pte.	97976	Machine Gun Corps	—	K. in A.
Fearnley, Duncan	Pte.	44641	K.O.Y.L.I.	—	K. in A.
Fearnley, E. W.	Pte.	1503	1st K.E. Horse	—	K. in A.
Fearnley, G. M.	Pte.	201899	1/5th Seaforth Highdrs.	—	D. of W.
Fearnley, G. W.	Pte.	1504	1st K.E. Horse	—	K. in A.
Fearnley, Jas. H.	Sgt.	7508	W. Yorks.	—	Died
Fearnley, John H.	Pte.	5152	5th Irish Lancers	—	K. in A.
Fearnley, Joshua	Pte.	202377	Highland Lt. Infty.	—	K. in A.
Fearnley, Levi	Rfm.	2648	1/8th W. Yorks.	—	K. in A.
Fearnley, Percy	L/Cpl.	266536	W. Yorks.	—	Died
Fearnley, Percy	Rfm.	4017	1/8th W. Yorks.	—	Died
Fearnley, Thos.	Pte.	2987	2/5th Northumb'l'd Fusrs.	—	Killed
Feasby, T. W.	Pte.	38685	Northumberland Fusrs.	—	Died P.O.W.
Feather, Ernest	Rfm.	13119	6th King's Royal Rifles	—	Died
Feather, Harry	Bdr.	32256	R.G.A.	—	K. in A.
Feeney, John W.	Rfm.	266445	2/7th W. Yorks.	—	K. in A.
Fell, Hubert	Rfm.	306765	2/8th W. Yorks.	—	Died
Fell, John Wm.	Pte.	24026	1st W. Yorks.	—	K. in A.
Fellowes, J. G.	Pte.	077368	R.A.S.C.	—	D. a. Dis.
Felstead, Arthur	Pte.	28223	2nd Grenadier Guards	—	K. in A.
Feltham, John E.	Pte.	200733	Norfolk	—	Died
Fenton, Bert	Pte.	161180	Labour Corps.	—	Died
Fenton, Ernest	Pte.	267009	W. Yorks.	—	K. in A.
Fenton, H.	R.S.M.	265102	1/7th W. Yorks.	—	K. in A.
Fenton, Herbert	C.S.M.	1610	1/7th W. Yorks	—	K. in A.
Fenton, Jas.	Pte.	7130	2nd W. Yorks.	—	Missing
Fenton, Jas.	Pte.		Canadians	—	Died
Fenton, Jas.	R.S.M.	5/4349	Training Reserve	—	K. in A.
Fenton, John	Pte.	56476	W. Yorks.	—	K. in A.
Fenton, John R.	Pte.	27871	W. Yorks.	—	Died
Fenton, Rowland T.	Cpl.	110428	Labour Corps.	—	D. a. Dis.
Fenton, Sam W.	A.B.	KW884	H.M.S. " Victory "	—	Drowned
Fenton, Walter	Pte.	36560	Royal Berks.	—	D. of W.
Fenwick, Geo. Wm.	Pte.	38269	15th W. Yorks.	—	K. in A.
Fenwick, Wm. T.	A.B.	J3846	Submarine E.41	—	Drowned

LEEDS ROLL OF HONOUR.

Name	Rank	No.	Regiment	Honours	How Died
Ferguson, Alfred	Cpl.	2107	1/5th W. Riding	—	Missing
Ferguson, Duncan	Rfm.	4854	2/7th W. Yorks.	—	K. in A.
Ferguson, Edward	Rfm.	268509	10th W. Yorks.	—	Missing
Ferguson, John	L/Cpl.	12870	18th W. Yorks.	—	Missing
Ferguson, Thos.	Rfm.	5257	1/8th W. Yorks.	—	D. of W.
Ferguson, Wm.	Rfm.	4117	2/8th W. Yorks.	—	K. in A.
Ferguson, Wm. T.	Cpl.	125667	R.A.S.C.	—	Died
Ferney, Chas.	Dvr.	47792	Royal Engineers	—	Died
Ferney, Jas.	Pte.	38497	York. & Lancs.	—	Died
Ferrand, Geo. M.	L/Cpl.	325	15th W. Yorks.	—	K. in A.
Fewkes, Walter	Gnr.	142882	R.G.A.	—	K. in A.
Fewson, Fred R.	Pte.	103398	Royal Fusiliers	—	Died
Fewster, Benj. H.	Sgt.	31157	E. Yorks.	—	K. in A.
Fewster, Jas.	Pte.	4593	4th Seaforth Highdrs.	—	Died
Fiddes, Wm.	Sgt.	8123	W. Riding	—	Died
Field, F. M.	Captain		7th E. Yorks.	—	K. in A.
Field, H. E.	Pte.	40927	10th Lancs. Fusiliers	—	K. in A.
Field, Henry	Rfm.	267266	2/7th W. Yorks.	—	Died
Field, Wm.	Cpl.	83631	R.F.A.	—	K. in A.
Fieldhouse, Llewellyn	Stkr.	K/54050	H.M.S. " Victory "	—	Died
Fielding, Edward	Pte.	39102	13th Manchester	—	D. of W.
Fielding, Geo.	Rfm.	205159	8th W. Yorks.	—	K. in A.
Fielding, Sydney H.	Cpl.	25598	W. Riding	—	Died
Fieldhouse, Thos. E.	Pte.		Manchester	—	K. in A.
Fields, Wm.	Cpl.	266275	2/7th W. Yorks.	—	Missing
Filbey, Thos.	Pte.	10346	3rd W. Riding	—	Missing
Fillingham, Arthur E.	Pte.	327	15th W. Yorks.	—	K. in A.
Finister, Thos. W.	Pte.	251888	Labour Corps	—	D. a. Dis.
Finklestein, G. W.	Pte.	026156	A.O.C.	—	K. in A.
Finley, Joseph H.	Pte.	176	21st W. Yorks.	—	Killed
Finley, Samuel	Pte.	28315	King's Own R. Lancs.	—	Died
Finnerty, Patrick	Pte.	9767	3rd W. Yorks.	—	D. a. Dis.
Finnerty, Wilfred	Lieut.		10th Lincoln	—	K. in A.
Finney, Herbert	Pte.		12th W. Yorks.	—	D. of W.
Finney, Walter	Rfm.	265397	2/7th W. Yorks.	—	K. in A.
Firbank, Ernest	Pte.	332535	Highland Light Infantry	—	K. in A.
Firby, Robert	Pte.	39779	W. Riding	—	K. in A.
Firmstone, Fred W.	Pte.	59654	Machine Gun Corps	—	K. in A.
Firn, Walter	Pte.	13202	10th W. Yorks.	—	K. in A.
Firth, Albert E.	Rfm.	2732	1/8th W. Yorks.	—	K. in A.
Firth, Arnold A.	Pte.	21062	W. Riding	—	Died
Firth, Chas.	Pte.	102039	R.A.S.C.	—	K. in A.
Firth, Denton	Pte.	26658	4th Grenadier Guards	—	K. in A.
Firth, E. A.	Pte.	419699	R.A.S.C.	—	D. a. Dis.
Firth, Edmund	Pte.	38835	25th Northumb'l'd Fusrs.	—	K. in A.
Firth, Ernest	A/C.S.M.	25529	1st K.O. Scottish Bordrs.	—	K. in A.
Firth, Harry	2/A.M.	63035	Royal Air Force	—	Died

LEEDS ROLL OF HONOUR.

Name	Rank	No.	Regiment	Honours	How Died
Firth, Herbert	L/Cpl.3/	17263	12th W. Yorks.	—	Died
Firth, Jas. A...	Pte.	1576	R.A.M.C.	—	D. a. Dis.
Firth, John	Pte.	12913	10th W. Yorks.	—	K. in A.
Firth, John	Pte.	401339	R.A.M.C.	—	D. of W.
Firth, Percy	Sgt.	6679	King's Royal Rifle Cps.	—	Killed
Firth, Percy	2nd Lieut.		2nd Yorks.	—	Died
Firth, Robt. B.	Pte.	M/09340	R.A.S.C.	—	Died
Firth, Thos.	Pte.	11085	K.O.Y.L.I.	—	K. in A.
Firth, Tom. L.	Rfm.	C12937	21st King's R. Rifle Cps.	—	Missing
Firth, Wm.	Pte.	12489	K.O.Y.L.I.	—	Killed
Firth, Wm.	Gnr.	129187	R.F.A.	—	D. of W.
Fish, Harry	Pte.	17360	2nd E. Yorks.	—	K. in A.
Fish, Horace	Pte.	41584	17th W. Yorks.	—	K. in A.
Fish, John	Dvr.	785138	R.F.A.	—	K. in A.
Fishburn, Albert	L/Cpl.	25935	2nd W. Yorks.	—	K. in A.
Fishburn, Alfred H.	Gnr.	785611	R.F.A.	—	K. in A.
Fishburn, Arthur S.	Pte.	19933	Durham Lt. Infantry	—	Died
Fishburn, Leonard	Pte.	4900	2/7th W. Yorks.	—	K. in A.
Fisher, Alexander	Pte.	41566	8th S. Staffs.	—	Missing
Fisher, Bertram	2nd Lieut.		Royal Air Force	—	Killed
Fisher, E.	Bdr.	796316	R.F.A.	—	K. in A.
Fisher, George	Sgt.	20755	Royal Air Force	—	Died
Fisher, Harold	L/Cpl.	240393	1/4th Yorks.	—	K. in A.
Fisher, Harry	Pte.	42708	S. Staffs.	—	Missing
Fisher, Henry	Pte.	21145	2nd W. Yorks.	—	K. in A.
Fisher, John	Rfm.	307730	1/8th W. Yorks.	—	Killed
Fisher, Sydney	Pte.	266096	W. Yorks.	—	K. in A.
Fisher, Wm. A.	Pte.	24000	16th Durham Lt. Infty.	—	Died
Fitton, Chas.	Rfm.	2071	8th W. Yorks.	—	D. a. Dis.
Fitton, Louis	Rfm.	3264	7th W. Yorks.	—	D. of W.
Fitzgibbon, Thos. F.	L/Cpl.	6233	W. Yorks.	—	K. in A.
Fitzpatrick, Arthur	Pte.	4139	Leinster	—	D. a. Dis.
Fitzpatrick, Edward	Spr.	277303	Royal Engineers	—	Died
Fitzpatrick, Walter	Dvr.	2267	8th W. Yorks.	—	Died
Fitzsimmons, Harry	Pte.	265028	2nd W. Yorks.	—	K. in A.
Flaherty, John	Pte.	8160	Royal Defence Corps	—	Killed
Flanagan, John	Pte.	8632	W. Yorks.	—	Died
Flanagan, John	Pte.	412161	10th W. Yorks.	—	K. in A.
Flanagan, Martin	Pte.	366114	R.A.S.C.	—	Died
Flanagan, Patrick	Pte.	1786	K.O.Y.L.I.	—	Died
Flannigan, Martin	Pte.	39782	1/4th W. Riding	—	K. in A.
Flathers, T. H.	Pte.	42142	S. Staffs.	—	Died
Flatley, John	Pte.	3186	13/17th W. Yorks.	—	Killed
Flatt, H.	2nd Lieut.		6th York. & Lancs.	—	K. in A.
Flaxington, W.	Rfm.	4406	4th King's R. Rifle Cps.	—	K. in A.
Fleetwood, Arthur	Pte.	260038	26th Northumb'l'd Fusrs.	—	K. in A.
Fleetwood, Edward	Gnr.	162007	R.G.A.	—	Died

LEEDS ROLL OF HONOUR.

Name	Rank	No.	Regiment	Honours	How Died
Fleetwood, Geo. Hy.	Pte.	34777	14th W. Yorks.	—	K. in A.
Fleming, Edward	Pte.	10190	2nd W. Riding	—	D. of W.
Fleming, John Wm.	Pte.	561	17th W. Yorks.	—	K. in A.
Fleming, Joseph	Dvr.	920	R.F.A.	—	K. in A.
Fleming, Samuel G.	Pte.	47362	22nd Northumb'l'd Fusrs.	—	D. of W.
Fleming, Thos.	Pte.	8553	2nd W. Yorks.	—	K. in A.
Flesher, Fredk. A.	Lieut.		2/6th Royal Warwicks.	—	D. of W.
Fletcher, Beaumont	L/Cpl.	290298	13th Royal Sussex	—	Died
Fletcher, C.	Pte.	403396	R.A.M.C.	—	K. in A.
Fletcher, E.	Pte.	368034	Labour Corps	—	K. in A.
Fletcher, E.	Pte.	76464	Notts. & Derby.	—	Missing
Fletcher, Edward	Pte.	33619	8th Yorks.	—	Killed
Fletcher, Edward S.	2nd Lieut.		2/6th W. Yorks.	—	K. in A.
Fletcher, G.	Pte.	240801	6th Lancs. Fusiliers	—	Killed
Fletcher, G.	Pte.	23925	W. Yorks.	—	K. in A.
Fletcher, G. H.	Pte.	306832	W. Yorks.	—	K. in A.
Fletcher, Henry	L/Cpl.	13549	K.O.Y.L.I.	—	K. in A.
Fletcher, James	P.C.	18358	H.M.S. " Invincible "	—	K. in A.
Fletcher, Jas. W.	Pte.	18911	6th W. Yorks.	—	K. in A.
Fletcher, Jos. H.	Pte.	40078	10th York. & Lancs.	—	Died
Fletcher, Norman D.	Pte.	24273	W. Yorks.	—	K. in A.
Fletcher, Richard	Pte.	30738	Labour Corps	—	Killed
Fletcher, Samuel T.	Pte.	5425	1/7th W. Riding	—	K. in A.
Fletcher, Stanley P.	Pte.	1275	15th W. Yorks.	—	K. in A.
Fletcher, Walter	Pte.	3111	W. Yorks.	—	Died
Fletcher, Wm. H.	L/Cpl.	206607	1/8th W. Yorks.	—	K. in A.
Flint, Geo.	L/Cpl.	3601	W. Riding	—	Killed
Flint, John	Pte.		15th W. Yorks.		Missing
Flint, Richard	Pte. M2/168140		R.A.S.C.	—	K. in A.
Flintoft, John Wm.	Pte.	2674	1/5th Durham Lt. Infty.	—	K. in A.
Flinton, J. H.	L/Cpl.	2914	1/7th W. Yorks.	—	K. in A.
Flockton, Fred	Pte.	341	15th W. Yorks.	—	Missing
Flockton, Harold	Pte.	276148	5/6th Royal Scots.	—	K. in A.
Flockton, John Wm.	Pte.	10636	10th W. Yorks.	—	K. in A.
Flower, Clifford	Dvr.	835827	R.F.A.	—	K. in A.
Flynn, Thos.	Pte.	73153	Machine Gun Corps	—	K. in A.
Flynn, Thos.	Rfm.	11565	2/7th W. Yorks.	—	K. in A.
Foggin, Geo.	Pte.	15237	2nd W. Yorks.	—	Died
Foggitt, A.	L/Cpl.	31393	8th E. Yorks.	—	Died
Foggitt, E.	Gnr.	117317	R.G.A.	—	K. in A.
Foggitt, Frank	L/Cpl.	1660	W. Yorks.	—	K. in A.
Foley, Leonard	Pte.	268402	8th W. Riding	—	Missing
Foley, Thos.	A.B.	3706	H.M.S. " Marlborough "	—	Drowned
Footit, Arthur	Sgt.	29691	13th Yorkshire	—	K. in A.
Ford, Albert E.	Pte.		W. Yorks.	—	Died
Ford, Benj.	Pte.		W. Riding	—	Died
Ford, Geo.	Rfm.	3273	7th W. Yorks.	—	K. in A.

LEEDS ROLL OF HONOUR.

Name	Rank	No.	Regiment	Honours	How Died
Ford, Geo. Wm.	Gnr.	806757	R.F.A.	—	Died
Ford, Herbert	Pte.	10373	1st K.O.Y.L.I.	—	K. in A.
Ford, Jas. A.	Pte.	9370	2nd E. Yorks.	—	Died
Ford, Thos.	Pte.	7409	W. Riding	—	K. in A.
Ford, W. T.	Sgt.	265006	W. Yorks.	—	K. in A.
Fordon, Chas. W.	Pte.	SE29335	Army Vetery. Corps	—	Died
Forrest, Arthur	Sgt.		Scots Guards	—	K. in A.
Forrest, Geo. S.	Pte.	31177	1st E. Yorks.	—	Missing
Forrest, Thos. S.	Pte.	335696	Royal Scots.	—	K. in A.
Forshaw, Edgar	Pte.	12881	6th K.O.Y.L.I.	—	Missing
Forth, R.	L/Cpl.			—	K. in A.
Foskett, Arthur E.	Pte.	1519	15th W. Yorks.	—	Missing
Foskett, Reginald	Pte.	42709	1st Leicester	—	Missing
Foster, Albert	Pte.	17304	10th Yorks.	—	Died
Foster, Arthur C.	Pte.	11720	10th W. Riding	—	K. in A.
Foster, Arthur E.	Pte.	4758	3/5th W. Yorks.	—	K. in A.
Foster, Claude	Pte.	41867	8th Northumb'l'd Fusrs.	—	K. in A.
Foster, Edgar	Sig.	J9194	H.M.S. B.13	—	Killed
Foster, Ernest	Pte.	28495	12th Durham Lt. Infty.	—	K. in A.
Foster, Frank	Pte.	28382	Grenadier Guards	—	K. in A.
Foster, Fred	Rfm.	8761	8th W. Yorks.	—	K. in A.
Foster, Fred	Pte.	776	21st W. Yorks.	—	K. in A.
Foster, Fredk.	Pte.	9745	2nd W. Riding	—	K. in A.
Foster, Harold	Pte.	1139	E. Yorks.	—	Died
Foster, Harry	1 C. B.	1916	H.M.S. " Invincible "	—	K. in A.
Foster, J. B.	2nd Lieut.		1/7th W. Yorks.	—	K. in A.
Foster, J. J.	L/Cpl.	23007	15th Cheshire	—	K. in A.
Foster, J. W.	L/Cpl.	451795	Labour Corps.	—	D. a. Dis.
Foster, John V.	Gnr.	775139	R.F.A.	—	K. in A.
Foster, Joseph	Pte.	202232	K.O. Scottish Borderers	—	K. in A.
Foster, Reginald	2nd Lieut.		Royal Air Force	—	K. in A.
Foster, Robert G.	Rfm.	2295	1/8th W. Yorks.	—	K. in A.
Foster, Thomas	Rfm.	3936	8th W. Yorks.	—	Died
Foster, Wm.	Pte.	350948	Durham Light Infantry	—	K. in A.
Foster, Wm.	Pte.	3298	Yorkshire	—	Died
Foster, Wm.	L/Cpl.	10591	Royal Dublin Fusiliers	—	Died
Foster, Wm. D.	Pte.	20235	15th Cheshire	—	K. in A.
Foster, Wm. T.	Pte.	200756	W. Riding	—	D. a. Dis.
Fotherby, Alfred	Pte.	36774	15th W. Yorks.	—	K. in A.
Fotherby, Jas.	Pnr.	83951	Royal Engineers	—	Died
Fothergill, Edwin	A.B.On/86166		H.M.S. " Hampshire "	—	Killed
Fothergill, Wilson	Rfm.	45430	Royal Irish Rifles	—	Killed
Foulis, Albert	Pte.	11341	9th Yorks.	—	D. of W.
Fountain, Ernest	Pte.	49654	1/6th W. Yorks.	—	Died
Fountain, Fred	Pte.	43717	W. Yorks.	—	K. in A.
Fountain, George	O.S.	5611	H.M.S. " Flirt "	—	Killed
Fountain, Joe	Rfm.	2318	1/8th W. Yorks.	—	K. in A.

LEEDS ROLL OF HONOUR

Name	Rank	No.	Regiment	Honours	How Died
Fountain, John	Pte.	287	Royal Marine Lt. Infty.	—	K. in A.
Fowler, B. E.	Lieut.		Machine Gun Corps	—	Missing
Fowler, Geo.	L/Cpl.	2067	7th W. Yorks.	—	K. in A.
Fowler, George	Pte.		W. Yorks.	—	Died
Fowler, H. A.	L/Cpl.	1360	15th W. Yorks.		K. in A.
Fowler, J. W.	Pte.	3660	Cameron Highlanders	—	K. in A.
Fowler, Jack J.	Pte.	16067	9th K.O.Y.L.I.	—	K. in A.
Fowler, Thomas	Pte.	11090	York. & Lancs.	—	Died
Fowler, Walter	Pte.	13638	9th K.O.Y.L.I.	—	Missing
Fox, Arthur	Pte.	17099	2/4th W. Riding	—	K. in A.
Fox, C. E.	Pte.	56166	10th W. Yorks.	—	K. in A.
Fox, Dick	C.Q.M.S.	15255	K.O.Y.L.I.	—	D. of W.
Fox, George	Pte.	64106	W. Yorks.	—	Died
Fox, George	Pte.	511	Grenadier Guards	—	K. in A.
Fox, Geo. E.	Pte.	118227	Machine Gun Corps	—	K. in A.
Fox, H.	Pte.	125975	Machine Gun Corps	—	K. in A.
Fox, Harold	Spr.	S/1109	Royal Engineers		Died
Fox, John	Pte.	1826	2nd K.O.Y.L.I.		K. in A.
Fox, John H.	Pte.	38362	16th W. Yorks.	—	Missing
Fox, Leonard	Rfm.	2695	1/7th W. Yorks.	—	K. in A.
Fox, Sam W.	Pte.	39442	11th W. Yorks.		Died
Fox, Thomas	Pte.	267192	W. Yorks.	—	K. in A.
Foxcroft, Fredk. M.	Pte.	316334	R.A.S.C.	—	K. in A.
Foxcroft, Harry	Pte.	24849	7th Yorks.	—	K. in A.
Foxon, Harold L.	A.B.	2506	H.M.S. "Stephen Furness"	—	Died
Fozard, Walter S.	Pte.	14254	2nd Scots Guards	—	Missing
Frain, John F.	Pte.	59138	9th W. Yorks.	—	K. in A.
France, Harry	Pte.	107280	51st W. Yorks.	—	Died
France, John	Pte.	S/1756	12th Rifle Brigade	—	K. in A.
France, Robert H.	Pte.	41585	15th W. Yorks.	—	K. in A.
Frankland, E.	Sgt.	199	R.A.M.C.	—	K. in A.
Frankland, Geo. S.	Rfm.	307076	1/8th W. Yorks.	—	Killed
Frankland, Raymond	Pte.	40885	Northumberland Fusrs.	—	K. in A.
Frankland, Walter	A/Sgt.	305335	1/8th W. Yorks.	—	Died
Franklin, Arthur	Pte.	3098	Dragoon Guards	—	D. a. Dis.
Franklin, Clifford	L/Cpl.	266211	1/7th W. Yorks.	—	K. in A.
Franklin, Horace P.	Pte.	220636	Royal Berks.	—	K. in A.
Franklin, N. W.	Pte.	37484	W. Yorks.	—	K. in A.
Franklin, Thos.	Pte.	21526	10th York. & Lancs.	—	K. in A.
Franklin, Wm.	Pte.	49629	W. Yorks.	—	Missing
Franklyn, Samuel	L/Bdr.	24744	R.G.A.	—	D. a. Dis.
Fraser, Clifford E.	Pte.	235788	21st Lancers	—	Died
Fraser, G.	Pte.	38865	25th Northumb'l'd Fusrs.	—	K. in A.
Fraser, Thomas	Rfm.	1872	7th W. Yorks.	—	K. in A.
Frear, John Wm.	Pte.	25228	Royal Warwicks.	—	D. of W.
Freedman, Joseph	Pte.	235130	9th K.O.Y.L.I.	—	K. in A.

LEEDS ROLL OF HONOUR.

Name	Rank	No.	Regiment	Honours	How Died
Freeman, F. G.	Rfm.	48964	8th W. Yorks.	—	K. in A.
Freeman, Harold	Pte.	268644	W. Yorks.	—	K. in A.
Freeman, Henry	Pte.	33014	15th W. Yorks.	—	Missing
Freeman, Herbert	Pte.	535399	1/15th London	—	K. in A.
Freeman, Jas. A.	Sig.	38588	W. Yorks.	—	K. in A.
Freeman, John	Dvr.	022756	R.A.S.C.	—	Died
Freeman, Tom F.	L/Cpl.	15587	9th W. Yorks.	—	K. in A.
Freeman, Wm. Hy.	Sgt.M2/	076258	R.A.S.C.	—	K. in A.
Freshwater, Wm. Hy.		J39931	H.M.S. "Black Prince"	—	K. in A.
Fretwell, John	Rfm.	242546	3/7th W. Yorks.	—	K. in A.
Frienze, Jack	Pte.	39246	Lancs. Fusiliers	—	K. in A.
Frieze, Archie	Pte.	41626	Highland Lt. Infty.	—	K. in A.
Frieze, Maurice	Pte.	35132	2nd W. Yorks.	—	K. in A.
Frieze, Simon	Pte.	44217	Essex	—	Died
Frobisher, Ernest	Rfm.	265267	7th W. Yorks.	—	K. in A.
Frosdick, Horace J.	Pte.	12305	6th Bedfords.	—	K. in A.
Frost, Joseph	Rfm.	3076	2/7th W. Yorks.	—	K. in A.
Frost, Oxley J.	Cpl.	R/7430	12th King's R. Rifle Cps.	—	K. in A.
Frow, Geo. R.	Pte.	33018	9th W. Yorks.	—	K. in A.
Fry, Jas. A.	Gnr.	162578	R.G.A.	—	K. in A.
Fryer, Albert	Rfm.	3221	8th London	—	D. of W.
Fryer, Albert	Pte.	9883	2nd W. Riding	—	K. in A.
Fryer, John L.	Cpl.	94797	R.G.A.	—	K. in A.
Fryer, Ralph	Pte.	2124	R. Guernsey Lt. Infty.	—	K. in A.
Fryer, Thos.	Sgt.	8311	2nd W. Yorks.	—	K. in A.
Fuller, Chas. Hy.	Pte.	5177	Scots Guards	—	Died
Fuller, Geo. E.	Sgt.	175876	R.A.F.	—	K. in A.
Funey, John W.	Rfm.	266445	2/7th W. Yorks.	—	Died
Funnemark, Wm.	Pte.	471570	Labour Corps.	—	D. a. Dis.
Furlong, Harry J.	Rfm.	306649	3/8th W. Yorks.	—	K. in A.
Furman, Percy	Pte.	401279	R.A.M.C.	—	K. in A.
Furness, Joseph	L/Cpl.	306183	2/8th W. Yorks.	—	Missing
Furniss, J. W.				—	K. in A.
Furniss, James	Pte.	36596	9th W. Yorks.	—	Missing
Furniss, James	Pte.	19985	1st W. Yorks.	—	K. in A.
Gabriel, Thomas	Pte.	1950	Machine Gun Corps	—	K. in A.
Gadd, William	Smn.		Royal Navy	—	K. in A.
Gadsby, Harold	Pte.	36781	1/4th K.O.Y.L.I.	—	K. in A.
Gadsby, Joseph	Pte.	8553	3rd W. Yorks.	—	K. in A.
Gaffigan, James	Rfm.	48618	1/8th W. Yorks.	—	K. in A.
Gaffney, William	L/Cpl.	12556	Yorks.	—	K. in A.
Gaines, Charles	Pte.	45541	K.O.Y.L.I.	—	Died
Gaines, J. P.	Rfm.	A3471	8th King's R. Rifle Cps.	—	D. of W.
Gale, Harry N.	Pte.	52207	17th W. Yorks.	—	Died
Gale, Sidney	Pte.	29475	Loyal N. Lancs.	—	Missing
Galinsky, Harry	Pte.	29459	1st W. Yorks.	—	K. in A.

LEEDS ROLL OF HONOUR.

Name	Rank	No.	Regiment	Honours	How Died
Gallagher, Ben	Pte.	25909	13th E. Yorks.	—	K. in A.
Gallagher, C. M.	Pte.	70388	R.A.M.C.	—	Died
Gallagher, F. J.	Sgt.	50794	Machine Gun Corps	—	K. in A.
Gallagher, J. J.	Sgt.	27874	9th Lancs. Fusiliers	—	K. in A.
Gallagher, James	Pte.	4/8539	15th W. Yorks.	—	Missing
Gallagher, James	Pte.	10951	W. Riding	—	K. in A.
Gallagher, John	Pte.	3/5827	8th E. Yorks.	—	K. in A.
Gallagher, Thomas	Cpl.	34234	K.O.Y.L.I.	—	K. in A.
Gallantree, Arthur W.	Pte.	9503	W. Yorks.	—	K. in A.
Galley, Alfred	Pte.	17124	W. Yorks.	—	K. in A.
Galli, Francis	Pte.	73	17th W. Yorks.	—	K. in A.
Gallivan, Thomas	Pte.		W. Yorks.	—	Died
Gallogley, James	Pte.	10698	Durham Light Infantry	—	Died
Gallop, Wm. Chas.	B.S.M.	21424	R.F.A.	—	K. in A.
Galloway, Edward	Pte.	108684	Royal Fusiliers	—	D. of W.
Galloway, Geo. A.	D.A.	14021	Royal Naval Reserve	—	Killed
Galloway, Walker	Pte.	43730	1/6th R. Warwicks.	—	K. in A.
Galvin, John	Pte.	10277	9th W. Yorks.	—	Missing.
Galvin, Thomas	Pte.	242085	13th E. Surrey	—	D. a. Dis.
Gamble, Fredk.	Pte.	8287	6th W. Yorks.	—	K. in A.
Gample, David	Rfm.	203778	2/7th W. Yorks.	—	K. in A.
Gannon, Anthony	Pte.	9691	2nd W. Riding	—	K. in A.
Gannon, Geo. Wm.	Cpl.	CH/18137	1st Royal Marines	M.M.	K. in A.
Gannon, Thos. P.	L/Cpl.	37379	W. Yorks.	—	K. in A.
Gant, Thos.	Pte.	202107	Leciester	—	K. in A.
Garb, Barnard	Pte.	23695	13th Yorks.	—	K. in A.
Garbutt, Alfred W.	Pte.	38675	16th W. Yorks.	—	K. in A.
Garbutt, C. M.	Pte.	4917	16th Lancers	—	Died
Garbutt, G.	L/Cpl.	129875	Royal Engineers	—	K. in A.
Garbutt, John Hy.	Pte.	37390	3rd W. Yorks.	—	K. in A.
Garbutt, Robert	Cpl.	7869	W. Yorks.	—	Killed
Garbutt, Robert S.	Pte.	016265	R.A.S.C.	—	Died
Garbutt, Wilfred	Pte.		Royal Fusiliers	—	Died
Gardiner, Clifford	Pte.	305266	W. Yorks.	—	K. in A.
Gardiner, Edmund A.	Dvr.	37006	Machine Gun Corps	—	D. of W.
Gardner, C.			W. Yorks	—	
Gardner, Harry	Pte.	260068	York. & Lancs.	—	K. in A.
Gardner, Jas. F.	L/Cpl.	27875	Lancs.	—	D. a. Dis.
Gardner, Jas. S.	Pte.	182340	Royal Engineers	—	K. in A.
Gardner, William	Pte.	41418	2/5th Royal Lancs.	—	K. in A.
Garforth, Alfred	Spr.	166405	Royal Engineers	—	K. in A.
Garland, Albert	Pte.	24382	K.O.Y.L.I.	—	K. in A.
Garnett, Edgerton	Pte.		15th W. Yorks.	—	K. in A.
Garnett, Ernest	Pte.	174562	R.F.A.	—	Died
Garnett, J. A.	Pte.	39317	N. Staffs.	—	Missing
Garnett, William	Rfm.	202428	20th Rifle Brigade	—	Killed
Garr, Benny	Pte.	23695	2nd Yorks.	—	K. in A.

LEEDS ROLL OF HONOUR.

Name	Rank	No.	Regiment	Honours	How Died
Garratt, Henry	Pte.	40812	10th Essex	—	D. of W.
Garratt, Wm.	L/Cpl.	14	R.A.M.C.	—	D. of W.
Garrett, Joseph	Bdr.	89963	R.F.A.	—	K. in A.
Garrigan, James	Pte.	43241	R.A.M.C.	—	Died
Garritt, J. C.	Lieut.		Durham Lt. Infantry	—	K. in A.
Garrity, Wm.	L/Cpl.	611134	Royal Engineers	—	Died
Garside, Edward	Pte.	213095	20th Rifle Brigade	—	D. a. Dis.
Garside, Walter	Sgt.	306489	1/8th W. Yorks.	—	K. in A.
Garth, Harold P.	Pte.	88935	8th Durham Lt. Infty.	—	K. in A.
Garton, Robert	Sgt.	598	10th Lincoln.	—	K. in A.
Garvey, John	L/Sgt.	52009	22nd Royal Fusiliers	—	K. in A.
Garvie, Oswald	Pte.	61765	R.A.M.C.	—	K. in A.
Gascoigne, Edward	Pte.	36971	Durham Lt. Infantry	—	K. in A.
Gatehouse, Walter	1/A.M.	309321	Royal Air Force	—	Died
Gatenby, Percy	Pte.	42800	9th Manchester	—	K. in A.
Gates, George	Sgt.	90202	R.F.A.	—	K. in A.
Gath, John W.	L/Cpl.	305246	2/8th W. Yorks.	—	K. in A.
Gathergood, A. H.	Pte.	27961	E. Yorks.	—	K. in A.
Gaughan, John	Pte.	13967	7th E. Kent	—	K. in A.
Gaunt, Arthur	Pte.	24869	9th W. Yorks.	—	K. in A.
Gaunt, Arthur	L/Cpl.	14819	6th York. & Lancs.	—	Missing
Gaunt, Clifford	Pte.	202239	2nd Lincoln	—	Died
Gaunt, Clifford	Gnr.	775813	R.F.A.	—	K. in A.
Gaunt, E.	2nd Lieut.		5th W. Yorks.	—	K. in A.
Gaunt, Fredk.	Sgt.	2043	7th Royal Munster Fusrs.	—	Died
Gaunt, Fred A.	Pte.	62101	W. Yorks.	—	K. in A.
Gaunt, Godfrey	Pte.	39400	10th W. Yorks.	—	K. in A.
Gaunt, John	Pte.	203211	1/4th Royal Scots Fusrs.	—	Missing
Gaunt, John E.	Pte.	111010	Labour Corps	—	D. a. Dis.
Gaunt, Jonas	Pte.	33435	16th W. Yorks.	—	K. in A.
Gaunt, Morris	Pte.	28032	12th W. Yorks.	—	K. in A.
Gaunt, P.	Pte.	A/785	King's Royal Rifle Cps.	—	K. in A.
Gaunt, Stanley	Pte.	307077	W. Yorks.	—	K. in A.
Gaunt, Walter	Sgt.	2329	1/7th W. Yorks.	—	K. in A.
Gavins, Joe	L/Cpl.	715	17th W. Yorks.	—	K. in A.
Gedge, John	Pte.	46266	York. & Lancs.	—	K. in A.
Geldard, Alfred	Dvr.	18811	R.F.A.	—	K. in A.
Geldard, Chas. E. B.	L/Cpl.	47163	22nd Northumb'l'd Fusrs.	—	K. in A.
Geldard, Harry	Pte.	27394	3rd E. Yorks.	—	Died
Geldard, Walter	Rfm.	266032	1/7th W. Yorks.	—	K. in A.
Geldart, Herbert	L/Cpl.	27901	12th W. Yorks.	—	K. in A.
Gelder, Charles	Pte.	21651	1/8th K.O. Scottish Bdrs.	—	D. of W.
Gelder, George	Pte.	20777	1st K.O. Scottish Bordrs.	—	K. in A.
Gelder, Jas. N.	C.S.M.	13013	10th W. Yorks.	—	K. in A.
Gelderd, Harry	Pte.	41419	2/5th R. Lancs.	—	K. in A.
George, Edward	Pte.	110393	Tank Corps.	—	K. in A.
George, R.	Bdr.	95909	R.F.A.	—	K. in A.

LEEDS ROLL OF HONOUR.

Name	Rank	No.	Regiment	Honours	How Died
George, Teddy	L/Cpl.	24429	1/7th W. Yorks.	—	K. in A.
Geraghty, James	Pte.	21461	York. & Lancs.	—	Died
Geraghty, Wm.	Pte.		York. & Lancs.	—	Died
Germaine, Leonard	Spr.	3668	2/1st Royal Engineers	—	K. in A.
Germaine, Wm.	Pte.	38647	Highland Lt. Infty.	—	Died
Gerraghty, Alfred	L/Cpl.	2991	W. Yorks.	—	K. in A.
Gerrard, John Wm.	Pte.	8540	4th W. Yorks.	—	K. in A.
Gibb, James	Pte.	64139	R.A.M.C.	—	K. in A.
Gibbons, Alfred	L/Cpl.	8423	7th W. Yorks.	—	K. in A.
Gibbons, James	Rfm.	306598	8th W. Yorks.	—	K. in A.
Gibbons, Thomas	O.S.	J62567	Royal Navy	—	Killed
Gibbs, Jacob	Pte.	1383	1/8th W. Riding	—	D. a. Dis.
Gibson, Albert	Pte.	21469	1st Northumb'l'd Fusrs.	—	D. of W.
Gibson, Archie	Pte.	7088	1st Cameron Highldrs.	—	K. in A.
Gibson, Arthur T.	Pte.	87534	Northumberland Fusrs.	—	Died
Gibson, Ernest	Pte.	60517	Welsh	—	K. in A.
Gibson, Ernest	Pte.	13780	W. Yorks.	—	K. in A.
Gibson, Frank T.	Pte.	24241	Yorks.	—	D. a. Dis.
Gibson, George	Gnr.	6193	R.F.A.	—	K. in A.
Gibson, George	Bdr.	23479	12th Royal Fusiliers	—	Missing
Gibson, George	Pte.	6802	Yorks.	—	K. in A.
Gibson, George	Pte.	8543	4th W. Yorks.	—	K. in A.
Gibson, Horace	Pte.	18705	W. Yorks.	—	K. in A.
Gibson, J. W.	Sgt.	11878	16th Lancs. Fusiliers	—	K. in A.
Gibson, John	Rfm.	307465	1/8th W. Yorks.	—	Missing
Gibson, John P.	Pte.	31965	16th W. Yorks.	—	K. in A.
Gibson, Thos. E.	2nd Lieut.		2/5th W. Yorks.	—	K. in A.
Gibson, Wm.	Pte.	33155	Labour Corps.	—	K. in A.
Gidlow, Sidney	Pte.	69126	Training Reserve	—	D. a. Dis.
Gieshen, John	Pte.	307459	W. Yorks.	—	K. in A.
Gilbank, Chas. W.	Rfm.	5032	2/7th W. Yorks.	—	K. in A.
Gilchrist, John A.	Cpl.	2182	8th W. Yorks.	—	K. in A.
Gilchrist, Wm.	Rfm.	3723	W. Yorks. T.F.	—	D. a. Dis.
Gilderdale, C.	Rfm.	307030	2/8th W. Yorks.	—	K. in A.
Gilderdale, Wm. Hy.	Spr.	1935	Australian Infantry	—	D. a. Dis.
Gilks, Jos. Hy.	Pte.	240763	Labour Corps	—	Died
Gill, A.	Dvr.	63303	R.F.A.	—	K. in A.
Gill, Arthur	L/Bdr.	775077	R.F.A.	—	K. in A.
Gill, Bernard	Sgt.	12385	15th W. Yorks.	—	D. of W.
Gill, Cornelius	Pte.	266837	W. Yorks.	—	Missing
Gill, Ernest	Pte.	38921	10th E. Yorks.	—	D. of W.
Gill, Ernest	Pte.	41380	2/5th Lincoln	—	Died
Gill, Fred	Pte.	6922	2nd W. Yorks.	—	Died
Gill, G. Wm.	Pte.	3/23980	Argyle & Sutherland Hdrs.	—	K. in A.
Gill, George	Rfm.	33751	8th W. Yorks.	—	K. in A.
Gill, Harry	C.S.M.	374	15th W. Yorks.	—	D. of W.
Gill, Herbert	Cpl.	2969	2/7th W. Yorks.	—	K. in A.

LEEDS ROLL OF HONOUR.

Name	Rank	No.	Regiment	Honours	How Died
Gill, John R.	Pte.	9415	W. Yorks.	—	K. in A.
Gill, S. J.	Pte.	29530	11th W. Yorks.	—	K. in A.
Gill, Thos. A.	Gnr.	108802	R.G.A.	—	K. in A.
Gill, Walter	S/Sgt.	060017	R.A.S.C.	—	Died
Gill, Wm.	Pte.	62096	15th W. Yorks.	—	K. in A.
Gillard, Wm.	Pte.	23489	Yorks.	—	K. in A.
Gillen, Jas.	Pte.	8164	Royal Defence Corps.	—	Died
Gilliam, W. F.	Pte.	75572	W. Yorks.	—	K. in A.
Gilligan, Charles	L/Cpl.	7294	W. Yorks.	—	K. in A.
Gilligan, D. C.	Pte.	33365	E. Lancs.	—	K. in A.
Gilligan, Jas.	Pte.	7647	W. Riding	—	K. in A.
Gilligan, Jas.	Pte.		W. Yorks.	—	Died
Gilligan, John	Smn.		Royal Navy	—	Died
Gilligan, Thomas	Sgt.		Canadians	—	Died
Gilling, A.	Pte.	7265987	R.A.S.C. (M.T.)	—	D. a. Dis
Gillon, Francis	Skr.	111202	H.M.S. " Invincible "	—	K. in A.
Gillon, Robert	Pte.	41621	3rd W. Yorks.	—	Died
Gillson, Albert	P.O.	T/38966	Royal Navy	—	K. in A.
Gillson, Wm.	Rfm.	267373	3/7th W. Yorks.	—	K. in A.
Gilpin, Herbert	Pte.	S/17698	1/6th Gordon Highdrs.	—	K. in A.
Gilyard, Thos. A.	Pte.	205098	W. Yorks.	—	Killed
Ginsberg, J.	Pte.	6144	Connaught Rangers	—	Died
Ginsberg, Samuel	Pte.	2102	22nd Royal Fusiliers	—	K. in A.
Girvin, E. O.	Gnr.	776847	R.F.A.	—	D. of W.
Givens, John Wm.	Dvr.M2/098458		R.A.S.C.	—	Died
Gladders, Wm. Edgar	Sgt.	378	15th W. Yorks.	—	K. in A.
Glass, E. R.	Rfm.	371157	London	—	K. in A.
Gleave, Fred	Dvr.	776003	R.F.A.	—	K. in A.
Gledden, Chas.	Pte.	25945	K.O.Y.L.I.	—	K. in A.
Gledhill, Arthur	Pte.	441451	Labour Corps	—	D. a. Dis.
Gledhill, Harry	Pte.	202618	W. Yorks.	—	K. in A.
Gledhill, Herbert	Dvr.	72939	Royal Engineers	—	Died
Gledhill, Jas. H.	Pte.	26181	13th E. Yorks.	—	Missing
Gledhill, John E.	Pte.	201527	Royal Scots Fusiliers	—	K. in A.
Gledhill, John Hy.	Dvr.	586637	R.F.A.	—	Died
Gledhill, Leonard F.	Pte.	37664	S. Lancs.	—	Died
Gledhill, Walter B.	Pte.	36748	K.O.Y.L.I.	—	Missing
Gledhill, Wm.	Gnr.	776848	R.F.A.	—	D. a. Dis.
Glenham, Thos. Wm.	Pte.	7985	Northumberland Fusrs.	—	Died
Glithero, Wm. P.	Gnr.	26112	R.F.A.	—	K. in A.
Glover, Albert	Pte.	267369	W. Yorks.	—	K. in A.
Glover, C. S.	Pte.	47277	12th W. Yorks.	—	K. in A.
Glover, Edwin	Pte.	202183	2/4th Leicester	—	K. in A.
Glover, Percy	Pte.	648	17th W. Yorks.	—	K. in A.
Glover, Wm.	Cpl.	25715	K.O.Y.L.I.	—	D. of. W.
Godber, Geo.	Sgt.	142245	Machine Gun Corps	—	Missing
Goddard, H.	W/M.	13440	H.M.S. " Queen Mary "	—	K. in A.

LEEDS ROLL OF HONOUR.

Name	Rank	No.	Regiment	Honours	How Died
Goddard, Samuel	Gnr.	17284	R.F.A.	—	K. in A.
Godfrey, James	Pte.	3/9620	8th Yorks.	—	K. in A.
Godfrey, James	Pte.	10208	E. Yorks.	—	K. in A.
Godson, Arthur	Pte.	381	15th W. Yorks.	—	D. of W.
Goff, Alfred R.	Gnr.	953	R.F.A.	—	Died
Goldberg, Henry	Pte.	556747	Labour Corps	—	Died
Goldberg, Herbert	L/Cpl.	12695	King's Royal Rifle Cps.	—	K. in A.
Golding, S.	Pte.	10007	W. Riding	—	D. of W.
Goldman, S.	2/A.M.	22013	Royal Air Force	—	Died
Goldsbury, Ernest	Pte.	10156	King's Royal Rifle Cps.	—	Missing
Goldstein, Harris	Pte.	335466	1/9th Royal Scots	—	K. in A.
Goldthorp, Harry	Rfm.	3311	1/7th W. Yorks.	—	K. in A.
Goldthorpe, Ewart	Gnr.	142877	R.G.A.	—	K. in A.
Goldthorpe, George	L/Cpl.	17/1710	10th W. Yorks.	—	K. in A.
Golesworthy, Walter C.	Gnr.	232840	R.F.A.	—	Died
Gomersall, Harry	Pte.	159524	Machine Gun Corps	—	K. in A.
Good, Wm. A.	Rfm.	4920	2/8th W. Yorks.	—	K. in A.
Goodall, Fred	Pte.	8547	4th W. Yorks.	—	D. of W.
Goodall, Fred	Rfm.	43549	King's Royal Rifle Cps.	—	Died
Goodall, Joseph	Pte.	7511	1st W. Yorks.	—	K. in A.
Goodall, Wm. H.	Pte.	3200	W. Riding	—	D. of W.
Goodchild, Francis T.	Gnr.	741511	R.F.A.	—	K. in A.
Goodchild, Joseph H.	Pte.	98882	Machine Gun Corps	—	K. in A.
Goodenham, Jas. L.	Pte.	76836	R.A.M.C.	—	Killed
Goodenough, R.	Pte.	15669	Yorks.	—	K. in A.
Goodhind, Fred	Pte.	22204	A. P. C.	—	K. in A.
Goodman, Ernest	Gnr.	104274	R.G.A.	—	K. in A.
Goodman, Eustace E.	Pte.	41292	Gordon Highlanders	—	K. in A.
Goodman, James	Pte.	98694	Machine Gun Corps	—	Died
Goodman, Samuel	Pte.	267009	1/10x. & Bucks. L.I.	—	K. in A.
Goodrick, J. J. S.	Sgt.	242201	2/6th S. Staffs.	—	K. in A.
Goodson, Fred	Pte.	27784	Lancs. Fusiliers	—	K. in A.
Goodson, Sam	Pte.	32651	York. & Lancs.	—	K. in A.
Goodson, Wm.	L/Cpl.	3748	7th W. Yorks.	—	K. in A.
Goodwill, Francis	Pte.	33696	W. Yorks.	—	K. in A.
Goodwill, G. Wm.	Pte.	15455	Yorks.	—	K. in A.
Goodwill, Stanley	Pte.	28067	14th W. Yorks.	—	K. in A.
Goodyear, Horace	Pte.	59603	W. Yorks.	—	K. in A.
Goodyer, Fred N.	Pte.	49553	1st W. Yorks.	—	K. in A.
Goom, Norman	Pte.	28049	3rd Grenadier Guards	—	K. in A.
Gordon, Alec M.	Captain		R.F.A.	—	K. in A.
Gordon, John Wm.	Pte.	653858	Labour Corps	—	D. a. Dis.
Gorman, Frank	Pte.	26291	Royal Dublin Fusiliers	—	K. in A.
Gorman, John	Pte.	17/647	11th W. Yorks.	—	K. in A.
Gornall, Chas. E.	Pte.	352827	9th Royal Scots.	—	K. in A.
Gosney, John	Pte.	13623	K.O.Y.L.I.	—	K. in A.
Gosney, Thos.	Gnr.	819	R.F.A.	—	K. in A.

LEEDS ROLL OF HONOUR.

Name	Rank	No.	Regiment	Honours	How Died
Gospel, Chas. Wm.	Pte.	6249	2/9th London	—	K. in A.
Goss, Jas. H.	Gnr.	25233	1/8th W. Yorks.	—	K. in A.
Gouarne, R. A.	Spr.	72389	Royal Engineers	—	K. in A.
Goucher, Edwin	Pte.	42358	3/6th W. Yorks.	—	K. in A.
Gough, Joseph	Pte.	47275	12th W. Yorks.	—	K. in A.
Gough, Norman	Pte.	1802	15th W. Yorks.	—	K. in A.
Gough, O. J.	Pte.	441452	Labour Corps	—	Died
Gould, Albert	Gnr.	109926	R.F.A.	—	D. of W.
Gould, Frank	Cpl.	40156	13th York. & Lancs.	—	D. of W.
Goulden, John	Rfm.	57091	8th W. Yorks.	—	K. in A.
Goulden, Joseph	Rfm.	305410	1/8th W. Yorks	—	Died
Goulding, Walter	Pte.	11492	9th W. Riding	—	K. in A.
Goulding, Wm.	Pte.	40364	1st Cameron Highdrs.	—	K. in A.
Govier, Benj.	Pte.	1071	14th York. & Lancs.	—	K. in A.
Goward, Wm.	L/Cpl.	59570	W. Surrey	—	Missing
Gower, Sidney	Pte.	1333	15th W. Yorks.	—	K. in A.
Gower, Thos. H.	C.S.M.	305674	W. Yorks.	M.M.	K. in A.
Gowland, Chas. E.	Sgt.	266016	1/7th W. Yorks.	—	K. in A.
Gozney, C. M.	Captain		1/15th London	—	K. in A.
Grady				—	Died
Graham, Clifford	Pte.	9017	W. Yorks.	—	Died
Graham, Harry	Pte.	39075	10th Northumb'rl'd Fusrs.	—	K. in A.
Graham, Leonard	A.L/Cpl.	305333	W. Yorks.	—	D. a. Dis.
Graham, Matthew	Pte.	21448	York. & Lancs.	—	Killed
Graham, W.	Pte.	35512	9th Dragoon Guards	—	K. in A.
Graham, Walter E.	Sgt.		12th King's Liverpool	—	D. of W.
Graham, Wm. G.	Pte.	24604	13th Yorks.	—	Died
Grainger, Geo.	Rfm.	2047	2/7th W. Yorks.	—	K. in A.
Grainger, John	Pte.	37272	11th W. Yorks.	—	D. of W.
Grainger, Wm.	Pte.	38546	12th W. Yorks.	—	K. in A.
Grand, H.	Pte.	2/15903	1st Middlesex	—	K. in A.
Granger, Arthur J.	Pte.	37438	9th W. Yorks.	—	Killed
Granger, J.	Pte.	11498	2nd W. Riding	—	K. in A.
Grant, Albert	Pte.	33377	18th W. Yorks.	—	Died
Grant, Cameron	Pte.	53226	Durham Light Infantry	—	K. in A.
Grant, G. H.	Pte.M2/	177639	R.A.S.C.	—	Died
Grant, Harry T.	Pte.	50021	Lincoln	—	K. in A.
Grant, John I.	Rfm.	30665	8th W. Yorks.	—	K. in A.
Grant, John W.	Rfm.	3212	1/7th W. Yorks.	—	K. in A.
Grant, Joseph	Pte.	40171	7th Royal Scots Fusrs.	—	K. in A.
Grant, Norman	L/Cpl.	2204	1/8th W. Yorks.	—	K. in A.
Grant, Richard	Pte.	48806	4th W. Yorks.	—	K. in A.
Grant, Squire	Rfm.	3947	1/7th W. Yorks.	—	K. in A.
Grantham, W.	Captain		1/4th W. Riding	—	D. of W.
Grasby, Geo. W.	Pte.	267199	W. Yorks.	—	K. in A.
Grassick, Chas. A.	Cpl.	464466	17th Highland Lt. Infty.	—	D. a. Dis.
Graves, Robert	Dvr.	222867	R.F.A.	—	Died

LEEDS ROLL OF HONOUR.

Name	Rank	No.	Regiment	Honours	How Died
Gray, Alfred	Pte.	28809	Reserve Cavalry	—	Died
Gray, Edwin	Pte.	181	19th W. Yorks.	—	K. in A.
Gray, George	Pte.	12294	19th Yorks.	—	K. in A.
Gray, Harry	Pte.	71939	R.A.M.C.	—	K. in A.
Gray, Harry	L/Bdr.	950337	R.G.A.	—	Died
Gray, Henry	Sgt.	265314	1/7th W. Yorks.	—	Killed
Gray, James	Cpl.	10486	King's Own R. Lancs.	—	K. in A.
Gray, John Wm.	Pte.	36121	Royal Defence Corps	—	D. a. Dis.
Gray, Percy	Pte.	24337	1st W. Yorks.	—	Missing
Grayham, H.	Sgt.	39002	Machine Gun Corps	—	K. in A.
Grayman, Sam	Pte.	J/901	Royal Fusiliers	—	Killed
Grayshon, Frank	Pte.	5600	Scots Guards	—	K. in A.
Grayshon, George	Pte.	39233	W. Yorks.	—	Killed
Grayson, Geo. H.	Pte.	39196	W. Yorks.	—	Missing
Grayson, Herbert	Pnr.	294711	Royal Engineers	—	K. in A.
Grayson, Randolph	Pte.	40302	18th W. Yorks.	—	K. in A.
Grayson, Thos.	P.O.	1020	Royal Marine Lt. Infty.	—	K. in A.
Grayson, Thos.	Pte.	12959	K.O.Y.L.I.	—	Missing
Grayson, Thos.	Pte.	9618	1st W. Yorks.	—	K. in A.
Greasley, Alfred R.	L/Sgt.	371	15th W. Yorks.	—	K. in A.
Greasley, Stanley E.	L/Cpl.	305216	1/8th W. Yorks.	—	K. in A.
Greason, Seth	Rfm.	39365	2/7th W. Yorks.	—	K. in A.
Greatrex, Fred	Sgt.	191264	Labour Corps	—	Died
Greatwich, Harry	L/Cpl.	2622	W. Yorks.	—	D. of W.
Greaves, A.	Pte.	77901	R.A.M.C.	—	K. in A.
Greaves, Albert	Cpl.	134803	Royal Engineers	—	K. in A.
Greaves, G. F.	Pte.	203751	5th Lancs. Fusiliers	—	K. in A.
Greaves, Geo. Wm.	Pte.	S/11860	Royal Highlanders	—	K. in A.
Greaves, Harry	Pte.	10085	10th W. Yorks.	—	D. a. Dis.
Greaves, Henry	Pte.	305853	11th W. Yorks.	—	Died
Greaves, John	2nd Lieut.		Royal Warwick	—	D. of W.
Greaves, John R.	Pte.	401318	R.A.M.C.	—	K. in A.
Greaves, John R.	Gnr.	20889	R.F.A.	—	K. in A.
Greaves, Percy	Pte.	24811	W. Yorks.	—	Died
Greaves, Thos. E.	Pte.	367495	Labour Corps	—	K. in A.
Greaves, Walter	Gnr.	64342	R.G.A.	—	K. in A.
Green, A. E.	Pte.	37480	16th W. Yorks.	—	K. in A.
Green, Arthur	Pte.	1464	Royal Marine Lt. Infty.	—	K. in A.
Green, Arthur	Cpl.	12037	7th K.O.Y.L.I.	—	D. of W.
Green, Ernest	Pte.	22939	11th Royal W. Surrey	—	K. in A.
Green, F.	Gnr.	6049	R.G.A.	—	K. in A.
Green, George	Pte.	24775	13th W. Yorks.	—	K. in A.
Green, George	A.B.	8418	Royal Naval Division	—	K. in A.
Green, Harry	Pte.	47388	R.G.A.	—	K. in A.
Green, Herbert	Pte.	23067	2nd York. & Lancs.	—	K. in A.
Green, Horace	Pte.	16669	2nd Northumb'l'd Fusrs.	—	K. in A.
Green, J. A.	L/Cpl.	179469	Labour Corps	—	K. in A.

LEEDS ROLL OF HONOUR.

Name	Rank	No.	Regiment	Honours	How Died
Green, John ..	A.B.	..239496	H.M.S. " Morning Star "	—	K. in A.
Green, Joseph	Pte.	5794	1/5th K.O.Y.L.I.	—	D. of W.
Green, Lawrence G. ..	Pte.	53077	2nd Manchester	—	Died
Green, Samuel	Pte.	40995	Scottish Highlanders ..	—	K. in A.
Green, Thos. W.	Pte.	24422	R.F.A. ..	—	K in A.
Green, William	Pte.	R/258886	G.S.C. ..	—	K. in A.
Greenberg, Philip	Pte.	..242578	W. Yorks.	—	Died
Greenfield, Benj.	Pte.	14287	12th W. Yorks.	—	K. in A.
Greenhalch, J.	Pte.	2289	11th Manchester	—	Died
Greenhalgh, B.	..	..	Canadians	..	
Greenhough, Arthur	Pte.	104	12th K.O.Y.L.I.	—	K. in A.
Greenhough, Wm.	Pte.	19620	2nd Leicester	—	D. of W.
Greenhough, Wm.	Pte.	..203313	K.O.Y.L.I.	—	K. in A.
Greenside, Harry	Pte.R/M266446		1/6th W. Yorks.	—	K. in A.
Greensmith, Turner ..	Pte.	8205	1st W. Yorks.	—	K. in A.
Greenway, Geo.	Pte.	42363	W. Yorks.	—	K. in A.
Greenwell, Wm.	Bmdr.	790044	R.F.A. ..	—	D. of W.
Greenwood, Albert E.	L/Cpl.	3547	K.O.Y.L.I.	—	K. in A.
Greenwood, Frank L.	Cpl.	41449	10th E. Yorks.	—	K. in A.
Greenwood, George ..	Sgt.	..288263	21st Canadian	—	K. in A.
Greenwood, H.	Pte.	21462	Northumberland Fusrs.	—	Killed.
Greenwood, Harry	Rfm.	3958	2/7th W. Yorks.	—	K. in A.
Greenwood, Henry ..	Pte.	..307448	1/6th W. Yorks.	—	Missing
Greenwood, Herbert	Pte.	8249	1st W. Yorks.	—	D. of W.
Greenwood, Herbert A.	Pte.	41420	Royal Lancs. ..	—	K. in A.
Greenwood, James ..	Rfm.	3716	2/7th W. Yorks.	—	D. of W.
Greenwood, James ..	Pte.	33998	Gordon Highlanders ..	—	Died
Greenwood, John	Pte.	..3/8284	1st W. Yorks.	—	K. in A.
Greenwood, John Thos.	Pte.	..240904	Royal Engineers	—	Died
Greenwood, John Wm.	Bmdr.	73117	R.F.A. ..	—	K. in A.
Greetham, Geo. Ed. ..	Stkr.	..	H.M.S. " Ardent "	—	Died
Gregg, Wm. ..	Gnr.	..775318	R.F.A. ..	—	K. in A.
Gregg, Wm. H.	L/Cpl.	10698	27th Northumb'l'd Fusrs.	—	K. in A.
Gregg, Wm. S.	Pte.	7409	1st E. Yorks. ..	—	Killed
Gregory, Horace	Cpl.	3347	Royal Air Force	—	Died
Gregory, John R.	Pte.	14059	13th Coldstream Guards	—	K. in A.
Greig, W. ..	Pte.	..105036	Northumberland Fusrs.	—	Died
Gresham, John	Pte.	..307459	2nd W. Yorks.	—	Died
Greville, Peter	Pte.	28756	12th W. Yorks.	—	Died
Grey, Christian	Pte.	649	17th W. Yorks.	—	D. of W.
Grey, George	Pte.	..	19th Yorks.	—	K. in A.
Greyman, Sam	Pte.	901	38th Royal Fusiliers ..	—	Killed
Greyson, T. ..	Pte.	11372	16th Lancs. Fusiliers	—	K. in A.
Gricewood, Clarence	Bmdr.	69475	R.G.A. ..	—	Died
Griffin, James	Pte.	..106773	Notts. & Derby	—	K. in A.
Griffin, Patrick	Pte.	16323	W. Yorks.	—	K. in A.
Griffiths, Charles	Pte.	60312	Machine Gun Corps	—	K. in A.

LEEDS ROLL OF HONOUR.

Name	Rank	No.	Regiment	Honours	How Died
Griffiths, David	Pte.	13255	9th K.O.Y.L.I.	—	K. in A.
Griffiths, Harry	Pte.	24786	13th Yorks.	—	K. in A.
Griffiths, John	Pte.	12567	9th W. Yorks.	—	Missing
Griffiths, Joseph	Pte.	120305	R.A.M.C.	—	D. a. Dis.
Griffiths, Robert B.	Spr.	368964	Royal Engineers	—	Died
Griffiths, Thos. H.	Pte.	35152	Yorks.	—	K. in A.
Grimes, Wm.	L/Cpl.	4093	1/8th W. Yorks.	—	K. in A.
Grimes, Wm.	Pte.	229	K.O.Y.L.I.	—	K. in A.
Grimshaw, Chas.	Rfm.	265301	7th W. Yorks.	—	Died
Grimshaw, Wm.	Pte.	10242	1st W. Yorks.	—	K. in A.
Grimson, Fredk.	Pte.	14376	Norfolk	—	D. a. Dis.
Grix, Robert A.	L/Cpl.	3/8265	7th Yorks.	—	K. in A.
Grogan, James	Cpl.	6365	Manchester	—	Died
Grogan, James	Pte.	25913	W. Yorks.	—	K. in A.
Grogan, W. L.	Bmdr.	61312	R.F.A.	—	K. in A.
Groves, Enoch	Pte.M2/153784		R.A.S.C.	—	Killed
Grundon, Percy	Pte.	31424	Northumberland Fusrs.	—	K. in A.
Grundy, Geoffrey S.	Pte.	1362	H.A.C.	—	K. in A.
Grundy, H. B.	Pte.	203386	5th Manchester	—	K. in A.
Grundy, Herod		13334	Military Police	—	Died
Gubby, Walter C.	R.S.M.	618	R.G.A.	—	K. in A.
Gudgeon, Albert	L/Cpl.	38268	15/17th W. Yorks.	—	K. in A.
Gudgeon, Alfred	Rfm.		1/8th W. Yorks.	—	K. in A.
Gurney, R. A.	Spr.		Royal Engineers	—	K. in A.
Guthrie, Arthur	C.E.R.A.	262915	H.M.S. " Pembroke "	—	D. a. Dis.
Guthrie, Fred	Pte.	17176	2nd W. Yorks.	—	K. in A.
Guthrie, Geo. G.	Pte.	65	17th W. Yorks.	—	K. in A.
Guthrie, Jas. A.	Pte.	10061	W. Yorks.	—	K. in A.
Guthrie, Samuel	Pte.	46775	K.O. Scottish Borderers	—	K. in A.
Guttridge, Albert	Cpl.	407	15th W. Yorks.	—	K. in A.
Guy, Leonard	Pte.	11935	10th K.O.Y.L.I.	—	Missing
Guy, Robert	Pte.	18176	1st K.O. Scottish Bordrs.	—	Missing
Hackers, Albert	Cpl.	203278	W. Riding	—	K. in A.
Hackett, Chas. H.	Rfm.	4715	King's Royal Rifle Cps.	—	K. in A.
Haddlesay, HerbertW.	Pte.	13960	King's Own R. Lancs.	—	K. in A.
Haddock, David	Pte.	29516	W. Yorks.	—	K. in A.
Haddock, George A.	Pte.	31355	E. Yorks.	—	K. in A.
Haddock, Percy	Pte.	37134	12th W. Yorks.	—	D. of W.
Hadwen, John	Pte.	21240	Labour Corps	—	K. in A.
Hague, Edward	Pte.	371289	Labour Corps	—	K. in A.
Hague, W.	Pte.	305735	Yorks.	—	Died
Haigh, Arthur	Dvr.	44	R.A.S.C.	—	Died
Haigh, Benjamin	Rfm.	2899	W. Yorks.	—	K. in A.
Haigh, C. T.	Sgt.	8879	2nd W. Yorks.	—	K. in A.
Haigh, Edward T.	Pte.	23393	Loyal N. Lancs.	—	K. in A.
Haigh, George	A.B.	R/1777	Royal Naval Division	—	Died

LEEDS ROLL OF HONOUR.

Name	Rank	No.	Regiment	Honours	How Died
Haigh, George	Pte.	9684	Machine Gun Corps	—	D. of W.
Haigh, George	Pte.	10599	W. Riding	—	Missing
Haigh, Harold	Pte.	11543	Seaforth Highlanders	—	K. in A.
Haigh, Harold	Pte.	33961	10th W. Yorks.	—	K. in A.
Haigh, Harold H.	Pte.	13230	K.O.Y.L.I.	—	K. in A.
Haigh, Henry	Pte.	232711	Labour Corps	—	K. in A.
Haigh, Joseph	Pte.	12896	9th K.O.Y.L.I.	—	K. in A.
Haigh, Tom	Pte.	4389	W. Yorks.	—	K. in A.
Haines, Thos.	Rfm.	265244	2/7th W. Yorks.	—	K. in A.
Haines, Walter	Pte.	26277	18th W. Yorks.	—	D. of W.
Hainsworth, Arthur	Pte.	23574	6th Dorset	—	K. in A.
Hainsworth, Arthur	Pte.	8618	2nd W. Yorks.	—	K. in A.
Hainsworth, F. J.	L/Cpl.	255603	9th W. Yorks.	—	K. in A.
Hainsworth, JohnWm.	Pte.	11801	6th K.O.Y.L.I.	—	K. in A.
Hainsworth, Joseph	Pte.	5690	10th W. Yorks.	—	K. in A.
Hainsworth, Joseph	Pte.	70386	R.A.M.C.	—	K. in A.
Hainsworth, Wm.	Pte.	202892	W. Yorks.	—	K. in A.
Haist, John	Sgt.	412	15th W. Yorks.	—	K. in A.
Haitwaite, Clifford	Pte.	38825	25th Northumb'l'd Fusrs.	—	Missing
Halden, Alfred	Pte.	308173	8th King's Irish L'vpool	—	K. in A.
Haldenby, Albert	L/Cpl.	305942	2/8th W. Yorks.	—	K. in A.
Hale, John W.	Pte.	19348	1st Northumb'l'd Fusrs.	—	D. of W.
Haley, Arthur L.	C.Q.M.S.	210417	R.A.S.C.	—	K. in A.
Haley, Bernard	Pte.	40176	14th York. & Lancs.	—	K. in A.
Haley, Edmund	Sgt.	8041	10th W. Yorks.	—	K. in A.
Haley, Ernest	Pte.	65415	S. Lancs.	—	Died
Haley, Henry	Pte.	15358	Royal Scots Fusiliers	—	K. in A.
Haley, Isaac	Pte.	308051	1/7th W. Riding	—	K. in A.
Haley, John	Pte.	36859	15th W. Yorks.	—	Missing
Haley, John	Gdsmn.	15433	Coldstream Guards	—	K. in A.
Haley, John	Pte.	13549	W. Yorks.	—	K. in A.
Haley, Michael	Pnr.	296022	Royal Engineers	—	Died
Haley, Thos.	Pte.	49507	12th W. Yorks.	—	K. in A.
Haley, Wm.	Pte.	32787	9th W. Yorks.	—	K. in A.
Hall, Arthur	Pte.	37316	16th W. Yorks.	—	K. in A.
Hall, Arthur	Pte.	39199	14th Durham Lt. Infty.	—	K. in A.
Hall, Arthur	Pte.	33930	6th K.O.Y.L.I.	—	K. in A.
Hall, Benjamin	Pte.	7474	1st E. Yorks.	M.M.	K. in A.
Hall, C.	Pte.	51443	R.A.M.C.	—	Died
Hall, Clifford	Rfm.	306235	2/8th W. Yorks.	—	K. in A.
Hall, Edward	Sgt.	17971	W. Yorks.	—	Died
Hall, Edward L.	Gdsmn.	8552	1st Scots Guards	—	K. in A.
Hall, Edwin	Pte.	290106	R.A.S.C.	—	D. a. Dis.
Hall, Ernest	L/Cpl.	19058	K.O.Y.L.I.	—	K. in A.
Hall, Fred	Pte.	451	21st W. Yorks.	—	Missing
Hall, Geoffrey	2nd Lieut.		2nd Middlesex	—	K. in A.
Hall, Geo. H.	L/Cpl.	18305	1st W. Yorks.	—	K. in A.

LEEDS ROLL OF HONOUR.

Name	Rank	No.	Regiment	Honours	How Died
Hall, H. S.	Pte.	62068	2nd York. & Lancs.	—	K. in A.
Hall, Harold	Pte.	350295	Highland Lt. Infantry	—	K. in A.
Hall, Herbert	Pte.	8362	4th W. Yorks.	—	K. in A.
Hall, John	Pte.	19776	17th W. Yorks.	—	K. in A.
Hall, John	Pte.	20525	W. Yorks.	—	Died
Hall, John C.	Pte.	374290	Labour Corps	—	D. a. Dis.
Hall, John H.	Pte.	3049	1/4th K. O. R. Lancs.	—	K. in A.
Hall, John R.	Pte.	40954	27th Northumb'l'd Fusrs.	—	K. in A.
Hall, John S.	Pte.	7374	E. Yorks.	—	K. in A.
Hall, Joseph	Pte.	24522	W. Yorks.	—	Died
Hall, Percy	Sgt.		Canadians	—	K. in A.
Hall, Stanley	Pte.	13988	W. Yorks.	—	K. in A.
Hall, Thos.	Pte.	14899	11th Durham Lt. Infty.	—	K. in A.
Hall, Willie	Rfm.	40871	2nd Scottish Rifles	—	Died
Hall, Wm.	Pte.	37576	E. Lancs.	—	K. in A.
Hall, Wm.	Pte.	20783	Highland Lt. Infantry	—	K. in A.
Hall, Wm. A.	Pte.	11786	9th K.O.Y.L.I.	—	K. in A.
Hall, Wm. H.	Dvr.	T4/45856	R.A.S.C.	—	Died
Hallad, A.	Pte.	12757	10th W. Yorks.	—	K. in A.
Hallah, Geo. A.	L/Cpl.	36219	15th Highland Lt. Infty.	—	K. in A.
Hallam, Geo.	Pte.	300070	18th W. Yorks.	—	K. in A.
Hallam, Harry	Pte.	21229	9th W. Yorks.	—	K. in A.
Hallam, Robt. W.	Rfm.	306004	2/8th W. Yorks.	—	K. in A.
Hallas, A. E.	Pte.	4316	Royal Fusiliers	—	K. in A.
Hallas, Fred	Rfm.	39266	2/7th W. Yorks.	—	K. in A.
Hallewell, James	Pte.	612517	London	—	K. in A.
Hallewell, Walter	Bdr.	382634	R.G.A.	—	D. of W.
Halliday, David E.	Spr.	126680	Royal Engineers	—	D. a. Dis.
Halliday, H.	Spr.	504747	Royal Engineers	—	D. a. Dis.
Halpine, Walter	Pte.	24511	W. Riding	—	D. of W.
Halstead, Tom	Pte.			—	Died
Halton, Chas.	Pte.	11531	K.O.Y.L.I.	—	K. in A.
Hamer, Arthur E.	Pte.	43864	1/4th Durham Lt. Infty.	—	Missing
Hamer, Henry	E.R.A.	M11436	H.M.S. " Invincible "	—	K. in A.
Hamilton, Bernard St. George	Lieut.		9th Highland Lt. Infty.	—	K. in A.
Hamilton, Gavin P.	Pte.	419	15th W. Yorks.	—	K. in A.
Hamilton, James L.	Pte.	41996	7th E. Yorks.	—	K. in A.
Hamilton, Tom	Dvr.	35934	R.F.A.	—	Died
Hammond, Sowden	Pte.	375977	15th Durham Lt. Infty.	—	K. in A.
Hammond, Walter	Cpl.	27962	Lancs. Fusiliers	M.M.	Died
Hammond, William	A.B.	J10508	H.M.S. " Bulwark "	—	K. in A.
Hammond, Willie	Pte.	38307	10th York. & Lancs.	—	K. in A.
Hammonds, J. T.	Pte.	43191	14th Durham Lt. Infty.	—	K. in A.
Hampshire, Harry	Pte.	36194	9th W. Yorks.	—	D. of W.
Hampshire, J. W.	Pte.	15439	9th W. Yorks.	—	K. in A.
Hampshire, J. W.	Pte.	57753	20th Manchester	—	K. in A.

LEEDS ROLL OF HONOUR.

Name	Rank	No.	Regiment	Honours	How Died
Hampson, George	Rfm.	2925	1/7th W. Yorks.	—	K. in A.
Hampson, James	Pte.	7679	S. Lancs.	—	Died
Hanakin, Thos.	Pte.	63217	Labour Corps	—	D. a. Dis.
Hanbey, Thos. H.	Pte.	29777	2/5th Warwick	—	Missing
Hancock, Geoffrey	L/Cpl.	422	15th W. Yorks.	—	K. in A.
Hancock, W. S.	Pte.	408272	R.A.M.C.	—	K. in A.
Handcock, Wm.	Sgt.	309472	Labour Corps	—	Died
Handley, John V.	Pnr.	142192	Royal Engineers	—	K. in A.
Haney, John	Cpl.	6509	3rd W. Yorks.	—	K. in A.
Haney, Peter	L/Cpl.	9754	W. Yorks.	—	K. in A.
Hangerton, W.	Pte.	810	R.A.M.C.	—	Drowned
Hanley, Arthur H.	Pte.	11158	Machine Gun Corps	—	D. a. Dis.
Hanlon, Frank	Pte.	425	15th W. Yorks.	—	Died
Hanlon, Harold F.	L/Cpl.	3768	W. Yorks.	—	Died
Hannan, Arthur	Pte.	35277	16th W. Yorks.	—	K. in A.
Hannan, James H.	Pte.	18018	12th Royal Fusiliers	—	K. in A.
Hansell, Walter	Pte.	15790	9th York. & Lancs.	—	K. in A.
Hansgate, Henry	Pte.	109094	Durham Lt. Infty.	—	D. a. Dis.
Hanshaw, John W.	Pte.	38607	Yorks.	—	Died
Hanson, Alfred	Rfm.	306224	1/8th W. Yorks.	—	Died
Hanson, Alfred	Pte.	241219	Yorks.	—	K. in A.
Hanson, Fred	Spr.	153951	Royal Engineers	—	K. in A.
Hanson, Joseph	Pte.	9342	3rd W. Yorks.	—	D. a. Dis.
Hanson, Walter	Gnr.	84450	R.G.A.	—	D. of W.
Hant, Cyril	Pte.	305559	10th W. Yorks.	—	K. in A.
Hara, Wm.	Sgt.	2575	Royal Munster Fusiliers	—	Died
Harcourt, Isiah	Spr.	82775	Royal Engineers	—	K. in A.
Hardaker, Percy	Pte.	17521	Northumberland Fusrs.	—	K. in A.
Hardcastle, Arthur	Pte.	31825	4th K.O. Scottish Bordrs.	—	K. in A.
Hardcastle, Bernard A.	Pte.	41793	21st W. Yorks.	—	K. in A.
Hardcastle, Chas.	L/Cpl.	305759	1/8th W. Yorks.	—	K. in A.
Hardcastle, Fred W.	Pte.	139811	Machine Gun Corps	—	K. in A.
Hardcastle, John T.	Pte.	1372	15th W. Yorks.	—	D. of W.
Hardcastle, John T.	Gnr.	36028	R.F.A.	—	D. a. Dis.
Hardcastle, John W.	Pte.	20877	2nd K.O.Y.L.I.	—	K. in A.
Hardcastle, Matthew	Tpr.	20884	Norfolk Yeomanry	—	D. a. Dis.
Hardcastle, Wm.	Gdsm.	14428	Coldstream Guards	—	K. in A.
Harding, Colin	Pte.	12168	3rd Royal Scots	—	Died
Harding, Fred W.	L/Cpl.	3239	1/8th W. Yorks.	—	K. in A.
Harding, James	Pte.	7817	K.O. Scottish Bordrs.	—	K. in A.
Harding, John E.	Rfm.		1/8th W. Yorks.	—	K. in A.
Harding, Joseph	Spr.	100707	Royal Engineers	—	Died
Harding, Thos.	Pte.	200416	1/5th K.O.Y.L.I.	—	K. in A.
Hardisty, Alfred	Pte.	54919	4th E. Yorks.	—	D. a. Dis.
Hardisty, John E.	Pte.	366291	Labour Corps.	—	Died
Hardley, John K.	Pte.	36692	W. Yorks.	—	Missing.
Hardman, Chas.	Pte.	2198	K.O.Y.L.I.	—	K. in A.

LEEDS ROLL OF HONOUR.

Name	Rank	No.	Regiment	Honours	How Died
Hardwick, Harry	Rfm.	2337	1/8th W. Yorks.	—	Died
Hardwick, J.	Cpl.	9494	3rd W. Kents.	—	K. in A.
Hardwick, John J.	Pte.	2366	W. Yorks.	—	D. of W.
Hardwick, Joseph	Pte.	205079	1/5th W. Yorks.	—	Missing
Hardwick, Wm.	Gdsm.	28391	Grenadier Guards	—	Died
Hardwick, Wm. C.	Pte.	1269	15th W. Yorks.	—	K. in A.
Hardy, Benjamin	Gnr.	108233	R.G.A.	—	D. of W.
Hardy, Ernest	Pte.	24778	10th W. Yorks.	—	Missing
Hardy, Frank	Pte.	428	15th W. Yorks.	—	K. in A.
Hardy, Herbert	Pte.	45058	1/5th Northumb'l'd Fus.	—	K. in A.
Hardy, Thos. H.	Pte.	25480	E. Yorks.	—	Missing
Hardy, Thorpe	Pte.	1047	17th W. Yorks.	—	D. of W.
Hardy, Wm.	Pte.	10721	6th W. Yorks.	—	K. in A.
Hare, Harry	Pte.	37691	21st W. Yorks.	—	D. of W.
Hargate, Christopher	Pte.	203781	W. Yorks.	—	Died
Hargrave, Chas.	Pte.	32840	16th W. Yorks.	—	K. in A.
Hargrave, Ernest	Pte.	202654	W. Yorks.	—	K. in A.
Hargrave, Fred W.	Pte.	350962	15th Durham Lt. Infty.	—	K. in A.
Hargrave, Herbert	Rfm.	24573	1/8th W. Yorks.	—	Missing
Hargrave, Herbert	Pte.	11299	Yorks.	—	Died
Hargrave, Herbert	Pte.	8407	W. Yorks.	—	K. in A.
Hargrave, Horace	Pte.	38305	York. & Lancs.	—	K. in A.
Hargrave, Richard	Pte.	8410	1st W. Yorks.	—	K. in A.
Hargrave, Robert	Sgt.	291571	1/8th Scots Rifles	—	K. in A.
Hargrave, Rowlatt	Pte.	307103	W. Yorks.	—	K. in A.
Hargrave, Wm.	Pte.	42861	Royal Scots	—	K. in A.
Hargreave, Joseph	Cpl.	34699	4th Yorks.	—	Died P.O.W.
Hargreaves, Edwin	Cpl.	38551	W. Ridings	—	K. in A.
Hargreaves, George	Rfm.	3987	1/7th W. Yorks.	—	K. in A.
Hargreaves, Harry B.	Pte.	3061	Australian Imp. Forces	—	Missing
Hargreaves, John W.	Pte.	129876	Royal Engineers	—	K. in A.
Hargreaves, John W.	Gnr.	151391	R.G.A.	—	K. in A.
Hargreaves, Joseph H.	Stkr. K	27211	H.M.S. " Hampshire "	—	K. in A.
Hargreaves, Leonard	Pte.	23571	Dorset	—	K. in A.
Hargreaves, Rowland	Dvr.	72457	Royal Engineers	—	D. of W.
Hargreaves, Samuel	Pte.	11995	Machine Gun Corps.	—	K. in A.
Hargreaves, Thos.	Dvr.	775637	R.F.A.	—	D. of W.
Hargreaves, Wm.	Rfm.	39761	1/7th W. Yorks.	—	Died
Hargreaves, Willie	Pte.	23055	8th Yorks.	—	K. in A.
Harker, Clifford	Pte.	20084	1st Royal Irish Rifles	—	Died
Harker, Hbt. J.	A.B.	KP436	Royal Naval Division	—	K. in A.
Harker, Richard	Pte.	24693	Lancs. Fusiliers	—	K. in A.
Harker, Walter	Gdsmn.	15237	Scots Guards	—	K. in A.
Harker, Wm. J.	L/Cpl.	8186	2nd Yorks.	—	K. in A.
Harkness, James	Rfm.	3428	8th W. Yorks.	—	K. in A.
Harland, John A.	Gnr.	96467	R.F.A.	—	K. in A.
Harland, Roland	Pte.	13838	11th W. Yorks.	—	K. in A.

LEEDS ROLL OF HONOUR.

Name	Rank	No.	Regiment	Honours	How Died
Harley, James W.	Dvr.	775569	R.F.A.	—	K. in A.
Harley, Percy	Pte.	41791	W. Yorks.	—	K. in A.
Harlow, Edward C.	Pte.	432	15th W. Yorks.	—	Missing
Harman, John W.	Pte.	205466	1/4th E. Yorks.	—	K. in A.
Harmar, Gerald	2nd Lieut.		9th N. Staffs.	—	K. in A.
Harmston, John	Pte.	241852	K.O.Y.L.I.	—	K. in A.
Harmsworth, Fred J.	Pte.	265603	W. Yorks.	—	K. in A.
Harper, Ezra	Pte.	36846	15th W. Yorks.	—	Missing
Harper, Harry	Pte.	202364	K.O.Y.L.I.	—	K. in A.
Harrington, Donald H.	Pte.	41330	Norfolk	—	K. in A.
Harrington, H.	Pte.	8446	1st Northumb'l'd Fusrs.	—	K. in A.
Harriman, Wilfred	Pte.	1021	Royal Marine Lt. Infty.	—	K. in A.
Harris, Albert	Cpl.	16003	9th K.O.Y.L.I.	—	K. in A.
Harris, Christopher S.	2nd Lieut.		6th W. Yorks.	—	K. in A.
Harris, Fredk.	Pte.	42536	Machine Gun Corps	—	K. in A.
Harris, H.	Pte.	2405	1/4th E. Yorks.	—	K. in A.
Harris, Harry	Pte.	43055	W. Yorks.	—	K. in A.
Harris, John H.	Pte.	4409	9th Cameron Highdrs.	—	K. in A.
Harris, Michael	Pte.	2447	E. Kent	—	K. in A.
Harris, Mick	Gnr.	111927	R.F.A.	—	Died
Harris, William	Cpl.	202196	5th K.O.Y.L.I.	M.M.	D. of W.
Harris, William	Pte.	351003	Durham Lt. Infantry	—	Died
Harrison, Albert	Pte.	62535	K.O.Y.L.I.	—	K. in A.
Harrison, Albert	Pte.	19518	K.O.Y.L.I.	—	K. in A.
Harrison, Arthur	Pte.	9472	2nd W. Riding	—	Missing
Harrison, Aubrey R.H.	Pte.	40017	York. & Lancs.	—	Died
Harrison, Ben	Pte.	307145	W. Yorks.	—	*K. in A.
Harrison, Chas.	Pte.	47284	12th W. Yorks.	—	K. in A.
Harrison, Chas.	Pte.	13000	9th W. Yorks.	—	K. in A.
Harrison, Chas. A.	Pte.	10290	3rd W. Riding	—	D. of W.
Harrison, Chas. W.	Pte.	71754	15th W. Yorks.	—	Missing
Harrison, E. W.	Pte.	36216	10th W. Yorks.	—	D. a. Dis.
Harrison, Ernest	Gnr.	143608	R.G.A.	—	K. in A.
Harrison, Fred	Pte.	1292	3rd K.O.Y.L.I.	—	K. in A.
Harrison, Fred	Rfm.	306554	2/8th W. Yorks.	—	K. in A.
Harrison, Fred S.	Pte.	39022	2/8th Lancs. Fusiliers	—	K. in A.
Harrison, G. Wm.	Sgt.	8932	York. & Lancs.	—	K. in A.
Harrison, George W.	Rfm.	3309	2/8th W. Yorks.	—	Acc. Killed
Harrison, George Wm.	Pte.	25687	W. Surrey	—	K. in A.
Harrison, James	Pte.	34290	9th W. Yorks.	—	K. in A.
Harrison, John	Pte.	7269	E. Yorks.	—	D. of W.
Harrison, John	A.B.	R5310	Royal Naval V. Res.	—	Died
Harrison, John W.	Pte.	268411	W. Riding	—	D. of W.
Harrison, Joseph	Pte.	196582	Labour Corps	—	Died
Harrison, Morris	Rfm.	268013	1/7th W. Yorks.	—	Died
Harrison, Oliver	Pte.	15761	9th W. Yorks.	—	K. in A.
Harrison, Sidney	Pte.	28424	6th S. Lancs.	—	D. of W.

LEEDS ROLL OF HONOUR.

Name	Rank	No.	Regiment	Honours	How Died
Harrison, Thomas	L/Cpl.	33132	21st W. Yorks.	—	K. in A.
Harrison, Walter	Pte.	23091	25th Northumb'l'd Fusrs.	—	K. in A.
Harrison, William	Pte.	20139	K.O.Y.L.I.	—	K. in A.
Harrison, William	L/Cpl.	37520	W. Yorks.	—	Died
Harrison, Wm.	Gnr.	82750	R.F.A.	—	K. in A.
Harrison, Wm. E.	Gnr.	143536	R.G.A.	—	Died
Harrison, Wm. R.	3/A.M.	119808	Royal Air Force	—	Died
Harrold, Thomas	Pte.	20570	2nd Border	—	Missing
Hart, Alfred	Pte.	41853	10th Northumb'l'd Fusrs.	—	K. in A.
Hart, Chas. E.	Cpl.	3087	1/8th W. Yorks.	—	K. in A.
Hart, Edward	Rfm.	3963	8th W. Yorks.	—	K. in A.
Hart, Ernest	Pte.	211886	Royal Air Force	—	Died
Hart, Ernest	Pte.	12495	10th K.O.Y.L.I.	—	K. in A.
Hart, Fredk.	L/Cpl.	8760	Border	—	K. in A.
Hart, Martin	L/Cpl.	3418	2/8th W. Yorks.	—	Died
Hart, Percy	RN 2	16352	H.M.S. " Kellingworth "	—	Died
Hart, Thomas	Pte.	8407	W. Yorks.	—	K. in A.
Hart, Wm.	Dvr.	01542	R.A.S.C.	—	Died
Hartley, Ben	Rfm.	266977	2/7th W. Yorks.	—	Died
Hartley, Bradshaw	Pte.	46200	13th York. & Lancs.	—	K. in A.
Hartley, Frank	Pte.	12937	8th K.O.Y.L.I.	—	K. in A.
Hartley, G. T.	Spr.	37162	Royal Engineers	—	K. in A.
Hartley, George	A/Cpl.	15351	Machine Gun Corps	—	K. in A.
Hartley, George	Cpl.		Northumberland Fusrs.	—	Died
Hartley, Herbert	Pte.	9774	3rd W. Yorks.	—	K. in A.
Hartley, John	Gnr.	75623	R.F.A.	—	Missing
Hartley, Joshua	Pte.	169579	Labour Corps	—	D. a. Dis.
Hartley, Percival	L/Cpl.	14031	Coldstream Guards	—	K. in A.
Hartley, William	2/A.M.	23440	Royal Air Force	—	Died
Hartman, Arthur	Pte.	44498	23rd Northumb'l'd Fus.	—	K. in A.
Hartnell, Cuthbert	Lieut.		1/8th W. Yorks.	—	K. in A.
Hartshorn, Arthur	Pte.	30507	York. & Lancs	—	D. a. Dis.
Hartshorn, George	Pte.	1323	17th W. Yorks.	—	K. in A.
Harvey, Ephraim E.	Pte.	21280	W. Yorks.	—	K. in A.
Harvey, Fredk.	Pnr.	607647	Royal Engineers	—	D. a. Dis.
Harvey, Henry	Pte.	6395	Connaught Rangers	—	K. in A.
Harvey, John	Sgt.	17389	6th York. & Lancs.	—	K. in A.
Harvey, John W.	Sgt.	12377	3rd W. Riding	—	K. in A.
Harvey, Reginald	Gnr.	99577	R.F.A.	—	K. in A.
Harvey, William	Pnr.	274696	Royal Engineers	—	D. a. Dis.
Harwood, Alfred	Pte.	21874	6th K.O.Y.L.I.	—	K. in A.
Harwood, Harry	Rfm.	34063	2/7th W. Yorks.	—	K. in A.
Harwood, James H.	Pte.	25694	6th K.O.Y.L.I.	—	K. in A.
Harwood, John	Pte.	2638	3rd K.O.Y.L.I.	—	Died
Harwood, Joseph	Pte.	36891	1st W. Yorks.	—	D. of W.
Haseltine, James J.	Pte.	412659	R.A.S.C.	—	Died
Hastings, George A.	Pte.	14827	10th Notts. & Derby	—	K. in A.

LEEDS ROLL OF HONOUR.

Name	Rank	No.	Regiment	Honours	How Died
Haswell, Arthur	1/A.M.	409822	R.A.F.	—	D. a. Dis.
Haswell, John C.	Pte.	84	17th W. Yorks.	—	K. in A.
Hatfield, John T.	Pte.	31778	W. Yorks.	—	D. of W.
Hatley, John	Sgt.	40253	17th W. Yorks.	—	K. in A.
Hatter, John T.	Pte.	1697	17th W. Yorks.	—	Died
Hatton, George W.	Pte.	27963	21st W. Yorks.	—	K. in A.
Hatton, Thomas	Pte.	17134	2nd Leicester	—	K. in A.
Haw, Thomas W.	Pte.	20328	13th Northumb'l'd Fus.	—	K. in A.
Haw, William	Spr.	521920	Royal Engineers	—	Died
Hawden, Geo. Albert	Pte.	5323	K.O.Y.L.I.	—	Died
Hawden, Harry	Pte.	10480	9th Royal Fusiliers	—	Missing
Hawes, Edward	Cpl.	305231	8th W. Yorks.	—	K. in A.
Hawes, Leonard	Pte.	238044	4th Northumbe'l'd Fus.	—	K. in A.
Hawke, John H.	Pte.	525	2/5th W. Yorks.	—	K. in A.
Hawkesworth, David	Pte.	1919	Yorks.	—	K. in A.
Hawkins, Chas. P.	Pte.	475810	Labour Corps.	—	K. in A.
Hawkins, Fred	Rfm.	39318	2/8th W. Yorks.	—	K. in A.
Hawkins, Kirby	Pte.	36960	9th W. Yorks.	—	K. in A.
Hawkins, Leonard	Pte.	7812	Royal Defence Corps	—	Died
Hawkins, Thomas	Pte.	266234	W. Yorks.	—	Died
Hawkins, William	Pte.	52341	10th Cheshire	—	K. in A.
Hawkins, William	Pte.	18534	9th W. Yorks.	—	K. in A.
Hawkridge, John W.	Pte.	15537	W. Riding	D.C.M.	K. in A.
Hawkshaw, Alfred S.	Dvr.	83283	R.F.A.	—	K. in A.
Hawkshaw, Chris. W.	Pte.	44820	Lincoln	—	K. in A.
Hawkyard, Arthur N.	Smn.	T53484	H.M.S. " Royal Sovereign "	—	Died
Hawkyard, Thomas	Pte.	38802	Northumberland Fusrs.	—	K. in A.
Hawxwell, Alfred	Pte.	132745	Royal Fusiliers	—	D. a. Dis.
Haxby, Robert	Rfm.	2784	8th W. Yorks.	—	D. of W.
Hay, Charles	Pte.	60760	25th Northumb'l'd Fusrs.	—	K. in A.
Hay, William B.	Pte.	19337	York. & Lancs.	—	K. in A.
Hayden, William	Pte.	11776	2/4th K.O.Y.L.I.	—	K. in A.
Hayes, Charles	Pte.	13449	10th W. Yorks.	—	K. in A.
Hayes, Horace W.	Sgt.	378	R.F.A.	—	K. in A.
Hayes, J.	Pte.	23271	6th York. & Lancs.	—	K. in A.
Hayes, Jesse	Pte.	22453	6th E. Lancs.	—	Died
Hayes, John	Pte.	201321	2nd W. Yorks.	—	K. in A.
Hayes, John	Sgt.	697671	Labour Corps	—	Died
Hayes, John T.	Pte.	23425	8th Yorks.	—	K. in A.
Hayes, Patrick	Cpl.	957	S. Lancs.	—	Died
Hayes, Richard	Pte.	103113	Machine Gun Corps	—	K. in A.
Hayes, Sidney	Rfm.	4732	3/7th W. Yorks.	—	K. in A.
Hayes, Walter	Pte.	25614	13th Yorks.	—	K. in A.
Hayes, Walter	Cpl.	24254	18th W. Yorks.	—	D. of W.
Hayes, Walter F.	L/Cpl.	29610	E. Yorks.	—	K. in A.

LEEDS ROLL OF HONOUR.

Name	Rank	No.	Regiment	Honours	How Died
Hayes, William	Cpl.	20536	2nd Yorks.	—	K. in A.
Hayhurst, John	Pte.		15th W. Yorks.	—	K. in A.
Hayle, William	Pte.	8593	3rd W. Yorks.	—	K. in A.
Haynes, John E.	Pte.	940	18th W. Yorks.	—	K. in A.
Haynes, Robert W.	Pte.	33112	18th W. Yorks.	—	K. in A.
Haythorne, George	Pte.	31133	1st E. Yorks.	—	K. in A.
Hayton, Edmund	Dvr.	4/083497	R.A.S.C.	—	Died
Hayton, Walter	Sgt.	885	17th W. Yorks.	—	K. in A.
Hayward, Frank	Pte.	38768	1/3rd Gloucester	—	K. in A.
Hayward, Lewis	Pte.	8398	3rd W. Yorks.	—	K. in A.
Hayward, William	Pte.	49244	10th W. Yorks.	—	K. in A.
Haywood, Alfred	Pte.	40267	8th K.O. Scottish Bdrs.	—	Missing
Hazelgrave, George W.	Pte.	51548	1st Cheshire	—	Missing
Hazelgrave, Thornton	Pte.	307385	W. Yorks.	—	Died
Head, Walter	Pte.	11574	Machine Gun Corps	—	D. of W.
Headlam, Harry	Rfm.	4473	7th W. Yorks.	—	D. of W.
Headley, Walter	Pte.	8784	Notts. & Derby.	—	K. in A.
Headlong, George	Pte.	50132	2nd Lincoln	—	K. in A.
Heald, Arthur	Pte.	656	W. Riding	—	D. of W.
Heald, Arthur J.	Pte.	9815	W. Yorks.	—	Died P.O.W.
Heald, George	Pte.	8128	Yorks.	—	K. in A.
Heald, George W.	Rfm.	305907	8th W. Yorks.	—	K. in A.
Healey, Edward	Cpl.	442	15th W. Yorks.	—	Missing
Healey, Fredk.	Cpl.	425	17th W. Yorks.	—	K. in A.
Healey, Leonard	A.B.		H.M.S. " Queen Mary "	—	K. in A.
Healy, Charles	C.S.M.	6002	2nd K.O.Y.L.I.	M.C.	Missing
Healy, Thomas	Pte.	12885	9th W. Riding	—	K. in A.
Heap, Herbert	Sgt.		21st King's R. Rifle Cps.	—	K. in A.
Heard, Thomas	Pte.	306342	12th W. Yorks.	—	K. in A.
Heath, Clifton A.	Pte.	44821	1st Lincolns.	—	Missing
Heathcote, George	L/Cpl.	12490	K.O.Y.L.I.	—	K. in A.
Heaton, Charles H.	Dvr.	251907	R.A.S.C.	—	Died
Heaton, H.	Pte.	43910	Inniskillen Fusiliers	—	K. in A.
Heaton, Herbert	Pte.	3402	W. Yorks.	—	Died
Hebden, John J.	Cpl.	41591	17th W. Yorks.	—	K. in A.
Hebden, Tom	Pte.	23906	10th W. Yorks.	—	K. in A.
Hebditch, James F.	L/Cpl.	503019	Royal Engineers	—	Died
Hector, Harry	Pte.	19076	York. & Lancs.	—	K. in A.
Heden, William E.	Pte.	1625	17th W. Yorks.	—	Died
Heeley, Fredk.	Gnr.	107321	R.F.A.	—	Died
Hefford, Wilfred	Pte.	33183	3rd W. Yorks.	—	K. in A.
Heffron, Thomas	Pte.	291255	Northumberland Fusrs.	—	K. in A.
Helstrip, Herbert	Gdsmn.	8381	Scots Guards	—	Died P.O.W.
Hemingbrough, Chas. A.	Pte.	444	15th W. Yorks.	—	Died
Hemingbrough, John	Pte.	13019	10th K.O.Y.L.I.	—	K. in A.
Hemingway, Alfred	Pte.	1331	17th W. Yorks.	—	K. in A.
Hemingway, Ernest	S/Sgt./Mjr.		R.A.S.C.	—	Died

LEEDS ROLL OF HONOUR.

Name	Rank	No.	Regiment	Honours	How Died
Hemingway, Fred W.	Pte.	76142	Durham Lt. Infantry	—	K. in A.
Hemingway, Harry B.	Pte.	36753	15th W. Yorks.	—	Missing
Hemingway, Job	Rfm.	1211	1st Rifle Brigade	—	K. in A.
Hemingway, Johnson	A/Sgt.	5925	1st W. Riding	—	K. in A.
Hemingway, T. H.	Pte.	269046	10th W. Riding	—	K. in A.
Hemingway, Wm. M.	Gnr.	283475	R.G.A.	—	K. in A.
Hemingway, W. W. C.				—	Died
Hemsley, George H.	Pte.	25844	W. Yorks.	—	K. in A.
Hemsley, Horace	Pte.	39511	2nd W. Yorks.	—	K. in A.
Hemsley, Hubert	L/Cpl.	10053	W. Yorks.	—	K. in A.
Hemsley, Leonard	Pte.	10017	W. Yorks.	—	D. a. Dis.
Hemsley, Walter	Sgt.	220	17th W. Yorks.	—	K. in A.
Hemsley, William	Pte.	336574	Royal Defence Corps.	—	Died
Hemsworth, Herbert	Rfm.	265264	7th W. Yorks.	—	Died
Henderson, F.	Pte.	12686	10th W. Yorks.	—	D. of W.
Henderson, George	Pte.	8184	2nd W. Riding	—	D. of W.
Henderson, Henry	Sgt.	267547	Seaforth Highlanders	—	K. in A.
Henderson, James	Dvr.	80787	R.F.A.	—	K. in A.
Henderson, James A.	Dvr.	223467	R.F.A.	—	Died
Heney, Joseph	Sgt.	126803	Royal Engineers	—	D. a. Dis.
Henry, Bernard	Dvr.	92839	R.F.A.	—	K. in A.
Henry, Ernest J.	Rfm.	5357	8th W. Yorks.	—	Missing.
Henry, Joseph	Pte.	537	15th W. Yorks.	—	K. in A.
Henry, Michael	Pte.	7110	Royal Irish Fusiliers	—	D. a. Dis.
Henry, Thomas	Pte.	22151	K.O.Y.L.I.	—	K. in A.
Henry, Thomas	Pte.	265541	W. Yorks.	—	K. in A.
Henson, Walter	Gnr.	104542	R.G.A.	—	D. a. Dis.
Hepburn, John	Dvr.	36205	R.F.A.	—	K. in A.
Hepple, L.	Pte.	171197	Machine Gun Corps	—	Died
Hepworth, Charles	Pte.	62729	6th W. Yorks.	—	D. of W.
Hepworth, Clifford	Pte.	40136	R.A.M.C.	—	D. of W.
Hepworth, Thomas	Pte.	30736	1st K.O. Scottish Brders.	—	K. in A.
Hepworth, William C.	Pte.	28926	Northumberland Fusrs.	—	D. of W.
Herbert, G. A.	Cpl.	266699	W. Yorks.	—	K. in A.
Herbert, George	Pte.	26610	10th W. Yorks.	—	K. in A.
Herley, John W.	Pte.	447	15th W. Yorks.	—	K. in A.
Herrington, Arthur	Sgt.	29353	Notts. & Derby	—	D. a. Dis.
Herrity, Andrew	Spr.	1177	Royal Engineers	—	Died
Herrod, John	Sgt.	3902304	S. Wales Borderers	—	K. in A.
Herson, George W.	Pte.	21044	15th W. Yorks.	—	Missing
Heseltine, James	Pte.	412659	R.A.S.C.	—	Died
Heseltine, John R.	O.S.	39067	H.M.S. " Defiance "	—	Died
Heseltine, Willie		M/7833	H.M.S. " Stephen Furness "	—	K. in A.
Heshon, Chas. J.	Pte.	10463	K.O.Y.L.I.	—	Missing
Hesketh, H. G.	Pte.	36610	10th W. Yorks.	—	D. of W.
Heslington, Reg. W.	Pte.	174901	R.A.S.C.	—	Died

LEEDS ROLL OF HONOUR.

Name	Rank	No.	Regiment	Honours	How Died
Heslington, Walter H.	Q.M.S.		Machine Gun Corps	—	Died
Hess, A.	Major		W. Yorks.	—	D. of W.
Hess, Henry	2nd Lieut. (Adjt.)		Middlesex	—	K. in A.
Hessay, Richd.	Pte.	203664	S. Staffs.	—	K. in A.
Hesselberg, Myer	Pte.	45981	11th Northumb'l'd Fus.	—	K. in A.
Hesseltine, James J.	Pte.	412659	R.A.S.C.	—	Died
Hewerdine, Henry	Pte.	8083	2nd Yorks.	—	K. in A.
Hewerdine, Joseph	Pte.	10351	2nd Yorks.	—	K. in A.
Hewison, Arthur	Pte.	17241	W. Yorks.	—	K. in A.
Hewison, Walter	Pte.		W. Yorks.	—	Died
Hewitt, Alfred	Pte.	17367	K.O.Y.L.I.	—	Died
Hewitt, Bernard	Pte.	23949	14th W. Yorks.	—	K. in A.
Hewitt, David	Pte.	26315	6th Cameron Highdrs.	—	K. in A.
Hewitt, George W.	Pte.	242317	2nd W. Yorks.	—	K. in A.
Hewitt, Harry E.	Gnr.	70282	R.G.A.	—	Died
Hewitt, Henry R.	Pte.	138675	Machine Gun Corps	—	K. in A.
Hewitt, Herbert	Sgt.	449	15th W. Yorks.	—	K. in A.
Hewitt, Marcus G.	Pte.	076118	R.A.S.C.	—	K. in A.
Hewitt, Wilfred	Pte.	148277	Machine Gun Corps	—	K. in A.
Hewitt, Willie	Pte.	4389	6th W. Riding	—	K. in A.
Heworth, Edgar B.	Pte.	120041	Labour Corps	—	Died
Hewson, Thomas	Pte.	10578	9th W. Yorks	—	Missing
Hey, Joseph	Gnr.	240868	R.F.A.	—	Died
Hey, W.	Pte.	19337	8th York. & Lancs.	—	K. in A.
Heyes, Nathan	Pte.	9260	16th W. Yorks.	—	Missing
Heyes, P.	Cpl.	957	S. Lancs.	—	Died
Heywood, Alan	Lieut.		Royal Air Force	—	Died
Hezmalhach, Eric	Gdsmn.	119044	Coldstream Guards	—	K. in A.
Hibbert, E. J.	L/Cpl.	84888	Machine Gun Corps	—	D. of W.
Hick, John	Pte.	33055	1st E. Yorks.	—	K. in A.
Hick, Wm.	Rfm.	266104	7th W. Yorks.	—	Died
Hickey, Daniel	Spr.	94517	Royal Engineers	—	Died
Hickey, Wm.	Pte.	12174	W. Yorks.	—	K. in A.
Hicks, Geo.	Gnr.	34902	R.F.A.	—	K. in A.
Hicks, Thomas W.	Pte.	859	21st W. Yorks.	—	K. in A.
Hickson, Laurie	Tpr.	1171	Household Cavalry	—	Died
Hickson, Lawrence	Pte.	457	15th W. Yorks.	—	K. in A.
Hickson, Sidney	Spr.	277142	Royal Engineers	—	D. a. Dis.
Hickson, William	3A.M.	185464	Royal Air Force	—	D. a. Dis.
Hield, Eustace J.	L/Cpl.	403508	R.A.M.C.	M.M.	K. in A.
Hield, Wm. C.	2nd Lieut.		Royal Air Force	—	K. in A.
Higginbottom, G.	Pte.	17842	7th Yorks.	—	K. in A.
Higginbottom, Joe F.	Pte.	1805	15th W. Yorks.	—	Missing
Higgins, Frank	Pte.	73742	K.O.Y.L.I.	—	D. of W.
Higgins, Harry	Cpl.	34370	2nd W. Yorks.	—	K. in A.
Higgins, James	Pte.	6815	York. & Lancs.	—	Died
Higgins, Peter	Pte.	202934	5th W. Yorks.	—	Died

LEEDS ROLL OF HONOUR.

Name	Rank	No.	Regiment	Honours	How Died
Higgs, Stanley	Pte.	30805	Welsh	—	Died
High, Aubrey R.	Pte.	40014	York. & Lancs.	—	Died
Higson, Alfred	Pte.	42167	S. Staffs.	—	Missing
Hildred, James	Pte.	7498	W. Yorks.	—	Died
Hiley, Allan	Pte.	12710	10th W. Riding	—	K. in A.
Hiley, Harry	Pte.	34591	W. Yorks.	—	K. in A.
Hiley, John C.	Bdr.	45433	R.F.A.	—	K. in A.
Hiley, Tom	Rfm.	4704	7th W. Yorks.	—	Missing
Hill, Albert E.	Pte.	13137	10th W. Yorks.	—	K. in A.
Hill, Alfred	Pte.	36734	12th E. Yorks.	—	Missing
Hill, Arthur	Pte.	612	17th W. Yorks.	—	Died
Hill, Charles	1Stkr.	109674	H.M.S. " Victory "	—	Died
Hill, Claude S.	Pte.	460	15th W. Yorks.	—	K. in A.
Hill, Ernest	A.M.	5719	Royal Air Force	—'	D. of W.
Hill, Fredk.	Pte.	25482	W. Yorks.	—	Died
Hill, Harold	L/Sgt.	15417	Somerset Lt. Infantry	—	K. in A.
Hill, Herbert	A.B.	Z115260	H.M.S. " Venerable "	—	Died
Hill, James	Pte.	817	W. Yorks.	—	Died
Hill, John	Spr.	283921	Royal Engineers	—	K. in A.
Hill, John B.	Pte.	306328	W. Yorks.	—	K. in A.
Hill, John R.	Pte.	1524	15th W. Yorks.	—	K. in A.
Hill, Joseph	Pte.	31677	Royal Army Vety. Cps.	—	Died
Hill, Robert	Pte.	1154	17th W. Yorks.	—	K. in A.
Hill, Squire E.	Pte.	33353	K.O.Y.L.I.	—	K. in A.
Hill, Thomas	Rfm.	266049	7th W. Yorks.	—	D. of W.
Hill, Thomas	L/Cpl.	16143	Lancs. Fusiliers	—	Died
Hill, William	Pte.	203118	Highland Lt. Infantry	—	K. in A.
Hills, Harry B.	Pte.	17222	1st Northumber'd Fusrs.	—	K. in A.
Himsworth, Harry	Rfm.	41063	1st Scottish Rifles	—	K. in A.
Hinchcliffe, Albert	Pte.	202191	Leicester	—	D. of W.
Hinchcliffe, John	Pte.	50056	2nd Lancs. Fusiliers	—	K. in A.
Hinchcliffe, John P.	Sgt.	305595	8th W. Yorks.	—	Died
Hinchcliffe, Samuel	Pte.	71899	Notts. & Derby.	—	K. in A.
Hinchsliff, Charles	Gdsmn.	8417	Scots Guards.	—	K. in A.
Hindle, Ernest	Pte.	22859	Royal W. Surrey	—	K. in A.
Hindley, Charles	Pte.	9279	2nd W. Yorks.	—	K. in A.
Hine, N. A. W.	Lieut.		W. Yorks.	—	Died
Hingerton, William	Pte.	810	R.A.M.C.	—	K. in A.
Hinsley, Harry	Pte.	403286	R.A.M.C.	—	D. of W.
Hinson, Walter	Pte.	37440	9th W. Yorks.	—	K. in A.
Hinton, Ernest H.	Stwd.	L/3046	H.M.S. " Cressy "	—	K. in A.
Hipkin, Albert P.	Sgt.	241759	York. & Lancs.	—	D. of W.
Hirsch, D. P.	Captain		Yorks.	V.C.	K. in A.
Hirst, Alfred	Pte.	10394	K.O.Y.L.I.	—	K. in A.
Hirst, Charles	Pte.	34902	25th Northumb'l'd Fus.	—	K. in A
Hirst, Chas. H.	Sgt.			—	K. in A
Hirst, Francis A.	Sgt.	6790	2nd West Yorks.	—	D. a. Dis.

LEEDS ROLL OF HONOUR.

Name	Rank	No.	Regiment	Honours	How Died
Hirst, Geo. E.	Pte.	18664	6th K.O.Y.L.I.	—	K. in A.
Hirst, Harry	Rfm.	3297	2/7th West Yorks.	—	K. in A.
Hirst, Harry	Gdsmn.	24348	Coldstream Guards	—	K. in A.
Hirst, J.	Pte.	8305	Northampton	—	K. in A.
Hirst, J.	Pte.	271945	Labour Corps	—	Died
Hirst, Jas.	Rfm.	306561	2/8th W. Yorks.	M.M.	K. in A.
Hirst, Stanley L.	2nd Lieut.		17th W. Yorks.	—	K. in A.
Hirst, Thos.	Pte.	24202	Labour Corps	—	K. in A.
Hirst, Thos.	Pte.	26530	9th K.O.Y.L.I.	—	K. in A.
Hirst, Thos.	Rfm.	265989	2/7th W. Yorks.	—	Died P.O.W.
Hirst, Thos.	Dvr.	775197	R.F.A.	—	K. in A.
Hirst, Thos. W.	L/Cpl.	4389	1/4th W. Riding	—	K. in A.
Hirst, Walter	Pte.	81023	Durham Light Infantry	—	K. in A.
Hitchen, Arthur B.	Rfm.	2804	7th W. Yorks.	—	K. in A.
Hitchen, Geo. H.	Pte.	1772	15th W. Yorks.	—	K. in A.
Hitchen, Geo. H.	Pte.	1082	19th W. Yorks.	—	K. in A.
Hitchen, Leonard	Gnr.	72662	R.G.A.	—	Died
Hitchins, Robert	Sgt.	8637	3rd W. Yorks.	—	K. in A.
Hoare, Alfred	Rfm.	4141	2nd King's R. Rifle Cps.	—	K. in A.
Hoban, John W.	Cpl.	265219	1/7th W. Yorks.	—	K. in A.
Hoban, Richard E.	O.S.	T54372	Royal Naval Division	—	K. in A.
Hoban, Thos.	Pte.	31142	Royal Defence Corps	—	Died
Hobday, Albert E.	Cpl.	305221	W. Yorks.	—	K. in A.
Hobson, Chas.	Pte.	8706	2nd W. Yorks.	—	K. in A.
Hobson, David	Sgt.	12870	K.O.Y.L.I.	—	K. in A.
Hobson, Ernest	Pte.	24925	12th W. Yorks.	—	D. of W.
Hobson, George	Rfm.	3934	1/8th W. Yorks.	—	K. in A.
Hobson, Harvey	Pte.	10510	9th W. Yorks.	—	Missing
Hobson, Jas.	Pte.	12796	K.O.Y.L.I.	—	K. in A.
Hobson, Leonard	A.B.	633	Royal Naval Division	—	K. in A.
Hockney, William	Pte.	34227	King's Own R. Lancs.	—	K. in A.
Hodge, Thomas P.	Pte.	36296	Duke of Cornwall L.I.	—	K. in A.
Hodges, Wm. A.	Sig.	19135	Yorks.	—	K. in A.
Hodgkinson, Richard	Rfm.	266126	2/7th W. Yorks.	—	K. in A.
Hodgkinson, Wm.	A.B.	34792	"H.M.S. Pembroke"	—	D. a. Dis.
Hodgkinson, Wm.	Pte.	196020	R.A.S.C.	—	Died
Hodgson, Alfred	Cpl.	201409	Seaforth Highlanders	—	K. in A.
Hodgson, Clifford	Pte.	25209	10th W. Yorks.	—	D. of W.
Hodgson, George	Rfm.	12083	King's R. Rifle Corps	—	K. in A.
Hodgson, Geo. R.	Pte.	41889	12th Northumb'l'd Fus.	—	K. in A.
Hodgson, Geo. W.	Pte.	49154	W. Yorks.	—	K. in A.
Hodgson, Harold	Pte.	30043	10th K.O.Y.L.I.	—	Died
Hodgson, Louis	Pte.	305754	10th W. Yorks.	—	K. in A.
Hodgson, Peter S.	Pte.	75398	R.A.M.C.	—	K. in A.
Hodgson, Robert	Pte.	20059	1st K.O. Scottish Brdrs.	—	K. in A.
Hodgson, Sam.	Rfm.	1487	1/8th W. Yorks.	—	K. in A.
Hodgson, Sml.	Pte.	13337	8th K.O.Y.L.I.	—	K. in A.

LEEDS ROLL OF HONOUR.

Name	Rank	No.	Regiment	Honours	How Died
Hodgson, Wilfred	Gnr.	85054	R.F.A.	—	D. of W.
Hoffman, W. J. F.	Pte.	17926	2nd Manchester	—	Died
Hogan, John	Pte.	12826	Labour Corps	—	D. of W.
Hogg, Godfrey G.	Pte.	202147	Leicester	—	K. in A.
Hogg, John Louis	Sgt.	468	15th W. Yorks.	—	Missing
Hogg, Richard W.	L/Sgt.	13829	11th W. Yorks.	—	K. in A.
Hogg, Royle	A/Cpl.	5111	3/4th Seaforth Highdrs.	—	D. of W.
Hogg, Thos.	Pte.	14796	9th K.O.Y.L.I.	—	Missing
Hogg, Wm. J.	Pte.	18827	W. Yorks.	—	Died
Holden, Alfred	Pte.	308173	King's Liverpool	—	D. of W.
Holden, Angus	Pte.	9997	E. Yorks.	—	K. in A.
Holden, F.	Pte.	65345	Machine Gun Corps	—	D. of W.
Holden, Hbt.	Pte.	31151	1st E. Yorks.	—	K. in A.
Holden, John E.	Rfm.	266342	2/7th W. Yorks.	—	K. in A.
Holden, Leonard	Dvr.	776853	R.F.A.	—	Died
Holden, Sml.	Pte.	4755	5th W. Yorks.	—	Missing
Holder, Harry	L/Cpl.	18154	W. Riding	—	Died
Holder, Willie	Rfm.	6186	King's Royal Rifle Cps.	—	D. of W.
Holderness, Arthur	Dvr.	401294	R.A.M.C.	—	K. in A.
Holdsworth, Arthur	Pte.	1713	2nd W. Yorks.	—	Died
Holdsworth, Edgar	Rfm.	307580	8th W. Yorks.	—	D. of W.
Holdsworth, Fred	Gnr.	144809	R.F.A.	—	K. in A.
Holdsworth, Harold	Pte.	43548	Durham Lt. Infantry	—	Died
Holdsworth, Hbt.	Pte.	10984	11th W. Yorks.	—	D. of W.
Holdsworth, Jas. W.	Pte.	10513	9th W. Yorks.	—	K. in A.
Holdsworth, Joe W.	Rfm.	6237	King's Royal Rifle Cps.	—	Died
Holdsworth, John S.	Pte.	363045	R.A.S.C.	—	Died
Holdsworth, Joseph	Pte.	21816	Labour Corps	—	D. a. Dis.
Holdsworth, Mark W.	Pte.	37613	W. Yorks.	—	K. in A.
Holdsworth, Wm. A.	Sgt.	776852	R.F.A.	—	K. in A.
Holehan, John	Pte.	7647	1st W. Yorks.	—	K. in A.
Holgate, Arthur	Pte.	34870	1st W. Yorks.	—	K. in A.
Holgate, Cecil	Pte.	38450	York. & Lancs.	—	Missing
Holgate, Chas. T.	Pte.	12948	9th K.O.Y.L.I.	—	K. in A.
Holgate, Herbt.	Dvr.	84122	Royal Engineers	—	K. in A.
Holgate, Hbt. A.	Sgt.		R. Canadians	—	K. in A.
Holgate, Joseph D.	L/Cpl.	8510	K.O. Scottish Bordrs.	—	K. in A.
Holl, E.	L/Cpl.	268237	8th W. Yorks.	—	Died
Holland, Arthur	Pte.	10228	2nd Yorks.	—	K. in A.
Holland, Edward	Pte.	21233	Labour Corps	—	Died
Holland, Ernest	Pnr.	214405	Royal Engineers	—	K. in A.
Holland, Geo. R.	Pte.	10117	Royal Fusiliers	—	K. in A.
Holland, Lazarus	Pte.	29461	1st W. Yorks.	—	K. in A.
Holland, Wm. B.	Cpl.	66371	Northumberland Fusrs.	—	Died
Holland, Wm. R. G.	Lieut.		10th W. Yorks.	M.C.	K. in A.
Holliday, Arthur	Pte.	1285	15th W. Yorks.	—	K. in A.
Holliday, Chas. H.	L/Cpl.	15607	2nd Royal Fusiliers	—	K. in A.

LEEDS ROLL OF HONOUR.

Name	Rank	No.	Regiment	Honours	How Died
Holliday, Clement	Rfm.	300048	8th W. Yorks.	—	K. in A.
Holliday, Fred	Pte.	13139	W. Yorks.	—	D. of W.
Holliday, Geo. R.	L/Cpl.	24488	3rd W. Yorks.	—	D. of W.
Holliday, Harry	Cpl.	38906	Northumberland Fusrs.	—	K. in A.
Holliday, John	L/Cpl.	2556	8th W. Yorks.	—	D. of W.
Holliday, John W.	Gnr.	270908	R.F.A.	—	K. in A.
Holliday, Thos.	Pte.	32848	17th W. Yorks.	—	Died
Holliday, Wilfred	Dvr.	152011	R.G.A.	—	K. in A.
Holliday, Wm.	Cpl.	3149	Yorks.	—	K. in A.
Holliday, Wm. H.	Bdr.	63313	R.F.A.	—	D. of W.
Hollings, Clarence	Pte.	37397	W. Yorks.	—	K. in A.
Hollings, David S.	Pte.	50453	10th Lancs. Fusrs.	—	K. in A.
Hollings, Wm. A.	Pte.	470	15th W. Yorks.	—	K. in A.
Hollingworth, G.	Pte.	267394	W. Yorks.	—	K. in A.
Hollingworth, Joseph	Pte.	18930	1st W. Yorks.	—	K. in A.
Hollingworth, Leonard	Pte.	92031	2nd Durham Lt. Infty.	—	K. in A.
Hollinsworth, Hbt.	Cpl.	24112	3rd Lancs. Fusrs.	—	K. in A.
Hollins, Arthur	Pte.	40987	Leicester	—	K. in A.
Hollis, Wm.	Pte.	2837	3rd York. & Lancs.	—	D. a. Dis.
Holmes, Albert	Pte.	307485	W. Yorks.	—	K. in A.
Holmes, Arthur N.	Pte.	202653	2/4th Leicester	—	K. in A.
Holmes, C. H.	Sgt.	4286	W. Yorks.	—	K. in A.
Holmes, Chas.	Pte.	8542	York. & Lancs.	—	Died
Holmes, Clifton	Pte.	21281	Royal Marine Lt. Infty.	—	K. in A.
Holmes, F. E.	1/A.M.	22781	Royal Air Force	—	Died
Holmes, Frank	Rfm.	306146	8th W. Yorks.	—	K. in A.
Holmes, Frank W.	Pte.	113951	R.A.S.C.	—	Died
Holmes, Fred	Spr.	476509	Royal Engineers	—	Missing
Holmes, Geo.	Sgt.	400	17th W. Yorks.	—	D. a. Dis.
Holmes, Harry	Sig.	49873	1st Lincoln	—	Died P.O.W.
Holmes, Hbt.	Pte.	59382	Welsh	—	D. of W.
Holmes, J. E.	Rfm.	5235	7th W. Yorks.	—	K. in A.
Holmes, Jas.	Rfm.	267111	5th W. Yorks.	—	K. in A.
Holmes, Jas Henry	Sgt.	256890	Labour Corps	—	Died
Holmes, Jas. M.	Pte.	263016	5th Loyal N. Lancs.	—	K. in A.
Holmes, John Wm.	Pte.	10926	2nd W. Riding	—	K. in A.
Holmes, Nelson	L/Cpl.	28845	8th E. Yorks.	—	K. in A.
Holmes, Norman	Sig.	202570	4th York. & Lancs.	—	K. in A.
Holmes, Peter	Pte.	142014	R.A.M.C.	—	Died
Holmes, R. L.	Pte.	1122	15th W. Yorks.	—	K. in A.
Holmes, R. V.	Rfm.	4288	7th W. Yorks.	—	K. in A.
Holmes, Robert	Pte.	57145	Lancs. Fusiliers	—	K. in A.
Holmes, Thomas	L/Cpl.	2302	Royal Munster Fusiliers	—	K. in A.
Holmes, Thomas	Pte.	7766	9th W. Yorks.	—	K. in A.
Holmes, Walter	Pte.	36044	24th Northumb'l'd Fus.	—	Died
Holmes, Wilfred	Pte.	217	17th Northumber'l'd Fus.	—	K. in A.
Holmes, William	Pte.	314111	Labour Corps	—	Died

LEEDS ROLL OF HONOUR.

Name	Rank	No.	Regiment	Honours	How Died
Holmes, William	Pte.	9575	W. Yorks.	—	D. a. Dis.
Holmes, William	Pte.	20004	15th Cheshire	—	K. in A.
Holroyd, Benj.	2nd Lieut.		5th Seaforth Highdrs.	—	K. in A.
Holroyd, Herbert	Pte.	689	17th W. Yorks.	—	Died
Holroyd, Isaac H.	Cpl.	25157	7th W. Yorks.	—	K. in A.
Holstead, Moses	Rfm.	305494	8th W. Yorks.	—	K. in A.
Holstead, Robert	Pte.	22463	E. Lancs.	—	K. in A.
Holt, Arthur N. I.	L/Cpl.	61363	Durham Light Infantry	—	K. in A.
Holt, E.	Pte.	268237	W. Yorks.	—	Died
Holt, Edwin	Pte.	5491	W. Yorks.	—	D. of W.
Holt, Harold C.	S/Smith	2704	R.F.A.	—	Died
Holt, Malcolm W.	L/Cpl.	268195	2nd W. Yorks.	—	K. in A.
Holt, Richard	Pte.	6841	4th W. Yorks.	—	K. in A.
Holt, William	Pte.	12343	10th W. Yorks.	—	K. in A.
Holt, William	L/Cpl.	1067	15th W. Yorks.	—	K. in A.
Holt, William	Pte.	23092	Northumberland Fusrs.	—	D. a. Dis.
Holt, William	Cpl.	9288	Seaforth Highlanders	—	K. in A.
Honour, Bruce	Pte.	43300	Bedford..	—	K. in A.
Hood, H.	Pte.	14231	5th W. Yorks.	—	K. in A.
Hood, H.	Pte.	53142	Lincoln	—	D. of W.
Hood, Herbert			W. Yorks.	—	K. in A.
Hook, Harry	Pte.	75	10th W. Yorks.	—	K. in A.
Hooley, Arthur	Pte.	12484	W. Yorks.	—	K. in A.
Hooley, John	Pte.	44948	York. & Lancs.	—	Died
Hooligham, John	Pte.	7647	W. Yorks.	—	K. in A.
Hoonan, R.	Pte.	10645	W. Riding	—	K. in A.
Hooper, Sidney F.	Lieut.		Wiltshire	—	K. in A.
Hoopern, Louis	A/Sgt.	41765	R.F.A.	—	K. in A.
Hopkin, Edmund	Pte.	475	15th W. Yorks.	—	K. in A.
Hopkins, Alfred	Pte.	49395	7th Lincoln	—	Missing
Hopkins, George	Pte.	18746	W. Yorks.	—	K. in A.
Hopkins, John H.	Pte.	1021	5th W. Yorks.	—	D. of W.
Hopkinson, Arthur	Pte.	42349	Worcester	—	Died
Hopper, Arthur	Cpl.	201865	5th Manchester	—	K. in A.
Hopper, Chas. C.	Pte.	78568	Tank Corps.	—	K. in A.
Hopps, Fred A.	Pte.	41860	Irish Fusiliers	—	K. in A.
Hopson, John G.	Pte.	241725	Highland Light Infantry	—	K. in A.
Horam, James	Pte.	202268	10th K.O.Y.L.I.	—	Missing
Horam, Jeremiah	Spr.	274976	Royal Engineers	—	D. a. Dis.
Horam, Thomas	Pte.	11510	K.O.Y.L.I.	—	K. in A.
Horam, Thomas	Pte.	27250	Army Vetery. Corps	—	D. a. Dis.
Horlick, Chas.	L/Cpl.	79975	3rd W. Yorks.	—	K. in A.
Horman, John W.	Pte.	205466	1/4th E. Yorks.	—	K. in A.
Horn, Fred	Pte.	11914	W. Yorks.	—	K. in A.
Hornby, Darius	Rfm.	3945	W. Yorks.	—	Died
Hornby, Frank	2/A.M.	51073	Royal Air Force	—	Died
Hornby, John	Pte.	125369	Royal Fusiliers	—	Died

LEEDS ROLL OF HONOUR

Name	Rank	No.	Regiment	Honours	How Died
Hornby, Samuel	Pte.	46241	12th Yorks.	—	K. in A.
Horne, Albert C.	Pte.	41534	Lincolns.	—	Missing
Horne, John	Pte.	31645	S. Lancs.	—	Died
Horne, Thomas	Pte.	652413	Labour Corps	—	Died
Horner, Albert	Spr.	180777	Royal Engineers	—	D. a. Dis.
Horner, Arthur	Pte.	208813	Royal Air Force	—	Died
Horner, Gilbert E.	L/Cpl.	2577	6th W. Riding	—	K. in A.
Horner, Karl C.	2nd Lieut.		Royal Air Force	—	K. in A.
Horner, Percy	Pte.	3066	Northumberland Fusrs.	—	Died
Horner, Samuel	Pte.	10006	2nd W. Riding	—	K. in A.
Horner, Thomas	Pte.	28518	Durham Lt. Infantry	—	K. in A.
Horner, William	Pte.	9059	2nd W. Riding	—	K. in A.
Horner, William	L/Cpl.	1068	17th W. Yorks.	—	K. in A.
Horney, Herbert	Pte.	15407	2nd Royal Scots	—	Died
Hornsby, Joseph	Pte.	38687	18th W. Yorks.	—	Died
Hornsey, Fredk. W.	Rfm.	36974	7th W. Yorks.	—	K. in A.
Hornsey, J. A.	Sgt.	1308	15th W. Yorks.	—	K. in A.
Horsfall, C. H.	Rfm.	266337	2/7th W. Yorks.	—	D. a. Dis.
Horsfall, Charles	Pte.	29462	Highland Lt. Infantry	—	K. in A.
Horsfall, Charles	Pte.	8214	2nd Yorks.	—	K. in A.
Horsfall, Ernest	Pte.	10095	3rd W. Yorks.	—	D. a. Dis.
Horsfall, George	Pte.	36366	2nd Yorks.	—	K. in A.
Horsfall, Joseph	Pte.	19106	7th K.O.Y.L.I.	—	K. in A.
Horsfall, L.	Pte.	20698	2nd K.O.Y.L.I.	—	K. in A.
Horsfall, Marmaduke	Pte.	202248	Leicester	—	K. in A.
Horsfall, William	Pte.	8950	K.O.Y.L.I.	—	Died
Horsfield, H. H.	Pte.	208603	5th W. Yorks.	—	K. in A.
Horsfield, John W.	Pte.	38942	25th Northumb'l'd Fusrs.	—	K. in A.
Horsman, Chas. J.	S/Sgt.	149404	R.A.S.C.	—	D. of W.
Horsman, F. A.	Pte.	60847	25th Northumb'l'd Fusrs.	—	K. in A.
Horsman, Horace		K17373	H.M.S. " Invincible "	—	K. in A.
Horton, George	Sgt.	162045	Labour Corps	—	D. a. Dis.
Horton, Samuel	Pte.	306352	W. Yorks.	—	K. in A.
Hatter, John T.	Pte.	1697	17th W. Yorks.	—	K. in A.
Hough, J.	Pte.	4274	S. Staffs.	—	D. of W.
Houghton, Harry	Pte.	64877	Machine Gun Corps	—	Died
Houghton, John	Gdsmn.	20100	Grenadier Guards	—	Died
Houlden, Chas. E.	Pte.	21456	K.O. Scottish Bordrs.	—	Died
Houlden, Joseph	Pte.	353124	Highland Lt. Infantry	—	K. in A.
Houlder, Wilfred	Gnr.	175677	R.G.A.	—	D. of W.
Houlgate, James W.	Pte.	242326	Seaforth Highlanders	—	K. in A.
Hoult, Albert	Pte.	29476	2/4th Dorsets	—	K. in A.
Housago, Arthur	Pte.	33000	15th W. Yorks.	—	K. in A.
Howard, David	Gnr.	18932	R.F.A.	—	K. in A.
Howard, Fred	Pte.	37261	3rd W. Yorks.	—	K. in A.
Howard, G. F.	2nd Lieut.		Royal Air Force	—	K. in A.
Howard, G. W.	Sgt.	104515	Royal Engineers	—	Died

LEEDS ROLL OF HONOUR.

Name	Rank	No.	Regiment	Honours	How Died
Howard, H. A.	Pte.	268420	W. Riding	—	K. in A.
Howard, James A. E.	A/Cpl.	13134	R.A.S.C.	—	D. a. Dis.
Howard, John E.	Rfm.	9139	King's Royal Rifle Cps.	—	Died
Howard, Joseph	Pte.	38362	25th Durham Lt. Infty.	—	K. in A.
Howard, Joseph	Pte.	7601	Yorks.	—	K. in A.
Howard, Richd. S.	Pte.	204708	10th W. Riding	—	K. in A.
Howard, Sidney I.	Pte.	50616	Camel Corps.	—	K. in A.
Howard, Thomas	Pte.	403060	R.A.M.C.	—	K. in A.
Howcroft, Ernest	Pte.	25899	K.O.Y.L.I.	—	Died
Howden, G. A.	Pte.	5323	4th K.O.Y.L.I.	—	K. in A.
Howden, John	Pte.	21240	Labour Corps	—	D. of W.
Howden, Joseph T.	Cpl.	66330	Durham Lt. Infantry	—	Died
Howe, Albert	Pte.	13700	Seaforth Highlanders	—	K. in A.
Howe, W. T.	2nd Lieut.		7th W. Yorks.	M.M.	K. in A.
Howe, Warwick	Pte.	23687	13th Yorks.	—	K. in A.
Howell, Francis	Pte.	15754	9th W. Yorks.	—	K. in A.
Howell, Fredk. E.	Gnr.	111787	R.F.A.	—	Died
Howell, Herbert	Pte.	765	17th W. Yorks.	—	Died
Howell, John W.	Pte.	11472	6th K.O.Y.L.I.	—	K. in A.
Howell, Thomas H.	A.B.	KP434	Royal Naval V. Res.	—	K. in A.
Howgate, James H.	Pte.	266626	W. Yorks.	—	Missing
Howgate, Wm. H.	Pte.	24512	2nd W. Riding	—	K. in A.
Howitt, Cecil J.	Sgt.	3269	7th W. Yorks.	—	K. in A.
Howitt, Frank	L/Cpl.	306789	8th W. Yorks.	—	D. of W.
Howley, Ernest	Pte.	12935	8th K.O.Y.L.I.	—	Missing
Howroyd, James L.	Sgt.	99591	R.F.A.	—	K. in A.
Howson, George	Pte.	15076	8th Northumb'l'd Fusrs.	—	K. in A.
Howson, William	Pte.	11792	8th W. Riding	—	K. in A.
Hoyle, Charles	Cpl.	6081	Notts. & Derby	—	K. in A.
Hoyle, Clarence	Pte.	32653	York. & Lancs.	—	Missing
Hoyle, John R.	Spr.	72239	Royal Engineers	—	Died
Hoyle, William	Pte.	8593	12th W. Yorks.	—	K. in A.
Huby, George E.	Gnr.	8454	R.G.A.	—	D. a. Dis.
Huby, George H.	Rfm.	305460	8th W. Yorks.	—	Missing
Hudson, F. H.	Pte.	1824	R.A.M.C.	—	Died
Hudson, Fred	Pte.	21563	Yorks.	—	D. a. Dis.
Hudson, Friend	Gnr.	192738	R.G.A.	—	K. in A.
Hudson, Harry	Rfm.	2060	7th W. Yorks.	—	K. in A.
Hudson, Horbin	Pte.	31176	E. Yorks.	—	K. in A.
Hudson, James A.	Pte.	19636	11th W. Yorks.	—	D. of W.
Hudson, John	Cpl.	2148	7th W. Yorks.	—	K. in A.
Hudson, John	Pte.	91225	Durham Light Infantry	—	K. in A.
Hudson, John	Pte.	7353	1st W. Yorks.	—	K. in A.
Hudson, Lawrence A.	A/Sgt.	716	10th Lincoln	—	D. of W.
Hudson, Percy	Pte.	5929	6th W. Riding	—	Died
Hudson, Robert A.	Lt. Colonel		8th W. Yorks.	D.S.O.	K. in A.
Hudson, Thomas H.	Pte.	360160	R.A.S.C.	—	Died

LEEDS ROLL OF HONOUR.

Name	Rank	No.	Regiment	Honours	How Died
Hudson, Thomas W.	Pte.	61913	Royal Scots	—	Died
Hudson, William	L/Cpl.	306068	8th W. Yorks.	—	K. in A.
Huffingley, Albert	Rfm.	1669	1/8th W. Yorks.	—	K. in A.
Huffington, Thomas	Captain		7th Yorks.	—	D. of W.
Huggan, George	L/Cpl.	436387	Labour Corps	—	D. a. Dis.
Huggins, Jim	Pte.	27809	Labour Corps	—	D. a. Dis.
Huggins, Walter	Pte.	41274	Training Reserve	—	D. a. Dis.
Hughes, F. R.	Pte.	5134	S.A. Scots. Infantry	—	K. in A.
Hughes, Fredk.	Sgt.	12012	21st King's R. Rifle Cps.	—	K. in A.
Hughes, George V.	Pte.	82157	Durham Light Infantry	—	K. in A.
Hughes, J. H. H.	Rfm.	300940	18th W. Yorks.	—	Missing
Hughes, J. W.	Pte.	8148	2nd S. Wales Borderers	—	D. of W.
Hughes, James			17th W. Yorks.	—	Died
Hughes, James	L/Cpl.	41479	17th W. Yorks.	—	Missing.
Hughes, James	Pte.	2087	K.O.Y.L.I.	—	K. in A.
Hughes, John	L/Cpl.	201549	4th Seaforth Highdrs.	—	Died
Hughes, John J.	Pte.	4162	15th W. Yorks.	—	K. in A.
Hughes, Robert S.	Pte.	288040	21st Northumb'l'd Fus.	—	K. in A.
Hughes, Walter	Pte.	35084	24th Northumb'l'd Fus.	—	K. in A.
Hughes, Wm.	Pte.	11986	K.O.Y.L.I.	—	Died
Hugill, J. C. J.	Sgt.	12656	Leicester	—	K. in A.
Huison, Walter	Pte.	37440	9th W. Yorks.	—	K. in A.
Hulbert, Wm.	Pte.	159514	Machine Gun Corps	—	D. a. Dis.
Hullah, Albert	Pte.	41615	19th Northumb'l'd Fus.	—	K. in A.
Hullah, Alfred	A/Sgt.	39300	R.F.A.	—	D. a. Dis.
Hullah, Arthur	Pte.	19757	10th W. Yorks.	—	K. in A.
Hullah, Fred	Pte.	42169	K.O.Y.L.I.	—	K. in A.
Hullah, G. A.	L/Cpl.	36219	Highland Light Infantry	—	K. in A.
Hulley, George	Stkr.	E26692	H.M.S. " Invincible "	—	K. in A.
Hulse, Harry	Sgt.	8143	9th W. Yorks.	—	K. in A.
Hume, Guess	Pte.	19521	Leicester	—	K. in A.
Hume, Robert	Pte.	675	21st W. Yorks.	—	K. in A.
Hummel, Raymond	2nd Lieut.		W. Yorks.	—	Died
Hummerston, Eric	Spr.	84112	Royal Engineers	—	K. in A.
Humphrey, Herbert	Rfm.	266573	1/7th W. Yorks.	—	K. in A.
Humphrey, J. D.	Pte.		11th Northumb'l'd Fus.	—	K. in A.
Humphries, Percy A.	Sgt.	6410	2nd Cheshire	—	K. in A.
Hunsley, Wm.	L/Sgt.	18792	7th K.O.Y.L.I.	—	K. in A.
Hunt, George	Pte.	202167	Leicester	—	Died
Hunt, Henry	Spr.	505362	Royal Engineers	—	D. a. Dis.
Hunt, J.	Pte.	28918	Leicester	—	K. in A.
Hunt, J.	Pte.	8861	15th Hussars	—	Missing
Hunt, J.	L/Cpl.	9745	10th E. Yorks.	—	Missing
Hunt, James	Pte.	2447	1/4th Lincoln	—	K. in A.
Hunt, John	Pte.	49805	W. Riding	—	K. in A.
Hunt, Richd. H.	Pte.	21575	3rd K.O.Y.L.I.	—	K. in A.
Hunt, Robert	Gnr.	168595	R.F.A.	—	Died

LEEDS ROLL OF HONOUR.

Name	Rank	No.	Regiment	Honours	How Died
Hunter, Archibald	Pte.	107521	Notts. & Derbys.	—	K. in A.
Hunter, Arthur	L/Cpl.	22609	20th Lancs. Fusiliers	—	Died
Hunter, C. W.	Pte.	82158	Durham Lt. Infantry	—	K. in A.
Hunter, Charles	Pte.	42568	S. Staffs.	—	K. in A.
Hunter, Ernest	Pte.	40778	2nd K.O.Y.L.I.	—	K. in A.
Hunter, G.	Rfm.	5049	R. Irish Rifles	—	K. in A.
Hunter, G. S...	Lieut.		R.A.S.C. (Att. R.B.)	M.C.	D. of W.
Hunter, Herbert	Pte.	25032	W. Yorks.	—	K. in A.
Hunter, Horace	Pte.	32587	E. Lancs.	—	K. in A.
Hunter, John H.	Pte.	488	15th W. Yorks.	—	K. in A.
Hunter, Samuel	Pte.	3270	3rd K.O.Y.L.I.	—	K. in A.
Hunton, John	L/Cpl.	18486	11th W. Yorks.	—	D. of W.
Hurd, Harry	Cpl.	10267	9th W. Yorks.	—	Died
Hurd, Samuel	Pte.	74415	2/7th Durham Lt. Infty.	—	Died
Hurford, Albert	A/Sgt.	50884	1st E. Yorks.	M.M. and Bar	K. in A.
Hurowitch, Michael	Pte.	266447	W. Yorks.	—	K. in A.
Hurrell, L. J.	Dvr.	131037	Royal Engineers	—	K. in A.
Hurst, Chas. H.	Sgt.	2439	W. Yorks.	—	K. in A.
Hurst, Chas. H.	Pte.	376823	2/6th Durham Lt. Infty.	—	K. in A.
Hurst, John A.	Sgt.	1619	17th W. Yorks.	—	K. in A.
Hurtley, John B.	Pte.	37170	W. Yorks.	—	D. of W.
Husken, George	Cpl.		W. Yorks.	—	Died
Hustwit, Albert	L/Cpl.	2274	Machine Gun Corps	—	K. in A.
Hutchings, Ernest H.	Dvr.	110226	R.A.S.C.	—	Died
Hutchinson, Arthur B.	L/Cpl.		Royal Engineers	—	Died
Hutchinson, G. W.	Pte.	12581	9th W. Yorks.	—	K. in A.
Hutchinson, George H.	Pte.	10691	6th Yorks.	—	K. in A.
Hutchinson, H.	Pte.	25193	1st W. Yorks.	—	K. in A.
Hutchinson, J. H.	Pte.	268326	W. Yorks.	—	K. in A.
Hutchinson, John	Rfm.	265959	2/7th W. Yorks.	—	Missing
Hutchinson, Louis	Pte.	24815	16th W. Yorks.	—	D. of W.
Hutchinson, Sidney	Pte.	27872	15th W. Yorks.	—	Missing
Hutchinson, Thomas	Pte.	1264	15th W. Yorks.	—	Missing
Hutchinson, Thomas	Pte.	10311	3rd W. Yorks.	—	D. a. Dis.
Hutton, George A.	Pte.		15th W. Yorks.	—	K. in A.
Hutton, Samuel	Gnr.	94144	R.G.A.	—	K. in A.
Hutton, Thomas W.	L/Sgt.	4155	W. Yorks.	—	K. in A.
Hutton, Walter H.	L/Cpl.	5636	Military Foot Police	—	K. in A.
Hyde, George	L/Cpl.	39454	2nd W. Yorks.	—	K. in A.
Hyman, Joseph	Pte.	37454	9th W. Yorks.	—	Died
Ibbetson, Frank	Sgt.	1972	1/7th W. Yorks.		K. in A.
Ibbetson, Geo.	Pte.	24021	2nd W. Yorks.	—	K. in A.
Ibbetson, John	Pte.	8415	9th W. Yorks.	—	Died
Ibbitson, Albert	Pte.	18507	6th York. & Lancs.	—	K. in A.
Ibbitson, Manassah	Pte.	16742	12th York. & Lancs.	—	K. in A.
Ibbotson, Thos.	Pte.	381	17th W. Yorks.	—	K. in A.

LEEDS ROLL OF HONOUR.

Name	Rank	No.	Regiment	Honours	How Died
Ibbotson, Walter	2/A.M.	405044	Royal Air Force	—	K. in A.
Ibbotson, Walter	Pte.	299869	2nd Cheshire	—	K. in A.
Iken, H.	Pte.	21852	Hampshire	—	Missing
Iles, Horace	Pte.	1784	W. Yorks.	—	K. in A.
Iles, Percy	Cpl.	270286	6th Royal Scots Fusrs.	—	K. in A.
Illingworth, Francis	Pte.	32588	13th E. Lancs.	—	K. in A.
Illingworth, J. H.	Pte.	263099	York. & Lancs.	—	Died
Illingworth, John	Pte.DM2/	096743	R.A.S.C.	—	K. in A.
Illingworth, Wm.	Pte.	60855	2nd W. Yorks.	—	Died
Impey, Walter J.	Pte.	144	W. Yorks.	—	K. in A.
Ingham, Ben	Pte.	17735	Yorks.	—	D. a. Dis.
Ingham, Chas. R.	Pte.	187	14th E. Yorks.	—	Missing
Ingham, John Thos.	Pte.	1559	5th W. Yorks.	—	Died
Ingham, Major	2nd Lieut.		W. Yorks.	—	K. in A.
Ingham, Sam	Engr.	F32334	H.M.S. " Coronation "	—	Died
Ingle, Ernest	Pte.	352193	8th Royal Scots Fusrs.	—	K. in A.
Ingle, Jas.	A/Cpl.	62730	Yorks. Lt. Infantry	—	Died
Ingleby, Harry	L/Sgt.	2771	1/7th W. Yorks.	—	D. of W.
Ingleson, Ernest	Pte.	501	15th W. Yorks.	—	K. in A.
Ingleson, Geo.	Pte.	4365	13th London	—	Died
Ingleson, Harry	Pte.	300057	18th W. Yorks.	—	K. in A.
Ingleson, Thos. B.	Cpl.	14527	Scots Guards	—	K. in A.
Ingram, Arthur M.	Pte.	61863	Durham Lt. Infantry	—	K. in A.
Ingram, John	Pte.	11615	10th W. Yorks.	—	K. in A.
Ingram, Jos.	Pte.	21022	K.O. Scottish Bordrs.	—	K. in A.
Ireland, J. K.	Captain		Royal Fusiliers	—	K. in A.
Ireland, W. G.	Pte.	2589	Yorks. Hussars	—	K. in A.
Ironsdale, Jacob	A.B.	30308	H.M.S. " Calypso "	—	Died
Irvine, Geo.	Pte.	12834	Labour Corps	—	Died
Irvine, Rbt.	Pte.	305683	2nd W. Yorks.	—	K. in A.
Irving, Geo.	Pte.	10885	6th K.O.Y.L.I.	—	K. in A.
Irving, Louis W.	Rfm.	19798	1/8th W. Yorks.	—	K. in A.
Isles, Fredk.	Dvr.	781029	R.F.A.	—	D. of W.
Isles, Henry	Pte.	268200	Labour Corps	—	D. a. Dis.
Isles, Horace	Pte.	1784	15th W. Yorks.	—	K. in A.
Ismay, Wm.	L/Cpl.	12012	11th W. Yorks.	—	K. in A.
Issatt, Geo.	Pte.	12480	6th K.O.Y.L.I.	—	D. of W.
Issatt, John	Pte.	33106	1/4th W. Riding	—	D. of W.
Issitt, Rennie	Pte.	20662	Middlesex	—	K. in A.
Ivers, Thos.	Pte.	87791	Yorks.	—	Died
Ives, Derick	Sub.-Lieut.		Royal Navy	—	Missing
Ives, Fredk. B.	Pte.	7200	R.A.M.C.	—	D. a. Dis.
Ives, Kenneth H.	2nd Lieut.		W. Yorks.	—	K. in A.
Ives, M.	Pte.	40203	16th W. Yorks.	—	K. in A.
Ives, Robert	Pte.	21509	K.O.Y.L.I.	—	K. in A.
Jackson, Albert E.	Pte.	202893	1/5th W. Yorks.	—	K. in A.

LEEDS ROLL OF HONOUR.

Name	Rank	No.	Regiment	Honours	How Died
Jackson, Alfred	Cpl.	10050	2nd W. Riding	—	D. of W.
Jackson, Alfred	Pte.	36786	2nd W. Yorks.	—	D. of W.
Jackson, Alfred	Pte.	77247	R.A.M.C.	—	K. in A.
Jackson, Arthur	Pte.	106811	N. Derbys.	—	Died
Jackson, Arthur	Pte.	29919	Ox. & Bucks.	—	Died
Jackson, Arthur	Cpl.	503	15th W. Yorks.	—	D. of W.
Jackson, Ben	Pte.	23992	9th K.O.Y.L.I.	—	K. in A.
Jackson, Ben	Rfm.	3392	2/8th W. Yorks.	—	K. in A.
Jackson, Chas. W.	Cpl.	23843	1/6th W. Yorks.	—	K. in A.
Jackson, Edward	Pte.	4160	1/6th W. Riding	—	D. of W.
Jackson, F. W.	Pte.	216880	1st Canadian M. Rifles	—	K. in A.
Jackson, Frank	Pte.	26182	E. Yorks.	—	Missing
Jackson, Frank	Pte.	26095	E. Yorks.	—	K. in A.
Jackson, Fred	Rfm.	4134	1/8th W. Yorks.	—	Died
Jackson, Geo.	P.O.	I.237459	H.M.S. " Indefatigable "	—	Drowned
Jackson, Geo. W.	Sgt.	775814	R.F.A.	—	K. in A.
Jackson, Geo. Wm.	Pte.	38328	9th W. Yorks.	—	Missing
Jackson, H. R.	Pte.	135170	52nd Canadians	—	Died
Jackson, Harold	Pte.	11683	10th W. Yorks.	—	K. in A.
Jackson, Harold M.	Pte.	CH/7298	Royal Marine Lt. Infty.	—	Drowned
Jackson, Harry	Rfm.	267671	1/7th W. Yorks.	—	Died
Jackson, Harry	Pte.	35531	6th K.O.Y.L.I.	—	Died
Jackson, Harry	Pte.	40923	27th Northumb'l'd Fus.	—	K. in A.
Jackson, Harry	Pte.	12750	11th W. Yorks.	—	K. in A.
Jackson, Henry H.	L/Cpl.	16880	Northumberland Fusrs.	—	K. in A.
Jackson, Henry S.	Spr.	147774	Royal Engineers	—	K. in A.
Jackson, Henry S.	L/Cpl.	507	15th W. Yorks.	—	Missing
Jackson, Herbert	Cpl.	93095	24th Royal Fusiliers	—	K. in A.
Jackson, Herbert W.	Pte.	—	W. Yorks.	—	K. in A.
Jackson, James	Pte.	33116	W. Riding	—	Died
Jackson, John	A/Sgt.	28252	W. Yorks.	—	K. in A.
Jackson, John	Pte.	13572	K.O.Y.L.I.	—	K. in A.
Jackson, John	Cpl.	23588	Royal Air Force	—	Died
Jackson, John T.	Wireman	17486	H.M.S. " Invincible "	—	K. in A.
Jackson, John W.	Cpl.	235790	9th K.O.Y.L.I.	—	K. in A.
Jackson, Lawrence	Pte.	18981	1st K.O. Scottish Bordrs.	—	K. in A.
Jackson, Louis B.	Gdsmn.	8916	Scots Guards	—	K. in A.
Jackson, Percy	Sgt.	8173	Northumberland Fusrs.	—	K. in A.
Jackson, Rbt.	Sgt.	2804	2/8th W. Yorks.	—	D. of W.
Jackson, S. F.	Lieut.	—	1/7th W. Yorks.	—	K. in A.
Jackson, Saml.	Pte.	18333	2nd W. Yorks.	—	Missing
Jackson, Squire	Pte.	48709	W. Yorks.	—	Died
Jackson, T.	Pte.	54402	Northumb'erland Fusrs.	—	D. a. Dis.
Jackson, Tom	Pte.	8386	Yorks.	—	Missing
Jackson, Tom	Pte.	306463	W. Yorks.	—	K. in A.
Jackson, Walter	Rfm.	4263	1/7th W. Yorks.	—	K. in A.
Jackson, Walter	Pte.	615	W. Yorks.	—	K. in A.

LEEDS ROLL OF HONOUR.

Name	Rank	No.	Regiment	Honours	How Died
Jackson, Walter	Pte.	602026	Labour Corps.	—	D. a. Dis.
Jackson, Wm.	Pte.	020185	R.A.S.C.	—	Died
Jackson, Wm. L.	L/Sgt.	31428	22nd Northumb'l'd Fus.	—	K. in A.
Jackson, Wilson	Pte.	202588	2/5th W. Yorks.	—	K. in A.
Jacobson, Abraham	Pte.	31876	1st W. Yorks.	—	K. in A.
Jacobs, Abey	Pte.	203474	4th E. Yorks.	—	K. in A.
Jacobs, B.	Rfm.	8017	1/12th London	—	K. in A.
Jacobs, Lawrence	Dvr.	775480	R.F.A.	—	K. in A.
Jacobs, Leonard	Pte.	202146	1/4th King's O.R. Lancs.	—	K. in A.
Jacquemot, Louis	Sgt.	18776	16th R. Scots.	—	Died
Jacques, Arthur	Spr.	606425	Royal Engineers	—	Died
Jacques, L. J. L.	L/Sgt.	22482	E. Yorks.	—	K. in A.
Jacques, Montrose	Pte.	22182	Royal Dublin Fusiliers	—	Died
Jaffe, Israel	Pte.	40956	K.O.Y.L.I.	—	K. in A.
Jaffer, Goodman	Rfm.	14667	20th King's R. Rifles	—	K. in A.
Jagger, Thos. S.	Pte.	615	21st W. Yorks.	—	K. in A.
Jagger, Wilfred	Pte.	28892	W. Yorks.	—	K. in A.
Jagger, Rbt. Wm.	L/Cpl.	1869	1/7th W. Yorks.	—	K. in A.
Jakeman, Chas.	Pte.	21328	9th W. Yorks.	—	K. in A.
Jakeman, Chas.	Pte.	42361	Lincoln	—	K. in A.
Jakeman, Fredk.	Gnr.	775619	R.F.A.	—	K. in A.
Jakeman, Wm.	Pte.	266387	West Yorks.	—	K. in A.
James, Arthur D.	Pte.	41353	6th Leicester	—	K. in A.
James, Edward	Pte.	26727	Lincoln	—	Died
James, Geo. P.	A/Cpl.	42957	Royal Air Force	—	Died
James, H. E. H.	Pte.	D/3224	Royal Dragoons	—	D. a. Dis.
James, Henry	S/Cpl.	11215	R.F.A.	—	K. in A.
James, Hbt. W.	Pte.	39209	2nd W. Yorks.	—	D. of W.
James, Robt K.	Lieut.		K.O.Y.L.I.	—	K. in A.
James, Wm.	Pte.	515	15th W. Yorks.	—	K. in A.
Jameson, Fred	Rfm.	5931	1/6th W. Yorks.	—	K. in A.
Jameson, Horace A.	Major		R.F.A.	M.C. and Bar	K. in A.
Jameson, J. Leslie	Lieut.		W. Riding	M.C.	K. in A.
Jameson, John	Pte.	27564	10th E. Warwick	—	Missing
Jamieson, John	Pte.	33666	1/8th R. Warwick	—	K. in A.
Janney, Harold	Pte.	41426	W. Yorks.	—	K. in A.
Jaques, George	2nd Lieut.		R.F.A.	—	K. in A.
Jaques, J.	L/Cpl.	101315	66th Canadians	—	K. in A.
Jaques, Leonard J. L.	A/Sgt.	22482	11th E. Yorks.	—	K. in A.
Jardine, Jas. W.	Rfm.	268054	1/7th W. Yorks.	—	K. in A.
Jardine, John I.	Pte.	44821	2/9th Manchester	—	K. in A.
Jarman, Harry	Pte.	204482	15th S. Lancs.	—	D. a. Dis.
Jarman, L. M.	Pte.	53198	Northumberland Fusrs.	—	Died
Jarman, Saml.	Pte.		Hampshire	—	Died
Jarman, Saml. W.	Gdsmn.	6295	2nd Scots Guards	—	K. in A.
Jarman, Walter	Cpl.	13098	22nd Labour Corps	—	D. of W.
Jarrett, Geo.	Pte.	20017	15th Cheshire	—	K. in A.

LEEDS ROLL OF HONOUR.

Name	Rank	No.	Regiment	Honours	How Died
Jarvis, Harry..	Pte.	52751	W. Yorks.	—	K. in A.
Jarvis, Thos...	Pte.	4803	W. Yorks.	—	Died
Jasper, Hbt. ..	Rfm.	305842	1/8th W. Yorks.	—	K. in A.
Jearsley, H. J.	Dvr.	49662	54th R.H.A.	—	K. in A.
Jeffcock, Clifford	Pte.	307762	Tank Corps	—	K. in A.
Jeffcock, Clifford	Pte.	5273	Royal Scots	—	K. in A.
Jefferson, Herbert L.	Pte.		7th Royal Fusiliers	—	D. of W.
Jefferson, John	L/Cpl.	9013	W. Yorks.	—	K. in A.
Jeffery, Geo. F.	Pte.	41232	11th W. Yorks.	—	K. in A.
Jeffery, Thos. W.	Pte.	181532	R.A.S.C. (M.T.)	—	Died
Jeffreys, Henry	Pte.	38193	17th W. Yorks.	—	K. in A.
Jeffreys, Sidney	Pte.	28315	King's Own Royal Lancs.	—	K. in A.
Jeffs, James ..	Pte.	16037	Yorks.	—	K. in A.
Jenkinson, Albert	Rfm.	25079	17th King's R. Rifle Cps.	—	D. of W.
Jenkinson, Ernest H.	Pte.	35902	2/4th K.O.Y.L.I.	—	Missing
Jenkinson, Francis V.	A/Cpl.M/337241		R.A.S.C. (M.T.)	—	Died
Jenkinson, Fredk. J.	Sgt.	401079	R A M.C	—	D. a. Dis.
Jenkinson, Harry	Pte.	62099	Royal Defence Corps..	—	D. a. Dis.
Jenkinson, Sidney	Pte.	522	15th W. Yorks.	—	K. in A.
Jenkinson, Wilfred	Pte.	19119	Yorks.	—	K. in A.
Jennings, Frank T.	Pte.	44180	Lincoln	—	K. in A.
Jennings, Geo.	Pte.	19020	W. Yorks.	—	K. in A.
Jennings, J. W.	L/Cpl.	1692	7th W. Yorks.	—	K. in A.
Jennings, Jas. S.	Pte.	408141	R.A.M.C.	—	K. in A.
Jennings, Wm. A.	Gdsmn.	2161	2nd Life Guards	—	K. in A.
Jepson, Frank	Rfm.	3087	1/7th W. Yorks.	—	K. in A.
Jepson, Jos. ..	Pte.	18127	2nd K.O.Y.L.I.	—	Missing
Jessop, Alfred	Pte.	31147	E. Yorks.	—	Died
Jessop, John Wm.	Pte.	1530	15th W. Yorks.	—	K. in A.
Jewitt, Lewis	1st Cl. C'ksm'te	12470	H.M.S. " Hampshire "	—	K. in A.
Jewitt, Reginald	Rfm.	2480	1/8th W. Yorks.	—	K. in A.
Jillings, Wm. A.	Pte.	305597	W. Yorks.	—	K. in A.
Jipson, Geo. Wm.	L/Cpl.	266671	W. Yorks.	—	Died
Jobson, D. E.	Pte.	8323	Royal Defence Corps ..	—	Died
Joel, Edward	Cpl.	3610	10th Hussars ..	—	K. in A.
Johns, Bertie	Rfm.	267146	2/7th W. Yorks.	—	D. of W.
Johns, Sml. ..	Pte.	23798	16th W. Yorks.	—	K. in A.
Johnson, A. ..	Rfm.	8/7740	13th Rifle Brigade	—	K. in A.
Johnson, A. ..	Pte.	209535	R.A.S.C.	—	Died
Johnson, Albert	Pte.	9776	W. Yorks.	—	Died
Johnson, Albert	Pte.	1461	W. Yorks.	—	D. a. Dis.
Johnson, Arthur	Pte.DM/096744		R.A.S.C. (M.T.)	—	K. in A.
Johnson, Arthur	Gnr.	72387	R.G.A. ..	—	K. in A.
Johnson, Arthur	1/A.M.	40318	Royal Air Force	—	D. a. Dis.
Johnson, C. W.	Pte.	50973	11th E. Yorks.	—	K. in A.
Johnson, Chas. H.	Pte.	1058	15th W. Yorks.	—	Missing

LEEDS ROLL OF HONOUR.

Name	Rank	No.	Regiment	Honours	How Died
Johnson, Edward	Rfm.	306619	1/8th W. Yorks.	—	K. in A.
Johnson, Edward	Pte.	22140	1/6th W. Yorks.	—	K. in A.
Johnson, Ernest A.	Pte.	37389	W. Yorks.	—	K. in A.
Johnson, Ernest	Pte.	8627	3rd W. Yorks	—	K. in A.
Johnson, F.	Spr.		Royal Engineers	—	K. in A.
Johnson, Frank	Pte.	151873	Labour Corps	—	K. in A.
Johnson, Frank	Rfm.	776	7th W. Yorks.	—	K. in A.
Johnson, Fred	Spr.	27208	Royal Engineers	—	K. in A.
Johnson, G.	Sgt.	505	15th W. Yorks.	—	K. in A.
Johnson, G. W.	Pte.	32266	Labour Corps	—	D. a. Dis.
Johnson, Geo.	B'dsm'n	14827	Royal Fusiliers	—	K. in A.
Johnson, Geo.	Cpl.	18775	K.O.Y.L.I.	—	K. in A.
Johnson, H.	Pte.	25553	Royal Welsh Fusrs.	—	Died
Johnson, H.	Pte.	22530	Northumberland Fusrs.	—	K. in A.
Johnson, H. E.	Rfm.	242571	1/7th W. Yorks.	—	K. in A.
Johnson, Harold	Pte.	350614	Durham Lt. Infantry	—	Missing
Johnson, Harold W.	Cpl.	36087	W. Yorks.	—	K. in A.
Johnson, Harry	Pte.	87258	Machine Gun Corps	—	Missing
Johnson, Harry	Pte.	21886	W. Yorks.	—	Died
Johnson, Herbert	Pte.	53216	19th Durham Lt. Infty.	—	K. in A.
Johnson, Herbert	L/Cpl.	266530	1/7th W. Yorks.	—	D. of W.
Johnson, Herbert	L/Cpl.	401436	R.A.M.C.	M.M.	D. of W.
Johnson, J.	Trmr.		H.M.S. " Duchess of Hamilton "	—	Drowned
Johnson, James	L/Cpl.	10713	York. & Lancs.	—	K. in A.
Johnson, James	Pte.	5233	Seaforth Highlanders	—	K. in A.
Johnson, James	Pte.	9137	2nd W. Yorks.	—	K. in A.
Johnson, James A.	Pte.	5367	W. Yorks.	—	D. of W.
Johnson, James A.	Sgt.	P627	Military Mtd. Police	—	Died
Johnson, James H.	L/Cpl.	29788	3rd K.O.Y.L.I.	—	K. in A.
Johnson, James W.	Rfm.	3073	8th W. Yorks.	—	Died
Johnson, John	L/Cpl.	*2965	Notts. & Derby.	—	K. in A.
Johnson, John Ed.	Pte.	40935	27th Northumb'l'd Fusrs.	—	K. in A.
Johnson, Joseph	Rfm.	4140	7th W. Yorks.	—	K. in A.
Johnson, Joseph L.	Pte.	4089753	R.A.S.C.	—	Killed
Johnson, Leonard	Pte.	30021	K.O.Y.L.I.	—	Died
Johnson, Louis	Pte.	SE29753	Royal Army Vet. Co.	—	Died
Johnson, Mark	L/Cpl.	17072	W. Yorks.	—	K. in A.
Johnson, Mark A.	Pte.	24680	13th Yorks.	—	K. in A.
Johnson, Raymond	Pte.	13843	W. Yorks.	—	Died
Johnson, Samuel	L/Cpl.	19887	15th Cheshire	—	D. of W.
Johnson, Sidney	Pte.	13592	K.O.Y.L.I.	—	Missing
Johnson, Sidney	Rfm.	10632	7th W. Yorks.	—	K. in A.
Johnson, Thos. E.	Pte.	33055	W. Yorks.	—	D. of W.
Johnson, Vernon	Pte.	1566	15th W. Yorks.	—	K. in A.
Johnson, W.	Pte.	7848	W. Yorks.	—	K. in A.
Johnson, Walter	Gnr.	8096	246th R.F.A.	—	K. in A.

LEEDS ROLL OF HONOUR.

Name	Rank	No.	Regiment	Honours	How Died
Johnson, Walter	Cpl.	408307	R.A.M.C.	—	K. in A.
Johnson, Walter	Rfm.	3885	1/8th W. Yorks.	—	K. in A.
Johnson, Willie	Pte.	44470	25th Northumb'l'd Fusrs.	—	K. in A.
Johnson, Wm.	2nd Lieut.		10th S. Staffs.	—	K. in A.
Johnson, Wm.	Pte.	44745	Lincoln	—	K. in A.
Johnson, Wm.	Gnr.	127199	R.G.A.	—	K. in A.
Johnson, Wm.	Pte.	242584	W. Yorks.	—	Died
Johnson, Wm.	Pte.	59921	6th Royal Welsh Fusrs.	—	K. in A.
Johnson, Wm.	Pte.	7848	4th W. Yorks.	—	D. a. Dis.
Johnson, Wm. H.	Pte.	15002	9th W. Yorks.	—	K. in A.
Johnston, Amos	Pte.	7984	Machine Gun Corps	—	K. in A.
Johnston, James	Pte.	81800	Durham Lt. Infantry	—	Died
Johnston, Norman	Pte.	23969	10th W. Yorks.	—	D. of W.
Johnstone, Wm.	Pte.	075543	R.A.S.C. (M.T.)	—	K. in A.
Jolley, Ernest	L/Cpl.	8967	W. Yorks.	—	K. in A.
Jolley, Tom	Pte.	33753	9th W. Yorks.	—	K. in A.
Jolliffe, Chas. H.	Cpl.	510683	Labour Corps	—	D. of W.
Jones, A. E.	2/A.M.	18470	Royal Air Force	—	Died
Jones, A. H.	Dvr.	775153	R.F.A.	—	K. in A.
Jones, Albert R.	Cpl.	73220	R.F.A.	—	Died
Jones, B.	Pte.	22081	K.O.Y.L.I.	—	Died
Jones, C. H.	Pte.	106813	Notts. & Derby.	—	D. of W.
Jones, Chas. E.	Dvr.	71726	R.F.A.	—	K. in A.
Jones, Deakin	Pte.	35688	8th Gloucester	—	Missing
Jones, E.	Pte.	49565	2/5th W. Yorks.	—	K. in A.
Jones, Edgar	Tpr.	H3103	20th Hussars	—	K. in A.
Jones, Edwin H.	Pte.	202969	1/4th York. & Lancs.	—	Died.
Jones, Ernest	Rfm.	3400	7th W. Yorks.	—	K. in A.
Jones, Ernest	Pte.	305798	W. Yorks.	—	K. in A.
Jones, F. V.	Pte.	30789	Northumberland Fusrs.	—	K. in A.
Jones, G. W.	L/Cpl.	41450	E. Yorks.	—	K. in A.
Jones, Geo. E.	Pte.	18961	8th Royal Irish Rifles	—	D. a. Dis.
Jones, George	Pte.	19455	Labour Corps	—	D. a. Dis.
Jones, Harold W.	Rfm.	2231	8th West Yorks.	—	K. in A.
Jones, Harry	Pte.	46566	K.O.Y.L.I.	—	Died
Jones, Hbt.	Pte.	5307	W. Yorks.	—	Died
Jones, J. W.	Sig.	775850	R.F.A.	—	K. in A.
Jones, Jas.	L/Cpl.	38850	4th N. Hants.	—	K. in A.
Jones, Jas. W.	Pte.	294135	Labour Corps	—	D. a. Dis.
Jones, John	Pte.	17943	7th K.O. Shropshire L.I.	—	K. in A.
Jones, Leonard	L/Cpl.	21949	W. Yorks.	—	D. of W.
Jones, Percy	Rfm.	5051	2/7th W. Yorks.	—	K. in A.
Jones, Percy	Rfm.	267200	W. Yorks.	—	K. in A.
Jones, Rbt. H.	Pte.	33050	2nd K.O.Y.L.I.	—	Died
Jones, Rbt. M.	Pte.	G/95111	Royal Fusiliers	—	Missing
Jones, Samson	Pte.	33360	18th W. Yorks.	—	D. a. Dia.
Jones, W.	Pte.	12067	7th K.O.Y.L.I.	—	Died

LEEDS ROLL OF HONOUR.

Name	Rank	No.	Regiment	Honours	How Died
Jones, Walter	A.B.	J40796	H.M.S. " Woolwich "..	—	K. in A.
Jones, Wm.	Rfm.	1682	1/7th W. Yorks.	—	K. in A.
Jones, Wm. R.	Rfm.	64140	8th W. Yorks.	—	K. in A.
Jordan, F.S.	Bdr.	111992	R.F.A.	—	D. of W.
Jordan, Jas.	Pte.	4739	1/5th W. Yorks.	—	Died
Jordan, Jas.	Cpl.	14678	10th W. Yorks.	—	K. in A.
Jordan, Louis	Pte.	31237	E. Yorks.	—	Died
Joseph, Marks	Pte.	267235	W. Yorks.	—	Died
Jowett, Chas.	Pte.	38783	16th W. Yorks.	—	Missing
Jowett, Ellis	L/Cpl.	15361	Hants.	—	Drowned
Jowett, Jas. A.	Gnr.	895653	R.F.A.	—	Missing
Jowett, Jos.	L/Cpl.	12733	W. Yorks.	—	D. a. Dis.
Jowett, William	Pte.	10516	Yorks.	—	Missing
Jowett, Wm.	Bdr.	73318	R.F.A.	—	D. of W.
Jowett, Willie	Pte.	110093	Royal Fusiliers	—	Died
Jowitt, Arthur	Pte.	40205	Cameron Highlanders	—	K. in A.
Jowitt, Lewis		12470	H.M.S. " Hampshire "	—	Drowned
Jowitt, Sidney	Pte.	144729	Machine Gun Corps	—	Died
Joy, Walter	Pte.	1794	1st W. Yorks.	—	K. in A.
Joy, Wilfred	Pte.	534	W. Yorks.	—	K. in A.
Joyce, Henry A.	B'dsm'n	4499	2nd Dragoon Guards	—	K. in A.
Joyce, Isaac	Pte.	20192	1st Loyal N. Lancs.	—	D. of W.
Joyce, John	Pte.	6698	2nd W. Yorks.	—	Missing
Jowsey, Chas. H.	Pte.	91233	Durham Light Infantry	—	K. in A.
Jowsey, Wilfred	Pte.	23578	6th Dorset	—	D. of W.
Joynes, Edwin	A/Sgt.	408233	R.A.M.C.	—	Died
Jubb, Albert	Pte.	43564	10th Lincoln	—	K. in A.
Jubb, Chas. W.	Gnr.	785844	R.F.A.	—	K. in A.
Jubb, Harry	Pte.	266673	W. Yorks.	—	K. in A.
Jubb, John	Pte.	10579	2nd W. Riding	—	K. in A.
Jubb, Walter	Pte.	39716	Lancs. Fusiliers	—	K. in A.
Judge, John	Dvr.	014692	R.A.S.C.	—	K. in A.
Julian, Wm.	Spr.	82903	Royal Engineers	—	D. a. Dis.
Kaberry, Walter	Pte.	27994	19th W. Yorks	—	Died
Kavanagh, Clifford	Pte.	90	17th W. Yorks.	—	K. in A.
Kay, Alfred	Pte.	41608	9th Norfolks.	—	Died
Kay, Ernest	Pte.	8490	W. Yorks.	—	K. in A.
Kay, Fred	Pte.	1930	1/6th W. Yorks.	—	Died
Kay, Geo.	Dvr.	775867	R.F.A.	—	D. a. Dis.
Kay, Geo.	Pte.	306416	W. Yorks.	—	K. in A.
Kay, J. R. C.	Pte.	241255	5th Seaforth Highdrs.	—	K. in A.
Kay, John	Rfm.	S/6174	Rifle Brigade	—	Died
Kay, Mark	Pte.		6th Cameron Highdrs.	Croix de Guerre	K. in A.
Kay, Rbt.	Pte.	44866	R.A.M.C.	—	K. in A.
Kay, Stanley B.	Captain		7th Yorks.	—	Died
Kay, Tom	Dvr.	84661	R.F.A.	—	K. in A.

LEEDS ROLL OF HONOUR.

Name	Rank	No.	Regiment	Honours	How Died
Kay, Wm.	Rfm.	1463	1/7th W. Yorks.	—	D. of W.
Kaye, Arthur	Pte.	36117	26th Royal Fusiliers	—	K. in A.
Kaye, Ben	Pte.	266852	W. Yorks.	—	K. in A.
Kaye, Bryan	Pte.	14662	8th W. Riding	—	K. in A.
Kaye, Chas.	Pte.	39300	W. Yorks.	—	K. in A.
Kaye, Geo. H.	Pte.	40880	27th Northumb'l'd Fus.	—	K. in A.
Kaye, Percy	Pte.	350983	Durham Lt. Infantry	—	Died
Kaye, Sidney	Pte.	20643	K.O.Y.L.I.	—	K. in A.
Keach, Naylor	Pte.	4525	2/4th York. & Lancs.	—	K. in A.
Kearn, Sidney	Rfm.	3080	1/8th W. Yorks.	—	K. in A.
Kearney, John	Pte.	9196	W. Riding	—	D. a. Dis.
Kearney, Wm. John	Pte.	10275	W. Yorks.	—	K. in A.
Kearsley, Harry	Cpl.	403031	R.A.M.C.	—	K. in A.
Keeble, H.	Pte.	10434	Durham Lt. Infantry	—	K. in A.
Keedy, John Rbt.	Pte.	89	17th W. Yorks.	—	K. in A.
Keedy, Thos. Henry	Pte.	10831	Yorks.	—	Missing
Keeley, Arthur		33549	Devon	—	Missing
Keeley, Fred	Gnr.	681622	R.F.A.	—	K. in A.
Keeligan, John	Pte.	37221	W. Yorks.	—	K. in A.
Keelty, Jas.	Pte.	37370	W. Yorks.	—	K. in A.
Keenan, Tom	Pte.	60425	10th W. Yorks.	—	K. in A.
Keene, Thos.	Pte.		W. Riding	—	Died
Keens, Albert	Pte.	24320	1st W. Yorks.	—	K. in A.
Keighley, Clifford	Cpl.	24199	16th W. Yorks.	—	K. in A.
Keighley, Joseph	Pte.	621	Royal Warwicks.	—	K. in A.
Keighley, Leonard	Pte.	37746	16th Highland Lt. Infty.	—	K. in A.
Keighley, Maurice K.	Pte.	318993	R.A.S.C. (M.T.)	—	Died
Keighley, Sml.	Pte.	300010	W. Yorks.	—	K. in A.
Keightley, Albert	Pte.	56510	W. Yorks.	—	K. in A.
Keilty, Tom			19th Hussars	—	K. in A.
Kell, Thos.	Rfm.	6513	1/8th W. Yorks.	—	D. of W.
Kelleghan, Edwd.	Sgt.	1891	Royal Irish Fusiliers	—	Died
Kellet, Saml. P.	Pte.	37654	9th W. Yorks.	—	K. in A.
Kellett, Alfred	Pte.	45362	Lincoln	—	K. in A.
Kellett, Ben	Pte.	24198	W. Yorks.	—	Died
Kellett, Ernest	Pte.	77775	W. Yorks.	—	K. in A.
Kellett, Harry	Rfm.	1503	1/8th W. Yorks.	—	Died
Kelly, Archibald	Pte.	4107	2/5th York. & Lancs.	—	D. of W.
Kelly, Ben	Pte.	20446	Army Cycle Corps	—	K. in A.
Kelly, Bernard	Spr.	82636	Royal Engineers	—	K. in A.
Kelly, Chas.	Pte.			—	Died
Kelly, Dennis	Pte.		W. Yorks.	—	Died
Kelly, Ernest	Cpl.	75393	Manchester	—	K. in A.
Kelly, Francis	Pte.	84542	W. Yorks.	—	Died
Kelly, Francis	Pte.	20541	Training Reserves	—	D. a. Dis.
Kelly, Jas.	Pte.	91127	Durham Lt. Infantry	—	Died
Kelly, Jas.	Pte.	333	Royal Marine Lt. Infty.	—	K. in A.

LEEDS ROLL OF HONOUR.

Name	Rank	No.	Regiment	Honours	How Died
Kelly, Jas.	Bdr.	1703	R.F.A.	—	K. in A.
Kelly, John	Pte.	39078	1/5th York. & Lancs.	—	K. in A.
Kelly, John T.	Gdsmn.	18994	Grenadier Guards	—	Died
Kelly, Joseph	Pte.	4028	W. Yorks.	—	Missing
Kelly, Laurence	Pte.	10404	2nd W. Yorks.	—	K. in A.
Kelly, Thos.	Pte.		W. Yorks.	—	Died
Kelly, Thos.	Gnr.	5837	H.M.S. " Queen Mary "	—	K. in A.
Kelly, Thos. S.	Pte.	260076	1/5th York. & Lancs.	—	K. in A.
Kelly, Walter	Pte.	1494	12th K.O.Y.L.I.	—	K. in A.
Kelly, Wm.	Pte.		W. Yorks.	—	Died
Kelsey, Edgar	Pte.	37382	12th W. Yorks.	—	K. in A.
Kelsey, F.	Pte.	36638	1/5th Essex	—	K. in A.
Kelsey, Jas.	Pte.	6907	Yorks.	—	K. in A.
Kemp, Bertram	Pte.	51651	18th Liverpool	—	K. in A.
Kemp, Edward H.	Sgt.	430787	7th Canadians M. Rifles	—	K. in A.
Kemp, Ernest	Pte.	23721	S. Wales Bordrs.	—	K. in A.
Kemp, Ernest H.	Pte.	29064	2nd W. Yorks.	—	D. of W.
Kemp, Horace	Pte.	75767	R.A.M.C.	—	D. a. Dis.
Kemp, John	Gnr.	775924	R.F.A.	—	D. of W.
Kemp, John Wm.	Pte.	22027	6th K.O. Scottish Brdrs.	—	K. in A.
Kemp, Richard A.	Pte.	35218	Machine Gun Corps	—	K. in A.
Kemp, Rbt.	Pte.	42703	10th Durham Lt. Infty.	—	Missing
Kemp, Sylvester	Pte.	307605	10th W. Yorks.	—	K. in A.
Kemp, Wm. T.	Spr.	138432	Royal Engineers	—	K. in A.
Kenally, Jos.	Sgt.	7623	Yorkshire	—	Died
Kendale, Wm.	Gnr.	127691	R.F.A.	—	K. in A.
Kendall, F. Albert V.	Cpl.	3416	17th Lancers	—	K. in A.
Kendall, Clarence	Bdr.	785926	R.F.A.	—	Died
Kendall, Frank	Cpl.		17th Lancers	—	K. in A.
Kendall, Jas.	Rfm.	2927	1/7th W. Yorks.	—	D. of W.
Kendall, John	Pte.	25557	Yorkshire	—	Killed
Kendall, John	Cpl.	51288	R.F.A.	—	K. in A.
Kendall, Jos.	Pte.	3/8642	W. Yorks.	—	K. in A.
Kendall, Percy	Pte.	9564	6th Yorks.	—	Missing
Kendrew, Arthur D.	Gnr.	155030	R.G.A.	—	Died
Kendrew, Harold	Pte.	368252	R.A.S.C.	—	K. in A.
Kendrick, Vere	Pte.	8093	13th Yorks.	—	K. in A.
Kennally, Jos.	Sgt.	9623	19th Yorks.	—	K. in A.
Kennedy, John	Gnr.	104082	R.G.A.	—	K. in A.
Kennedy, Matthew W.	Sgt.	83640	Royal Engineers	—	D. a. Dis.
Kennedy, Patrick	Sgt.	16488	12th W. Yorks.	—	K. in A.
Kennett, Sam	Pte.	11983	10th K.O.Y.L.I.	—	D. of W.
Kenney, Thos. W.	A/Sgt.	268168	W. Yorks.	—	D. a. Dis.
Kenny, Albert	Pte.	34299	W. Riding	—	K. in A.
Kenny, Edward	Pte.	119809	R.A.M.C.	—	Died
Kenny, John	Pte.	10958	1/5th W. Yorks.	—	Killed
Kenny, John	Pte.	14254	W. Yorks.	—	K. in A.

LEEDS ROLL OF HONOUR.

Name	Rank	No.	Regiment	Honours	How Died
Kenny, John ..	Pte. ..		W. Riding	—	Died
Kenny, John ..	Pte. ..	10735	K.O.Y.L.I.	—	K. in A.
Kenny, John ..	Sgt. ..	48939	R.G.A.	—	K. in A.
Kent, Benj. ..	L/Cpl.	301704	W. Yorks.	—	K. in A.
Kent, Frank ..	Gnr.	L/19006	R.F.A.	—	K. in A.
Kent, Frank ..	Pte. ..		W. Yorks.	—	Died
Kent, Joseph	L/Cpl.	6044	Oxford & Bucks L. I. ..	—	Missing
Kent, W. R. ..	Pte. ..	78968	Royal W. Surrey ..	—	K. in A.
Kenworthy, Harry ..	Sgt.	S/4157127	R.A.S.C.	—	Died
Kenworthy, John E.B.	Pte. ..	32234	S. Lancs.	—	D. of W.
Kenyon, Ernest	L/Cpl.	401222	R.A.M.C.	—	D. of W.
Kenyon, Wm.	Pte. ..	15350	Royal Army Vet. Corps	—	Died
Kerbotsom, Joe		663	21st W. Yorks. ..	—	K. in A.
Kerr, Geo. S.	Pte. ..	16302	K.O. Scottish Borderers	—	Died
Kerr, Henry ..	Rfm. ..	307450	8th W. Yorks. ..	—	Died
Kerr, John ..	Dvr. ..	88417	R.F.A.	—	Died
Kerry, Sml. ..	Pte. ..	14672	12th W. Yorks. ..	—	K. in A.
Kershaw, Clifford	Pte. ..	31801	2nd W. Yorks. ..	—	Killed
Kershaw, Frank	Pte. ..	28265	9th W. Yorks. ..	—	K. in A.
Kerrshaw, Fred S. ..	Pte. ..	34183	W. Yorks.	—	Died
Kershaw, J. P.	Pte. ..	504871	Labour Corps	—	D. a. Dis.
Kershaw, John	Bdr. ..	2898	R.G.A.	—	K. in A.
Kershaw, John		2289	11th Manchester ..	—	K. in A.
Kershaw, John E. ..	Gnr. ..	796589	R.F.A.	—	Died
Kershaw, Sam	Cpl. ..	266289	7th W. Yorks. ..	—	D. of W.
Kershaw, Willie	Rfm. ..	48239	Rifle Brigade	—	D. a. Dis.
Kerton, Sidney	Sgt. ..	15/548	W. Yorks.	—	Killed
Kester, Wm. ..	Gnr. ..	52854	R.H.A.	—	K. in A.
Kettle, Arthur	Rfm. ..	265671	W. Yorks.	—	Died
Kettlewell, Geo.	Rfm. ..	267001	7th W. Yorks. ..	—	Missing
Kettlewell, Harry ..	Pte. ..	38540	2/5th W. Yorks. ..	—	D. of W.
Kettlewell, John H. ..	Rfm. ..	38615	7th W. Yorks. ..	—	Died
Kettlewell, John W.	Pte. ..	8945	W. Yorks.	—	Died
Kettlewell, Jos.	L/Cpl.	2176	8th W. Yorks. ..	—	D. of W.
Kettlewell, Percy H.	Sgt. ..	3354	1st Northumb'l'd Fusrs.	—	K. in A.
Kew, Lester ..	Pte. ..	50802	11th Lancs. Fusiliers ..	—	K. in A.
Key, Ernest ..	L/Cpl.	39267	2nd W. Yorks. ..	—	Missing
Key, Henry ..	Gnr. ..	143329	R.G.A.	—	Died
Keywood, Arthur E.	Bdr. ..	850280	R.F.A.	—	Died
Keyworth, Jos.	Pte. ..	26285	2nd Lancs. Fusiliers ..	—	K. in A.
Kidd, Ernest ..	Pte. ..	117252	Machine Gun Corps ..	—	Died
Kidd, Maurice H. ..	Pte. ..	6/7311	Training Reserves ..	—	K. in A.
Kidd, Wm. ..	Pnr. ..	83817	Royal Engineers ..	—	D. a. Dis.
Kierce, Jos. ..	Pte. ..	50567	K.O.Y.L.I.	—	Missing
Kilburn, Herbert ..	Pte. ..	91239	Durham Light Infantry	—	K. in A.
Kilburn, Percy	Pte. ..	1944	W. Yorks.	—	K. in A.
Kilburn, Thos.	Pte. ..	12234	8th Yorks.	—	K. in A.

LEEDS ROLL OF HONOUR.

Name	Rank	No.	Regiment	Honours	How Died
Kilby, John W.	Pte.	15722	Labour Corps	—	K. in A.
Kilkenny, A. C.	Spr.	72364	Royal Engineers	—	Died
Kilkenny, Edward P. L.	L/Cpl.	19/227	7th W. Yorks.	—	Died P.O.W.
Killen, Horace	Pte.	549	15th W. Yorks	—	D. of W.
Killen, John W.	Pte.	550	W. Yorks.	—	K. in A.
Killeen, Wm. L.	Pte.	1471	17th W. Yorks.	—	K. in A.
Killerby, F. J.	Sgt.	551	15th W. Yorks.	—	K. in A.
Killingbeck, Josh.	Pte.	35833	R.A.M.C.	—	K. in A.
Killion, Tom	A.M.	47213	R.A.F.	—	Died
Kilroy, John	Pte.	23824	Cameron Highdrs.	—	D. of W.
Kilvington, Chas.	Pte.	32289	16th W. Yorks.	—	K. in A.
Kinder, Arthur	Gdsmn.	6132	1st Irish Guards	—	K. in A.
Kinder, Geo. G.	Captain		2/8th W. Yorks.	M.C.	K. in A.
King	Pte.	11628	10th W. Yorks.	—	K. in A.
King, Alfred	Gdsmn.	7118	3rd Scots Guards	—	Died
King, Arthur	Rfm.	12308	King's Royal Rifle Cps.	—	K. in A.
King, F.	Spr.	69334	Royal Engineers	—	K. in A.
King, Frank	Pte.	197050	Labour Corps	—	Died
King, Fred	Pte.	23959	W. Yorks.	—	D. a. Dis.
King, Fredk. W.	Sgt.	93187	R.F.A.	—	K. in A.
King, Herbert	Pte.	32307	16th W. Yorks.	—	K. in A.
King, Herbert	Lieut.		R.A.O.C.	—	K. in A.
King, Jas.	Pte.	3400	Loyal N. Lancs.	—	Died
King, John	Pte.	12901	7th K.O.Y.L.I.	—	K. in A.
King, John	Pte.	45147	South Wales Borderers	—	D. of W.
King, John G.	Pte.	46896	2/4th Leicester	—	Died
King, Michael	Pte.	14585	East Kent	—	K. in A.
King, Percy J.	2nd Lieut.			—	K. in A.
King, Robert	Pte.		10th W. Yorks.	—	K. in A.
King, S. W.	Rfm.	10512	King's Royal Rifle Cps.	—	K. in A.
King, Saml.	A.B.	WNK132	H.M.S. "Good Hope"	—	K. in A.
King, Walter J.	Pte.	39447	2nd W. Yorks.	—	Missing
King, Wm.	Rfm.	5588	King's Royal Rifle Cps.	—	K. in A.
King, Willie	Pte.	1365	W. Yorks.	—	K. in A.
Kingdom, Arthur	Pte.	10353	9th W. Yorks.	—	K. in A.
Kingdom, Robert	Cpl.	21345	W. Yorks.	—	K. in A.
Kingsley, John Thos.	Rfm.	306711	2/8th W. Yorks.	—	K. in A.
Kingswood, George	L/Cpl.	306735	8th W. Yorks.	—	K. in A.
Kingswood, John Wm.	Pte.	77322	R.A.M.C.	—	K. in A.
Kingswood, Walter	Pte.	63652	W. Yorks.	—	K. in A.
Kipling, Wm. Thos.	S.B.	4772	H.M.S. "Hague"	—	K. in A.
Kirby, Jas.	Pte.	11520	K.O. Scottish Borderers	—	K. in A.
Kirby, Norman	Rfm.	37668	3/8th W. Yorks.	—	K. in A.
Kirby, T. H.	Cpl.		R.F.A.	—	K. in A.
Kirk, Albert	L/Cpl.	3939	2/7th W. Yorks.	—	D. of W.
Kirk, Arthur	Rfm.	268204	3/8th W. Yorks.	—	K. in A.
Kirk, Chas.	Rfm.	7346	7th W. Yorks.	—	D. of W.

LEEDS ROLL OF HONOUR.

Name	Rank	No.	Regiment	Honours	How Died
Kirk, Geo.	L/Cpl.	29556	17th W. Yorks.	—	Missing
Kirk, J. E.	Gnr.	117334	R.G.A.	—	Died
Kirk, Jas. A.	Pte.	40014	9th Royal Irish Rifles	—	K. in A.
Kirk, John	L/Cpl.	356172	10th Liverpool	—	K. in A.
Kirk, John R.	Pte.	1243	15th W. Yorks.	—	K. in A.
Kirk, Lawrence	L/Cpl.	3000	1/7th W. Yorks.	—	D. of W.
Kirk, Leonard	Gnr.	165978	R.F.A.	—	Died
Kirk, R.	Pte.		15th W. Yorks.	—	K. in A.
Kirk, Rbt. W.	Pte.	1442	20th Hussars	—	Died
Kirk, Wm.	Pte.	12026	W. Yorks.	—	Died
Kirkbride, Fredk.	Pte.	26209	W. Yorks.	—	K. in A.
Kirkbright, Tom	Cpl.	8187	18th Hussars	—	K. in A.
Kirkby, Harry	Spr.	484167	Royal Engineers	—	Died
Kirkby, John	Pte.	73206	9th York. & Lancs.	—	D. of W.
Kirkham, Henry T.	Gnr.	795426	R.F.A.	—	D. a. Dis.
Kirkley, Wm.	Pte.	77030	R.A.M.C.	—	K. in A.
Kirkwood, Clifford	Pte.	12844	10th W. Yorks.	—	K. in A.
Kirkwood, Cyril	Rfm.	5341	8th W. Yorks.	—	Died
Kirkwood, Ernest	Rfm.	5249	W. Yorks.	—	D. a. Dis.
Kitchen, Ernest	Pte.	47281	12th W. Yorks.	—	K. in A.
Kitchen, Geo.	L/Cpl.	22735	K.O. Scottish Borderers	—	K. in A.
Kitchen, Richard	Pte.	555	15th W. Yorks.	—	Missing
Kitchen, Rbt. S.	L/Cpl.	25474	13th Yorks.	—	K. in A.
Kitching, Arthur W.	Pte.	27636	7th K.O. Shropshire L.I.	—	K. in A.
Kitching, Harry	Tpr.	18255	E.R. Yeomanry	—	K. in A.
Kitching, John	Fitter	98822	R.F.A.	—	D. of W.
Kitching, Jos. B.	Pte.	205100	5th W. Yorks.	—	K. in A.
Kitson, Harry B.	Rfm.	8807	King's Royal Rifle Cps.	—	K. in A.
Kitson, Hbt.	Pte.	17730	1st W. Yorks.	—	K. in A.
Kitson, J.	Pte.	200094	K.O.Y.L.I.	—	Died
Kitson, W.	Pte.	55162	R.A.M.C.	—	K. in A.
Kitson, William	Pte.	53447	W. Yorks.	—	K. in A.
Knapton, Frank	Pte.	23705	2nd Yorks.	—	K. in A.
Knapton, Geo. H.	Rfm.	4881	2/7th W. Yorks.	—	K. in A.
Knight, Albert	2 Shipwt.	M12558	H.M.S. " Dolphin "	—	K. in A.
Knight, James	Gnr.	152827	R.F.A.	—	D. of W.
Knight, Matthew B.	L.Smn.	230546	H.M.S. " Christopher "	—	Died
Knight, Osborne	Pte.	1792	11th W. Yorks.	—	K. in A.
Knight, Wm.	Spr.	164353	Royal Engineers	—	Died
Knock, F. T.	Pte.	432128	49th Canadians	—	Died
Knock, Frank	Pte.	28047	Loyal N. Lancs.	—	Died
Knockton, George	Pte.	53450	W. Yorks.	—	K. in A.
Knopwood, Thomas	Pte.	11925	7th K.O.Y.L.I.	—	K. in A.
Knowles, Albert	Pte.	15/1614	11th W. Yorks.	—	K. in A.
Knowles, Arthur	L/Cpl.	202798	Durham Lt. Infantry	—	K. in A.
Knowles, Fred	Rfm.	6001	1/5th W. Yorks.	—	D. of W.
Knowles, Horace	Dvr.	307586	R.G.A.	—	K. in A.

LEEDS ROLL OF HONOUR.

Name	Rank	No.	Regiment	Honours	How Died
Knowles, Joseph	L/Sgt.	3300	1/7th W. Yorks.	—	K. in A.
Knowles, Noah	Gnr.	45181	R.F.A.	—	D. of W.
Knowles, Rowland	Gnr.	144	R.G.A.	—	K. in A.
Knowles, Wm. C.	Gnr.	165724	R.F.A.	—	Died
Knowlson, A.	Bdr.	32663	R.H.A.	—	Died
Knowlson, J. W.	1 Ck's Mte.	11659	H.M.S. " Hampshire "	—	K. in A.
Knutton, Thomas	Gdsmn.	8312	Scots Guards	—	K. in A.
Kramer, A.	Pte.	20010	York. & Lancs.	—	Died
Kyne, Thomas G.	Pte.	999	21st W. Yorks.	—	K. in A.
Lacey, Joseph	L/Cpl.	11192	1st Sherwood Forstrs.	—	K. in A.
Lacey, O. A.	Pte.	46531	1/4th Yorks.	—	Died
Lacy, James	Pte.	24818	1t5h W. Yorks.	—	K. in A.
Lacy, Willie	Rfm.	1725	2/8th W. Yorks.	—	K. in A.
Ladley, Charles W.	Pte.	38678	16th W. Yorks.	—	K. in A.
Lafbery, Sidney T.	Pte.	25186	Cheshire	—	K. in A.
Laffen, James	L/Cpl.	12844	K.O.Y.L.I.	—	K. in A.
Laid, George	Pte.	8622	1st W. Yorks.	—	K. in A.
Laidlaw, John	Pte.	517715	Labour Corps	—	K. in A.
Laidlaw, Robert	Gnr.	477504	R. Canadian Arty.	—	D. of W.
Laing, Edward	L/Cpl.	3011	1/8th W. Yorks.	—	D. of W.
Laing, Fred	Pte.	39955	1/4th Seaforth Highdrs.	—	K. in A.
Laird, George	Pte.	3/8622	1st W. Yorks.	—	K. in A.
Lake, Alfred	Pte.	34044	9th W. Yorks.	—	K. in A.
Lake, John	Pte.	53277	K.O.Y.L.I.	—	K. in A.
Lake, Thomas W.	Pte.	565	15th W. Yorks.	—	Missing
Lalley, James E.	Rfm.	263039	1/8th W. Yorks.	—	D. of W.
Lalley, John	Pte.	3660	1st W. Yorks.	—	K. in A.
Lamb, Fred	Gdsmn.	7889	Scots Guards	—	Died
Lamb, Geo. M.	Pte.	38568	12th W. Yorks.	—	K. in A.
Lamb, R. H.	Pte.	47887	15th Canadians	—	K. in A.
Lamb, Thomas	Pte.	306962	W. Yorks.	—	Died
Lamb, William		1364	15th W. Yorks.	—	Missing
Lambert, Arthur	Cpl.	16/57	Royal Warwick	—	K. in A.
Lambert, David L.	Bdr.	775191	R.F.A.	—	K. in A.
Lambert, Horace	Pte.	20093	1st K.O. Scottish Bordrs.	—	K. in A.
Lambert, John R.	Gnr.	111228	R.F.A.	—	K. in A.
Lambert, John W.	Dvr.	1107	R.F.A.	—	K. in A.
Lambert, Richard	Sgt.	7463	6th Yorks.	—	K. in A.
Lambert, Tom	Sgt.	5654	2nd Yorks.	—	K. in A.
Lambert, Thomas	Pte.	11682	10th W. Yorks.	—	K. in A.
Lambert, W. H.	Pte.	66088	Machine Gun Corps	—	Died
L'Amie, Herbert	Sdlr.	103459	R.F.A.	—	Died
Lancaster, Fredk.	Pte.	567	15th W. Yorks.	—	K. in A.
Lancaster, George H.	Rfm.	5409	1/8th W. Yorks.	—	Died
Lancaster, J.	Cpl.	48869	R.G.A.	—	K. in A.
Lancaster, Walter	Sgt.	3/8251	2nd Yorks.	—	K. in A.

LEEDS ROLL OF HONOUR.

Name	Rank	No.	Regiment	Honours	How Died
Land, Clifford	Rfm.	2/37297	2nd Rifle Brigade	—	Died
Landreth, Harold	Pte.	24633	1st W. Yorks.	—	K. in A.
Lane, George	Pte.	40376	1st Cameron Highdrs.	—	K. in A.
Lane, Tom W.	A.B.	B/5128/SS	Royal Naval Reserve	—	K. in A.
Lang, Mark	Sgt.	3547	8th W. Yorks.	—	K. in A.
Lang, Wm. E.	Gnr.	118174	R.G.A.	—	K. in A.
Langley, Arthur	Pte.	37536	1/6th W. Yorks.	—	K. in A.
Langley, Harold	Pte.	401049	R.A.M.C.	—	K. in A.
Langshaw, Albert	Pte.	230	12th Northumb'l'd Fusrs.	—	K. in A.
Langstaff, Clifford	Pte.	1237	15th W. Yorks.	—	K. in A.
Lannan, Patrick	Gnr.	12646	R.G.A.	—	D. a. Dis.
Lappage, William	Sgt.	8262	6th Yorks.	—	Missing
Lapping, Everett	Gnr.	93706	R.F.A.	—	Died
Lapping, John	Sgt.	10493	York. & Lancs.	—	K. in A.
Larkin, Fredk.	Spr.	564335	Royal Engineers	—	Died
Larvin, David	L/Cpl.	3868	2/7th W. Yorks.	—	K. in A.
Larvin, Jas.	Rfm.	17919	8th W. Yorks.	—	K. in A.
Laurence, Edwin	Pte.	51031	K.O.Y.L.I.	—	Missing
Laurie, Horace J.	A.B.	67528	H.M.S. "Canada"	—	Died
Laverack, Ernest C.	Gnr.	143325	R.G.A.	—	K. in A.
Laverack, Francis W.	A.B.	J12812	H.M.S. "Amphion"	—	K. in A.
Laverack, Tom	Pte.	4047	Australian	—	K. in A.
Lavine, Hyman	Pte.	48928	W. Yorks.	—	Drowned
Law, Charlie	Pte.	267102	1st W. Yorks.	—	K. in A.
Law, Clifford	L/Bdr.	19407	R.F.A.	—	Died
Law, Frank	L/Cpl.	268251	2nd W. Yorks.	—	K. in A.
Law, Henry B.	Pte.	60821	W. Yorks.	—	Died
Law, Walter	Rfm.	266171	2/7th W. Yorks.	—	K. in A.
Lawford, Joseph	Pte.	4802	1/7th W. Riding	—	D. of W.
Lawless, Peter	Pte.	G6158	7th Royal Fusiliers	—	K. in A.
Lawn, Geoffrey	Cpl.	202953	1/4th Yorks.	M.M.	K. in A.
Lawrence, Edwin	Pte.	51031	5th K.O.Y.L.I.	—	K. in A.
Lawrence, Fred	Pte.	268799	1st W. Yorks.	—	K. in A.
Lawrence, Harry	Rfm.	4197	1/8th W. Yorks.	—	K. in A.
Lawrence, Harry	Pte.	2796	W. Yorks.	—	K. in A.
Lawrence, J. H.	Pte.	98720	Royal Engineers	—	Died
Lawrence, John	Gdsmn.	8313	2nd Scots Guards	—	K. in A.
Lawrence, Jos.	Pte.	202419	2/5th Durham Lt. Infty.	—	K. in A.
Lawrence, Joseph					Died
Lawrence, Jos. Henry	Pte.	30154	2nd K.O.Y.L.I.	—	K. in A.
Lawrence, Richard	Gnr.	95923	R.F.A.	—	D. of W.
Lawrence, Walter	Pte.	40894	5th Cameron Highdrs.	—	K. in A.
Lawson, Allan	Pte.	4924	1/5th W. Yorks.	—	K. in A.
Lawson, Arthur A.	2nd Lieut.		Tank Corps	—	Killed
Lawson, Ernest	Cpl.	41637	17th W. Yorks.	—	K. in A.
Lawson, F.	Rfm.	265819	2/7th W. Yorks.	—	Missing
Lawson, Geo. Wm.	2nd Lieut.		5th Yorks.	—	K. in A.

LEEDS ROLL OF HONOUR.

Name	Rank	No.	Regiment	Honours	How Died
Lawson, Jas.	Pte.	44171	Northumberland Fusrs.	—	K. in A.
Lawson, Jas. W.	Pte.	8839	1st York. & Lancs.	—	K. in A.
Lawson, Jos.	Pte.	260062	1st Monmouth	—	Missing
Lawson, Reginald	Pte.	29623	W. Yorks.	—	Died
Lawson, Wilfred	Pte.	41594	17th W. Yorks.	—	K. in A.
Lawton, Ernest	Rfm.	4969	2/8th W. Yorks.	—	K. in A.
Lawton, Geo. E.	Pte.	260043	1/5th Northumb'l'd Fusrs.	—	Missing
Lawton, John W.	Pte.	402226	W. Yorks.	—	Missing
Lawton, Wm.	Pte.	266839	W. Yorks.	—	K. in A.
Lax, Arthur	Pte.	36373	10th Yorks.	—	Died
Lax, Donald			W. Yorks.	—	K. in A.
Laycock, Arthur C.	2/A.M.	75208	Royal Air Force	—	Drowned
Laycock, Benj.	Pte.	20083	Royal Fusiliers	—	K. in A.
Laycock, Donald S.	2nd Lieut.		A.F.A.	—	D. of W.
Laycock, John	Rfm.	265980	1/7th W. Yorks.	—	K. in A.
Laycock, W.	Pte.	166458	Labour Corps	—	Died
Laycock, W.	L/Cpl.	14259	Scots Guards	—	Died
Layfield, Harry	Pte.	25075	W. Yorks.	—	K. in A.
Laylor, —				—	Died
Layt, Clifford	Pte.	13427	W. Yorks.	—	K. in A.
Layton, Ernest	Rfm.	3356	8th W. Yorks.	—	K. in A.
Lazenby, J.	Pte.	22910	W. Riding	—	K. in A.
Lea, Clarence	Pte.	23885	10th W. Yorks.	—	D. of W.
Leach, David	Spr.	474676	Royal Engineers	—	K. in A.
Leach, J.	Rfm.	9595	2nd R. Irish Rifles	—	Died
Leach, Rbt.	Dvr.	107487	R.F.A.	—	D. a. Dis.
Leadbeater, C.	Cpl.	9252	Rifle Brigade	—	Died
Leadbeater, C. T.	Pte.	17722	1st W. Yorks.	—	K. in A.
Leadbeater, John	Rfm.	4717	3/7th W. Yorks.	—	Died
Leaf, Chris.	Pte.	25003	3rd W. Yorks.	—	K. in A.
Leaf, Ernest	Gnr.	786049	R.F.A.	—	D. of W.
Leaf, J. W.	Spr.	362792	Royal Engineers	—	D. a. Dis.
Leaf, Jas.	Pte.	16744	York. & Lancs.	—	D. a. Dis.
Leaf, John Rbt.	Gnr.	12025	R.F.A.	—	Died
Leak, Arthur	L/Cpl.	266883	W. Yorks.	—	D. of W.
Leak, Wilfred	Pte.		Northumberland Fusrs.	—	K. in A.
Leake, Cyril J.	L/Cpl.	5299	9th Northumb'l'd Fusrs.	—	K. in A.
Leake, Geo.	A.B.	Z/11544	H.M.S. "Pembroke"	—	Died
Leake, Harold	Pte.	11722	W. Riding	—	K. in A.
Leake, Sml.	Pte.	20752	2nd K.O.Y.L.I.	—	K. in A.
Lealand, Horace	2/A.M.	247990	Royal Air Force	—	K. in A.
Leary, Bernard	Pte.		Canadians	—	Died
Leatham, Geo. W.	Pte.	25656	W. Yorks.	—	Died
Leatherbarrow, W.			9th W. Yorks	—	
Leckenby, Ernest	Rfm.	267172	1/7th W. Yorks.	—	K. in A.
Leckenby, Herbert	Pte.	61094	36th Northumb'l'd Fus.	—	K. in A.
Ledgard, Arthur	Pte.	26210	W. Yorks.	—	Missing

LEEDS ROLL OF HONOUR.

Name	Rank	No.	Regiment	Honours	How Died
Ledgard, Leonard	Rfm.	3796	1/8th W. Yorks.	—	K. in A.
Ledger, Arthur	L/Cpl.	293	Royal Marine Lt. Infty.	—	K. in A.
Lee, Alfred	Sgt.	14784	K.O.Y.L.I.	M.M.	Died
Lee, Alfred	Gdsmn.	23650	Grenadier Guards	—	K. in A.
Lee, Alfred	Pte.	60867	Northumberland Fusrs.	—	Died
Lee, Chas.	A.B.	J20266	H.M.S. " Queen Mary "	—	K. in A.
Lee, Clifford	L/Bdr.	775290	R.F.A.	—	Died
Lee, Edgar	Pte.	409433	R.A.S.C.	—	Died
Lee, Edward	Rfm.	268017	W. Yorks.	—	Died
Lee, Edward	L/Cpl.	8003	1st W. Yorks.	—	K. in A.
Lee, Frank S.	Lieut.		Rifle Brigade	—	Died
Lee, Fred	Pte.	33366	6th W. Yorks.	—	K. in A.
Lee, Fred		353123	Highland Light Infantry	—	Died
Lee, Geo. H. W.	L/Cpl.	2133	1/7th W. Yorks.	—	K. in A.
Lee, Harry	Pte.	21449	W. Yorks.	—	K. in A.
Lee, Harry	Pte.	242555	1/6th Yorks.	—	K. in A.
Lee, Harry	Pte.	2/184445	R.A.S.C. (M.T.)	—	Died
Lee, Harry	Pte.	36423	K.O.Y.L.I.	—	K. in A.
Lee, Jas. A.	Sgt.	3/1747	8th K.O.Y.L.I.	—	K. in A.
Lee, Jas.	L/Cpl.	2986	W. Yorks.	—	K. in A.
Lee, Jas.	Rfm.	266431	2/7th W. Yorks.	—	K. in A.
Lee, John	Pte.	42804	9th Manchester	—	K. in A.
Lee, John R.	Pte.	64000	2nd Border	—	K. in A.
Lee, Joseph	Pte.R	4089753	R.A.S.C.	—	Killed
Lee, Joshua	Pte.	14740	K.O.Y.L.I.	—	Missing
Lee, Mark	L/Cpl.		W. Yorks.	—	Died
Lee, Percy	Pte.	15938	1st Royal Scots	—	D. a. Dis.
Lee, Rbt.	2/A.M.	23682	Royal Air Force	—	Died
Lee, Thos.	Pte.	96	17th West Yorks.	—	K. in A.
Lee, Thos. H.	Spr.	479980	Royal Engineers	—	Died
Lee, Val. M.	L/Cpl.	3677	2/8th W. Yorks.	—	K. in A.
Lee, Wm.	Pte.	3403	2nd Northumb'l'd Fusrs.	—	K. in A.
Leech, Jas.	L/Cpl.	9595	Royal Irish Rifles	—	K. in A.
Leech, Squire	Pte.	416218	Labour Corps	—	D. a. Dis.
Leedham, Geo. C.	Pte.	21815	K.O. Scottish Borderers.	—	D. a. Dis.
Leeman, Joseph P.	Pte.	13193	Royal Dublin Fusiliers	—	K. in A.
Leeming, Sam	Pte.	435255	52nd Canadians	—	Died
Lees, Alfred	Pte.	40025	2nd York. & Lancs.	—	K. in A.
Lees, Jos. F.	Pte.	2046	R.A.S.C. (M.T.)	—	D. a. Dis.
Leffly, Leonard	L/Cpl.	33688	17th W. Yorks.	—	K. in A.
Leigh, Thos.	Pte.	45455	K.O.Y.L.I.	—	Drowned
Leigh, Tom	Gnr.	30457	R.F.A.	—	K. in A.
Leighton, Ernest	Pte.	42173	S. Staffs.	—	D. of W.
Leizabram, Philip	Pte.	306862	W. Yorks.	—	K. in A.
Lemmon, Alfred D.	Pte.	1453	London	—	D. of W.
Leng, Harry	Bdr.	251246	R.F.A.	—	Died
Lengthorne, William	Pte.	32007	2/5th York. & Lancs.	—	K. in A.

LEEDS ROLL OF HONOUR.

Name	Rank	No.	Regiment	Honours	How Died
Lennahan, Arthur	Pte.	10950	W. Yorks.	—	K. in A.
Lennahan, John	Rfm.	24301	7th Yorks.	—	K. in A.
Lennon, Gordon H.	Pte.	14829	11th Royal Fusiliers	—	K. in A.
Lennox, Francis W.	Pte.	586	15th W. Yorks.	—	Died
Lenton, Chas. Wm.	Pte.	1849	1/5th Yorks.	—	K. in A.
Leonard, David	C.S.M.	265183	W. Yorks.	—	D. a. Dis.
Leonard, Patrick	Pte.	8118	1st W. Yorks.	—	K. in A.
Leonard, Thos.	Pte.	7948	Yorks.	—	Missing
Leslie, C. E.	Sgt.	63640	2nd Canadians	—	Died
Leslie, Harold	Dvr.	233227	R.F.A.	—	D. a. Dis.
Lester, Arthur	Pte.	4061	9th York. & Lancs.	—	K. in A.
Letby, Rbt.	Pte.	19780	15th W. Yorks.	—	K. in A.
Lethem, John	Lieut.		R.F.A.	—	K. in A.
Leuchter, Douglas	Pte.	1616	11th W. Yorks.	—	K. in A.
Levenson, Harry	Rfm.	S11583	Rifle Brigade	—	Missing
Lever, Harry	Pte.CH/S/1370		Royal Marine Lt. Infty.	—	D. of W.
Leverington, Arthur	L/Cpl.	53356	W. Yorks.	—	Died
Levi, Abe	Pte.	10639	3rd W. Riding	—	K. in A.
Levi, Barnet	Pte.	25660	10th W. Yorks.	—	K. in A.
Levi, Barney	Pte.	41119	W. Yorks.	—	Died
Levi, Dan	Pte.	242685	W. Yorks.	—	K. in A.
Levi, Louis	Pte.	24065	10th W. Yorks.	—	K. in A.
Levi, Reuben	Pte.	40139	Royal Scots Fusiliers	—	K. in A.
Levitt, Harold	Pte.	202757	1/5th W. Yorks.	—	Died
Levitt, Harry	Gnr.	776005	R. Highldrs. & R.F.A.	—	D. a. Dis.
Levitt, Louis	Gnr.	775807	R.F.A.	—	Died
Levitt, Thos.	Pte.	57796	Northumberland Fusrs.	—	K. in A.
Levy, Geo. A.	Pte.	267609	W. Yorks.	—	K. in A.
Lewis, Albert E.	Pte.	4301	W. Yorks.	—	K. in A.
Lewis, Arthur L.	Rfm.	41471	1/8th W. Yorks.	—	Died
Lewis, Ben	Pte.	5104	2/7th W. Yorks.	—	K. in A.
Lewis, Denis H.	Sgt.	34515	R.F.A.	—	Died
Lewis, Harry	Pte.	45478	K.O.Y.L.I.	—	Died
Lewis, Harry	Gnr.	127171	R.F.A.	—	Missing
Lewis, Harry	Sgt.	19379	Royal Fusiliers	—	K. in A.
Lewis, Fredk. R.	Pte.	587	15th W. Yorks.	—	D. of W.
Lewis, Jas.	Rfm.	4065	1/8th W. Yorks.	—	K. in A.
Lewis, Nathan	Pte.	278792	Argyle & Suther. Highdrs.	—	K. in A.
Lewis, Vincent	Pte.	404	R.A.M.C.	—	Died
Ley, Albert E.	Spr.	350195	Royal Engineers	—	K. in A.
Liddell, Albert E.	A.B.	S25199	H.M.S. "Monmouth"	—	Died
Light, Geo.	Rfm.	4032	1/7th W. Yorks.	—	K. in A.
Lightfoot, Albert	Pte.	7907	2nd W. Yorks.	—	K. in A.
Lightfoot, Harry	Sgt.	266959	1/7th W. Yorks.	—	K. in A.
Lightfoot, Harry	Rfm.	3915	1/8th W. Yorks.	—	K. in A.
Lightfoot, Herbert	Pte.	21104	K.O.Y.L.I.	—	K. in A.
Liley, Ernest	Armr.	11050	H.M.S. "Malaya"	—	K. in A.

LEEDS ROLL OF HONOUR.

Name	Rank	No.	Regiment	Honours	How Died
Lilley, Arnold L.	Pte.	282133	Highland Lt. Infantry	—	K. in A.
Lilley, Leonard J.	Pte.	387969	R.A.S.C.	—	Died
Lilleyman, Horace B.	Sgt.	7204	2nd Yorks.	—	K. in A.
Lillie, Frank W.	2nd Lieut.		9th K.O.Y.L.I.	—	D. of W.
Lillis, John	Q.M.S.	90427	R.G.A.	—	D. a. Dis.
Limbert, Arthur	Spr.	98769	Royal Engineers	—	Died
Limbert, Geo.	Sgt.	2618	1/8th W. Yorks.	—	K. in A.
Limbert, Wm.	Pte.	40046	Royal Innisk. Fusrs.	—	K. in A.
Lincoln, Ernest	Pte.	52567	K.O.Y.L.I.	—	Died
Lindekvist, Harold	L/Cpl.	14426	2nd Scots Guards	—	K. in A.
Linecar, Leonard			15th W. Yorks.	—	K. in A.
Lines, Jos. J.	Pte.	205557	Royal W. Kent	—	K. in A.
Linfoot, Terence E.	L/Cpl.	305828	10th W. Yorks.	—	K. in A.
Ling, Chas. Jos.	Gdsmn.	16554	Coldstream Guards	—	D. of W.
Lingard, Fred	Dvr.	50730	R.F.A.	—	D. a. Dis.
Lingley, Frank	Rfm.	266458	2/7th W. Yorks.	—	K. in A.
Linley, Albert	Pte.	31169	E. Yorks.	—	K. in A.
Linley, Chas.	Pte.	9687	2nd K.O.Y.L.I.	—	K. in A.
Linley, Ernest	Pte.	60967	W. Yorks.	—	K. in A.
Linley, E.	3/A.M.	197854	Royal Air Force	—	Killed
Linley, Leonard	Stkr.	K6852	H.M.S. " Niger "	—	K. in A.
Linley, Sam	Pte.	7600	6th Yorks.	—	Missing
Linley, Wm.	Cpl.	11844	7th Yorks.	—	Missing
Linley, Wm.	Pte.	11962	6th Yorks.	—	K. in A.
Linnecor, Leonard L.	Pte.	38122	15th W. Yorks.	—	Missing
Lipchinsky, Sam R.	Rfm.	39321	1/7th W. Yorks.	—	K. in A.
Lipman, Morris	Pte.	1017	W. Yorks.	—	K. in A.
Lishman, John	L/Cpl.	13892	E. Kent	—	K. in A.
Lister, Arthur	Sgt.	12430	10th W. Yorks.	M.M.	D. of W.
Lister, Arthur	Pte.	4061	9th York. & Lancs.	—	K. in A.
Lister, Benj. W.	Pte.	28431	6th S. Lancs.	—	K. in A.
Lister, Chas. Henry	L/Cpl.	98432	Royal Engineers	—	K. in A.
Lister, Edward	2/A.M.	31117	Royal Air Force	—	Died
Lister, Geo.	A.B.	SS/6623	H.M.S. " Osiris "	—	K. in A.
Lister, Geo. B.	Rfm.	4159	3/8th W. Yorks.	—	K. in A.
Lister, Geo. S.	Pte.		York. & Lancs.	—	K. in A.
Lister, Harry	Pte.	24657	Machine Gun Corps	—	K. in A.
Lister, Horsman	Gnr.	95038	R.G.A.	—	Died
Lister, Jas.	Pte.	55067	1/6th North Staffs.	—	K. in A.
Lister, John M.	Pte.	268711	W. Yorks.	—	Died
Lister, Jos. E.	Pte.	8521	W. Yorks.	—	K. in A.
Lister, Jos. E.	Pte.	41937	E. Yorks.	—	K. in A.
Lister, Morris C.	Cpl.	241809	1/5th K.O.Y.L.I.	—	K. in A.
Lister, Thos.	Pte.	23831	Cameron Highlanders	—	Missing
Lister, Wilfred	Rfm.	39579	7th W. Yorks.	—	Died
Lister, Wm. P.	Rfm.	267936	1/7th W. Yorks.	—	K. in A.
Lister, Wm. C.	Cpl.	60936	Northumberland Fusrs.	—	K. in A.

LEEDS ROLL OF HONOUR.

Name	Rank	No.	Regiment	Honours	How Died
Litherland, J. C.	Sgt.	11281	6th Border	D.C.M.	K. in A.
Little, Chas. Henry	Pte.	84912	2/5th Liverpool	—	K. in A.
Little, Chas. R.	Pte.	50674	12th W. Yorks.	—	K. in A.
Little, Geo. B.	Rfm.	2515	1/8th W. Yorks.	—	K. in A.
Littlehales, Frank G.	Pte.	22007	11th E. Yorks.	—	K. in A.
Littlewood, John W.	Pte.	464211	Labour Corps	—	Died
Littlewood, Wilson	Rfm.	53767	1/7th W. Yorks.	—	K. in A.
Liversedge, Frank	Bdr.	26925	R.F.A.	—	K. in A.
Liversedge, John Wm.	Pte.	516	21st W. Yorks.	—	D. a. Dis.
Liversedge, Rbt.	Pte.	20141	9th K.O.Y.L.I.	—	D. of W.
Liversedge, Wm.	Pte.	33317	1st Lincoln	—	K. in A.
Liversidge, Albert	2nd Lieut.		15th W. Yorks.	—	D. of W.
Liversidge, Benj.	Pte.	31442	3rd Northumb'l'd Fus.	—	K. in A.
Lloyd, Arthur E.	Pte.		R.A.M.C.	—	K. in A.
Lobley, Raymond	Pte.	307541	W. Yorks.	—	K. in A.
Lock, Geo. Wm.	Pte.	32048	15th W. Yorks.	—	K. in A.
Lockham, Jas.	Pte.	5989	2/8th Royal Scots	—	Died
Lockham, Jas.	Pte.	67463	Labour Corps	—	K. in A.
Lockwood, Dennis	Pte.	406272	Labour Corps	—	D. a. Dis.
Lockwood, Harold	L/Cpl.	266496	2nd W. Yorks.	—	K. in A.
Lockwood, Harry	Pte.	29519	10th W. Yorks.	—	K. in A.
Lockwood, Hbt.	Pte.	20641	1st K.O. Scottish Bords.	—	K. in A.
Lockwood, Jas. S.	Pnr.	360401	Royal Engineers	—	K. in A.
Lockwood, Jos. H.	Pte.	307569	W. Yorks.	—	K. in A.
Lockwood, Willie	Gdsmn.	8946	2nd Scots Guards	—	K. in A.
Lodge, Cyril	Pte.	60846	W. Yorks.	—	K. in A.
Lodge, Harry W.	Rfm.	2153	1/7th W. Yorks.	—	K. in A.
Lodge, Leonard	Pte.	483	20th Durham Lt. Infty.	—	K. in A.
Lodge, Robt.	Pte.	139287	Labour Corps	—	D. a. Dis.
Loft, David	Gnr.	129911	R.F.A.	—	K. in A.
Lofthouse, Alfred	Pte.	16260	1st W. Yorks.	—	K. in A.
Lofthouse, Henry	Cpl.	305708	1/8th W. Yorks.	—	Died
Lofthouse, Jas. W.	Gnr.	18894	R.G.A.	—	K. in A.
Lofthouse, Jas. Wm.	Gnr.	72966	R.F.A.	—	K. in A.
Loftus, Jas.	Pte.	1543	5th W. Yorks.	—	D. a. Dis.
Loftus, Patrick	Pte.	27282	10th Royal Dublin Fus.	—	D. of W.
Logan, Thos.	C/Sgt.	4611	Northumberland Fusrs.	—	Died
Logg, Wm.	Dvr.	9258	R.F.A.	—	Died
Lolley, Geo. A.	Pte.	202799	1/4th E. Yorks.	—	K. in A.
Long, Fred	Pte.	19497	2nd Yorks.	—	Missing.
Long, James	Pte.	22396	12th Northumb'l'd Fus.	—	K. in A.
Long, Joseph	Cpl.	6395	S. Wales Borderers	—	D. a. Dis.
Long, Joseph	Rfm.	306365	1/8th W. Yorks.	—	K. in A.
Long, Lawrence H.	Sgt.	241862	K.O.Y.L.I.	—	K. in A.
Long, William	Gnr.	113761	R.G.A.	—	K. in A.
Longbottom, Arnold V.	Rfm.	33716	Rifle Brigade	—	K. in A.
Longbottom, E. B.	Lieut.		7th W. Yorks.	—	K. in A.

LEEDS ROLL OF HONOUR.

Name	Rank	No.	Regiment	Honours	How Died
Longbottom, H.	Pte.		4th Hussars	—	K. in A.
Longbottom, Herbert	Pte.	21334	9th W. Yorks.	—	K. in A.
Longbottom, Herbert	Pte.	22044	Machine Gun Corps	—	D. of W.
Longbottom, Hbt. W.	Pte.	31189	1st Devonshire	—	K. in A.
Longbottom, Horace	Pte.	12159	W. Yorks.	—	K. in A.
Longbottom, Percy	Pte.	12810	W. Yorks.	—	Missing
Longbottom, Thos.	A.B.	SS/5420	H.M.S. " Roxburgh "	—	Died
Longbottom, W.	Pte.	204920	1/4th W. Riding	—	Missing
Longbottom, Walter	Pte.	22127	3rd W. Yorks.	—	K. in A.
Longbottom, Wm.	Pte.	21898	Yorks.	—	Died
Longden, Chas.	Pte.	19461	2nd Leicester	—	Died
Longden, Jas. R.	Pte.	310103	9th Lancers	—	K. in A.
Longfellow, Arthur	Rfm.	266811	1/7th W. Yorks.	—	K. in A.
Longfellow, Harry	Pte.	103347	R.A.S.C.	—	Died
Longfield, Leonard	Pte.	5439	Yorks.	—	K. in A.
Longfield, Percy	Sgt.	1687	W. Yorks.	—	K. in A.
Longfield, Sidney P.	Rfm.	535339	15th London	—	K. in A.
Longley, Ernest	Pte.	601	16th W. Yorks.	—	K. in A.
Longley, W.	Sig.			—	Died
Longley, William	Pte.	8178	2nd Yorks.	—	K. in A.
Longron, Alfred J.	Rfm.	307068	1/8th W. Yorks.	—	Died
Longshaw, Albert	Pte.	230	13th Northumb'l'd Fus.	—	K. in A.
Longster, Thos. G.	Rfm.	300118	7th W. Yorks.	—	K. in A.
Lonsdale, Herbert	L/Cpl.	305047	W. Yorks.	—	K. in A.
Looms, Jas. Arthur	Pte.	4834	3/5th K.O.Y.L.I.	—	K. in A.
Lord, E.	Pte.	66535	Northumberland Fusrs.	—	K. in A.
Lord, Ernest	1 Stkr.	K29294	H.M.S. " Tipperary "	—	K. in A.
Lord, Ernest	Gnr.	138566	R.F.A.	—	K. in A.
Lord, George E.	Pte.	7101	1st Lincoln	—	K. in A.
Lord, Henry	Pte.	203843	12th W. Yorks.	—	K. in A.
Lord, Joseph R.	Pte.	339821	Labour Corps	—	D. a. Dis.
Lord, Walter	Boy	J48653	H.M.S. " Vanguard "	—	K. in A.
Lorriman, John	Pte.	30668	K.O.Y.L.I.	—	K. in A.
Lorriman, R. H.	Pte.	458761	Labour Corps	—	D. a. Dis.
Lothergtom, John W.	Pte.	31154	1st E. Yorks.	—	K. in A.
Loughran, Thos.	Pte.	6559	Royal Irish	—	K. in A.
Loughton, Geo. W.	Pte.	1323	15th W. Yorks.	—	K. in A.
Loveday, Harry	Pte.	195537	Labour Corps	—	D. a. Dis.
Loveday, Wm.	Spr.	280162	Royal Engineers	—	Died
Lowe, Arthur	Pte.	26691	Gordon Highlanders	—	K. in A.
Lowe, Jos. H.	Pte.	823	W. Yorks.	—	Died
Lowe, Leonard	CQMS	1166459	Labour Corps	—	Died
Lowe, Richard	Pte.	268429	2/7th W. Riding	—	D. of W.
Lowe, Richard	Sgt.	1699	17th W. Yorks.	—	D. of W.
Lowery, Michael	Pte.	9097	W. Yorks.	—	K. in A.
Lowery, Thos.	Pte.	242768	2/5th W. Riding	—	Died
Lowes, Harold	Pte.	12995	10th W. Yorks.	—	K. in A.

LEEDS ROLL OF HONOUR.

Name	Rank	No.	Regiment	Honours	How Died
Lowes, John ..	.. Pte. ..	13016	10th W. Yorks.	—	Died
Lowrey, James ..	.. Pte. ..	27938	12th W. Yorks.	—	K. in A.
Lowrey, Samuel	.. Pte. ..	25775	2nd K.O.Y.L.I.	—	Missing
Lowther, Henry	.. Rfm. ..	7982	4th King's R. Rifle Cps.	—	Missing
Luby, John Thos.	.. Pte. ..	13896	K.O.Y.L.I.	—	K. in A.
Lucas, Frank	.. Pte. ..	17687	10th Royal Fusiliers ..	—	Killed
Lucas, Harold	.. Pte. ..	266653	1st W. Yorks.	—	K. in A.
Lucas, Harold J.	.. Cpl. ..	8005	2nd K.O. Scottish Brds.	—	K. in A.
Lucas, Joseph	.. Rfm. ..	266957	1st W. Yorks.	—	K. in A.
Lucas, Richard	.. Pte. ..	1398	Royal Defence Corps	—	Died
Ludgate, Allan	.. Gdsmn.	6045	1st Scots Guards	—	K. in A.
Lumb, Fredk.	.. Gdsmn.	7889	1st Scots Guards	—	K. in A.
Lumb, Harry V.	.. L/Cpl.	141861	Royal Engineers	—	K. in A.
Lumb, Thos. D.	.. Tpr. ..		Yorks. Hussars	—	K. in A.
Lumb, Wilfred D.	.. Pte. ..		15th W. Yorks.	—	D. of W.
Lumb, Wm. H.	.. Pnr.WR/	20119	Royal Engineers	—	Died
Lumby, H. ..	.. Pte. ..	534435	15th London ..	—	K. in A.
Lumby, Harry S.	.. Pte. ..	266628	W. Yorks.	—	K. in A.
Lumley, Robert H.	.. Rfm. ..	5113	2/7th W. Yorks.	—	K. in A.
Lumley, William	.. Pte. ..	32006	1/5th York. & Lancs.	—	Died
Lund, Albert V.	.. Pte. ..	53014	2nd W. Yorks.	—	K. in A.
Lund, Henry ..	.. Rfm. ..	5035	2/8th W. Yorks.	—	D. of W.
Lund, John Wm.	.. L/Cpl.	3585	2/7th W. Yorks.	—	K. in A.
Lunn, David ..	.. Sgt. ..	30550	7th Border	—	K. in A.
Lunn, Geo. ..	.. Bdr. ..	58758	R.G.A. ..	—	D. of W.
Lunn, Harry ..	.. Pte. ..	5058	W. Yorks.	—	K. in A.
Lunt, Jas. ..	.. L/Cpl.	72371	Royal Engineers	—	Died
Luntley, Fredk. C.	.. Pte. ..	1670	1st W. Yorks.	—	K. in A.
Lupton, C. R.	.. Captain		Royal Air Force	.. D.S.C.	K. in A.
Lupton, Clifford	.. Pte. ..	44815	8th Manchester	—	K. in A.
Lupton, F. A.	.. Major		W. Yorks.	—	K. in A.
Lupton, Harry	.. L/Cpl.	45192	South Staffs. ..	—	Missing
Lupton, Harry R.	.. Rfm. ..	8967	King's Royal Rifle Cps.	—	K. in A.
Lupton, L. M.	.. Lieut.		R.F.A. ..	—	K. in A.
Lupton, M. ..	.. Capt.		W. Yorks.	—	K. in A.
Lupton, Ronald	.. Dvr. ..	84138	Royal Engineers	—	Died
Lupton, Thos. H.	.. 1 Stkr.	K7916	H.M.S. " Queen Mary "	—	K. in A.
Lupton, Wm. P.	.. Pte. ..	838	W. Yorks.	—	K. in A.
Lye, Harry ..	.. Rfm. ..	2519	8th W. Yorks.	—	K. in A.
Lye, Hbt. J. ..	.. L/Cpl.	3978	King's Royal Rifle Cps.	—	K. in A.
Lynch, Fredk. W.	.. L/Cpl.	39283	21st W. Yorks.	—	K. in A.
Lynch, John ..	.. Rfm. ..		Rifle Brigade ..	—	D. a. Dis.
Lynch, Joseph	.. Pte. ..	34004	W. Yorks.	—	Died P.O.W.
Lynch, Stephen	.. Pte. ..	28947	K.O. Scottish Borderers	—	Died
Lynch, William	.. Pte. ..	61040	King's Liverpool	—	Died
Lyner, Jas. ..	.. Pte. ..	6289	London	—	K. in A.
Lynes, Gerald	.. Cpl. ..	18567	11th W. Yorks.	—	K. in A.

LEEDS ROLL OF HONOUR.

Name	Rank	No.	Regiment	Honours	How Died
Lynes, Harry	Sgt.	94	17th W. Yorks.	—	K. in A.
Lynn, Martin	A/Cpl.	8318	1st W. Yorks.	—	K. in A.
Lyon, Francis W.	Pte.	20753	K.O.Y.L.I.	—	K. in A.
Lyon, Luke	Rfm.	2273	1/7th W. Yorks.	—	K. in A.
Lyons, Jas.	Pte.	266786	W. Yorks.	—	K. in A.
Lyons, John	Sgt.	9867	W. Riding	—	Missing
Lyons, John	Pte.	10567	3rd E. Yorks.	—	D. a. Dis.
Lyons, John	Pte.	42802	2/9th Manchester	—	K. in A.
Lyson, Thos. H.	Pte.	7653	1st W. Yorks.	—	K. in A.
Lyth, Geo.	Pte.	266363	W. Yorks.	—	K. in A.
Lythe, Harry	Gnr.		52nd Canadian	—	K. in A.
McAndrew, James	Pte.	37036	9th W. Yorks.	—	K. in A.
McAndrew, A.	Pte.	39164	Northumberland Fusrs.	—	D. a. Dis.
McArthur, A.	Pte.	9890	1st E. Yorks.	—	D. of W.
Macaulay, W. H.	Sgt.	608	15th W. Yorks.	—	K. in A.
Maccabe, Albert	Pte.	12729	10th W. Yorks.	—	K. in A.
McCamman, Geo. F.	Pte.	8979	2nd W. Yorks.	—	K. in A.
McCaragher, Chas. P.	Pte.	6058	9th Leinster	—	K. in A.
McCarthy, Owen	Pte.	23600	1st W. Yorks.	—	K. in A.
McCarthy, Tom	Pte.	266136	2nd W. Yorks.	—	K. in A.
McClean, Wm.	A.B.	J10446	H.M.S. " Princess Irene "	—	K. in A.
McClymont, Jos.	Pte.	241301	Seaforth Highlanders	—	K. in A.
McConnell, Herbert	L/Cpl.	3555	Military M. Police	—	Died
McCrea, John	Spr.	140743	Royal Engineers	—	D. of W.
McCrudden, A. W. R.	2nd Lieut.		15th W. Yorks.	—	Died
McCullagh, Frank	Sgt.	628	15th W. Yorks.	—	K. in A.
McCullogh, David	Pte.	27017	4th S. Wales Bordrs.	—	K. in A.
McCulloch, Fred	Pte.	25654	22nd Manchester	—	D. of W.
McCulloch, James J.	Pte.	12028	10th W. Yorks.	—	K. in A.
McCulloch, Wm.	Sgt.	23812	1st Royal Lancs.	—	K. in A.
McDermott, Edward	Pte.	9382	1st W. Yorks.	—	K. in A.
McDermott, Geo.	Pte.	38178	3rd W. Yorks.	—	K. in A.
McDermott, Michael	Pte.	14283	W. Yorks.	—	D. of W.
McDermott, Patrick	Pte.	17229	Northumberland Fusrs.	—	K. in A.
McDermott, Timothy	Ptr.	21984	W. Yorks.	—	Missing
McDonald, Albert	Sgt.	265031	1/7th W. Yorks.	—	K. in A.
McDonald, Michael	Pte.	112749	R.A.S.C.	—	D. a. Dis.
McDonald, Thos.	Rfm.	4453	1/7th W. Yorks.	—	Died
McDonald, Thos.	Pte.	10280	9th W. Yorks.	—	Missing
McDonald, Wm.	Pte.	8628	2nd W. Yorks.	—	K. in A.
McDonnell, Edward	Pte.	412903	13th Canadian Highdrs.	—	Died
McDowell, Wilfred	Pte.	265820	W. Yorks.	—	Died
Mace, Herbert	Pte.	8424	2nd Yorks.	—	K. in A.
McEwan, David G.	2nd Lieut.		10th Welsh	—	K. in A.
McEwan, Robt. W.	Pte.	629	15th W. Yorks.	—	K. in A.
McFadden, Joseph	Sgt.	18248	Royal Welsh Fusrs.	—	Drowned

LEEDS ROLL OF HONOUR.

Name	Rank	No.	Regiment	Honours	How Died
McFarlane, Wm.	L/Cpl.	33927	Loyal N. Lancs.	—	K. in A.
McGarry, James	Pte.	30870	Lincoln	—	D. a. Dis.
McGill, James	Sgt.	2488	R.F.A.	—	D. of W.
McGill, James D.	Rfm.	42414	2/8th W. Yorks.	—	K. in A.
McGlynn, J.	Pte.	17251	W. Riding	—	K. in A.
McGowan, Edward	Pte.	15170	Munster Fusrs.	—	K. in A.
McGowan, Francis	O.S.		H.M.S. " Hampshire "	—	K. in A.
McGowan, John	Pte.	7555	2nd Yorks.	—	K. in A.
McGowan, Percy N...	L/Cpl.	781705	Canadian Exped. Force	—	K. in A.
McGrail, James	Pte.	13887	W. Riding	—	Died
McGregor, Chas.	Pte.	1341	1/6th W. Yorks.	—	K. in A.
McGregor, Geo.	Sgt.	8721	2nd W. Yorks.	—	K. in A.
McGregor, Geo.	Pte.	26042	12th Northumb'l'd Fusrs.	—	K. in A.
McGuiness, John	Pte.	6806	Royal Sussex	—	Died
McGuiness, John	AirCfm.	F18897	Royal Navy	—	D. a. Dis.
McGuiness, John R...	Pte.	368655	Labour Corps	—	K. in A.
McGuire, Dennis	Pte.	28336	7th E. Yorks.	—	K. in A.
McGuire, James E.	Cpl.	265350	W. Yorks.	—	K. in A.
McGuire, Walter	Pte.			—	Died
McGuire, Wilfred J.	Pte.	29703	Labour Corps	—	K. in A.
McGuirk, James	Pte.	15922	K.O.Y.L.I.	—	D. of W.
McGwynn, Patrick	Sgt.	702109	20th W. Yorks.	—	D. a. Dis.
McHale, James	Pte.	40790	South Staffs.	—	K. in A.
Machan, Edgar	A.S.	J20116	H.M.S. " Invincible "	—	K. in A.
Machen, Frank S.	Pte.	50555	12th W. Yorks.	—	K. in A.
Machin, F. W.	Pte.	33900	W. Riding	—	K. in A.
Machin, James	Pte.	263016	Loyal N. Lancs.	—	K. in A.
McHugh, John	Cpl.	41989	8th W. Yorks.	—	K. in A.
McIntyre, Cormick	Rfm.	306018	2/8th W. Yorks.	—	K. in A.
McIntyre, Duncan	A.B.	66420	H.M.S. " Victory "	—	K. in A.
McIntyre, John	Pte.	9640	W. Riding	—	D. of W.
McJury, John	Pte.	45381	1/4th York. & Lancs.	—	K. in A.
Mack, Wm.	Sgt.	9389	2nd Seaforth Highldrs.	—	K. in A.
Mackay, Eric S.	Pte.	53686	W. Yorks.	—	K. in A.
Mackay, Wm.	Sgt.	17825	2nd W. Yorks.	—	K. in A.
McKenna, James	Pte.	423275	233rd Labour Compy.	—	Died
Mackenzie, James	Pte.	13907	E. Kent	—	K. in A.
McKenzie, Robt.	Pte.	T40617	R.A.S.C.	—	Died
McKie, Walter	Gnr.	13540	R.F.A.	—	Died
McKillen, Daniel	Pte.	40556	Scottish Rifles	—	Died
McLaren, Guy B.	Pte.	41622	Northumberland Fusrs.	—	D. of W.
McLaughlin, Arthur	Pte.	13761	Army Cyclist Corps	—	K. in A.
McLaughlin, Francis Y.	Cpl.	0/21967	Royal Air Force	—	Died
McLean, John H.	Pte.	1906	1st W. Yorks.	—	K. in A.
McLoughlin, Hugh	Cpl.	1910	K.O.Y.L.I.	—	Died
McLoughlin, James	Pte.		9th W. Yorks.	—	K. in A.
McLoughlin, James	Pte.	2085	5th Leicester	—	D. of W.

LEEDS ROLL OF HONOUR.

Name	Rank	No.	Regiment	Honours	How Died
McLoughlin, James	Rfm.	2302	1/8th W. Yorks.	—	D. of W.
McLoughlin, John	Pte.	30021	1st E. Yorks.	—	Died
McLoughlin, Joseph	Pte.	12827	8th K.O.Y.L.I.	—	K. in A.
McLoughlin, Joseph	Pte.	13117	W. Yorks.	—	K. in A.
McMahon, John	Pte.	12120	12th W. Yorks.	—	K. in A.
McMahon, Thos.	Sgt.	58392	R.F.A.	—	K. in A.
McManns, Geo.	Pte.	38577	W. Riding	—	D. of W.
McManus, Francis	Pte.	105	17th W. Yorks.	—	K. in A.
McManus, Francis	Pte.	10647	W. Riding	—	D. of W.
McManus, Herbert	Pte.	202278	3/5th W. Yorks.	—	K. in A.
McMaster, Arthur	Pte.	10349	2nd W. Riding	—	K. in A.
McMillan, Albert	Pte.	21452	11th Northumb'l'd Fusrs.	—	K. in A.
McMillan, Chas. M.	Lieut. Pilot		Royal Air Force	—	K. in A.
McMillan, Wm.	Rfm.	43197	1/8th W. Yorks.	—	D. of W.
McMillen, Benjamin D.	Rfm.	4345	1/8th W. Yorks.	—	K. in A.
McNab, Alfred	Rfm.	1493	1/8th W. Yorks.	—	K. in A.
McNamee, Lawrence	Pte.	S/20774	Gordon Highlanders	—	D. a. Dis.
McNeil, Edward	Cpl.	41443	7th E. Yorks.	—	K. in A.
McNeil, Harold	L/Cpl.	265906	10th W. Yorks.	—	K. in A.
McNeill, Wm.	Pte.	61501	Royal Defence Corps.	—	Died
McNeney, John	Pte.	10165	3rd Durham Lt. Infty.	—	Died
McNichol, John	Pte.	35963	1st Northumb'l'd Fusrs.	—	Died
McNiff, Peter	Pte.	7743	2nd York. & Lancs.	—	Died
McNulty, Wm. H.	L/Cpl.	8118	1st W. Yorks.	—	K. in A.
Macpherson, Henry D.	2nd Lieut.		Royal Air Force	—	K. in A.
Madden, Thos.	Rfm.	265942	2/7th W. Yorks.	—	K. in A.
Maddra, Thos.	Pte.	34173	9th W. Yorks.	—	K. in A.
Madin, Geo. T.	Pte.	27566	Machine Gun Corps	—	K. in A.
Magee, Joseph	Pte.	11681	W. Yorks.	—	K. in A.
Magee, Thos.	Pte.	7403	1st Royal Irish Fusrs.	—	K. in A.
Maguire, Dennis	Pte.	28336	7th E. Yorks.	—	K. in A.
Mahoney, Jos. F.	Pte.	1521	17th W. Yorks.	—	Died
Main, Albert B.	Pte.	20494	2nd Leicester	—	K. in A.
Mair, Fredk. S.	L/Cpl.	32407	10th W. Yorks.	—	K. in A.
Maisey, Harold C.	2nd Lieut.		Royal Naval Air Service	—	Missing
Makin, Arthur L.	L/Sgt.	3639	2/7th W. Yorks.	—	K. in A.
Makin, Edward	Pte.	42757	2/7th Manchester	—	K. in A.
Makin, Geo.	Gdsmn.	8726	Scots Guards	—	K. in A.
Makin, Walter	L/Cpl.	2625	1/7th W. Yorks.	D.C.M.	K. in A.
Makin, Walter	Pte.	39918	2/5th W. Yorks.	—	K. in A.
Malcolm, Archibald H.	2nd Lieut.		K.O. Scottish Bordrs.	—	K. in A.
Malcolm, Ernest	Pte.	10406	2nd W. Riding	—	Missing
Malkin, Albert	Cpl.	13498	8th York. & Lancs.	—	K. in A.
Malkin, Ernest	Pte.	3218	W. Yorks.	—	Died
Mallaby, Arthur E.	Pte.	26326	12th W. Yorks.	—	K. in A.
Mallinson, Albert	Pte.	29477	8th Border	—	Died P.O.W.
Mallinson, Albert	Rfm.	48242	Rifle Brigade	—	K. in A.

LEEDS ROLL OF HONOUR.

Name	Rank	No.	Regiment	Honours	How Died
Mallinson, G. S.	Cpl.		Royal Engineers	—	K. in A.
Mallinson, Jos. S.	Pte.	612549	19th City of London	—	Missing
Mallinson, P. S.	Pte.		Royal Fusiliers	—	K. in A.
Mallory, Albert C.	Pte.	203521	1/4th K.O.Y.L.I.	—	Died
Malone, Wm.	Pte.	202256	2/4th Lincoln	—	K. in A.
Maloney, Cornelius	L/Cpl.	10897	1st K.O. Scottish Bordrs.	—	K. in A.
Maloney, Wm. A.	Pte.	110544	Labour Corps	—	Died
Maltas, Ernest	Pte.	64882	K.O.Y.L.I.	—	K. in A.
Maltby, Percy	Rfm.		1/7th W. Yorks.	—	K. in A.
Maltby, Tom	Pte.		Northants.	—	K. in A.
Manby, James	Pte.	6615	1st W. Yorks.	—	K. in A.
Mangham, Jos.	Pte.	9948	8th W. Riding..	—	Missing
Mangham, Thos.	Pte.	82861	Durham Lt. Infantry..	—	D. a. Dis.
Mankin, James H. W.	Spr.	237617	Royal Engineers	—	Died
Manley, James	Pte.	34316	2nd Welsh Fusrs.	—	Died
Manley, James	Pte.	101631	1st W. Yorks.	—	Missing
Manley, Patrick	Pte.	10976	10th W. Yorks.	—	K. in A.
Mann, Albert M.	Pnr.	72499	Royal Engineers	—	K. in A.
Mann, Chas.	Pte.	36375	10th Yorks.	—	K. in A.
Mann, Cyril	Pte.	37313	W. Yorks.	—	K. in A.
Mann, Ernest..	Spr.	476527	Royal Engineers	—	K. in A.
Mann, Geo. H.	Teleg.	1378	Royal Naval V. Res.	—	Died
Mann, Harold	L/Cpl.	305528	1/8th W. Yorks.	—	K. in A.
Mann, Harry	Pte.	427593	Labour Corps	—	K. in A.
Mann, Harry	Pte.	16379	1st W. Yorks.	—	K. on A.
Mann, Herbert	Pte.	23790	15th W. Yorks.	—	Died P.O.W.
Mann, Herbert	L/Cpl.	305205	2/8th W. Yorks.	—	K. in A.
Mann, James	L/Cpl.	632737	20th City of London	—	K. in A.
Mann, James A.	Cpl.	25277	15th W. Yorks.	—	Missing
Mann, Leonard	Rfm.	266549	3/7th W. Yorks.	—	K. in A.
Mann, Leonard	Gdsmn.	26717	Grenadier Guards	—	Died
Mann, Richard	Rfm.	265092	1/7th W. Yorks.	—	K. in A.
Mann, Tom	Rfm.	2809	7th W. Yorks.	—	K. in A.
Mann, Walter	Pte.	10089	3rd W. Yorks.	—	Died
Manners, Frank	Pte.	41978	22nd Northumb'l'd Fus.	—	K. in A.
Manning, James	Pte.	7792	1st W. Yorks.	—	K. in A.
Mansley, Geo.	Pte.	S/40721	1/7th Gordon Highdrs.	—	Died
Manton, Ernest	Gdsmn.	7219	Scots Guards	—	Died P.O.W.
March, Wm. M.	L/Cpl.	34277	W. Yorks.	—	K. in A.
Marchant, Bernard	Sgt.	84549	R.F.A.	—	K. in A.
Marchant, John	A.B.	KP844	Royal Naval Division	—	Died
Marchant, Francis S.	Lieut.		Border	—	K. in A.
Marchant, Tom	Pte.	25793	2nd K.O.Y.L.I.	—	K. in A.
Marchant, Wm.	Cpl.	612	W. Yorks.	—	K. in A.
Marchington, J. D.	Pte.	141967	Canadian Infantry	—	Died
Markham, Walter	Pte.	401420	R.A.M.C.	—	D. of W.
Markinson, Wm. E.	Pte.	36044	11th Royal Fusiliers	—	K. in A.

LEEDS ROLL OF HONOUR.

Name	Rank	No.	Regiment	Honours	How Died
Marks, David	Cpl.	41046	Royal Dublin Fusiliers	—	Died
Marks, Ernest G.	Pte.	27958	1/5th W. Yorks.	—	K. in A.
Marks, Eustace H.	Pte.	45176	14th Worcester	—	K. in A.
Marks, Horace W.	Pte.	78289	R.A.M.C.	—	D. of W.
Marlow, Fred	Pte.	11637	W. Riding	—	K. in A.
Marr, James	Pte.	12746	W. Yorks.	—	K. in A.
Marr, Wm.	Pte.	21657	10th W. Yorks.	—	K. in A.
Marriner, Leonard	Gnr.	154894	R.F.A.	—	D. of W.
Marriott, Arthur	Pte.	314840	Labour Corps	—	Died
Marriott, Geo.	Gnr.	94806	Tank Corps	—	D. a. Dis.
Marriott, Joseph	Pte.	39437	2nd W. Yorks.	—	Missing
Marsden, Clifford	Pte.	41641	W. Yorks.	—	Died
Marsden, Ernest	L/Sgt.	2127	1/7th W. Yorks.	—	K. in A.
Marsden, Ernest	Pte.	18722	9th W. Yorks.	—	Missing
Marsden, Geo.	Gnr.	29927	R.F.A.	—	Died
Marsden, Harold	2nd Lieut.		3rd W. Riding	—	Died
Marsden, Harry	Rfm.	4845	W. Yorks.	—	Died
Marsden, Herbert	Gnr.	5972	R.F.A.	—	D. a. Dis.
Marsden, Joseph	Pte.	19560	2nd Leicester	—	K. in A.
Marsden, Joseph	Pte.	385	17th W. Yorks.	—	K. in A.
Marsden, Rowland	Pte.	15965	K.O.Y.L.I.	—	K. in A.
Marsden, Samuel	Pte.	41135	11th W. Yorks.	—	K. in A.
Marsden, Thornton	Pte.		1/5th W. Yorks.	—	K. in A.
Marsden, Wm.	Pte.	34229	1/5th K.O.Y.L.I.	—	Died
Marsh, Horace	Pte.	77744	Durham Light Infantry	—	D. a. Dis.
Marsh, Thos.	Pte.	102107	Notts. & Derby	—	K. in A.
Marshall, Alfred	Sgt.	7207	W. Yorks.	—	Died
Marshall, Chas. E.	Pte.	202250	Highland Lt. Infantry	—	Died
Marshall, Ernest	Pte.	917	17th W. Yorks.	—	D. of W.
Marshall, Ernest	Pte.	64883	K.O.Y.L.I.	—	K. in A.
Marshall, George	Cpl.	305406	1/8th W. Yorks.	—	K. in A.
Marshall, George	Gdsmn.	23281	Grenadier Guards	—	K. in A.
Marshall, Geo. Y.	Pte.	4412	2/15th London	—	D. of W.
Marshall, Harold	Pte.	38724	K.O.Y.L.I.	—	K. in A.
Marshall, Harold	L/Cpl.	307126	2/5th W. Yorks.	—	K. in A.
Marshall, Harry	Pte.	17755	W. Yorks.	—	D. a. Dis.
Marshall, Henry	Pte.	271547	Royal Scots	—	K. in A.
Marshall, Horace	Pte.	2718	1/6th W. Riding	—	K. in A.
Marshall, James	Rfm.	3177	7th W. Yorks.	—	K. in A.
Marshall, John	L/Cpl.	15310	W. Riding	—	Died
Marshall, John J.	L/Cpl.	32374	W. Yorks.	—	Died
Marshall, Joseph	L/Cpl.	23323	13th Yorks.	—	D. of W.
Marshall, Richard H.	Pte.	13488	12th W. Yorks.	—	K. in A.
Marshall, Samuel	Pte.	46248	York. & Lancs.	—	Died
Marshall, Sydney	Pte.	75768	R.A.M.C.	—	D. of W.
Marshall, Thos. W.	A.B.	J58619	H.M.S. " Bacchant "	—	Died
Marshall, W.	Pte.	140569	Machine Gun Corps	—	Died

LEEDS ROLL OF HONOUR.

Name	Rank	No.	Regiment	Honours	How Died
Marshall, Walter	Rfm.	S/8061	Rifle Brigade	—	K. in A.
Marshall, Wilfred	Pte.	42542	Machine Gun Corps	—	K. in A.
Marshall, Wm.	Pte.	284816	Labour Corps	—	D. a. Dis.
Marsland, Harold	Rfm.	307542	1/8th W. Yorks.	—	K. in A.
Marsland, Roger	E.R.A.	M28419	Royal Navy	—	D. a. Dis.
Marston, Ernest	Pte.	20517	K.O.Y.L.I.	—	K. in A.
Martin, Chas. A.	Rfm.	306853	2/8th W. Yorks.	—	K. in A.
Martin, Chas. H.	L/Sgt.	13233	K.O.Y.L.I.	—	K. in A.
Martin, George	Rfm.	48820	1/8th W. Yorks.	—	K. in A.
Martin, G. W.	Major		17th Northumb'l'd Fusrs. (late 1st W. Yorks.)	—	K. in A.
Martin, John	Pte.	9926	3rd W. Yorks.	—	K. in A.
Martin, Joseph	Gdsmn.	8475	2nd Scots Guards	—	Missing
Martin, Thos.	Pnr.	293903	Royal Engineers	—	D. a. Dis.
Martin, W.	Pte.	130479	551st Labour Compy.	—	Died
Martin, Wm.	Pte.	17533	Labour Corps	—	Died
Marvell, Cyril	Pte.	15810	9th W. Yorks.	—	K. in A.
Marwood, George	L/Cpl.	2716	1/7th W. Yorks.	—	K. in A.
Marwood, Joseph	Rfm.	2014	1/7th W. Yorks.	—	K. in A.
Maskill, Geo. H.	Dvr.	18794	R.F.A.	—	Died
Maskill, James E.	Pte.	25835	2nd W. Yorks.	—	K. in A.
Mason, Arthur	Pte.	203187	W. Yorks.	—	K. in A.
Mason, Chas. H.	Pte.	3319	2/6th City of London	—	K. in A.
Mason, Cyril	Sig.	175339	R.G.A.	—	D. a. Dis.
Mason, Ernest F.	Rfm.	3370	7th W. Yorks.	—	K. in A.
Mason, Fred	Pte.	38180	17th W. Yorks.	—	K. in A.
Mason, Fred	Pte.	306896	Labour Corps	—	D. a. Dis.
Mason, Haman	L/Cpl.	2236	W. Yorks.	—	K. in A.
Mason, Herbert H. J.	L/Cpl.	621	15th W. Yorks.	—	Missing
Mason, John	Pte.	1195	19th W. Yorks.	—	D. a. Dis.
Mason, John	Spr.		5th Canadian	—	K. in A.
Mason, John Wm.	Pte.	35188	9th W. Yorks.	—	Missing
Mason, Leonard	Pte.	10930	4th W. Yorks.	—	K. in A.
Mason, Matthew	Pte.	426	1st Northumb'l'd Fusrs.	—	Missing
Mason, Percy	Pte.	2435	1/5th W. Yorks.	—	K. in A.
Mason, R. H.	Pte.	13718	Lincoln	—	D. of W.
Mason, T.	Pte.	202338	R.A.S.C.	—	Died
Mason, Wm.	Gnr.	75041	R.F.A.	—	K. in A.
Mason, Wm.	L/Cpl.	32737	7th Yorks.	—	Missing
Masser, Chas. H.	Pte.	268019	W. Yorks.	—	K. in A.
Massey, John	Pte.	2794	2nd Yorks.	—	K. in A.
Massey, Wm.	Pte.	14139	11th W. Yorks.	—	K. in A.
Masterman, H. W.	Pte.	155465	R.A.S.C. (M.T.)	—	Died
Mather, Edward	Sgt.	9601	2nd W. Yorks.	—	K. in A.
Mather, Harold	Pte.	49766	9th Liverpool	—	D. of W.
Mathers, Edward	Pte.	7278	1st Leicester	—	K. in A.
Mathers, Francis H.	Pte.	25282	Duke of Cornwall L.I.	—	K. in A.

LEEDS ROLL OF HONOUR.

Name	Rank	No.	Regiment	Honours	How Died
Mathers, Gilbert	Gdsmn.	8128	2nd Scots Guards	—	Missing
Mathers, James	Q.M.S.	5599	8th W. Yorks.	—	Died
Mathers, T.	L/Sgt.	8857	2nd E. Yorks.	—	K. in A.
Mathers, Wm.	Pte.	25657	2nd Yorks.	—	Died
Mathews, Walter	Pte.	18905	K.O.Y.L.I.	—	K. in A.
Matkin, James	Pte.	26654	Northumberland Fusrs.	—	Died
Matterson, Wm.	Pte.	25821	K.O.Y.L.I.	—	Missing
Matthewman, Willie	Pte.	569	17th W. Yorks.	—	K. in A.
Matthews, A.	Rfm.	47652	Rifle Brigade	—	K. in A.
Matthews, James	Pte.	1077	17th W. Yorks.	—	K. in A.
Matthews, John	Gnr.	141725	R.G.A.	—	K. in A.
Matthews, Walter	Pte.	20415	10th Gloucester	—	D. of W.
Matthews, Wm.	Pte.	112829	R.A.M.C.	—	K. in A.
Mattison, Alfred	Pte.	6969	2nd Yorks.	—	K. in A.
Mattock, Joe S.	Pte.	11225	Royal Fusiliers	—	K. in A.
Maude, G.	Pte.	55511	R.A.M.C.	—	Died
Maude, John	Rfm.	1787	1/8th W. Yorks.	—	K. in A.
Maude, Thos.	Pte.	115278	Labour Corps	—	D. of W.
Maudsley, John	Pnr.	303329	Royal Engineers	—	Died
Maudsley, Thos. Wm.	Pte.	37106	9th W. Yorks.	—	K. in A.
Maundrill, Wilfred H.	Pte.	21947	3rd E. Yorks.	—	Died
Mawman, Harold	Pte.	28443	S. Lancs.	—	Died
Mawman, Walter	Pte.	25970	5th Wilts.	—	K. in A.
Mawn, Lawrence	Pte.	4308	Cameron Highlanders	—	K. in A.
Mawson, David	Pte.	65074	K.O.Y.L.I.	—	K. in A.
Mawson, Edwin	Dvr.	62874	R.F.A.	—	Died
Mawson, John Wm.	L/Cpl.	21087	1st W. Yorks.	—	D. of W.
Mawson, Wm.	Cpl.	242964	1/6th W. Yorks.	—	K. in A.
Maxwell, Robt. T.	L/Sgt.	20579	Yorks.	—	D. a. Dis.
Maxwell, Robt. V.	Pte.	241888	2/6th W. Yorks.	—	Died
May, Alfred	L/Cpl.	8220	2nd W. Yorks.	—	K. in A.
May, Clement	Pte.	32857	16th W. Yorks.	—	D. of W.
May, Thos. A.	Pte.	13755	12th W. Yorks.	—	Died
Mayer, John	Dvr.	72898	R.F.A.	—	K. in A.
Mayhew, John E. M.	Pte.	10398	1st K.O.Y.L.I.	—	Died
Maynard, George	Sgt.	9787	3rd W. Yorks.	—	Died
Mayne, Bertie	Gnr.	775210	R.F.A.	—	K. in A.
Mayne, Geo. W.	Cpl.	3484	2/8th W. Yorks.	—	D. of W.
Mazza, Anthony	Rfm.	305962	2/8th W. Yorks.	—	Died
Mazza, Dominick	Pte.		K.O.Y.L.I.	—	K. in A.
Mazza, Francis	Pte.	18906	7th K.O.Y.L.I.	—	K. in A.
Mazza, Joseph	L/Sgt.	305895	2/8th W. Yorks.	—	K. in A.
Mead, James	Pte.	11367	W. Riding	—	K. in A.
Meadley, Geo.	Pte.	24605	13th Yorks.	—	K. in A.
Meadows, Edward	L/Cpl.	206670	1/7th W. Yorks.	—	Died
Meakin, John T.	Pte.	19450	12th W. Yorks.	—	K. in A.
Meavis, Francis B.	Rfm.	266271	2/7th W. Yorks.	—	Died

LEEDS ROLL OF HONOUR.

Name	Rank	No.	Regiment	Honours	How Died
Medd, Tom	Pte.	12032	W. Yorks.	—	K. in A.
Medley, Walter	Rfm.	267241	2/7th W. Yorks.	—	K. in A.
Mee, Walter F.	Pte.	702139	23rd London	—	D. of W.
Meechan, Henry H.	Gdsmn.	8629	2nd Scots Guards	M.M.	K. in A.
Meegan, John	Rfm.	4705	2/8th W. Yorks.	—	K. in A.
Meegan, Thos.	L/Cpl.	27797	W. Yorks.		Died
Meek, Bernard	L/Cpl.	8518	9th Northumb'l'd Fus.	—	K. in A.
Meek, Ernest	Rfm.	2071	7th W. Yorks.	—	K. in A.
Meeks, Walter	Pte.	33762	15th W. Yorks.	—	D. of W.
Meeson, Arthur	L/Cpl.	B633	15th W. Yorks.	—	K. in A.
Meggiton, James J.	Pte.	9137	2nd W. Yorks.	—	K. in A.
Megson, Henry	Pte.	3/26896	S. Wales Borderers	—	K. in A.
Megson, Robert	Gnr.	795569	R.F.A.	—	K. in A.
Melia, Edward	Pte.	34852	12th Yorks.	—	K. in A.
Melia, Francis	L/Bdr.	220556	R.G.A.	—	K. in A.
Melia, Joseph	Pte.	656924	Labour Corps	—	D. a. Dis.
Melia, Wm.	Pte.	13496	Machine Gun Corps	—	K. in A.
Mellard, R. Lawrence	Sgt.	1881	15th W. Yorks.	—	K. in A.
Mellor, Fred	Rfm.	4427	3/7th W. Yorks.	—	D. a. Dis.
Mellor, Harry	Sgt.	1104	15th W. Yorks.	—	Missing
Mellor, Joe	L/Cpl.	3799	3/8th W. Yorks.	—	K. in A.
Melton, Ernest	Pte.	39860	3rd W. Yorks.	—	K. in A.
Mence, Horace W.	Spr.	144545	Royal Engineers	—	Died
Mennell, Thos.	Bdr.	745864	R.F.A.	—	K. in A.
Mennell, Wm.	Pte.	37024	W. Yorks.	—	K. in A.
Mercer, Alfred S.	2nd Lieut.		R.F.A.	—	K. in A.
Merchant, J.	Gnr.	18929	R.F.A.	—	K. in A.
Meredith, Arthur	Pte.	37386	Royal Scots	—	K. in A.
Merrell, Chas. Wm.	Pte.	8964	20th Hussars	—	K. in A.
Merritt, Edgar	Pte.	60858	W. Yorks.	—	K. in A.
Merritt, George	L/Cpl.	8326	2nd W. Yorks.	—	D. of W.
Merritt, George	Pte.	27905	12th W. Yorks.	—	D. of W.
Merry, W.			Northumberland Fusrs.	—	K. in A.
Merson, Harry	Rfm.	2959	1/7th W. Yorks.	—	K. in A.
Mervin, Thos.	Pte.		K.O. Scottish Borderers	—	Died
Metcalf, Wm. Henry	Pte.	18143	11th K.O.Y.L.I.	—	Died
Metcalfe, Albert	Pte.	56506	10th W. Yorks.	—	K. in A.
Metcalfe, Clifford	Pte.	630	15th W. Yorks.	—	Missing
Metcalfe, E.	Pte.	32125	2nd Durham Lt. Infty.	—	K. in A.
Metcalfe, Fred	Pte.	44154	Durham Light Infantry	—	Died
Metcalfe, Geo. H.	Smn.	207310	H.M.S. " Fortune "	—	K. in A.
Metcalfe, Geo. Wm.	Pte.	123056	Machine Gun Corps	—	D. a. Dis.
Metcalfe, James	Sgt.	265018	7th W. Yorks.	—	D. a. Dis.
Metcalfe, John E.	Rfmn.	266329	2/7th W. Yorks.	—	Missing
Metcalfe, John Wm.	Gnr.	58609	R.G.A.	—	Died
Metcalfe, Leonard	Pte.	31425	Northumberland Fusrs.	—	K. in A.
Metcalfe, Peter R.	Sgt.	4476	W. Yorks.	—	K. in A.

LEEDS ROLL OF HONOUR.

Name	Rank	No.	Regiment	Honours	How Died
Metcalfe, Reginald	Cpl.	305254	2/7th W. Riding	—	K. in A.
Metcalfe, Robert L.	Pte.	134098	Machine Gun Corps	—	D. a. Dis.
Metcalfe T.	Rfm.	2457	W. Yorks.	—	Died
Metcalfe, Thos. G.	Pte.	43059	10th W. Yorks.	—	K. in A.
Metcalfe, Walter	Rfm.	306613	3/8th W. Yorks.	—	K. in A.
Metcalfe, Walter H.	Cpl.	13763	12th W. Yorks.	—	K. in A.
Metcalfe, Wm.	L/Sgt.	7930	1st W. Yorks.	—	Died
Metcalfe, Wm.	Pte.	13086	W. Riding	—	Missing
Metcalfe, Wm. H.	Pte.	10627	2nd Yorks.	—	K. in A.
Mewis, Harry A. E.	A/Sgt.R/33663		King's Royal Rifle Cps.	—	K. in A.
Micklethwaite, Arthur	Pte.	203565	1/5th W. Yorks.	—	Missing
Micklethwaite, Chas. A.	Pte.	4090	W. Yorks.	—	K. in A.
Middleton, Arthur	Pte.	1632	6th K.O.Y.L.I.	—	K. in A.
Middleton, Ernest	Gdsmn.	15005	Scots Guards	—	D. of W.
Middleton, Fredk.	Gnr.	127521	R.F.A.	—	D. of W.
Middleton, Harry	Pte.	21334	Machine Gun Corps	—	K. in A.
Middleton, Herbert	Pte.	13044	10th W. Yorks.	—	K. in A.
Middleton, Joe	Pte.	7679	10th W. Yorks.	—	Missing
Middleton, Percival V.	Pte.	30364	E. Yorks.	—	K. in A.
Middleton, Rawdon	Drmr.	10086	1st Royal Highlanders	—	K. in A.
Middleton, Samuel	R.S.M.	19822	10th York. & Lancs.	—	K. in A.
Middleton, Wm.	Pte.	41137	S. Staffs.	—	Died
Midgeley, Thos. P.	Dvr.	84937	R.F.A.	—	Died
Midgley, Alfred	Pte.	844	17th W. Yorks.	—	K. in A.
Midgley, B. W.	Pte.	1925	W. Yorks.	—	K. in A.
Midgley, Edgar	Spr.	160259	Royal Engineers	—	D. of W.
Midgley, Edward	Dvr.	82176	R.F.A.	—	K. in A.
Midgley, Ellis R.	2nd Lieut.		1/5th K.O.Y.L.I.	—	K. in A.
Midgley, Fred	Pte.	307135	W. Yorks.	—	K. in A.
Midgley, Geo. Wm.	L/Cpl.	11775	1st King's Liverpool	—	K. in A.
Midgley, John Thos.	Cpl.	267841	6th Northumb'l'd Fusrs.	—	K. in A.
Midgley, Norman W.	Dvr.	63242	R.F.A.	—	K. in A.
Milburn, Fred	Rfm.	37046	2/7th W. Yorks.	—	K. in A.
Milburn, Herbert	Rfm.	49601	2/7th W. Yorks.	—	Killed
Midgley, James	C.S.M.	6361	6th R.W. Surrey	—	K. in A.
Miles, Frank	L/Cpl.	G777	Military M. Police	—	Died
Miller, A.	Pte.	467	17th W. Yorks.	—	Killed
Miller, Alfred E.	Pte.	263649	Royal Air Force	—	D. a. Dis.
Miller, Andrew	Pte.	34377	18th W. Yorks.	—	Missing
Miller, Fred Wm.	Dvr.	73063	R.F.A.	—	Drowned
Miller, Herbert	Pte.	5/70462	Training Reserve	—	Died
Miller, John A.	L/Cpl.	15/647	W. Yorks.	—	Missing
Miller, John Hy.	Pte.	16747	York. & Lancs.	—	K. in A.
Miller, Norman	Rfm.	2814	7th W. Yorks.	—	K. in A.
Miller, T.	Dvr.	5797	R.F.A.	—	Died
Milligan, Arthur Wm.	Pte.	266903	6th Seaforth Highdrs.	—	K. in A.
Mills, Alfred	L/Cpl.	18313	1/5th W. Yorks.	—	K. in A.

LEEDS ROLL OF HONOUR.

Name	Rank	No.	Regiment	Honours	How Died
Mills, Archibald	Pte.	12923	7th K.O.Y.L.I.	—	K. in A.
Miller, Arthur	Rfm.	306885	2/8th W. Yorks.	—	K. in A.
Mills, Arthur	L/Cpl.	2297	W. Yorks.	—	Died
Mills, Frank	Pte.	38545	15th W. Yorks.	—	K. in A.
Mills, J. W.	Pte.	159148	18th Canadians	—	Died
Mills, James A.	Pte.	19107	K.O.Y.L.I.	—	Died
Mills, Joseph	Pte.	53192	Lincoln	—	Missing
Mills, Joseph	Pte.	266543	9th W. Yorks.	—	K. in A.
Mills, Samuel	2nd Lieut.		2nd K.O.Y.L.I.	—	K. in A.
Millson, Harry	Pte.	265771	W. Yorks.	—	K. in A.
Milne, Douglas H.	Captain		Cameron Highdrs.	—	K. in A.
Milner, Arthur	Pte.	195169	Labour Corps	—	Died
Milner, Arthur F.	L/Cpl.	26021	1st County of London	—	K. in A.
Milner, Harry	Rfm.	266650	1/7th W. Yorks.	—	K. in A.
Milner, Harry	Pte.	48617	K.O.Y.L.I.	—	Died
Milner, Henry	Cpl.	117151	Royal. Engineers	—	D. a. Dis.
Milner, J. W.	Sgt.	266328	York. & Lancs.	—	K. in A.
Milner, J. W.	S.W./1	116848	H.M.S. "Black Prince"	—	Died
Milner, John	L/Cpl.	15253	Yorks.	—	Missing
Milner, John Wm.	Pte.	1785	15th W. Yorks.	—	K. in A.
Milner, Robt. V.	Pte.	1284	Royal Marine Lt. Infty.	—	K. in A.
Milner, Samuel	Cpl.	J/38809	King's Royal Rifle Cps.	—	K. in A.
Milner, Wm.	Pte.	11025	Labour Corps...	—	Died
Milnes, Edmund	A.B.	1312	H.M.S. "Good Hope"	—	K. in A.
Milnes, Fredk.	Pte.	651	15th W. Yorks.	—	Missing
Milnes, H. A. E.	2nd Lieut.		New Zealand	—	K. in A.
Milnes, J.	A.B.	206965	H.M.S. "Hague"	—	K. in A.
Milnes, Willie	Rfm.	306920	2/8th W. Yorks.	—	K. in A.
Milton, John	Sgt.	27828	W. Yorks.	—	K. in A.
Minnithorpe, Chas. A.	Pte.	10587	9th W. Yorks.	—	K. in A.
Mirande, Ernest A.	Pte.	33900	Lincoln	—	K. in A.
Missett, James	Q.M.S.	6564	1st W. Yorks.	—	Died
Missitt, John Ed.	Pte.	7479	1st W. Yorks.	—	K. in A.
Mitchell, Arthur B.	L/Cpl.	39957	18th York. & Lancs.	—	D. of W.
Mitchell, Arthur R.	Pte.	62094	2/4th K.O.Y.L.I.	—	D. of W.
Mitchell, Chas. H.	2nd Lieut.		6th W. Yorks.	—	K. in A.
Mitchell, Dan.	Pte.	16547	Royal Scots Fusiliers	—	Died
Mitchell, Frank	Pte.	76975	W. Yorks.	—	Died
Mitchell, George	Pte.	38528	10th W. Yorks.	—	K. in A.
Mitchell, Harry	Pte.	18129	12th W. Yorks.	—	K. in A.
Mitchell, Herbert	Pte.	306417	9th W. Yorks.	—	K. in A.
Mitchell, Herbert	Pte.	3/7543	3rd W. Yorks.	—	K. in A.
Mitchell, Herbert	Pte.	24474	W. Yorks.	—	K. in A.
Mitchell, Horace	Stkr.	26493	H.M.S. "Glasgow"	—	Died
Mitchell, James S.	Bdr.	152279	R.F.A.	—	K. in A.
Mitchell, John	Pte.	51080	E. Yorks.	—	K. in A.
Mitchell, John Ed.	Pte.	32906	W. Yorks.	—	K. in A.

LEEDS ROLL OF HONOUR.

Name	Rank	No.	Regiment	Honours	How Died
Mitchell, Lawrence	Pte.	240695	1/5th Yorks.	—	D. of W.
Mitchell, Phillip	Pte.	326257	Royal Scots Fusiliers	—	K. in A.
Mitchell, Samuel	Pte.	102185	Machine Gun Corps	—	K. in A.
Mitchell, Thos.	Pte.	34175	W. Yorks.	—	Died P.O.W.
Mitchell, Wm.	Sgt.	12339	10th W. Yorks.	—	K. in A.
Mitchell, Wm. J.	Pte.	2001	K.O.Y.L.I.	—	K. in A.
Mitton, Arthur	Pte.	27851	W. Yorks.	—	K. in A.
Moate, R. A.	Gnr.	84059	R.G.A.	—	K. in A.
Moffat, Edward	Bdr.	930	Australian F.A.	—	Died
Moffitt, Edwin	Dvr.	218966	R.F.A.	—	Died
Moffitt, John E.	Pte.	10398	1st K.O.Y.L.I.	—	Died
Molan, John	Pte.	4760	2/5th K.O.Y.L.I.	—	K. in A.
Moll, R. I.	Gdsmn.	9696	Scots Guards	—	Died
Mollan, Robt. H.	Pte.	7719	2nd W. Riding	—	K. in A.
Mollitt, John Wm.	L/Cpl.	266631	1/7th W. Yorks.	—	K. in A.
Molloy, John	Pte.		Lincoln	—	Died
Molloy, John	Cpl.	265464	1/7th W. Yorks.	—	K. in A.
Monaghan, Thos.	Pte.	12889	K.O.Y.L.I.	—	Missing
Monaghan, Wm.	Pte.	25542	13th Yorks.	—	K. in A.
Money, Herbert	Pte.	11851	Yorks.	—	K. in A.
Mongan, Joseph	Pte.		R.A.M.C.	—	Died
Mongan, Wm.	Pte.	33552	2nd Yorks.	—	K. in A.
Monkman, Clifford D.	Rfm.	265568	1/7th W. Yorks.	—	K. in A.
Monteith, Fred G.	Pte.	366861	Northumberland Fusrs.	—	K. in A.
Montgomery, G. G.	A/Sgt.	306609	Canadian Air Force	—	Died
Moody, Albert	Rfm.	266364	3/8th W. Yorks.	—	K. in A.
Moody, John W.	Sgt.	11692	10th W. Yorks.	M.M.	K. in A.
Moody, Joseph S.	Pte.	19143	10th Yorks.	—	K. in A.
Moody, S.	Rfm.	203130	King's Royal Rifle Cps.	—	K. in A.
Moon, Thos.	L/Cpl.	31483	12th E. Yorks.	—	K. in A.
Moorby, James L.	Pte.	18061	10th W. Yorks.	—	K. in A.
Moorby, John Wm.	Pte.	14214	11th W. Yorks.	—	K. in A.
Moorby, Robt.	Pte.	1117	15th W. Yorks.	—	Missing
Moore, Albert	Pte.	50609	E. Yorks.	—	K. in A.
Moore, Alfred	Pte.	23491	E. Yorks.	—	K. in A.
Moore, Arnold	L/Cpl.	28293	7th E. Yorks.	—	K. in A.
Moore, Clifford	Pte.	1897	15th W. Yorks.	—	Missing
Moore, Fred	Pte.	8334	9th W. Yorks.	—	K. in A.
Moore, Furrell	Pte.	8901	Machine Gun Corps.	—	K. in A.
Moore, Geo. A.	Pte.	17783	Royal Dublin Fusrs.	—	Died
Moore, John Wm.	Sgt.	5896	10th King's R. Rifle Cps.	—	K. in A.
Moore, Percy	Pte.	7292	1/6th W. Yorks.	—	D. of W.
Moore, Reginald J.	Spr.	72122	Royal Engineers	—	Died
Moore, Vincent	Pte.	202671	W. Yorks.	—	K. in A.
Moore, Wm. H.	Pte.	12126	Dorset	—	D. a. Dis.
Moore, Wm. S.	L/Cpl.	10577	9th W. Yorks.	—	Missing
Moorhouse, Thos. Ed.	Sgt.	268	11th Middlesex	—	K. in A.

LEEDS ROLL OF HONOUR.

Name	Rank	No.	Regiment	Honours	How Died
Moorhouse, Walter	Captain		2nd W. Yorks.	—	K. in A.
Moran, Chas. F.	Pte.	10463	K.O.Y.L.I.	—	K. in A.
Moran, Edward	Pte.	40143	Royal Scots Fusiliers	—	D. of W.
Moran, Frank	Pte.	31190	1st E. Yorks.	—	K. in A.
Moran, James	Pte.	25904	W. Yorks.	—	Died
Moran, James	Rfm.	305137	1/8th W. Yorks.	—	K. in A.
Moran, John E.	Pte.	13762	10th W. Yorks.	—	Missing
Moran, John P.	Pte.	26841	W. Riding	—	Died
Moran, John W.	Pte.	1576	17th W. Yorks.	—	K. in A.
Moran, Patrick	A.B.	917	Royal Navy	—	K. in A.
Moran, Thos.	Spr.	213342	Royal Engineers	—	K. in A.
Morant, Norman	2nd Lieut.		2nd Yorks.	—	D. of W.
Morby, Wm. H.	Cpl.	6457	1st Leicester	—	K. in A.
Morcambe, Eddie	Pte.	38429	K.O.Y.L.I.	—	K. in A.
Morgan, Ambrose S.	Pte.	32584	8th York. & Lancs.	—	K. in A.
Morgan, Ernest	Pte.	10466	Royal W. Kent	—	Died
Morgan, Frank	Dvr.	282453	R.A.S.C.	—	Died
Morgan, Hubert	Pte.	20948	Dorset	—	K. in A.
Morgan, John	Pte.	64433	Northumberland Fusrs.	—	K. in A.
Morgan, John Wm.	Pte.	23166	Queen's Royal W. Surrey	—	K. in A.
Morgan, John Wm.	Pte.	375833	Durham Lt. Infantry	—	D. a. Dis.
Morgan, Lawrence	Pte.		W. Yorks.	—	Died
Morgan, Michael	Pte.	3972	W. Yorks.	—	Died
Morisoli, Edwin	2A.C.	284478	Royal Air Force	—	Died
Morley, A. E.	Pte.	44105	12th Durham Lt. Infty.	—	K. in A.
Morley, Alfred	Rfm.	268102	2/8th W. Yorks.	—	K. in A.
Morley, Austin	Pte.	14131	11th W. Yorks.	—	K. in A.
Morley, Chas.	Pte.	28433	S. Lancs.	—	K. in A.
Morley, Chas. Wm.	Pte.	17179	W. Yorks.	—	Died
Morley, Clifford	Pte.	8456	2nd W. Yorks.	—	K. in A.
Morley, Fred	Pte.	7816	1st W. Yorks.	—	K. in A.
Morley, Fredk. F.	Pte.	32995	15th W. Yorks.	—	Missing
Morley, J.	Pte.	69168	1/5th Northumb'l'd Fusrs.	—	Died
Morley, Lawrence	Pte.	13224	K.O.Y.L.I.	—	K. in A.
Morley, Robert	Pte.	140573	Machine Gun Corps	—	K. in A.
Morley, Stewart	Sig.	2788	1/8th W. Yorks.	—	K. in A.
Morley, Thos. Wm.	Dvr.	338980	Royal Engineers	—	Died
Morrell, Gilbert A.	Pte.	28620	R.A.M.C.	—	K. in A.
Morrell, Hardy	Pte.	1205	K.O.Y.L.I.	—	K. in A.
Morrell, James	Rfm.		1/8th W. Yorks.	—	K. in A.
Morrell, Tom	Pte.	195543	Labour Corps	—	K. in A.
Morris, Alfred	Pte.	526539	50th Canadn. M. Rifles	—	Died
Morris, Arthur	Pnr.	83733	Royal Engineers	—	K. in A.
Morris, Chas.	Pte.	3052	W. Yorks.	—	K. in A.
Morris, E.	A/Sgt.	40299	9th W. Yorks.	—	K. in A.
Morris, Edward	Pte.	37014	1st Northumb'l'd Fusrs.	—	K. in A.
Morris, George	Pte.	4907	Labour Corps	—	D. a. Dis.

LEEDS ROLL OF HONOUR.

Name	Rank	No.	Regiment	Honours	How Died
Morris, Harry	Pte.	106829	Notts & Derby	—	D. of W.
Morris, Henry	Dvr.	213373	R.A.S.C.	—	Died
Morris, James Wm.	Pte.	9738	2nd W. Riding	—	Died
Morris, John	Pte.	18941	9th K.O.Y.L.I.	—	K. in A.
Morris, Joseph	Pte.	36202	25th Northumb'l'd Fusrs.	—	Missing
Morris, Stanley B.	Gdsmn.	13969	3rd Grenadier Guards	—	K. in A.
Morris, Thos.	Pte.	117944	Royal Engineers	—	K. in A.
Morris, Wm. V.	Pte.	100063	11th Royal Fusiliers	—	D. of W.
Morrison, James	L/Cpl.	45935	12th W. Yorks.	—	K. in A.
Morrison, Thos. A.	Pte.	277955	7th Argy. & Suth. Highdrs.	—	K. in A.
Morrison, Wm. G.	Rfm.	62769	W. Yorks.	—	K. in A.
Morritt, Walter	Pte.	32852	16th W. Yorks.	—	Missing
Morritt, Wm.	Pte.	42013	7th E. Yorks.	—	K. in A.
Mortimer, Arthur	Pte.	202247	12th Highland Lt. Infty.	—	K. in A.
Mortimer, Edward	L/Cpl.	12184	Yorks.	—	K. in A.
Mortimer, Ernest S.	Spr.	279824	Royal Engineers	—	D. a. Dis.
Mortimer, Fred	Pte.	24345	W. Yorks.	—	D. of W.
Mortimer, Harry	Pte.	28076	1st W. Yorks.	—	K. in A.
Mortimer, John	Pte.	44894	R.A.M.C.	—	D. of W.
Mortimer, Percy	L/Cpl.	28833	K.O.Y.L.I.	—	Died
Mortimer, Wm.	Pte.	40184	15th W. Yorks.	—	D. of W.
Mortlock, Percy	A.B.	3822	Royal Naval Division	—	K. in A.
Morton, Chas.	Pte.	7970	4th W. Riding	—	K. in A.
Morton, Albert	Pte.	201423	1/4th Seaforth Highdrs.	—	D. of W.
Morton, Arthur	Pte.	20699	Yorks.	—	K. in A.
Morton, Arthur	Pte.	10640	10th W. Yorks.	—	K. in A.
Morton, Chas.	Pte.	235295	1/4th Yorks.	—	K. in A.
Morton, Harry	Pte.	8787	4th W. Yorks.	—	Died
Morton, Henry	Pte.	8650	K.O. Scottish Borderers	—	D. of W.
Morton, J. W.	Pte.	287641	Labour Corps	—	Died
Morton, James R.	Pte.	658	17th W. Yorks.	—	K. in A.
Morton, John	Pte.	22472	W. Yorks.	—	K. in A.
Morton, Sidney	Pte.	40830	16th Manchester	—	K. in A.
Morton, Thos.	Pte.	2652	W. Yorks.	—	Died
Morton, Wm.	2nd Lieut.		5th S. Staffs.	—	Died
Moscrop, Edwin	Pte.	52748	1st E. Yorks.	—	Died
Mosedale, James	Pte.	27891	9th Lancs. Fusiliers	—	K. in A.
Moses, Edward H.	Pte.	10729	4th W. Yorks.	—	K. in A.
Moses, George	L/Cpl.	30218	Inniskilling Fusiliers	—	Died
Moses, Harry	Pte.	40065	Royal Irish Fusiliers	—	Missing
Mosey, Richard	Pte.	56224	W. Yorks.	—	Died
Mosley, Ammon	Pte.	265213	W. Yorks.	—	K. in A.
Mosley, Geo. Wm.	Pte.	12919	6th K.O.Y.L.I.	—	K. in A.
Mosley, John	Pte.	19376	K.O.Y.L.I.	—	K. in A.
Mosley, John Wm.	Pte.	203788	1/5th W. Yorks.	—	K. in A.
Mosley, Raymond	Pte.	22729	Lancs. Fusiliers	—	K. in A.
Moss, A.	Pte.	55394	Northumberland Fusrs.	—	K. in A.

LEEDS ROLL OF HONOUR.

Name	Rank	No.	Regiment	Honours	How Died
Moss, Albert	Rfm.	265162	1/7th W. Yorks.	—	K. in A.
Moss, Amos	Pte.	34151	2nd W. Yorks.	—	K. in A.
Moss, G. James	Pte.	59725	Northumberland Fusrs.	—	K. in A.
Moss, Geo. Hy.	Pte.	8979	9th W. Yorks.	—	K. in A.
Moss, Harold	Pte.	11120	K.O.Y.L.I.	—	K. in A.
Moss, Hy. W.	O.S.	J84318	Royal Navy	—	Died
Moss, Herbert	Sgt.	305383	1/8th W. Yorks.	—	Died P.O.W.
Moss, Joe	Pte.	64156	W. Yorks.	—	K. in A.
Moss, Joe A.	Rfm.	3387	1/8th W. Yorks.	—	K. in A.
Moss, John C.	L/Cpl.	265208	W. Yorks.	D.C.M.	D. a. Dis.
Moss, R. Arthur	Cpl.	S/40364	R.A.S.C.	—	D. a. Dis.
Moss, Samuel	Pte.	265711	W. Yorks.	—	K. in A.
Moss, Tom	Cpl.	775785	R.F.A.	—	D. of W.
Moss, Thos. A.	Pte.	202112	2/4th Leicester	—	K. in A.
Mountain, Harry	L/Cpl.	28801	7th K.O.Y.L.I.	—	K. in A.
Mountain, Horace	Pte.	14695	1/7th Gordon Highdrs.	—	K. in A.
Mountain, John Wm.	L/Sgt.	24708	16th W. Yorks.	—	D. of W.
Mountain, Wm.	Dvr.	186599	R.F.A.	—	D. a. Dis.
Mower, John Wm.	Rfm.	39768	1/7th W. Yorks.	—	K. in A.
Mower, Robert	Pte.	56429	W. Yorks.	—	K. in A.
Moxon, Alfred	Pte.	201641	Seaforth Highlanders	—	Died
Moxon, Arthur	Pte.	357238	R.A.S.C.	—	Died
Moxon, John	Pte.	32585	York. & Lancs.	—	K. in A.
Mudd, Frank	Pte.	3485	18th W. Yorks.	—	K. in A.
Muff, John E.	L/Cpl.	8747	W. Yorks.	—	Died
Mugg, Clifford	Pte.	21903	Northumberland Fusrs.	—	K. in A.
Muir, Wm.	L/Cpl.	2416	7th Royal Highdrs.	—	K. in A.
Muir, Wm. A.	Cpl.	9864	Royal Irish	—	K. in A.
Muirhead, James	Pte.	100612	R.A.M.C.	—	K. in A.
Muldowney, James	Pte.	41890	Northumberland Fusrs.	—	K. in A.
Mulhern, James	Pte.	15585	Machine Gun Corps	—	Died
Mulholland, Wm. A.	L/Cpl.	201796	2/5th W. Yorks.	—	K. in A.
Mullaney, Francis	Pte.	1608	W. Yorks.	—	D. of W.
Mullarkey, Bernard	Cpl.	64136	R.F.A.	—	K. in A.
Mulley, Albert	Sgt.	41389	17th W. Yorks.	—	K. in A.
Mulligan, James	Pte.	27876	W. Yorks.	—	Died
Mullins, John	Pte.	7696	9th W. Yorks.	—	Missing
Mullins, John G.	Pte.	201705	2/5th W. Yorks.	—	K. in A.
Mullow, Alfred	Rfm.	3928	7th W. Yorks.	—	K. in A.
Mulvaney, Thos. J.	Sgt.	265343	1/7th W. Yorks.	—	Died
Mumby, Wm.	Sgt.	8138	W. Yorks.	—	K. in A.
Munro, Alexander	Pte.	31968	Durham Light Infantry	—	K. in A.
Munro, James	Pte.	117	17th W. Yorks.	—	D. of W.
Munro, R.	Rfm.	40159	King's Royal Rifle Cps.	—	K. in A.
Munton, Fred	Cpl.	366473	2/7th W. Yorks.	—	Missing
Murfitt, Albert	Pte.	20568	2nd K.O. Scottish Bords.	—	K. in A.
Murgatroyd, Alfred	Sgt.	8971	E. Yorks.	—	K. in A.

LEEDS ROLL OF HONOUR.

Name	Rank	No.	Regiment	Honours	How Died
Murphy, James	Pte.	75643	Machine Gun Corps	—	Died
Murphy, John	Pte.	34388	York. & Lancs.	—	Died
Murphy, John	Pte.	2949	Northumberland Fusrs.	—	K. in A.
Murphy, Patrick	Pte.	20787	Royal Dublin Fusiliers	—	K. in A.
Murphy, Thos.	Pte.	76584	R.A.M.C.	—	Died
Murphy, Wm. S.	Pte.	36883	10th W. Yorks.	—	K. in A.
Murray, Clifford	L/Cpl.	12312	1st K.O.Y.L.I.	—	Missing
Murray, Daniel	Condr.	3864	R.A.O.C.	—	K. in A.
Murray, Edmund	Sgt.	4870	Machine Gun Corps	—	K. in A.
Murray, Felix	L/Cpl.	13286	K.O.Y.L.I.	—	D. of W.
Murray, James	Pte.	27932	12th W. Yorks.	—	K. in A.
Murray, James	Cpl.	6365	Manchester	—	Died
Murray, Joseph	Rfm.	2042	1/7th W. Yorks.	—	D. a. Dis.
Murray, Thos.	Pte.	40270	Cameron Highlanders	—	K. in A.
Murray, Thos.	Pte.	16121	8th W. Riding	—	K. in A.
Murray, Wm...	Pte.	47349	Northumberland Fusrs.	—	Missing
Murray, Wm...	Pte.	20815	Northumberland Fusrs.	—	D. of W.
Musgrave, Arthur	Rfm.	306009	8th W. Yorks.	—	K. in A.
Musgrave, Ernest	Rfm.	4178	1/7th W. Yorks.	—	K. in A.
Musgrave, Geo. E.	Pte.	29042	Border	—	Died
Musgrave, John	Pte.	7435	R. Guernsey Lt. Infty.	—	Died
Musgrave, Joseph	Pte.	667	15th W. Yorks.	—	Missing
Musgrave, Jos. Wm...	Dvr.	35956	R.F.A.	—	K. in A.
Musgrave, Samuel	Pte.	7157	9th E. Yorks.	—	Missing
Musgrave, Wm.	Rfm.	265924	1/7th W. Yorks.	—	K. in A.
Musson, Reginald H.	Pte.	27750	King's Shropshire L.I.	—	K. in A.
Mustard, C. F. C.	Pte.	15838	8th Loyal N. Lancs.	—	Missing
Mutlow, Alfred H.	Rfm.	3928	2/7th W. Yorks.	—	Died
Mutter, Edward	Pte.	28240	10th E. Yorks.	—	D. of W.
Myco, Harry	Pte.	12771	10th W. Yorks.	—	K. in A.
Myers, David F.	C.S.M.	499	1/8th Yorks.	—	K. in A.
Myers, Fred	Pte.	37818	17th W. Yorks.	—	K. in A.
Myers, Harold	Pte.	29001	2nd W. Yorks.	—	Missing
Myers, John H.	Pte.	91255	Durham Light Infantry	—	K. in A.
Myers, Lawrence	Cpl.	1287	18th W. Yorks.	—	K. in A.
Myers, Samuel H.	Pte.	43924	14th Durham Lt. Infty.	—	K. in A.
Myers, Tom	Pte.	106017	Royal Air Force	—	K in A.
Myers, Thomas H.	Pte.	35187	W. Yorks.	—	Died
Myers, William	A.B.	28447	H.M.S. " Brooke "	—	Drowned
Myers, Wm. B.	Pte.	467	Royal Defence Corps	—	K. in A
Myland, John E.	Pnr.	298011	Royal Engineers	—	D. of W.
Naden, John	Pte.	702225	Labour Corps.	—	Died
Naiff, Alfred	Pte.	34928	W. Yorks.	—	Died
Naylor, Abraham	Pte.	29538	2nd W. Yorks.	—	K. in A.
Naylor, Albert	Pte.	3077	York. & Lancs.	—	K. in A.
Naylor, Arthur	Rfm.	4011	1/8th W. Yorks.	—	K. in A.

LEEDS ROLL OF HONOUR.

Name	Rank	No.	Regiment	Honours	How Died
Naylor, Arthur	Rfm.	40206	1/7th W. Yorks.	—	K. in A.
Naylor, B. M.	Pte.	26675	K.O.Y.L.I.	—	Died
Naylor, Chas...	L/Cpl.	25181	W. Yorks.	—	K. in A.
Naylor, Edward	Pte.	32349	3rd W. Yorks.	—	K. in A.
Naylor, Herbert	Pte.	36807	16th W. Yorks.	—	K. in A.
Naylor, Hiram	Pte.	21556	3rd York. & Lancs.	—	K. in A.
Naylor, James	Pnr.	273973	Royal Engineers	—	Died
Naylor, John	L/Cpl.	235538	W. Riding	—	Died
Naylor, John	Pte.	63318	K.O.Y.L.I.	—	K. in A.
Naylor, Joseph	Spr.	82765	Royal Engineers	—	Died
Naylor, Leonard	Pte.	28435	S. Lancs.	—	Died
Naylor, Merrit	Pte.	34510	10th W. Yorks.	—	K. in A.
Naylor, Reg...	Pte.	36772	16th W. Yorks.	—	D. of W.
Naylor, Robt. C.	Pte.	861	R.A.M.C.	—	D. a. Dis.
Naylor, Samuel	Pte.	129640	Royal Engineers	—	K. in A.
Naylor, Wilfred	A/LCpl.	14373	Military Foot Police	—	Died
Naylor, Wilfred	Gnr.	73125	R.F.A.	—	K. in A.
Naylor, Wm.	Pte.	41023	7th K.O.Y.L.I.	—	K. in A.
Neal, Thos.	Pte.	268260	1/5th W. Yorks.	—	K. in A.
Neal, Thos. A.	Pte.	24985	E. Yorks.	—	K. in A.
Neal, Walter	L/Cpl.	835	R.A.S.C.	—	D. of W.
Neary, Patrick	Rfm.	41599	1/7th W. Yorks.	—	Died
Needham, Christopher	1Stkr.	K27007	H.M.S. " Flirt "	—	Drowned
Needham, Ernest	Bglr.	22614	K.O.Y.L.I.	—	Died
Neep, Walter S.	Pte.	46220	13th York. & Lancs.	—	K. in A.
Neil, S. T. A.	Captain		15th W. Yorks.	—	K. in A.
Neild, Cyril	Rfm.	305982	2/8th W. Yorks.	—	Died P.O.W.
Nelsey, Fred	Sig.	36638	1/5th Essex	—	K. in A.
Nelsey, Herbert	Pte.	25312	15th W. Yorks.	—	Missing
Nelsey, Louis	Pte.	3943	4th Cameron Highdrs.	—	K. in A.
Nelson, Arthur L.	A/Sgt.	1083	15th W. Yorks.	—	Died
Nelson, Frank M.	O.L.	TZ11676	Royal Naval V. Res.	—	Died
Nelson, John	Rfm.	1724	7th W. Yorks.	—	Died
Nelson, Wm.	Cpl.		Canadian Lt. Infantry	—	D. of W.
Nettleton, Arnold	Pte.	15456	9th W. Yorks.	—	K. in A.
Nettleton, Arthur	Rfm.	1495	7th W. Yorks.	—	K. in A.
Nettleton, Arthur	L/Cpl.	265055	1/7th W. Yorks.	—	K. in A.
Nettleton, Harold	Pte.	15456	9th W. Yorks.	—	K. in A.
Nettleton, Harry	Pte.	20218	2/4th Leicester	—	K. in A.
Nettleton, Joe	Pte.	203414	Cameron Highlanders	—	K. in A.
Neville, Jas. W.	Pte.	5782	1st Royal Dragoons	—	Died
Nevins, John	Pte.	201866	W. Yorks.	—	Died
Newall, John T.	Pte.	35518	K.O.Y.L.I.	—	K. in A.
Newbould, John	Dvr.	1098	R.F.A.	—	K. in A.
Newboult, B.	Pte.	18892	W. Riding	—	Died
Newby, Osborne	Pte.	22053	Durham Lt. Infantry	—	K. in A.
Newell, Banks	Sgt.	776881	R.F.A.	—	Died

LEEDS ROLL OF HONOUR.

Name	Rank	No.	Regiment	Honours	How Died
Newell, Edmund	Pte.	1909	K.O.Y.L.I.	—	K. in A.
Newell, Sam	L/Cpl.	680	15th W. Yorks.	—	D. of W.
Newham, P.	Pte.	51664	Lincoln	—	K. in A.
Newing, John	A/Cpl.	12863	2/8th W. Yorks.	—	K. in A.
Newing, Jonathan	Pte.	9480	3rd W. Yorks.	—	K. in A.
Newland, Louis		J19324	H.M.S. " Queen Mary "	—	K. in A.
Newlove, Chas.	Pte.	12936	6th K.O.Y.L.I.	—	K. in A.
Newman, Ernest	Pte.	21065	Grenadier Guards	—	K. in A.
Newman, George	Pte.	40534	15th W. Yorks.	—	Missing
Newman, Wm.	Pte.	11094	K.O.Y.L.I.	—	Died
Newsome, Arthur	Pte.	1222	2nd Welsh	—	K. in A.
Newsome, Arthur	Pte.	282163	10/11th Highland L.I.	—	K. in A.
Newsome, Clifford	Pte.	2945	Machine Gun Corps	—	Died
Newsome, Clifford W.	2nd Lieut.		Royal Fusiliers	—	K. in A.
Newsome, Frank	Pte.	19900	Cheshire	—	K. in A.
Newsome, Friend	Pte.	36748	3rd W. Yorks.	—	Died
Newsome, Geo. A.	Sgt.	34941	R.F.A.	—	K. in A.
Newsome, H.	Pte.	350985	Durham Light Infantry	—	Missing
Newsome, Harry	Pte.	651	W. Yorks.	—	K. in A.
Newsome, Horace	Pte.	42614	9th N. Staffs.	—	K. in A.
Newsome, J. W.	Dvr.	775634	R.F.A.	—	D. of W.
Newsome, James W.	Pte.	23754	9th Yorks.	—	K. in A.
Newsome, John W. L.	Cpl.	606245	Royal Engineers	—	Died
Newton, Albert	Pte.	32185	2nd W. Yorks.	—	Missing
Newton, Charles	Pte.	6494	1st Scots Guards	—	D. P.O.W.
Newton, Charles	Pte.	49769	1st W. Yorks.	—	K. in A.
Newton, Clifford	Pte.	202765	1/5th W. Yorks.	—	K. in A.
Newton, G. W.	Pte.	42807	9th Manchester	—	Died
Newton, George	L/Cpl.	18223	4th W. Yorks.	—	K. in A.
Newton, George W.	L/Cpl.		W. Yorks.	—	Died
Newton, James	Pte.	36849	W. Yorks.	—	K. in A.
Newton, James	Pte.	39766	4th W. Yorks.	—	K. in A.
Newton, T.	Pte.	8345	Royal Defence Corps	—	Died
Newton, Thomas	Pte.	1906	W. Yorks.	—	Missing
Newton, William	Pte.	546127	R.A.M.C.	—	Died
Nichol, John G.	Pte.	38937	Northumberland Fusrs.	—	K. in A.
Nicholls, Herbert A.	L/Cpl.	24202	A.P.C.	—	Died
Nicholls, Thomas	Pte.	120	17th W. Yorks.	—	Died
Nicholls, W.	Rfm.	4558	3/7th W. Yorks.	—	Died
Nichols, Edwin	Pte.	37220	K.O.Y.L.I.	—	K. in A.
Nichols, Fred	Pte.	471	17th W. Yorks.	—	K. in A.
Nichols, Harold	Gnr.	41315	R.F.A.	—	K. in A.
Nicholls, Harry	Pte.	34298	K.O.Y.L.I.	—	K. in A.
Nichols, Robert E.	Pte.	43170	10th W. Yorks.	—	K. in A.
Nichols, Thomas	A/Sgt.	12872	7th K.O.Y.L.I.	—	K. in A.
Nichols, Thomas W.	Rfm.	2893	1/8th W. Yorks.	—	D. of W.
Nichols, William	Pte.	54884	W. Yorks.	—	K. in A.

LEEDS ROLL OF HONOUR.

Name	Rank	No.	Regiment	Honours	How Died
Nichols, Wm. E.	Rfm.	4615	1/8th W. Yorks.	—	K. in A.
Nicholson, Alfred	Pte.	311776	W. Yorks.	—	Died
Nicholson, Edward	Rfm.	305096	1/8th W. Yorks.	M.M.	Died
Nicholson, Edwin A.	Pte.	60850	2nd W. Yorks.	—	K. in A.
Nicholson, George	Pte.				
Nicholson, George H.	Pte.	9516	Lincoln	—	Died
Nicholson, Harry	Pte.	291835	1/7th Northumb'l'd Fus.	—	K. in A.
Nicholson, Harry M.	L/Cpl.	407010	R.A.M.C.	—	Died
Nicholson, Herman	Pte.	60164	16th Royal W. Fusrs.	—	K. in A.
Nicholson, James	Pte.	45142	11th Lancs. Fusiliers	—	Missing
Nicholson, Joseph	Pte.	12730	W. Yorks.	—	K. in A.
Nicholson, Richard	Pte.	6046	2nd W. Riding	—	D. P.O.W.
Nicholson, Richard J.	A/Cpl.	100	Canadian Grenadiers	—	Died
Nicholson, Robert	1/A.C.	238590	Royal Naval Air Service	—	Died
Nicholson, Thomas	Cpl.	60714	Northumberland Fusrs.	—	K. in A.
Nicholson, W.	Pte.	235246	2/5th Gloucesters.	—	K. in A.
Nicholson, Walter	Rfm.	306200	2/8th W. Yorks.	—	K. in A.
Nicholson, Wilfred N.	Pte.	60860	W. Yorks.	—	K. in A.
Nicholson, William	Pte.	9676	W. Yorks.	—	K. in A.
Nicholson, William	Pte.	403456	R.A.M.C.	—	Died
Nickolson, Ed. P.	Pte.	51835	K.O.Y.L.I.	—	Died
Nickolson, George	Pte.	19136	Border	—	K. in A.
Nickson, G. S.	Pte.	268532	W. Yorks.	—	K. in A.
Nield, Thomas	Pte.	40706	12th Royal Scots	—	K. in A.
Nixon, George	Pte.	242428	6th W. Yorks.	—	Missing
Noble, Albert	Rfm.	4495	W. Yorks.	—	Died
Noble, Alfred	Pte.	3777	Northumberland Fusrs.	—	K. in A.
Noble, Arthur	Gnr.	5762	R.F.A.	—	K. in A.
Noble, Frank I.	Rfm.	306314	3/8th W. Yorks.	—	K. in A.
Noble, Fred	Pte.	19929	K.O.Y.L.I.	—	Died
Noble, Herbert	Sgt.	775698	R.F.A.	—	K. in A.
Noble, J. W.	Pte.	268254	11th R. Warwick	—	K. in A.
Noble, James	Pte.	23288	13th Durham Lt. Infty.	—	K. in A.
Noble, Jesse	Pte.	63624	21st W. Yorks.	—	K. in A.
Noble, Percy H.	L/Sgt.	305184	W. Yorks.	—	K. in A.
Noble, Sam	Pte.	52249	Durham Light Infantry	—	K. in A.
Nolan, Francis	Pte.	7298	1/6th W. Yorks.	—	K. in A.
Nolan, Frank	Pte.	27321	Labour Corps	—	Died
Nolan, John	Pte.	4760	2/5th K.O.Y.L.I.	—	Acc. Killed.
Nolan, Peter F.	Gnr.	127173	R.F.A.	—	D. of W.
Nolan, Tom	Pte.	275572	Royal Engineers	—	Died
Noon, Thomas	Pte.	1491	W. Yorks.	—	Died
Norman, G. B.	Spr.	224547	Royal Engineers	—	K. in A.
Norman, R.	Pte.	24119	2nd Yorks.	—	K. in A.
Norman, Saml. W.	Gnr.	2554	R.F.A.	—	D. of W.
Normington, Arthur	Pte.	1374	18th W. Yorks.	—	Died
North, Curtis	Pte.	25249	W. Yorks.	—	K. in A.

LEEDS ROLL OF HONOUR.

Name	Rank	No.	Regiment	Honours	How Died
North, George	Dvr.	795843	R.F.A.	—	K. in A.
North, Harold	Pte.	306745	1/6th W. Yorks.	—	K. in A.
North, J. W.	Flt/Sgt.	14475	Royal Air Force	—	Died
North, James	Pte.	38900	Northumberland Fusrs.	—	K. in A.
North, James D. M.	A.B.	J38818	H.M.S. " Queen Mary "	—	Drowned
North, John A.	Pte.	224270	R.A.S.C.	—	Died
North, Joseph	Pte.	201741	Seaforth Highlanders	—	K. in A.
North, Robert	Rfm.	267326	1/7th W. Yorks.	—	K. in A.
Northard, George	Gnr.	103921	R.G.A.	—	K. in A.
Northfield, E.	Pte.	15730	9th W. Yorks.	—	K. in A.
Norton, Frank H.	Gnr.	348604	R.G.A.	—	K. in A.
Norton, Harry	Rfm.	6753	Rifle Brigade	—	D. of W.
Norton, Fredk.	Rfm.	300013	1/8th W. Yorks.	—	Missing
Norton, James A.	Rfm.	267071	2/7th W. Yorks.	—	K. in A.
Norton, William	L/Cpl.	3542	K.O.Y.L.I.	—	K. in A.
Nossiter, Chas. E.	Pte.	33907	K.O.Y.L.I.	—	K. in A.
Nott, Bernard T.	Rfm.	2062	1/8th W. Yorks.	—	K. in A.
Nott, Fred	L/Cpl.	21927	Yorks.	—	Drowned
Nottingham, Benj.	Pte.	10359	2nd W. Yorks.	—	K. in A.
Nowell, Walter	Rfm.	3453	1/7th W. Yorks.	—	D. of W.
Nowland, Ernest	Rfm.	307606	1/8th W. Yorks.	—	K. in A.
Nowland, Fred	Stkr.	K26357	H.M.S. " Hampshire "	—	K. in A.
Nowland, George	Cpl.	1353	17th W. Yorks.	—	K. in A.
Nowland, Henry	Pte.	10900	Royal Defence Corps	—	Died
Nowland, Lewis	A.B.	J19324	H.M.S. " Queen Mary "	—	Drowned
Nowland, Walter	Cpl.	10473	K.O.Y.L.I.	—	Died
Nowland, W.	Pte.	40247	18th W. Yorks.	—	K. in A.
Noyland, E.	Pte.	28537	E. Yorks.	—	K. in A.
Nugent, George	Pte.	1306	Northumberland Fusrs.	—	K. in A.
Nunns, —	—	8238	Yorks. Hussars	—	K. in A.
Nunns, Sam	Spr.	83692	Royal Engineers	—	K. in A.
Nunns, W. N.	Pte.	14338	Border	—	K. in A.
Nunwick, E. A.	Rfm.	307381	1/8th W. Yorks.	—	Died
Nussey, John	Cpl.	44455	Northumberland Fusrs.	—	K. in A.
Nuttall, Clifford	Rfm.	265751	2/7th W. Yorks.	—	K. in A.
Nuttall, L.	Pte.	52857	W. Yorks.	—	K. in A.
Nutter, Albert	Pte.	34846	Royal Scots Fusiliers	—	Died
Nutter, W.	Cpl.	13380	Dorset	—	K. in A.
Nyman, Harry	Pte.	10975	W. Yorks.	—	K. in A.
Oakes, Frank	Pte.	26335	W. Yorks.	—	Died
Oakes, J. A.	Pte.	235139	2/6th Warwick	—	Died
Oakes, Robert	Pte.	10646	W. Riding	—	Died
Oakley, Chas. E.	Rfm.	265558	7th W. Yorks.	—	Missing
Oates, Albert	Pte.	16780	York. & Lancs.	—	Died
Oates, Arthur	Pte.	12160	10th W. Yorks.	—	Died
Oates, George A.	Pte.	8670	W. Yorks.	—	Died
Oates, Harold	Gnr.	775080	R.F.A.	—	K. in A.

LEEDS ROLL OF HONOUR.

Name	Rank	No.	Regiment	Honours	How Died
Oates, Harry B.	Pte.	93668	Royal Welsh Fusiliers	—	K. in A.
Oates, Herbert	Rfm.	41136	11th W. Yorks.	—	K. in A.
Oates, James H.	Pte.	13634	K.O.Y.L.I.	—	K. in A.
Oates, Joseph	Pte.	162952	R.A.S.C.	—	Died
O'Brien, Chas.	1/A.M.	92120	Royal Air Force	—	Died
O'Brien, Fred M.	Pte.	41400	17th W. Yorks.	—	K. in A.
O'Brien, John T.	Pte.		W. Yorks.	—	Died
O'Brien, Michael	Rfm.	596	Royal Irish Fusiliers	—	Died
O'Brien, T.	Pte.	36921	Training Reserve	—	Died
O'Boyle, Peter	Sgt.	9402	W. Yorks.	—	K. in A.
Ockleton, James	Pte.	17402	Coldstream Guards	—	K. in A.
Ockleton, Robert	Pte.	34264	Northumberland Fusrs.	—	K. in A.
O'Connor, Terence	A/Sgt.	9981	Machine Gun Corps	—	Died
O'Connor, Thomas	Rfm.	306129	1/8th W. Yorks.	—	K. in A.
Oddis, Charles	Pte.	267282	W. Yorks.	—	K. in A.
Oddy, Banj.	L/Cpl.	3161	1/5th W. Yorks.	—	K. in A.
Oddy, Charles	Pte.	43200	4th Durham Lt. Infty.	—	Missing
Oddy, Ernest	Rfm.	305887	2/8th W. Yorks.	—	K. in A.
Oddy, H. L.	L/Cpl.	21518	Highland Light Infantry	—	K. in A.
Oddy, Herbert	L/Cpl.	10695	K.O. Royal Lancs.	—	K. in A.
Oddy, Herbert	Pte.	49276	1st W. Yorks.	—	K. in A.
Oddy, Walter	Pte.	33941	W. Yorks.	—	K. in A.
Oddy, William	Pnr.	167365	Royal Engineers	—	K. in A.
Odell, Alfred F.	Pte.	2547	5th Northumb'l'd Fusrs.	—	K. in A.
Odgers, Hugh P.	Sgt.	691	15th W. Yorks.	—	K. in A.
O'Donnell, James	Pte.	265282	W. Yorks.	—	K. in A.
O'Donnell, James	Pte.	358980	Labour Corps	—	Died
O'Donnell, Samuel	Pte.	10357	12th W. Yorks.	—	K. in A.
O'Donnell, William	Pte.	7647	K.O. Scottish Bordrs.	—	K. in A.
Ogden, Harry	Pte.	23279	K.O. Scottish Bordrs.	—	K. in A.
Ogden, J. W.	Sgt.	265766	2/7th Yorks.	—	Died
Ogilvie, John	Cpl.	20984	3rd E. Yorks.	—	K. in A.
Ogle, Henry	Spr.	83606	Royal Engineers	—	Missing
Ogone, Peter	Pte.	39034	2/5th W. Yorks.	—	K. in A.
O'Grady, Daniel	Pte.	5059	W. Yorks.	—	D. of W.
O'Grady, Thomas	L/Cpl.	24986	15th W. Yorks.	—	D. of W.
O'Grady, William	Pte.	20609	5th W. Yorks.	—	Died
Oldridge, William	L/Bdr.	796236	R.F.A.	—	K. in A.
Oldroyd, William	Pte.	97797	Machine Gun Corps	—	Missing
Oliver, Edward	Rfm.	4753	1/7th W. Yorks.	—	Missing.
Oliver, Ernest	Cpl.	265193	8th W. Yorks.	—	Died .
Oliver, Harry	Pte.	9605	2nd W. Riding	—	Died
Oliver, Walter	L/Cpl.	201243	1/4th Seaforth Highdrs.	—	K. in A.
Olley, Clare	Pte.	21039	W. Yorks.	—	K. in A.
Ombler, James P.	Gnr.	186275	R.F.A.	—	Died
O'Neill, William	Pte.		W. Yorks.	—	Died
O'Neill, John	Pte.	267002	2nd W. Yorks.	—	K. in A.

LEEDS ROLL OF HONOUR.

Name	Rank	No.	Regiment	Honours	How Died
O'Neill, John H.	Stkr.	K19431	H.M.S. " Queen Mary "	—	Drowned
O'Neill, Joseph	Pte.	72134	Training Reserve	—	Died
O'Neill, Patrick	Pte.	32095	15th W. Yorks.	—	K. in A.
O'Neill, Wm.	Spr.	200281	Royal Engineers	—	K. in A.
Onions, James W.	Pte.	305475	11th W. Yorks.	—	Died
Oram, Regd. J.	Sgt.	128331	R.A.S.C.	—	Died
Orange, James E.	Pte.	40680	K.O.Y.L.I.	—	K. in A.
Ord, George	Dvr.	770696	R.F.A.	—	K. in A.
Orgill, Thomas	Pte.	23600	Yorkshire	—	K. in A.
O'Rourke, John	Pte.	14623	Machine Gun Corps	—	Died
Orpin, Wm. J.	Pte.	34188	9th W. Yorks.	—	Missing
Orton, Sidney	Pte.	075697	R.A.S.C. (M.T.)	—	Died
Osborne, Henry	Sgt.	270012	1/7th W. Yorks.	—	Died
Osborne, Isaac	Sgt.	997	R.G.A.	—	K. in A.
O'Shoughnessy, Alfd.	Rfm.	1412	1/8th W. Yorks.	—	Died
Ossett, Harry	Pte.	30808	2/4th E. Lancs.	—	K. in A.
Ostcliffe, Harry	L/Cpl.	11761	1st Liverpool	—	K. in A.
Ostler, Ernest	L/Cpl.	44160	Machine Gun Corps	—	K. in A.
O'Sullivan, Daniel	Pte.	351179	22nd Durham Lt. Infty.	—	K. in A.
Othick, Harry	Bdr.	96262	R.F.A.	—	Died
Ott, Will. F.	Cpl.	39928	11th Cheshire	—	K. in A.
Otter, Joseph K.	Pte.	5770	City of London	—	K. in A.
Oughtbridge, Robt.	F. Cad.	110656	Royal Air Force	—	Died
Outram, Chas. R.	Pte.	24944	1st Highland Lt. Infty.	—	K. in A.
Overend, W.	Pte.	376369	Durham Lt. Infantry	—	Died
Overton, Wm.	L/Cpl.	343	W. Yorks.	—	Died
Owbridge	Bdr.	4126	R.F.A.	—	Acc. Killed
Owen, Alfred	Pte.	13560	10th K.O.Y.L.I.	—	K. in A.
Owen, Frank	Pte.		W. Yorks.	—	Died
Owen, Francis	Pte.	795975	R.F.A.	—	K. in A.
Owen, Harry	Pte.	67654	Machine Gun Corps	—	K. in A.
Owram, James H.	Gnr.	50191	R.G.A.	—	K. in A.
Oxley, Gilbert	E.R.A.2/	271718	Sub. " D " 6 H.M.S. " Vulcan "	—	Died
Oxley, Ormond	Pte.	7868	3rd W. Yorks.	—	K. in A.
Oxley, Samuel	L/Cpl.	8268	3rd Yorks.	—	K. in A.
Oxley, Stanley	Pte.	19978	15th Cheshire	—	Died
Oxley, Walter	Pte.	37673	3rd W. Yorks.	—	K. in A.
Pacey, Chas. F.	Pte.	24764	13th Cheshire	—	K. in A.
Packer, Leonard	Rfm.	12082	King's Royal Rifle Cps.	—	K. in A.
Padden, —		6875	1st W. Yorks.	—	K. in A.
Paddison, John Wm.	Spr.	189362	Royal Engineers	—	Died
Padgett, Horace	Pte.	306355	W. Yorks.	—	K. in A.
Padgett, Horace	Pte.	16680	2nd K.O. Scottish Brdrs.	—	Died
Padgett, Oliver	Pte.	1899	S. Wales Borderers	—	K. in A.
Padley, Herbert	Rfm.	3367	1/7th W. Yorks.	—	Died

LEEDS ROLL OF HONOUR.

Name	Rank	No.	Regiment	Honours	How Died
Page, Frank	Pte.	56511	10th W. Yorks.	—	K. in A.
Page, H.	Rfm.	A204573	King's Royal Rifle Cps.	—	K. in A.
Page, Hubert	A.B.	6040	Royal Naval V. Res.	—	Missing
Page, Wilfred	Pte.	31984	15th W. Yorks.	—	Missing
Page, William	L/Cpl.	22007	K.O. Scottish Bordrs.	—	Died
Paget, Fredk. R.	Pte.	1522	12th E. Yorks.	—	K. in A.
Pakenham, Chas. R.	Sgt.	41714	3rd Toronto	—	K. in A.
Paley, H. L.	Pte.	7636	1/13th Kensington	—	K. in A.
Paley, Lawrence	Pte.		W. Yorks.	—	K. in A.
Paley, Rowland	2/A.M.	63156	Royal Air Force	—	Died
Paley, Walter	Pte.			—	K. in A.
Palliser, Harold L.	P.O. 1st Cls.		H.M.S. "Intrepid"	—	K. in A.
Pallister, Harry	Pte.	306942	W. Yorks.	—	K. in A.
Palmer, Albert	Pte.	17755	8th K.O. Scottish Brdrs.	—	K. in A.
Palmer, Harold	Pte.	8186	11th W. Yks.	—	K. in A.
Palmer, John H.	Spr.	180150	Royal Engineers	—	K. in A.
Palmer, John Wm.	Pte.	1584	16th W. Yorks.	—	K. in A.
Pankhurst, Horace	Rfm.	4272	3/8th W. Yorks.	—	D. of W.
Pankhurst, Leonard	Pte.	16512	10th W. Riding	—	D. a. Dis.
Pannett, Arthur	Pte.	1428	W. Yorks.	—	K. in A.
Pannett, Arthur	Pte.	1361	15th W. Yorks.	—	Missing
Panther, Horace	Pte.	1115	15th W. Yorks.	—	Missing
Pape, Chas. B.	Pte.	60847	W. Yorks.	—	Died
Pape, James	Pte.		15th W. Yorks.	—	K. in A.
Pape, John W.	Cpl.	13847	Royal Engineers	—	K. in A.
Parish, Fred			2/9th Manchester	—	K. in A.
Park, Richard	Pte.	350710	R.A.S.C.	—	Died
Parker, A. L.	Pte.	32399	15th W. Yorks.	—	D. of W.
Parker, Albert	A.B.	771	Royal Navy	—	Died
Parker, Albert E.	Pte.	33264	2nd W. Yorks.	—	K. in A.
Parker, Arthur	Cpl.	82337	R.F.A.	—	K. in A.
Parker, Arthur	Cpl.	21354	Northumberland Fusrs.	—	K. in A.
Parker, Arthur	Cpl.	266461	1/7th W. Yorks.	—	K. in A.
Parker, Arthur Y.	Pte.	21218	12th W. Yorks.	—	K. in A.
Parker, Chas. A.	Pte.	25837	W. Yorks.	—	K. in A.
Parker, Clifford	Sgt.	101798	29th Durham Lt. Infty.	—	K. in A.
Parker, Elijah	Pte.	53038	W. Yorks.	—	K. in A.
Parker, Frank	Pte.	29016	11th W. Yorks.	—	Died
Parker, Fred	L/Sgt.	740	R.A.S.C.	—	Died
Parker, George	Trmr.	85 TS	H.M.S. "Jasper"	—	Missing
Parker, George	L/Cpl.	20733	2nd Yorks.	—	K. in A.
Parker, George	Gnr.	11418	R.F.A.	—	Died
Parker, Harold G.	Pte.	1456	17th W. Yorks.	—	K. in A.
Parker, Harry	Pte.	401447	R.A.M.C.	—	Died
Parker, Harry	Pte.	15142	6th Yorks.	—	K. in A.
Parker, Harry	Pte.	40022	9th Royal Irish Fusrs.	—	K. in A.
Parker, Henry	Pte.	563812	Labour Corps	—	D. a. Dis.

LEEDS ROLL OF HONOUR.

Name	Rank	No.	Regiment	Honours	How Died
Parker, Joseph	Rfm.	244	1/8th W. Yorks.	—	K. in A.
Parker, J.	Pte.	12142	W. Yorks.	—	K. in A.
Parker, J. B.	Sgt.	18257	13th Gloucesters.	—	K. in A.
Parker, J. Stanley	Lieut.		1/7th W. Yorks.	—	K. in A.
Parker, James E.	Sgt.	31363	R.F.A.	—	K. in A.
Parker, John	Pte.	29959	E. Yorks.	—	K. in A.
Parker, John	L/Cpl.	24827	9th W. Yorks.	—	K. in A.
Parker, John A.	Pte.	9034	3rd W. Yorks.	—	K. in A.
Parker, John W.	2nd Lieut.		1/5th W. Yorks.	M.C.	K. in A.
Parker, Leonard	Spr.	502744	Royal Engineers	—	Died
Parker, Robert	Rfm.	266492	1/7th W. Yorks.	—	D. a. Dis.
Parker, Tom	Pte.	33933	25th Northumb'l'd Fus.	—	D. of W.
Parker, William	Pte.	34667	Lancaster	—	K. in A.
Parker, William	Gnr.	64539	R.F.A.	—	D. of W.
Parker, Wm. B.	Pte.	25732	15th W. Yorks.	—	Missing
Parkin, Charles	Pte.	42045	W. Yorks.	—	D. of W.
Parkin, Fred	Rfm.	12708	21st King's R. Rifle Cps.	—	K. in A.
Parkin, George E.	Pte.	48688	W. Yorks.	—	K. in A.
Parkin, Harry	Rfm.	300075	1/7th W. Yorks.	—	Died
Parkin, Jim A.	Pte.	26726	Lincoln	—	Died
Parkin, John	Dvr.	320	17th W. Yorks.	—	K. in A.
Parkin, Sam A.	Pte.	40256	18th W. Yorks.	—	Died
Parkin, William	Pte.	1624	15th W. Yorks.	—	Missing
Parkin, William	Pte.	41000	Norfolk	—	K. in A.
Parkinson, Charles	Pte.	202449	Highland Light Infty.	—	Died
Parkinson, Ernest	L/Cpl.	307613	2/7th W. Riding	—	Missing
Parkinson, J.	Pte.	65744	Northumberland Fusrs.	—	K. in A.
Parkinson, James	Pte.	19125	9th W. Yorks.	—	Missing
Parkinson, Leonard	Pte.	58813	Machine Gun Corps	—	K. in A.
Parkinson, Matthew	Pte.	10734	K.O.Y.L.I.	—	K. in A.
Parkinson, Norman	Pte.	15098	Royal Fusiliers	—	D. a. Dis.
Parkinson, Robert	Rfm.	265642	7th W. Yorks.	—	K. in A.
Parnell, W. E.	Pte.	204700	Royal Scots Fusiliers	—	K. in A.
Parr, Fred	Pte.	3507	W. Yorks.	—	K. in A.
Parrott, Alfred	Pte.	43041	Seaforth Highdrs.	—	Missing
Parrott, Fredk.	Pte.	3961	8th Northumb'l'd Fus.	—	K. in A.
Parrott, Thomas	Pte.	8190	Yorks.	—	D. a. Dis.
Parrott, William	Pte.	52176	Middlesex	—	Died
Parry, Edward	Pte.	306008	1/6th W. Yorks.	—	Missing
Parry, W.	Pte.	10723	W. Yorks.	—	K. in A.
Parsons, A.	Cpl.	598	K.O.Y.L.I.	—	Died
Parsons, Ben W.	Pte.	111872	R.A.S.C.	—	D. a. Dis.
Parsons, Herbert	2nd Lieut.		14th Royal Scots	—	K. in A.
Parsons, Walter	Pte.	19545	Gordon Highlanders	—	K. in A.
Partridge, Ernest	Pte.	160	21st W. Yorks.	—	K. in A.
Partridge, Henry	Rfm.	1846	1/8th W. Yorks.	—	K. in A.
Pashley, Edgar	Pnr.	83708	Royal Engineers	—	Died

LEEDS ROLL OF HONOUR.

Name	Rank	No.	Regiment	Honours	How Died
Patchett, Ed. S.	Pte.	157467	Royal Air Force	—	D. a. Dis.
Pateman, J.	C.S.M.	066299	R.A.S.C.	—	K. in A.
Paterson, George	C.Q.M.S.	30517	W. Yorks.	—	K. in A.
Patrick, Fred	A.B.	TZ11598	Royal Naval V. Reserve	—	Died
Patrick, Fred	Sgt.	1020	W. Yorks.	—	Died
Patrick, G.	Cpl.	13178	W. Yorks.	—	K. in A.
Patrick, Samuel P.	Pte.		Royal Marine Lt. Infty.	—	K. in A.
Patterson, T. G.	Pte.	103140	Machine Gun Corps	—	K. in A.
Pattinson, Albert	Pte.	22402	Northumberland Fusrs.	—	K. in A.
Pattinson, Chas.	C.S.M.	6090	W. Yorks.	—	K. in A.
Pattinson, Robt.	Rfm.	306468	W. Yorks.	—	Died
Pattison, Albert	Pte.	194984	Labour Corps	—	Died
Pattison, J. G.	Pte.	880	21st W. Yorks.	—	Died
Pattison, Harry	Spr.	23480	Royal Engineers	—	K. in A.
Pattison, Thomas W.	L/Cpl.	265153	1/7th W. Yorks.	—	K. in A.
Paul, Alfred	Pte.	708	15th W. Yorks.	—	D. of W.
Paul, Thomas	Pte.	1757	15th W. Yorks.	—	K. in A.
Paul, Walter	Pte.	13580	9th K.O.Y.L.I.	—	K. in A.
Pawson, Arthur	Pte.	10359	9th W. Yorks.	—	K. in A.
Pawson, Benj.	Rfm.	25394	1/7th W. Yorks.	—	Died
Pawson, Edward	Pte.	31095	E. Yorks.	—	Died
Pawson, George W.	Gnr.	111229	R.F.A.	—	D. of W.
Pawson, Harry	Rfm.	201496	13th Rifle Brigade	—	Missing
Pawson, Percival	A/Sgt.	266370	7th W. Yorks.	—	K. in A.
Pawson, Robert	Pte.	35127	2nd W. Yorks.	—	K. in A.
Pawson, Stanley	Pte.	16658	3rd Hants. Infantry	—	K. in A.
Paylor, Ernest	Pte.	49744	W. Yorks.	—	Died
Payne, Eli	Pte.	40750	2nd Royal Innisk. Fusrs.	—	K. in A.
Payne, Ernest H.	Pte.	34389	York. & Lancs.	—	K. in A.
Payne, Fred G.	Pte.	34334	18th W. Yorks.	—	Missing
Payne, James V.	Pte.	1355	15th W. Yorks.	—	K. in A.
Peace, J.	2Pte.	126854	Royal Air Force	—	Died
Peacock, Arthur E.	Rfm.	305508	1/8th W. Yorks.	—	K. in A.
Peacock, Clarence	Pte.	5349	Scottish Horse	—	K. in A.
Peacock, Herbert E.	C.S.M.	265079	1/7th W. Yorks.	—	Missing
Peacock, John	Sgt.	307334	Tank Corps	—	K. in A.
Peacock, Robt. Wm.	Pte.	22614	Lancs. Fusiliers	—	Died
Peacock, Thomas G.	Rfm.	266437	2/7th W. Yorks.	—	K. in A.
Peaker, Chas. E.	Pte.	23914	W. Yorks.	—	K. in A.
Peaker, W.	Pte.	242093	K.O. Scottish Bordrs.	—	K. in A.
Peaker, Walter	Pte.	42306	1st W. Yorks.	—	K. in A.
Pearce, Andrew	Pte.	41625	Northumberland Fusrs.	—	D. of W.
Pearce, Edward J.	Rfm.	2778	7th W. Yorks.	—	K. in A.
Pearce, Frank	Pte.	45922	W. Yorks.	—	K. in A.
Pearcy, Arthur	Pte.	456089	Labour Corps	—	D. a. Dis.
Pearcy, Wm. F.	Pte.	39928	15th Cheshire	—	K. in A.
Pears, John	Pte.	36611	E. Yorks.	—	Died

LEEDS ROLL OF HONOUR.

Name	Rank	No.	Regiment	Honours	How Died
Pearse, Geo. P.	Rfm.	266927	2/7th W. Yorks.	—	Died
Pearse, Wm. J.	Gnr.		R.G.A.	—	K. in A.
Pearson, Albert	Cpl.	305104	W. Yorks.	—	K. in A.
Pearson, Alex. F.	Pte.	40834	16th W. Yorks.	—	K. in A.
Pearson, Alf.	Pte.	20734	2nd Yorks.	—	D. of W.
Pearson, Archie J.	Pte.	31103	1st E. Yorks.	—	K. in A.
Pearson, Arthur	Pte.	618	21st W. Yorks.	—	D. of W.
Pearson, Arthur	Pte.	20591	10th Yorks.	—	K. in A.
Pearson, Chas. F.	Pte.		2nd Royal Fusiliers	—	D. of W.
Pearson, Edwin	Pte.	21807	K.O.Y.L.I.	—	K. in A.
Pearson, Edwin J.	C.S.M.	9050	York. & Lancs.	—	Died
Pearson, Geo.	Cpl.	17722	York. & Lancs.	—	D. a. Dis.
Pearson, Geo.	Pte.	164938	R.A.S.C.	—	Died
Pearson, Harry	Rfm.	306763	2/8th W. Yorks.	—	K. in A.
Pearson, J.			R.F.A.	—	Died
Pearson, James	Pte.	449661	Labour Corps	—	Died
Pearson, James	Dvr.T4/213407		R.A.S.C.	—	Died
Pearson, Joseph	Cpl.	8657	15th W. Yorks.	—	K. in A.
Pearson, Percy	Pte.	32945	Royal Scots	—	K. in A.
Pearson, Reginald	2nd Lieut.		5th W. Yorks.	—	K. in A.
Pearson, Samuel	Cpl.	143815	R.A.S.C.	—	Died
Pearson, Tom	Pte.	11950	6th K.O.Y.L.I.	—	K. in A.
Pearson, Walter	L/Cpl.	37006	17th W. Yorks.	—	K. in A.
Pearson, Wm.	Rfm.	4169	1/8th W. Yorks.	—	D. of W.
Pease, James H.	Pte.	40630	12th Middlesex	—	K. in A.
Pease, Leonard	Pte.	236020	9th W. Yorks.	—	K. in A.
Pease, T.	Pte.	306156	W. Yorks.	—	Died
Pease, Walter	Pte.	47765	12/13th Northumb. Fusrs.	—	K. in A.
Peat, Harold	Pte.	51035	K.O.Y.L.I.	—	K. in A.
Peat, Reginald	Pte.	202266	4th Lincoln	—	Died
Peck, Willie	Rfm.	2193	1/8th W. Yorks.	—	K. in A.
Peech, Lawrence	Pte.	659	21st W. Yorks.	—	Died
Peech, Robt.	Pte.	235792	York. & Lancs.	—	D. a. Dis.
Peel, Benjamin H. L.	Cpl.	39391	21st W. Yorks.	—	D. of W.
Peel, C. F.	L/Cpl.	1309	15th W. Yorks.	—	Missing
Peel, Clarence T.	Rfm.	97044	King's Royal Rifle Cps.	—	K. in A.
Peel, Harry	Pte.	8328	3rd W. Yorks.	—	K. in A.
Peel, Joseph	Pte.	12304	11th K.O.Y.L.I.	—	K. in A.
Peirse, Sidney E.	2nd Lieut.		Australian	—	Died
Peirson, Bertie	Pte.	60717	25th Northumb'l'd Fusrs.	—	K. in A.
Pemberton, Albert	Pte.	266179	W. Yorks.	—	K. in A.
Pemberton, G. W.	Sgt.	1918	1/8th W. Yorks.	—	K. in A.
Pemberton, Harry	Pte.	6458	1st W. Yorks.	—	K. in A.
Pemberton, John R.	Rfm.	3535	1/7th W. Yorks.	—	D. a. Dis.
Pemberton, Sydney	Pte.	17843	W. Yorks.	—	Died
Penchion, John	Pte.	13517	25th Royal Fusiliers	—	Died
Pendlebury, Richard	Cpl.	479541	4th W. Riding.	—	Died

LEEDS ROLL OF HONOUR.

Name	Rank	No.	Regiment	Honours	How Died
Peniket, Edward	Rfm.	1651	8th W. Yorks.	—	K. in A.
Peniston, Herbert	Pte.	8331	11th W. Yorks.	—	D. of W.
Peniston, Wm.	Pte.	306186	W. Yorks.	—	K. in A.
Pennington, Frank	Sgt.	365391	W. Yorks.	—	K. in A.
Pennington, Harold	Rfm.	5366	8th W. Yorks.	—	Died
Pennington, Mark	Pte.	26872	10th W. Yorks.	—	K. in A.
Pennington, Wm.	Pte.	25308	W. Yorks.	—	D. of W.
Penny, Edward	Rfm.	5011	7th W. Yorks.	—	K. in A.
Penny, Robert	L/Cpl.	15313	8th W. Riding	—	K. in A.
Penrose, Ernest	Pte.	235918	9th W. Yorks.	—	K. in A.
Pepper, Bertram J.	Cpl.	786074	R.F.A.	—	K. in A.
Pepyat, Edgar	L/Cpl.	265204	1/7th W. Yorks.	—	K. in A.
Percival, Walter	Pte.	34874	Yorks.	—	Died P.O.W.
Perfect, Ernest D.	A/Sgt.	13096	11th W. Yorks.	—	K. in A.
Perfect, F. R.	Sgt.	S4/250926	R.A.S.C.	—	Died
Perkin, Cyril	Pte.	18663	10th W. Riding	—	K. in A.
Perkin, William	Pte.M2/139291		R.A.S.C.	—	Died
Perkins, George	Pte.	331101	Royal Scots	—	Died
Perkins, J. D.	Rfm.		1/7th W. Yorks.	—	K. in A.
Perray, Percy	Pte.	27850	16th W. Yorks.	—	K. in A.
Perray, Sidney	Pte.	50671	2nd Lancs. Fusiliers	—	K. in A.
Perry, A.	Pte.	281828	22nd Royal Fusiliers	—	K. in A.
Perry, John	Pte.	10402	Yorks.	—	K. in A.
Perry, Percy	Pte.	88323	Machine Gun Corps	—	Missing
Petch, George	Rfm.	3351	1/7th W. Yorks.	—	K. in A.
Petch, James T.	Pte.	350989	Durham Light Infantry	—	D. of W.
Petch, William	Cpl.	201955	8th W. Yorks.	—	K. in A.
Peterkin, Alfred	Pte.	41402	W. Yorks.	—	K. in A.
Peters, Joseph	Gnr.		R.F.A.	—	Died
Petrie, Géorge	Stkr.	L8115	H.M.S. " Penarth "	—	Drowned
Phanp, George W.	Pte.	265283	Oxford & Bucks.	—	K. in A.
Phelan, Thomas	Rfm.	5299	7th W. Yorks.	—	K. in A.
Phillips, Chas. H.	L/Cpl.	11526	K.O. Scottish Borderers	—	K. in A.
Phillips, John	Pte.	10566	Labour Corps	—	D. a. Dis.
Phillips, Joseph	Pte.	11161	2nd W. Riding	—	K. in A.
Phillips, Percy	Pte.	332579	Highland Light Infantry	—	K. in A.
Phillips, Richard	Pte.	7731	1st W. Yorks.	—	K. in A.
Phillipson, F.	Rfm.	306277	1/8th W. Yorks.	—	Died
Phillis, E.	Pte.	36160	20th Northumb'l'd Fus.	—	K. in A.
Phillpotts, George	Pte.	300059	18th W. Yorks.	—	Missing
Pick, Clarence	Gnr.	191419	R.G.A.	—	Died
Pick, Harry	Pte.	52531	Middlesex	—	K. in A.
Pick, Henry	Wireman	32640	H.M.S. " Victory "	—	Died
Pick, Nathaniel	Gnr.	58456	R.G.A.	—	D. a. Dis.
Pick, Wm. H.	L/Cpl.	3302092	Highland Light Infantry	—	D. a. Dis.
Pickard, Arthur	Pte.	441053	2nd Can. M. Rifles	—	D. of W.
Pickard, Berkeley R.	Pte.	32104	8th York. & Lancs.	—	K. in A.

LEEDS ROLL OF HONOUR.

Name	Rank	No.	Regiment	Honours	How Died
Pickard, Charles	Pte.	37347	W. Yorks.	—	K. in A.
Pickard, F. G.	Sgt.	5713	1st W. Yorks.	—	Died
Pickard, G.	Rfm.	306730	1/8th W. Yorks.	—	K. in A.
Pickard, G. F.	Pte.	59088	K.O.Y.L.I.	—	Died
Pickard, Harry	Pte.	28891	2/5th W. Yorks.	—	Died
Pickard, John R.	Pte.	49724	W. Yorks.	—	Died
Pickard, Regnld. W.	Sgt.	201415	2/6th W. Yorks.	—	K. in A.
Pickard, Sam	Pte.	2226	W. Yorks.	—	K. in A.
Pickard, William	L/Cpl.	98509	Royal Engineers	—	K. in A.
Pickering, Joseph	Pte.		Northumberland Fusrs.	—	K. in A.
Pickering, Richd.	Cpl.	5783	R.F.A.	—	Died
Pickersgill, Albert E.	2ndP.O.	294	H.M.S. "Hawke"	—	K. in A.
Pickersgill, Alfred	Pte.	3/10127	10th Yorks.	—	K. in A.
Pickersgill, Charles	Pte.	10971	W. Yorks.	—	K. in A.
Pickersgill, G. W.	Pte.	6343	19th London	—	K. in A.
Pickersgill, John	Gnr.	246439	7th R.H.A.	—	Died
Pickett, Chas. S.	Pte.	G/62387	9th Royal Fusiliers	—	D. a. Dis.
Pickett, John W.	Cpl.	265586	3/7th W. Yorks.	—	K. in A.
Pickles, Clifford C.			R.A.M.C.	—	D. a. Dis.
Pickles, Ellis E.	Pte.	83924	Royal Fusiliers	—	Died
Pickles, Fred	L/Cpl.	305334	8th W. Yorks.	—	Died
Pickles, George	Pte.	S/40850	R.A.S.C.	—	Died
Pickles, Jack	Pte.	21382	Northumberland Fusrs.	—	Died
Pickles, Norman S.	Cpl.	2004	Australian Infantry	—	Died
Pickles, Phillip D.	Surgeon		H.M.S. "Russell"	—	Died
Pickles, Thomas	Pte.	5365	W. Yorks.	—	K. in A.
Pickles, Walter	Pte.	32367	15th W. Yorks.	—	Missing
Pickles, William	Pte.	10435	2nd W. Riding	—	K. in A.
Pickthall, R.	Cpl.	48577	W. Yorks.	—	Missing
Pickup, Fred H.	Pte.	1094	15th W. Yorks.	—	K. in A.
Pickup, Thomas	Pte.	30295	E. Yorks.	—	K. in A.
Pierce, John R.	Pte.	15824	Notts. & Derby.	—	K. in A.
Pierce, Joseph	Pte.	2381	York. & Lancs.	—	K. in A.
Piercy, Ernest H.		J61860		—	Died
Pigg, Robert	A/S.M.	4363	19th Royal Lancs.	—	K. in A.
Pilkington, Thomas	Pte.	1429	15th W. Yorks.	—	K. in A.
Pilling, Herbert W.	Pte.	3909	R.A.S.C.	—	D. a. Dis.
Pilling, Horace	Pte.	41401	15th W. Yorks.	—	K. in A.
Pillinger, Harold	Pte.	21929	13th W. Yorks.	—	K. in A.
Pinches, Arthur	Pte.	202170	K.O.Y.L.I.	—	Died
Pinches, Samuel P.	Pte.	19453	9th W. Yorks.	—	K. in A.
Pincott, Albert H.	O.S.	Z5938	Royal Navy	—	Missing
Pinder, Chas.	Pte.	21206	1/5th York. & Lancs.	—	Died
Pinder, Ernest	A.B.	15611	H.M.S. "Dal-Louise"	—	Died
Pinder, Harold	Pte.	300032	18th W. Yorks.	—	K. in A.
Pinder, Norman R.	Pte.	38195	W. Yorks.	—	D. of W.
Pink, Clifford R.	Rfm.	305580	1/8th W. Yorks.	—	Died

LEEDS ROLL OF HONOUR.

Name	Rank	No.	Regiment	Honours	How Died
Pinkney, Harry	Gdsmn.	2391	3rd Dragoon Guards	—	Died
Pitch, George	Rfm.	3351	1/7th W. Yorks.	—	K. in A.
Pitts, Albert	Pte.	3/8563	2nd W. Yorks.	—	K. in A.
Pitts, J. R.	Pte.	10105	2nd W. Yorks.	—	Died
Place, Thomas	L/Cpl.	259977	Royal Engineers	—	Died
Place, Walter	Sgt.	9936	1st W. Yorks.	—	Died
Place, William	Pte.	46529	1/4th Yorks.	—	K. in A.
Place, William	Pte.	25331	10th W. Yorks.	—	K. in A.
Plackett, Harry	Sgt.	305413	1/8th W. Yorks.	—	K. in A.
Plannett, Arthur	Pte.	17777	W. Yorks.	—	K. in A.
Platt, Herbert	Pte.	40031	York. & Lancs.	—	K. in A.
Platts, Harold	Gnr.	151119	R.G.A.	—	K. in A.
Platts, Harold	A/Cpl.	37974	Machine Gun Corps	—	K. in A.
Platts, Wm. E.	Pte.	164762	R.A.S.C.	—	K. in A.
Plews, Edwin	Pte.	241107	Yorks.	—	K. in A.
Plowman, Arthur	Pte.	1540	15th W. Yorks.	—	K. in A.
Plowman, George A.	Pte.	106861	Notts. & Derby.	—	K. in A.
Plowman, George T.	Rfm.	4463	1/8th W. Yorks.	—	K. in A.
Plowman, R. H.	1Clk.	98673	Royal Air Force	—	Died
Plows, Chas. P.	Pte.	200089	3rd W. Yorks.	—	K. in A.
Pocklington, Hbt. C.				—	K. in A.
Poe, Arthur	Pte.	24415	W. Yorks.	—	D. of W.
Pogotto, Anthony	Cpl.	25854	1st W. Yorks.	—	K. in A.
Pogrund, Sam	Sig.	16237	Machine Gun Corps	—	Drowned
Pogson, John	Rfm.	2872	1/8th W. Yorks.	—	K. in A.
Pogson, Samuel	Pte.	9171	10th W. Yorks.	—	D. of W.
Pollard, Arthur	2nd Lieut.		6th Notts. & Derby.	—	K. in A.
Pollard, B.	Pte.	36834	9th W. Yorks.	—	K. in A.
Pollard, Chas.	Gdsmn.	8413	Scots Guards	—	Died
Pollard, Clifford	Pte.	53250	11th Durham Lt. Infty.	—	Died
Pollard, Herbert	Pte.	36932	W. Yorks.	—	D. of W.
Pollard, James H.	Pte.	305646	2nd W. Yorks.	—	Died
Pollard, Joseph H.	Pte.	51148	E. Yorks.	—	K. in A.
Pollard, Wilfred	Pte.	95582	7th Tank Corps	—	Died
Pollard, Wm. C.	Pte.	38055	15th W. Yorks.	—	Missing
Pollington, John	Rfm.	306716	2/8th W. Yorks.	—	K. in A.
Pollitt, Geoffrey J.	Pte.	336599	R.A.S.C. (M.T.)	—	Died
Poole, Arthur	Gdsmn.	20185	3rd Grenadier Guards	—	Missing
Poole, George F.	Pte.	41209	11th W. Yorks.	—	K. in A.
Poole, H.	Pte.	13569	K.O. Scottish Bordrs.	—	K. in A.
Poole, Henry	Pte.	106864	Notts. & Derby	—	Missing
Poole, Thos.	Dvr.	L/5381	R.F.A.	—	K. in A.
Poole, Thos. L.	Gdsmn.	8947	Scots Guards	—	Died
Popple, W.	Pte.	242368	6th W. Yorks.	—	Died
Popplewell, F.	Cpl.	8076	27th Northumb'l' Fus.	—	K. in A.
Popplewell, Herbert P.	Pte.	8331	11th W. Yorks.	—	K. in A.
Porritt, Albert E.	Rfm.	45705	King's Royal R. Cps.	—	Died

LEEDS ROLL OF HONOUR.

Name	Rank	No.	Regiment	Honours	How Died
Porritt, Albert J.	O.S.	J75943	H.M.S. " Rambling Rose "..	—	Died
Porteous, Herbert	Pte.	463327	Labour Corps ..	—	D. a. Dis.
Porter, David	L/Cpl.	33182	1/7th W. Yorks.	—	K. in A.
Potter, Chris.	Rfm.	4113	1/7th W. Yorks.	—	D. of W.
Potter, Ernest H.	Cpl.	18891	York. & Lancs.	—	K. in A.
Potter, Geo.	Pte.	66560	Northumberland Fusrs.	—	Died
Potter, Geo.	Pte.	21120	2nd York. & Lancs.	—	K. in A.
Porter, Geo. L.	Rfm.	4771	2/7th W. Yorks.	—	K. in A.
Potter, J. H. S.	Gnr.	231173	R.F.A.	—	Died
Potter, John	L/Cpl.	6514	Military Foot Police	—	Died
Potter, Thos.	L/Cpl.	31686	10th Essex	—	Died
Potterton, Henry	2nd Lieut.		2/6th W. Yorks.	—	K. in A.
Potts, Alfred	Pte.	33007	Lincoln	—	Missing
Potts, Fred A.	Pte.	307718	1/8th Warwick	—	K. in A.
Potts, Henry G.	Gnr.	796238	R.F.A.	—	K. in A.
Potts, Thos.	Pte.	37780	4th W. Yorks.	—	D. of W.
Potts, Wm. E.	2nd Lieut.		2/8th W. Yorks.	M.M.	K. in A.
Poulter, Clayton	Gdsmn.	16447	1st Scots Guards	—	K. in A.
Poulter, Joseph N. L.	L.S.		H.M.S. " Princess Irene "	—	K. in A.
Pounder, Benj. W.	Lieut.		W. Riding	—	K. in A.
Powell, Fred	Pte.	2137	Liverpool	—	K. in A.
Powell, Geo. W.	L/Cpl.	12500	1st Liverpool	—	K. in A.
Powell, John	Gnr.	127318	R.F.A.	—	Died
Powell, Joseph	Pte.	15240	1st Royal Munster Fus.	—	K. in A.
Powell, Walter	Sgt.	2086	1/7th W. Yorks.	—	K. in A.
Powell, Walter N.	Pte.	31140	1st E. Yorks.	—	K. in A.
Power, Alan M.	Pte.	732	15th W. Yorks.	—	K. in A.
Power, Thaddeus	Pte.	257222	15th Yorks.	—	Died
Pratt, Alfred S.	Rfm.	34891	King's Royal Rifle Cps.	—	D. of W.
Pratt, Chas.	L/Cpl.	612574	19th London	—	K. in A.
Pratt, Ernest	L/Cpl.	32843	16th W. Yorks.	—	K. in A.
Pratt, Geo .W.	1 Stkr.SS10034		H.M.S. " Cressy "	—	K. in A.
Pratt, Gilbert R.	Pte.	238042	21st Northumb'l'd Fus.	—	K. in A.
Pratt, Henry C. W.	Pte.	29154	2nd W. Yorks.	—	K. in A.
Pratt, Herbert H.	Rfm.	41411	7th W. Yorks.	—	K. in A.
Pratt, Thos. H.	Pte.	401285	R.A.M.C.	—	K. in A.
Pratt, Wm.	Rfm.	5164	2/7th W. Yorks.	—	Missing
Pratten, Chas. H.	Pte.	17054	10th Scots Rifles	—	Missing
Preece, John L.	L/Cpl.	734	W. Yorks.	—	D. a. Dis.
Prendergast, Michael	Pte.	14486	12th W. Yorks.	—	D. of W.
Prendville, John Wm.	Pte.	28793	K.O. Scottish Borderers	—	D. of W.
Prentice, Arthur	Pte.	40835	16th W. Yorks.	—	K. in A.
Prest, Edgar	Pte.	8246	W. Yorks.	—	K. in A.
Preston, Abraham	Pte.	38310	York. & Lancs.	—	Died
Preston, F. W.	Gnr.	111997	R.F.A.	—	D. a. Dis.
Preston, Geo.	Pte.	260010	6th K.O.Y.L.I.	—	K. in A.

LEEDS ROLL OF HONOUR.

Name	Rank	No.	Regiment	Honours	How Died
Preston, Harry	Pte.	12728	10th W. Yorks.	—	K. in A.
Preston, Henry	R.S.M.	1071	W. Yorks.	—	Died
Preston, Herbert	Pte.	41380	26th Northumb'l'd Fus.	—	K. in A.
Preston, Lindley	Bdr.	L12130	R.F.A.	—	K. in A.
Preston, Wm. B.	Pte.	5345	E. Kent	—	K. in A.
Preston, Wm. G.	Pte.	35091	24th Northumb'l'd Fus.	—	K. in A.
Pretty, Ernest D.	Pte.	746	2nd Yorks.	—	K. in A.
Price, Clifford	Cpl.	41445	E. Yorks.	—	K. in A.
Price, John	Sgt.	10113	12th W. Yorks.	—	D. of W.
Price, Louis	Rfm.	306925	2/8th W. Yorks.	—	Died
Price, Thos.	Pte.	12192	5th Yorks.	—	D. of W.
Pridmore, Harry	Gnr.	99538	R.F.A.	—	Died
Priestley, Harry	Pte.	47262	12th W. Yorks.	—	K. in A.
Priestley, Harry J.	Pte.	28800	W. Yorks.	—	K. in A.
Priestley, John W.	Cpl.	19796	8th Yorks.	—	K. in A.
Priestley, Laurie	Pte.	40908	27th Northumb'l'd Fus.	—	K. in A.
Priestley, Leonard	Pte.	49092	K.O.Y.L.I.	—	Died
Priestley, Robert W.	Pte.	735	W. Yorks.	—	K. in A.
Priestley, Walter	Pte.	63096	2nd W. Yorks.	—	K. in A.
Priestley, William	Stkr.	31827	H.M.S. "Tartar"	—	K. in A.
Priestman, Arthur S.	Dvr.	881698	R.F.A.	—	D. a. Dis.
Priestman, Wilfred	Pte.	242194	S. Staffs.	—	K. in A.
Prince, Charles	Pte.	41108	11th W. Yorks.	—	K. in A.
Prince, George	Pte.	24367	41st Labour Co.	—	D. of W.
Prince, Thomas	Pte.	40592	6th Yorks.	—	D. of W.
Prince, Wm.	Pte.	37637	12th W. Yorks.	—	K. in A.
Pringle, Henry N.	Pte.	31400	9th Northumb'l'd Fusrs.	—	K. in A.
Pritchard, Alfred	Pte.	3279	5th W. Yorks.	—	Died
Proctor, Albert R.	Pte.	202980	1/4th K.O.Y.L.I.	—	D. of W.
Proctor, Frank	Rfm.	54936	1/8th W. Yorks.	—	K. in A.
Proctor, H. S.	Pte.	15184	2nd W. Riding..	—	Died
Proctor, Harry	Pte.	155788	Machine Gun Corps	—	Died
Proctor, Herbert	Pte.	29098	2nd W. Yorks.	—	Missing
Proctor, Horace	Pte.	33694	9th W. Yorks.	—	D. of W.
Proctor, Misgeley	A.B.		H.M.S. "Hawke"	—	K. in A.
Proctor, Percy	Gnr.	151958	R.G.A.	—	Died
Proctor, Ralph V.	L/Cpl.	737	W. Yorks.	—	K. in A.
Proctor, Thomas	Pte.	14700	12th W. Yorks.	—	K. in A.
Proctor, Wm.	Pte.	3/8995	1st Yorks.	—	Died
Proud, Ernest	Pte.	266167	10th W. Yorks.	—	K. in A.
Prudames, Samuel M.	C.Q.M.S.	25457	2nd W. Yorks..	—	D. a. Dis.
Prudhoe, John W.	Pte.	8987	W. Yorks.	—	K. in A.
Pullan, Arthur	A.B.	5301	H.M.S. "Vanguard"	—	K. in A.
Pullan, Edgar	Sig.	89853	R.G.A.	—	D. a. Dis.
Pullan, Joseph	Pte.	4506	W. Yorks.	—	Acc. Dr'ned.
Pullan, Wm. H.	A.B.	TZ10843	Royal Naval V. Res.	—	K. in A.
Pullan, Wm. W.	Rfm.	3381	2/7th W. Yorks.	—	K. in A.

LEEDS ROLL OF HONOUR.

Name	Rank	No.	Regiment	Honours	How Died
Pullein, Harold J.	2nd Lieut.		25th Northumb'l'd Fus.	—	K. in A.
Pulleyne, Richd. I.	Lieut.		Royal Navy	D.S.O. D.S.C.	Died
Purcell, William	Sdler.	95939	R.F.A.	—	Died
Purchon, Thomas H. H.	Gdsmn.	17725	Gordon Highlanders	—	D. a. Dis.
Purnell, Herbert	Sgt.	20754	6th Yorks.	—	Died
Pybus, Fred	Pte.	35201	Machine Gun Corps	—	D. of W.
Quarton, Carl. B.	Pte.	10603	W. Riding	—	K. in A.
Quarton, Harry	Pte.	38916	Northumberland Fusrs.	M.M.	K. in A.
Queenan, Thomas	L/Sgt.	9958	1st W. Yorks.	—	K. in A.
Quiat, Alex	Pte.	71706	Machine Gun Corps	—	K. in A.
Quigley, Isaac	Cpl.	1106	15th W. Yorks.	—	K. in A.
Quinn, James	Pte.	8764	2nd W. Yorks.	—	Died
Quinn, John	Cpl.	19882	15th Cheshire	—	K. in A.
Quinn, John J.	A/Sgt.	310715	Royal Engineers	—	Died
Quinn, Lawrence	Pte.	4695	5th Seaforth Highdrs.	—	Died
Race, Ernest	Pte.	29151	2nd W. Yorks.	—	K. in A.
Race, John	A/L.Cpl.	18683	K.O.Y.L.I.	—	D. of W.
Race, Wm.	L/Cpl.	1737	1/5th W. Yorks.	—	K. in A.
Radcliffe, John Wm.	Pte.	21928	11th W. Yorks.	—	K. in A.
Radwell, W.	Pte.	79012	1/22nd London	—	K. in A.
Raftery, James	L/Cpl.	42170	W. Yorks.	—	K. in A.
Ragan, John	Gnr.	50826	R.G.A.	—	K. in A.
Raggett, Cyril	Cpl.	1945	K.O.Y.L.I.	—	Missing
Ragsdale, George	Pte.	8671	W. Yorks.	—	Died
Rainbow, Francis L.	Pte.	9131	6th Middlesex	—	K. in A.
Rainey, John C.	L/Cpl.	25166	W. Yorks.	—	D. of W.
Rainford, Horace	Dvr.	40121	R.F.A.	—	K. in A.
Raistrick, Ernest	Pte.	22050	1st W. Yorks.	—	D. of W.
Raistrick, Henry	Dvr.	T4/25255	R.A.S.C.	—	Died
Rakusen, Harry	Pte.	32837	1/6th W. Yorks.	—	K. in A.
Ralphs, Arthur	Lieut.		Royal Air Force	—	K. in A.
Ramsdale, Tom	Pte.	14787	K.O.Y.L.I.	—	K. in A.
Ramsden, Arthur	Rfm.	3678	1/7th W. Yorks.	—	K. in A.
Ramsden, Arthur	Pte.	133	W. Yorks.	—	Died
Ramsden, Edward	Pte.	172433	53rd Durham Lt. Infty.	—	Died
Ramsden, Harry	Pte.	26739	45th Labour Co.	—	K. in A.
Ramsden, Harry	L/Cpl.	19980	1st K. O. Scottish Brdrs.	—	K. in A.
Ramsden, James	Pte.		10th W. Yorks.	—	K. in A.
Ramsey, Arthur	Pte.	28695	Royal Inniskilling Fus.	—	Died
Ramsey, John J.	Pte.	21372	Northumberland Fusrs.	—	K. in A.
Randall, Arthur	Pte.	20114	Leicester	—	D. a. Dis.
Randall, J.	Pte.	1298	12th K.O.Y.L.I.	—	K. in A.
Randall, J. E.	Pte.	75459	1st W. Yorks.	—	K. in A.
Randall, J. W.	Pte.	16022	10th Scots Rifles	—	K. in A.
Randall, Walter	Pte.	57510	Northumberland Fusrs.	—	K. in A.

LEEDS ROLL OF HONOUR.

Name	Rank	No.	Regiment	Honours	How Died
Randerson, Thos. Hy.	Pte.	40026	9th Royal Irish Fusrs.	—	Killed
Rands, George	Pte.	37762	York. & Lancs.	—	Died
Ransom, John Wm.	Pte.	25774	2nd W. Yorks.	—	K. in A.
Ransome, Geoffrey C.	Lieut.		10th Yorks.	—	D. of W.
Rasson, Achille	Cpl.	1176	Belgian Army	—	K. in A.
Ratchford, Myles	Pte.	84570	W. Yorks.	—	Died
Ratcliffe, Chas.	L/Cpl.	2903	7th W. Yorks.	—	D. of W.
Ratcliffe, George	Pte.	5438	Lincoln	—	K. in A.
Ratcliffe, Geo. H.	Pte.	40756	6th Yorks.	—	Missing
Ratcliffe, James E.	Rfm.	692246	2/7th W. Yorks.	—	K. in A.
Ratcliffe, John W.	Pte.	21928	11th W. Yorks.	—	D. of W.
Ratcliffe, Wm.	Pte.	265473	7th Yorks.	—	K. in A.
Rathmell, Leslie	Rfm.	1877	2/7th W. Yorks.	—	K. in A.
Rathmell, William	Dvr.	75652	R.F.A.	—	K. in A.
Rawcliffe, Fredk.	Pte.	42811	9th Manchester	—	K. in A.
Rawe, Arthur	Pte.	307070	W. Yorks.	—	K. in A.
Rawling, Arthur	Gnr.	775545	R.F.A.	—	K. in A.
Rawling, Edward N.	Rfm.	306384	1/8th W. Yorks.	—	Died
Rawlings, William	Sgt.	2393	R.G.A.	—	K. in A.
Rawnsley, Edward S.	Pte.	164920	R.A.S.C. (M.T.)	—	Died
Rawnsley, Fredk.	Rfm.	2736	1/7th W. Yorks.	—	K. in A.
Rawnsley, Fredk. W.	Pte.	60706	Northumberland Fusrs.	—	K. in A.
Rawnsley, George	Pte.	41062	1st Scottish Rifles	—	D. of W.
Rawnsley, Thos.	Pte.	305770	9th W. Yorks.	—	K. in A.
Rawson, Albert	Rfm.	205142	1/8th W. Yorks.	—	K. in A.
Rawson, James S.	Pte.	20806	2nd W. Yorks.	—	K. in A.
Rawson, Joseph	Cpl.	864	1st W. Riding	—	K. in A.
Rawson, R.	L/Cpl.	26534	12th Highland Lt. Infty.	—	K. in A.
Rawson, Sam.	Pte.	27399	10th E. Yorks.	—	K. in A.
Ray, Fredk.	Pte.	40789	Norfolks	—	Died
Rayfield, Sidney	Pte.	745	15th W. Yorks.	—	K. in A.
Rayner, Ernest	Pte.	31067	W. Riding	—	Died
Rayner, Fred	L/Cpl.	13127	1st W. Yorks.	—	K. in A.
Rayner, Fredk.	Pte.	746	15th W. Yorks.	—	K. in A.
Rayner, Harold	2nd Lieut.		5th E. Yorks.	—	D. of W.
Rayner, James	Pte.	3/8763	1st W. Yorks.	—	K. in A.
Rayner, Percival	Pte.	33943	14th W. Yorks.	—	K. in A.
Rayner, William	Gnr.	75614	R.F.A.	—	K. in A.
Rayner, Wm. H.	Pte.	47355	Lancs. Fusiliers	—	D. in A.
Raynor, Geo.	Rfm.	6752	5th Rifle Brigade	—	K. in A.
Read, Chas.	Lieut.		A.P.W.O. Yorks.	—	K. in A.
Read, David	Pte.	11502	2nd W. Riding	—	K. in A.
Read, Richard	Sgt.	34165	7th S. Lancs.	—	K. in A.
Reader, Robt.	Pte.	24079	2nd W. Yorks.	—	K. in A.
Reader, Wm.	Pte.	45920	12th W. Yorks.	—	K. in A.
Ream, Norman S.	Pte.	761966	Artists' Rifles	—	K. in A.
Reardon, Owen	Pte.	12156	3rd King's R. Rifle Cps.	—	Died

LEEDS ROLL OF HONOUR.

Name	Rank	No.	Regiment	Honours	How Died
Reason, Leonard	L/Cpl.	2831	W. Yorks.	—	K. in A.
Reddin, Wm.	Pte.	265261	1/5th W. Yorks.	—	Died P.O.W.
Redding, Edwin	Pte.	8016	4th W. Yorks.	—	Missing
Reddington, Anthony	Pte.	18405	1st W. Yorks.	—	K. in A.
Reddington, Thos.	Pte.	13799	12th W. Yorks.	—	K. in A.
Reddyhoff, Harold	Dvr.	795022	R.F.A.	—	K. in A.
Reddyhoff, Tom C.	L/Cpl.	3173	W. Yorks.	—	K. in A.
Redfearn, A.	Pte.	675130	21st Canadian	—	K. in A.
Redfearn, T. J.	A/Sgt.	6184	1st W. Riding	—	K. in A.
Redford, Wm.	Pte.	10563	2nd Royal Lancs.	—	K. in A.
Redman, Robt.	Pte.	10040	Labour Corps	—	Died
Redman, Robt.	Pte.	27977	4th Liverpool	—	K. in A.
Redshaw, Geo. A.	Gdsmn.	20180	Grenadier Guards	—	K. in A.
Redshaw, Herbert			2nd W. Yorks.	—	K. in A.
Redshaw, James	Pte.	201693	2/5th W. Yorks.	—	K. in A.
Redshaw, Leonard	L/Cpl.	749	15th W. Yorks.	—	K. in A.
Redshaw, Robt.	Pte.	1994	W. Yorks.	—	K. in A.
Redshaw, Thos. S.	Dvr.	268130	R.F.A.	—	Missing
Redshaw, Thos. Wm.	Pte.	9463	1st Northumb'l'd Fusrs.	—	K. in A.
Redshaw, Winn	Pte.	42010	10th Northumb'l'd Fusrs.	—	D. of W.
Reed, Bernard	A/Captain		15th W. Yorks.	—	K. in A.
Reed, Clarence	L/Cpl.	12313	10th K.O.Y.L.I.	—	K. in A.
Reed, Geo. E.	L/Cpl.	310944	Warwick	—	K. in A.
Reed, John	Pte.	214227	Labour Corps	—	D. a. Dis.
Reed, John H.	Pte.	41299	Royal Scots Fusrs.	—	K. in A.
Reed, Richard H.	L/Cpl.	307092	2/8th Sherwood Forstrs.	—	K. in A.
Reeder, Leonard	Pte.	4421	6th Highland Lt. Infty.	—	D. a. Dis.
Regan, Arthur	Pte.	266707	W. Yorks.	—	K. in A.
Regan, Chas.	Pte.	7661	W. Yorks.	—	K. in A.
Regan, Joseph	Pte.	2131	1st Manchester	—	K. in A.
Reid, —	Sgt.	9820	2nd W. Riding	—	K. in A.
Reid, John	Pte.	214227	Labour Corps	—	D. a. Dis.
Reid, Squire	Pte.	22283	2nd W. Yorks.	—	K. in A.
Reid, Thos.	Pte.	47287	W. Yorks.	—	K. in A.
Reilly, Robt. F.	Rfm.	550639	2/16th Q. Westmnst. Rfles	—	Died
Relph, Rowland	Pte.	19364	15th Cheshire	—	D. of W.
Relton, Frank W.	Dvr.	2221	R.F.A.	—	Died
Remmer, Geo. A.	L/Cpl.	40993	9th W. Yorks.	—	K. in A.
Render, Henry	Pte.	20095	1st K.O. Scottish Bdrs.	—	K. in A.
Render, Henry R.	Dvr.T4/247875		R.A.S.C.	—	D. a. Dis.
Render, Herbert	Pte.	15621	W. Yorks.	—	K. in A.
Rennard, Frank	Pte.	46631	11th Northumb'l'd Fusrs.	—	K. in A.
Rennard, T. M. C.	Pte.	95748	R.A.M.C.	—	Died
Rennison, Fred	L/Cpl.	265237	9th W. Yorks.	—	K. in A.
Rennison, Walter	Sgt.	9583	W. Yorks.	—	Died
Rennison, Willie	Rfm.	4226	3/8th W. Yorks.	—	K. in A.
Renton, Henry M.	Pte.	21988	11th W. Yorks.	—	K. in A.

LEEDS ROLL OF HONOUR.

Name	Rank	No.	Regiment	Honours	How Died
Renton, Norman	Pte.	12079	K.O.Y.L.I.	—	K. in A.
Reuben, Morris	Pte.	33097	15th W. Yorks.	—	K. in A.
Reucroft, John W.	Pte.	71701	Machine Gun Corps	—	K. in A.
Reucroft, Robt. L.	Pte.	40897	K.O.Y.L.I.	—	K. in A.
Reucroft, Tom	Pte.	2545	1/6th W. Riding	—	K. in A.
Reveley, Wm.	Sgt.	1606	17th W. Yorks.	—	K. in A.
Reynard, James	Pte.	28344	E. Yorks.	—	Died
Reynard, Walter	Pte.	14743	10th K.O.Y.L.I.	—	Missing
Reyner, Burnett	Pte.	754	15th W. Yorks.	—	K. in A.
Reynolds, Chas. H.	Pte.	25214	2nd W. Yorks.	—	K. in A.
Reynolds, Fred	Sgt.	152182	R.A.S.C. (M.T.)	—	K. in A.
Rhodes, A.	Pte.	38782	W. Yorks.	—	D. of W.
Rhodes, Arthur	Gnr.	157737	R.G.A.	—	Died
Rhodes, Barclay	Pte.	12459	2nd K.O.Y.L.I.	—	K. in A.
Rhodes, Cecil W.	Pte.	62798	W. Yorks.	—	K. in A.
Rhodes, Ephraim	Pte.	76272	22nd Durham Lt. Infty.	—	Missing
Rhodes, Fred	Pte.	780	21st W. Yorks.	—	Missing
Rhodes, Geo.	Pte.	81969	Durham Lt. Infantry	—	K. in A.
Rhodes, Geo. E.	Pte.	39949	12th Durham Lt. Infty.	—	K. in A.
Rhodes, John S.	Pte.	140576	8th Machine Gun Corps	—	K. in A.
Rhodes, Harold	Pte.	92919	King's Liverpool	—	Died
Rhodes, Harry	Rfm.	307119	1/8th W. Yorks.	—	K. in A.
Rhodes, Harry	Pte.	1547	W. Yorks.	—	K. in A.
Rhodes, Herbert	Sgt.	1746	1/8th W. Yorks.	—	K. in A.
Rhodes, Herbert	Pte.	10773	9th W. Yorks.	—	K. in A.
Rhodes, James H.	Pte.	24810	W. Yorks.	—	D. of W.
Rhodes, John Ed.	Pte.	57512	Royal Fusiliers	—	K. in A.
Rhodes, John Wm.	L/Cpl.	33089	W. Yorks.	—	D. a. Dis.
Rhodes, Percy	Pte.	4588	W. Yorks.	—	D. of W.
Rhodes, Walter	Pte.	1901	11th W. Yorks.	—	D. of W.
Rhodes, Walter	Pte.	14729	K.O.Y.L.I.	—	K. in A.
Rhudstein, Soloman	Pte.	47940	W. Yorks.	—	K. in A.
Rich, Fred	Bdr.	126790	R.G.A.	—	D. of W.
Richards, G.	Dvr.	19999	R.F.A.	—	K. in A.
Richards, Wm. Ed.	Pte.	48613	W. Yorks.	—	D. of W.
Richardson, B. J.	2nd Lieut.		W. Yorks.	—	K. in A.
Richardson, Ernest	Rfm.	16913	18th W. Yorks.	—	K. in A.
Richardson, Ernest	L/Cpl.	24465	W. Yorks.	—	K. in A.
Richardson, Ernest	Pte.	7282	Welsh	—	K. in A.
Richardson, Frank	Pte.	16036	K.O.Y.L.I.	—	Missing
Richardson, Frank	Pte.	1415	17th W. Yorks.	—	K. in A.
Richardson, Fred L.	Cpl.	33758	15th W. Yorks.	—	K. in A.
Richardson, Geo. W.	Pte.M2/	166709	R.A.S.C.	—	K. in A.
Richardson, Guy B.	A.B.		Hawke Bttn. R.N.	—	K. in A.
Richardson, H.	Pte.	49768	W. Yorks.	—	K. in A.
Richardson, Harold	Rfm.	2304	1/8th W. Yorks.	—	K. in A.
Richardson, Harry	Pte.	14818	K.O.Y.L.I.	—	Missing

LEEDS ROLL OF HONOUR.

Name	Rank	No.	Regiment	Honours	How Died
Richardson, Henry	2/Pte.	275481	Royal Air Force	—	K. in A.
Richardson, Herbert	Rfm.	24434	3/7th W. Yorks.	—	Missing
Richardson, James	Pte.	8126	W. Yorks.	—	K. in A.
Richardson, James A.	Pte.	1717	17th W. Yorks.	—	Missing
Richardson, James Hy.	Pte.	4086	1st Border	—	D. of W.
Richardson, James Wm.	Pte.	203847	12th W. Yorks.	—	D. of W.
Richardson, Joseph	A.B.	T15833	H.M.S. " Canada "	—	K. in A.
Richardson, Lewis T.	Pte.	32831	W. Yorks.	—	Died
Richardson, P. T.	Pte.	37857	9th W. Yorks.	—	K. in A.
Richardson, Percy	Pte.	33354	9th W. Yorks.	—	K. in A.
Richardson, Peter	Dvr.	786345	R.F.A.	—	K. in A.
Richardson, Regd. R.	Pte.	235304	1/4th W. Riding	—	K. in A.
Richardson, Richard	Pte.	7451	Royal Welsh Fusiliers	—	K. in A.
Richardson, Rowland	Pte.	49721	Lincoln	—	K. in A.
Richardson, Sam	Pte.	28238	W. Yorks.	—	K. in A.
Richardson, Sidney B.	Pte.	760	15th W. Yorks.	—	Missing
Richardson, Thos.	Pte.	3/6076	E. Yorks.	—	K. in A.
Richardson, Tom	Pte.	2791	12th W. Yorks.	—	K. in A.
Richardson, Walter	Pte.	458	17th W. Yorks.	—	K. in A.
Riches, F. G. T.	Pte.	48820	Innis. Fusiliers	—	Died
Richmond, Fredk.	Sgt.	7435	6th Yorks.	—	Missing
Richmond, Harry	Pte.	266157	W. Yorks.	—	Died
Richmond, Thos. Wm.	A/Cpl.	19039	6th Yorks.	—	K. in A.
Richmond, Wm.	Pte.	72840	Royal Engineers	—	D. a. Dis.
Rider, Albert	Pte.	60909	Northumberland Fusrs.	—	K. in A.
Rider, Albert	Dvr.	2/16910	R.A.S.C.	—	K. in A.
Rider, Alfred	Pte.	21027	6th K.O.Y.L.I.	—	K. in A.
Rider, Arthur S.	Pte.	19770	26th Royal Fusiliers	—	K. in A.
Rider, Harry	Spr.	98554	Royal Engineers	—	Died
Rider, John W.	Rfm.	38536	2/7th W. Yorks.	—	K. in A.
Rider, Thos.	Pte.	36980	9th W. Yorks.	—	K. in A.
Ridley, Albert E.	Pnr.	354110	Royal Engineers	—	Died
Ridley, Fred B.	Pte.	35294	4th W. Yorks.	—	K. in A.
Ridley, Herbert	Pte.	32808	12th Royal Scots Fusrs.	—	K. in A.
Ridsdale, Frank E.	Sig.	306273	2/8th W. Yorks.	—	D. of W.
Ridyard, Samuel	Rfm.	267407	1/7th W. Yorks.	—	K. in A.
Rigby, Abraham	Rfm.	8918	King's Royal Rifle Cps.	—	Died
Rigby, Alec.	Rfm.	3917	1/8th W. Yorks.	—	D. of W.
Riggle, Phillip	Pte.	307056	W. Yorks.	—	K. in A.
Rilchester, James	Pte.	1989	W. Yorks.	—	Died
Riley, Abraham	Pte.	263022	1/6th W. Yorks.	—	Died
Riley, Abraham	Pte.	74	Northumberland Fusrs.	—	K. in A.
Riley, Allen	Pte.	38869	1st W. Yorks.	—	K. in A.
Riley, Chas. Hy.	Gnr.	66050	R.F.A.	—	K. in A.
Riley, Harry	L/Cpl.	266147	2/7th W. Yorks.	—	Missing
Riley, Harry S.	Sgt.	15711	18th Lancs. Fusiliers	—	K. in A.
Riley, James	Pte.	7599	Yorks.	—	K. in A.

LEEDS ROLL OF HONOUR.

Name	Rank	No.	Regiment	Honours	How Died
Riley, John	Rfm.	1965	1/8th W. Yorks.	—	Died
Riley, John	Pte.	15771	W. Yorks.	—	K. in A.
Riley, Joseph	Cpl.	6804	3rd W. Riding	—	K. in A.
Riley, Maurice	Pte.	28303	E. Yorks.	—	Died
Riley, Sam	Cpl.	12133	6th Yorks.	—	K. in A.
Riley, Stanley	Cpl.	8530	3rd E. Yorks.	—	K. in A.
Riley, Thos.	Pte.	64541	R.G.A.	—	K. in A.
Riley, Walker	Pte.	41272	Royal Lancs.	—	D. of W.
Riley, Walter	Pte.	63241	Lancs. Fusiliers	—	Died
Riley, Wilfred	Pte.	10633	10th W. Yorks.	—	K. in A.
Riley, William	Gnr.	2846	R.F.A.	—	Died
Riley, Willie	L/Cpl.	44897	10th Northumb'l'd Fus.	—	Died
Riley, Wm. G.	Pte.	305713	W. Yorks.	—	K. in A.
Rimington, Arthur	Gnr.	167825	R.F.A.	—	K. in A.
Rimmington, C.	Pte.	29824	Lincoln	—	K. in A.
Ripley, Joseph	Pte.	235793	York. & Lancs.	—	K. in A.
Ripley, William	Pte.	38754	2nd K.O.Y.L.I.	—	K. in A.
Ritchie, Wm. J.	Pte.	69023	Northumberland Fusrs.	—	K. in A.
Roan, James	Pte.	10446	W. Yorks.	—	Missing
Roberts, Arthur	Pte.	196301	R.A.S.C.	—	Drowned
Roberts, Arthur	Pte.	6069	Yorks.	—	D. a. Dis.
Roberts, Benjamin	Pte.	24419	2nd W. Yorks.	—	D. of W.
Roberts, Birdsell	Lieut.		9th W. Yorks.	—	K. in A.
Roberts, Chas.	Pte.	65272	4th Royal Fusiliers	—	K. in A.
Roberts, Chris. R.	Gnr.	186475	R.F.A.	—	Died
Roberts, Fred	Pte.	37976	W. Yorks.	—	Missing
Roberts, George	Cpl.	330874	Royal Scots	M.M.	K. in A.
Roberts, George	Spr.	476866	Royal Engineers	—	D. of W.
Roberts, Geo. A.	Pte.	81138	1/5th Durham Lt. Infty.	—	K. in A.
Roberts, Geo. P.	Pte.	47382	19th Manchester	—	K. in A.
Roberts, Harry	Pte.	51557	Northumberland Fusrs.	—	K. in A.
Roberts, Harry	Sgt.	33892	R.F.A.	—	K. in A.
Roberts, Henry	Pnr.	211545	Royal Engineers	—	K. in A.
Roberts, Herbert	Pte.	28409	S. Lancs.	—	Died
Roberts, J. H.	Bdr.	1245	R.F.A.	—	Died
Roberts, James	Pte.	35522	Yorks.	—	K. in A.
Roberts, John	Pte.	38643	16th W. Yorks.	—	K. in A.
Roberts, John W.	2 A.M.	113357	Royal Air Force	—	D. a. Dis.
Roberts, Joseph	Pte.	115300	Labour Corps	—	K. in A.
Roberts, Joseph	Pte.	78705	Durham Light Infantry	—	K. in A.
Roberts, L. L.	Pte.	204676	Royal Air Force	—	Died
Roberts, Matthew	S.Smith	45572	R.F.A.	—	Died
Roberts, Percy B.			H.M.S. " Hampshire "	—	Drowned
Roberts, Robert	Pte.	10145	2nd W. Yorks.	—	K. in A.
Roberts, William	Pte.	267570	W. Yorks.	—	Died
Roberts, William	Dvr.	204878	R.F.A.	—	D. of W.
Roberts, William	Pte.	27401	E. Yorks.	—	D. a. Dis.

LEEDS ROLL OF HONOUR.

Name	Rank	No.	Regiment	Honours	How Died
Roberts, Willie	Pte.	9506	1st Royal Irish Rifles	—	K. in A.
Robertshaw, Richard	Pte.	4912	London	—	K. in A.
Robertshaw, T. H.	Pte.	34887	W. Yorks.	—	D. a. Dis.
Robertshaw, Thos.	Pte.	7460	York. & Lancs.	—	D. a. Dis.
Robertshaw, Thos. F.	Pte.	10346	3rd W. Riding	—	Missing
Robertson, Allan	Lieut.		2/5th Northumb'l'd Fus.	—	Died
Robertson, David	Pte.	21049	15th Cheshire	—	K. in A.
Robertson, Harry	Pte.	71999	R.A.M.C.	—	K. in A.
Robinson, Alfred	Pte.	270109	16th Royal Scots	—	K. in A.
Robinson, Alfred	Pte.	559829	Royal Engineers	—	D. a. Dis.
Robinson, Arthur	Gnr.	801119	R.F.A.	—	D. of W.
Robinson, Arthur	Pte.	26737	45th Labour Co.	—	K. in A.
Robinson, Arthur	L/Cpl.		4th Middlesex	—	K. in A.
Robinson, Arthur	Pte.	42035	Yorks.	—	K. in A.
Robinson, Arthur	Pte.	79403	Durham Light Infantry	—	Died
Robinson, Cornelius	Pte.	33113	Oxford & Bucks. L.I.	—	K. in A.
Robinson, Edward	Sgt.	266507	W. Yorks.	—	D. a. Dis.
Robinson, Ernest L.	Pte.	769	15th W. Yorks.	—	K. in A.
Robinson, Frank	Pte.	307376	5th W. Yorks.	—	Died
Robinson, Fred	Pte.	3/10304	W. Riding	—	Missing
Robinson, Fred Wm.	Pte.	3259	Royal Marine Lt. Infty.	—	K. in A.
Robinson, George	Pte.	305978	W. Yorks.	—	D. a. Dis.
Robinson, George	Pte.	4724	W. Yorks.	—	Died
Robinson, George	Gnr.	127233	R.F.A.	—	K. in A.
Robinson, George	Rfm.	4013	3/8th W. Yorks.	—	K. in A.
Robinson, George	L/Cpl.	9273	W. Yorks.	—	Died
Robinson, Harold	Pte.	202184	Seaforth Highlanders	—	Died
Robinson, Harold	Pte.	S/26310	Cameron Highlanders	—	Missing
Robinson, Harry	Pte.	20839	K.O. Scottish Bordrs.	—	K. in A.
Robinson, Harry	Pte.	37240	K.O.Y.L.I.	—	D. of W.
Robinson, Herbert	Pte.	19883	W. Yorks.	—	K. in A.
Robinson, James E.	Pte.	350	R.A.M.C.	—	D. a. Dis.
Robinson, John H.	Pte.	27809	9th Lancs. Fusiliers	—	Missing
Robinson, John Wm.	Gnr.	20270	R.F.A.	—	K. in A.
Robinson, Joseph A.	Pte.	29121	W. Yorks.	—	Died
Robinson, Joe	Pte.	12301	K.O.Y.L.I.	—	K. in A.
Robinson, Jos. T.	Pte.	48864	W. Yorks.	—	Died
Robinson, Joshua	1Stkr.		H.M.S. "Good Hope"	—	K. in A.
Robinson, Leonard	Pte.	30396	E. Yorks.	—	K. in A.
Robinson, Marcus	Pte.	60188	Northumberland Fusrs.	—	K. in A.
Robinson, Matthew	Pte.	6453	S. Wales Borderers	—	K. in A.
Robinson, Percival	Pnr.	133831	Royal Engineers	—	K. in A.
Robinson, Percy	Pte.	49883	Liverpool	—	K. in A.
Robinson, Percy	Rfm.	1990	1/8th W. Yorks.	—	K. in A.
Robinson, Percy	Gnr.	186671	R.F.A.	—	D. a. Dis.
Robinson, Samuel	Pte.	40836	16th W. Yorks.	—	K. in A.
Robinson, Sydney	Pte.	2138	Notts. & Derby.	—	Missing

LEEDS ROLL OF HONOUR.

Name	Rank	No.	Regiment	Honours	How Died
Robinson, Tom	Pte.	140942	Machine Gun Corps	—	Died
Robinson, Thos. H.	RQMS.	11255	9th W. Riding	—	D. A. Dis.
Robinson, Thos. Wm.	L/Cpl.	200004	5th Durham Lt. Infty.	—	Died
Robinson, Walter	Pte.	241842	2/5th K.O.Y.L.I.	—	K. in A.
Robinson, William	Pte.	241971	2nd Scottish Rifles	—	K. in A.
Robinson, Wm. A.	Gnr.	64337	R.G.A.	—	D. a. Dis.
Robinson, Wm. W.	Pte.	5100	1/5th Welsh	—	Died
Robshaw, James	Pte.	20656	Yorks.	—	K. in A.
Robshaw, John	Pte.	12190	6th Yorks.	—	K. in A.
Robshaw, Joseph A.	Pte.	3548	2nd Northumb'l'd Fusrs.	—	K. in A.
Robshaw, Samuel	Pte.	12473	2nd K.O.Y.L.I.	—	K. in A.
Robshaw, Thos. A.	A.B.	1494	H.M.S. "Good Hope"	—	K. in A.
Robson, Albert	Pte.	44516	Essex	—	K. in A.
Robson, Arthur	Pte.	37030	9th W. Yorks.	—	K. in A.
Robson, Ernest C.	Pte.	29235	3rd W. Yorks.	—	D. a. Dis.
Robson, F. W.	Lieut.		5th Machine Gun Corps	—	K. in A.
Robson, George	Pte.	1300	15th W. Yorks.	M.M.	K. in A.
Robson, Geo.	Rfm.	20558	King's Royal Rifle Cps.	—	K. in A.
Robson, Herbert E.	Pte.	69024	Northumberland Fusrs.	—	Died
Robson, John C.	Pte.	4690	Seaforth Highlanders	—	K. in A.
Robson, John Wm.	Pte.	61058	8th Liverpool	—	D. of W.
Robson, Walter	Pte.	38689	2nd W. Yorks.	—	Missing
Roche, Jos. H.	Pte.	76059	Durham Lt. Infantry	—	K. in A.
Roddy, Joseph	Pte.	140889	21st Machine Gun Corps	—	K. in A.
Roddy, Wm.	Pte.	42108	Northumberland Fusrs.	—	Died
Rodgers, Arthur	2Stkr.	K48056	H.M.S. "Victory"	—	Killed
Rodgers, Austin	Pte.	1031	3rd W. Riding	—	D. a. Dis.
Rodgers, Charles	Pte.	47097	26th Northumb'l'd Fusrs.	—	D. of W.
Rodgers, Charles	Pte.	242161	W. Yorks.	—	Died
Rodgers, Geo. H.	Pte.	37448	W. Yorks.	—	Died
Rodgers, Harry	Pte.	44614	13th Northumb'l'd Fusrs.	—	K. in A.
Rodgers, Joseph	Pte.	401287	R.A.M.C.	—	D. of W.
Rodley, Hedley	Pte.	409	17th W. Yorks.	—	K. in A.
Rodley, Richard	Cpl.	305283	W. Yorks.	—	D. a. Dis.
Rodwell, James W.	Pte.	79012	1/22nd London	—	K. in A.
Roebuck, E.	Pte.	204658	20th Durham Lt. Infty.	—	K. in A.
Rogan, J. G.	Sgt.	7572	1/9th London	—	K. in A.
Rogan, John	Pte.	24071	2/6th W. Riding	—	K. in A.
Rogan, Wm.	Pte.	21580	2nd Highland Lt. Infty.	—	K. in A.
Rogers, Arthur D.	Pte.	772	15th W. Yorks.	—	K. in A.
Rogers, Herbert	Pte.	13068	11th W. Yorks.	—	K. in A.
Rogers, James H.	Pte.	13642	9th K.O.Y.L.I.	—	D. of W.
Rogers, Walter	Dvr.	063355	R.A.S.C.	—	K. in A.
Rogerson, Geo.	Pte.	81668	1/5th Durham Lt. Infty.	—	K. in A.
Rollinson, Alfred A.	L/Cpl.	181363	Royal Engineers	—	K. in A.
Rollinson, Arthur	Pte.	47296	W. Yorks.	—	K. in A.
Rollinson, Harold	Gnr.	176964	R.G.A.	—	K. in A.

LEEDS ROLL OF HONOUR.

Name	Rank	No.	Regiment	Honours	How Died
Rollinson, Herbert	Pte.	23892	K.O.Y.L.I.	—	K. in A.
Rollinson, John G.	Pte.	14011	E. Kent	—	Died
Rollinson, Willie	Spr.	136198	Royal Engineers	—	K. in A.
Ronham, Wm.	Pte.	11927	1/4th K.O.Y.L.I.	—	K. in A.
Rooke, Albert	Pte.	16519	12th W. Yorks.	—	Died
Rooms, Maurice	Pte.	51881	Lincoln	—	K. in A.
Roper, George	O.S.	J58200	H.M.S. "Naneric"	—	D. a. Dis.
Roper, Herbert	Pte.	22370	11th W. Yorks.	—	D. of W.
Rosanberg, Bernard	Pte.	40025	9th Royal Irish Fusrs.	—	K. in A.
Roscoe, Ernest	2nd Lieut.		17th W. Yorks.	—	Killed
Rose, George	L/Cpl.	10998	9th Scottish Rifles	—	K. in A.
Rose, John Hy.	Pte.	849	17th W. Yorks.	—	D. a. Dis.
Roseman, Myer	Pte.	9269	W. Yorks.	—	K. in A.
Rosenberg, Abraham	Pte.	34958	51st Machine Gun Corps	—	K. in A.
Rosenberg, Joe	Rfm.	13468	King's Royal Rifle Cps.	—	Missing
Rosenberg, Leslie	O.S.	YZ10143	H.M.S. "President"	—	Drowned
Rosenbloom, Abraham	Pte.	29528	1st W. Yorks.	—	K. in A.
Rosenblum, Marks	Dvr.	156284	R.F.A.	—	K. in A.
Rosendale, Horace	Pte.	34186	9th W. Yorks.	—	K. in A.
Rosendale, Jacob	L/Cpl.	3969	1/7th W. Yorks.	—	D. of W.
Rosendale, Joseph	L/Cpl.	13886	K.O.Y.L.I.	—	K. in A.
Rosendale, Richard	S.Maj.	6585	8th E. Yorks.	—	D. of W.
Rosendale, Robinson	Pte.	14760	K.O.Y.L.I.	—	D. of W.
Rosenthall, H.	Pte.	28/34	16th Northumb'l'd Fusrs.	—	K. in A.
Rosindale, Fredk. W.	L/Cpl.	6632	6th E. Yorks.	—	K. in A.
Ross, Harry	Pte.	10640	W. Riding	—	Died
Ross, Henry	Pte.	11118	2nd K.O. Scottish Bdrs.	—	Died
Ross, Herbert	A.B.	226497	H.M.S. "Lynx"	—	Died
Ross, Hugh	Pte.	203437	K.O.Y.L.I.	—	K. in A.
Ross, Johnson	Pte.	12985	Machine Gun Corps	—	K. in A.
Rossington, Fredk.	Pte.	21955	Labour Corps	—	K. in A.
Rothery, Fred	Bdr.	73020	R.F.A.	—	D. of W.
Rothery, James	Pte.	1316	W. Yorks.	—	K. in A.
Rothery, John Hy.	Pte.	325995	Royal Scots Fusiliers	—	K. in A.
Rothery, Vincent	Pte.	62199	W. Yorks.	—	Died P.O.W.
Rothery, Wilkinson	Spr.	11547	13th Royal Fusiliers	—	K. in A.
Rothwell, Arthur	Rfm.	2560	1/8th W. Yorks.	—	D. of W.
Rothwell, John	Sgt.	6917	W. Yorks.	—	K. in A.
Rouhan, Thos.	Pte.	80408	K.O.Y.L.I.	—	K. in A.
Roulstone, G. W.	Sgt.	44193	Machine Gun Corps	—	K. in A.
Roundell, Arthur	Pte.	2292	W. Yorks.	—	K. in A.
Roundhill, John	Pte.	10105	2nd W. Yorks.	—	Died
Rounding, William	Pte.	29174	Labour Corps	—	D. of W.
Rourke, Francis	L/Cpl.	8229	W. Yorks.	—	K. in A.
Rourke, Pat.	Pte.	37367	10th W. Yorks.	—	K. in A.
Rouse, Ernest	Cpl.	776	15th W. Yorks.	—	Died
Routledge, Harry	Pte.	12282	13th Yorks.	—	Died

LEEDS ROLL OF HONOUR.

Name	Rank	No.	Regiment	Honours	How Died
Routledge, William	Sgt.	83900	Royal Engineers	—	D. a. Dis.
Rowan, Andrew	Rfm.	3000	1/8th W. Yorks.	—	K. in A.
Rowan, Michael	L/Cpl.	8660	W. Yorks.	—	K. in A.
Rowe, Herbert	Sgt.	S360003	R.A.S.C.	—	D. a. Dis.
Rowell, Harold	Pte.	78442	13th Durham Lt. Infty.	—	Died
Rowland, Thos.	Rfm.	267190	2/7th W. Yorks.	—	Missing
Rowland, Thos.	Rfm.	1324	8th W. Yorks.	—	K. in A.
Rowley, Chas. Ed.	O.S.	53/7738	H.M.S. " Temeraire "	—	K. in A.
Rowley, James W.	Pte.	21149	8th K.O.Y.L.I.	—	K. in A.
Rowley, Wm.	Rfm.	307047	2/8th W. Yorks.	—	Died
Rowntree, Herbert	Pte.	311604	R.A.S.C.	—	Drowned
Rowthorn, W. E.	Rfm.	4926	2/8th W. Yorks.	—	D. of W.
Royce, Thos.	Pte.	9467	Northumberland Fusrs.	—	K. in A.
Rubenstein, Chas.	Pte.	38836	25th Northumb'l'd Fusrs.	—	K. in A.
Ruckworth, John A.	Pte.	23339	8th Yorks.	—	K. in A.
Rudd, Fredk...	Pte.	514595	Labour Corps	—	D. a. Dis.
Rudd, Sydney	Pte.	36836	W. Yorks.	—	K. in A.
Ruddick, Jlohn Thos.	Rfm.	11453	King's Royal Rifle Cps.	—	K. in A.
Rudkin, Willie	Pte.	1701	15th W. Yorks.	—	K. in A.
Rudstein, Soloman	Pte.	47940	18th W. Yorks.	—	Missing
Rumbelow, John R.	Dvr.	223866	R.H.A.	—	K. in A.
Rummer, Geo. A.	L/Cpl.	40993	W. Yorks.	—	Died
Rusby, Joseph	Pte.	38089	15th W. Yorks.	—	Missing
Rush, Thos. Hy.	Sgt.	30	R.F.A.	—	K. in A.
Rushby, William	Pte.	52376	Cheshire	—	Died
Rushfirth, Austin	Gnr.	80456	R.F.A.	—	D. of W.
Rushfirth, James	Pte.	170049	Labour Corps	—	D. a. Dis.
Rushforth, Harold	Pte.	519271	Labour Corps	—	Died
Rushforth, John	Rfm.	4099	1/8th W. Yorks.	—	Killed
Rushforth, Lister	Pte.	306978	2nd W. Yorks.	—	D. of W.
Rushworth, Chas.	Pte.	33626	Royal Defence Corps	—	Died
Rushworth, Geo. A.	Tpr.	1989	Fife & Forfar Yeomanry	—	K. in A.
Rushworth, James	A.B.	Z9028	Royal Naval Res.	—	Died
Rushworth, John Wm.	Pte.	32453	13th W. Yorks.	—	Died
Rushworth, Thos. Hy.	L/Cpl.	22412	8th Northumb'l'd Fusrs.	—	K. in A.
Russell, F.	Sgt.	306280	10th W. Yorks.	—	K. in A.
Russell, Frank S.	Pte.	203657	1/4th York. & Lancs.	—	K. in A.
Russell, Fred	Pte.	55664	York. & Lancs.	—	K. in A.
Russell, Jas. Wm.	Pte.	10725	4th W. Yorks.	—	K. in A.
Russell, John	Pte.	10270	9th W. Yorks.	—	Missing
Russell, Wm. Hy.	K.W.	531	Royal Naval V. Res.	—	K. in A.
Ruston, Albert	Rfm.	78285	8th W. Yorks.	—	K. in A.
Ruston, Thos.	Pte.	24061	K.O.Y.L.I.	—	D. of W.
Rutherford, Abraham	Rfm.	267050	2/7th W. Yorks.	—	Died
Rutherford, Mark	Lieut.		Tank Corps	—	K. in A.
Rutter, Alb. H.	Pte.	27471	S. Staffs.	—	Died
Rutter, G. M.	Rfm.	306398	8th W. Yorks.	—	K. in A.

LEEDS ROLL OF HONOUR.

Name	Rank	No.	Regiment	Honours	How Died
Ryall, Chas. R.	Rfm.	2620	1/7th W. Yorks.	—	D. of W.
Ryan, Bernard	Pte.	14980	16th W. Yorks.	—	K. in A.
Ryan, Edward	Pte.	569540	12th Durham Lt. Infty.	—	D. a. Dis.
Ryan, Fredk.	Sgt.	779	15th W. Yorks.	—	D. of W.
Ryan, Geo. W.	Pte.	28002	12th W. Yorks.	—	Missing
Ryan, Joseph	Cpl.	9321	6th Yorks.	—	K. in A.
Ryan, Patrick	Gdsmn.	12562	Scots Guards	—	K. in A.
Ryan, Wm.	Dvr.	62746	R.F.A.	—	K. in A.
Ryan, Wm.	Pte.	4955	9th Lancers	—	K. in A.
Ryans, Albert	L/Cpl.	21383	Royal Highlanders	—	K. in A.
Rycroft, Geo. Hy.	Pte.	12705	W. Riding	—	K. in A.
Ryder, Albert	Gnr.	65383	R.G.A.	—	D. a. Dis.
Ryder, Herbert	Gnr.	775804	R.F.A.	—	D. of W.
Ryder, John Wm.	Pte.	36395	8th Northumb'l'd Fus.	—	D. of W.
Sacofsky, M.	Pte.	28555	Leicester	—	Missing
Sadler, Leonard	Pte.	401422	R.A.M.C.	—	D. of W.
Sadler, Thomas	Pte.	12121	W. Yorks.	—	K. in A.
Sagar, E.	Gnr.	165908	R.F.A.	—	Died
Sager, Percy	Pte.	19180	2nd Suffolk	—	Died
Sales, Joseph	Pte.	410144	948th Labour Co.	—	D. a. Dis.
Salmon, Wm.	Pte.	16125	3rd King's R. Rifle Cps.	—	K. in A.
Sammons, Thomas	Pte.	45950	12th Northumb'l'd Fus.	—	K. in A.
Sample, John Wm.	A.B.	J24146	H.M.S. " Black Prince "	—	Died
Sampson, John E.	Pte.	37816	17th W. Yorks.	—	Died P.O.W.
Sampson, Joseph	Pte.	165712	Labour Corps	—	K. in A.
Sampson, Thomas H.	Sgt.	M/2216	Royal Engineers	—	Died
Samuel, Abey N.	Pte.	35666	K.O.Y.L.I.	—	D. of W.
Samuels, Harry	Pte.	40966	1st S. Staffs.	—	K. in A.
Sandaver, Reginald	Pte.	81671	5th Durham Lt. Infty.	—	K. in A.
Sandays, Wm. R.	Pte.	DM2/163110	R.A.S.C. (M.T.)	—	Killed
Sanders, Albert	Pte.	41638	Northumberland Fusrs.	—	K. in A.
Sanderson, Ernest	Pte.	6007	Highland Light Infantry	—	K. in A.
Sanderson, Frank	Pte.	23970	14th W. Yorks.	—	D. of W.
Sanderson, Jas. A.	Gnr.	127718	R.F.A.	—	Died
Sanderson, Jas. W.	Pte.	55986	10th W. Yorks.	—	K. in A.
Sanderson, John	Pte.	1708	W. Yorks.	—	K. in A.
Sanderson, Richard	Pte.	49664	W. Yorks.	—	K. in A.
Sanderson, Wm. Jas.	Pte.	28213	1st Royal Scots	—	K. in A.
Sandford, Jas.	Pte.	7504	W. Yorks.	—	K. in A.
Sandiforth, Arthur	Pte.	7938	W. Yorks.	—	K. in A.
Sandiforth, Arthur	Pte.	2967	1/5th W. Riding	—	K. in A.
Sandiforth, Ernest	Pte.	13730	K.O.Y.L.I.	—	K. in A.
Sandiforth, Frank	Sgt.	775032	R.F.A.	—	K. in A.
Sandiforth, Fred	Pnr.		New Zealand	—	K. in A.
Sandland, Robert D.	Q.M.S.		W. Yorks.	—	Died
Sands, Percival	Pte.	127484	Training Reserve	—	Died

LEEDS ROLL OF HONOUR.

Name	Rank	No.	Regiment	Honours	How Died
Sands, S.	Q.M.S.	5949	W. Riding	—	Died
Sanofski, Israel	Pte.	202186	W. Yorks.	—	Died
Sang, Fred Wm.	Pte.	41753	Essex	—	K. in A.
Saperia, Louis	Pte.	41458	9th W. Yorks.	—	K. in A.
Sarginson, Wm.	Pte.	19117	9th Yorks.	—	K. in A.
Sattenstall, Wm.	Gnr.	301687	Tank Corps	—	K. in A.
Saunders, Harold M.	Lieut.		11th E. Lancs.	—	K. in A.
Saunders, Jack	Pte.	9463	Northumberland Fusrs.	—	K. in A.
Saunders, Reginald	Gnr.	168644	R.F.A.	—	Died
Savage, Norman	Gnr.	94146	R.G.A.	—	K. in A.
Saville, Benj.	Pte.	205496	10th Royal W. Kent	—	Killed
Saville, Fred	Pte.	7217	1st W. Yorks.	—	K. in A.
Saville, Jas. H.	Pte.	19805	W. Yorks.	—	K. in A.
Saville, Jesse	Pte.	20430	K.O. Scottish Borderers	—	K. in A.
Saville, Louis	Pte.	43236	5th Durham Lt. Infty.	—	Died
Saville, Rufus W.	Pte.	242335	E. Surrey	—	K. in A.
Saville, Tom W.	Pte.	106	12th K.O.Y.L.I.	—	K. in A.
Sawyer, Albert W.	Pte.	28150	Grenadier Guards	—	K. in A.
Sawyer, Geo. Wm.	Rfm.	1740	7th W. Yorks.	—	D. a. Dis.
Saville, Harry	Sig.	786085	R.F.A.	—	Died
Saxton, George	Rfm.	1336	1/7th W. Yorks.	—	D. of W.
Saxton, Maurice	Pte.	7405	2nd W. Riding	—	D. of W.
Sayer, Harold	Cpl.	403125	R.A.M.C.	—	Died
Sayer, James A.	Pte.	5/41005	Cameron Highlanders	—	D. of W.
Sayles, G.W.	Pte.	8588	12th Lancers	—	K. in A.
Saynor, Frank	L/Cpl.	306322	1/8th W. Yorks.	—	K. in A.
Saynor, Lionel	Gnr.	192052	R.G.A.	—	Died
Saynor, Wm.	L/Cpl.	1351	15th W. Yorks.	—	K. in A.
Scaife, John T.	Pte.	22604	Durham Light Infantry	—	K. in A.
Scales, Walter	Pte.	107210	Royal Fusiliers	—	Died
Scarce, John B.	Rfm.	267140	1/7th W. Yorks.	—	K. in A.
Scargill, H.	Pte.	88120	W. Yorks.	—	Died
Scarr, Reg. G.	2nd Lieut.		12th W. Yorks.	—	K. in A.
Scarth, Geo.	Pte.	37014	16th W. Yorks.	—	K. in A.
Scarth, John Wm.	Pte.	18437	16th W. Yorks.	—	Missing
Scatcherd, Edward	Rfm.	2731	1/7th W. Yorks.	—	K. in A.
Scatcherd, Fredk.	Spr.	84160	Royal Engineers	—	K. in A.
Scatcherd, Jos.	Pte.	37966	74th Machine Gun Corps	—	K. in A.
Scawboard, Tom	Pte.	1545	15th W. Yorks.	—	Missing
Schimeld, Thos.	Rfm.	1187	1/8th W. Yorks.	—	K. in A.
Schofield, Albert	Pte.	202605	King's Liverpool	—	K. in A.
Schofield, Frank E.	Cpl.	775979	R.F.A.	—	Died
Schofield, George	Gnr.	10660	R.G.A.	—	K. in A.
Schofield, George	Rfm.	1729	1/7th W. Yorks.	—	K. in A.
Schofield, Geo. Wm.	Bmdr.	65857	R.F.A.	—	D. of W.
Schofield, H.	Pte.	475201	27th Canadian	—	K. in A.
Schofield, Harry	Pte.	12420	11th W. Yorks.	—	K. in A.

LEEDS ROLL OF HONOUR.

Name	Rank	No.	Regiment	Honours	How Died
Schofield, Harry	L/Cpl.	10972	10th W. Yorks.	—	K. in A.
Schofield, James	Rfm.	205545	7th W. Yorks.	—	D. of W.
Schofield, John Hy.	Dvr.	82464	R.F.A.	—	K. in A.
Schofield, Joseph S.	Pte.	10973	W. Yorks.	—	K. in A.
Schofield, Lawrence	Pte.	241420	W. Yorks.	—	K. in A.
Schofield, Tom	Pte.	3117	1st S. African Infty.	—	Died
Schofield, Walter B.	Pte.	235243	1/5th W. Yorks.	—	K. in A.
Schofield, Wm. I.	L/Cpl.	47344	25th Northumb'l'd Fus.	—	K. in A.
Scholefield, Harry	2nd Lieut.		1/4th K.O.Y.L.I.	—	D. of W.
Scholes, Walter	Pte.	60702	Northumberland Fusrs.	—	K. in A.
Scholey, Albert	Pte.	38363	25th Durham Lt. Infty.	—	D. a. Dis.
Scholey, Alfred	Pte.	41407	17th W. Yorks.	—	Killed
Scholey, Fred	Pte.	J/52186	8th Middlesex	—	K. in A.
Scholey, Clifford	Pte.	H/8971	15th Hussars	—	K. in A.
Scholey, George	Gnr.	108770	R.G.A.	—	K. in A.
Scholey, George	Spr.	83834	Royal Engineers	—	K. in A.
Scholey, James	Rfm.	5266	1/7th W. Yorks.	—	K. in A.
Scholey, James	Rfm.	1823	1/7th W. Yorks.	—	K. in A.
Schutz, Clarence	Sgt.	43	1/7th W. Yorks.	—	K. in A.
Scobey, Francis H.	Dvr.	81215	R.F.A.	—	K. in A.
Scoffield, Freeman	Rfm.	1636	1/7th W. Yorks.	—	K. in A.
Scott, Albert	Pte.	694764	Labour Corps	—	Died
Scott, Albert	Pte.	13231	K.O.Y.L.I.	—	D. of W.
Scott, Arthur	Pte.	7813	1st W. Yorks.	—	D. of W.
Scott, Arthur	Cpl.	791	15th W. Yorks.	—	Died
Scott, Benj.	Rfm.	6230	18th King's R. Rifle Cps.	—	K. in A.
Scott, Clarence	L.Tel.	J31016	H.M.S. " Torrent "	—	K. in A.
Scott, Edward	L/Cpl.	14375	12th W. Yorks.	—	K. in A.
Scott, Fred	Pte.	S/11310	Rifle Brigade	—	K. in A.
Scott, Fred	Pte.	792	15th W. Yorks.	—	K. in A.
Scott, George	Sgt.	11492	Scots Guards	—	D. a. Dis.
Scott, Harold	Rfm.	377875	P.O. Rifles	—	D. a. Dis.
Scott, James	Stkr.	109399	Royal Navy	—	D. a. Dis.
Scott, James			H.M.S. " Woolwich "	—	Died
Scott, John	Rfm.	3152	W. Yorks.	—	D. a. Dis.
Scott, John E.	L/Cpl.	1070	15th W. Yorks.	—	K. in A.
Scott, John Wm.	Pte.	5/8548	2nd W. Yorks.	—	K. in A.
Scott, John Wm.	Pte.	12862	K.O.Y.L.I.	—	K. in A.
Scott, Leonard	Pte.	260545	W. Yorks.	—	K. in A.
Scott, Leonard	Pte.	G/52162	Middlesex	—	Died
Scott, Malcolm W.	Pte.	268195	W. Yorks.	—	Died
Scott, Thomas	Rfm.	1934	7th W. Yorks.	—	D. a. Dis.
Scott, Walter R.	Eng. 1 Grade		Royal Naval Air Service	—	Died
Scott, William	Pte.	112676	R.A.S.C.	—	D. a. Dis.
Scott, Wm. E.	S.M.	590	1/7th W. Yorks.	M.M.	K. in A.
Scott, Wm. H.	Pte.	7409	1st E. Yorks.	—	K. in A.
Scriminger, Ernest	Pte.	7899	2nd W. Yorks.	—	Died P.O.W.

LEEDS ROLL OF HONOUR

Name	Rank	No.	Regiment	Honours	How Died
Scrubbs, Arthur	Pte.	26099	10th E. Yorks.	—	K. in A.
Scrubbs, J. T.	Cpl.	36149	Northumberland Fusrs.	—	K. in A.
Scruton, Henry	Pte.	8612	1st York. & Lancs.	—	K. in A.
Scruton, John	Pte.	76278	Durham Lt. Infantry	—	K. in A.
Scully, John	L/Cpl.	10512	W. Yorks.	—	K. in A.
Scupham, Arthur	Pte.	33058	4th W. Yorks.	—	K. in A.
Scurr, Leonard	L/Cpl.	41845	10th Northumb'l'd Fus.	—	K. in A.
Seaman, Alfred T.	Pte.	26246	9th Yorks.	—	D. of W.
Season, Chas.	Pte.	10403	Border	—	K. in A.
Secker, Wilfred	Pte.	2900	1/5th W. Yorks.	—	K. in A.
Seddon, Fred	Pte.	25160	W. Yorks.	—	D. of W.
Seddon, Norman	Pte.	4059	2/5th K.O.Y.L.I.	—	K. in A.
Sedgwick, Frank	Pte.	38811	Northumberland Fusrs.	—	K. in A.
Sedgwick, George	Pte.	306167	W. Yorks.	—	K. in A.
Sedgwick, John	Sgt.	9080	9th Yorks.	—	K. in A.
Sedgwick, Lawrence	Pte.	49799	Royal Fusiliers	—	K. in A.
Sedgwick, Leonard	Pte.	16432	W. Yorks.	—	D. of W.
Sedgwick, Thos. Wm.	Gdsmn.	11710	Scots Guards	—	Drowned
Sedgwick, Wm.	L/Cpl.	160296	Royal Engineers	—	Drowned
Sedman, Cecil	L/Cpl.	133359	9th W. Yorks.	—	K. in A.
Seed, J. Wm.	Pte.	41637	Northumb'l'd Fus.	—	K. in A.
Seed, Wm. Hy.	Gnr.	795746	R.F.A.	—	K. in A.
Sefton, H.	Rfm.	203058	7th Rifle Brigade	—	K. in A.
Sefton, W.	Pte.	200088	W. Yorks.	—	Died
Selby, Albert	Cpl.	7950	Yorkshire	—	Died
Selby, George	Pte.	48119	Yorkshire	—	K. in A.
Selby, Wm.	A.C. 2	147028	Royal Air Force	—	D. a. Dis.
Self, George	Pte.	77376	Durham Lt. Infantry	—	D. of W.
Sellers, David	Pte.	17842	Northumberland Fusrs.	—	K. in A.
Sellers, Tom R.	Pte.	5071	Royal Defence Corps.	—	D. a. Dis.
Sen, J. N.	Pte.	795	15th W. Yorks.	—	K. in A.
Seneschall, Herbert	Cpl.	6136	Lincoln	—	K. in A.
Senior, Charles	Pte.	37716	16th W. Yorks.	—	K. in A.
Senior, Chas. F.	Pte.	36475	17th W. Yorks.	—	K. in A.
Senior, George	Pte.	22918	10th Highland Lt. Infty.	—	K. in A.
Senior, Harry	Pte.	42777	K.O.Y.L.I.	—	K. in A.
Senior, Herbert	Gnr.	214380	R.F.A.	—	K. in A.
Senior, James	Pte.	44480	25th Northumb'l'd Fus.	—	K. in A.
Senior, Joe	Pte.	36233	Northumberland Fusrs.	—	D. a. Dis.
Senior, John	Pte.	11616	K.O.Y.L.I.	—	K. in A.
Senior, Joseph	L/Cpl.	305236	3/8th W. Yorks.	—	K. in A.
Senior, Sylvester	Pte.	65210	K.O.Y.L.I.	—	Died
Senior, Thos. A.	L/Cpl.		6th Dorset	—	K. in A.
Senior, Thos. Ed.	Pte.	32405	16th W. Yorks.	—	K. in A.
Senior, Walter	A.B.	SS9186	Royal Navy	—	K. in A.
Senior, Wm. G.	Pte.	35888	1/5th K.O.Y.L.I.	—	K. in A.
Sergeant, Robert J.	Pte.	291967	Middlesex	—	Died

LEEDS ROLL OF HONOUR.

Name	Rank	No.	Regiment	Honours	How Died
Seward, Arthur	Pte.	29180	Labour Corps	—	K. in A.
Seward, Wm.	Rfm.	16591	King's Royal Rifle Corps	—	K. in A.
Sewell, B. C.	Dvr.	73512	R.F.A.	—	Died
Sewell, Wilfred	Sgt.	800	15th W. Yorks.	—	K. in A.
Shackleton, C. E.	Dvr.	309533	R.A.S.C.	—	D. a. Dis.
Shackleton, Ernest	L/Cpl.	9849	1st W. Yorks.	—	K. in A.
Shackleton, Hy. L. N.	Gdsmn.	14809	Scots Guards	—	K. in A.
Shackleton, Sydney	Pte.	82484	Durham Light Infantry	—	Died
Shakespear					
Shann, Allan W.	2nd Lieut.		8th W. Yorks.	—	K. in A.
Shann, John W.	Lieut. Act. Ad.		10th Yorks.	—	K. in A.
Shann, John Wm.	Pte.	203944	1/4th Seaforth Highdrs.	—	K. in A.
Shann, Thos. E.	Sgt.	75085	Royal Engineers	—	Died
Shannon, Geo. E.	Pte.	19453	York. & Lancs.	—	K. in A.
Sharp, Albert	Pte.	854	17th W. Yorks.	—	Died
Sharp, Alfred	Rfm.	307735	W. Yorks.	—	K. in A.
Sharp, Clarence	Pte.	31170	E. Yorks.	—	Missing
Sharp, Frank	Pte.	1039	15th W. Yorks.	—	Missing
Sharp, Fred	Pte.	20/501	Durham Light Infantry	—	Died
Sharp, Harold	Pte.	27214	16th W. Yorks.	—	Died
Sharp, Harry	Pte.	72789	Notts. & Derby	—	K. in A.
Sharp, Harry	Pte.	1898	W. Yorks.	—	K. in A.
Sharp, James	Sgt.	99147	6th K.O.Y.L.I.	—	Died
Sharp, James			W. Yorks.	—	Died
Sharp, Jas.	L/Sgt.	6818	12th W. Yorks.	—	K. in A.
Sharp, Leonard	Pte.	4399	4th Seaforth Highdrs.	—	K. in A.
Sharp, Wm. A.	Pte.	43204	W. Yorks.	—	D. of W.
Sharpe, Arthur	Pte.	4918	1st H.A.C.	—	K. in A.
Sharpe, Chas. Hy.	Pte.		9th Norfolk	—	K. in A.
Sharples, Jas.	Cpl.	804	15th W. Yorks.	—	Missing
Sharples, Wm.	Pte.	49246	10th Lancs. Fus.	—	K. in A.
Shaw, Alfred	Spr.	107941	Royal Engineers	—	K. in A.
Shaw, Alfred B.	Clk.	M/22794	H.M.S. " Glatton "	—	K. in A.
Shaw, Arthur	Pte.	376510	15th Durham Lt. Infty.	—	K. in A.
Shaw, Benj.	Pte.	201069	1/4th Welsh	—	Missing
Shaw, Chas.	Rfm.	39403	1/8th W. Yorks.	—	K. in A.
Shaw, David	Pte.	202034	W. Yorks.	—	K. in A.
Shaw, Ernest	Rfm.	522	7th W. Yorks.	—	Died
Shaw, Frank	L/Cpl.	11104	K.O. Scottish Borderers	—	K. in A.
Shaw, Fred	Pte.	203163	W. Yorks.	—	K. in A.
Shaw, Fred	Dvr.	107262	Royal Engineers	—	Died
Shaw, Fred	Pte.	88129	W. Yorks.	—	K. in A.
Shaw, George	Pte.	23978	12th W. Yorks.	—	K. in A.
Shaw, George	Pte.	91282	Durham Light Infantry	—	K. in A.
Shaw, Geo. H.	Rfm.	R/9011	King's Royal Rifle Cps.	—	K. in A.
Shaw, Geo. H.	L/Cpl.	13756	10th W. Yorks.	—	D. of W.
Shaw, Harry	Pte.	47500	1st Leicester	—	Died

LEEDS ROLL OF HONOUR.

Name	Rank	No.	Regiment	Honours	How Died
Shaw, James	L/Cpl.	8015	1st W. Yorks.	—	K. in A.
Shaw, Jas. H.	Pte.	34286	16th Northumb'l'd Fus.	—	Died
Shaw, John	Pnr.	240764	Royal Engineers	—	Died
Shaw, John J.	Pte.	1951	15th W. Yorks.	—	K. in A.
Shaw, Jos. H.	Gnr.	775597	R.F.A.	—	Died
Shaw, Robert W.	Pte.	592685	1/18th London	—	D. a. Dis.
Shaw, Thomas	Rfm.	305925	2/8th W. Yorks.	—	Missing
Shaw, Thos. H.	Pte.	401123	R.A.M.C.	—	D. of W.
Shaw, Tom	Pte.	20804	K.O.Y.L.I.	—	D. of W.
Shaw, W.	Pte.	1306	15th W. Yorks.	—	K. in A.
Shaw, Walter	2 Pte.	248972	Royal Air Force	—	K. in A.
Shaw, Walter C.	Pte.	806	15th W. Yorks.	—	K. in A.
Shaw, Wm. John	Gdsmn.	8189	1st Scots Guards	—	K. in A.
Sheard, Alfred J.	Spr.	71888	Royal Engineers	—	Died
Sheard, Arthur	S.Sgt.	408011	R.A.M.C.	—	Died
Sheard, Arthur	Pte.	35263	9th W. Yorks.	—	K. in A.
Sheard, E.	Sgt.	477	17th W. Yorks.	—	K. in A.
Sheard, Harold	Pte.	245119	Durham Light Infantry	—	K. in A.
Sheard, James	Rfm.	306887	2/8th W. Yorks.	—	K. in A.
Sheard, James	Pte.	69211	2nd Devons	—	Died
Sheard, John	Pte.	2650	Northumberland Fusrs.	—	K. in A.
Sheard, John L.	Pte.	809	15th W. Yorks.	—	D. of W.
Sheard, Joseph	Pte.	91289	Durham Light Infantry	—	K. in A.
Shearon, Jas. Ed.	Pte.	4/7964	1st W. Yorks.	—	K. in A.
Shearsmith, Wm. Edwin	Bmdr.	775724	R.F.A.	—	Killed
Shepherd, Arthur S.	Cpl.	13089	11th W. Yorks.	—	K. in A.
Shepherd, Bertram	Pte.	23847	York. & Lancs.	—	K. in A.
Shepherd, Charles	Pte.	306102	W. Yorks.	—	K. in A.
Shepherd, Edward	Pte.	203453	York. & Lancs.	—	K. in A.
Shepherd, George	Pte.	2077	W. Yorks.	—	K. in A.
Shepherd, Norman L.	Rfm.	62805	1/7th W. Yorks.	—	K. in A.
Shepherd, Walter R.	Bglr.	10579	2nd K.O.Y.L.I.	—	K. in A.
Sheppard, Chas. W. S.	Pte.	54037	W. Yorks.	—	K. in A.
Sherlock, Henry	L/Cpl.	83658	Royal Engineers	—	D. of W.
Sherman, Solomon	Rfm.	5151	2/8th W. Yorks.	—	K. in A.
Sherrard, Robert	A.Bs.	R3524	Drake Btn. Royal Navy	—	D. of W.
Sherwin, Hugh	Pte.	781	17th W. Yorks.	—	K. in A.
Sherwood, Herbert	Pte.	DM2/169470	R.A.S.C.	—	K. in A.
Shields, Horace	Rfm.	5500	W. Yorks.	—	K. in A.
Shillito, Alfred	Pte.	37290	1/5th W. Yorks.	—	Missing
Shillito, Tom	L/Cpl.	267366	W. Yorks.	—	K. in A.
Shinn, J. W.	L/Cpl.	29456	1/7th W. Yorks.	—	Missing
Shipman, Edward	Pte.	10362	10th W. Yorks.	—	K. in A.
Shipman, Wm.	Pte.	50452	N. Staffs.	—	Missing.
Shippen, Albert	Pte.	24243	W. Yorks.	—	K. in A.
Shippen, Harry	Pte.	23141	11th Northumb'l'd Fus.	—	K. in A.
Shippen, Tom	L/Cpl.	8572	2nd W. Yorks.	—	K. in A.

LEEDS ROLL OF HONOUR.

Name	Rank	No.	Regiment	Honours	How Died
Shipstone, Ernest	Pte.	4/8344	W. Yorks.	—	D. of W.
Shires, Harry	Pte.	42574	1/10th Manchester	—	K. in A.
Shires, Leonard	Pte.	31060	19th Manchester	—	Missing
Shires, Wm.	Pte.	20953	K.O. Scottish Borderers	—	D. a. Dis.
Shoesmith, Harry	Pte.	2910	23rd London	—	K. in A.
Shoesmith, John	Pte.	C16474	Royal Sussex	—	D. of W.
Shoesmith, Wm. C.	Bmdr.	776018	R.F.A.	—	K. in A.
Short, T. T.	Pte.	19448	Northampton	—	Died
Shortell, Ernest	Pte.	7722	2nd W. Yorks.	—	Died
Shouksmith, Harold W.	Pte.	40845	16th W. Yorks.	—	K. in A.
Shubotham, John	Pte.	12045	10th K.O.Y.L.I.	—	K. in A.
Shuter, Herbert	L/Cpl.	267441	1/7th W. Yorks.	—	Killed
Shuter, Robert	Pte.	1221	K.O. Scottish Borderers	—	D. a. Dis.
Shutt, F.	Pte.	25622	K.O.Y.L.I.	—	K. in A.
Shutt, Harry	Pte.	26769	Labour Corps	—	K. in A.
Shutt, John Ed.	Gnr.	778615	R.F.A.	—	K. in A.
Sibley, Ben.	Cpl.	9303	16th King's R. Rifle Cps.	—	Missing
Sibson, Geo.	Pte.	23479	22nd Royal Fusiliers	—	Missing
Sibson, George	L/Cpl.	20054	6th Training Reserve	—	Died
Siddle, Arthur	Pte.	245212	Durham Light Infantry	—	Died
Siddle, Edward	Sgt.	37	8th W. Yorks.	—	D. a. Dis.
Sidebottom, Ben	Rfm.	300061	1/8th W. Yorks.	—	K. in A.
Sidebottom, Chas.	A/Cpl.	2005	Lincoln	—	Died
Sidebottom, James	Pte.	18582	W. Yorks.	—	Died
Sienesi, S. C.	A.B.	209400	H.M.S. "Petard"	—	Died
Sigsworth, Wm. H.	Pte.	125533	R.A.M.C.	—	Died
Silberg, Manuel	Pte.	10929	9th W. Riding	—	K. in A.
Silcock, C. C.	Sgt.	43292	Canadian Field Artillery	—	D. of W.
Silcock, Fred	Rfm.	2996	8th W. Yorks.	—	K. in A.
Silcock, William	Pte.	39896	2nd W. Yorks.	—	K. in A.
Silcock, William	Sgt.	266945	1/7th W. Yorks.	—	Missing
Silverman, Henry	2 A.M.	22010	Royal Air Force	—	D. a. Dis.
Silverstone, Sanuel	Pte.	214011	Labour Corps	—	Died
Silverwood, Albert	Pte.	7145	K.O.Y.L.I.	—	K. in A.
Silverwood, Herbert	Cpl.	45266	R.F.A.	—	K. in A.
Simmonds, Ed. J.	Pte.	29902	2nd Dorset	—	K. in A.
Simmons, George	Bmdr.	82183	R.F.A.	—	K. in A.
Simmons, George	Pte.	21313	K.O. Scottish Borderers	—	K. in A.
Simmons, Geo. Jas.	Gnr.	196423	R.F.A.	—	K. in A.
Simmons, Herbert	Pte.	201577	1/4th Royal Lancs.	—	D. of W.
Simmons, John Ed.	Pte.	21772	10th Worcester	—	Missing
Simms, Sydney G.	Sig.	306216	8th W. Yorks.	—	K. in A.
Simon, Barnett	Pte.	298288	R.A.S.C.	—	Died
Simon, Chas.	Pte.	20020	15th Cheshire	—	K. in A.
Simon, Chas. R.	Sgt.	193	1/7th West Yorks.	—	K. in A.
Simon, Harry	Cpl.	20396	R.F.A.	—	D. of W.
Simon, Sidney	Spr.	73311	Royal Engineers	—	D. of W.

LEEDS ROLL OF HONOUR.

Name	Rank	No.	Regiment	Honours	How Died
Simpkins, Arthur W.	Captain		8th W. Yorks.	—	K. in A.
Simpson, Arthur	Pte.	41624	13th Royal Scots	—	Missing
Simpson, Charles	Sig.	306072	2/8th W. Yorks.	—	K. in A.
Simpson, E.	Pte.	38270	W. Yorks.	—	K. in A.
Simpson, E. C.	Captain		H.M.S. " Transylvania "	M.C.	Drowned
Simpson, Edward	Pte.	53229	2/5th Lincoln	—	K. in A.
Simpson, F. R.	Pte.	80517	Durham Light Infantry	—	K. in A.
Simpson, Frank	A.B.	J/31130	Royal Navy	—	K. in A.
Simpson, Geo. W.	Pte.	235869	K.O.Y.L.I.	—	Died
Simpson, Henry		6801	2nd Durham Lt. Infty.	—	K. in A.
Simpson, Herbert	Gnr.	34265	R.F.A.	—	K. in A.
Simpson, J. H.			Royal Engineers	—	Died
Simpson, James	Pte.	20820	3rd K.O.Y.L.I.	—	K. in A.
Simpson, John	Pte.	1430	R.A.S.C.	—	K. in A.
Simpson, John	Pte.	37671	9th W. Yorks.	—	D. of W.
Simpson, John	Rfm.	8217	7th W. Yorks.	—	Died
Simpson, John E.	Pte.	PO/18289	Royal Marine Lt. Infty.	—	Died
Simpson, John T.		8787	1st Northumb'l'd Fusrs.	—	K. in A.
Simpson, Joseph	Pte.	55419	21st Northumb'l'd Fus.	—	K. in A.
Simpson, Joseph	Pte.	2138	W. Yorks.	—	D. a. Dis.
Simpson, Jos. W.	L/Cpl.	2323	1/8th W. Yorks.	—	K. in A.
Simpson, Leonard S.	Spr.	484043	Royal Engineers	—	Died
Simpson, Percy	Pte.	37305	W. Yorks.	—	K. in A.
Simpson, Robert	Pte.	13218	Cameron Highlanders	—	K. in A.
Simpson, Samuel	Pte.	375471	Durham Light Infantry	—	Died
Simpson, T.	Pte.	45322	K.O.Y.L.I.	—	K. in A.
Simpson, Tom	Pte.	T/251944	R.A.S.C.	—	K. in A.
Simpson, Wm.	Pte.	2538	3rd York. & Lancs.	—	K. in A.
Simpson, Wm.	Sgt.	268454	1/8th W. Yorks.	—	K. in A.
Sims, A. A.	Pte.	265767	15th W. Yorks.	—	K. in A.
Sims, Chas. A.	Pte.	18096	10th W. Yorks.	—	K. in A.
Sims, John	Rfm.	267031	1/7th W. Yorks.	—	K. in A.
Sims, Sidney, G.	Rfm.	306216	8th W. Yorks.	—	K. in A.
Sinclair, Harry	Gnr.	142691	R.G.A.	—	Died
Sinclair, John W.	Rfm.	306856	8th W. Yorks.	—	K. in A.
Sinclair, Samuel	Pte.	7513	W. Riding	—	K. in A.
Singleton, John	S.Sgt.		Canadian O.C.	—	K. in A.
Singleton, Thos.	Pte.	629	21st W. Yorks.	—	K. in A.
Sinkinson, Henry	Pte.	333902	Highland Lt. Infantry	—	Died
Sirr, Edward	Pte.	202736	Highland Lt. Infantry	—	K. in A.
Sissons, Robert	Cpl.	15313	8th W. Riding	—	K. in A.
Sitlington, Chas. Hy.	L/Cpl.	11670	1st Liverpool	—	D. of W.
Skellington, Wm.	Rfm.	267101	2/7th W. Yorks.	—	K. in A.
Skelton, Chas. A.	Rfm.	S/6750	1st Rifle Brigade	—	K. in A.
Skelton, F.	Lieut.		Royal Air Force	—	K. in A.
Skelton, John	Rfm.	5348	12th King's R. Rifle Cps.	—	D. of W.
Skelton, Sydney	Pte.	37161	10th W. Yorks.	—	K. in A.

LEEDS ROLL OF HONOUR.

Name	Rank	No.	Regiment	Honours	How Died
Skerrit, Ross ..	A/Cpl.S/	11110	8th Rifle Brigade	—	K. in A.
Skilbeck, Hy. Chas.	L/Cpl.	28990	1st W. Yorks.	—	K. in A.
Skipper, Horace	L/Cpl.	8257	1st W. Yorks.	—	D. of W.
Skipsey, F. ..	Rfm.	305345	1/8th W. Yorks.	—	K. in A.
Skirrow, Wm. A.	Pte.	260009	3/4th W. Riding	—	D. of W.
Slack, John P.	Pte.	29105	13th W. Yorks.	—	K. in A.
Sladden, John	Pte.	1063	21st W. Yorks.	—	Died
Slater, Benj. ..	Pte.	884	Seaforth Highlanders ..	—	K. in A.
Slater, Cyril ..	Pte.	37740	W. Yorks. ..	—	K. in A.
Slater, F. ..	Pnr.	118929	Royal Engineers	—	K. in A.
Slater, Fred ..	W.Tel.	36567	H.M.S. " Valour "	—	K. in A.
Slater, Fred ..	Pte.	37009	W. Yorks. ..	—	K. in A.
Slater, Joseph	Pte.	4/7901	W. Yorks.	—	K. in A.
Slater, Tom B.	Cpl.	37691	Northumberland Fusrs.	—	Died
Sleight, John Wm.	Cpl.	13782	W. Yorks. ..	—	Died
Slicer, Louis ..	Rfm.	45199	Rifle Brigade ..	—	Died
Slinger, Chas...	Pte.		17th W. Yorks.	—	D. of W.
Slinger, Edward	Pte.	202190	4th Welsh Fusiliers ..	—	K. in A.
Sloan, Peter ..	Pte.	32113	21st W. Yorks. ..	—	K. in A.
Sloane, Robert	Pte.	40157	1st Royal Scots Fusrs.	—	Died
Sloman, Leopold A.	Pte.	202279	2/4th Lincoln ..	—	K. in A.
Slunker, John Wm.	L/Cpl.	1284	1/8th W. Yorks.	—	K. in A.
Smales, Ben ..	Sgt.	2631	2nd King's R. Rifle Cps.	—	K. in A.
Smales, Jas. W.	Pte.	66539	K.O.Y.L.I.	—	K. in A.
Smalley, Rowland	1/Stkr.		H.M.S. " Black Prince "	—	K. in A.
Smalley, Walter	Pte.	60251	19th Northumb'l'd Fus.	—	Missing
Smalley, Wm. Hy.	Spr.	477204	Royal Engineers	—	Died
Smallpage, Percy	Pte.	242285	2/6th W. Yorks.	—	K. in A.
Smart, Bertie..	Pte.	36966	3rd W. Yorks.	—	K. in A.
Smart, Geo. H.	Gnr.	312709	R.F.A.	—	D. a. Dis.
Smart, Harry..	Pte.	41926	27th Northumb'l'd Fus.	—	Killed
Smart, Jas. ..	Bugler.	1691	1/7th W. Yorks. ..	—	D. of W.
Smart, Robert	Bmdr.	186162	R.F.A.	—	K. in A.
Smethers, John	Pte.	268470	2/6th W. Yorks.	—	Killed
Smickersgill, Geo. A.	Pte.	919	17th W. Yorks.	—	K. in A.
Smiles, Jas. ..	Pte.	6056	W. Yorks. ..	—	D. of W.
Smillie, Geo. A.	Pte.	55314	W. Yorks. ..	—	K. in A.
Smillie, Joseph	Pte.	6053	1/5th W. Yorks.	—	D. of W.
Smith, Albert	Pte.	44632	Lincolns. ..	—	K. in A.
Smith, Albert	Rfm.	4372	1/7th W. Yorks.	—	Killed
Smith, Albert	Spr.	79341	Royal Engineers ..	—	Died
Smith, Albert	Pte. CH/	19671	Royal Marine Lt. Infty.	—	K. in A.
Smith, Albert	Pte.	24347	9th K.O.Y.L.I. ..	—	Missing
Smith, Albert	Stkr.SS/	114387	H.M.S. " Hampshire "	—	K. in A.
Smith, Albert E.	Pte.	1283	1/4th W. Riding ..	—	K. in A.
Smith, Alex. ..	Pte.	267371	6th Seaforth Highdrs.	—	K. in A.
Smith, Alf. ..	S.Smith	772549	R.F.A.	—	Killed

LEEDS ROLL OF HONOUR.

Name	Rank	No.	Regiment	Honours	How Died
Smith, Alonzo	Pte.	2785	1/5th Royal Lancs.	—	K. in A.
Smith, Arthur	1 Stkr.	107875	H.M.S. "Hannibal"	—	Died
Smith, Arthur	Rfm.	3824	2/7th W. Yorks.	—	K. in A.
Smith, Arthur	L/Cpl.	143	R.A.M.C.	—	D. of W.
Smith, Arthur	Pte.	40853	16th W. Yorks.	—	Killed
Smith, Arthur	Pte.	28967	Yorks.	—	K. in A.
Smith, Arthur	Pte.	163859	R.A.S.C.	—	D. a. Dis.
Smith, Arthur	Rfm.	266403	2/7th W. Yorks.	—	K. in A.
Smith, Arthur H.	Pte.	941	21st W. Yorks.	—	K. in A.
Smith, Arthur H.	Pte.	21978	8th S. Staffs.	—	K. in A.
Smith, Arthur Wm.	Gnr.	L/5843	R.F.A.	—	D. a. Dis.
Smith, Benj.	L/Cpl.	6491	2nd Yorks.	—	K. in A.
Smith, Chas.	Rfm.	2365	1/8th W. Yorks.	—	K. in A.
Smith, Chas.	L/Cpl.	3047	1/7th W. Yorks.	—	K. in A.
Smith, Chas.	Pte.	25323	16th W. Yorks.	—	K. in A.
Smith, Chas. A.	2nd Lieut.		1/2nd Leicester	D.C.M.	K. in A.
Smith, Chas. E.	Pte.	260013	6th K.O.Y.L.I.	—	Missing
Smith, Chas. H.	Rfm.	48888	1/8th W. Yorks.	—	K. in A.
Smith, Chas. Wm.	Pte.	78466	Durham Lt. Infantry	—	Died
Smith, Clifford	Pte.	52198	K.O. Liverpool	—	K. in A.
Smith, Clifford	Gnr.	99893	R.F.A.	—	D. of W.
Smith, Cornelius	Pte.	266837	W. Yorks.	—	Missing
Smith, Dennis S.	Pte.	81027	Durham Lt. Infantry	—	K. in A.
Smith, E.	C.S.M.	6261	10th W. Yorks.	—	K. in A.
Smith, Edgar	Pte.	16172	2nd E. Yorks.	—	Missing
Smith, Edgar	Dvr.	1651	R.A.S.C.	—	D. of W.
Smith, Edward	Sgt.	11769	10th W. Riding	—	K. in A.
Smith, Edwin	Pte.	100894	5th Training Res.	—	K. in A.
Smith, Ernest	Pte.	16991	Yorks.	—	K. in A.
Smith, Ernest	Pte.		6th K.O.Y.L.I.	—	K. in A.
Smith, Ernest M.	Pte.	37223	16th W. Yorks.	—	K. in A.
Smith, Ernest W.	Pte.	41029	Norfolks	—	K. in A.
Smith, Francis	Pte.	40519	8th S. Staffs.	—	K. in A.
Smith, Frank	Pte.	1590	17th W. Yorks.	—	K. in A.
Smith, Fred	Pte.	15009	York. & Lancs.	—	Died
Smith, Fred	Pte.	1603	1/5th Yorks.	—	K. in A.
Smith, Fred	Pte.	9025	3rd W. Yorks.	—	K. in A.
Smith, Fred	Pte.	25035	W. Yorks.	—	Died
Smith, Fredk.	Rfm.	15212	1/8th W. Yorks.	—	D. of W.
Smith, Fredk.	Sgt.	305161	8th W. Yorks.	—	D. a. Dis.
Smith, Fredk. E.	Pte.	55715	York. & Lancs.	—	D. of W.
Smith, Fred W.	Gnr.	127411	R.G.A.	—	Died
Smith, George	Rfm.	1556	1/8th W. Yorks.	—	K. in A.
Smith, George	Pte.	10644	K.O. Scottish Bordrs.	—	K. in A.
Smith, George	L/Cpl.	265864	W. Yorks.	—	K. in A.
Smith, George	Pte.	403393	R.A.M.C.	—	Killed
Smith, George	Pte.	265292	2nd W. Yorks.	—	Killed

LEEDS ROLL OF HONOUR.

Name	Rank	No.	Regiment	Honours	How Died
Smith, George	Gnr.	34902	R.F.A.	—	K. in A.
Smith, George	Pte.	267027	W. Riding	—	Missing
Smith, George	Pte.	17023	6th Royal Scots Fusrs.	—	K. in A.
Smith, George	Pte.	42985	2/8th Manchester	—	K. in A.
Smith, George	Pte.	21922	K.O. Scottish Bordrs.	—	K. in A.
Smith, George A.	Pte.	31153	1st E. Yorks.	—	K. in A.
Smith, George B.	Pte.	31436	16th Northumb'l'd Fusrs.	—	K. in A.
Smith, George E.	Gnr.	82161	R.F.A.	—	D. of W.
Smith, George H.	Pte.	423	21st W. Yorks.	—	K. in A.
Smith, George Wm.	Pte.	41737	K.O.Y.L.I.	—	Died
Smith, H.	Captain Adjt.		15th W. Yorks.	M.C.	K. in A.
Smith, Harold V.	Pte.	80915	Durham Lt. Infantry	—	Died
Smith, Harry	Dvr.	776898	R.F.A.	—	Killed
Smith, Harry	Pte.	41784	1st W. Yorks.	—	K. in A.
Smith, Harry	Rfm.	305514	1/8th W. Yorks.	—	Killed
Smith, Harry	L/Cpl.	24072	Royal Sussex	—	K. in A.
Smith, Harry	Pte.	238234	5th Lancs. Fusiliers	—	K. in A.
Smith, Harry	Cpl.	22612	Lancs. Fusiliers	—	Missing
Smith, Harry	Pte.	21046	10th W. Yorks.	—	K. in A.
Smith, Henry			K.O.Y.L.I.	—	K. in A.
Smith, Henry	Pte.	202590	1st Royal Scots Fusrs.	—	Killed
Smith, Henry	Pte.	51309	Somerset Lt. Infty.	—	K. in A.
Smith, Herbert	Pte.	10761	12th W. Yorks.	—	K. in A.
Smith, Herbert F.	Gnr.	338622	R.G.A.	—	Died
Smith, Horace	Rfm.	897185	King's Royal Rifle Cps.	—	D. a. Dis.
Smith, James	Rfm.	3033	W. Yorks.	—	Died
Smith, James	Rfm.	4482	1/7th W. Yorks.	—	Died
Smith, James	Pte.	28251	10th W. Yorks.	—	Died
Smith, James	Pte.	47643	R.A.M.C.	—	D. a. Dis.
Smith, James	Pte.	B/12722	10th Durham Lt. Infty.	—	K. in A.
Smith, Jas. A.	Pte.	21041	13th W. Yorks.	—	Died
Smith, Jas. A.	Pnr.	28066	Royal Engineers	—	D. of W.
Smith, Jas. E.	Pte.	36673	W. Yorks.	—	Died
Smith, Jas. E.	Pte.	56365	10th W. Yorks.	—	D. of W.
Smith, Jas. F.	Spr.	398861	Royal Engineers	—	K. in A.
Smith, John	Pte.	15421	9th W. Riding	—	Missing
Smith, John	Rfm.	4534	1/7th W. Yorks.	—	D. a. Dis.
Smith, John A.	Pte.	209632	3rd W. Yorks.	—	K. in A.
Smith, John Ed.	L/Cpl.	22788	Machine Gun Corps	—	K. in A.
Smith, John E.	Pte.	117394	R.A.S.C. (M.T.)	—	Died
Smith, John J.	Pte.	12147	9th Lancers	—	Died
Smith, John Thos.	Pte.	5628	3rd W. Yorks.	—	K. in A.
Smith, John Wm.	Pte.	24212	3rd W. Yorks.	—	Died P.O.W.
Smith, John W.	Gdsmn.	19299	1st Coldstream Guards	—	K. in A.
Smith, John W.	Rfm.	7055	1st Rifle Brigade	—	Missing
Smith, Joseph	Pte.	62779	K.O.Y.L.I.	—	Died
Smith, Joseph	Pte.	8656	2/7th W. Riding	—	Killed

LEEDS ROLL OF HONOUR.

Name	Rank	No.	Regiment	Honours	How Died
Smith, Joseph	Pte.	265638	7th W. Yorks.	—	K. in A.
Smith, Joseph	Pte.	3281	7th W. Yorks.	—	K. in A.
Smith, Joseph W.	L/Cpl.	202138	Seaforth Highlanders	—	K. in A.
Smith, Lawrence E.	Sgt. P.	629	Military Mounted Police	—	Died
Smith, Leonard	Pte.	203180	1/5th W. Yorks.	—	K. in A.
Smith Leonard	Gdsmn.	15290	Scots Guards	—	K. in A.
Smith, Mark	Pte.	202147	2/5th W. Yorks.	—	K. in A.
Smith, Nathaniel	Pte.	26142	W. Riding	—	D. of W.
Smith, Norman	Pte.	111547	Tank Corps	—	K. in A.
Smith, Norman	Pte.	2718	W. Yorks.	—	Killed
Smith, Percy	L/Cpl.	13612	2/4th K.O.Y.L.I.	—	K. in A.
Smith, Percy	Pte.	24154	9th W. Yorks.	—	D. of W.
Smith, Percy A.	Pte.	7030	Northumberland Fusrs.	—	K. in A.
Smith, Ralph	Rfm.	2782	8th W. Yorks.	—	K. in A.
Smith, Randolph	Pte.	224736	Labour Corps	—	K. in A.
Smith, Robert	Pte.	32594	8th York. & Lancs.	—	K. in A.
Smith, Rbt. B.	Pte.	720	Royal Marine Lt. Infty.	—	K. in A.
Smith, Roland C.	L/Cpl.	11520	1st King's Liverpool	—	K. in A.
Smith, S.	Pte.	7951	Yorks.	—	K. in A.
Smith, Sam	Sgt.	2137	1/8th W. Yorks.	—	Missing
Smith, Samuel	Pte.	40014	Royal Defence Corps	—	Killed
Smith, Samuel	Pte.	22896	Royal W. Surrey	—	K. in A.
Smith, Samuel	Pte.	T/274633	R.A.S.C. (M.T.)	—	Died
Smith, Samuel	Pte.	23077	Northumberland Fusrs.	—	K. in A.
Smith, Samuel G.	Pte.	26116	9th Loyal N. Lancs.	—	Died
Smith, Stanley	Pte.	1849	19th W. Yorks.	—	K. in A.
Smith, Stephen	S. Maj.	6261	10th W. Yorks.	—	K. in A.
Smith, Sydney	Pte.	12176	7th Yorks.	—	K. in A.
Smith, Sydney	Pte.	27937	W. Yorks.	—	K. in A.
Smith, T.	Gnr.	34929	R.F.A.	—	Died
Smith, Thos.	Pte.	97880	Northumberland Fusrs.	—	D. a. Dis.
Smith, Thos. A. P.	Pte.	41373	Leicester	—	Died
Smith, Thos. B.	Cpl.	9347	Yorks.	—	Died
Smith, Thos. Wm.	Pte.	23956	5th Cameron Highdrs.	—	K. in A.
Smith, Tom	Pte.	9094	W. Riding	—	Died
Smith, Tom	L/Cpl.	8356	9th W. Yorks.	—	K. in A.
Smith, W.	Pte.	41217	11th W. Yorks.	—	K. in A.
Smith, Walter	Pte.	284843	Labour Corps	—	Died
Smith, Walter	Gnr.	881922	R.F.A.	—	K. in A.
Smith, Wilfred	Cpl.	7135	King's Royal Rifle Cps.	—	K. in A.
Smith, Wm.	Pte.	203088	K.O.Y.L.I.	—	Died
Smith, Wm.	Pte.	27415	Royal Warwick	—	Missing
Smith, Wm.	Pte.	440777	Labour Corps	—	Died
Smith, Wm.	Rfm.	266481	8th W. Yorks.	—	Died
Smith, Wm.	Sgt.	72281	Royal Engineers	—	Died
Smith, Wm.	A.B.	R/3766	Royal Naval Division	—	Died
Smith, Wm.	Pte.	1632	19th W. Yorks.	—	D. a. Dis.

LEEDS ROLL OF HONOUR.

Name	Rank	No.	Regiment	Honours	How Died
Smith, Wm.	Pte.	24153	4th W. Yorks.	—	K. in A.
Smith, Wm.	Pte.	21899	7th K.O. Scottish Brds.	—	K. in A.
Smith, Wm. Chas.	1 Stkr.		H.M.S. "Trenchant"	—	Died
Smith, Wm. Hy.	Dvr.	101419	R.F.A.	—	Died
Smith, Wm. H.	Pte.	240882	1/6th W. Yorks.	—	K. in A.
Smith, Wm. H.	Pte.	14543	E. Kent	—	K. in A.
Smithson, A.	Gdsmn.	6582	Coldstream Guards	—	Killed
Smithson, Arthur	Pte.	211029	Labour Corps	—	Died
Smithson, Clifford	Pte.	33116	2nd W. Yorks.	—	Died
Smithson, Fred	Pte.	19071	2nd W. Yorks.	—	Missing
Smithson, Fredk. L.	Pte.	267321	11th W. Yorks.	—	K. in A.
Smithson, Harry	Pte.	220113	8th E. Yorks.	—	Died
Smithson, Herbert	L/Cpl.	36476	1/5th W. Yorks.	—	Killed
Smithson, Joe	Pte.	21428	2nd W. Yorks.	—	K. in A.
Smithson, Thos. Hy.	Rfm.	4550	1/7th W. Yorks.	—	K. in A.
Smyth, A. Ed.	Pte.	24068	10th W. Yorks.	—	D. of W.
Snedkir, Wm.	Sgt.	13819	10th York. & Lancs.	—	K. in A.
Snell, Harold	Pte.	202674	2/5th W. Yorks.	—	Missing
Snow, Ephraim	Pte.	16326	K.O.Y.L.I.	—	K. in A.
Snowball, Jas. R.	Pte.	202276	2/4th Lincoln	—	K. in A.
Snowden, Herbert	Pnr.	83972	Royal Engineers	—	Died
Snowden, John Ed.	L/Sgt.	265684	1/7th W. Yorks.	—	K. in A.
Snowden, Richard	Pte.	21703	W. Yorks.	—	Died
Snowden, Walter J.	Pte.	301007	5th W. Yorks.	—	Died
Snowdon, John	Ftr.	155894	R.F.A.	—	Killed
Solomon, Maxwell	Gdsmn.	7449	1st Scots Guards	—	K. in A.
Somers, Wm. R.	Pte.	202189	1/4th Royal Welsh Fus.	—	K. in A.
Sones, Ernest	A/Cpl.	42365	W. Yorks.	—	K. in A.
Sotheran, Geo. H.	Gdsmn.	8681	1st Scots Guards	—	K. in A.
Southern, Fred	Pte.	380874	W. Yorks.	—	Died
Southward, Edward	Pte.	834	15th W. Yorks.	—	K. in A.
Southwell, W.	Sgt.	265754	W. Yorks.	—	Died
Southwick, Geo.	Pte.	11813	K.O.Y.L.I.	—	K. in A.
Southwick, Thos.	Sgt.	21844	R.A.M.C.	—	Died
Southworth, Thos.	Pte.	15847	W. Yorks.	—	D. of W.
Sowden, Clarence	Pte.	41003	6th K.O.Y.L.I.	—	Killed
Sowden, Fred	Pte.	5475	W. Yorks.	—	K. in A.
Sowden, Geo. F.	Pte.	14828	K.O.Y.L.I.	—	Died
Sowden, Harold	Gnr.	890	R.F.A.	—	Killed
Sowden, John	Pte.	78077	Royal Fusiliers	—	Died
Sowden, Lawrence	Pte.	38789	22nd Northumb'l'd Fus.	—	K. in A.
Sowden, Wm. H.	L/Cpl.	21/300	W. Yorks.	—	D. a. Dis.
Sowerby, Geo. R.	Pte.	34667	York. & Lancs.	—	K. in A.
Sowery, Thos.	Pte.	242768	W. Riding	—	Died
Sowrey, John R.	Pte.	34578	9th W. Yorks.	—	K. in A.
Sowrey, Thos. A.	Pte.		R.A.M.C.	—	K. in A.
Sowry, Arthur	Pte.	15639	15th W. Yorks.	—	K. in A.

LEEDS ROLL OF HONOUR.

Name	Rank	No.	Regiment	Honours	How Died
Sowter, Thos.	Pte.	220663	1st Royal Berks.	—	K. in A.
Spall, Geo. A.	Pte.	298253	Labour Corps	—	Died
Sparling, Samuel	Pte.	53232	Lincoln	—	Missing
Sparks, William Henry	Pte.		2nd Hampshire	—	K. in A.
Speak, Oliver	Pte.	66578	K.O.Y.L.I.	—	Died
Speechley, Arthur	Rfm.	306207	8th W. Yorks.	—	K. in A.
Speed, Thos. W.	Pte.	39137	2nd W. Yorks.	—	K. in A.
Speed, Wm.	Pte.	4435	W. Yorks.	—	K. in A.
Speight, C. A.	Pte.	584	17th W. Yorks.	—	K. in A.
Speight, Frank	Pte.	42285	6th Leicester	—	K. in A.
Speight, George	Pte.	267735	3/4th Seaforth Highdrs.	—	K. in A.
Speight, Harper	Pte.	28502	Loyal N. Lancs.	—	Missing
Speight, Harry	Sgt.	306265	W Yorks.	—	K. in A.
Speight, Harry	Pte.	418359	Canadian Black Watch	—	D. a. Dis.
Speight, John	Pte.	25536	2nd W. Yorks.	—	Killed
Speight, John	Pte.	39343	2nd W. Yorks.	—	Killed
Speight, John Wm.	Gnr.	77406	R.F.A.	—	D. of W.
Speight, Joshua	Pte.	S/11534	7th Seaforth Highdrs.	—	K. in A.
Speight, Leonard	Sgt.	3100	1st Northumb'l'd Fus.	—	K. in A.
Speight, Sam	Cpl.	10849	7th K.O.Y.L.I.	—	K. in A.
Speight, Thos.	Pte.	20775	16th Cheshire	—	K. in A.
Speight, Walter	Pte.	40035	York. & Lancs.	—	K. in A.
Speight, Wm.	Pte.	20012	5th Wiltshire	—	K. in A.
Speight, Wm.	Pte.	21272	K.O.Y.L.I.	—	D. of W.
Spellman, Thos.	Rfm.	266338	1/7th W. Yorks.	—	K. in A.
Spence, Arthur	Pte.	23977	K.O.Y.L.I.	—	K. in A.
Spence, Benj.	Pte.	10344	9th W. Yorks.	—	Missing
Spence, Ernest A.	Cpl.	32179	R.F.A.	—	K. in A.
Spence, J. R.	Pte.	16564	7th K.O. Scottish Bords.	—	K. in A.
Spence, Sydney	Pte.	31650	Royal Highlanders	—	Died
Spence, Wm. Hy.	Pte.	40842	16th W. Yorks.	—	K. in A.
Spencer, Arthur	Pte.	63637	W. Yorks.	—	K. in A.
Spencer, Arthur	Pte.	300034	18th W. Yorks.	—	Missing
Spencer, Charles	L/Cpl.	11367	11th King's R. Rifle Cps.	—	K. in A.
Spencer, Edwin B.	Dmr.	9862	W. Yorks.	—	K. in A.
Spencer, Frank	Pte.	10507	Liverpool	—	Died
Spencer, Fred	Rfm.	4134	1/8th W. Yorks.	—	K. in A.
Spencer, Fredk.	Pte.	47493	2/8th Lancs. Fusiliers	—	Missing
Spencer, Fred W.	Gnr.	83978	R.F.A.	—	D. of W.
Spencer, George	Pte.	20233	Leicester	—	Died
Spencer, George	Rfm.	15434	King's Royal Rifle Corps	—	K. in A.
Spencer, Miles	Pte.	266777	W. Yorks.	—	Died
Spencer, Percy	Pte.	34788	10th K.O.Y.L.I.	—	K. in A.
Spencer, Reg. A.	Gdsmn.	8588	2nd Scots Guards	—	Died P.O.W.
Spencer, Samuel M.	Cpl.	10396	King's Royal Rifle Corps	—	Died
Spencer, Wm.	Pte.	7949	4th W. Yorks.	—	K. in A.
Spencer, Wm.	Pte.	62810	W. Yorks.	—	Died

LEEDS ROLL OF HONOUR.

Name	Rank	No.	Regiment	Honours	How Died
Spiby, Clifford	Pte.	269993	Labour Corps	—	Died
Spilg, Wm.	Pte.	330256	6th Highland Lt. Infty.	—	K. in A.
Spink, Arthur	Pte.	46227	13th York. & Lancs.	—	K. in A.
Spink, Harry	Pte.	8900	11th Royal Warwicks.	—	K. in A.
Spink, James	Rfm.	202826	Rifle Brigade	—	D. a. Dis.
Spink, William	Cpl.	19304	9th K.O.Y.L.I.	—	Died
Spinks, Albert	Pte.	883	21st W. Yorks.	—	K. in A.
Spivey, Alfred	Pte.	11049	E. Yorks.	—	Died
Splain, Timothy	S.Smith.	20413	R.F.A.	—	Died
Spofforth, F. P.	Pte.	10124	11th W. Yorks.	—	K. in A.
Spoors, Harry	Pte.	7994	Machine Gun Corps	—	D. of W.
Spowage, Harold	Pte.	993	2nd W. Yorks.	—	K. in A.
Sprittles, Harry	Rfm.	35268	12th King's R. Rifle Cps.	—	K. in A.
Spurr, David	A.B.	SS4971	H.M.S. " Charon "	—	Died
Spurr, Harry	Pte.	37256	W. Yorks.	—	K. in A.
Spurr, John	L/Cpl.	4417	W. Yorks.	—	K. in A.
Spurr, John	Pte.	33114	18th W. Yorks.	—	Missing
Spurr, Samuel	L/Cpl.	24867	15th W. Yorks.	—	Killed
Squire, Clifford B.	Dvr.	T4/253718	R.A.S.C.	—	Died
Squire, Tom	Rfm.	39785	1/8th W. Yorks.	—	Died
Squires, George	Pte.	11188	K.O.Y.L.I.	—	K. in A.
Stabler, Percy	C.S.M.	23524	Leicester	—	K. in A.
Stables, John	S.Smith.	1809	R.F.A.	—	K. in A.
Stacey, Arthur	Pte.	315740	Northumberland Fusrs.	—	D. a. Dis.
Stacey, J. H.	Pte.	201536	W. Yorks.	—	Died
Stacey, Jas. W.	Pte.	261039	Royal Air Force	—	D. a. Dis.
Stackhouse, Fred	Sgt.	16029	17th King's R. Rifle Cps.	—	K. in A.
Stainsby, Walter	Pte.	210045	W. Yorks.	—	K. in A.
Stainthorpe, Sidney	Pte.	41922	Northumberland Fusrs.	—	K. in A.
Stammers, G. F.	Pte.	78708	Durham Light Infantry	—	K. in A.
Stammers, Wm.	Spr.	72141	Royal Engineers	—	Killed
Stamp, E. J.	Cpl.	17198	W. Yorks.	—	K. in A.
Stamp, Geo. Wm.	L/Cpl.	83462	W. Yorks.	—	Died
Stamper, Ernest	Pte.	31201	13th Yorks. & Lancs.	—	K. in A.
Stancliffe, Chas. J.	Pte.	408220	R.A.M.C.	—	K. in A.
Stancliffe, Wm. A.	Pte.	305890	W. Yorks.	—	K. in A.
Standage, Albert	L/Cpl	265246	1/7th W. Yorks.	—	K. in A.
Standage, Ben. R.	Pte.	57549	York. & Lancs.	—	K. in A.
Standage, Robert	Pte.	34487	9th K.O.Y.L.I.	—	K. in A.
Standhaven, Harry	Pte.	4832	K.O.Y.L.I.	—	K. in A.
Stanhope, Chas.	Gnr.	167368	R.G.A.	—	Died
Staniland, A.	Pte.	202501	Royal Highlanders	—	Died
Staniland, Richard E.	Pte.	266546	2/6th Northumb'l'd Fus.	—	D. of W.
Stanley, Chas.	A/Cpl.	21703	Loyal N. Lancs.	—	Died
Stanley, Chas. E.	Pte.	2637	W. Yorks.	—	K. in A.
Stanley, Fred	Pte.	239078	Labour Corps	—	K. in A.
Stannard, George	Pte.	42815	9th Manchester	—	Missing

LEEDS ROLL OF HONOUR.

Name	Rank	No.	Regiment	Honours	How Died
Stansfield, Edgar	Pte.	34703	3rd Lincoln	—	D. a. Dis.
Stansfield, Sidney	Rfm.	4609	1/8th W. Yorks.	—	K. in A.
Stansfield, Thos.	Rfm.	46108	8th W. Yorks.	—	K. in A.
Stansfield, Thos.	Pte.	43202	10th W. Yorks.	—	Missing
Stansfield, Walter	Pte.	25096	1st W. Yorks.	—	Died
Stanton, Anthony	Pte.	9786	York. & Lancs.	—	K. in A.
Stanton, John	Pte.	7401	W. Riding	—	K. in A.
Stanton, Wilfred	Pte.	41133	25th Durham Lt. Infty.	—	K. in A.
Stapleton, A. Chas.	Cpl.	99894	R.F.A.	—	K. in A.
Stathers, Fredk.	Dvr.	52239	R.F.A.	—	K. in A.
Stavely, Arthur	L/Sgt.	266714	W. Yorks.	—	K. in A.
Stawman, Clifford	Pte.	21098	8th K.O. Scottish Bords.	—	K. in A.
Stawman, Harry	Pte.	21097	8th K.O. Scottish Bords.	—	K. in A.
Stead, A. E.	Pte.	21285	8th K.O.Y.L.I.	—	D. of W.
Stead, Alfred	Pte.	306929	W. Yorks.	—	K. in A.
Stead, Chas.	Rfm.	306690	1/8th W. Yorks.	—	K. in A.
Stead, Chas. B.	Lieut.		W. Yorks.	—	K. in A.
Stead, Edmund	O.Tel.	J/35189	H.M.S. "Hampshire"	—	Killed
Stead, Fred	Pte.	69214	Northumberland Fusrs.	—	K. in A.
Stead, G. W.	Pte.	38882	1/4th Northumb'l'd Fus.	—	Died P.O.W.
Stead, Geo. E.	Pte.	33087	16th Royal Scots	—	Killed
Stead, H. K.	Rfm.	5016	1/7th W. Yorks.	—	D. of W.
Stead, Harold	Pte.	47494	Lancs. Fusiliers	—	K. in A.
Stead, Harry	Pte.	72180	W. Yorks.	—	Died
Stead, Harry	Pte.	37255	9th W. Yorks.	—	K. in A.
Stead, Harry	Pte.	266282	W. Yorks.	—	D. a. Dis.
Stead, Herbert	Cpl.	270546	Royal Engineers	—	D. a. Dis.
Stead, J. W.	Pte.	35217	Army Vet. Corps	—	Died
Stead, J. Wm.	Pte.	33845	13th W. Yorks.	—	K. in A.
Stead, John	Pte.	1774	W. Yorks.	—	K. in A.
Stead, John H.	Dvr.	10845	R.F.A.	—	K. in A.
Stead, Lawrence	Pte.	24224	W. Yorks.	—	K. in A.
Stead, R.	C.Q.M.S.	1475	Yorks. Hussars	—	K. in A.
Stead, Wilfred	Dvr.	62783	R.F.A.	—	K. in A.
Stead, Wm. M.	Q.M.S.	800	7th W. Yorks.	—	Killed
Stead, Willie	L/Cpl.	23959	5th Cameron Highdrs.	—	K. in A.
Stead, Willie W.	Lieut.		17th W. Yorks.	—	K. in A.
Steel, Edmund	Pte.	12840	Machine Gun Corps	—	Missing.
Steel, John J.	Pte.	39882	K.O.Y.L.I.	—	K. in A.
Steel, John R. A.	Pte.	1181	15th W. Yorks.	—	K. in A.
Steel, Reg.	Pte.	49467	1st Lincoln	—	K. in A.
Steel, Rbt.	L/Cpl.	21202	W. Yorks.	—	K. in A.
Steele, Thos. J.	Pte.	125715	R.A.M.C.	—	Died
Steele, Wm.	Pte.	49864	4th Royal Scots Fusrs.	—	K. in A.
Steels, Thos. R.	Rfm.		8th W. Yorks.	—	K. in A.
Steer, Wm.	Sgt.	62661	7th W. Yorks.	—	K. in A.
Steinberg, Abraham	Pte.	41609	W. Yorks.	—	Died

LEEDS ROLL OF HONOUR.

Name	Rank	No.	Regiment	Honours	How Died
Steinberg, Isaac	Pte.	40287	3/4th Cameron Highdrs.	—	Killed
Steinberg, I. John	A/Sgt.	27384	R.A.F.	—	K. in A.
Steinberg, Jack	2nd Lieut.		R.A.F.	—	Killed
Steinburg, Moses L.	Pte.	M/352777	R.A.S.C.	—	K. in A.
Stendell, Geo. F.	Pte.	270	15th W. Yorks.	—	Missing
Stephens, Alfred	Pte.	35544	K.O.Y.L.I.	—	Died
Stephens, Geo.	Pte.	20212	2nd K.O.Y.L.I.	—	Died
Stephenson, C.	Pte.	112179	R.A.M.C.	—	Died
Stephenson, Chas.	Pte.	26770	Labour Corps	—	Died
Stephenson, Chas. Wm.	Pte.	37458	16th W. Yorks.	—	Missing
Stephenson, Eric A.	2nd Lieut.		3rd Yorks.	—	K. in A.
Stephenson, Ernest	Pte.	105151	R.A.M.C.	—	Died
Stephenson, George	Pte.	38316	York. & Lancs.	—	Died
Stephenson, Geo.	Pte.	33441	W. Yorks.	—	D. of W.
Stephenson, Hanson	Pte.	035999	Royal Army Vet. Corps	—	Died
Stephenson, J.	Pte.	235268	W. Yorks.	—	Missing
Stephenson, Jeremiah	Cpl.	3241	1/7th W. Yorks.	—	K. in A.
Stephenson, Jim	Pte.	69215	Northumberland Fusrs.	—	Died
Stephenson, John Wm.	Pte.		R.A.M.C.	—	D. of W.
Stephenson, Leonard	Pte.	44130	Lincoln	—	K. in A.
Stephenson, Norman	Pte.	38537	12th W. Yorks.	—	K. in A.
Stephenson, Ralph	Bmdr.	100332	R.G.A.	—	K. in A.
Stephenson, Walter	Gnr.	775151	R.F.A.	—	K. in A.
Sterne, Donald	Pte.	26628	W. Riding	—	Missing
Sterry, Geo. F.	Pte.	18217	K.O. Scottish Bordrs.	—	Died
Stevens, Amos.	Pte.	953	17th W. Yorks.	—	K. in A.
Stevens, Michael	Pte.	1338	K.O.Y.L.I.	—	Missing
Stevens, W. N.	Pte.	14620	2nd W. Riding	—	Died
Stevenson, H.	Pte.	11300	4th Royal Scots Fusrs.	—	Died
Stevenson, Harry	L/Cpl.	202117	Leicester	—	D. a. Dis.
Stevenson, Norman	Pte.	7081	Canadian	—	K. in A.
Stevenson, Wm. L.	L/Cpl.	331183	Yorks. Hussars	—	Died
Steward, Hbt.	Pte.	7168	Durham Light Infantry	—	K. in A.
Stewart, Alfred	Pte.	45277	York. & Lancs.	—	Killed
Stewart, Chas.	Pte.	305211	W. Yorks.	—	K. in A.
Stewart, Chas. E.	2nd Lieut.		Manchester	—	K. in A.
Stewart, J. W.	Pte.	34809	Northumberland Fusrs.	—	K. in A.
Stewart, Jas.	Pte.	25786	2nd West Yorks.	—	K. in A.
Stewart, Jas.	Pte.	61	W. Yorks.	—	K. in A.
Stewart, (or Stuart) Jas. H.	Pte.	56326	W. Yorks.	—	K. in A.
Stewart, John	Cpl.	201248	Seaforth Highlanders	—	K. in A.
Stewart, John S.	Pte.	5076	Royal Defence Corps	—	D. a. Dis.
Stewart, John Wm.	Pte.	41634	2nd Lincoln	—	K. in A.
Stewart, Leonard	Dmr.	18415	2nd W. Yorks.	—	K. in A.
Stewart, Leslie T.	L/Cpl.	1594	22nd Royal Fusiliers	—	Died
Stewart, Walter	Pte.	32461	1st W. Yorks.	—	Died

LEEDS ROLL OF HONOUR.

Name	Rank	No.	Regiment	Honours	How Died
Stewart, Walter	Pte.	157379	R.A.S.C.	—	Died
Stewart, William	Pte.	1327	15th W. Yorks.	—	Died
Stewart, Wm. Arthur	Pte.	11082	8th W. Riding	—	K. in A.
Stilwell, Clifford S.	Pte.	1224	18th W. Yorks.	—	Died
Stillwell, Arthur	Dvr.	T4/213379	R.A.S.C.	—	K. in A.
Stirk, Harry	Pte.	24585	1st W. Yorks.	—	K. in A.
Stirk, Jas.	Spr.	83578	Royal Engineers	—	K. in A.
Stirk, Saml.	Pte.	73111	Machine Gun Corps	—	K. in A.
Stirk, Walter	Rfm.	7705	1st King's R. Rifle Cps.	—	D. of W.
Stock, Reginald	Spr.	20379	Royal Engineers	—	Died
Stockdale, Ernest	Pte.	78718	Durham Light Infantry	—	K. in A.
Stockhill, G.	Gnr.	81155	R.F.A.	—	K. in A.
Stockhill, Jas.	Cpl.	21402	2nd Northumb'l'd Fus.	—	K. in A.
Stocks, Clifford	Pte.	57846	Lancs. Fusiliers	—	K. in A.
Stocks, Douglas	L/Cpl.	12288	Yorks.	—	K. in A.
Stocks, Harold	Pte.	2085	16th Cheshire	—	K. in A.
Stocks, Irwin A.	Pte.	77864	9th Durham Lt. Inftry.	—	K. in A.
Stocks, John W.	Sgt.	787	17th W. Yorks.	—	K. in A.
Stocks, Joseph	Pte.	21684	K.O.Y.L.I.	—	Died
Stocks, Oscar	Pte.	59887	W. Yorks.	—	K. in A.
Stocks, Selwin J.	Pte.	71017	Machine Gun Corps	—	K. in A.
Stocks, Walter J.	Pte.	144	W. Yorks.	—	K. in A.
Stockwell, John	Dvr.	73078	R.F.A.	—	Died
Stodel, Jack	Pte.	10821	8th W. Riding	—	K. in A.
Stoker, Wm.	Gnr.	28398	R.G.A.	—	K. in A.
Stokie, Edwin	Sgt.	12627	Labour Corps	—	Died
Stokoe, Crawford	Pte.	855	15th W. Yorks.	—	K. in A.
Stone, Barnett	Pte.	558321	Labour Corps	—	D. a. Dis.
Stone, Wm.	Rfm.	306615	1/8th W. Yorks.	—	K. in A.
Stoner, Leonard	Pte.	7476	10th Northumb'l'd Fus.	—	K. in A.
Stones, Albert	Rfm.	1740	1/8th W. Yorks.	—	K. in A.
Stones, Clifford	Pte.	82500	Durham Light Infantry	—	K. in A.
Stones, George	Pte.	19794	York. & Lancs.	—	Died
Stones, Hbt. G.	Pte.	24319	6th Yorks.	—	K. in A.
Stones, Michael	Spr.	15946	Royal Engineers	—	Died
Stones, Willie	Pte.	53238	Durham Light Infantry	—	K. in A.
Storer, F.	Gnr.	45453	R.F.A.	—	D. of W.
Storey, Arthur	Cpl.	41647	17th Yorks.	—	K. in A.
Storey, Arthur	Tpr.	76198	1/1st Derby Yeom.	—	Died
Storey, Clarence S.	Gnr.	66570	R.F.A.	—	K. in A.
Storey, Cyril	Cpl.	10179	9th W. Yorks.	—	K. in A.
Storey, Harold	Rfm.	266475	1/7th W. Yorks.	—	K. in A.
Storey, Jas. H.	Pte.	13546	K.O.Y.L.I.	—	K. in A.
Storey, John	Rfm.	41447	King's Royal Rifle Corps	—	K. in A.
Storr, Joseph	Pte.	3924	W. Yorks.	—	Missing
Storr, Robert	Pte.	113150	Labour Corps	—	K. in A.
Storr, Wm.	Rfm.	10163	King's Royal Rifle Corps	—	K. in A.

LEEDS ROLL OF HONOUR.

Name	Rank	No.	Regiment	Honours	How Died
Story, Arthur W.	Gnr.	107559	R.F.A.	—	Died
Stothard, Harry	Pte.	022624	R.A.O.C.	—	Died
Stott, Henry	Pte.	19949	K.O. Scottish Bordrs.	—	K. in A.
Stott, Jas. A.	Rfm.	305877	1/7th W. Yorks.	—	K. in A.
Stott, Jas. Ed.	Pte.	72247	Royal Defence Corps	—	Died
Stott, Kenneth	Disp'sr.	98034	R.A.M.C.	—	Died
Stott, Vincent E.	Pte.	48774	W. Yorks.	—	K. in A.
Stowe, Ernest	Pte.	10773	10th W. Yorks.	—	K. in A.
Strachan, David L.	Captain		3/6th W. Yorks.	—	Died
Strangeway, Clifford	L/Cpl.	24015	2nd W. Yorks.	—	K. in A.
Strangeway, J. S.	Pte.	2219	W. Yorks.	—	K. in A.
Strangeways, Ernest	Pte.	38834	16th W. Yorks.	—	Missing
Strangeways, Herbert	Pte.	44809	2/9th Manchester	—	K. in A.
Straw, Lawrence	Trpr.	5015	18th Hussars.	—	K. in A.
Straw, Lionel E. V.	Pte.	8329	4th W. Yorks.	—	D. a. Dis.
Stringer, Alfred	Gdsmn.	8729	1st Scots Guards	—	Died
Stringer, Ernest	Pte.	G63149	7th London	—	K. in A.
Stringer, Willie	Pte.	202597	5th S. Wales Borderers	—	Died
Stringfellow, Fredk. A.	A.B.	KW932	Royal Naval Division	—	Died
Strothard, Raymond	Pte.	78473	Durham Light Infantry	—	Died
Strother, Jesse D.	Pte.	266981	W. Yorks.	—	K. in A.
Stuart, Geo. Wm.	Sgt.	6805	2nd Scots Guards	—	K. in A.
Stubb, H.	Pte.	37524	W. Yorks.	—	D. of W.
Stubbs, Ernest	Pte.	562966	Labour Corps	—	D. a. Dis.
Stubbs, Henry	Gnr.	151999	R.F.A.	—	Died
Stubbs, John	Rfm.	266417	2/7th W. Yorks.	—	Died
Stubbs, Wm.	Pte.	205066	25th Northumb'l'd Fus.	—	Killed
Stubley, Albert M.	Pte.	66574	1/4th Northumb'ld Fus.	—	Died
Studd, Ernest	A.B.	J/22070	Royal Navy	—	K. in A.
Studd, James	Pte.	241221	N. Staffs.	—	K. in A.
Studley, Chas. C.	2nd Lieut.		1/8th W. Yorks.	—	K. in A.
Stumbles, Edgar A.	Gnr.	2764	R.F.A.	—	D. of W.
Suffill, John	Rfm.	5663	1/7th W. Yorks.	—	Died
Sugden, A.	Pte.	30404	Lancs.	—	K. in A.
Sugden, Albert	Rfm.	6677	4th Royal Brigade	—	K. in A.
Sugden, Geo.	Pte.	399891	Labour Corps	—	Died
Sugden, Gilbert	L/Cpl.	265383	W. Yorks.	—	Died
Sugden, Horace	Pte.	89204	Training Reserve	—	Died
Sugden, James	Rfm.	3286	1/8th W. Yorks.	—	K. in A.
Sugden, Lewis	Pte.	19947	13th W. Yorks.	—	D. of W.
Sugden, Willie	Pte.	47278	12th W. Yorks.	—	K. in A.
Suggitt, Wm.	Pte.	40283	W. Yorks.	—	K. in A.
Sulch, Harry	Pte.	53276	9th Cheshire	—	Died P.O.W.
Sullivan, Chas.	Pte.	75721	24th Royal Fusiliers	—	K. in A.
Sullivan, F. P.	Pte.	37163	W. Yorks.	—	K. in A.
Sullivan, Michael	Pte.	291726	Labour Corps	—	K. in A.
Sullivan, Michael C.	C.S.M.	13146	Oxford & Bucks L.I.	—	K. in A.

LEEDS ROLL OF HONOUR.

Name	Rank	No.	Regiment	Honours	How Died
Summers, Chas. H.	Rfm.	268024	1/7th W. Yorks.	—	K. in A.
Summers, John	Pte.	6725	W. Yorks.	—	D. of W.
Summers, Thos. A.	Pte.	49341	10th W. Yorks.	—	K. in A.
Summerscales, A. Norman	Pte.	861	15th W. Yorks.	—	K. in A.
Summerscales, Harry	Rfm.	4244	1/7th W. Yorks.	—	K. in A.
Summerscales, J. Stanley	Pte.	862	15th W. Yorks.	—	K. in A.
Summersgill, George	Pte.	76303	R.A.M.C.	—	K. in A.
Sunderland, Edward	Pte.	21261	12th Northumb'l'd Fus.	—	K. in A.
Sunderland, Fred C.	Pte.	268426	1/6th W. Riding	—	Died
Sunderland, Herbert W.	Pte.	C864	15th W. Yorks.	—	K. in A.
Sunderland, Ralph	Rfm.	266309	2/7th W. Yorks.	—	K. in A.
Sunley, Abraham	Pte.	241840	2/5th K.O.Y.L.I.	—	K. in A.
Sunter, George	Sgt.	8030	1st W. Yorks.	—	K. in A.
Sunter, R.	Pte.	35003	W. Riding	—	K. in A.
Sutcliffe, Chas. F.	L/Cpl.	36976	Cheshire	—	D. a. Dis.
Sutcliffe, Ernest	Rfm.	266230	1/7th W. Yorks.	—	K. in A.
Sutcliffe, George	Dvr.	79054	R.F.A.	—	K. in A.
Sutcliffe, George	Pte.	305523	11th W. Yorks.	—	K. in A.
Sutcliffe, Harold	Cpl.	202450	Highland Light Infantry	—	K. in A.
Sutcliffe, Harry	L/Cpl.	40255	18th W. Yorks.	—	K. in A.
Sutcliffe, Harry	Rfm.	13202	16th King's R. Rifle Cps.	—	K. in A.
Sutcliffe, Oswald	2nd Lieut.		1/4th K.O.Y.L.I.	—	K. in A.
Sutcliffe, Paul	Dvr.	63349	R.F.A.	—	D. of W.
Sutcliffe, Peter	Pte.	37532	17th W. Yorks.	—	K. in A.
Sutherland, Alex.	Gdsmn.	9242	2nd Scots Guards	—	K. in A.
Sutherland, Horace	Pte.	7042	R.A.S.C.	—	D. a. Dis.
Sutterby, E. W.	Pte.	187395	Labour Corps	—	Died
Sutton, Harry	Rfm.	8728	4th King's R. Rifle Cps.	—	K. in A.
Sutton, Percy	Sgt.	29674	Machine Gun Corps	—	Died
Sutton, Robert	A.B.	20245	H.M.S. " Queen Mary "	—	K. in A.
Swaby, Chas. S.	Pte.	26020	E. Yorks.	—	K. in A.
Swaby, John	Pte.	317078	R.A.S.C. (M.T.)	—	K. in A.
Swailes, James	L/Cpl.	11182	K.O. Scottish Borderers	—	Died
Swain, Albert	L/Cpl.	12758	11th W. Yorks.	—	K. in A.
Swainson, Harold	L/Cpl.	265189	7th W. Yorks.	—	K. in A.
Swale, Chas. L.	Pte.	4897	1/5th W. Yorks.	—	Missing
Swales, Arthur	2 A.M.	47095	Royal Air Force	—	D. a. Dis.
Swales, John	Pte.	301394	Royal Scots	—	Died
Swales, Samuel	Pte.	35257	5th Yorks.	—	Died P.O.W.
Swallow, Alfred	Cpl.	306975	8th W. Yorks.	—	K. in A.
Swallow, James	Pte.	300035	18th W. Yorks.	—	K. in A.
Swan, William	Cpl.	34407	York. & Lancs.	—	Missing
Swann, E. G.	Pte.	11675	10th W. Yorks.	—	D. of W.
Swann, John R.	Pte.	2466	Royal Marine Lt. Infty.	—	D. a. Dis.
Swann, Tom Y.	Pte.	17599	Labour Corps	—	Died

LEEDS ROLL OF HONOUR.

Name	Rank	No.	Regiment	Honours	How Died
Swarbreck, Thomas P.	Rfm.	305127	2/8th W. Yorks.	—	K. in A.
Sweating, Ed.	L/Cpl.	8119	K.O. Scottish Borderers	—	Died
Sweeney, John	Pte.	10034	W. Yorks.	—	Died
Sweeney, Joseph	Pte.	11076	18th Hussars	—	Missing
Sweeting, E. D. A.	Pte.	1652	15th W. Yorks.	—	Died
Swift, Allan W.	Pte.	15868	2/5th W. Yorks.	—	K. in A.
Swift, Geo. K.	Gnr.	21413	R.G.A.	—	K. in A.
Swift, Harold.	Spr.	84025	Royal Engineers	—	Died
Swift, Joseph	Pte.	28940	Leicester	—	D. a. Dis.
Swift, Michael	1 Stkr.K/24961		H.M.S. " Queen Mary "	—	K. in A.
Swift, Thomas M.	Pte.	41261	8th Suffolks	—	Missing
Swift, Wm. H.	Pte.	38814	17th W. Yorks.	—	K. in A.
Swinburn, Harold	Pte.	202927	W. Riding	—	K. in A.
Swinnerton, Robt. H.	Pte.	528079	R.A.M.C.	—	D. a. Dis.
Swinson, Robert	Rfm.	267052	W. Yorks.	—	D. a. Dis.
Swithenbank, James W.	Spr.	132651	Royal Engineers	—	Died
Sykes, Albert	Pte.	203869	12th W. Yorks.	—	K. in A.
Sykes, Chas. H.	Pte.	20806	K.O. Scottish Borderers	—	D. a. Dis.
Sykes, Craven	Pte.	35295	14th W. Yorks.	—	K. in A.
Sykes, Edward	Gnr.	776343	R.F.A.	—	Died
Sykes, Harry	Pte.	50134	Lancs. Fusiliers	—	Died
Sykes, Hubert	Pte.	268410	W. Riding	—	K. in A.
Sykes, Joe	Gnr.	166835	R.G.A.	—	K. in A.
Sykes, John Wm.	Pte.	1688	1/4th Northants.	—	K. in A.
Sykes, Joseph W.	Pte.	11630	W. Riding	—	K. in A.
Sykes, Leonard	Pte.	29409	R.A.M.C.	—	Died
Sykes, M.	Pte.	250708	Durham Light Infantry	—	Died
Sykes, Richard	A.B.	KP733	Royal Naval V. Reserve	—	Killed
Sykes, Tatton	Pte.	267654	Seaforth Highlanders	—	K. in A.
Sykes, Thomas H.	Pte.	216752	R.A.S.C.	—	K. in A.
Sykes, Wm. C.	L/Cpl.	19164	15th W. Yorks.	—	Missing
Tadman, John C.	Sgt.	305707	W. Yorks.	—	K. in A.
Taggart, Isaac R.	Rfm.	306780	2/8th W. Yorks.	—	K. in A.
Talbot, Chas.	Pte.	182636	Labour Corps	—	Died
Talbot, Horace	L/Cpl.	268178	2nd W. Yorks.	—	K. in A.
Tallant, Chas.	Pte.	17722	W. Yorks.	—	K. in A.
Tallents, Frank	Pte.	28636	9th W. Yorks.	—	K. in A.
Tamblin, Arthur	Pte.	8882	Lancs. Fusiliers	—	Died
Tarpey, John	Pte.	31963	Royal Irish Fusiliers	—	D. a. Dis.
Tarpey, Thos.	Pte.	354147	R.A.S.C.	—	D. a. Dis.
Tarpey, Walter	Cpl.	4677	W. Riding	—	Died
Tarry, Wm. S.	Dvr.	253854	R.A.S.C.	—	K. in A.
Tasker, Harry P.	Rfm.	4349	3/8th W. Yorks.	—	D. of W.
Tasker, Harry W.	E.R.A.	18021	Royal Navy	—	Killed
Tate, Alfred L.	Pte.	131082	Machine Gun Corps	—	K. in A.
Tate, Chas. A.	Pte.	208659	W. Yorks.	—	K. in A.

LEEDS ROLL OF HONOUR.

Name	Rank	No.	Regiment	Honours	How Died
Tate, Edgar	Pte.	18099	K.O. Scottish Borderers	—	K. in A.
Tate, Ernest A.	Pte.	25612	13th Yorks.	—	K. in A.
Tate, Geo.	Pte.	17298	W. Riding	—	D. of W.
Tate, Geo. A.	Pte.	38810	Northumberland Fusrs.	—	K. in A.
Tate, Harry	L/Cpl.	21249	9th W. Yorks.	—	K. in A.
Tate, Jas. L.	Rfm.	534930	London	—	K. in A.
Tate, John E.	Pte.	24542	11th W. Yorks.	—	D. of W.
Tate, Percy	Gnr.	72485	R.G.A.	—	K. in A.
Tate, Tom	Dvr.	209149	Royal Engineers	—	Died
Tate, T.	Pte.	425778	1st Canadian M. Rifles	—	K. in A.
Tattersfield, Harry	Gnr.	140365	R.F.A.	—	K. in A.
Tayler, Phillip	Pte.	2190	Royal Fusiliers	—	Died
Taylor, Albert	Pte.	49038	1/5th W. Yorks.	—	Missing
Taylor, Alfred	Pte.	11838	6th Yorks.	—	K. in A.
Taylor, Allan	Pte.	35568	16th W. Yorks.	—	Missing
Taylor, Allan W.	Pte.		15th W. Yorks.	—	K. in A.
Taylor, Arthur	Pte.	44215	27th Northumb'l'd Fus.	—	K. in A.
Taylor, Arton R.	Pte.	64317	15th W. Yorks.	—	K. in A.
Taylor, Bert	L/Cpl.	876	15th W. Yorks.	—	D. of W.
Taylor, C.	L/Cpl.	8905	E. Lancs.	—	K. in A.
Taylor, Chas.	Pte.	161	17th W. Yorks.	—	K. in A.
Taylor, Chas. E.	C.Mate.	M10541	H.M.S. " King George V."	—	Died
Taylor, Claude R. P.	Pte.	41220	11th E. Yorks.	—	K. in A.
Taylor, Cyril	L/Cpl.	1390	17th W. Yorks.	—	K. in A.
Taylor, E.	Pte.	265400	1/5th W. Yorks.	—	Died P.O.W.
Taylor, Edward	Pte.	8033	2nd Canadians	—	D. of W.
Taylor, Ernest	Pte.	36398	4th Yorks.	—	K. in A.
Taylor, Ernest	L/Sgt.	10960	8th W. Riding	—	K. in A.
Taylor, Ernest	Pte.	49744	W. Yorks.	—	Died
Taylor, Francis S.	Pte.	34883	9th W. Yorks.	—	K. in A.
Taylor, Frank	Pte.	1834	W. Yorks.	—	D. a. Dis.
Taylor, Frank	L/Cpl.	268251	W. Yorks.	—	K. in A.
Taylor, Fred	Pte.	878	W. Yorks.	—	K. in A.
Taylor, Fred	Pte.	52345	9th Cheshire	—	K. in A.
Taylor, Fredk.	Rfm.	2794	2/8th W. Yorks.	—	K. in A.
Taylor, Fredk.	A.B.	TZ/9716	Royal Naval V. Reserve	—	K. in A.
Taylor, Geo.	Pte.	8206	W. Yorks.	—	K. in A.
Taylor, Geo.	Pte.	4431	2/5th York. & Lancs.	—	K. in A.
Taylor, Geo.	Pte.	141	R.A.M.C.	—	Died
Taylor, Geo.	Pnr.	116843	Royal Engineers	—	K. in A.
Taylor, Geo.	Pte.	1677	19th W. Yorks.	—	D. a. Dis.
Taylor, Geo. E.	Pte.	2344	Manchester	—	K. in A.
Taylor, Geo. M.	Lieut.		R.A.M.C.	—	K. in A.
Taylor, Geo. W.	Pte.	26616	1st W. Yorks.	—	K. in A.
Taylor, Harold	Pte.	42366	W. Yorks.	—	K. in A.
Taylor, Harold D.	Gnr.	128044	R.F.A.	—	K. in A.
Taylor, Harry	Pte.	31250	E. Yorks.	—	K. in A.

LEEDS ROLL OF HONOUR.

Name	Rank	No.	Regiment	Honours	How Died
Taylor, Harry	Pte.	24284	W. Yorks.	—	K. in A.
Taylor, Herbert	Pte.	301771	Durham Light Infantry	—	Died P.O.W.
Taylor, Jas.	Pte.	17079	W. Yorks.	—	K. in A.
Taylor, John A.	Pte.	8721	1st W. Yorks.	—	K. in A.
Taylor, John B.	Pte.	702316	23rd London	—	Missing
Taylor, John Edward	Pte.	276184	1/7th Durham Lt. Infty.	—	K. in A.
Taylor, John Wm.	Pte.	12679	4th W. Yorks.	—	K. in A.
Taylor, Joseph	Pte.	16487	W. Yorks.	—	K. in A.
Taylor, Joseph T.	Pte.	3209	K.O.Y.L.I.	—	K. in A.
Taylor, L.	Pte.	21111	Cheshire	—	Died
Taylor, Lawrence	Pte.	1474	W. Yorks.	—	K. in A.
Taylor, N.	Gnr.	559	4th W. Riding	—	K. in A.
Taylor, Oliver	Pte.	23874	W. Yorks.	—	K. in A.
Taylor, Oliver	Spr.	159605	Royal Engineers	—	K. in A.
Taylor, Percy	Pte.	213184	Royal Highlanders	—	K. in A.
Taylor, Reginald	L/Cpl.	38295	Gloucester	—	Missing
Taylor, Richard	Rfm.	1988	1/8th W. Yorks.	—	D. of W.
Taylor, Rbt. Wm.	Gdsmn.	15611	Scots Guards	—	K. in A.
Taylor, Rbt. Wm.	L/Cpl.	484096	Royal Engineers	—	D. a. Dis.
Taylor, Sydney	Pte.	8400	2nd Yorks.	—	Died
Taylor, Sydney	Pte.	115329	Labour Corps	—	K. in A.
Taylor, Sylvester H.	Pte.	159664	Machine Gun Corps	—	K. in A.
Taylor, Thomas	Pte.	8673	1st E. Yorks.	—	K. in A.
Taylor, Thomas	Pte.	10854	W. Riding	—	K. in A.
Taylor, Thomas	Pte.	115333	Labour Corps	—	Died
Taylor, Tom	Pte.	330849	8th Royal Scots	—	K. in A.
Taylro, Tom	L/Cpl.	266751	2/7th W. Yorks.	—	K. in A.
Taylor, Walter	Pte.	3707	Seaforth Highlanders	—	K. in A.
Taylor, Walter	Pte.	77841	R.A.M.C.	—	K. in A.
Taylor, Walter	1 Stkr.K/25682		H.M.S. "Wellington"	—	K. in A.
Taylor, Wilfred	Rfm.	1987	1/8th W. Yorks.	—	K. in A.
Taylor, Wm.	Rfm.	21710	1/8th W. Yorks.	—	K. in A.
Taylor, Wm.	Pte.	36831	W. Yorks.	—	K. in A.
Taylor, Wm. B.	Dvr.	149409	R.F.A.	—	K. in A.
Taylor, Wm. H.	L/Sgt.	2849	1/8th W. Yorks.	—	Missing
Taylor, Wm. H.	Sgt.	595	21st Northumb'l'd Fus.	—	Died
Taylor, Wm. H.	Pte.	22152	Yorks.	—	K. in A.
Tayne, Jas.	Spr.	482219	Royal Engineers	—	K. in A.
Tayne, Jos.	Pte.	50936	11th E. Yorks.	—	K. in A.
Teague, Chas.	L/Cpl.	1023	21st W. Yorks.	—	K. in A.
Teakle, Wm. G.	Pte.	52165	Middlesex Regt.	—	K. in A.
Teal, Harry	Gnr.	5051	R.G.A.	—	D. a. Dis.
Teal, Jos. T.	Pte.	9559	2nd W. Yorks.	—	K. in A.
Teale, A.	Pte.	59961	21st Canadian	—	K. in A.
Teale, Albert	Pte.	9544	1st W. Yorks.	—	D. of W.
Teale, Chas.	Cpl.	11717	1st King's Liverpools	—	K. in A.
Teale, Edgar A.	Pte.	133780	R.A.S.C.	—	Died

LEEDS ROLL OF HONOUR.

Name	Rank	No.	Regiment	Honours	How Died
Teale, Sydney	Rfm.	4596	1/7th W. Yorks.	—	K. in A.
Teale, William	Pte.	45913	12th Northumb'l'd Fus.	—	K. in A.
Tebbs, E.	Pte.	42603	Leicesters.	—	K. in A.
Tebbs, Willie	Sgt.	116	Royal Engineers	—	Died
Teed, Geo. Wm.	Pte.	319619	Labour Corps	—	Died
Telper, Geo. D.	Pte.	40952	Cameron Highlanders	—	K. in A.
Telford, Geo.	Cpl.	99176	R.F.A.	—	K. in A.
Tempest, David	Pte.	12135	18th W. Yorks.	—	K. in A.
Tempest, Horace	Pte.	23799	4th W. Yorks.	—	D. of W
Tempest, John Wm.	Stkr.	299815	H.M.S. " Defence "	—	Died
Tempest, Samuel	Sgt.		1st W. Yorks.	—	K. in A.
Tempest, Thomas	Dvr.	795856	R.F.A.	—	Killed
Temple, Arthur	Pte.	401129	R.A.M.C.	—	K. in A.
Temple, Geo. H.	Pte.	35223	Machine Gun Corps	—	K. in A.
Temple, Henry H.	L/Cpl.	33373	9th W. Yorks.	—	K. in A.
Temple, Jas. A.	Pte.	19267	8th E. Yorks.	—	K. in A.
Temple, Joseph	Pte.	401913	Labour Corps	—	Died
Temple, Rowland	Pte.	518	Northumberland Fusrs.	—	K. in A.
Temple, Thos.	Pte.	23196	W. Yorks.	—	D. a. Dis.
Templeton, John C.	L/Sgt.	5896	Yorks.	—	Died
Tennant, Gilbert	Pte.	28016	Lancs. Fusiliers	—	Died
Tennant, Isaac R.	Bdr.	283486	R.G.A.	—	Died
Tennant, Richard	Pte.	8629	2nd Manchester	—	K. in A.
Terry, Clifford H.	Rfm.	3084	1/7th W. Yorks.	—	K. in A.
Tetley, Cecil	Pte.	12170	10th W. Yorks.	—	D. a. Dis.
Tetley, Harry	Gnr.	775430	R.F.A.	—	D. a. Dis.
Thackeray, Fred	Rfm.	28599	King's Royal Rifle Cps.	—	Died
Thackeray, Harry	Pte.	10022	W. Riding	—	Missing
Thackeray, Reginald	Cpl.	98370	Royal Engineers	—	K. in A.
Thackery, Fredk.	Pte.	65058	Worcester	—	Died
Thackrah, Banjamin	Pte.	202878	20th Rifle Brigade	—	K. in A.
Thackrah, Walter	Pte.	102218	Machine Gun Corps	—	K. in A.
Thackrah, Wm.	Cpl.	2132	W. Yorks.	—	K. in A.
Thackrah, W. H.	Pte.	5051	4th Gordon Highdrs.	—	K. in A.
Thackray, Chas.	Pte.	21604	W. Yorks.	—	Missing
Thackray, Edward	Pte.	020550	R.A.O.C.	—	D. a. Dis.
Thackray, Geo.	Rfm.	266765	1/7th W. Yorks.	—	K. in A.
Thackray, Harry	Pte.	5094	W. Yorks.	—	K. in A.
Thackray, Herbert	Rfm.	270262	1/7th W. Yorks.	—	K. in A.
Thackray, Joseph C.	Gnr.	96336	R.F.A.	—	K. in A.
Thackray, Joseph	L/Cpl.	7367	Scots Guards	—	D. of W.
Thackray, Thos. H.	Bmdr.	128084	R.F.A.	—	K. in A.
Thackray, Wm. H.	2nd Lieut.		5th R.I. Lancers	—	K. in A.
Thackwray, John	Sgt.	265862	W. Yorks.	—	K. in A.
Theakstone, Walter	Pte.	46205	17th W. Yorks.	—	K. in A.
Thewlis, Clarence	Pte.	27431	Royal Warwicks.	—	K. in A.
Thipsey, Thos.	Rfm.	305345	1/8th W. Yorks.	—	K. in A.

LEEDS ROLL OF HONOUR.

Name	Rank	No.	Regiment	Honours	How Died
Thirkettle, Herbert J.	Pte.	166176	Durham Light Infantry	—	Died
Thirkill, Geo. H.	Pte.	10048	W. Riding	—	K. in A.
Thomas, Aaron	Pte.	10674	W. Riding	—	K. in A.
Thomas, Albert H.	Gnr.	224652	R.F.A.	—	D. a. Dis.
Thomas, Arthur	Pte.	24976	W. Yorks.	—	K. in A.
Thomas, Chas.	Pte.	50699	Northants.	—	K. in A.
Thomas, Geo. Wm.	Gnr.	63998	R.F.A.	—	K. in A.
Thomas, Harold	Pte.	1549	15th W. Yorks.	—	K. in A.
Thomas, J. A.	Pte.	2990	1/5th W. Riding	—	K. in A.
Thomas, John Wm.	Pte.	284726	Labour Corps	—	K. in A.
Thomas, Phillip E.	Cpl.	40071	Devons.	—	Died
Thomas, Richard E.	Pte.	33635	Royal Defence Corps.	—	K. in A.
Thomas, Wm.	Gnr.	301690	Tank Corps	—	D. a. Dis.
Thompson, A. E.	Pte.	66915	Northumberland Fusrs.	—	K. in A.
Thompson, Alban R.	Pte.	39773	1/6th W. Yorks.	—	Missing
Thompson, Albert	Spr.	84109	Royal Engineers	—	Died
Thompson, Albert	Pte.	017768	R.A.O.C.	—	D. a. Dis.
Thompson, Alfred	Pte.	4263	Northumberland Fusrs.	—	Died
Thompson, Arthur	Sman.		S.S. "Mabel Baird"	—	Died
Thompson, Arthur	Pte.	20499	Army Cyclist Corps	—	K. in A.
Thompson, Benjamin	Pte.	260086	York. & Lancs.	—	K. in A.
Thompson, C. F.	Pte.	34383	18th W. Yorks.	—	Missing
Thompson, Chas.	Rfm.	306691	2/8th W. Yorks.	—	K. in A.
Thompson, Chas.	Rfm.	266035	2/7th W. Yorks.	—	K. in A.
Thompson, Chas. H.	Gnr.	192533	R.G.A.	—	K. in A.
Thompson, Clarence S.	L/Cpl.	27705	W. Yorks.	—	D. a. Dis.
Thompson, Edmund C.	Rfm.	267592	3/7th W. Yorks.	—	K. in A.
Thompson, Ernest	Rfm.	5241	1/7th W. Yorks.	—	D. of W.
Thompson, Ernest	Pte.	110650	Labour Corps	—	K. in A.
Thompson, Ernest H.	Dvr.	18994	R.F.A.	—	D. a. Dis.
Thompson, Frank	Pte.	131	Royal Marine Lt. Infty.	—	K. in A.
Thompson, Frank M.	Pte.	21112	W. Yorks.	—	K. in A.
Thompson, Fred	Rfm.	306287	2/8th W. Yorks.	—	K. in A.
Thompson, Fredk. W.	Cpl.	56089	R.A.M.C.	—	K. in A.
Thompson, Geo.	Pte.	42987	Manchester	—	K. in A.
Thompson, Geo.	Pte.	8247	2nd W. Yorks.	—	D. of W.
Thompson, Geo. A.	Pte.	9551	W. Riding	—	K. in A.
Thompson, Harold	Pte.	403216	R.A.M.C.	—	K. in A.
Thompson, Harry	Pte.	413	17th W. Yorks.	D.C.M.	K. in A.
Thompson, Harry	Bmdr.	73144	R.F.A.	—	K. in A.
Thompson, Harry	Pte.	249	W. Yorks.	—	K. in A.
Thompson, Harry	Pte.	17228	W. Riding	—	K. in A.
Thompson, Harry	Pte.	261442	R.A.S.C.	—	Died
Thompson, Harry W.	L/Sgt.	7337	W. Yorks.	—	K. in A.
Thompson, Henry	Cpl.	8990	Durham Light Infantry	—	K. in A.
Thompson, Henry	Pte.	17928	W. Riding	—	K. in A.
Thompson, Herbert	Rfm.	41815	1/7th W. Yorks.	—	K. in A.

LEEDS ROLL OF HONOUR.

Name	Rank	No.	Regiment	Honours	How Died
Thompson, Herbert	Pte.	669	W. Yorks.	—	Missing
Thompson, Horace C.	L/Cpl.	028967	R.A.O.C.	—	D. of W.
Thompson, James	Pte.	11584	K.O.Y.L.I.	—	K. in A.
Thompson, James	Pte.	10928	Royal Defence Corps	—	Died
Thompson, James A.	Spr.	47587	Royal Engineers	—	Died
Thompson, James D.	Pte.	890	W. Yorks.	—	K. in A.
Thompson, James E.	1 A.M.	106375	Royal Air Force	—	Died P.O.W.
Thompson, James W.	Pte.	1575	Northumberland Fusrs.	—	K. in A.
Thompson, John	Dvr.	111245	R.F.A.	—	K. in A.
Thompson, John W.	Cpl.	273725	Royal Engineers	—	D. a. Dis.
Thompson, John W.	Pte.	7584	W. Yorks.	—	K. in A.
Thompson, Joseph					K. in A.
Thompson, Joseph	Pte.	12131	W. Yorks.	—	K. in A.
Thompson, Joseph	L/Sgt.	12858	W. Yorks.	—	K. in A.
Thompson, Joseph	Pte.	7610	Yorks.	—	K. in A.
Thompson, Joseph	Pte.	19869	York. & Lancs.	—	Missing
Thompson, Leonard	Tel.	J34769	R.N H.M.S. "Vala"	—	K. in A.
Thompson, Richard G.	Sgt.	330335	Gloucester Hussars	—	K. in A.
Thompson, Robert	Rfm.	2190	W. Yorks.	—	Died
Thompson, Robert P.	L./S.	239905	Royal Navy	—	K. in A.
Thompson, Samuel		4593	W. Yorks.	—	K. in A.
Thompson, Sidney C.	Rfm.	306766	2/8th W. Yorks.	—	K. in A.
Thompson, Sydney	L/Cpl.	1571	W. Yorks.	—	K. in A.
Thompson, Sydney J.	Pte.	30509	York. & Lancs.	—	Died
Thompson, William	Pte.	12678	W. Yorks.	—	K. in A.
Thompson, William	Pte.	38443	K.O.Y.L.I.	—	K. in A.
Thompson, William	L/Cpl.	20597	10th Yorks.	—	K. in A.
Thompson, William	Pte.	17227	8th W. Riding	—	K. in A.
Thompson, William B.	Pte.	28106	2nd W. Yorks.	—	K. in A.
Thompson, William E.	Pte.	21487	6th K.O.Y.L.I.	—	D. of W.
Thompson, William E.	Pte.	38821	Northumberland Fusrs.	—	K. in A.
Thompson, William E.	Sgt.	8883	E. Yorks.	—	K. in A.
Thompson, William G.	Pte.	37708	W. Yorks.	—	K. in A.
Thompson, William H.	Pte.	12872	1/5th W. Yorks.	—	K. in A.
Thompson, William H.	Pte.	13316	K.O.Y.L.I.	—	K. in A.
Thorley, Lionel	Pte.	26706	3rd W. Yorks.	—	Died
Thorley, Thomas W.	Pte.	8636	2nd W. Yorks.	—	K. in A.
Thorn, James D.	Pte.	18937	10th W. Yorks.	—	K. in A.
Thornhill, Arthur W.	Pte.	25650	W. Yorks.	—	D. of W.
Thornton, Arthur	Pte.	41022	7th K.O.Y.L.I.	—	K. in A.
Thornton, C.	Sgt.	849	20th Rifle Brigade	—	Died
Thornton, Claude A.M.	2nd Lieut.		7th W. Yorks.	—	K. in A.
Thornton, Edward	Pte.	405444	R.A.M.C.	—	K. in A.
Thornton, Ernest	Dvr.	126512	R.H.A.	—	Died
Thornton, Henry	Pte.	8638	11th W. Yorks.	—	K. in A.
Thornton, Herbert	Pte.	49368	W. Yorks.	—	K. in A.
Thornton, John		58902	8th Durham Lt. Infty.	—	K. in A.

LEEDS ROLL OF HONOUR.

Name	Rank	No.	Regiment	Honours	How Died
Thornton, John E.	L/Cpl.	15622	8th W. Riding	—	Died
Thornton, Reginald	L/Cpl.	33131	W. Yorks.	—	K. in A.
Thornton, Robert W.	Sgt.	205503	Durham Light Infantry	—	K. in A.
Thornton, William	Rfm.	307495	8th W. Yorks.	—	K. in A.
Thornton, William	Pte.	24592	Yorks.	—	K. in A.
Thornton, William	Rfm.	305928	2/8th W. Yorks.	—	K. in A.
Thorp, Thomas		130749	R.A.S.C.	—	Died
Thorpe, Albert	Pte.	375503	Durham Light Infantry	—	Died
Thorpe, H.	Gnr.	775402	R.F.A.	—	Died
Thorpe, John W.	Pte.	47459	Bedford	—	K. in A.
Thorpe, Thomas W.	Pte.	36471	16th W. Yorks.	—	Died
Thorpe, Thomas W.	Pte.	23774	2nd W. Yorks.	—	K. in A.
Threapleton, Fred	Pnr.	274088	Royal Engineers	—	K. in A.
Threapleton, Joseph	Pte.	17979	W. Yorks.	—	K. in A.
Threlfall, Thomas	Pte.	141395	Royal Air Force	—	Died
Thrippleton, Cecil M.	L/Cpl.	201621	1/4th Seaforth Highdrs.	—	K. in A.
Thrippleton, Joseph	Pte.	42532	S. Staffs.	—	K. in A.
Thrupp, Thomas	Sgt.	19202	9th Worcester	—	K. in A.
Thurlow, Thomas	Pte.	15700	1st Royal Scots Fusrs.	—	K. in A.
Tibbs, Walter	Pte.	946	8th Aus. Imp. Force	—	K. in A.
Tidds, Albert	Pte.	38956	Northumberland Fusrs.	—	K. in A.
Tierney, James	Spr.	251775	Royal Engineers	—	Died
Tiffany, Joe	Pnr.	98392	Royal Engineers	—	Died
Tiffany, John	Pte.	607791	Labour Corps	—	Died
Tiffany, Leonard	Pte.	5/43036	Seaforth Highlanders	—	K. in A.
Tilley, Geo. W. L.	Stkr.	7660	Royal Navy	—	K. in A.
Tillotson, Ernest	Pte.	44159	Machine Gun Corps	—	K. in A.
Tillotson, James W.	Pte.	13996	9th K.O.Y.L.I.	—	K. in A.
Tillotson, John A.	L/Cpl.	2791	2nd Northumb'l'd Fus.	—	D. of W.
Tillotson, Joseph	L/Cpl.	266637	1/7th W. Yorks.	—	Missing
Tillotson, Thos. H.	Gdsmn.	15361	2nd Coldstream Guards	—	K. in A.
Tillotson, Thos. W.	Pte.	15/897	W. Yorks.	—	K. in A.
Tillotson, Wm.	Pte.	11836	6th Yorks.	—	Missing
Timblin, Edward	Pte.	10286	W. Yorks.	—	Died
Timms, Robert	Pte.	899	15th W. Yorks.	—	K. in A.
Tindall, Chas.	Pte.	21191	K.O.Y.L.I.	—	K. in A.
Tindall, G. Robt.	L/Cpl.	300772	3rd Res. W. Yorks.	—	D. of W.
Tindall, James	Pte.	29955	Royal Scots Fusiliers	—	Died
Tindall, John C.	Rfm.	1888	8th W. Yorks.	—	K. in A.
Tindell, Alfred	Spr.	13752	Royal Engineers	—	K. in A.
Tingle, Walter	Pte.	7954	9th W. Yorks.	—	K. in A.
Tinker, R. H.	L/Cpl.	235020	W. Yorks.	—	K. in A.
Tiplady, Henry W.	Pte.	63302	1/4th K.O.Y.L.I.	—	K. in A.
Tipling, Clifford	Pte.	R258933	R.A.S.C.	—	Died
Tipper, Joseph	Pte.	13236	8th K.O.Y.L.I.	—	Missing
Tipple, Fredk. G.	Pte.	48820	Iniskilling Fusiliers	—	K. in A.
Tippler, E. E.	L/Cpl.	43702	W. Yorks.	—	K. in A.

LEEDS ROLL OF HONOUR.

Name	Rank	No.	Regiment	Honours	How Died
Tobin, James	Pte.	235247	2/4th Gloucester	—	K. in A.
Tobin, Peter	Pte.	7919	12th Scottish Rifles	—	Died
Tobin, Thomas	Pte.		Gloucester	—	Died
Todd, Albert	Pte.	31850	W. Yorks.	—	K. in A.
Todd, Edward	Pte.	11674	W. Riding	—	Died
Todd, George	Pte.	37938	18th Yorks.	—	Died
Todd, John E.	Pte.	199124	46th Canadians	—	K. in A.
Todd, Robt. E.	Pte.	16525	Royal Lancs.	—	K. in A.
Todd, Sidney	Pte.	902	W. Yorks.	—	K. in A.
Todd, Wilfred	Pte.	62820	W. Yorks.	—	K. in A.
Todd, William	L/Cpl.	307470	W. Yorks.	—	K. in A.
Todd, Wm. C.	L/Sgt.	10759	10th Scottish Rifles	—	K. in A.
Tolan, James	Pte.	15504	W. Riding	—	Missing
Tollenache, Edwin	Pte.	4696	Seaforth Highlanders	—	K. in A.
Tolmon, Edward	L/Cpl.	3956	3/4th Seaforth Highdrs.	—	K. in A.
Tolson, Frank	Gnr.	775676	R.F.A.	—	D. of W.
Tolson, Robt. H.	Captain		15th W. Yorks.	—	K. in A.
Tolson, Samuel W.	Pte.	17258	9th W. Yorks.	—	K. in A.
Tomlinson, Arthur		775157	R.F.A.	—	K. in A.
Tomlinson, Ernest	2nd Lieut.		Lincoln	—	K. in A.
Tomlinson, George	Pte.	33173	Training Reserve	—	K. in A.
Tomlinson, Harry	Pte.	36034	24th Northumb'l'd Fus.	—	K. in A.
Tomlinson, James	Pte.	12770	Lincoln	—	K. in A.
Tomlinson, John T.	Pte.	49681	W. Yorks.	—	K. in A.
Tomlinson, Joseph	Pte.	41219	11th W. Yorks.	—	K. in A.
Tomlinson, Louis De Witt	Pte.	86364	17th King's Liverpool	—	K. in A.
Tomlinson, Vernon	Gnr.	14680	R.F.A.	—	K. in A.
Tomlinson, Vincent	Cpl.	795006	R.F.A.	—	K. in A.
Tomlinson, Walter	Pte.	47479	K.O.Y.L.I.	—	K. in A.
Tomlinson, Wilfred	Sgt.	32915	10th Lincoln	—	K. in A.
Tomlinson, William	Sig.	23963	Cameron Highlanders	—	K. in A.
Tomlinson, Wm.	Pte.	11464	King's Liverpool	—	Died
Tompolsky, Myer	Pte.	267261	W. Yorks.	—	K. in A.
Toms, Richard	Gnr.	776353	1st W. Riding R.F.A.	—	K. in A.
Tonks, Amos	Rfm.	4208	1/8th W. Yorks.	—	K. in A.
Tooke, Bernard	Captain		15th W. Yorks.	—	K. in A.
Topham, A.	Pte.	1305	25th Northumb'l'd Fus.	—	D. of W.
Topham, Henry	Pte.	18460	W. Yorks.	—	Died
Topham, Percy	Pte.	14244	W. Yorks.	—	Died
Topping, Frank	Pte.	306687	W. Yorks.	—	K. in A.
Tordoff, Harry	L/Bmdr.	122140	R.F.A.	—	Died
Tordoff, Harry	A/Cpl.	28883	2nd W. Yorks.	—	K. in A.
Tose, Thomas W.	Rfm.	267402	1/7th W. Yorks.	—	Died
Tottie, Robert	Pte.	1636	15th W. Yorks.	—	Died
Tough, James	Cpl.	1581	1/7th W. Yorks.	—	K. in A.
Toulson, Daniel	Pte.	3419	1st York. & Lancs.	—	K. in A.

LEEDS ROLL OF HONOUR.

Name	Rank	No.	Regiment	Honours	How Died
Toulson, Harold	Tmr.	TS6488	Royal Navy	—	Died
Toulson, William	Pte.	12762	10th W. Yorks.	—	K. in A.
Towend, J. W.	Pte.	4512	W. Yorks.	—	K. in A.
Towle, J.	Pte.	41940	York. & Lancs.	—	K. in A.
Towlers, Ernest	L/Cpl.	703	17th W. Yorks.	—	K. in A.
Town, Chas. A.	Captain		11th W. Yorks.	M.C.	K. in A.
Townend, David	Pte.	13019	10th W. Yorks.	—	K. in A.
Townend, Edgar	Pte.	8346	4th W. Yorks.	—	Died
Townend, Harry	Pte.		Lincoln	—	Died
Townend, John T.	Rfm.	305845	2nd W. Yorks.	—	Missing
Townend, Leonard	Dvr.	111477	R.F.A.	—	Died
Townend, Peter	Pte.	266679	W. Yorks.	—	K. in A.
Townend, Tom	Pte.	7171	1/9th Durham Lt. Infty.	—	K. in A.
Townend, William	Sig.	201823	R.F.A.	—	K. in A.
Towns, James H.	L/Cpl.	158	17th W. Yorks.	—	K. in A.
Townsend, David	Dvr.	T/259763	R.A.S.C.	—	K. in A.
Townsend, Ernest	Pte.	17512	Manchester	—	Died
Townsend, Harry	Lieut.		R.F.A.	—	Died
Townsend, Harry	Pte.	7774	2/5th Northumb'l'd Fus.	—	K. in A.
Townsin, Alfred	Pte.	38318	York. & Lancs.	—	Missing
Townsley, Albert V.	Pte.	6483	W. Yorks.	—	Died
Townsley, Alfred	Rfm.	2423	2/7th W. Yorks.	—	K. in A.
Townsley, Alfred B.	Pte.	265040	W. Yorks.	—	Missing
Townsley, Arthur		11230	W. Riding	—	K. in A.
Townsley, Brian H.	2nd Lieut.		2/9th W. Yorks.	—	K. in A.
Townsley, Ernest	Pte.	32924	15th W. Yorks.	—	Missing
Townsley, Herbert A.	2nd Lieut.		R.A.F.	—	K. in A.
Townsley, John C.	Pte.	202902	10th W. Yorks.	—	K. in A.
Townsley, Joseph	Pte.	11499	9th W. Riding	—	K. in A.
Townsley, Richard S.	Pte.	49478	7th Lincoln	—	K. in A.
Towse, Herbert	Pte.	31435	25th Northumb'l'd Fus.	—	K. in A.
Toyne, Frank	Cpl.	TS/8277	R.A.S.C.	—	Died
Trainer, Chas. H.	Pte.	75165	W. Yorks.	—	K. in A.
Trainer, Willie	Gnr.	111945	R.F.A.	—	K. in A.
Tranmer, Walter	Pte.	22841	2nd Yorks.	—	K. in A.
Travis, Arthur	Rfm.	3647	2/7th W. Yorks.	—	K. in A.
Trenan, Wm.	Rfm.	3256	King's Royal Rifle Cps.	—	Died
Tringhan, George	Pte.	25426	Royal W. Surrey	—	Died
Trippett, Harold	Pte.	75324	Northumberland Fusrs.	—	Died
Tronsdale, J. H.	Rfm.	3923	3/7th W. Yorks.	—	K. in A.
Trotter, Ed.	Pte.	334380	212th Labour Co.	—	Died
Troughton, John	Rfm.	265518	1/7th W. Yorks.	—	K. in A.
Troughton, Thomas W.	L/Cpl.	21110	16th Cheshire	—	K. in A.
Trousdale, Jacob	A.B.	30308	H.M.S. " Calypso "	—	K. in A.
Trousdale, John H.	Rfm.	8151	7th W. Yorks.	—	Died
Trout, Tom	Sgt.	241248	2/5th York. & Lancs.	—	K. in A.
Trow, George R.	Pte.	33018	9th W. Yorks.	—	K. in A.

LEEDS ROLL OF HONOUR.

Name	Rank	No.	Regiment	Honours	How Died
Trowsdale, Fred	Pte.	41194	11th W. Yorks.	—	K. in A.
Truscott, Percy I.	Pte.	1655	Warwick	—	K. in A.
Tucker, Chas. H.	Pte.	34215	9th W. Yorks.	—	K. in A.
Tucker, Douglas	Pte.	4579	2/5th W. Yorks.	—	K. in A.
Tuckwell, William	Pte.	16135	Northumberland Fusrs.	—	K. in A.
Tuffy, Percival T.	Wireman		H.M.S. " Penn "	—	Died
Tuke, Frank	Pte.	401389	R.A.M.C.	—	K. in A.
Tunley, Herbert	Pte.	202137	6th Leicester	—	K. in A.
Tunnington, John T.	L/Cpl.	265502	W. Yorks.	—	Died
Tunstall, Jack	Pte.	245201	Durham Lt. Infantry	—	Died
Tunstall, Samuel	Pte.	15318	9th Yorks.	—	K. in A.
Turham, C.	Pnr.	83702	Royal Engineers	—	K. in A.
Turnbull, John	L/Sgt.	345	King's Royal Rifle Cps.	—	K. in A.
Turnbull, Robt.	Cpl.	7754	48th Machine Gun Corps	—	K. in A.
Turnbull, Wm.	Rfm.	27469	Rifle Brigade	—	K. in A.
Turner, Albert	Pte.	22431	12th W. Yorks.	—	K. in A.
Turner, Albert E.	L/Cpl.	2335	8th W. Yorks.	—	K. in A.
Turner, Albert E.	Pte.	21058	W. Yorks.	—	K. in A.
Turner, Bert	Pte.	1790	15th W. Yorks.	—	Missing
Turner, Chas. E.	Sgt.	28033	12th W. Yorks.	—	K. in A.
Turner, Chas. G.	Pte.	25945	K.O.Y.L.I.	—	K. in A.
Turner, Chas. H.	Cpl.	17197	1st W. Yorks.	—	Missing
Turner, Ernest W.	Pte.	22603	Lancs. Fusiliers	—	K. in A.
Turner, Frank	Sgt.	19373	Cheshire	—	K. in A.
Turner, Fred	Pte.	28288	E. Yorks.	—	K. in A.
Turner, Fredk.	Gdsmn.	23547	1st Grenadier Guards	—	K. in A.
Turner, George	Pte.	26982	4th S. Wales Borderers	—	K. in A.
Turner, Henry	Pte.	69234	Northumberland Fusrs.	—	K. in A.
Turner, Herbert		289	17th W. Yorks.	—	K. in A.
Turner, Hubert N.	Lieut.		19th W. Yorks.	—	K. in A.
Turner, James	Pnr.	83777	Royal Engineers	—	K. in A.
Turner, James	Pte.	1824	K.O.Y.L.I.	—	Died
Turner, John	Sgt.	9500	W. Yorks.	—	K. in A.
Turner, John H.	Gdsmn.	7956	Scots Guards	—	Missing
Turner, John N.	Rfm.	266724	1/7th W. Yorks.	—	K. in A.
Turner, Joseph	Pte.	21217	Northumberland Fusrs.	—	Missing
Turner, Joseph H.	Spr.	83846	Royal Engineers	—	Died
Turner, R.	Pte.	158514	Machine Gun Corps	—	Died
Turner, Robert	Pte.	6073	1st Northumb'l'd Fus.	—	K. in A.
Turner, Thomas	Spr.	446	Royal Engineers	—	K. in A.
Turner, Thomas	Sgt.	10724	W. Yorks.	—	K. in A.
Turner, Thomas	L/Cpl.	17833	1/5th W. Yorks.	—	D. of W.
Turner, Tom	Pte.	34161	1st W. Yorks.	—	Died
Turner, W.	Sgt.	25774	14th Canadians	—	Died
Turner, Walter	Pte.	40045	Worcester	—	Died
Turnpenny, Wm. C.	Pte.	265706	W. Yorks.	—	K. in A.
Turton, Walter	Pte.	60944	25th Northumb'l'd Fus.	—	K. in A.

LEEDS ROLL OF HONOUR.

Name	Rank	No.	Regiment	Honours	How Died
Turver, James	L/Cpl.	2889	1/7th W. Yorks.	—	Died
Tuting, Harry	Pte.	10771	W. Yorks.	—	Died
Twigg, Tom	Pte.	24067	K.O.Y.L.I.	—	Missing
Twyford, Thomas	Pte.	21372	K.O. Scottish Borderers	—	K. in A.
Tyne, Walter	Pte.	260051	Northumberland Fusrs.	—	K. in A.
Tyreman, Walter	Pte.	201729	Seaforth Highlanders	—	K. in A.
Umpleby, Thomas	Pte.	47282	W. Yorks.	—	K. in A.
Umpleby, Walter	Pte.	7176	1/9th Durham Lt. Infty.	—	K. in A.
Umpleby, Wm.	L/Cpl.	9227	2nd W. Yorks.	—	K. in A.
Uncless, Bernard	Pte.	37498	W. Yorks.	—	K. in A.
Underhill, George	Dvr.	786106	R.F.A.	—	Died
Underhill, James		118052	R.A.S.C. (M.T.)	—	Died
Underwood, Harold	Pte.	39537	2nd W. Yorks.	—	K. in A.
Upton, Alfred	Pte.	305496	W. Yorks.	—	K. in A.
Upton, John	Pte.	39480	Leicester	—	Died
Usherwood, Henry	Pte.	419783	Labour Corps	—	Died
Vale, John E.	Pte.	78430	Durham Light Infantry	—	K. in A.
Valentine, Francis	Pte.	17195	5th Gordon Highdrs.	—	K. in A.
Valentine, Geo. H.	Pte.	37459	16th W. Yorks.	—	Missing
Valette, Louis	Pte.		50th Australian L.I.	—	K. in A.
Valters, Jas. F.	Pte.	69235	Northumberland Fusrs.	—	Died
Vant, Thos.	Pte.	28346	E. Yorks.	—	K. in A.
Varey, Cecil	L/Cpl.	23788	2nd W. Yorks.	—	K. in A.
Varey, Edward	Pte.	48733	3rd W. Yorks.	—	K. in A.
Varey, John H.	Pte.	19149	9th Northumb'l'd Fus.	—	K. in A.
Varley, Albert	Pte.	52384	Lancs. Fusiliers	—	K. in A.
Varley, Arthur	Pte.	307651	W. Yorks.	—	K. in A.
Varley, Harry	Pte.	3942	W. Yorks.	—	K. in A.
Varley, Joseph	Pte.	241791	3/5th K.O.Y.L.I.	—	K. in A.
Varley, Richard	Pte.	40955	Northumberland Fusrs.	—	Died
Varty, Wm. E.	Bmdr.	28308	R.G.A.	—	K. in A.
Vasey, Harry	Pte.	242310	W. Yorks.	—	K. in A.
Vasey, William	L/Cpl.	1408	1/8th W. Yorks.	—	Missing
Vaughan, Alfred	Pte.	612286	Labour Corps	—	D. a. Dis.
Vaughan, Arthur T.	A/Sgt.	7259	R.F.A.	—	K. in A.
Vause, J. G.	Lieut.		15th W. Yorks.	—	Died
Vause, Thomas C.	2nd Lieut.		1/8th W. Yorks.	—	K. in A.
Veal, Harry	Sgt.	185	R.G.A.	—	K. in A.
Venning, Benj.	Pte.	11149	West Yorks.	—	Killed
Verity, Alfred	Pte.	24362	2nd W. Yorks.	—	K. in A.
Verity, Charles	Pte.	30300	10th E. Yorks.	—	K. in A.
Verity, F. W.	L/Cpl.	37343	3rd W. Yorks.	—	K. in A.
Vernon, Allen	Pte.	48908	W. Yorks.	—	K. in A.
Verrent, William	Gnr.	39623	R.F.A.	—	Died
Vevers, George	Pte.	9420	9th W. Yorks.	—	Died

LEEDS ROLL OF HONOUR.

Name	Rank	No.	Regiment	Honours	How Died
Vickerman, H.	Pte.	24407	W. Yorks.	—	D. a. Dis.
Vickers, Ben	Rfm.	3433	2/8th W. Yorks.	—	K. in A.
Vickers, Benj. P.	Pte.	22169	6th Royal Lancs.	—	K. in A.
Vickers, Chas.	Spr.	98382	Royal Engineers	—	K. in A.
Vickers, Ernest	L/Cpl.	8174	W. Yorks.	—	Died
Vickers, Joseph	Pte.	9680	W. Yorks.	—	Died
Vickers, L. P.	A/Cpl.	44097	Lincolns.	—	K. in A.
Vickers, Wm. Hy.	Pte.	50605	1/8th Lancs. Fusrs.	—	K. in A.
Victor, C.	Pte.	39128	W. Yorks.	—	K. in A.
Vince, W. W.	C.S.M.	918	W. Yorks.	—	K. in A.
Vine, Harold W.	Pte	29595	8th Border	—	Killed
Viney, James	Pte.		K.O.Y.L.I.	—	Died
Virgo, Thomas W.	Pte.	34050	9th W. Yorks.	—	K. in A.
Vollans, Charles	Cpl.	304558	R.A.S.C.	—	K. in A.
Vollans, Harry	Gdsmn.	28256	Grenadier Guards	—	D. of W.
Vyner, G. E.	Pte.	8364	10th W. Yorks.	—	K. in A.
Vyner, Willie	Gnr.	79613	R.F.A.	—	K. in A.
Waddington, Arthur B.	A.B.	10979	S.S. " Traveal "	—	Killed
Waddington, Arthur B.	Pte.	10637	8th Royal Fusiliers	—	Missing
Waddington, Edward	Pte.	24322	W. Yorks.	—	Died
Waddington, Harold	Rfm.	3520	2/7th W. Yorks.	—	K. in A.
Waddington, Henry	A.B.	Z8970	Royal Naval V. Reserve	—	D. of W.
Waddington, Herbert	Pte.	13152	10th W. Yorks.	—	K. in A.
Waddington, Herbert	Pte.		W. Riding	—	K. in A.
Waddington, Joseph	Pte.	14536	3rd Dorset	—	Died
Waddington, Rowland	Pte.	25712	W. Yorks.	—	K. in A.
Waddle, Geo. Wm.	Pte.	23980	12th W. Yorks.	—	K. in A.
Wade, Ernest	Pte.	23639	9th W. Yorks.	—	K. in A.
Wade, Harry	Pte.	24461	3rd W. Yorks.	—	K. in A.
Wade, James	Pte.	039942	R.A.O.C.	—	D. a. Dis.
Wade, Sydney	Pte.	26131	W. Yorks.	—	K. in A.
Wade, Walter	Cpl.	305412	1st W. Yorks.	—	K. in A.
Wadkin, Henry	Pte.	77920	Durham Light Infantry	—	K. in A.
Wadman, Vincent H.	Pte.	8149	18th Royal Fusiliers	—	K. in A.
Wadsworth, Alfred	Pte.	32981	16th W. Yorks.	—	Missing
Wadsworth, Geo.	Pte.	38675	York. & Lancs.	—	K. in A.
Wadsworth, James	L/Cpl.	11300	K.O.Y.L.I.	—	K. in A.
Wadsworth, William	Rfm.	202925	7th Rifle Brigade	—	K. in A.
Waggett, Ernest L.	Pte.	81360	Royal Fusiliers	—	Died
Wagstaff, Robt. H.	Pte.	20515	8th Yorks.	—	K. in A.
Wagstaff, Thos.	Spr.	72904	Royal Engineers	—	D. of W.
Wain, Wm. Hy.	Pte.	69456	Labour Corps	—	Died
Wainfor, Nelson	Pte.	12198	9th W. Yorks.	—	K. in A.
Wainwright, Albert	Gnr.	5545	R.F.A.	—	K. in A.
Wainwright, Arthur	L/Cpl.	10770	W. Yorks.	—	D. P.O.W.
Wainwright, Ernest	L/Cpl.	1332	17th W. Yorks.	—	K. in A.

LEEDS ROLL OF HONOUR.

Name	Rank	No.	Regiment	Honours	How Died
Wainwright, Geo.	Pte.	40428	6th Cameron Highdrs.	—	D. of W.
Wainwright, James	Cpl.	1812	9th K.O.Y.L.I.	—	Missing
Wainwright, Mark	Pte.	15618	2/6th W. Yorks.	—	K. in A.
Wainwright, Tom	Pte.	15835	Machine Gun Corps	—	K. in A.
Wainwright, Wm.	Sgt.	9227	2nd Lancs. Fusiliers	—	K. in A.
Wainwright, Willie	Rfm.	5337	1/8th W. Yorks.	—	K. in A.
Waite, Arthur	Spr.	82768	Royal Engineers	—	K. in A.
Waite, G. H.	Pte.	7238	Royal Fusiliers	—	Missing
Waite, George	Pte.	13765	Royal Fusiliers	—	Died
Waite, Harry	Pte.	644405	Labour Corps	—	D. a. Dis.
Waite, John	Pte.	695193	Labour Corps	—	D. a. Dis.
Waite, Percy	Pte.	35322	1st W. Yorks.	—	D. of W.
Waite, Roland	Cpl.	201320	4th Seaforth Highdrs.	—	K. in A.
Waite, Wilfred	Pte.	40465	Cameron Highlanders	—	D. a. Dis.
Waite, Wm.	Pte.	G52180	1/8th Middlesex	—	Killed
Wake, Wm.	Pte.	10380	9th W. Yorks.	—	D. of W.
Wakefield, Chas.	Pte.	21585	Yorks. Regt.	—	Died
Walbank, Leonard	Pte.	11472	11th W. Yorks.	—	Died
Walden, Percy	Pte.	35096	Northumberland Fusrs.	—	K. in A.
Walder, Michael	Pte.	175	2nd W. Yorks.	—	Died
Wales, Richard	Pte.	11619	8th W. Riding	—	K. in A.
Walker, Albert	Pte.	38197	15th W. Yorks.	—	K. in A.
Walker, Albert	Pte.	44925	K.O.Y.L.I.	—	Missing
Walker, Albert	Pte.	6120	1/8th Durham Lt. Infty.	—	K. in A.
Walker, Alfred	Pte.	31291	E. Yorks.	—	K. in A.
Walker, Alfred Hy.	Pte.	118425	R.A.S.C.	—	Died
Walker, Andrew	Cpl.	11612	12th W. Yorks.	—	K. in A.
Walker, Arthur	Cpl.	11290	7th Yorks.	—	K. in A.
Walker, Arthur	Gnr.	781386	R.F.A.	—	K. in A.
Walker, B.	Pte.	34999	7th E. Yorks.	—	K. in A.
Walker, Chas.	Pte.	38566	17th W. Yorks.	—	D. of W.
Walker, Chas.	Pte.	44444	Machine Gun Corps	—	D. a. Dis.
Walker, Chas. Owen	Pte.	40077	Royal Irish Fusrs.	—	K. in A.
Walker, Clifford	Cpl.	12992	W. Yorks.	—	K. in A.
Walker, Edgar	Sgt.	268262	1/8th W. Yorks.	—	K. in A.
Walker, Edgar	Pte.	235794	2/4th York. & Lancs.	—	Missing
Walker, Edgar	Rfm.	2214	8th W. Yorks.	—	K. in A.
Walker, Edgar	Dvr.	199957	R.A.S.C.	—	Died
Walker, Ernest	Gnr.	95967	R.F.A.	—	K. in A.
Walker, Ernest	Pte.	930	15th W. Yorks.	—	K. in A.
Walker, Ernest D.	Pte.	81644	Durham Light Infantry	—	K. in A.
Walker, Francis	Gnr.	72754	R.F.A.	—	K. in A.
Walker, Francis W.	Pte.	25569	15th W. Yorks.	—	Missing
Walker, Frank	Sgt.	265969	W. Yorks.	—	K. in A.
Walker, Fred	Pte.	7691	E. Yorks.	—	Died
Walker, Fred	C.Q.M.S.	5417	W. Yorks.	—	Died
Walker, Fredk. Wm.	A.B.	SS5300	H.M.S. "Narborough"	—	Drowned

LEEDS ROLL OF HONOUR.

Name	Rank	No.	Regiment	Honours	How Died
Walker, Harry	Pte.	260037	26th Northumb'l'd Fus.	—	D. of W.
Walker, Geo.	Pte.	265209	11th W. Yorks.	—	K. in A.
Walker, Geo.	Pte.	45343	King's Liverpool	—	K. in A.
Walker, Geo.	Pte.	31941	2nd Scots Rifles	—	Missing
Walker, Geo.	Pte.	53216	K.O.Y.L.I.	—	K. in A.
Walker, Geo.	Pte.	242371	1st W. Yorks.	—	K. in A.
Walker, Geo. H.	Pte.	43956	8th Lincoln	—	K. in A.
Walker, H.	Pte.	55856	York. & Lancs.	—	K. in A.
Walker, Harold	Gnr.	775840	R.F.A.	—	D. of W.
Walker, Harry	Pte.	23390	E. Yorks.	—	K. in A.
Walker, Harry	L/Cpl.	11685	2/7th W. Yorks.	—	K. in A.
Walker, Harry	Pte.	18303	W. Yorks.	—	D. of W.
Walker, Harry	L/Cpl.	267666	W. Yorks.	—	Died
Walker, Harry C.	Pte.	238036	21st Northumb'l'd Fus.	—	K. in A.
Walker, Henry	Pte.	32894	16th W. Yorks.	—	Missing
Walker, Henry	Pte.	201670	3/4th Seaforth Highdrs.	—	K. in A.
Walker, Herbert	Rfm.	7125	7th W. Yorks.	—	K. in A.
Walker, Herbert	Pte.	38481	1st York. & Lancs.	—	K. in A.
Walker, Herbert	L/Cpl.	202005	King's Royal Rifle Cps.	M.M.	D. of W.
Walker, J. F.	Pte.	29729	E. Yorks.	—	K. in A.
Walker, James	Pte.	27051	4th S. Wales Borderers	—	K. in A.
Walker, Jas. Wm.	Pte.	43824	10th W. Yorks.	—	K. in A.
Walker, John	Pte.	267947	1/6th Royal Highlanders	—	Missing
Walker, John C.	2nd Lieut.		1/5th W. Yorks.	—	K. in A.
Walker, John Chas.	Dvr.	119001	R.F.A.	—	D. a. Dis.
Walker, John Wm.	Pte.	17791	1st W. Yorks.	—	K. in A.
Walker, Joseph	Pte.	15485	6th Yorks.	—	K. in A.
Walker, Joseph	Rfm.	1955	8th W. Yorks.	—	K. in A.
Walker, Joseph	Pte.	38435	Yorks.	—	K. in A.
Walker, Joseph W.	L/Cpl.	5137	2/7th W. Yorks.	—	K. in A.
Walker, Lawrence	L/Cpl.	368064	W. Yorks.	—	K. in A.
Walker, Leslie	Pte.	90160	Machine Gun Corps	—	D. a. Dis.
Walker, Oliver B.	Pte.	1860	15th W. Yorks.	—	Missing
Walker, Percy	Spr.	182998	Royal Engineers	—	D. a. Dis.
Walker, Percy	Pte.	205107	W. Yorks.	—	K. in A.
Walker, Robert	1 A.M.	4950	Royal Air Force	—	Died
Walker, Samuel	Pte.	7178	Durham Light Infantry	—	K. in A.
Walker, Samuel	Pte.	15246	26th Labour Co.	—	K. in A.
Walker, Samuel	L/Cpl.	301471	2nd Royal Scots	—	K. in A.
Walker, Sidney	Gnr.	154524	R.G.A.	—	K. in A.
Walker, Smith	Pte.	39430	W. Yorks.	—	Missing
Walker, T. J.	Cpl.	1444	6th Rifle Brigade	—	K. in A.
Walker, Thos.	Pte.	24019	7th K.O.Y.L.I.	—	Missing
Walker, Thos. G.	Pte.	33038	1/5th W. York.	—	K. in A.
Walker, Walter	Pte.	345309	Durham Light Infantry	—	K. in A.
Walker, Walter	Cpl.	265823	W. Yorks.	—	Died
Walker, Walter S.	Pte.	31411	9th Northumb'l'd Fus.	—	K. in A.

LEEDS ROLL OF HONOUR.

Name	Rank	No.	Regiment	Honours	How Died
Walker, William	Pte.	1519	W. Yorks.	—	Died
Walker, William	Sgt.	9713	10th W. Yorks.	—	K. in A.
Walker, William	Pte.	4621	W. Yorks.	—	Missing
Walker, William	Pte.	48627	15th W. Yorks.	—	Killed
Walker, William	Pte.	38739	3rd Leicester	—	Killed
Walker, William	B.Q.M.S.	27015	R.F.A.	—	K. in A.
Walker, William	Pte.	408262	R.A.M.C.	—	D. a. Dis.
Wallace, Herbert	Pte.		R.A.S.C.	—	D. of W.
Wallace, John	Gnr.	162465	R.G.A.	—	Died
Wallace, Wm. W.	Pte.	57585	York. & Lancs.	—	K. in A.
Waller, Frank	Pte.	32414	9th W. Yorks.	—	K. in A.
Wallis, Arthur	Cpl.	4514	3/7th W. Yorks.	—	Died
Wallis, Clifford	Rfm.	2196	7th W. Yorks.	—	K. in A.
Wallis, William	Pte.	265523	9th W. Yorks.	—	K. in A.
Wallis, William	Sig.	24429	9th K.O.Y.L.I.	—	D. of W.
Walls, George	Pte.	14117	9th W. Yorks.	—	K. in A.
Walls, James	Pte.	13639	K.O.Y.L.I.	—	K. in A.
Walls, Jas. E. B.	Rfm.	1710	1/8th W. Yorks.	—	K. in A.
Walpole, Joe	Rfm.	4248	2/8th W. Yorks.	—	K. in A.
Walpole, Newland	Pte.	306906	W. Yorks.	—	K. in A.
Walpole, William	Pte.	13257	K.O.Y.L.I.	—	K. in A.
Walsh, Edward	Pte.	7643	W. Yorks.	—	D. of W.
Walsh, George	Pte.	26649	K.O.Y.L.I.	—	Died
Walsh, John	Sgt.	9180	1st Scots Guards	—	K. in A.
Walsh, Joseph	Pte.	22119	6th Northants.	—	K. in A.
Walsh, Michael	Pte.	40152	Royal Scots Fusiliers	—	K. in A.
Walsh, Oswald H.	Pte.	535216	15th County of London	—	K. in A.
Walsh, Richard	Pte.	268464	W. Yorks.	—	K. in A.
Walsh, Thos.	Dvr.	306315	R.A.S.C.	—	Died
Walsh, Thos.	Pte.	12299	W. Yorks.	—	Died
Walsh, Thos.	Pnr.	274799	Royal Engineers	—	Died
Walsh, Wm. N.	Pte.	3219	7th W. Yorks.	—	K. in A.
Walsworth, Friend	Pte.	58560	18th Liverpool	—	Missing
Walter, Maurice	Cpl.	1432	15th W. Yorks.	—	Died
Walters, Fredk. R.	Pte.	51384	E. Yorks.	—	K. in A.
Walters, Thos. Wm.	Gnr.	52599	R.F.A.	—	K. in A.
Walton, A.	Rfm.	3589	1/7th W. Yorks.	—	Died
Walton, Albert	A.B.	J29140	H.M.S. " Swordfish "	—	Died
Walton, Alfred V.	Pte.	25291	W. Yorks.	—	D. a. Dis.
Walton, Arthur	Rfm.	3355	1/7th W. Yorks.	—	K. in A.
Walton, Eric H.	Pte.	4820	K.O.Y.L.I.	—	Missing
Walton, Fred	Pte.	15768	11th W. Yorks.	—	K. in A.
Walton, Herbert	Gdsmn.	8149	1st Scots Guards	—	D. of W.
Walton, Herbert	Pte.	34223	17th W. Yorks.	—	K. in A.
Walton, James E.	Pte.	24886	W. Yorks.	—	K. in A.
Walton, John	Spr.	343295	Royal Engineers	—	Died
Walton, John	Pte.	459202	Labour Corps	—	Died

LEEDS ROLL OF HONOUR.

Name	Rank	No.	Regiment	Honours	How Died
Walton, Joseph	Rfm.	1422	2/8th W. Yorks.	—	K. in A.
Walton, Joseph	Pte.	11785	Machine Gun Corps	—	K. in A.
Walton, Percy	Pte.	80975	1/8th Durham Lt. Infty.	—	D. of W.
Walton, Sid.	Cpl.	948	15th W. Yorks.	—	K. in A.
Walton, Sidney G.	Pte.	41044	Norfolk	—	K. in A.
Wane, Christopher	O.S.	40880	H.M.S. " Diligence "	—	Died
Want, Geo.	L/Cpl.	203181	10th W. Yorks.	—	K. in A.
Warbrick, Allen S.	Pte.	57487	10th W. Yorks.	—	Died
Warburton, Alfred E.	Spr.	275772	Royal Engineers	—	K. in A.
Warcup, James T.	Pte.	32748	Norfolk	—	K. in A.
Ward, Albert	Pte.	52183	Middlesex	—	Missing
Ward, Alec	2nd Lieut.		15th W. Yorks.	—	K. in A.
Ward, Alfred	Pte.	22394	3rd W. Yorks.	—	D. a. Dis.
Ward, Archer W.	Pte.	306332	W. Yorks.	—	Died
Ward, Arthur	L/Cpl.	8675	1st W. Yorks.	—	D. of W.
Ward, Arthur	Dvr.	7535	R.F.A.	—	K. in A.
Ward, Benjamin	Rfm.	14288	13th King's R. R. Corps.	—	K. in A.
Ward, Chas. E.	Rfm.	4976	2/7th W. Yorks.	—	K. in A.
Ward, Clifford	Dvr.	775653	R.F.A.	—	D. a. Dis.
Ward, E. G.	Cpl.	7375	Royal Air Force	—	Died
Ward, Emmanuel	Pte.	8193	4th W. Yorks.	—	K. in A.
Ward, Ernest	L/Cpl.	201865	Seaforth Highlanders	—	Missing
Ward, Ernest C.	Stkr.	21342	Royal Naval Division	—	K. in A.
Ward, Fredk.	Pte.	55442	Northumberland Fusrs.	—	K. in A.
Ward, Frank	Pte.	201722	Northumberland Fusrs.	—	K. in A.
Ward, George	Pte.	20859	1st K.O. Scottish Bords.	—	K. in A.
Ward, Harold	Sgt.	589064	17th London	—	K. in A.
Ward, Herbert	Pte.	403312	R.A.M.C.	—	K. in A.
Ward, Herbert	L/Cpl.	3922	3/8th W. Yorks.	—	Missing
Ward, J.	Pte.	142448	Machine Gun Corps	—	K. in A.
Ward, John	Rfm.	300037	18th W. Yorks.	—	K. in A.
Ward, John H.	Sgt.	31716	R.G.A.	—	K. in A.
Ward, John Thos.	Pte.	22479	1/5th W. Yorks.	—	K. in A.
Ward, John Wm.	Pte.	31409	Northumberland Fusrs.	—	D. of W.
Ward, Joseph	Pte.	199972	Royal Air Force	—	D. a. Dis.
Ward, Richard	Pte.	23912	10th W. Yorks.	—	K. in A.
Ward, Ronald	BQMS	775292	R.F.A.	—	K. in A.
Ward, Sam	Rfm.	1627	1/8th W. Yorks.	—	K. in A.
Ward, Walter	Pte.	57616	Liverpool	—	D. of W.
Ward, Wm.	Rfm.	3508	King's Royal Rifle Cps.	—	K. in A.
Ward, William	Cpl.	79154	R.F.A.	—	K. in A.
Wardale, Thos.	Pte.	1751	W. Yorks.	—	K. in A.
Wardle, Henry	Pte.	17722	6th Yorks.	—	K. in A.
Wardle, James K.	Lieut.		15th W. Yorks.	—	D. of W.
Wardle, Richard	Cpl.	6954	2nd W. Riding	—	K. in A.
Wardle, Thos.	Rfm.	206060	Rifle Brigade	—	D. a. Dis.
Wardley, George	Pte.	10468	2nd Yorks.	—	K. in A.

LEEDS ROLL OF HONOUR.

Name	Rank	No.	Regiment	Honours	How Died
Wardman, John	Pte.	202292	2/4th Lincoln	—	D. of W.
Wardman, Levi	Pte.	9280	1st Yorks.	—	Died
Ware, Lawrence C.	O.S.	664	Royal Naval Division	—	Died
Waring, George	Pte.	44914	Training Reserve	—	K. in A.
Waring, Horace	Pte.	942	15th W. Yorks.	—	K. in A.
Waring, James Hy.	Pte.	9458	W. Riding	—	D. a. Dis.
Waring, John	Captain		20th Manchester	—	K. in A.
Warne, Wm. A.	Pte.	305776	1/6th W. Yorks.	—	Died P.O.W.
Warner, John	Pte.	13171	12th W. Yorks.	—	K. in A.
Warner, Wm.	Pte.	34394	8th York. & Lancs.	—	K. in A.
Warr, Geo. H. G.	Pte.	407040	R.A.M.C.	—	Died
Warren, Samuel A.	Pte.	1857	15th W. Yorks.	—	K. in A.
Warren, Thos.	Pte.	18541	1st Border	—	K. in A.
Warrener, Ernest	Spr.	287938	Royal Engineers	—	D. a. Dis.
Warrington, Arthur	L/Cpl.	28752	10th W. Yorks.	—	K. in A.
Warrington, Chas. A.	Pte.	201746	8th Northumb'l'd Fus.	—	K. in A.
Warrior, Herbert	Pte.	28309	Royal Lancs.	—	K. in A.
Warrior, Thos. Wm.	Rfm.	7707	16th King's R. R. Cps.	—	K. in A.
Wasey, Geo. Hy.	Pte.	22184	K.O.Y.L.I.	—	K. in A.
Washington, Fredk.	Pte.	19628	1st E. Yorks.	—	Died
Waterfield, Thos.	Dvr.	786413	R.F.A.	—	K. in A.
Waterhouse, Edgar	Pte.	36847	9th W. Yorks.	—	K. in A.
Waterhouse, Edward	Rfm.	307806	1/6th W. Yorks.	—	K. in A.
Waterhouse, H.	Pte.	242643	2nd W. Yorks.	—	K. in A.
Waterhouse, Harry	Pte.	38807	Northumberland Fusrs.	—	K. in A.
Waterhouse, Herbert	Pte.	25475	1st E. Yorks.	—	K. in A.
Waterhouse, John	Rfm.	43655	King's Royal Rifle Cps.	—	K. in A.
Waterhouse, Thos.	Pte.	4747	1/4th Seaforth Highdrs.	—	K. in A.
Waterland, Fred	Pte.	266604	6th Northumb'l'd Fus.	—	Died
Waterman, Wm.	Rfm.	267116	2/7th W. Yorks.	—	D. of W.
Waters, Alfred	Pte.	4890	W. Yorks.	—	Died
Waters, Willie	Sgt.	8204	W. Yorks.	—	K. in A.
Waterton, Chas.	L/Cpl.	17727	5th K. Shropshire L.I.	—	K. in A.
Waterton, Wm.	Pte.	24563	11th W. Yorks.	—	D. of W.
Waterworth, Horace	Gnr.	775519	R.F.A.	—	K. in A.
Waterworth, Walter	Pte.	235349	8th York. & Lancs.	—	K. in A.
Watford, John H.	Pte.	24686	1st W. Yorks.	—	K. in A.
Watkin, Alfred	Pte.	21294	Northumberland Fusrs.	—	K. in A.
Watkin, James	Pte.	266548	Northumberland Fusrs.	—	K. in A.
Watkins, Fred	Gnr.	127871	R.F.A.	—	Died
Watkins, Herbert	Gnr.	64986	R.F.A.	—	Died
Watkinson, Bertie	Cpl.	24653	13th Yorks.	—	D. of W.
Watkinson, Emmanuel	Pte.	368727	W. Yorks.	—	K. in A.
Watkins, Ernest	Pte.	32649	Northumberland Fusrs.	—	K. in A.
Watkinson, Harold	Pte.	33967	W. Yorks.	—	Killed
Watkinson, Harold	Pte.	32896	15th W. Yorks.	—	K. in A.
Watkinson, John	Pte.	31806	16th W. Yorks.	—	D. of W.

LEEDS ROLL OF HONOUR.

Name	Rank	No.	Regiment	Honours	How Died
Watkinson, Robert	Pte.	7911	1st W. Yorks.	—	Missing
Watkinson, Samuel S.	Pte.	3508	1/6th R. Warwick	—	K. in A.
Watmough, Fred	Pte.	12627	8th York. & Lancs.	—	K. in A.
Watmough, O. O.	2nd Lieut.		W. Riding	—	K. in A.
Watson, Albert	Pte.	1730	W. Yorks.	—	Died
Watson, Arthur	Pte.	T/9346	10th Royal W. Kent	—	K. in A.
Watson, Arthur	Pte.	716	8th Royal Fusiliers	—	K. in A.
Watson, Chas.	L/Cpl.	10174	W. Yorks.	—	K. in A.
Watson, Ernest	Pte.	10928	2nd W. Yorks.	—	K. in A.
Watson, Ernest	Sgt.	32447	6th W. Yorks.	—	K. in A.
Watson, Ernest	Pte.	43868	Royal Scots	—	K. in A.
Watson, F. Wm.	C.S.M.	5441	2/5th K.O.Y.L.I.	D.C.M M.C.	K. in A.
Watson, Frank	Pte.	25534	W. Yorks.	—	K. in A.
Watson, Fredk. J.	Pte.	38914	2/4th Royal Berks.	—	K. in A.
Watson, Geo.	Pte.	9704	1st W. Yorks.	—	Died P.O.W.
Watson, Geo.	Pte.	161197	Machine Gun Corps	—	D. a. Dis.
Watson, George	Pte.	13288	K.O.Y.L.I.	—	Died
Watson, Geo. H.	L/Cpl.	749	13th Cheshire	—	Died
Watson, Harry	L/Cpl.	949	W. Yorks.	—	K. in A.
Watson, Harry	Rfm.	2853	8th W. Yorks.	—	K. in A.
Watson, Herbert	Pte.	39428	2nd W. Yorks.	—	Died
Watson, Hugh	Pte.	9586	11th Hussars	—	K. in A.
Watson, James	Fmn.	00003	H.M.S. "Macedonia"	—	Died
Watson, James	Pte.	70631	A.D.C.	—	Died
Watson, James	Cpl.	15309	9th Yorks.	—	K. in A.
Watson, John	Pte.	852	Lincoln	—	K. in A.
Watson, Joseph H.	Pte.	21084	K.O. Scottish Borderers	—	Died
Watson, Lawrence	Cpl.	193098	Royal Engineers	—	K. in A.
Watson, Samuel	C.S.M.	13079	11th Hussars	—	Died
Watson, Seth	Pte.	2784	2nd S. Lancs.	—	Killed
Watson, Thos.	Sgt.	10809	Royal Defence Corps.	—	Died
Watson, Thos. Ed.	Pte.	21082	W. Yorks.	—	K. in A.
Watson, Walter	Dvr.	810	R.A.S.C.	—	Died
Watson, Wilson	Pte.	17725	York. & Lancs.	—	K. in A.
Watterson, Gerald	2nd Lieut.		E. Lancs.	—	K. in A.
Watts, Albert	Pte.	21676	1st K.O. Scottish Brds.	—	K. in A.
Watts, Chas. R.	Pte.	56494	W. Yorks.	—	D. of W.
Waud, Wilfred E.	Lieut.		7th Northumb'l'd Fus.	—	K. in A.
Waugh, R. W. G.	L.S.	197535	Royal Navy	—	K. in A.
Webb, Albert	A/Sgt.	23801	9th W. Yorks.	—	Died
Webb, Chas.	Pte.	861	17th W. Yorks.	—	K. in A.
Webb, Francis W.	L/Cpl.	48578	1/8th W. Yorks.	—	Missing
Webb, Geo. A.	Pte.	5564	24th Canadian	—	K. in A.
Webber, Jesse	Pte.	15259	Yorks.	—	K. in A.
Webster, Arthur	Gnr.	161974	R.G.A.	—	K. in A.
Webster, Frank A.	2nd Lieut.		1/4th Gloucester	M.C.	K. in A.
Webster, George	Pte.	263133	2/4th W. Riding	—	D. of W.

LEEDS ROLL OF HONOUR.

Name	Rank	No.	Regiment	Honours	How Died
Webster, George	Pte.	59700	W. Yorks.	—	Died
Webster, Gresham	Dvr.	194479	R.F.A.	—	Died
Webster, Harry	Pte.	1912	Yorks.	—	K. in A.
Webster, Herbert W.	Pte.	360585	R.A.S.C.	—	Died
Webster, Jack	Pte.	47221	9th W. Yorks.	—	K. in A.
Webster, John P.	Lieut.		9th K.O.Y.L.I.	—	K. in A.
Webster, Lawrence	A.B.	KP435	Royal Naval V. Reserve	—	K. in A.
Webster, Matthew W.	Bmdr.	795547	R.F.A.	—	Died
Webster, Michael H.	Lieut.		16th W. Yorks.	—	K. in A.
Webster, Samuel	Pte.	242919	1/6th W. Yorks.	—	D. of W.
Webster, Thos.	Pte.	17249	W. Yorks.	—	K. in A.
Webster, Thos.	Pte.	34541	W. Yorks.	—	D. a. Dis.
Weetman, Howard	Pte.	59118	K.O.Y.L.I.	—	Died
Welburn, Frank	Pte.	16666	York. & Lancs.	—	D. a. Dis.
Welham, William	Pte.	2185	Suffolk	—	Died
Welldon, Herbert A.	Pte.	10687	Labour Corps	—	K. in A.
Wells, Fredk. G.	Rfm.	43617	King's Royal Rifle Cps.	—	D. a. Dis.
Wells, Geo. E.	Pte.	265353	W. Yorks.	—	D. a. Dis.
Wells, Geo. S.	Pte.	31373	Royal Welsh Fusiliers	—	K. in A.
Wells, Geo. W.	Pte.	265941	10th W. Yorks.	—	Died
Wells, Hy. H.	Pte.	31372	Royal Welsh Fusiliers	—	K. in A.
Wells, John	Pte.	42822	9th Manchester	—	K. in A.
Wells, John H.	Pte.	204188	2/7th Northumb'l'd Fus.	—	Died
Wells, Patrick T.	Pte.	1641	W. Yorks.	—	K. in A.
Wells, Walter	Pte.	44234	10th K.O.Y.L.I.	—	D. of W.
Wells, Wm. Hy.	Cpl.	2803	8th W. Yorks.	—	K. in A.
Welsey, Fredk.	Pte.	36638	1/5th Essex	—	K. in A.
Welsh, John Wm.	Pte.	267243	W. Yorks.	—	D. a. Dis.
Welsh, Joseph	Pte.		W. Yorks.	M.M.	Died
Wentworth, Frank	Pte.	6118	1/8th Durham Lt. Infty.	—	Missing
Wentworth, Stanley	Pte.	30511	E. Yorks.	—	K. in A.
Wesley, John	Pte.	2110	Machine Gun Corps	—	K. in A.
West, Chas. H.	Pte.	707801	9th Durham Lt. Infty.	—	K. in A.
West, Fredk.	Pte.	5773	1st W. Yorks.	—	K. in A.
West, Norman F.	L/Cpl.	965	15th W. Yorks.	—	K. in A.
West, Robert	Pte.	41229	11th W. Yorks.	—	D. of W.
West, Vernon	Sgt.	38591	9th K.O.Y.L.I.	—	K. in A.
West, Wilfred H.	Pte.	38863	2nd Lincoln	—	Died
Westerman, Arthur	Pte.	8117	2nd W. Yorks.	—	K. in A.
Westerman, Arthur	Pte.	15150	8th Yorks.	—	D. of W.
Westerman, George	Cpl.	10287	Yorks.	—	K. in A.
Westerman, Samuel	Pte.	10861	8th W. Riding	—	Died
Westerman, Thos.	Pte.	32755	K.O.Y.L.I.	—	K. in A.
Westerman, Wm. Hy.	Gnr.	36093	R.F.A.	—	Died
Westfield, Wm. A.	Rfm.	27140	1/8th W. Yorks.	—	K. in A.
Westley, Geo. W.	S.Smith	841193	R.F.A.	—	Died
Westmorland, John	Rfm.	267045	1/7th W. Yorks.	—	Missing

LEEDS ROLL OF HONOUR.

Name	Rank	No.	Regiment	Honours	How Died
Westmoreland, Victor	Pte.	2558	K.O.Y.L.I.	—	K. in A.
Westnutt, Alfred	Pte.	828	Royal Marine Lt. Infty.	—	K. in A.
Westoby, Chas. F.	S.Smith	45279	R.F.A.	—	D. a. Dis.
Weston, Alfred	A.B.	R/5317	Royal Naval V. Reserve	—	D. of W.
Westwood, Adam	Pte.	39397	2nd W. Yorks.	—	Missing
Wetherall, Arthur	2nd Lieut.		Lancs. Fusiliers	D.C.M.	K. in A.
Wetherall, Wm.	Gdsmn.		Grenadier Guards	—	Missing
Wetherill, Fredk.	Dvr.	12449	R.F.A.	—	K. in A.
Wetherill, Jas. W.	Rfm.	305815	1/8th W. Yorks.	—	K. in A.
Wharfe, John Wm.	Rfm.	305552	1/8th W. Yorks.	—	D. a. Dis.
Wharton, Eric F.	L/Cpl.	42998	8th Lincoln	—	Died
Wharton, Fred	Pte.	190778	R.A.S.C.	—	K. in A.
Wharton, Sydney	Rfm.	305169	1/8th W. Yorks.	—	K. in A.
Wheater, Joseph	Pte.	388079	Labour Corps	—	Died
Wheatley, Arthur	Lieut.		K.O. Royal Lancs.	—	K. in A.
Wheatley, Tom N.	Cpl.	28763	W. Yorks.	—	Died
Wheeler, Harry	Pte.	13304	K.O.Y.L.I.	—	Missing
Wheelhouse, Arthur	Sgt.	731	7th W. Yorks.	—	K. in A.
Wheelhouse, Fredk. O.	L/Cpl.	19428	Suffolk	—	K. in A.
Wheelhouse, Thos. Wm.	Pte.	9492	W. Yorks.	—	K. in A.
Whelan, Wilfred	Pte.		W. Yorks.	—	Died
Whelan, Wm.	Gnr.	96572	R.F.A.	—	D. of W.
Wheller, Ronald F. S.	Pte.	41293	K.O. Royal Lancs.	—	K. in A.
Whetstone, Walter	Pte.	63858	W. Yorks.	—	K. in A.
Whetstone, Walter	Pte.	19386	Cheshire	—	Died
Whincup, John R.	S.Maj.	121305	Machine Gun Corps	—	Died
Whiston, Samuel	Cpl.	1703	1/7th W. Yorks.	—	K. in A.
Whitaker, Arthur	L/Cpl.	307824	8th W. Yorks.	—	Died
Whitaker, Bernard	L/Cpl.	9458	York. & Lancs.	—	K. in A.
Whitaker, Chas.	Pte.	76819	R.A.M.C.	—	D. of W.
Whitaker, Christopher	L/Cpl.	297	17th W. Yorks.	—	D. of W.
Whitaker, Ernest	L/Cpl.	10177	2nd W. Yorks.	—	K. in A.
Whitaker, Fred	Spr.	29809	Royal Engineers	—	Died
Whitaker, Gordon S.	Pte.	37457	16th W. Yorks.	—	K. in A.
Whitaker, Harold	L/Cpl.	1815	1st W. Yorks.	—	D. of W.
Whitaker, Harry	Dvr.	781146	R.F.A.	—	K. in A.
Whitaker, Herbert	Pte.		Northumberland Fusrs.	—	Died
Whitaker, John	Dvr.	1689	R.F.A.	—	Died
Whitaker, John	Dvr.	222910	R.F.A.	—	K. in A.
Whitaker, John	Pte.	42361	2/6th W. Yorks.	—	Died
Whitaker, John Wm.	Pte.	19943	10th W. Yorks.	—	K. in A.
Whitaker, Leslie	L/Cpl.	12468	1st K.O.Y.L.I.	—	K. in A.
Whitaker, Samuel	Pte.	25636	W. Yorks.	—	D. of W.
Whitaker, Samuel	A/Sgt.	971	15th W. Yorks.	—	K. in A.
Whitaker, Thos.	Pte.	46647	Northumberland Fusrs.	Croix de Guerre	Died
Whitaker, Thos.	Pte.	270280	W. Yorks.	—	Died
Whitaker, W.			R.A.F.	—	

LEEDS ROLL OF HONOUR.

Name	Rank	No.	Regiment	Honours	How Died
Whitaker, Wm. Hy.	Rfm.	306103	8th W. Yorks.	—	K. in A.
White, Albert	Rfm.	306043	8th W. Yorks.	—	K. in A.
White, Albert	Pte.	48043	1/5th W. Yorks.	—	K. in A.
White, Albert	Sgt.	31141	E. Yorks.	—	Died
White, Albert	Pte.	14236	12th W. Yorks.	—	Died
White, Alfred Wm.			H.M.S. "Hawke"	—	Drowned
White, Arthur	Rfm.	306398	1/8th W. Yorks.	—	K. in A.
White, Arthur	Sgt.	2051	8th W. Yorks.	—	K. in A.
White, Chas.	Pte.	25148	15th W. Yorks.	—	Died P.O.W.
White, Chas.	Pte.	78907	W. Yorks.	—	Died P.O.W.
White, Clarence A.	Pte.	62893	W. Yorks.	—	K. in A.
White, Cyril	L/Cpl.	11729	1st King's Liverpool	—	K. in A.
White, Edward	Pte.	12858	10th W. Yorks.	—	K. in A.
White, Geo. E.	Pte.	6383	19th City of London	—	D. of W.
White, Geo. Rbt.	Pte.	13423	10th W. Yorks.	—	K. in A.
White, Harry	Rfm.	305224	8th W. Yorks.	—	Missing
White, Harry				—	K. in A.
White, Herbert	Pte.	32644	8th York. & Lancs.	—	K. in A.
White, John Wm.	Pte.	372113	R.A.S.C.	—	K. in A.
White, Joseph J.	Gnr.	14601	Royal Marine Artillery	—	K. in A.
White, Norman	Pte.	19740	Royal Scots Fusiliers	—	K. in A.
White, Sidney	Pte.	49023	E. Yorks.	—	Died
White, T. C.	Pte.	32225	10th York. & Lancs.	—	K. in A.
White, Walter	Cpl.	959	15th W. Yorks.	—	Missing
White, Wilfred	Rfm.	39351	1/7th W. Yorks.	—	K. in A.
White, Wm.	Rfm.	2659	7th W. Yorks.	—	K. in A.
White, Wm.	Pte.	8857	1st Leinster	—	Missing
White, Wm.	Pte.	8482	W. Yorks.	—	K. in A.
White, Wm. H.	Pte.	46759	Yorks.	—	K. in A.
Whitehead, Arthur	Pte.	202647	W. Yorks.	—	K. in A.
Whitehead, Ernest	Gnr.	2598	R.F.A.	—	K. in A.
Whitehead, Ernest	Pte.	62808	K.O.Y.L.I.	—	K. in A.
Whitehead, ErnestWm.	Pte.	10048	W. Riding	—	Died
Whitehead, Frank H.	Pte.	338017	R.A.S.C.	—	Died
Whitehead, H.	Sig.	796098	R.F.A.	—	Died P.O.W.
Whitehead, Herbert	L/Cpl.	13070	2nd W. Yorks.	—	Died
Whitehead, James L.	Cpl.	300099	10th W. Yorks.	—	K. in A.
Whitehead, James L.W.	Pte.	306285	W. Yorks.	—	K. in A.
Whitehead, Joe	Rfm.	13207	9th King's R. R. Cps.	—	K. in A.
Whitehead, John S.	Pte.	960	W. Yorks.	—	K. in A.
Whitehead, Thos.	Pte.	20517	17th Army Cycling Cps.	—	K. in A.
Whitehead, Tom	Gnr.	776030	R.F.A.	—	D. of W.
Whitehead, Walter	Pte.	62264	K.O.Y.L.I.	—	K. in A.
Whitehead, Willie	L/Cpl.	305836	1/8th W. Yorks.	—	K. in A.
Whiteley, Chas.	Pte.	23896	10th W. Yorks.	—	K. in A.
Whiteley, Ernest	Gnr.	888	R.F.A.	—	K. in A.
Whiteley, H.	Sgt.	96358	R.F.A.	—	D. of W.

LEEDS ROLL OF HONOUR.

Name	Rank	No.	Regiment	Honours	How Died
Whiteley, Herbert	Pte.	351748	9th Royal Scots	—	Died
Whiteley, James	Pte.	51569	Machine Gun Corps	—	K. in A.
Whiteley, John T.	Pte.	25045	1st King's Liverpool	—	K. in A.
Whiteley, John W.	1 A.M.	6237	Royal Air Force	—	K. in A.
Whiteley, Joseph	L/Cpl.	306521	W. Yorks.	—	K. in A.
Whiteley, Leonard	Sgt.	2547	1st Northumb'l'd Fus.	—	K. in A.
Whiteley, Leonard R.	L/Cpl.	975	15th W. Yorks.	—	Missing
Whiteley, Phillip	Pte.	9126	2nd W. Yorks.	—	K. in A.
Whiteley, Stanley	Pte.	10548	1st R. Munster Fusiliers	—	K. in A.
Whiteley, Sydney	O.S.	J61741	H.M.S. " Partridge "	—	K. in A.
Whitelock, John A.	Gnr.	785254	R.F.A.	—	Died
Whitelock, Wm. R.	Pte.	71043	Durham Light Infantry	—	Died
Whitelow, Harry	Pte.	38261	15th W. Yorks.	—	K. in A.
Whiteron, Guy R.	Pte.	32533	1/8th Royal Scots	—	K. in A.
Whitewick, Clarence H.	Cpl.	309275	W. Yorks.	—	K. in A.
Whitfield, George	Dvr.	98366	Royal Engineers	—	D. a. Dis.
Whitfield, James	Pte.	26438	R.A.S.C.	—	K. in A.
Whitfield, Wm.	Pte.	12842	Machine Gun Corps	—	K. in A.
Whitham, Albert	Gnr.	166234	R.F.A.	—	K. in A.
Whitham, Harry C.	Pte.	55440	Northumberland Fusrs.	—	K. in A.
Whitley, Benjamin	Pte.	3/2702	K.O.Y.L.I.	—	D. a. Dis.
Whitley, George	Pte.	1493	15th W. Yorks.	—	K. in A.
Whitley, Walter	Pte.	32602	8th York. & Lancs.	—	K. in A.
Whittaker, Albert	Rfm.	2904	8th W. Yorks.	—	Died
Whittaker, Ernest	Rfm.	267404	1/7th W. Yorks.	—	K. in A.
Whittaker, Geo. H.	Pte.	96082	R.A.M.C.	—	Died
Whittaker, Herbert	Pte.	437	21st W. Yorks.	—	D. a. Dis.
Whittaker, Joseph	A.B.	HP125	R.N.R. Anson Batt.	—	K. in A.
Whittaker, Joseph	Sgt.	10699	Royal Engineers	M.M.	K. in A.
Whittingham, Thos. C.	Pte.	66968	9th Royal Fusiliers	—	K. in A.
Whittieston, Harry	Pte	137441	Machine Gun Corps	—	K. in A.
Whitty, Fred	Pte.	15290	Yorkshire	—	K. in A.
Whitwell, Harry	Gnr.	216390	R.G.A.	—	K. in A.
Whitworth, Fred	A.B.	TZ7681	Royal Navy	—	K. in A.
Whitworth, Fred	Pte.	43536	19th Durham Lt. Infty.	—	K. in A.
Whitworth, George	Pte.	591	17th W. Yorks.	—	K. in A.
Whitworth, Wm.	Pte.	40292	9th W. Yorks.	—	K. in A.
Whomack, Arthur	Rfm.	17175	8th W. Yorks.	—	Missing
Whomack, Israel	Pte.	17692	W. Yorks.	—	K. in A.
Wicks, George	Pte.	178	17th W. Yorks.	—	K. in A.
Wicks, Herbert	L/Cpl.	S/27055	Royal Highlanders	—	D. a. Dis.
Widd, Horace	Dvr.	26346	R.F.A.	—	K. in A.
Widdas, George	Pte.	21352	2nd W. Yorks.	—	D. of W.
Widdup, Arnold	L/Cpl.	28293	7th E. Yorks.	—	K. in A.
Wieblitz, A.	Pte.	31150	E. Yorks.	—	D. of W.
Wiggington, John J.	Pte.	48831	2nd Worcester	—	K. in A.
Wiggins, Arthur	Pte.	11940	King's Liverpool	—	K. in A.

LEEDS ROLL OF HONOUR.

Name	Rank	No.	Regiment	Honours	How Died
Wigglesworth, Frank W.	Pnr.	98476	Royal Engineers	—	D. a. Dis.
Wigglesworth, Fred	Pte.	28413	6th S. Lancs.	—	Died
Wigglesworth, James	Pte.	8137	2nd W. Yorks.	—	K. in A.
Wigglesworth, Jas. W.	Pte.	12293	10th W. Yorks.	—	K. in A.
Wight, Alfred	Pte.	78736	Durham Light Infantry	—	D. a. Dis.
Wightman, Alfred A.	Pte.	35629	12th W. Yorks.	—	D. a. Dis.
Wightman, John	L/Cpl.	41612	17th W. Yorks.	—	D. a. Dis.
Wigley, Wm. R.	Pte.	66925	13th Northumb'l'd Fus.	—	D. of W.
Wilby, Harry	Pte.	35541	6th K.O.Y.L.I.	—	Died
Wilby, Wm. C.	Pte.	632	17th W. Yorks.	—	K. in A.
Wilcher, Harold	2nd Lieut.		10th K.O.Y.L.I.	—	D. of W.
Wilcher, Leslie R. V.	2nd Lieut.		R.F.A.	—	Died
Wilcock, Albert V.	Pte.	29246	10th W. Riding	—	Missing
Wilcock, Arthur B.	Pte.	35	W. Yorks.	—	Missing
Wilcocks, Fredk. T.	Sig.	11918	8th Yorks.	—	K. in A.
Wilcox, Arthur B.		19135	17th W. Yorks.	—	Missing
Wild, Arthur	2nd Lieut.		16th Durham Lt. Infty.	—	K. in A.
Wild, Henry	Pte.	35538	6th K.O.Y.L.I.	—	Died
Wild, Leonard	Gdsmn.	15658	Coldstream Guards	—	K. in A.
Wilde, Fredk.	C.S.M.	7991	2nd York. & Lancs.	—	K. in A.
Wilde, John Ed.	Pte.	38666	York. & Lancs.	—	D. of W.
Wilde, Wm.	Pte.	285	10th Y. Works.	—	D. of W.
Wildman, Joseph C.	Pte.	24237	10th W. Yorks.	—	K. in A.
Wildman, Walter	Pte.	25870	1st E. Yorks.	—	K. in A.
Wildon, Alfred Wm.	Pte.	28875	12th Yorks.	—	K. in A.
Wilkes, Fred	Pte.	1440	15th W. Yorks.	—	Died
Wilkins, Fredk. T.	Boy	38940	H.M.S. " Natal "	—	K. in A.
Wilkins, George	Cpl.	21552	Royal Welsh Fusiliers	—	K. in A.
Wilkins, Harry	Pte.	268769	21st W. Yorks.	—	D. of W.
Wilkins, John R.	L/Sgt.	46919	N. Staffs.	—	K. in A.
Wilkins, Wm.	Pte.	9302	2nd W. Yorks.	—	K. in A.
Wilkinson, Albert E.	Pte.	65291	4th Royal Fusiliers	—	K. in A.
Wilkinson, Cedric A.	A.B.	F2670	H.M.S. " Iris "	—	K. in A.
Wilkinson, Chas.	Pte.	9276	4th W. Yorks.	—	D. of W.
Wilkinson, Chas. H.	A/Bdr.	32700	R.F.A.	—	D. a. Dis.
Wilkinson, Daniel	Pte.	34871	8th Staffs.	—	K. in A.
Wilkinson, Edward C.	L/Cpl.	36510	W. Yorks.	—	K. in A.
Wilkinson, Edward L.	3rd Officer		R.N. Transport Service	—	Killed
Wilkinson, Ernest	Pte.	28999	W. Yorks.	—	Died
Wilkinson, Frank L.	L/Cpl.	31149	1st E. Yorks.	—	K. in A.
Wilkinson, Fred	Pte.	9554	1st York. & Lancs.	—	K. in A.
Wilkinson, Fred	Gnr.	2017	R.F.A.	—	K. in A.
Wilkinson, Fredk. N.	L/Cpl.	72096	Royal Engineers	—	Died
Wilkinson, Geo. Hy.	Pte.	53586	York. & Lancs.	—	K. in A.
Wilkinson, Harold	3 A.M.	122464	Royal Air Force	—	Died
Wilkinson, Harold	Pte.	50849	E. Yorks.	—	K. in A.
Wilkinson, J. A.	Pte.	29515	W. Yorks.	—	K. in A.

LEEDS ROLL OF HONOUR.

Name	Rank	No.	Regiment	Honours	How Died
Wilkinson, James	Pte.	33636	Royal Defence Corps	—	Died
Wilkinson, John	Pte.	62838	2nd W. Yorks.	—	Died
Wilkinson, John Wm.S.	Pte.	35217	Army Vet. Corps	—	Killed
Wilkinson, Joseph	Rfm.	1705	W. Yorks.	—	D. a. Dis.
Wilkinson, Joseph	Pte.	24112	Yorks.	—	K. in A.
Wilkinson, Joseph	Pte.	57430	Lancs. Fusiliers	—	K. in A.
Wilkinson, Jos. H.	A/Cpl.	983	15th W. Yorks.	—	Died
Wilkinson, Lewis H.	E.R.A.	N4474	H.M.S. "Maidstone"	—	Died
Wilkinson, Robert	L/Cpl.	4844	W. Yorks.	—	Died
Wilkinson, Stephen	Pte.	3462	Lancs. Fusiliers	—	K. in A.
Wilkinson, Sydney	Pte.	11625	K.O.Y.L.I.	—	K. in A.
Wilkinson, Sydney	Pte.	7694	1st W. Yorks.	—	D. of W.
Wilkinson, Thos.Wm.M.	Lieut.		8th Yorks.	—	K. in A.
Wilkinson, W.	Pte.	4180	W. Yorks.	—	K. in A.
Wilkinson, Wm.	L/Cpl.	1194	15th W. Yorks.	—	D. of W.
Wilkinson, Wm.	Sgt.	359	1/7th W. Yorks.	—	K. in A.
Wilks, Edward	Pte.	407942	Labour Corps	—	Died
Wilks, Enoch	Pte.	8085	Royal Defence Corps	—	D. a. Dis.
Wilks, James	Sgt.	25203	Machine Gun Corps	—	Died P.O.W.
Wilks, Walter	Pte.	33061	16th W. Yorks.	—	K. in A.
Wilks, Wm.	Pte.	41466	17th W. Yorks.	—	K. in A.
Willacy, Harry W.	1 Boy	J42418	H.M.S. "Invincible"	—	K. in A.
Willans, Guy R.	2nd Lieut.		Lancs. Fusiliers	—	K. in A.
Willans, Harold	Rfm.	2867	7th W. Yorks.	—	D. of W.
Willerton, Geo. W.	Pte.	41225	W. Yorks.	—	K. in A.
Willerton, Harold C.	Pte.	11310	Machine Gun Corps	—	Missing
Willey, John W.	Pte.	57666	Liverpool	—	K. in A.
Willey, Norman	L/Cpl.	36671	9th W. Yorks.	—	K. in A.
Willey, Thos. A. E.	2nd Lieut.		15th W. Yorks.	—	K. in A.
Williams, Albert	Pte.	401427	R.A.M.C.	—	K. in A.
Wil'iams, Chas. Hy.	Pte.	34205	9th W. Yorks.	—	K. in A.
Williams, Chas. Wm.	Pte.	37878	17th W. Yorks.	—	K. in A.
Williams, Edward T.	Pte.	85952	Royal Air Force	—	Died
Williams, Frank	Gnr.	781081	R.F.A.	—	D. of W.
Williams, Fredk.	L/Cpl.	14515	Military Foot Police	—	Died
Williams, Harold	2 Stkr.	21975	H.M.S. "Good Hope"	—	Died
Williams, Harry	S.Smith.	147802	R.F.A.	—	K. in A.
Williams, Harry	Pte.	927	17th W. Yorks.	—	K. in A.
Williams, Harry P.	Gnr.	9377	R.F.A.	—	K. in A.
Williams, John	Pte.	3065950	11th W. Yorks.	—	K. in A.
Williams, John Thos.	Gnr.	40204	R.F.A.	—	D. a. Dis.
Williams, R. A.	Sgt.	12233	W. Yorks.	—	K. in A.
Williamson, Alfred E.	Pte.	75035	2/5th Durham Lt. Infty.	—	Died
Williamson, Bertram	L/Cpl.	9667	King's Royal Rifle Cps.	—	K. in A.
Williamson, Cecil	Rfm.	2/7870	King's Royal Rifle Cps.	—	K. in A.
Williamson, George	Pte.	72675	9th Machine Gun Corps	—	D. of W.
Williamson, George	Pte.	37017	9th W. Yorks.	—	K. in A.

LEEDS ROLL OF HONOUR.

Name	Rank	No.	Regiment	Honours	How Died
Williamson, Harold	Pte.	41042	9th Norfolk	—	D. of W.
Williamson, Harry	Pte.	34077	9th W. Yorks.	—	K. in A.
Williamson, James H.	Gnr.	3672	R.G.A.	—	K. in A.
Williamson, John Alf.	Pte.	54688	16th R. Welsh Fusiliers	—	K. in A.
Williamson, Wilfred	Sig.	17/359	W. Yorks.	—	D. of W.
Williamson, William	Rfm.	201514	19th Rifle Brigade	—	K. in A.
Williamson, William	L.Stkr.	109588	H.M.S. " Bulwark "	—	Drowned
Willis, W. J.	Sgt.	284060	R.G.A.	—	D. a. Dis.
Willison, Edwin	Spr.	84014	Royal Engineers	—	K. in A.
Willman, Herbert	Pte.	12323	K.O.Y.L.I.	—	K. in A.
Wilman, J. N.	Pte.	19364	1st Worcester	—	K. in A.
Willows, George	Pte.	42699	W. Yorks.	—	K. in A.
Wills, Arthur B.	Pte.	46650	11th Northumb'l'd Fus.	—	Died
Willson, Frank	Gnr.	31143	R.G.A.	—	Died
Wilshaw, A. C. S.	L/Cpl.	15005	Lincoln	—	Died
Wilshire, Geo. Wm.	L/Cpl.	38531	1st Lancs. Fusiliers	—	D. of W.
Wilson, Albert	Pte.	39344	2nd W. Yorks.	—	Killed
Wilson, Albert	Pte.	56353	W. Yorks.	—	K. in A.
Wilson, Albert	Pte.	28048	Labour Corps	—	K. in A.
Wilson, Albert	Rfm.	4923	1/8th W. Yorks.	—	K. in A.
Wilson, Albert	Pte.	35427	8th Lincoln	—	D. of W.
Wilson, Alex. D.	Pte.	501476	5th W. Yorks.	—	D. a. Dis.
Wilson, Alex. G.	Pte.	7488	Yorkshire	—	K. in A.
Wilson, Alfred	Dvr.	75063	R.F.A.	—	Died
Wilson, Arthur	Pte.	2612	W. Yorks.	—	K. in A.
Wilson, Arthur	P.O.	J/32277	H.M.S. " Hampshire "	—	Drowned
Wilson, B.	Pte.	28102	2nd W. Yorks.	—	K. in A.
Wilson, Benj. J.	Stkr.	20850	H.M.S. " Hampshire "	—	Drowned
Wilson, Bernard	Pte.	2152	W. Yorks.	—	K. in A.
Wilson, Bernard	Rfm.	4698	1/8th W. Yorks.	—	K. in A.
Wilson, Bertie	Pte.	28102	W. Yorks.	—	K. in A.
Wilson, Chas.	Pte.	32948	K.O.Y.L.I.	—	K. in A.
Wilson, Clarence	Rfm.	2742	1/7th W. Yorks.	—	K. in A.
Wilson, Clifford	Pte.	719	K.O.Y.L.I.	—	K. in A.
Wilson, Dennis	Pte.	70940	1/5th Durham Lt. Infty.	—	K. in A.
Wilson, Edgar F.	Pte.	28280	21st W. Yorks.	—	K. in A.
Wilson, Edward	Sgt.	265548	1/7th W. Yorks.	—	K. in A.
Wilson, Edward	Bmdr.	775232	R.F.A.	—	D. of W.
Wilson, Edward M.	A/2nd En. Lt.		S.S. " Constantine "	—	Died
Wilson, Edwin	Pte.	27892	12th W. Yorks.	—	K. in A.
Wilson, Ernest	Pte.	1433	15th W. Yorks.	—	Missing
Wilson, Ernest	Pte.	306947	W. Yorks.	—	Died
Wilson, F.	Spr.	1215	Royal Engineers	—	K. in A.
Wilson, Frank N. E.	Pte.	988	15th W. Yorks.	—	K. in A.
Wilson, Fred	Dvr.	127301	R.F.A.	—	K. in A.
Wilson, Fred	Pte.	111	12th W. Yorks.	—	Died
Wilson, Fred	Rfm.	300018	18th W. Yorks.	—	Missing

LEEDS ROLL OF HONOUR.

Name	Rank	No.	Regiment	Honours	How Died
Wilson, Fred	Spr.	1215	W. Riding R.E.	—	K. in A.
Wilson, Fred Wm.	Pte.	41954	Northumberland Fusrs.	—	Died
Wilson, George	Pte.	990	15th W. Yorks.	—	Died
Wilson, Geo. H.	Gnr.	95872	R.F.A.	—	K. in A.
Wilson, Harold	Pte.	78486	Durham Light Infty.	—	K. in A.
Wilson, Harry	Pte.	24550	1st W. Yorks.	—	K. in A.
Wilson, Hy. B.	Pte.	266499	W. Yorks.	—	D. of W.
Wilson, Herbert	Rfm.	40869	1/8th W. Yorks.	—	D. of W.
Wilson, Herbert	Pte.	44040	10th Durham Lt. Infty.	—	K. in A.
Wilson, Herbert	Rfm.	2082	7th W. Yorks.	—	K. in A.
Wilson, Hugh S.	Rfm.	200928	Rifle Brigade	—	Missing
Wilson, I. C.	Pte.	33973	W. Riding	—	Died
Wilson, J.	A.B.	R6468	Royal Naval V. Reserve	—	K. in A.
Wilson, J. L.	L/Cpl.	106252	2/5th Notts. & Derby	—	Died
Wilson, J. W. H.	Pte.	12310	10th W. Yorks.	—	D. of W.
Wilson, James	Rfm.	375395	8th City of London	—	K. in A.
Wilson, James H.	Pte.	10639	W. Yorks.	—	Died
Wilson, James H.	Dvr.	30258	R.A.S.C.	—	D. a. Dis.
Wilson, Jas. Wm.	Pte.	75593	R.A.M.C.	—	Died
Wilson, Jesse	Sgt.	20646	1/7th Cheshire	—	K. in A.
Wilson, John	Pte.	333	17th W. Yorks.	—	K. in A.
Wilson, John	Rfm.	42415	2/8th W. Yorks.	—	K. in A.
Wilson, John	Dvr.	796713	R.F.A.	—	Died
Wilson, John	Pte.	116	2nd K.O.Y.L.I.	—	K. in A.
Wilson, John R.	L/Cpl.	5945	Dragoon Guards	—	K. in A.
Wilson, John W.	Gdsmn.	7169	2nd Scots Guards	—	K. in A.
Wilson, John Wm.	Pte.	1635	1st W. Yorks.	—	K. in A.
Wilson, John Wm.	L/Cpl.	2491	1/8th W. Yorks.	—	D. of W.
Wilson, Jonathan	L/Sgt.	17451	8th Seaforth Highdrs.	—	K. in A.
Wilson, Joseph	Pte.	6879	R.A.M.C.	—	Died
Wilson, Joseph	Pte.	36790	18th W. Yorks.	—	K. in A.
Wilson, Joseph	Rfm.	4056	King's Royal Rifle Cps.	—	K. in A.
Wilson, Joseph	Spr.	480258	Royal Engineers	—	K. in A.
Wilson, Joseph M.	Pte.	32947	York. & Lancs.	—	K. in A.
Wilson, Lawrence	Pte.	37362	10th W. Yorks.	—	D. of W.
Wilson, Marshall	Gnr.	141171	R.F.A.	—	Died
Wilson, Norman	2nd Lieut.		Royal Air Force	—	K. in A.
Wilson, Percy	Dvr.	480523	Royal Engineers	—	Died
Wilson, Percy	Pte.	49628	W. Yorks.	—	Missing
Wilson, Percy	Pte.	32622	Royal Scots	—	K. in A.
Wilson, Richard T.	L/Cpl.	42988	5th North Staffs.	—	K. in A.
Wilson, Robert	Gdsmn.	12815	Scots Guards	—	K. in A.
Wilson, Rowland L.	Pte.	1914	26th Royal Fusiliers	—	Missing
Wilson, Sam	Pte.	40681	K.O.Y.L.I.	—	K. in A.
Wilson, Sidney	Gnr.	100198	R.G.A.	—	K. in A.
Wilson, T.	Pte.	42792	W. Yorks.	—	K. in A.
Wilson, T.	Spr.	258349	Royal Engineers	—	Killed

LEEDS ROLL OF HONOUR.

Name	Rank	No.	Regiment	Honours	How Died
Wilson, Walter	Pte.	78733	6th Durham Lt. Infty.	—	Died P.O.W.
Wilson, Walter	Pte.	115345	Labour Corps	—	K. in A.
Wilson, Wilfred	1 Stkr.	K34811	Royal Naval V. Reserve	—	Died
Wilson, William	Pte.	26993	S. Wales Borderers	—	K. in A.
Wilson, William	Pte.	20034	Highland Lt. Infantry	—	K. in A.
Wilson, Wm. H.	A/Cpl.	343793	Labour Corps	—	K. in A.
Wilson, Wm. N.	Pte.	202693	1/5th W. Yorks.	—	K. in A.
Wilton, F.	Pte.		5th Canadian	—	K. in A.
Wimbles, Fred	Rfm.	306642	1/8th W. Yorks.	—	K. in A.
Windle, Norman	Spr.	106899	Royal Engineers	—	K. in A.
Windross, Joss.	Pte.	64333	W. Yorks.	—	Died
Windsor, Arthur	Pte.	3766	W. Yorks.	—	K. in A.
Windsor, Geo. W.	Pte.	21230	1st Northumb'l'd Fus.	—	D. of W.
Windsor, Herbert	Pte.	4556	2/5th Gloucester	—	K. in A.
Windsor, James C.	Rfm.	305285	2/8th W. Yorks.	—	K. in A.
Windsor, James E.		200986	4th E. Yorks.	—	Died
Windsor, John H.	Spr.	480466	Royal Engineers	—	Died
Winebloom, Ed. St. Clair	Bmdr.	775789	R.F.A.	—	K. in A.
Wineley, Fred	Pte.	1832	W. Yorks.	—	K. in A.
Wingfield, Victor J.	Pte.	66062	Machine Gun Corps	—	K. in A.
Winn, Arthur	Pte.	S/9808	Royal Highlanders	—	K. in A.
Winn, Herbert	A.B.	5740	Royal Naval V. Reserve	—	Died
Winn, Thos.	Pte.		W. Yorks.	—	Died
Winn, Wm.	Pte.	202143	12th W. Yorks.	—	Died P.O.W.
Winsett, S. Henry	Sdlr.T4/	211054	R.A.S.C.	—	D. a. Dis.
Winspear, Thomas	Sgt.	R/384044	R.A.S.C.	—	K. in A.
Winter, Andrew	Pte.	15041	9th W. Yorks.	—	K. in A.
Winter, Harry	A.B.	KP/482	Royal Naval Division	—	K. in A.
Winterburn, Samuel	Pte.	12931	8th K.O.Y.L.I.	—	K. in A.
Winterburn, Walter	Pte.	63450	K.O.Y.L.I.	—	Died
Winteringham, R. Hy.	Pte.	7836	4th W. Yorks.	—	K. in A.
Wise, Harold	Pte.	24881	13th W. Yorks.	—	Missing
Wise, Robert	Pte.	16520	7th K.O. Scottish Brdrs.	—	K. in A.
Wissler, Max. T.	L/Cpl.	1000	15th W. Yorks.	—	Missing
Witherley, Thos. W.	Spr.	158387	Royal Engineers	—	Died
Witty, Arthur	Cpl.	266336	1/7th W. Yorks.	—	Killed
Witty, Arthur	Pte.	35611	10th K.O.Y.L.I.	—	K. in A.
Witty, Fred Percy	Dvr.	20375	R.F.A.	—	Died
Witty, Harold K.	Pte.	45452	K.O.Y.L.I.	—	Died
Witty, Herbert	Pte.	44211	Machine Gun Corps	—	D. of W.
Wix, Clifford,	Pte.	38830	25th Northumb'l'd Fus.	—	K. in A.
Woffenden, Edward	Pte.	1003	15th W. Yorks.	—	D. of W.
Woffenden, Tom	L/Cpl.	7575	W. Yorks.	—	K. in A.
Wolfe, Harry	Pte.	6647	5th W. Yorks.	—	D. of W.
Wolstenholme, Alfred	Pte.	41698	7th Leicester	—	K. in A.
Wolstenholme, Chas. S.	Captain		12th Durham Lt. Infty.	—	K. in A.

LEEDS ROLL OF HONOUR.

Name	Rank	No.	Regiment	Honours	How Died
Wolstenholme, James	Pte.	182220	Labour Corps	—	D. a. Dis.
Wolstenholme, W.	L/Cpl.	19044	2nd W. Yorks.	—	K. in A.
Wolstenholme, Wm. H.	Pte.	61802	S. Wales Borderers	—	D. a. Dis.
Womack, George	2/A.M.	31049	Royal Air Force	—	Killed
Wood, A. S.	Pte.	30404	Loyal N. Lancs.	—	K. in A.
Wood, Albert Ed.	Sgt.	243523	4th Yorks.	—	K. in A.
Wood, Alex.	Pte.	16266	W. Yorks.	—	D. of W.
Wood, Alfred	Pte.	305545	11th W. Yorks.	—	K. in A.
Wood, Alfred	Pte.	82530	Durham Light Infantry	—	K. in A.
Wood, Alfred Jas.	Pte.	38375	York. & Lancs.	—	Died
Wood, Arthur	Pte.	M/286752	R.A.S.C.	—	K. in A.
Wood, Arthur	Pte.	65170	Machine Gun Corps	—	D. of W.
Wood, Arthur E.	Pte.	57432	Lancs. Fusiliers	—	Died
Wood, Arthur Ed.	Sgt.	1008	15th W. Yorks.	M.M.	D. of W.
Wood, Benj.	Gnr.		R.G.A.	—	D. of W.
Wood, Benj. F.	Pte.	1011	15th W. Yorks.	—	Died
Wood, Chas.	Pte.	25263	W. Yorks.	—	D. a. Dis.
Wood, Chas. R.	Rfm.	36688	3/8th W. Yorks.	—	K. in A.
Wood, David A.	Rfm.	4565	3/7th W. Yorks.	—	Died
Wood, Edgar	Pte.	12189	Yorks.	—	K. in A.
Wood, Edward	Pte.	40342	18th W. Yorks.	—	K. in A.
Wood, Edwin Jas.	Pte.	40136	Royal Fusiliers	—	Died
Wood, Edwin K.	Cpl.	47616	Essex	—	K. in A.
Wood, Ephraim	Pte.	21227	W. Yorks.	—	D. of W.
Wood, Frank	Rfm.	43613	King's Royal Rifle Cps.	—	K. in A.
Wood, Fred	Pte.	266531	W. Yorks.	—	K. in A.
Wood, Fredk. W.	Pte.	1013	15th W. Yorks.	—	Died
Wood, George	Rfm.	4436	1/7th W. Yorks.	—	K. in A.
Wood, George	L/Cpl.	56669	11th W. Yorks.	—	K. in A.
Wood, George	Pte.	203578	2/5th W. Yorks.	—	K. in A.
Wood, George H.	Pte.	18576	7th K.O.Y.L.I.	—	K. in A.
Wood, George S.	Sgt.	243523	Yorks.	—	K. in A.
Wood, George S.	L/Cpl.		Lancs. Hussars	—	Killed
Wood, Godfrey	Pte.	1414	15th W. Yorks.	—	K. in A.
Wood, Harry	Gdsmn.	5562	2nd Scots Guards	—	K. in A.
Wood, Harry	Pte.	92081	Durham Light Infantry	—	K. in A.
Wood, Henry C.	Sgt.	265217	1/7th W. Yorks.	—	K. in A.
Wood, Herbert A.				—	Died
Wood, Herbert L.	Pte.	267348	W. Yorks.	—	K. in A.
Wood, Herbert T.	Pte.	20839	E. Kent	—	Missing
Wood, J. C.	Pte.	513447	Royal Canadians	—	Died
Wood, J. C.	Sgt.	237003	25th Northumb'l'd Fus.	—	K. in A.
Wood, J. N.	Pte.	38569	12th W. Yorks.	—	Died
Wood, J. W. S.	Pte.	41614	17th W. Yorks.	—	Died
Wood, John	Rfm.	235200	2/7th W. Yorks.	—	K. in A.
Wood, John	Rfm.	835200	2/7th W. Yorks.	—	Died
Wood, John	Pte.	49494	Lincoln	—	K. in A.

LEEDS ROLL OF HONOUR.

Name	Rank	No.	Regiment	Honours	How Died
Wood, John	Pte.	302636	Durham Light Infantry	—	K. in A.
Wood, John A.	Cpl.	1015	15th W. Yorks.	—	D. a. Dis.
Wood, John W.	Cpl.	20516	Army Cycling Corps	M.M.	K. in A.
Wood, John Wm.	Pte.	351749	9th Royal Scots	—	Died
Wood, Joseph	Pte.	471619	Labour Corps	—	D. a. Dis.
Wood, Joseph	Rfm.	C/136	King's Royal Rifle Cps.	—	K. in A.
Wood, Joseph	L/Cpl.	61635	2nd W. Yorks.	—	K. in A.
Wood, Leonard	Cpl.	62345	Royal Defence Corps	—	Died
Wood, Leslie	Rfm.	R/13007	1st King's R. Rifle Cps.	—	D. of W.
Wood, Leslie	Cpl.	301461	Royal Engineers	—	K. in A.
Wood, Percy	Pte.	1328	15th W. Yorks.	—	K. in A.
Wood, Robert	Pte.	1017	15th W. Yorks.	—	D. of W.
Wood, Samuel	Rfm.	7699	8th Rifle Brigade	—	Died
Wood, Stanley	Pte.	60845	W. Yorks.	—	K. in A.
Wood, Thomas	Pte.	5534	W. Riding	—	K. in A.
Wood, Thomas	Pte.	2/295632	R.A.S.C.	—	D. a. Dis.
Wood, Thomas	Pte.	34543	13th W. Yorks.	—	D. a. Dis.
Wood, Thomas	Pte.	3/7225	8th E. Yorks.	—	K. in A.
Wood, Thomas	Pte.	20757	5th W. Yorks.	—	D. a. Dis.
Wood, Thos. E.	Pnr.	155480	Royal Engineers	—	K. in A.
Wood, Thos. S.	Pte.	355	16th W. Yorks.	—	K. in A.
Wood, W. D.	Gnr.	23633	R.G.A.	—	K. in A.
Wood, Walter	Sgt.	5376	2nd Yorks.	—	D. a. Dis.
Wood, Walter F.	Pte.	69069	Training Reserve	—	Died
Wood, William	Cpl.	13470	Army Pay Corps	—	D. a. Dis.
Wood, William	Cpl.	6839	W. Riding	—	K. in A.
Wood, William	Cpl.	8344	3rd W. Yorks.	—	D. a. Dis.
Wood, Wm. E.	Pte.	22478	K.O.Y.L.I.	—	Died
Wood, Wm. Hy.	C.S.M.	31871	W. Yorks.	—	K. in A.
Wood, Wm. S.	Pte.	470328	R.G.A.	—	K. in A.
Woodall, Stephen H.	Pte.	50515	12th W. Yorks.	—	K. in A.
Woodbridge, George	Pte.	47416	Royal Defence Corps	—	D. a. Dis.
Woodcock, Ernest	Rfm.	266834	1/7th W. Yorks.	—	D. of W.
Woodcock, Gilbert	Pte.	313621	Labour Corps	—	D. a. Dis.
Woodcock, Henry	Sgt.	11755	2nd K.O. Scottish Bdrs.	—	K. in A.
Woodcock, John	Pte.	32601	York. & Lancs.	—	K. in A.
Woodcock, Victor J.	Lieut.		Royal Air Force	—	K. in A.
Woodhead, Arthur	Rfm.	39211	1/7th W. Yorks.	—	K. in A.
Woodhead, Ernest	Pte.	24534	Royal W. Kents.	—	K. in A.
Woodhead, Fred	Pte.	40035	9th Royal Irish Fusrs.	—	Missing
Woodhead, Harold	Pte.	41337	10th Notts. & Derby	—	D. of W.
Woodhead, John Thos.	Sgt.	265379	1/7th W. Yorks.	—	K. in A.
Woodhead, Jos. A.	Dvr.	775345	R.F.A.	—	K. in A.
Woodhead, Richard	Pte.	10084	W. Yorks.	—	K. in A.
Woodhead, Tom	Dvr.	73666	R.F.A.	—	Died
Woodhead, Tom L.	Pte.	24480	Labour Corps	—	K. in A.
Woodhead, Wm.	Pte.	43725	W. Riding	—	D. a. Dis.

LEEDS ROLL OF HONOUR.

Name	Rank	No.	Regiment	Honours	How Died
Woodhead, Wm.	Pte.	63973	W. Yorks.	—	K. in A.
Woodhead, Wm.	Pte.	28114	1/6th W. Yorks.	—	K. in A.
Woodhouse, Arch. B.			Royal Naval Division	—	Died
Woodhouse, Arthur	Rfm.	8377	King's Royal Rifle Cps.	—	K. in A.
Woodhouse, Benj. E.	Pte.	12455	K.O.Y.L.I.	—	K. in A.
Woodhouse, Chas. C.	Pte.	203870	K.O.Y.L.I.	—	Died
Woodhouse, George	Pte. T4/250995		R.A.S.C.	—	Died
Woodhouse, Geo. C.	Pte.	65295	4th Royal Fusiliers	—	Died
Woodhouse, Laurence	Pte.	39122	8th Lancs. Fusiliers	—	K. in A.
Wooding, Jas. J.	Pte.	263043	Northumberland Fusrs.	—	K. in A.
Woodliffe, John	Pte.	5970	Royal Marines	—	K. in A.
Woodlock, Alfred	Pte.	68214	K.O.Y.L.I.	—	Died
Woodridge, George	Pte.	47416	Royal Defence Corps	—	Died
Woodruff, Thos. F.	Pte.	19007	K.O.Y.L.I.	—	K. in A.
Woodruff, Wm. H.	Rfm.	2176	1/7th W. Yorks.	—	K. in A.
Woodruffe, Wm. G.	Pte.	13338	K.O. Royal Lancs.	—	Died
Woods, Fred	Pte.	28317	7th E. Yorks.	—	K. in A.
Woods, Gilbert	Pte.	31968	16th W. Yorks.	—	K. in A.
Woods, Sydney G.	Bmbdr.	35292	R.F.A.	—	D. of W.
Woodward, Joseph	Pte.	11307	6th K.O.Y.L.I.	—	K. in A.
Woodward, Percy	Rfm.	306819	2/8th W. Yorks.	—	Died
Woodward, Samuel	Pte.	32895	16th W. Yorks.	—	K. in A.
Woodward, Wm. B.	Rfm.	14162	2nd King's R. Rifle Cps.	—	K. in A.
Woof, John H.	L/Cpl.	306621	W. Yorks.	—	K. in A.
Woolen, Wm. John	A.S.M.	20572	R.G.A.	—	K. in A.
Wooler, Chas. A.	A/Captain		10th W. Yorks.	—	D. of W.
Wooler, Herbert S.	2nd Lieut.		12th W. Yorks.	—	K. in A.
Wooler, Rupert B.	Lieut.		12th W. Yorks.	—	K. in A.
Woolhouse, Edward	Cpl.	267315	2/7th W. Yorks.	—	D. of W.
Woollard, Geo. W.	Rfm.	306952	2/8th W. Yorks.	—	K. in A.
Wooller, William	Pte.	1516	12th E. Yorks.	—	D. of W.
Woolley, William	Pte.	73361	Machine Gun Corps	—	K. in A.
Wordsworth, Josh. H.	Pte.	56271	Essex	—	K. in A.
Worfolk, E. P.	Spr.	182778	Royal Engineers	—	Died
Wormald, Edward	Gnr.	108773	R.G.A.	—	D. of W.
Wormald, George	Pte.	12019	9th W. Yorks.	—	Missing
Wormald, Harry	Gnr.	108852	R.G.A.	—	K. in A.
Wormald, Joseph	Sgt.	21220	1st Northumb'l'd Fus.	—	K. in A.
Wormald, Walter	Cpl.	23317	16th W. Yorks.	—	K. in A.
Worrall, Herbert	Lieut.		1/6th W. Yorks.	—	K. in A.
Worrall, Sydney	Pte.	201053	2/10th London	—	K. in A.
Worrall, Wm.	Pte.	21213	3rd W. Yorks.	—	Died
Worsley, Ernest	Pte.	268513	W. Yorks.	—	Died
Worsnop, Albert	Pte.	27712	9th Lancs. Fusiliers	—	D. of W.
Worsnop, Albert	Pte.	307148	W. Yorks.	—	Died
Worsnop, Andrew	A.B.	1497	Royal Naval Division	—	Died
Worsnop, Edgar	Lieut.		W. Yorks.	—	D. of W.

LEEDS ROLL OF HONOUR.

Name	Rank	No.	Regiment	Honours	How Died
Worsnop, Harry	Pte.	229005	London	—	Died
Worsnop, Harry	L/Cpl.	33190	9th W. Yorks.	—	D. of W.
Worsnop, John Wm.	Pte.	1018	21st W. Yorks.	—	Died P.O.W.
Worsnop, Roy	Rfm.	265860	1/7th W. Yorks.	—	Died P.O.W.
Worsnop, Tom	Pte.	21778	W. Yorks.	—	K. in A.
Worsnop, Wm. C.	Pte.	13633	K.O.Y.L.I.	—	Died
Worsnop, Wm. W.	Pte.	50982	Durham Light Inftary	—	Died
Worth, Jas. W.	2nd Lieut.		6th W. Yorks.	D.C.M. & M.C.	D. of W.
Worth, John H.	Pte.	37834	8th E. Yorks.	—	K. in A.
Worth, John W.	Pte.	12974	W. Yorks.	—	K. in A.
Worth, Roland	Pte.	34827	16th W. Yorks.	—	K. in A.
Worthy, Frank	Dvr.	028878	R.F.A.	—	Killed
Worthy, Herbert	Dvr.	892	R.F.A.	—	K. in A.
Wragby, Leonard	Pte.	39304	12th W. Yorks.	—	Killed
Wraith, Albert	Pte.	45930	12th W. Yorks.	—	K. in A.
Wrathall, Ernest	Pte.	16525	9th K.O.Y.L.I.	—	Killed
Wray, Albert	Sgt.	23138	6th Dorset	—	Died
Wray, Donald	A/Cpl.	86441	Royal Engineers	—	K. in A.
Wray, Frank	Cpl.	72713	Royal Engineers	—	Died
Wray, Harry	C.S.M.	7764	11th W. Yorks.	—	Died
Wray, Henry E.	Pte.	21825	W. Yorks.	—	D. of W.
Wray, Herbert	Pte.	26645	W. Riding	—	Missing
Wray, Leonard	Dvr.	119695	Machine Gun Corps	—	Died
Wray, Samuel	Sgt.	28017	9th Lancs. Fusiliers	—	D. of W.
Wrigglesworth, J. H.	L/Cpl.	2714	1/7th W. Yorks.	—	K. in A.
Wrigglesworth, Thomas	Rfm.	306286	2/8th W. Yorks.	—	K. in A.
Wright, Albert	Pte.	19023	Labour Corps	—	K. in A.
Wright, Chas.	Bmdr.	165918	R.F.A.	—	K. in A.
Wright, Ernest	Pte.	21514	11th W. Yorks.	—	Died
Wright, Ernest	Pte.	205117	5th W. Yorks.	—	K. in A.
Wright, Frank	Pte.	24398	W. Yorks.	—	Died
Wright, George	L/Cpl.	306282	2/8th W. Yorks.	—	K. in A.
Wright, Geo. C.	L/Cpl.	67139	1st Notts. & Derby	—	K. in A.
Wright, Geo. F.	Pte.	8972	3rd W. Yorks.	—	Died
Wright, Geo. W.	Pte.	7602	2nd Yorks.	—	K. in A.
Wright, Harry	Pte.	24476	W. Yorks.	—	K. in A.
Wright, Harry E.	Pte.	72543	2nd W. Yorks.	—	D. a. Dis.
Wright, Herbert	Pte.	125602	Machine Gun Corps	—	Died
Wright, John	Pte.	19946	9th W. Yorks.	—	Missing
Wright, John	Pte.	1218	K.O.Y.L.I.	—	K. in A.
Wright, John A.	Pte.	72372	9th Cheshire	—	K. in A.
Wright, Joseph	Gnr.	796456	R.F.A.	—	Died
Wright, Joseph	Pte.	14129	11th W. Yorks.	—	K. in A.
Wright, Joseph	Gdsmn.	15071	1st Scots Guards	—	K. in A.
Wright, Leonard	Gnr.	151584	R.F.A.	—	K. in A.
Wright, Reg.	Spr.	160393	Royal Engineers	—	K. in A.
Wright, Thos. B.	Pte.	46652	11th Northumb'l'd Fus.	—	K. in A.

LEEDS ROLL OF HONOUR.

Name	Rank	No.	Regiment	Honours	How Died
Wright, Wm.	Rfm.	266196	2/7th W. Yorks.	—	Killed
Wright, Wm.	Pte.	34073	13th Yorks.	—	K. in A.
Wright, Wm. A.	Pte.	1638	11th Northumb'l'd Fus.	—	K. in A.
Wrighton, Ernest	Pte.	235803	2/4th York. & Lancs...	—	K. in A.
Wrigley, Geo. A.	Pte.	24253	W. Yorks.	—	K. in A.
Wyatt, Gilbert	Pte.	27079	S. Wales Borderers	—	K. in A.
Wyers, Robert	Pte.	305918	W. Yorks.	—	Died
Wylde, Harry	A/Sgt.	7970	Royal Munster Fusrs.	—	K. in A.
Wynn, James	Pte.	P7610	Military Foot Police	—	D. a. Dis.
Wynnard, Martin	Pte.	4886	3/4th K.O.Y.L.I.	—	Died
Yaffin, Jack	Pte.	40301	18th W. Yorks.	—	K. in A.
Yarborough, Harry	Rfm.	5353	1/8th W. Yorks.	—	K. in A.
Yardley, Norman	Pte.	34917	Royal Army Vet. Corps	—	Died
Yarmovsky, Jacob	Pte.	31879	W. Yorks.	—	K. in A.
Yates, Frank	Gdsmn.	8219	2nd Scots Guards	—	K. in A.
Yates, George	Pte.	26707	Wiltshire	—	K. in A.
Yates, Geo. H.	A/Sgt.	20883	K.O.Y.L.I.	—	K. in A.
Yates, J. P.	Pte.	427950	Canadian Highlanders	—	K. in A.
Yates, Reg.	Pte.	24115	W. Yorks.	—	K. in A.
Yeadon, Albert H.	Pte.	376523	27th Durham Lt. Infty.	—	K. in A.
Yeadon, Hbt. D.	Pte.	6500	K.O.Y.L.I.	—	K. in A.
Yearby, Richard	Pte.	7309	1st W. Yorks.	—	K. in A.
York, John Wm.	Pte.	403143	R.A.M.C.	—	Died
Young, Arthur	Rfm.	1275	1/8th W. Yorks.	—	Died
Young, Chas.	A/BQMS.	796432	R.F.A.	—	K. in A.
Young, Frank E.	Dvr.	45409	R.F.A.	—	K. in A.
Young, Harry	Dvr.	796012	R.F.A.	—	Died
Young, Harry	Pte.	9357	W. Yorks.	—	K. in A.
Young, Jas. Wm.		6760	Royal Naval Air Service	—	Died
Young, Robert	Pte.	28631	S. Lancs.	—	K. in A.
Young, Sydney	Pte.	3055	5th W. Yorks.	—	K. in A.
Young, Thos.	Pte.	57587	York. & Lancs.	—	K. in A.
Young, Willie	Sgt.	72329	Royal Engineers	—	Died
Young, Wm.	Pte.	6437	1st W. Yorks.	—	K. in A.
Zimmerman, Fred	Pte.	267202	W. Yorks.	—	Died

www.ingramcontent.com/pod-product-compliance
Lightning Source LLC
Chambersburg PA
CBHW052039220426
43663CB00012B/2379